CATULLUS

CATULLUS

A COMMENTARY BY

C. J. FORDYCE

PROFESSOR OF HUMANITY
IN THE
UNIVERSITY OF GLASGOW

OXFORD
AT THE CLARENDON PRESS

Oxford University Press, Amen House, London E.C.4

GLASGOW NEW YORK TORONTO MELBOURNE WELLINGTON
BOMBAY CALCUTTA MADRAS KARACHI LAHORE DACCA
CAPE TOWN SALISBURY NAIROBI IBADAN ACCRA
KUALA LUMPUR HONG KONG

FIRST PUBLISHED 1961
REPRINTED LITHOGRAPHICALLY AT THE
UNIVERSITY PRESS, OXFORD
FROM CORRECTED SHEETS OF THE FIRST EDITION
1965

PRINTED IN GREAT BRITAIN

PREFACE

THIS edition is intended to meet the need for an English commentary for general school and university use. By permission of the Delegates of the Clarendon Press the Oxford text has been reprinted; a few poems which do not lend themselves to comment in English have been omitted.

My thanks are due to Mr. R. A. B. Mynors, who drew my attention to some recent work bearing on the history of the text, to Mr. G. W. Williams, who gave much of the commentary the benefit of his stimulating criticism, and to Mr. R. G. Austin, who read the whole; to his exact scrutiny and his meticulous latinity I am very greatly indebted.   C. J. F.

CONTENTS

INTRODUCTION

THE LIFE OF CATULLUS

APART from what his poems can tell us our information about Catullus' life is of the slenderest. Of the biography by Suetonius nothing has survived except the two facts which St. Jerome, in his expansion of Eusebius' chronicle, may be supposed to have derived from it. St. Jerome records his birth at Verona under the year 87 B.C. and his death at Rome, in his thirtieth year, under the year 57. The second date cannot be true; Catullus was certainly alive in 55. He mentions the second consulship of Pompey (113. 2), which fell in 55, and the Porticus Pompei (55. 6), which was built in that consulship, and two clear allusions to Caesar's invasion of Britain (11. 12, 29. 4; cf. 45. 22) must belong to the latter part of that year or the beginning of the next. On the other hand he has no reference to any event later than 55. If the figure of thirty is right (and it is perhaps more likely to be reliable than the dates; the age at which a man died was often recorded on his tombstone), Jerome or his source must have antedated his birth and his death by at least three years. There can be no certainty, but it is a reasonable hypothesis that he was born in 84 B.C.[1]

His birthplace was in the populous and prosperous region between the foothills of the Alps and the Po which in his time was not politically part of Italy; it belonged to one of the two provinces of Gaul. The Etruscans who had established themselves in it had

---

[1] The fact that, as Munro pointed out, 87 was the year of L. Cornelius Cinna's first consulship and 84 the year of his fourth and last is a possible explanation of the error.

been dislodged in the fourth century by a Celtic invasion of Gauls from the North; its towns were either (like
Mantua) of Etruscan or (like Verona itself) of Gallic
foundation. In 223–222 B.C., after repelling an invasion
by these Cisalpine Gauls, the Romans had penetrated
their country and established outposts in it, and when
the defeat of Hannibal left them free to attend to the
Northern frontier, they continued the series of military
colonies to maintain order among the tribes and defend
the Alpine passes against invaders from the North. The
development of the Cisalpine region and its resources by
Roman enterprise had been proceeding for more than
a century when it was constituted a province after the
Social Wars. The towns south of the Po received Roman
citizenship under a settlement made by Cn. Pompeius
Strabo in 89, but the Transpadanes were left a stage
behind. Their larger towns had only the restricted
status of the *ius Latinum*, and it was not until 49, when
Catullus was dead and his fellow countryman Virgil a
grown man, that they realized their long-cherished ambition and acquired full citizenship. In Catullus' time
many Roman citizens had found a home in the country
and a livelihood in its commerce; by then, probably, the
economy of the towns at any rate was largely romanized
and Gallic was no longer spoken there, but the region
retained a vigorous self-consciousness[1]—to Catullus it is
'the Province' (43. 6) and the Transpadanes are 'my
own people' (39. 13)—and had its own traditions, its
own ways of speech,[2] and its own cultural life.

[1] Even in the next century, when all political differences had long
vanished, those absentee Cisalpines, the two Plinys, are proud of
their Transpadane blood.

[2] We know from Quintilian (i. 5. 8) of one word, *ploxenum*, which
Catullus brought with him from beyond the Po; *basium* may be
another (see on 5. 6). If we may trust Servius (on *Geo.* i. 104), in the
mature Virgil there were traces of the idiom of his Northern boyhood.

Of Catullus' origins his name tells us nothing; for all that it implies, his ancestors are as likely to have been immigrant settlers from the South as romanized Gauls.[1] His family was certainly of high standing in the province; his father was in the habit of entertaining Caesar when he was governor (Suet. *Jul.* 73) and the villa at Sirmio on Lake Garda (31) was presumably a family property. A brother, to whom he was devoted, died in Asia Minor (65. 5 ff.; 68. 19 ff.; 101), where he may have been on official duty or in an unofficial employment such as Catullus had in Bithynia. The poet's background must have been the security and means of a local upper class.

Where he had his schooling and laid the foundations of his scholarship we do not know. The province had its own famous *grammatici*, teachers of literature; Suetonius (*Gramm.* 3) speaks of three, all Greeks, who settled and worked there. One of the most eminent of Italian *grammatici*, Valerius Cato, who counted for much in the development of the new movement in poetry—'Latina Siren', one of his pupils called him, 'qui solus legit et facit poetas'—came from the province; he taught, it seems, three of Catullus' contemporaries, Cinna, Furius Bibaculus, and Ticidas, and Catullus may have been another of the poets he made.[2] Virgil, some fifteen years later, when he had outgrown the resources of Cremona, was sent first to Milan, the largest town in the province, and then to Rome; Catullus may have

---

For peculiarities of Cisalpine pronunciation see Quintilian i. 5. 12 (an orator from Placentia; cf. Cic. *Brut.* 172) and i. 7. 24 (Livy and Asconius, both from Patavium).

[1] His *cognomen* has been thought to be Celtic (Schulze, *Latein. Eigennamen*, 23²), but if it is a derivative of *Cato*, which itself is a derivative of *catus*, it is as Italic as they are.

[2] For Valerius Cato see Suet. *Gramm.* 11; he may be the Cato of poem 56.

done likewise. We do not know how, or when, he came to Rome, but it was there that he fell under the spell of the woman he calls Lesbia, the inspiration of the poems for which he has been best remembered. She was married, and if, as there are grounds for believing, she was the famous Clodia, the wife of Metellus Celer, the connexion with her must have begun by 59 B.C., when Metellus died.[1] Catullus' last message to her (11) was written in 55 or 54; between, there is a dateless story of sunshine and passing shadows, then disillusion, torture, and despair. Only one event in his life can be dated with some confidence—his visit to Asia Minor, where he went (probably with his friend Cinna) as a member of the *cohors* of the governor of Bithynia, C. Memmius, a man of literary tastes who followed the common practice of attaching to his official household young men who shared them (see on 10. 10). Memmius was praetor in 58 B.C. and his term of propraetorship in Bithynia was probably from the spring of 57 to the spring of 56. Poems 46, 4, and 31 can be referred to the stages of Catullus' homeward journey and poem 4 was written soon after his return.

Rome was his home, as he says himself (68. 34 ff.)—though he had a country house also, on the Sabine side of Tibur (44)—but he did not lose touch with the North. He was back in Verona after his brother's death (68. 27), and it was to his beloved Sirmio that he went when he returned from his Bithynian adventure. Some of his occasional verses are concerned with the local life of the province, its gossip, and its scandals; 17, 67, and 100 are clearly such, and there may be others: when he wrote them there is no knowing. His father's influence may have helped to give him his footing in Rome, or the friendship of Cisalpines, like Cornelius Nepos, who were already established there; when we see him there, he is

[1] On the identification of Lesbia see below, pp. xiv–xviii.

already in the heart of the sophisticated society of his day. The list of his friends shows how fully he had been admitted to that society; besides Cornelius Nepos (1), there are his admired Calvus (14, 53), the distinguished son of a distinguished father, Cinna (10. 30) his ideal of the scholar-poet, Cornificius (38), poet and critic of oratory, Hortensius (65), Cicero's rival in the courts, perhaps Torquatus (61), the spokesman for Epicurean-ism in Cicero's *De Finibus*, perhaps Quintilius Varus (10), another Cisalpine, later the friend of Horace and Virgil.[1] It is a world of which we know a great deal from Cicero, especially in his Letters, though even he gives us no more than an inkling of the complicated and ever-changing web of personal relations. Most of these friends of Catullus—and others besides whose names appear in the poems, like Memmius and Sestius (44)—were in Cicero's circle, but Cicero never mentions Catullus and Catullus' lines to Cicero (49) are equivocal without a context; perhaps, if Cicero's correspondence with Nepos and with Calvus had survived,[2] it would have thrown some light on Catullus' story. In Catullus himself we catch a glimpse of other aspects of his generation—the uninhibited vitality and the irrespon-sible frivolities of a privileged young intelligentsia, its intense enthusiasm for the 'joyous discipline' of poetry,[3] its snobberies, its catchwords, and its conventions. The serious issues of social and political life in a disintegrat-ing society do not concern him; he is too much of an

[1] Perhaps also Caelius Rufus: see below, pp. xv f.

[2] At least two books of letters to Nepos and at least two of letters to Calvus were current in antiquity.

[3] Gavin Douglas's phrase is suggestive. The student of Catullus may find some useful analogies in the literature of the court of James IV; there also intoxication with a new world of poetry, full of sensitiveness and full of art, is combined with the boisterous gusto of scurrilous personalities which are not always to be taken at face value.

individualist. His attacks on Caesar and Pompey are personal, not political, prompted by the indignation of an exclusive fastidiousness at the rise of upstarts to wealth and power and at the patrons to whom they owed it. He sees Mamurra swaggering about Rome—or Verona, it may be, when he was there with Caesar's troops—and flings some lines of vicious abuse at Caesar (29, 57), the same man whose exploits beyond the Alps can fire his romantic imagination (11. 9 ff.). He does not look beyond the mood of the moment.

LESBIA

Propertius ii. 34. 87 f.:
> haec quoque lasciui cantarunt scripta Catulli,
> Lesbia quis ipsa notior est Helena.

Ovid, *Tristia* ii. 427 f.:
> sic sua lasciuo cantata est saepe Catullo
> femina cui falsum Lesbia nomen erat.

Martial viii. 73. 8:
> Lesbia dictauit, docte Catulle, tibi.

Even without Ovid we might well have guessed that Lesbia was a pseudonym. What Lesbia's real name was we know from Apuleius (*Apol.* 10) who, defending himself on the charge of giving fictitious names to his loves, says 'eadem opera accusant C. Catullum quod Lesbiam pro Clodia nominat'; like the others which he quotes— Ticidas' Perilla for Metella, Propertius' Cynthia for Hostia, Tibullus' Delia for Plania—the pseudonym conforms to the practice[1] of half-concealing a real name under a fictitious one of the same metrical value.

The Italian humanist Victorius was the first[2] to suggest identifying this Clodia with a Clodia of Catullus'

---

[1] Pointed out by Bentley on Hor. *Od.* ii. 12. 13; Gallus' Lycoris for Cytheris is another example.

[2] In his *Variae Lectiones* (1553), xvi. 1.

time of whom we have a vivid picture from another source, Cicero's speech *Pro Caelio*. She was the daughter of Appius Claudius Pulcher, the consul of 79 B.C., who left behind him an impoverished family of three daughters, of whom she was the second, and three sons, of whom P. Clodius Pulcher, Cicero's enemy, was the youngest. Her ancestry was patrician (her mother was a daughter of Q. Caecilius Metellus Balearicus), but she shared in the revolutionary concerns of her younger brother and she and her sisters seem to have adopted the popular form of their gentile name with which he advertised his political affiliations.[1] All three sisters made good marriages. The eldest married Q. Marcius Rex, the youngest L. Licinius Lucullus; the second was the wife of her cousin, the dull and pompous Q. Metellus Celer, who after being praetor in 63 B.C. went as governor to Cisalpine Gaul the next year. During his absence and after his return Clodia's scandalous behaviour was the talk of Rome and when early in 59 B.C., shortly after the end of his consulship, Metellus died, gossip alleged that she had poisoned him. In the same year she found a new favourite in M. Caelius Rufus, Cicero's gifted, cynical, and wayward protegé, who was making a name for himself as an orator and cutting a figure in fashionable society. Caelius had finally broken with her, to the relief of his friends, by 56, when she sought her revenge on him by engineering the charge of *uis* on which Cicero's ingenious advocacy secured his acquittal. The result of the trial seems to have been the end of Clodia's career and she is not heard of again.

[1] She appears as Clodia in all our texts except one—a letter from Cicero to her husband (*Fam.* v. 2. 6): the two elder brothers remained Claudii. For some words the 'homely' forms with *o* for *au* became generally current (e.g. *sodes* from *si audes*, *focale* beside *fauces*); Cicero uses others in his letters (e.g. *oricula*, *loreola*); cf. Suet. *Vesp.* 22, an anecdote of the rustic Vespasian, who said *plostra* for *plaustra*.

Nothing that we know of this Clodia is inconsistent with the identification. Lesbia was married and her husband was alive (68. 146, 83. 1) when the intimacy with Catullus began; the poems give the impression that she was of some social position. This Clodia was older than Catullus—perhaps by as much as ten years—but Caelius was younger than he was, and Cicero shows her emancipation, her looks, and her accomplishments sweeping young men off their feet. And Catullus' last merciless picture of the Lesbia who has betrayed him (11. 17–20, 58) is the picture which Cicero, with an advocate's calculated irony, gives of Clodia, 'mulier non solum nobilis uerum etiam nota', and her way of life.

Two poems have been adduced to confirm the identification. One is 79, which is concerned with someone whom Catullus calls 'Lesbius'. If Lesbia is Clodia, then Lesbius, it is reasonably argued, is a Clodius: the first words, Lesbius est pulcer, have point if there is a reference to P. Clodius' inherited cognomen, with which Cicero, the inveterate punster, makes play again and again,[1] and the charges against Lesbius which are implied are of the sort which were current against Clodius.[2] The other is 77, which is addressed to one Rufus, a false friend who has wrecked Catullus' happiness by stealing his love from him. This Rufus, it is suggested, is M. Caelius Rufus, and it was he who supplanted Catullus in Clodia's favours. If this poem could be taken by itself, the argument would be very plausible, and another poem addressed to a Rufus, a piece of harmless scurrility (69), need not affect it. But there are also two poems addressed to a Caelius. One (100) is a message

---

[1] Att. i. 16. 10 'pulcellus puer', ii. 22. 1 'pulcellum nostrum', in Clodium et Curionem fr. 25 'sed credo postquam speculum tibi adlatum est, longe te a pulcris abesse sensisti'.

[2] Cic. Har. Resp. 42, 59, Sest. 16.

of good wishes and thanks to Caelius for friendship shown in Catullus' own love affairs; the other (58) is a scathing exposure of Lesbia's degradation. Both are written as to a friend. Poem 58 might be supposed to have been written to Caelius Rufus after he had suffered the same disillusionment as Catullus. But poem 100 does not seem to fit the story at all; besides, the Caelius of 100 belongs to Verona and we know of nothing to connect Caelius Rufus with that place. It is not impossible that Catullus sent verses to two different Caelii, poem 58 to Caelius Rufus, his friend and former rival, and poem 100 to some other Caelius at Verona, but one cannot build much on such an hypothesis.

The identification is not proved, though the combined evidence makes it not unlikely. Lesbia may be some other Clodia. The spelling of the name points to Clodia Metelli and her sisters. Lesbia cannot have been Clodia Marcii, whose husband was dead by 61; nor can she have been Clodia Luculli,[1] who had been divorced in 66; neither had a *uir* at the time when Catullus can be supposed to have written poem 68. If she was not Clodia Metelli, we do not know who she was.[2] If the identification were firmly based, we could arrange the pattern of Catullus' life with a little more assurance. It is tempting to see the beginnings of the story in 'the Province' and the positions of Clodia's husband and Catullus' father there, and to think of Caelius and Catullus as fellow-members of Clodia's coterie, sharing the fascination of those flashing eyes and that fatal smile. But we cannot accept the identification, as some scholars have been tempted to do, for the sake of a chronology. If we do

---

[1] As Rothstein argued (*Philol.* lxxviii [1923], 1 ff.), followed by Maas (*C.Q.* xxxvi [1942], 79 ff.).

[2] That negative conclusion is argued by G. Giri, *Riv. Indo-Gr.-Ital.* vi (1922), 161 ff., *Athenaeum* vi (1928), 183 ff.

not know who Lesbia was, that does not greatly matter; what matters far more is a passion of such loyal intensity that, though only twenty-five of Catullus' poems, nearly all short, are concerned with Lesbia—only some 250 lines out of more than two thousand—she has survived the centuries with him.

CATULLUS AND 'ALEXANDRIANISM'[1]

The Greek poetry of the Hellenistic age, a literature of scholarship whose beginnings had been associated with the great library of Alexandria and the court of the Ptolemies, had made its impact on Rome in the second century. The first signs of its influence are to be seen in a handful of love epigrams in elegiacs, crude in their execution but clearly hellenistic in their inspiration, which we have from poets writing towards the end of the century—Lutatius Catulus, consul in 102 B.C., one of whose pieces is a translation of an epigram of Callimachus, Porcius Licinus, and Valerius Aedituus. A little later Laevius was experimenting with lyric metres and bizarreries of language in poems to which he gave the characteristically Alexandrian title of *Erotopaegnia*, and even, perhaps, introducing into Latin the hellenistic absurdities of pattern-poems.

These were in some sense the forerunners of a group of poets writing about the middle of the first century. Of that group Catullus is the only surviving representative and it is fair to conclude from the way in which his successors speak of him that he was its most outstanding member. We know from him, and from some traces they have left, who some of the others were—Calvus,

---

[1] This brief general account is intended to put the work of Catullus in perspective; for detail see the introductions to the several poems, especially 62, 63, 64, 66, and 68.

whose name is linked with Catullus' by later poets, Cinna, Cornificius, Ticidas, Furius Bibaculus. Of the work of these[1] we have fragments, meagre but sometimes revealing. Others again, no doubt, have vanished without a trace: but for some warm words from Catullus himself (35), we should never have heard of Caecilius of Comum. These were the poets whom Cicero called the 'moderns'—οἱ νεώτεροι (*Att.* vii. 2. 1: see on 64. 3) or *noui poetae* (*Orat.* 161: see on 116. 8)—who broke violently away from the old established tradition of Latin poetry, the epic and tragic tradition of Ennius, which Cicero himself admired and continued, and brought to poetry a new style and spirit, individual, subjective, and romantic, and new standards of technique. Why the revolution happened when it did, and what were the conditions, or the personal influences, that lay behind it, we have not the evidence to determine. But the connexion of a number of these new poets with Cisalpine Gaul, that remote, self-conscious, and highly developed province, may well be no accident, and it is probably not fanciful to ascribe a determining part in the development of their new poetry to the shadowy figure of the scholar, teacher, and poet Valerius Cato. Three of them speak warmly of him and his work and the terms in which they speak make the direction of his interest clear; he is *doctus*, writing for *docti*, and *doctrina*, 'taste', is the watchword of the new movement. Much of what these poets brought into Latin poetry came from Alexandria; just how much, our fragmentary knowledge of its vast literature does not allow us to say. From it they learned the lesson of form and pattern and the

---

[1] They used the same forms as Catullus: besides Cinna's *Zmyrna* (95) there were narrative poems by Calvus (*Io*) and Cornificius (*Glaucus*); Calvus and Ticidas wrote hymenaeals in glyconics; Calvus and Cinna used the scazon and all of them the hendecasyllable.

lesson of taking pains. But, if they were like Catullus, they were far from being slavish followers and they were far from depending on Alexandria alone. Writing in 45 B.C., some years after Catullus' death, Cicero, in an impassioned tribute to Ennius, brusquely dismisses the new poets as *cantores Euphorionis* (*Tusc. Disp.* iii. 45), but the first of them, at any rate, had not read only Euphorion and his like. Catullus translated Callimachus, but he translated Sappho too. That they were modern they knew, and they proudly and vigorously asserted it: Catullus' eulogy of Cinna (95), his persecution of a Suffenus (22) or a Volusius (36), his practical joke with Calvus (14) are all manifestoes of the new poetic creed—art for art's sake and perfection of shape and finish in small things. But in two respects they stood in sharp contrast to the Greek Alexandrians. For one thing, they were revolutionaries. The poetry of Alexandria, coming at the end of a long poetic history, was a literature of exhaustion, seeking novelty, in form and matter, because, as Callimachus said, everything had been done before. These Italian poets were leading a movement of revolt, dissatisfied with what had been done before them and with accepted standards of taste. For another, they were not academic observers of human emotion, detached from life; they not only wrote about human passions but felt them.

Alexandria has left its mark most clearly on the Peleus and Thetis (64), but it is only one of the strands that make up the texture of the poem. The subjective handling of the story and the complexity of the pattern are Alexandrian, and so are the mannerisms which hellenistic poets had developed to suit their purpose and their public—the precious allusion to which the learned reader can respond, the arresting devices of apostrophe and anaphora and exclamation, the novel tricks of rhythm. But much of his technique Catullus inherits from the old epic tradition; conventions of vocabulary, forms of phrase, alliteration—these he derives from the old poets and shares with their descendants, Lucretius and Cicero. And much he owes to no predecessor—not only the conciseness of form in that elaborate balancing of words within the line which was a lasting contribution to poetic style but an intimacy of feeling of which the sentimental diminutive, now first put to the service of high poetry, is a token. The blending of these strands is very clearly seen on a smaller scale in the elegiac poem 68. There pattern is at its most intricate and ingenious and allusion is pursued to the verge of pedantry; but there the traditional and un-Greek ornament of alliteration is employed in greatest profusion and there too the simplest of language is charged with the deepest feeling. Some hellenistic original must lie behind the conception of the Attis (63), a superb *tour de force* in its adaptation of Latin to an exacting metrical form; but the technique and the imaginative power of the language in which it is displayed are as much Catullus' own as the swing and the sparkle of the glyconic hymenaeal (61).

Doctrina, in its double aspect of awareness of a literary past and scrupulous concern for precision of form, is not less essential to the short lyric poems and the epigrams. Some of these pieces, perhaps, were tossed off on the spur of the moment to meet an occasion or to indulge a mood; but not so many as might at first sight appear. The intimacy of the address, to Calvus, or Varus, or Fabullus, is itself an artifice; these confidences were written to be read by other eyes within an admiring coterie. The lament for a dead bird (3), the invitation to dinner (13), the lines on a superannuated ship (4)—all these have prototypes in hellenistic epigram: Catullus knows them and their conceits, but with them his imagination has made something new, something immediate and personal and unmistakably Italian. The charming gaiety of the poem on Acme and Septimius (45) conceals a calculated nicety of pattern; the lines on Lesbia's kisses (7), the pitiful renunciation (11), the greeting to Sirmio (31), and the squib on Volusius' clumsy verses (36) are not less spontaneous because they turn to account, in earnest or in play, the romantic power of a name. The hendecasyllable came from Alexandria, as its name of Phalaecian reminds us; out of it Catullus makes a perfect vehicle for the brisk raciness or the pathetic simplicity of common Latin speech.

THE LATER HISTORY OF THE POEMS

On Virgil, his younger contemporary and his fellow-Transpadane, the influence of Catullus is very strong; borrowings and unmistakable verbal echoes show clearly how the longer poems were stored in his mind. Three times he takes a whole line from Catullus, altering only a word or two, and turns it to a new use;[1] again and again he introduces Catullan phrases and rhythms, sometimes in a context which recalls Catullus,[2] sometimes with a change of setting which suggests that the reminiscence was unconscious.[3] And there are echoes of thought as well as echoes of language; the pathetic similes with which he describes the deaths of Euryalus (*Aen*. ix. 435–7) and Pallas (xi. 68–70) recall Catullus' images of the cut and withered flower (11. 22, 62. 39).

---

[1] *Aen*. iv. 316—Cat. 64. 141, *Aen*. vi. 460—Cat. 66. 39, *Aen*. vii. 302—Cat. 64. 156.

[2] e.g. *Ecl*. 4. 46—Cat. 64. 327, *Aen*. vi. 27–30—Cat. 64. 113–15.

[3] e.g. *Geo*. i. 203 'atque illum in praeceps prono rapit alueus amni'—Cat. 65. 23 'atque illud prono praeceps agitur decursu'; *Aen*. iv. 599 'confectum aetate parentem'—Cat. 68. 119; *Aen*. xi. 581 'multae illam . . . optauere'—Cat. 62. 42.

Horace's one mention of Catullus is a disparaging reference, not to him, but to the contemporary littérateur who apes the 'advanced' modern school and ignores the virtues of the classics, 'simius iste / nil praeter Caluum et doctus cantare Catullum' (*Sat.* i. 10. 19). He was no doubt out of sympathy with the violent enthusiasm of the 'new' poets and the rebellious zest with which a Calvus or a Catullus flouted convention both in his writing and in his way of life; it may be, too, that he was less inclined to ignore their scurrilous attacks on Caesar than their victim himself had been.[1] But he did not disdain to read and remember Catullus' work in the lyric forms which he himself perfected. The sapphic ode to Septimius (i. 22) has echoes of Catullus' two poems in the same metre; the shape of Horace's second stanza is a reminiscence of poem 11 and his *dulce ridentem* came to him from poem 51. The repeated *otium* of ii. 16. 1–6 plainly recalls the stanza of Catullus which appears at the end of poem 51,[2] and the openings of the Diana odes (i. 21. 1–4, iii. 22. 1–4) have Catullus' poem 34 behind them.[3]

One of the occasional poems was well enough known to be the subject of a parody, probably soon after it was written. In the tenth poem of the *Catalepton*, the collection of verses, very much in the Catullan manner, which is attributed to the young Virgil (and some of which may be Virgil's work), Catullus' address to his yacht (4) is ingeniously turned to fit a *nouveau riche* of Cisalpina;

---

[1] Tac. *Ann.* iv. 34. 8 'carmina Bibaculi et Catulli referta contumeliis Caesarum leguntur: sed ipse diuus Augustus, ipse diuus Iulius et tulere ista et reliquere, haud facile dixerim moderatione magis an sapientia'; cf. Suet. *Iul.* 73.

[2] There is a curious piece of evidence for the popular currency of this stanza in Catullus' own time, or soon after it, in the witticism of Publilius Syrus at a party where Catullus' phrase was joked about: Macrobius ii. 7. 6 'ioculari super cena exorta quaestione quidnam esset "molestum otium", alio aliud opinante ille "podagrici pedes" dixit'.   [3] See also nn. on 29. 6–7, 42. 24.

whoever wrote it, the *jeu d'esprit* comes from Catullus' native province. The sixth poem of the same collection quotes (or misquotes) Catullus' 'socer generque, perdidistis omnia' (29. 24) as a familiar line.

The first century A.D. was an age of light verse and it was Catullus' lighter verses that were then remembered. His fellow-countryman the elder Pliny, dedicating his *Natural History* to Vespasian, quotes a hendecasyllable from the dedication to Cornelius Nepos (1. 3–4), deliberately altering it to conform to the stricter metrical fashion of his own time;[1] in the younger Pliny Catullus is still paired with Calvus, as he had been a century before, but his *meus Catullus* (i. 16. 5, iv. 27. 4) points to a particular personal devotion. For Quintilian, who quotes Catullus four times,[2] the lines on Arrius and his aspirates (84) are 'famous' (i. 5. 20 *nobile epigramma*). To Martial *tener Catullus* is the acknowledged master of hendecasyllable and scazon; his own ambition is to rank second to him and to do for his native Bilbilis what Catullus has done for Verona. His favourites are the *passer*-poems (2, 3) and the *basia*-poems (5, 7),[3] but he draws on the lyrics freely for turns and phrases.

Catullus was still part of the equipment of the man of letters and his readers in the second century. Apuleius (to whom we owe Lesbia's real name) quotes him twice for his own fantastic purposes (*Apologia*, 6, 11); Gellius

---

[1] *Praef.* 1 'namque tu solebas nugas esse aliquid meas putare—ut obiter emolliam Catullum conterraneum meum . . . ille enim, ut scis, permutatis prioribus syllabis duriusculum se fecit quam uolebat existimari a Veraniolis suis et Fabullis'. By Pliny's time a spondaic first foot had become the norm (in Martial it is invariable), and the iambus offends him.

[2] 29. 1–2 (without author's name), 62. 45 (where he guarantees the text), 86. 4, 93. 2 (where he has forgotten the author's name).

[3] There is a double allusion in xi. 6. 14–16: 'da nunc basia, sed Catulliana: / quae si tot fuerint quot ille dixit, / donabo tibi passerem Catulli.'

discusses the text of poem 27, testifying that it had been corrupted by his day, and quotes 92 to clear up a point of language. Thereafter Catullus shared the fate of authors whose works were not in the school syllabus: copies were not in demand and the transmission of his text became precarious. But through the darkening ages there is a thin stream of quotation, probably at second hand, in the grammarians and lexicographers down to Isidore in the seventh century, the learned Spanish bishop who gathered up in his encyclopaedia many fragments of antiquity which would otherwise have perished: he quotes, for their antiquarian interest, two scraps of Catullus, and his false ascription of one of them to Calvus is perhaps a last echo of the literary tradition which associated Catullus and his friend (*Etymol.* vi. 12. 3, xix. 33. 3).

After Isidore such few Catullan tags as appear anonymously in medieval writings are derived from glossaries and compilations. In the next seven centuries there are only two evidences of the existence of a text of Catullus. The first comes in the ninth century, when the manuscript now called Codex Thuaneus,[1] an anthology of Latin poetry, was written; it contains poem 62 with the title 'Epithalamium Catulli'. The second is in the middle of the tenth century, when the see of Verona was held, very insecurely, by a remarkable man, the Fleming Rather,[2] who in the course of a stormy career found time not only to read such authors as Plautus and Catullus but also to organize the *scriptorium* of Verona and to play an important part in the trans-

---

[1] From the name of a former owner, the scholar Jacques de Thou (1553–1617).

[2] On Rather and his work see Giuseppe Billanovich in *Italia Medioevale e Humanistica* ii (1959), 103 ff.; he shows that Rather not only supervised the writing of the Laurentianus 63. 19 of Livy but wrote part of it himself.

mission of the first decade of Livy. In 965 he wrote in a sermon 'Catullum nunquam antea lectum . . . lego' (Migne, *Patr. Lat.* cxxxvi, col. 752).

After Rather darkness falls on Catullus again and lasts till the latter part of the thirteenth century. Towards the end of that century, or early in the fourteenth, a lawyer of Padua, Hieremias de Montagnone, copied seven extracts from Catullus (with references to their position in a text) into an anthology which he called *Compendium Moralium Notabilium*, and in 1329 an anonymous Veronese included part of poem 22 (with title) in a similar compilation, *Liber Florum Moralium Auctoritatum*. So, in the unexpected role of a moral preceptor, which he is made to share with Ovid and Martial, Catullus enters the modern world.

The clue to this sudden emergence of an author who had been unknown for more than 300 years is given by an epigram which appears in two of our earliest surviving manuscripts, copied into them from their common source with an ascription to Benvenuto Campesani, a Lombard from Vicenza who died in 1323 (see p. 82); three couplets, put into the mouth of Catullus himself, declare that a manuscript of his poems was restored to his native Verona by a fellow-countryman. The lines do not reveal where the book was found or who the finder was; it was probably the book which Rather read and (since the first line need no more be taken literally than the last) it was probably in the Cathedral Library at Verona, left there by Rather when he had to abandon his see in 968. In any case, that manuscript, thus recovered only to be lost again before long (it seems) for ever, was the unique source from which our text of Catullus is derived.

The three surviving fourteenth-century manuscripts are the descendants of that lost Veronese archetype (denoted by the symbol **V**), and from their readings its text has to be recovered. They are Oxoniensis (**O**: Canonicianus Class. Lat. 30 in the Bodleian Library), Parisinus (**G**: now Lat. 14137 in the Bibliothèque Nationale, formerly in the library of the Abbey of St. Germain-des-Prés—hence its symbol), and Romanus (**R**: Ottobonianus Lat. 1829 in the Vatican Library).[1] **O**, the oldest, was copied directly from the archetype by an ignorant but conscientious scribe who had the virtue of trying to copy faithfully what he did not understand. **G**, which carries the date 1375 in a subscription, and **R**, which was probably written somewhat later, were derived from **V** through a common intermediary (**X**) whose scribe, more literate and enterprising than the writer of **O**, often used his judgement on what he saw and offered alternative readings which **G** and **R** preserve. For poem 62 we have another witness in the ninth-century Thuaneus (**T**: now Lat. 8071 in the Bibliothèque Nationale), whose errors (notably the omission after l. 32) show that it represents the same tradition.

Petrarch had read the new Catullus by 1347, perhaps in the Verona manuscript, perhaps in a copy of his own; that Catullus does not appear among those 'special books' (*libri peculiares*) which he constantly reread is not surprising, since the absence of divisions between the poems, which were written for long stretches without a break, combined with a multitude of corruptions, must have made much of the text difficult or even unintelligible.[2] Of the errors which **O**, **G**, and **R** inherited from **V** a large number were removed by the correctors

---

[1] Specimens of O, G, and T are given by Chatelain in *Paléographie des classiques latins* (Paris, 1884–92), plates xiv–xva, of R by W. G. Hale (its discoverer) in *Amer. Journ. of Archaeology*, 2nd ser., i (1897), plate i.

[2] See B. L. Ullman, *Studies in the Italian Renaissance* (Rome, 1955), pp. 117 ff., 194 ff.

of **G** and **R** (**g**, **r**: one of the correctors of **R** was Coluccio Salutati (1331–1406), chancellor of Florence, who owned it[1]) and by the writers of the copies made from **O**, **G**, or **R** in the fifteenth century. About a hundred of these are extant; the strata into which they have been divided by the editor of the text are indicated in the list of *sigla* (p. xxix). Many more errors were corrected by the humanists of the late fifteenth century and the sixteenth whose work appears in the series of printed editions beginning in 1472—first the Italians, Calphurnius (1481), Parthenius (1485), Avantius (1495, 1502, 1534), Palladius (1496), Baptista and Alexander Guarinus (1521), then Muretus (1554), Statius (1566), and Scaliger (1577), the first editor in northern Europe. More serious than the errors of **V** are its omissions: by the time when it was copied the text was mutilated. Not only are there omissions of several lines within three poems[2] and of a single line in four others;[3] there is evidence that whole poems had perished. The lines 14*b* are clearly the remnant of a lost poem; 2*b* looks like a fragment of the same kind; and the last four lines of 51 are probably another.

[1] Billanovich (see p. xxv n. 2 above) gives strong ground for believing that the writer of G was another eminent man of affairs, Antonio da Legnago, chancellor to the ruler of Verona.

[2] After 61. 78 and 107, 62. 32, 68. 46 (and probably 141).

[3] After 34. 2, 51. 7, 64. 23, 65. 8; the third of these, which was not obvious, was revealed, and partially repaired, by the accident that half of the missing line had been quoted by the fourth-century Verona Scholia on Virgil.

SIGLA

CODICES:

   V = archetypum (fons communis codd. O et X)

   O = Oxoniensis Canonicianus class. lat. 30 s. XIV

   X = fons communis codd. G et R

      G = Parisinus lat. 14137 anni MCCCLXXV

      R = Vaticanus Ottobonianus lat. 1829 s. XIV ex.

   T = Parisinus lat. 8071 s. IX (*continet carmen lxii*)

   OI = O *nondum correctus, similiter GI RI.*

FONTES CONIECTVRARVM MANV SCRIPTI:

   r = corrector(es) cod. R

   m = Venetus Marcianus lat. xii. 80 (4167) s. XV in.

   g = corrector(es) cod. G

Coniecturae e codicibus recentioribus ductae his notis insignitae sunt:

   α = nescio quis ante annum MCCCCXII

β =	,,	,,	,,	MCCCCXXIV
γ =	,,	,,	,,	MCCCCLII
δ, ϵ =	,,	,,	medium s. XV	
ζ, η =	,,	,,	annum MCCCCLX	
θ =	,,	,,	,,	MCCCCLXVIII

FONTES CONIECTVRARVM TYPIS IMPRESSI:

1472 = editio Veneta anni MCCCCLXXII; *1473* = Parmensis a. 'LXXIII; *ed. Rom.* = anonyma a. circa 'LXXV; *Calph(urnius)* = Vicentina a. 'LXXXI; *Parth(enius)* = Brixiensis a. 'LXXXV; *Auantius* = Emendationes eius a. 'XCV; *Pall(adius)* = Veneta a. 'XCVI; *Aldina* = Veneta a. MDII; *Guarinus* = Veneta a. MDXXI; *Auantius*[3] = Veneta apud Trincauellium a. circa MDXXXV.

CATVLLI CARMINA

I

Cvi dono lepidum nouum libellum
arida modo pumice expolitum?
Corneli, tibi: namque tu solebas
meas esse aliquid putare nugas
iam tum, cum ausus es unus Italorum   5
omne aeuum tribus explicare cartis
doctis, Iuppiter, et laboriosis.
quare habe tibi quidquid hoc libelli
qualecumque; quod, ⟨o⟩ patrona uirgo,
plus uno maneat perenne saeclo.   10

2

Passer, deliciae meae puellae,
quicum ludere, quem in sinu tenere,
cui primum digitum dare appetenti
et acris solet incitare morsus,
cum desiderio meo nitenti   5

---

1. 1 *citat Ausonius eclogarum* i. 1 (*p.* 120 *Schenkl, p.* 86 *Peiper*); 1–2 *Isidorus etymologiarum* vi. 12. 3; 1, 2 *et* 4 *Marius Victorinus, ars gramm.* (*p.* 148 *Keil*), *Caesius Bassus de metris* (*p.* 261 *K.*), *Terentianus de metris* 2562–4 (*p.* 401 *K.*); *cf. Atilium Fortunatianum* (*p.* 298 *K.*).   2 *Seruius ad Vergili aen.* xii. 587 'in pumice' autem masculino genere posuit . . . licet Catullus dixerit feminino.   3–4 *Plinius hist. nat.* i *praef.* 1 namque tu solebas nugas esse aliquid meas putare, ut obiter emolliam Catullum conterraneum meum.
2. 1 *citant Caesius Bassus* (*p.* 260 *K.*), *Atilius Fort.* (*p.* 293 *K.*), *fragmentum quod Censorini dicitur de metris* (*p.* 614 *K.*).

---

1. 2 arida *ex Seruio Itali*: arido *V*   5 tum . . . es *ε*: tamen . . . est *V*   8 tibi habe *V*: *corr.* *η*   libelli *al.* mei *X* (*al.* mei *del.* *r*)   9 o *add.* *θ*   qualecunque quidem est, patroni ut ergo *Bergk*   10 perire *O*
2. 3 cui *O* (*in margine*) *r*: qui *V*   appetenti *r*: at petenti *V* (*al.* patenti *X*, *al.* parenti *g*)

carum nescio quid lubet iocari,
et solaciolum sui doloris,
credo, ut tum grauis acquiescat ardor:
tecum ludere sicut ipsa possem
et tristis animi leuare curas!   10

2ᵇ

*   *   *

tam gratum est mihi quam ferunt puellae
pernici aureolum fuisse malum
quod zonam soluit diu ligatam.

3

LVGETE, o Veneres Cupidinesque,
et quantum est hominum uenustiorum:
passer mortuus est meae puellae,
passer, deliciae meae puellae,
quem plus illa oculis suis amabat.   5
nam mellitus erat suamque norat
ipsam tam bene quam puella matrem,
nec sese a gremio illius mouebat,
sed circumsiliens modo huc modo illuc
ad solam dominam usque pipiabat;   10

2ᵇ. 3 *citat Priscianus, inst.* i. 22 quod z. s. d. ligatam; *cf. Carm. epigr.* 1504. 49 (*Buecheler*) zonulam ut soluas diu ligatam.

---

6 karum *V*   libet *V* (al. iubet *O*)   7 et *V*: ut *B. Guarinus*
8 tum . . . acquiescat *B. Guarinus*: cum . . . acquiescet *V* (*locus nondum expeditus*)   9 tecum al. secum *O*   ludere al. luderem *G*
(luderem *fortasse O1*)   posse *Vossius* (*deinde* curas,)
   2ᵇ. *Ad* 2. 10: ' *Post hoc carmen in codice antiquissimo et manu scripto ingens sequitur fragmentum*' *A. Guarinus*   3 ligatam (*in margine* '*erat* negatam') *r*, ligatam al. negatam *m*, al. ligatam *add. g*: negatam *V*
   3. 9 circum siliens *rg*: circum silens *V* (al. siliens *O*)   illuc *O*,
illuc mouebat *X* (*corr. rg*)   10 pipiabat *codd. Harl. et Brix. in margine* (*idem Vossius*), pipilabat *ζη*: piplabat *V*

qui nunc it per iter tenebricosum
illud, unde negant redire quemquam.
at uobis male sit, malae tenebrae
Orci, quae omnia bella deuoratis:
tam bellum mihi passerem abstulistis.   15
o factum male! o miselle passer!
tua nunc opera meae puellae
flendo turgiduli rubent ocelli.

4

PHASELVS ille, quem uidetis, hospites,
ait fuisse nauium celerrimus,
neque ullius natantis impetum trabis
nequisse praeterire, siue palmulis
opus foret uolare siue linteo.   5
et hoc negat minacis Hadriatici
negare litus insulasue Cycladas
Rhodumque nobilem horridamque Thraciam
Propontida trucemue Ponticum sinum,
ubi iste post phaselus antea fuit   10

---

3. 12 *citat Seneca, ludus de morte Claudii* 11. 6; *cf. Carm. epigr.*
1504. 11. 16 *Cf. Carm. epigr.* 1512. 4 o factum male, Myia, quod
peristi.

4. *imitatur auctor carminis Vergiliani catalepton* 10.   1 *citant
Marius Victorinus(p.* 134 *K. et alibi), Terentianus de metris* 2277
(*p.* 393 *K.*), '*Censorini*' *de metris* (*p.* 612 *K.*).   25–26 *Priscianus,
inst.* ix. 49; 25–27 *Charisius* (*p.* 252 *K.*) *et Diomedes* (*p.* 344 *K.*).

---

11 tenebricosum *Parth.*: tenebrosum *V*   12 illud *V* (al. illuc *O*)
14 orci quae *r*: orcique *V* (al. quae *G*)   bella, *supra scripto* id est
pulcra *OG*(*V ?*)   16 o (*1⁰*) *r*: bonum *V*   o miselle *1473*: bonus ille
V (bellus ille *r*)

4. 2 ait *Calph.*: aiunt *V*   celerrimus *Parth.*: celer(r)imum *V*
3 ullius *Calph.*: illius *V*   trabis *Auantius* (trabis *ante* impetum *iam
Calph.*): tardis *V*   4 nequisse *θ*: neque esse *V*   4–5 siue
. . . siue *r*: sine . . . sine *V*   6 negant *r*   minacis *r*: mina
ei *V*   8 traciam *r*: tractam *V*

comata silua; nam Cytorio in iugo
loquente saepe sibilum edidit coma.
Amastri Pontica et Cytore buxifer,
tibi haec fuisse et esse cognitissima
ait phaselus: ultima ex origine 15
tuo stetisse dicit in cacumine,
tuo imbuisse palmulas in aequore,
et inde tot per impotentia freta
erum tulisse, laeua siue dextera
uocaret aura, siue utrumque Iuppiter 20
simul secundus incidisset in pedem;
neque ulla uota litoralibus deis
sibi esse facta, cum ueniret a mari
nouissimo hunc ad usque limpidum lacum.
sed haec prius fuere: nunc recondita 25
senet quiete seque dedicat tibi,
gemelle Castor et gemelle Castoris.

5

VIVAMVS, mea Lesbia, atque amemus,
rumoresque senum seueriorum
omnes unius aestimemus assis!
soles occidere et redire possunt:
nobis cum semel occidit breuis lux, 5
nox est perpetua una dormienda.
da mi basia mille, deinde centum,
dein mille altera, dein secunda centum,
deinde usque altera mille, deinde centum.
dein, cum milia multa fecerimus, 10

11 cytorio η, citherio r: citeorio V (citeono O) 13 cytore η,
cithori r: citheri V 14 cognotissima V 17 tuas X 20 uocare cura V: corr. r 23 a mari r`(-rei Lachmann): amaret V
24 nouissimo ζη: -ime V 25 hoc X (corr. r) 27 castor r:
castrum O, castrum al. castorum X
5. 3 estinemus O, extimemus X 8 dein mille Aldina, deinde
mi rmg: deinde mille V dein Aldina, da rmg: deinde V 10 dein
η: deinde V

conturbabimus illa, ne sciamus,
aut ne quis malus inuidere possit,
cum tantum sciat esse basiorum.

7

QVAERIS, quot mihi basiationes
tuae, Lesbia, sint satis superque.
quam magnus numerus Libyssae harenae
lasarpiciferis iacet Cyrenis
oraclum Iouis inter aestuosi   5
et Batti ueteris sacrum sepulcrum;
aut quam sidera multa, cum tacet nox,
furtiuos hominum uident amores:
tam te basia multa basiare
uesano satis et super Catullo est,   10
quae nec pernumerare curiosi
possint nec mala fascinare lingua.

8

MISER Catulle, desinas ineptire,
et quod uides perisse perditum ducas.
fulsere quondam candidi tibi soles,
cum uentitabas quo puella ducebat
amata nobis quantum amabitur nulla.   5
ibi illa multa cum iocosa fiebant,
quae tu uolebas nec puella nolebat,
fulsere uere candidi tibi soles.
nunc iam illa non uolt: tu quoque inpote⟨ns noli⟩,

---

11 conturbauimus V: corr. θ   13 tantum r: tantus V
7. 1 quot α: quod V   4 lasarpici feris al. fretis X, lasarpici
fecis O   tyrenis O, tyrrenis ut uidetur G1, tyrenis al. cyrenis
Rmg   5 oradum V: corr. r   6 batti ed. Rom.: beati O,
beati al. beari X   9 basia] basiei O, basiei al. basia X
  8. 4 quo rmg: quod V   6 cum V: tum Rmg   9 impotens
r: inpote V (imp- X)   noli om. V: add. Auantius

nec quae fugit sectare, nec miser uiue,   10
sed obstinata mente perfer, obdura.
uale, puella. iam Catullus obdurat,
nec te requiret nec rogabit inuitam.
at tu dolebis, cum rogaberis nulla.
scelesta, uae te, quae tibi manet uita?   15
quis nunc te adibit? cui uideberis bella?
quem nunc amabis? cuius esse diceris?
quem basiabis? cui labella mordebis?
at tu, Catulle, destinatus obdura.

9

VERANI, omnibus e meis amicis
antistans mihi milibus trecentis,
uenistine domum ad tuos penates
fratresque unanimos anumque matrem?
uenisti. o mihi nuntii beati!   5
uisam te incolumem audiamque Hiberum
narrantem loca, facta, nationes,
ut mos est tuus, applicansque collum
iucundum os oculosque suauiabor.
o quantum est hominum beatiorum.   10
quid me laetius est beatiusue?

10

VARVS me meus ad suos amores
uisum duxerat e foro otiosum,
scortillum, ut mihi tum repente uisum est,
non sane illepidum neque inuenustum.
huc ut uenimus, incidere nobis   5
sermones uarii, in quibus, quid esset

---

15 uae *B. Venator*: ne *V*   18 cui *X*, cum *O*
9. 1 uerani ζ: ueranni *V*   e *om. O*   2 antistans *Auantius*:
antistas *V* (antistes *r*)   4 unanimos η: uno animo *V*   anumque *Faernus*: sanamque *O*, suamque *al.* sanam *X*   9 suabior *V*:
corr. ζη
10. 1 uar(r)us γ: uarius *V*   mens *OG1*   3 tum *Gr*: tunc *V*

iam Bithynia, quo modo se haberet,
et quonam mihi profuisset aere.
respondi id quod erat, nihil neque ipsis
nec praetoribus esse nec cohorti   10
cur quisquam caput unctius referret,
praesertim quibus esset irrumator
praetor, nec faceret pili cohortem.
'at certe tamen,' inquiunt 'quod illic
natum dicitur esse, comparasti   15
ad lecticam homines.' ego, ut puellae
unum me facerem beatiorem,
'non' inquam 'mihi tam fuit maligne,
ut, prouincia quod mala incidisset,
non possem octo homines parare rectos.'   20
at mi nullus erat nec hic neque illic,
fractum qui ueteris pedem grabati
in collo sibi collocare posset.
hic illa, ut decuit cinaediorem,
'quaeso' inquit 'mihi, mi Catulle, paulum   25
istos commoda: nam uolo ad Serapim
deferri.' 'mane,' inquii puellae,
'istud quod modo dixeram me habere,
fugit me ratio: meus sodalis—
Cinna est Gaius—is sibi parauit.   30
uerum, utrum illius an mei, quid ad me?
utor tam bene quam mihi pararim.
sed tu insulsa male et molesta uiuis,
per quam non licet esse neglegentem.'

7 se *r*: posse *V*   8 et quoniam *O*, et quoniam al. quonam
X: ecquonam *Statius*, *fortasse recte* (*cf.* 28. 6)   aere ζ: here *V*
9 neque ipsis *1472*, nec ipsis ζη: neque nec in ipsis *V* (al. neque ipsis
nec *G*, al. neque ipsis *R*), neque in ipsis *mg*   10 nec (*1º*) *om. R*
(al. nec *in margine*): nunc *Westphal*   11 referet *R*   13 nec *O*,
non al. nec *X* facerent *r*   16 leticam hominis *V*   22 fractum
qui *r*: fractumque *V*   24 decuit θ: docuit *V*   26 com(m)oda
X, comodam *O*   sarapim al. -e- (*i.e.* serapim) *G*   27 deserti *O*,
deserti al. deferri *X*   inquii *Scaliger*: me inquit *V*   30 cinna
est caius *1473*: cuma est grauis *V*   31 ad *r*: a *V*   33 tu insulsa *r*: tulsa *O*, tu insula *X*

II

Fvri et Aureli, comites Catulli,
siue in extremos penetrabit Indos,
litus ut longe resonante Eoa
  tunditur unda,
siue in Hyrcanos Arabasue molles,   5
seu Sagas sagittiferosue Parthos,
siue quae septemgeminus colorat
  aequora Nilus,
siue trans altas gradietur Alpes,
Caesaris uisens monimenta magni,   10
Gallicum Rhenum horribile aequor ulti-
  mosque Britannos,
omnia haec, quaecumque feret uoluntas
caelitum, temptare simul parati,
pauca nuntiate meae puellae   15
  non bona dicta.
cum suis uiuat ualeatque moechis,
quos simul complexa tenet trecentos,
nullum amans uere, sed identidem omnium
  ilia rumpens;   20
nec meum respectet, ut ante, amorem,
qui illius culpa cecidit uelut prati
ultimi flos, praetereunte postquam
  tactus aratro est.

12

Marrvcine Asini, manu sinistra
non belle uteris: in ioco atque uino

tollis lintea neglegentiorum.
hoc salsum esse putas? fugit te, inepte:
quamuis sordida res et inuenusta est.   5
non credis mihi? crede Pollioni
fratri, qui tua furta uel talento
mutari uelit: est enim leporum
differtus puer ac facetiarum.
quare aut hendecasyllabos trecentos   10
exspecta, aut mihi linteum remitte,
quod me non mouet aestimatione,
uerum est mnemosynum mei sodalis.
nam sudaria Saetaba ex Hiberis
miserunt mihi muneri Fabullus   15
et Veranius: haec amem necesse est
ut Veraniolum meum et Fabullum.

13

CENABIS bene, mi Fabulle, apud me
paucis, si tibi di fauent, diebus,
si tecum attuleris bonam atque magnam
cenam, non sine candida puella
et uino et sale et omnibus cachinnis.   5
haec si, inquam, attuleris, uenuste noster,
cenabis bene; nam tui Catulli
plenus sacculus est aranearum.
sed contra accipies meros amores
seu quid suauius elegantiusue est: 10
nam unguentum dabo, quod meae puellae

4 salsum al. falsum G, falsum al. salsum OR (cf. 14. 16, 30. 1)
7 frater O   8 uoluit O   9 differtus Passerat: dissertus O,
disertus X   13 est mnemosinon Calph.: est nemo sinum X,
nemo est sinum O   14 settaba O, sethaba X   ex hiberis 1472
(-eis Lachmann): exhibere V   15 numeri O, numeri al. muneri
X   16 hec al. hoc R   amem δ: ameni V (almeni R1)   17 ut
θ: et V
    13. 6 inquam δ: unquam V   8 saculus V   9 meros X,
meos O   10 quid γ: qui O, qui al. quod X

donarunt Veneres Cupidinesque,
quod tu cum olfacies, deos rogabis,
totum ut te faciant, Fabulle, nasum.

14

Ni te plus oculis meis amarem,
iucundissime Calue, munere isto
odissem te odio Vatiniano:
nam quid feci ego quidue sum locutus
cur me tot male perderes poetis?   5
isti di mala multa dent clienti,
qui tantum tibi misit impiorum.
quod si, ut suspicor, hoc nouum ac repertum
munus dat tibi Sulla litterator,
non est mi male, sed bene ac beate,   10
quod non dispereunt tui labores.
di magni, horribilem et sacrum libellum!
quem tu scilicet ad tuum Catullum.
misti, continuo ut die periret,
Saturnalibus, optimo dierum!   15
non non hoc tibi, false, sic abibit.
nam, si luxerit, ad librariorum
curram scrinia, Caesios, Aquinos,
Suffenum, omnia colligam uenena,
ac te his suppliciis remunerabor.   20
uos hinc interea ualete abite

14. 9 *Martianus Capella* iii. 229 hoc etiam Catullus quidam, non insuauis poeta, commemorat dicens 'munus dat tibi Sylla litterator'. 15 *Macrobius, sat.* ii. 1. 8 'Sat. opt. dierum', ut ait Veronensis poeta.

14. 1 ni δ (nei *Lachmann*): ne *V*   5 male *1472*: malis *V*
6 dent ζη: dant *V*   9 sulla δ: si illa *V*   10 mi η: mi(c)hi *V*
14 misti η: misisti *V*   15 opimo al. optimo *X*, oppinio *O*
16 hoc γδ: hec *V*   false *OR*, salse al. false *G*   sic γδ: fit *OG*, sit
Rmg   abibit *rmg*: adhibit *O*, adbibit *X*   17 luserit al. -x- *G*
18 curram δ: curam *O*, cur tam *X*   scrinea *Rmg*   19 suphe-
num *1472*: suffenam *V*   20 ac α: hac *V*   tibi hiis supplitus *O*

illuc, unde malum pedem attulistis,
saecli incommoda, pessimi poetae.

14^b

Si qui forte mearum ineptiarum
lectores eritis manusque uestras
non horrebitis admouere nobis,

*   *   *

17

O Colonia, quae cupis ponte ludere longo,
et salire paratum habes, sed uereris inepta
crura ponticuli axulis stantis in rediuiuis,
ne supinus eat cauaque in palude recumbat:
sic tibi bonus ex tua pons libidine fiat,   5
in quo uel Salisubsali sacra suscipiantur,
munus hoc mihi maximi da, Colonia, risus.
quendam municipem meum de tuo uolo ponte
ire praecipitem in lutum per caputque pedesque,
uerum totius ut lacus putidaeque paludis   10
liuidissima maximeque est profunda uorago.
insulsissimus est homo, nec sapit pueri instar
bimuli tremula patris dormientis in ulna.
cui cum sit uiridissimo nupta flore puella
et puella tenellulo delicatior haedo,   15
adseruanda nigerrimis diligentius uuis,

23 secli η: seculi V

14^b. *a praecedentibus seiunxerunt B. Guarinus et Auantius.* 'In
codice antiquo non leguntur hic' nescio quis in cod. Parisino lat. 8458
saec. xv exeuntis; similiter Romanus Corsinianus 43. D. 20

17. 1 o culonia que δ (colonia quae θ): oculo in aque V   ludere
ed. Rom. (loedere *Scaliger*): ledere V   3 axulis *Hand* (acsuleis
Ellis), assulis *Statius*: ac sulcis V   stantis *Vossius*: tantis V
6 suscipiant V: corr. *Auantius*   10 putidaeque θ: pudiceque V
paludis η: paludes V   14 cui cum *Pall.* (quoi cum *Scaliger*, quoi
iam θ): cui iocum V   15 et δ: ut V   edo V

ludere hanc sinit ut lubet, nec pili facit uni,
nec se subleuat ex sua parte, sed uelut alnus
in fossa Liguri iacet suppernata securi,
tantundem omnia sentiens quam si nulla sit usquam; 20
talis iste meus stupor nil uidet, nihil audit,
ipse qui sit, utrum sit an non sit, id quoque nescit.
nunc eum uolo de tuo ponte mittere pronum,
si pote stolidum repente excitare ueternum,
et supinum animum in graui derelinquere caeno, 25
ferream ut soleam tenaci in uoragine mula.

22

SVFFENVS iste, Vare, quem probe nosti,
homo est uenustus et dicax et urbanus,
idemque longe plurimos facit uersus.
puto esse ego illi milia aut decem aut plura
perscripta, nec sic ut fit in palimpseston 5
relata: cartae regiae, noui libri,
noui umbilici, lora rubra membranae,
derecta plumbo et pumice omnia aequata.
haec cum legas tu, bellus ille et urbanus
Suffenus unus caprimulgus aut fossor 10
rursus uidetur: tantum abhorret ac mutat.
hoc quid putemus esse? qui modo scurra
aut si quid hac re scitius uidebatur,
idem infaceto est infacetior rure,

17. 19 *citat sub uoce 'suppernati' Festus p.* 396 *L.*

---

17 uni al. uim *R*   18 se *1472*: me *V*   19 superata *V*: *corr.*
Statius   21 meus *V*: merus *Passerat* (*fortasse recte*; *cf.* 13. 9)
nil] nichil *V*   22 qui *V*: quid *mg*   23 nunc cum *X* (al. hunc
eum *R*), nunc uolo *O*   24 potest olidum *V*: *corr. Victorius*
excitare ζη: exitare *V*   25 delinquere *X*   26 mulla *X*
22. 3 idemque al. itemque *G*   5 sic δ: sit *V*   palimpsesto
1473, -ton *Marcilius*: palmisepto *V*   6 noui *1473* (nouei *Lachmann*),
nouem β: noue *V*   7 membrane *V*: membrana *Auantius*   8 derecta *Statius*: detecta *V*   13 scitius *L. Mueller*, tritius *Pontanus*,
tersius *Peiper*: tristius *V*   14 infacetior θ: infaceto *V*

simul poemata attigit, neque idem unquam   15
aeque est beatus ac poema cum scribit:
tam gaudet in se tamque se ipse miratur.
nimirum idem omnes fallimur, neque est quisquam
quem non in aliqua re uidere Suffenum
possis. suus cuique attributus est error;   20
sed non uidemus manticae quod in tergo est.

23

FVRI, cui neque seruus est neque arca
nec cimex neque araneus neque ignis,
uerum est et pater et nouerca, quorum
dentes uel silicem comesse possunt,
est pulcre tibi cum tuo parente   5
et cum coniuge lignea parentis.
nec mirum: bene nam ualetis omnes,
pulcre concoquitis, nihil timetis,
non incendia, non graues ruinas,
non facta impia, non dolos ueneni,   10
non casus alios periculorum.
atqui corpora sicciora cornu
aut siquid magis aridum est habetis
sole et frigore et esuritione.
quare non tibi sit bene ac beate?   15
a te sudor abest, abest saliua,
mucusque et mala pituita nasi.
hanc ad munditiem adde mundiorem,

22. 21 *citat Porphyrion ad Horati serm.* ii. 3. 299.

---

15 neque *X*, uel neque nec *O* (*cf.* 23. 2)   16 ac *β*: ha *V*
17 tamquam *V*: *corr.* *r*   18 neque *X*, nec *O*
23. 1 Furei *V*   seruo *O*, seruo al. seruus *X* (*post* est *R1*)
2 neque (*1⁰*)] al neque *O*, animal neque *X* (*habuitne* nec al. neque *V ?*)
7 nec *G* (ni *g*), ne *O*, ne al. nec *R*   9 ruinas *G*, minas *OR*
10 facta *V*: fata *g*, furta *Haupt* (*cf.* 68. 140)   12 atqui *η*: aut
qui *V*   13 aridum magis *V*: *corr.* *1472*   15 sit *O*, si *X*
16 abest *alterum om. O*   17 muc(c)usque *ζη*: muccusue *V*

quod culus tibi purior salillo est,
nec toto decies cacas in anno;   20
atque id durius est faba et lapillis,
quod tu si manibus teras fricesque,
non umquam digitum inquinare posses.
haec tu commoda tam beata, Furi,
noli spernere nec putare parui,   25
et sestertia quae soles precari
centum desine: nam sat es beatus.

24

O QVI flosculus es Iuuentiorum,
non horum modo, sed quot aut fuerunt
aut posthac aliis erunt in annis,
mallem diuitias Midae dedisses
isti, cui neque seruus est neque arca,   5
quam sic te sineres ab illo amari.
'qui? non est homo bellus?' inquies. est:
sed bello huic neque seruus est neque arca.
hoc tu quam lubet abice eleuaque:
nec seruum tamen ille habet neque arcam.   10

26

FVRI, uillula uestra non ad Austri
flatus opposita est neque ad Fauoni
nec saeui Boreae aut Apheliotae,
uerum ad milia quindecim et ducentos.
o uentum horribilem atque pestilentem!   5

19 cuius *V*: cuius al. culus *R*, culus al. cuius *mg*   21 lupillis
Gulielmius   24 tu *η*: tua *V*   27 sat es beatus *Calph.*, satis
beatu's *Bergk*: satis beatus *V*

24. 1 es *η*: est *V*   2 quot *β*: quod *V*   4 Midae dedisses
Vossius: mi dededisses *O*, mi dedisses *X*   5 qui *V* (qui al. cui
Rmg) neque (*1º*)] nec *O*, neque *G* (al. nec *add. g*), nec al. neque *Rm*
neque (*2º*)] nec al. neque *R*   7 qui *X*, quid *O*   9 hec *G*
quam *O*, qua *G*, quam al. qua *R*

26. 1 uestra *O*, nostra *X*   2 *uersum om. O*   fauonii *X*

27

MINISTER uetuli puer Falerni
inger mi calices amariores,
ut lex Postumiae iubet magistrae
ebrioso acino ebriosioris.
at uos quo lubet hinc abite, lymphae,   5
uini pernicies, et ad seueros
migrate. hic merus est Thyonianus.

29

QVIS hoc potest uidere, quis potest pati,
nisi impudicus et uorax et aleo,
Mamurram habere quod comata Gallia
habebat uncti et ultima Britannia?
cinaede Romule, haec uidebis et feres?   5
et ille nunc superbus et superfluens
perambulabit omnium cubilia,
ut albulus columbus aut Adoneus?

---

27. 1–4 *Aulus Gellius* vi. 20. 6 (*ut correxit Haupt*) Catullus quoque
elegantissimus poetarum in hisce uersibus 'Minister . . . magistrae /
ebria. acina (ebriose ac in *codd.*) ebriosioris', cum dicere 'ebrio'
(ebriosi *codd.*) posset, quod erat usitatius acinum in neutro genere
appellare, amans tamen hiatus illius Homerici suauitatem 'ebriam'
(ebriosam *codd.*) dixit propter insequentis 'a' litterae concentum.
qui 'ebriosa' (ebrios *codd.*) autem Catullum dixisse putant aut 'ebrioso'
('ebriosos' *codd.*)—nam id quoque temere scriptum inuenitur—in
libros scilicet de corruptis exemplaribus factos inciderunt.

29. 1–2 *citat Quintilianus, inst. orat.* ix. 4. 141; *cf. Suetonium, diu.
Iul.* 73.   3 *Plinius, hist. nat.* xxxvi. 48 hic namque est
Mamurra Catulli Veronensis carminibus proscissus, quem . . . domus
ipsius clarius quam Catullus dixit habere quidquid habuisset Comata
Gallia.

---

27. 2 inger *Parth. ex Gellio*: ingere *V*   4 ebriose (-sae *1473*, -so
agnoscit Gellius) acino *V*: ebria acina *Haupt*, ebriosa acina *Parth.*
5 at *X*, ad *O*   quod iubet *V*: *corr.* θ
  29. 3 mamurram θ: nam murram *V*   4 uncti *Faernus*, ante
Statius: cum te *V*   7 perambulauit *V*: *corr.* ζ   8 adoneus
Statius: ydoneus *V* (idon- *R*)

cinaede Romule, haec uidebis et feres?
es impudicus et uorax et aleo.   10
eone nomine, imperator unice,
fuisti in ultima occidentis insula,
ut ista uestra diffututa mentula
ducenties comesset aut trecenties?
quid est alid sinistra liberalitas?   15
parum expatrauit an parum elluatus est?
paterna prima lancinata sunt bona,
secunda praeda Pontica, inde tertia
Hibera, quam scit amnis aurifer Tagus:
nunc Galliae timetur et Britanniae.   20
quid hunc malum fouetis? aut quid hic potest
nisi uncta deuorare patrimonia?
eone nomine †urbis opulentissime†
socer generque, perdidistis omnia?

30

ALFENE immemor atque unanimis false sodalibus,
iam te nil miseret, dure, tui dulcis amiculi?
iam me prodere, iam non dubitas fallere, perfide?
nec facta impia fallacum hominum caelicolis placent.
quae tu neglegis ac me miserum deseris in malis.   5
eheu quid faciant, dic, homines cuiue habeant fidem?

---

29. 24 *Cf. librum Vergilianum Catalepton* 6. 6 gener socerque perdidistis omnia.

---

13 uestra ζ: nostra *V*   diffututa η: diffutura *V*   14 comesset
r: comerset *O*, comeset *X*   15 alid *Statius*: alit *V*   16 parum
(*1º*) *X*, partum *O*   17 prima *Auantius³ et, teste Statio, Hadri-
anus*: primum *V*   19 libera *O*   scit *O*, sit *X*   amnis δ: amni
V   20 nunc γ (*repugnantibus tamen numeris*): hunc *V*   timetur *Froehlich*: timet *V*   21 hic α: hinc *V*   23 urbis o piissime
Lachmann, orbis, o piissimei *Haupt*

30. 1 alphene *V*   false δ: salse *V*   2 nil *1472*: nichil *V*
3 non *codex Antenoris Balbi*: non me *V*   *Post hunc uersum duos
excidisse credidit Ellis*   5 quae] que *V*: quos *B. Guarinus*, quod
L. Mueller   6 eheu *Pall.*: o heu *V*   dic *Auantius³*, dice
Ellis: dico *V*   cuiue *rmg*: cuine *V*

certe tute iubebas animam tradere, inique, ⟨me⟩
inducens in amorem, quasi tuta omnia mi forent.
idem nunc retrahis te ac tua dicta omnia factaque
uentos irrita ferre ac nebulas aereas sinis.　　　　10
si tu oblitus es, at di meminerunt, meminit Fides,
quae te ut paeniteat postmodo facti faciet tui.

31

Paene insularum, Sirmio, insularumque
ocelle, quascumque in liquentibus stagnis
marique uasto fert uterque Neptunus,
quam te libenter quamque laetus inuiso,
uix mi ipse credens Thuniam atque Bithunos　　　5
liquisse campos et uidere te in tuto.
o quid solutis est beatius curis,
cum mens onus reponit, ac peregrino
labore fessi uenimus larem ad nostrum,
desideratoque acquiescimus lecto?　　　　　　10
hoc est quod unum est pro laboribus tantis.
salue, o uenusta Sirmio, atque ero gaude
gaudente, uosque, o Lydiae lacus undae,
ridete quidquid est domi cachinnorum.

34

Dianae sumus in fide
puellae et pueri integri:

7 me *add. B. Guarinus et Auantius*　　　8 tuta omnia β: omnia O,
omnia tuta X　　　9 idem O, inde G, inde al. idem R　　　10 uento
V: *corr.* δ　　　11 at ζη: ut V　　　meminerunt] meminere, at *e codice
nescio quo Muretus*

31. 3 neptumnus X　　　4 libente V: *corr.* β　　　5 mi η: mihi V
crederis G (al. credens *add. g*)　　　Thuniam *Schwabe* (thyniam *iam B.
Guarinus*): thimiam V　　　Bithunos *Schwabe* (bithynos *iam m*, -inos
g): bithinios V　　　12 hero al. bero R　　　13 gaudente *Bergk*: gaude
O, gaudete X　　　uosque (*nisi potius* uosque o) η: uos quoque V

⟨Dianam pueri integri⟩
  puellaeque canamus.
o Latonia, maximi   5
magna progenies Iouis,
quam mater prope Deliam
  deposiuit oliuam,
montium domina ut fores
siluarumque uirentium   10
saltuumque reconditorum
  amniumque sonantum:
tu Lucina dolentibus
Iuno dicta puerperis,
tu potens Triuia et notho es   15
  dicta lumine Luna.
tu cursu, dea, menstruo
metiens iter annuum,
rustica agricolae bonis
  tecta frugibus exples.   20
sis quocumque tibi placet
sancta nomine, Romulique,
antique ut solita es, bona
  sospites ope gentem.

35

Poetae tenero, meo sodali,
uelim Caecilio, papyre, dicas
Veronam ueniat, Noui relinquens
Comi moenia Lariumque litus.
nam quasdam uolo cogitationes   5

---

34. 3 *uersum om. V*: Dianae pueri integri '*in uetustiore exemplari inuentum*' *restituit Pall.* (*idem teste Perreio Pontanus*), Dianam *Auantius*[3]   8 deposuit *V*: *corr. Pall.*   12 amniumque *cod. Pisaurensis*: omniumque *V* (omnium *X*)   sonantium *V*: *corr. Pall.*   15 notho es *V* (*al.* et noto es *Rmg*): notho's (*et* solita's *u.* 23) *L. Mueller*   17 menstrua *V*: *corr. B. Guarinus*   21 sis quecumque t. placet *O*, scis quecumque t. placent *X* (*al.* sis quocumque t. placet *Rmg*)

35. 2 cecilio *V* (occilio *O*)   4 menia *Rmg*: ueniam *O*, meniam *G*

amici accipiat sui meique.
quare, si sapiet, uiam uorabit,
quamuis candida milies puella
euntem reuocet, manusque collo
ambas iniciens roget morari.   10
quae nunc, si mihi uera nuntiantur,
illum deperit impotente amore.
nam quo tempore legit incohatam
Dindymi dominam, ex eo misellae
ignes interiorem edunt medullam.   15
ignosco tibi, Sapphica puella
musa doctior; est enim uenuste
Magna Caecilio incohata Mater.

36

ANNALES Volusi, cacata carta,
uotum soluite pro mea puella.
nam sanctae Veneri Cupidinique
uouit, si sibi restitutus essem
desissemque truces uibrare iambos,   5
electissima pessimi poetae
scripta tardipedi deo daturam
infelicibus ustulanda lignis.
et hoc pessima se puella uidit
iocose lepide uouere diuis.   10
nunc o caeruleo creata ponto,
quae sanctum Idalium Vriosque apertos
quaeque Ancona Cnidumque harundinosam

35. 12 *citat Charisius* (*p.* 134 *K.*).

11 mihi si *R*   12 inpotente ζη *et* amore *rmg* (*ita Charisius*): im-
potentem amorem *V*   13 legit *1472*: eligit *O*, elegit *X*   incohatam *B. Guarinus*, inchoatam *Pall.*: indotatam *V*   18 cecilia *V*:
corr. 1473

36. *1 et* 20 annales uolusi *θ*: anuale (annuale *X*) suo lusi *V*
5 dedissemque *V: corr. Auantius*   10 ioco se lepido *Scaliger*   diuis
ζη: se diuis *V*   11 o *om. O*   poncto *O*, punto *X*   12 adalium
O, adalium al. ydalium *X*   utriosque al. uriosque *G*   13 gnidum-
que *V*

colis quaeque Amathunta quaeque Golgos
quaeque Durrachium Hadriae tabernam,   15
acceptum face redditumque uotum,
si non illepidum neque inuenustum est.
at uos interea uenite in ignem,
pleni ruris et inficetiarum
annales Volusi, cacata carta.   20

38

MALEST, Cornifici, tuo Catullo,
malest, me hercule, et laboriose,
et magis magis in dies et horas.
quem tu, quod minimum facillimumque est,
qua solatus es allocutione?   5
irascor tibi. sic meos amores?
paulum quid lubet allocutionis,
maestius lacrimis Simonideis.

39

EGNATIVS, quod candidos habet dentes,
renidet usque quaque. si ad rei uentum est
subsellium, cum orator excitat fletum,
renidet ille; si ad pii rogum fili
lugetur, orba cum flet unicum mater,   5
renidet ille. quidquid est, ubicumque est,
quodcumque agit, renidet: hunc habet morbum,
neque elegantem, ut arbitror, neque urbanum.

14 colis quaeque ζη: colisque *V*   golgos *H. Barbarus* (*teste Mureto ad* 64. 96): alcos *V*   15 durachium *V*   18 uenite al.
uenire *R*   19 ruris *Pall.*: turis *V*

38. 1 malest *Lachmann* (male est *iam Calph.*): male est si *V*
cornifici *Auantius*: carnifici *V*   2 malest *Lachmann*: male si *V*
(male est si *r*); *cf.* 62. 8   et *V*: ei et *Lachmann,* et est *Sillig*

39. 2 si] sei *O,* seu *G,* seu ai. sei *R*   3 subsellum *O,* subsellum *X*   excitat orator *V*: *corr. θ*   4 pii *X* (al. impii *Rmg*),
impii *O*   rogum α: regum *V*   filii *V*

quare monendum est ⟨te⟩ mihi, bone Egnati.
si urbanus esses aut Sabinus aut Tiburs   10
aut pinguis Vmber aut obesus Etruscus
aut Lanuuinus ater atque dentatus
aut Transpadanus, ut meos quoque attingam,
aut quilubet, qui puriter lauit dentes,
tamen renidere usque quaque te nollem: 15
nam risu inepto res ineptior nulla est.
nunc Celtiber ⟨es⟩: Celtiberia in terra,
quod quisque minxit, hoc sibi solet mane
dentem atque russam defricare gingiuam,
ut, quo iste uester expolitior dens est,   20
hoc te amplius bibisse praedicet loti.

40

QVAENAM te mala mens, miselle Rauide,
agit praecipitem in meos iambos?
quis deus tibi non bene aduocatus
uecordem parat excitare rixam?
an ut peruenias in ora uulgi?   5
quid uis? qualubet esse notus optas?
eris, quandoquidem meos amores
cum longa uoluisti amare poena.

39. 11 *Liber Glossarum* (*Glossaria Latina* i. 443 *Lindsay, Corpus Gloss. Lat.* **v.** 233 *Goetz*) pinguis: crassus. nam obesus plus est quam pinguis. Catulus ait 'aut pinguis ubera aut obesus et grossus'. 19 *Apuleius, apol.* 6 ut ait Catullus . . . 'dentem atque russam pumicare gingiuam'.

9 mon. est te *Maehly*, mon. te est *Spengel*, monendus es *Calph.* 11 pinguis *ex glossario Lindsay*: parcus *V*   etruscus *g*: et truscus *V* (al. etruscus *Rm*)   12 lamiuinus *V*: *corr. m*   13 ut ε: aut *V*   14 pariter al. puriter *R*   17 es *add. Corr. de Allio* 19 rusam *V*   20 noster *O*   expolitior *g*: expolitor *V* (al. expolitior *Rm*)   21 loti *cod. Pisaurensis*: lotus *V*
40. 1 raude *Itali*   3 auocatus *V*: *corr. mg*   5 peruenamus *V*: *corr. θ*   8 pena *O*, poema *G*, poema al. poena *Rmg*

41

AMEANA puella defututa
tota milia me decem poposcit,
ista turpiculo puella naso,
decoctoris amica Formiani.
propinqui, quibus est puella curae, 5
amicos medicosque conuocate:
non est sana puella, nec rogare
qualis sit solet aes imaginosum.

42

ADESTE, hendecasyllabi, quot estis
omnes undique, quotquot estis omnes.
iocum me putat esse moecha turpis,
et negat mihi nostra reddituram
pugillaria, si pati potestis. 5
persequamur eam et reflagitemus.
quae sit, quaeritis? illa, quam uidetis
turpe incedere, mimice ac moleste
ridentem catuli ore Gallicani.
circumsistite eam, et reflagitate, 10
'moecha putida, redde codicillos,
redde, putida moecha, codicillos!'
non assis facis? o lutum, lupanar,
aut si perditius potes quid esse.
sed non est tamen hoc satis putandum. 15
quod si non aliud potest, ruborem
ferreo canis exprimamus ore.

42. 5 *Charisius* (*p.* 97 *K.*) haec pugillaria saepius neutraliter dicit idem Catullus in hendecasyllabis.

---

41. 1 A me an a *V, uix sanabile* defutura *R* 4 formani *V*: *corr. rmg* 5 puelle *V*: *corr.* δ 6 conuocare *V*: *corr. 1472* 8 aes *Froehlich*: et *V*
 42. 3 locum *O*, locum al. iocum *X* 4 nostra *Auantius*[3]: uestra *V* 7 illam *X* (*corr. r*) 8 mimice *Turnebus*: mirmice *V* 9 catulli *V*: *corr.* β 12 *uersum om. R1* 15 satis hoc *R*

conclamate iterum altiore uoce
'moecha putida, redde codicillos,
redde, putida moecha, codicillos!'   20
sed nil proficimus, nihil mouetur.
mutanda est ratio modusque uobis,
siquid proficere amplius potestis:
'pudica et proba, redde codicillos.'

43

SALVE, nec minimo puella naso
nec bello pede nec nigris ocellis
nec longis digitis nec ore sicco
nec sane nimis elegante lingua,
decoctoris amica Formiani.   5
ten prouincia narrat esse bellam?
tecum Lesbia nostra comparatur?
o saeclum insapiens et infacetum!

44

O FVNDE noster seu Sabine seu Tiburs
(nam te esse Tiburtem autumant, quibus non est
cordi Catullum laedere; at quibus cordi est,
quouis Sabinum pignore esse contendunt),
sed seu Sabine siue uerius Tiburs,   5
fui libenter in tua suburbana
uilla, malamque pectore expuli tussim,
non inmerenti quam mihi meus uenter,
dum sumptuosas appeto, dedit, cenas.
nam, Sestianus dum uolo esse conuiua,   10

21 nil *1473*: nichil *V*   nihil] nil *g*   22 uobis *θ*: nobis *V*
43. 8 seclum *Rmg*: sedum *V*   et] atque *mg*
  44. 2 cum quibus *G1*   4 pignoris *V*: *corr.* δ   7 malamque
p. expuli tussim *cod. Edinensis anni mccccxcv* (expui *Scaliger*): aliam-
que p. expulsus sim *V*   8 meus uenter *Faernus*: mens uertur *V*
10 festianus *O*   conuiuia *X* (*corr. gr*)

orationem in Antium petitorem
plenam ueneni et pestilentiae legi.
hic me grauedo frigida et frequens tussis
quassauit usque, dum in tuum sinum fugi,
et me recuraui otioque et urtica.   15
quare refectus maximas tibi grates
ago, meum quod non es ulta peccatum.
nec deprecor iam, si nefaria scripta
Sesti recepso, quin grauedinem et tussim
non mi sed ipsi Sestio ferat frigus,   20
qui tunc uocat me, cum malum librum legi.

45

ACMEN Septimius suos amores
tenens in gremio 'mea' inquit 'Acme,
ni te perdite amo atque amare porro
omnes sum assidue paratus annos,
quantum qui pote plurimum perire,   5
solus in Libya Indiaque tosta
caesio ueniam obuius leoni.'
hoc ut dixit, Amor sinistra ut ante
dextra sternuit approbationem.
    at Acme leuiter caput reflectens   10
et dulcis pueri ebrios ocellos
illo purpureo ore suauiata,
'sic', inquit 'mea uita Septimille,
huic uni domino usque seruiamus,
ut multo mihi maior acriorque   15
ignis mollibus ardet in medullis.'

---

11 oratione (-nem X) minantium V: corr. Status   petitorum rmg
13 hoc O   grauido V: corr. δ   19 sexti recepso ed. Rom.: sestire
cepso V   quin ζ: qui V   20 mi] mihi V   sectio V (al. sestio
R)   21 legi Lachmann: legit V
    45. 1 ac men X   septimios O, septimos X   3 perditi V:
corr. r   5 potest V: corr. r   9 dextram ζη   approbationem θ:
-one V (locus nondum expeditus)   10 at acme r: ad hac (hanc
X) me V   12 sauiata r: saniata V   13 septimille r: septi-
nulle V (al. septinuelle R)   14 uno X (corr. rmg)

hoc ut dixit, Amor sinistra ut ante
dextra sternuit approbationem.
    nunc ab auspicio bono profecti
mutuis animis amant amantur.   20
unam Septimius misellus Acmen
mauult quam Syrias Britanniasque:
uno in Septimio fidelis Acme
facit delicias libidinesque.
quis ullos homines beatiores   25
uidit, quis Venerem auspicatiorem?

46

I AM uer egelidos refert tepores,
iam caeli furor aequinoctialis
iucundis Zephyri silescit aureis.
linquantur Phrygii, Catulle, campi
Nicaeaeque ager uber aestuosae: 5
ad claras Asiae uolemus urbes.
iam mens praetrepidans auet uagari,
iam laeti studio pedes uigescunt.
o dulces comitum ualete coetus,
longe quos simul a domo profectos   10
diuersae uarie uiae reportant.

47

PORCI et Socration, duae sinistrae
Pisonis, scabies famesque mundi,
uos Veraniolo meo et Fabullo
uerpus praeposuit Priapus ille?

17 sinistra ut *r*: sinistrauit *V*   18 dextra *1472*: dextram *V*
21 septumius *V*   agmen *V*: *corr. r*   22 siriasque *V* (syr- *X*):
corr. γδ   24 libidinisque *X* (*corr. r*)
    46. 1 uere gelidos *V*: *corr. θ*   3 aureis *V* (auris *r*)   5 uber
Auantius: ruber *V*   estuose *r*: estuore *V*   10 quos *r*: quo
V (quoque *R*)   11 diuerse uarie *V*: diuersae uariae *uulgo*
    47. 2 mundae *Buecheler*   4 proposuit *V*: *corr. r*

uos conuiuia lauta sumptuose 5
de die facitis, mei sodales
quaerunt in triuio uocationes?

49

DISERTISSIME Romuli nepotum,
quot sunt quotque fuere, Marce Tulli,
quotque post aliis erunt in annis,
gratias tibi maximas Catullus
agit pessimus omnium poeta, 5
tanto pessimus omnium poeta,
quanto tu optimus omnium patronus.

50

HESTERNO, Licini, die otiosi
multum lusimus in meis tabellis,
ut conuenerat esse delicatos:
scribens uersiculos uterque nostrum
ludebat numero modo hoc modo illoc, 5
reddens mutua per iocum atque uinum.
atque illinc abii tuo lepore
incensus, Licini, facetiisque,
ut nec me miserum cibus iuuaret
nec somnus tegeret quiete ocellos, 10
sed toto indomitus furore lecto
uersarer, cupiens uidere lucem,
ut tecum loquerer simulque ut essem.
at defessa labore membra postquam
semimortua lectulo iacebant, 15
hoc, iucunde, tibi poema feci,

49. 7 omniums *R*   patronus *Or*, patronum *X*
50. 2 in meis *V*: inuicem *Sabellicus*, '*an* in tueis?' *Schwabe*
5 ludebat al. le- *R*   7 abiit *V*: corr. *r*   8 lacini *V*   facetiisque *r*: faceti tuique *V*   10 sompnus *r*: somnos *V*   12 uersare-
tur *V*: corr. *r*   13 omnem *X* (al. essem *add. Rmg*); *cf.* 63. 90
14 at *α*: ad *V*

ex quo perspiceres meum dolorem.
nunc audax caue sis, precesque nostras,
oramus, caue despuas, ocelle,
ne poenas Nemesis reposcat a te.   20
est uemens dea: laedere hanc caueto.

51

ILLE mi par esse deo uidetur,
ille, si fas est, superare diuos,
qui sedens aduersus identidem te
     spectat et audit

dulce ridentem, misero quod omnis   5
eripit sensus mihi: nam simul te,
Lesbia, aspexi, nihil est super mi

     .   .   .

lingua sed torpet, tenuis sub artus
flamma demanat, sonitu suopte   10
tintinant aures, gemina teguntur
     lumina nocte.

otium, Catulle, tibi molestum est:
otio exsultas nimiumque gestis:
otium et reges prius et beatas   15
     perdidit urbes.

---

50. 18 *Seruius ad Vergili aen.* iv. 409 Catullus cauĕre dixit (*cf.* 61.
145).

---

18 caue sis *Pall.*, caueas *r*: caueris *V*   19 ocello *V*: *corr. B.
Guarinus*   20 nemesis δε: ne messis *V*   resposcat *O*, reposcat *G*, reponat *R*   21 uehemens *V*
   51. 1 mi *rg*: mi(c)hi *V*   par θ: impar *V*   3/4 te / spectat
rg: / te spectat *V*   5 misero quod *g*: miseroque *V* (al. quod *Rm*)
8 *uersum om.* V: quod loquar amens *exempli gratia suppleuit Parth.,
alii alia*   10 flamma *r*: flamina *V*   11 tintiant *O*, tintinant
Gr, tintinnat *R*   12 limina *X*   13-16 *hos uu. fragmentum
carminis deperditi esse censuerunt Statius, alii* (*haud scio an recte*)
13 catuli *O*, catulli *X*: *corr.* θ

52

QVID est, Catulle? quid moraris emori?
sella in curuli struma Nonius sedet,
per consulatum peierat Vatinius:
quid est, Catulle? quid moraris emori?

53

RISI nescio quem modo e corona,
qui, cum mirifice Vatiniana
meus crimina Caluos explicasset,
admirans ait haec manusque tollens,
'di magni, salaputium disertum!'   5

55

ORAMVS, si forte non molestum est,
demonstres ubi sint tuae tenebrae.
te Campo quaesiuimus minore,
te in Circo, te in omnibus libellis,
te in templo summi Iouis sacrato.   5
in Magni simul ambulatione
femellas omnes, amice, prendi,

52. 2 *citant Marius Victorinus (p.* 136 *K.*), *Caesius Bassus de
metris (p.* 257 *K.); cf. Plinium, hist. nat.* xxxvii. 81, *Boethium de con-
solatione philosophiae* iii. 4.
53. 5 *Seneca, controuersiarum* vii. 4 (19) 7 erat enim (Caluus) paruolus statura, propter quod etiam Catullus in hendecasyllabis uocat
illum 'salaputtium disertum'.

---

52. 1 *et* 4 emori η: mori *V*   2 struma *V*: scrofa *Mar. Vict.*   nonius
ex Plinio Parth.: nouius *V*   3 peierat *r*: perierat *V*   uacinius *X*
53. 1 e ζ: et *V*   3 meos *V*: *corr. r*   crimina al. carmina *X* (?),
carmina *m*   caluus *r*   4 manusque al. inanius *R*   5 salaputium
ε: salapantium *V* (al. salapputium *R*)   disertum ζη: desertum *V*
55. 1 molestus es *V*: *corr.* β   3 quaesiuimus in *V*: in *del.*
Scaliger, ante Campo *traiecit Sillig*; quaesimus in *Birt*   te quaesiuimus in minore campo η   4 in (*1º*)] id *O*, id al. in *X*   libellis *vix sanum*: ligellis *B. Guarinus*   7 prehendi *X*

quas uultu uidi tamen sereno.
†aueltet†, sic ipse flagitabam,
Camerium mihi pessimae puellae.   10
quaedam inquit, nudum reduc . . .
'en hic in roseis latet papillis.'
sed te iam ferre Herculei labos est;
tanto te in fastu negas, amice.
dic nobis ubi sis futurus, ede   15
audacter, committe, crede luci.
nunc te lacteolae tenent puellae?
si linguam clauso tenes in ore,
fructus proicies amoris omnes.
uerbosa gaudet Venus loquella.   20
uel, si uis, licet obseres palatum,
dum uestri sim particeps amoris.

58

CAELI, Lesbia nostra, Lesbia illa,
illa Lesbia, quam Catullus unam
plus quam se atque suos amauit omnes,
nunc in quadriuiis et angiportis
glubit magnanimi Remi nepotes.   5

8 sereno β, serenas δ: serena V   9 auelte sic V: auelli sinite
Auantius   10 camerum *r*   pessime V   11 quedam *Or*,
quendam X   reduc V: sinum recludens *Riese*   12 en *r*, hem *g*:
em V   hic R: hec V   13 herculis *r*   14 te in V: ten
Muretus   16 audacter (audaciter O) hoc V: hoc *hinc summouit
1472*   crede al. crude X   luci *cod. Vaticanus lat.* 1608 *anni
mcccclxxix* (lucei *Scaliger*): lucet V   18 tenens V: *corr. r*
19 prohicies O, proijcies X   22 uestri V (al. nostri X)   sim *cod.
Pisaurensis*, sim ego *Auantius*: sis V

58[1 nostra R, uestra *OG*   4 quadruuiis G, quadriuis R   5 magnanimi Remi *Vossius*, -imos Remi *cod. Vat. lat.* 1608 *et Calph.*:
magna amiremini (adm- X) V

58ᵇ

Non custos si fingar ille Cretum,
non Ladas ego pinnipesue Perseus,　　　　　3
non si Pegaseo ferar uolatu,　　　　　　　　2
non Rhesi niueae citaeque bigae;
adde huc plumipedas uolatilesque,　　　　　5
uentorumque simul require cursum,
quos iunctos, Cameri, mihi dicares:
defessus tamen omnibus medullis
et multis languoribus peresus
essem te mihi, amice, quaeritando.　　　　　10

60

Nvm te leaena montibus Libystinis
aut Scylla latrans infima inguinum parte
tam mente dura procreauit ac taetra,
ut supplicis uocem in nouissimo casu
contemptam haberes, a nimis fero corde?　　　5

61

Collis o Heliconii
cultor, Vraniae genus,
qui rapis teneram ad uirum
uirginem, o Hymenaee Hymen,
o Hymen Hymenaee;　　　　　　　　　　5

58ᵇ. *post* 55. 12 *collocant paucissimi codd. recentiores, post* 55.
13 *ed. Rom., post* 55. 22 *Aldina*　　　　*uersus* 3, 2 *hoc ordine Muretus*
3 primipes *V* (*al.* pinnipes *Rmg*)　　　　4 niuee *G*, uinee *OR*　　　niueis
citisque bigis *Muretus*　　　　7 iunctos *g*: uictos *O*, uinctos *X*
　　60. 1 libissinis *O*, libisinis *X*: *corr. Scaliger*　　　　2 scylla *ε*: silla *V*
4 suplicus *O*, suppliciis *X*　　　5 contentam *OI*, conteptam *X*
　　61. 1 bellicon iei *O*, eliconei *X*　　　　4 hymen *om. V*: *add. Gr*
5 hymen (*om. G*) o hymenee hymen *V*: *corr. Aldina* (Hymen o *alii*)

cinge tempora floribus
suaue olentis amaraci,
flammeum cape laetus, huc
huc ueni, niueo gerens
    luteum pede soccum;   10

excitusque hilari die,
nuptialia concinens
uoce carmina tinnula,
pelle humum pedibus, manu
    pineam quate taedam.   15

namque Iunia Manlio,
qualis Idalium colens
uenit ad Phrygium Venus
iudicem, bona cum bona
    nubet alite uirgo,   20

floridis uelut enitens
myrtus Asia ramulis
quos Hamadryades deae
ludicrum sibi roscido
    nutriunt umore.   25

quare age, huc aditum ferens,
perge linquere Thespiae
rupis Aonios specus,
nympha quos super irrigat
    frigerans Aganippe.   30

ac domum dominam uoca
coniugis cupidam noui,
mentem amore reuinciens,
ut tenax hedera huc et huc
    arborem implicat errans.   35

7 amarici *V*: *corr. O*   8 flameum *V*   12 continens *V*,
concines *r*   13 tinnuula *V*: *corr. gr*   15 spineam *Parth.*
16 iunia *V*: Vibia *Syme*   manlio *θ*: mallio *V*   21 uelut] uult
O (*cf. uu.* 102, 187)   24 ludricum *V*: *corr. R*   rosido *V*   31 ac
V: ad *r*   33 reuincens *V*: *corr. ε*   34 hac et hac *r*

uosque item simul, integrae
uirgines, quibus aduenit
par dies, agite in modum
dicite, o Hymenaee Hymen,
   o Hymen Hymenaee;   40

ut lubentius, audiens
se citarier ad suum
munus, huc aditum ferat
dux bonae Veneris, boni
   coniugator amoris.   45

quis deus magis est ama-
tis petendus amantibus?
quem colent homines magis
caelitum, o Hymenaee Hymen,
   o Hymen Hymenaee?   50

te suis tremulus parens
inuocat, tibi uirgines
zonula soluunt sinus,
te timens cupida nouos
   captat aure maritus.   55

tu fero iuueni in manus
floridam ipse puellulam
dedis a gremio suae
matris, o Hymenaee Hymen,
   o Hymen Hymenaee.   60

nil potest sine te Venus
fama quod bona comprobet,

38 in nodum *V* (al. in modum *R*)   40 o hymenee (hymen o *r*)
hymenee hymen *V*   46/47 est ama-/tis *Bergk*, anxiis / est *Haupt*:
amatis / est *V*   *Inter* 49 *et* 50 *exhibuit V* comperarier (conpera-
ries *O*) ausit (cf. *uu*. 65, 70, 75): *del. r*   50 o hymen (hymen o *r*)
hymenee hymen *V*   51 suis tremulus η: sui si remulus *V* (suis
remulus *r*, sui si remus al. remulus *m*, al. remus *add. g*)   55 maritos
V: *corr. Muretus*   58–60 dedis a g. s. matris / o hymenee hymen
hymenee (o hymenee *mg*) *V*   61 nil *rmg*: nichil *V*

commodi capere, at potest
te uolente. quis huic deo
   compararier ausit?   65

nulla quit sine te domus
liberos dare, nec parens
stirpe nitier; at potest
te uolente. quis huic deo
   compararier ausit?   70

quae tuis careat sacris,
non queat dare praesides
terra finibus: at queat
te uolente. quis huic deo
   compararier ausit?   75

claustra pandite ianuae.
uirgo adest. uiden ut faces
splendidas quatiunt comas?

.   .   .   .

  .   .   .   .   (80)

.   .   .   .

.   .   .   .   .   .

tardet ingenuus pudor,
quem tamen magis audiens   80
   flet quod ire necesse est.   (85)

flere desine. non tibi, Aurunculeia, periculum est
ne qua femina pulcrior
clarum ab Oceano diem   85
   uiderit uenientem.   (90)

talis in uario solet
diuitis domini hortulo

---

68 nitier β: uities, O, uicier X   77 ades *Schrader*   *Post·*
u. 78 *lacunam quattuor uersuum statuunt edd.*   82 arunculeia X
88 ortullo V (ortulo *Rmg*)

stare flos hyacinthinus.
sed moraris, abit dies: 90
  ⟨prodeas noua nupta.⟩   (95)

prodeas noua nupta, si
iam uidetur, et audias
nostra uerba. uiden? faces
aureas quatiunt comas: 95
  prodeas noua nupta.   (100)

non tuus leuis in mala
deditus uir adultera,
probra turpia persequens,
a tuis teneris uolet   100
  secubare papillis,   (105)

lenta sed uelut adsitas
uitis implicat arbores,
implicabitur in tuum
complexum. sed abit dies: 105
  prodeas noua nupta.   (110)

o cubile, quod omnibus

  .   .   .   .

  .   .   .   .

    .   .   .   .

  candido pede lecti.   (115)

quae tuo ueniunt ero,
quanta gaudia, quae uaga   110
nocte, quae medio die
gaudeat! sed abit dies:
  prodeas noua nupta.   (120)

tollite, ⟨o⟩ pueri, faces:
flammeum uideo uenire.   115

89 iactintinus *O*, iacintinus *X*   90 (*idem* 105, 112) abiit *V*   91 *uer-
sum om. V*: *add. Aldina*   94 uiden *θ*, uide ut *Parth.*: uiden (uideri
O) ut *V*   99 probra turpia *Calph.*: procatur pia *V*   102 sed
O, -que *X*: qui *Aldina*, quin *Auantius*[3]   uelut] uult *O*   *Post*
107 *lacunam trium uersuum statuunt edd.*   110, 111 quae *r*: -que
V   114 o *add. r*   115 flamineum *V* (flammineum *O*)

ite concinite in modum
'io Hymen Hymenaee io,
   io Hymen Hymenaee.'   (125)

ne diu taceat procax
Fescennina iocatio,   120
nec nuces pueris neget
desertum domini audiens
   concubinus amorem.   (130)

da nuces pueris, iners
concubine! satis diu   125
lusisti nucibus: lubet
iam seruire Talasio.
   concubine, nuces da.   (135)

sordebant tibi uilicae,
concubine, hodie atque heri: 130
nunc tuum cinerarius
tondet os. miser a miser
   concubine, nuces da.   (140)

diceris male te a tuis
unguentate glabris marite   135
abstinere, sed abstine.
io Hymen Hymenaee io,
   ⟨io Hymen Hymenaee.⟩   (145)

scimus haec tibi quae licent
sola cognita, sed marito   140
ista non eadem licent.
io Hymen Hymenaee io,
   io Hymen Hymenaee.   (150)

117, 118, 116 *hoc ordine X*; 117, 116 *omisso uersu* 118 *O*
118 (*idem semper in sequentibus*) io *in fine add. V*   119 taceat *r*:
taceatis *V*   120 fosceninna *O*   iocatio *Heinsius*: locatio *V*
(locutio *m*, al. locutio *add. g*)   125 diu] domini *O*   127 iam]
nam *O*   129 iulice *O*, uillice *X*   132 miser a] misera *O*, miser
ah *X*   134 diceris *1473*: diceres *V*   male *Gr*, malle *ORmg*
138 *add.* β   143 *om. O*

nupta, tu quoque quae tuus
uir petet caue ne neges,   145
ni petitum aliunde eat.
io Hymen Hymenaee io,
    io Hymen Hymenaee.   (155)

en tibi domus ut potens
et beata uiri tui,   150
quae tibi sine seruiat
(io Hymen Hymenaee io,
    io Hymen Hymenaee)   (160)

usque dum tremulum mouens
cana tempus anilitas   155
omnia omnibus annuit.
io Hymen Hymenaee io,
    io Hymen Hymenaee.   (165)

transfer omine cum bono
limen aureolos pedes   160
rasilemque subi forem.
io Hymen Hymenaee io,
    io Hymen Hymenaee.   (170)

aspice intus ut accubans
uir tuus Tyrio in toro   165
totus immineat tibi.
io Hymen Hymenaee io,
    io Hymen Hymenaee.   (175)

illi non minus ac tibi
pectore uritur intimo   170

144 tuis *X*   146 ni *V* (ne *R in margine*)   148 *om. V*: *add.*
Rmg   151 seruiat *Parth.*: seruit *V* (fine seruit *r*)   153 (*et*
158, 163) *om. O*   155 anilitas *η*: anilis (ann- *X*) etas *V*   161
nassilemque *O*, rass- *X*: *corr. rmg*   subi *r*: sibi *V*   164 intus
Statius: unus *V*   169 ac *R*: hac *V*   170 uritur *V* (urimur
Rm, al. urimur *add. g*)

flamma, sed penite magis.
io Hymen Hymenaee io,
    io Hymen Hymenaee.   (180)

mitte brachiolum teres,
praetextate, puellulae: 175
iam cubile adeat uiri.
io Hymen Hymenaee io,
    io Hymen Hymenaee.   (185)

⟨uos⟩, bonae senibus uiris
cognitae bene feminae,   180
collocate puellulam.
io Hymen Hymenaee io,
    io Hymen Hymenaee.   (190)

iam licet uenias, marite:
uxor in thalamo tibi est,   185
ore floridulo nitens,
alba parthenice uelut
    luteumue papauer.   (195)

at, marite, ita me iuuent
caelites, nihilo minus   190
pulcer es, neque te Venus
neglegit: sed abit dies:
    perge, ne remorare.   (200)

non diu remoratus es:
iam uenis. bona te Venus   195

175 puellule η: puelle V   176 adeant X   179 uos *add.*
Auantius uiris *cod. Leidensis anni mccccliii*: unis V   180 bene
Calph. (beue *iam ed. Rom.*): berue V   181 puellulam η: puellam V   185 tibi est *Bentley*: est tibi V   187 uelut β: uult
O, uultu X (al. uult g)   189–93 *post u.* 198 V: *huc reuocauit
Scaliger*   189 ad maritum tamen iuuenem V: *corr. Scaliger*
191 pulcher es '*alii' apud Robortellum*: pulcre res V   neque
θ: nec V   192 abiit V   193 rememorare X   194 remoratus *Calph.*: remota O, remorata X

iuuerit, quoniam palam
quod cupis cupis et bonum
   non abscondis amorem.   (205)

ille pulueris Africi
siderumque micantium   200
subducat numerum prius,
qui uestri numerare uolt
   multa milia ludi.   (210)

ludite ut lubet, et breui
liberos date. non decet   205
tam uetus sine liberis
nomen esse, sed indidem
   semper ingenerari.   (215)

Torquatus uolo paruulus
matris e gremio suae   210
porrigens teneras manus
dulce rideat ad patrem
   semihiante labello.   (220)

sit suo similis patri
Manlio et facile insciis   215
noscitetur ab omnibus,
et pudicitiam suae
   matris indicet ore.   (225)

talis illius a bona
matre laus genus approbet,   220

---

196 iuuerit *θ*: inuenerit *V*   197 cupis cupis *OR(V?)*, cupis capis *Gr*   198 abscondas *V*: *corr.* *ζη*   199 africi *Heinsius* (-cei *Lachmann*): ericei *V*   202 uestri *β* (uostri *Itali*): nostri *V* uult *Calph.*: uolunt *V*   203 ludi *ed. Rom.* (ludei *Scaliger*): ludere *V*   204 ludite ut *Parth.* (ut iam *Calph.*): et ludite et *V* (et 2⁰ *del. r*)   208 ingenerati *O*   209 torcutus *O*   210 e] et *O* 213 semihiante *Scaliger*: sed mihi ante *V*   215 maulio *O*, manlio *X*: mallio *δ*   insciis *r* (-ieis *Lachmann*): insciens *V*   215/16 omnibus / nosc. ab insciis *Dawes*   217 suae *Calph.*, suo *r*: suam *V* 219/20 bona matre / laus *V*

qualis unica ab optima
matre Telemacho manet
    fama Penelopeo.   (230)

claudite ostia, uirgines:
lusimus satis. at boni   225
coniuges, bene uiuite et
munere assiduo ualentem
    exercete iuuentam.   (235)

62

VESPER adest, iuuenes, consurgite: Vesper Olympo
exspectata diu uix tandem lumina tollit.
surgere iam tempus, iam pinguis linquere mensas,
iam ueniet uirgo, iam dicetur hymenaeus.
Hymen o Hymenaee, Hymen ades o Hymenaee!   5

Cernitis, innuptae, iuuenes? consurgite contra;
nimirum Oetaeos ostendit Noctifer ignes.
sic certest; uiden ut perniciter exsiluere?
non temere exsiluere: canent quod uincere par est.
Hymen o Hymenaee, Hymen ades o Hymenaee!   10

Non facilis nobis, aequales, palma parata est;
aspicite, innuptae secum ut meditata requirunt.

---

221 ab *om. O*   222 thelamacho *O*, theleamaco *X*   223 peno-
lopeo *X*   224 hostia *V*   225 at boni ζη: ad bonlei *O*,
ad bolnei *X* (al. bonei *Rmg*)   226 bene uiuite *r*: bone uite *V*
227 assiduo ζη: assidue *V*   228 exercere *O*
62. (*adest codex Paris. lat.* 8071, *olim Thuaneus = T*)   Epithalamium Catulli *praescribit T*   *Versui* 1 *adscribit* Turba
uirorum *X* (uirum *R*); *uu.* 6, 11, 20, 32, 39 Puelle; *uu.* 26, 49 Iuuenes
3 pingues *X*   liquere *O*   6 consurgi eretera *T*   7 oeta eos
T, hoc· eos *V*   ignes *Pall.*: imbres *T*, imber *V*   8 certest
Haupt (certe est *iam Statius*): certes ·i· (id est) *T*, certe si *V* (certe
rmg)   9 quod *T*, quo *V*   uincere *B. Guarinus*: uisere *TV*
par est *T*, parent *V*   11 nobis *V*, nobilis *T*   (a)equalis *TV*
12 aspice *O*   que (querunt *O1*) secum *V*   meditata requirunt
Tr: meditare querunt *V*

non frustra meditantur: habent memorabile quod sit;
nec mirum, penitus quae tota mente laborant.
nos alio mentes, alio diuisimus aures;   15
iure igitur uincemur: amat uictoria curam.
quare nunc animos saltem conuertite uestros;
dicere iam incipient, iam respondere decebit.
Hymen o Hymenaee, Hymen ades o Hymenaee!

Hespere, quis caelo fertur crudelior ignis?   20
qui natam possis complexu auellere matris,
complexu matris retinentem auellere natam,
et iuueni ardenti castam donare puellam.
quid faciunt hostes capta crudelius urbe?
Hymen o Hymenaee, Hymen ades o Hymenaee!   25

Hespere, quis caelo lucet iucundior ignis?
qui desponsa tua firmes conubia flamma,
quae pepigere uiri, pepigerunt ante parentes,
nec iunxere prius quam se tuus extulit ardor.
quid datur a diuis felici optatius hora?   30
Hymen o Hymenaee, Hymen ades o Hymenaee!

Hesperus e nobis, aequales, abstulit unam.

  .   .   .   .

  .   .   .   .

namque tuo aduentu uigilat custodia semper;
nocte latent fures, quos idem saepe reuertens,
Hespere, mutato comprendis nomine Eous.   35
at lubet innuptis ficto te carpere questu.

---

13 habent] hunc *O*   memora psile *T*   14 *om. V, ex Thuaneo
primus recepit Muretus*   15 nos *V*, non *T*   17 nunc *T*, non *V*
conuertite *T*, committite *V*   20 quis *T*, qui *V*   22 auelle *T*
25 kymeno kymeneae kymenades o kymeneae (*et similia in sequentibus*) *T*   26 quis *T*, qui *V*   27 firmes *V*, fines *T*   28 quae *T*,
quo *V* (quod *r*)   uir *T*   29 uinxere *O*   30 a *om. T*
32 equales *V* (equalem *rmg*), aequalis *T*   *Post u.* 32 *lacunam statuit
Auantius*[3]   35 comprendis *V* (comprehendis *X*), comperendis *T*
eous *Schrader*: eospem *T*, eosdem *V*   36 at libet *V*, adlucet *T*

quid tum, si carpunt, tacita quem mente requirunt?
Hymen o Hymenaee, Hymen ades o Hymenaee!

Vt flos in saeptis secretus nascitur hortis,
ignotus pecori, nullo conuolsus aratro,
quem mulcent aurae, firmat sol, educat imber;   40
multi illum pueri, multae optauere puellae:
idem cum tenui carptus defloruit ungui,
nulli illum pueri, nullae optauere puellae:
sic uirgo, dum intacta manet, dum cara suis est;   45
cum castum amisit polluto corpore florem,
nec pueris iucunda manet, nec cara puellis.
Hymen o Hymenaee, Hymen ades o Hymenaee!

Vt uidua in nudo uitis quae nascitur aruo,
numquam se extollit, numquam mitem educat uuam, 50
sed tenerum prono deflectens pondere corpus
iam iam contingit summum radice flagellum;
hanc nulli agricolae, nulli coluere iuuenci:
at si forte eadem est ulmo coniuncta marito,
multi illam agricolae, multi coluere iuuenci: 55
sic uirgo dum intacta manet, dum inculta senescit;
cum par conubium maturo tempore adepta est,
cara uiro magis et minus est inuisa parenti.
⟨Hymen o Hymenaee, Hymen ades o Hymenaee!⟩   58b

---

62. 45 *Quintilianus, inst. orat.* ix. 3. 16 Catullus in Epithalamio:
'dum innupta manet, dum cara suis est', cum prius 'dum' significet
'quoad', sequens 'usque eo'.

---

37 quittum *T*, quid (quod al. quid *X*) tamen (al. tum *R*) *V* carpiunt
T quem a *T*, quam *V* 40 conuolsus *T*, conclusus *O*, contusus *Gr*
(*quid R1, latet*) 41 quae mulcens aure firma *T* *Post u.* 41 *uersum unum excidisse censuit Spengel* 43, 44 *om. T*; *seruauit V*
(*om. O*) 45 dum cara α: tum (cum *R1*) cara *TV* suis est *T*, sui
sed *V* (suis sed *r*) 49 ut *V*, et *T* 50 numquam mitem
(uitem *O*) educat *V*, quam muniteam ducat *T* 51 deflectens *V*,
perflectens *T* 53 nulli coluere (coll- *X*) *V*, multi acoluere *T*
54 at si *V*, apsi *T* marita *T* 55 acoluere *T*, accol- *V* 56 intacta *TV*: innupta (*cf. Quintil. ad u.* 45 *laudatum*) *Weber* dum
(2°) *V*, tum *T* 58 cara *r*: cura *TV* 58b *add. Muretus*

Et tu ne pugna cum tali coniuge, uirgo.
non aequom est pugnare, pater cui tradidit ipse,   60
ipse pater cum matre, quibus parere necesse est.
uirginitas non tota tua est, ex parte parentum est;
tertia pars patrist, pars est data tertia matri,
tertia sola tua est: noli pugnare duobus,
qui genero sua iura simul cum dote dederunt.   65
Hymen o Hymenaee, Hymen ades o Hymenaee!

63

SVPER alta uectus Attis celeri rate maria,
Phrygium ut nemus citato cupide pede tetigit
adiitque opaca siluis redimita loca deae,
stimulatus ibi furenti rabie, uagus animis,
deuolsit ili acuto sibi pondera silice,   5
itaque ut relicta sensit sibi membra sine uiro,
etiam recente terrae sola sanguine maculans,
niueis citata cepit manibus leue typanum,
typanum tuum, Cybebe, tua, mater, initia,
quatiensque terga tauri teneris caua digitis   10
canere haec suis adorta est tremebunda comitibus.
'agite ite ad alta, Gallae, Cybeles nemora simul,
simul ite, Dindymenae dominae uaga pecora,

---

63. 1 *citant Marius Victorinus* (*p.* 154 *K.*) *et Terentianus de metris*
2900 (*p.* 411 *K.*).   2 *Caesius Bassus de metris* (*p.* 262 *K.*).

---

59 tua *T*   ne *B. Guarinus*: nec *TV*   60 equom *T*, equo *V*
61 ipse *om. RI*   62 *uersum om. T*   63 pars patrist *Haupt*,
pars patris est *Muretus*: patris *T*, pars patri *V*   pars est *T*, est
O, data pars *X*   64 solit tu est noli tuignare *T*
63. 1 actis *V*   celeri *θ*: celere *V*   4 ibi *Auantius*[3]: ubi *V*
animis *Lachmann*, animi *Parth.*: amnis *V*   5 deuolsit *Haupt*:
deuoluit *V*   ilei *Bergk*: iletas *V*   pondera silice *Auantius*:
pondere silices *V*   7 maculas *V*: *corr.* ζη   8, 9 typanum
Scaliger: timpanum (tymp- *semel X*) *V*   9 tuom *Lachmann*:
tubam *V* Cybebe *Sillig* (Cybebes *iam Bentley*): cibeles *V*   tua
Calph.: tu *V*   10 quatiensque α: quatiens quod *V*   tauri ζ (-rei
Lachmann): tauri et *V*   12 (*similiter* 68 *et* 76) cibelles *O*, cibeles
X   13 dindimenee *mg*   pectora *V*: *corr. Auantius* (*cf.* 77)

aliena quae petentes uelut exules loca
sectam meam exsecutae duce me mihi comites   15
rapidum salum tulistis truculentaque pelagi,
et corpus euirastis Veneris nimio odio,
hilarate erae citatis erroribus animum.
mora tarda mente cedat: simul ite, sequimini
Phrygiam ad domum Cybebes, Phrygia ad nemora deae, 20
ubi cymbalum sonat uox, ubi tympana reboant,
tibicen ubi canit Phryx curuo graue calamo,
ubi capita Maenades ui iaciunt hederigerae,
ubi sacra sancta acutis ululatibus agitant,
ubi sueuit illa diuae uolitare uaga cohors,   25
quo nos decet citatis celerare tripudiis.'
  simul haec comitibus Attis cecinit notha mulier,
thiasus repente linguis trepidantibus ululat,
leue tympanum remugit, caua cymbala recrepant,
uiridem citus adit Idam properante pede chorus.   30
furibunda simul anhelans uaga uadit animam agens
comitata tympano Attis per opaca nemora dux,
ueluti iuuenca uitans onus indomita iugi;
rapidae ducem sequuntur Gallae properipedem.
itaque, ut domum Cybebes tetigere lassulae,   35
nimio e labore somnum capiunt sine Cerere.
piger his labante languore oculos sopor operit;
abit in quiete molli rabidus furor animi.
sed ubi oris aurei Sol radiantibus oculis

38 *citat sub uoce 'rabidus' Festus p.* 338 *L.*

---

14 alienaque *V*   loca *B. Guarinus*: loca celeri *V*   15 execute
V (excute *r*)   16 pelage *Victorius*   17 euitastis *Om*   18 herae
citatis *Auantius*, aere citatis *Lachmann* (aere *iam 1473*): erocitatis *O*,
crocitatis *X* (al. ere citatis *R*)   an animum *V*: *corr. ε*   19 cedit
G (cedat al. cedit *g*)   20 (*similiter* 35, 84, 91) Cybebes *Bentley*:
cibelles *O*, cibeles *X*   23 menade sui *V*   ederigere *Calph.*: ei
derigere *V*   27 actis *ζη*: atris *V*   notha *O*, nota *X*: noua *η*
28 thiasus *δ*: thiasis *O*, -iis *X*   31 animam agens *Lachmann*:
animagens *V* (*quid G1, non liquet*)   32 actis *V*   33 iugi
1472: luci *V*   34 rapide *V*   propere pedem *V*: *corr. B. Venator*
38 abiit *X*   mollis *V*: *corr. θ*   39 horis aurei *V*: *corr. θ*

lustrauit aethera album, sola dura, mare ferum, 40
pepulitque noctis umbras uegetis sonipedibus,
ibi Somnus excitam Attin fugiens citus abiit;
trepidante eum recepit dea Pasithea sinu.
ita de quiete molli rapida sine rabie
simul ipsa pectore Attis sua facta recoluit, 45
liquidaque mente uidit sine quis ubique foret,
animo aestuante rusum reditum ad uada tetulit.
ibi maria uasta uisens lacrimantibus oculis,
patriam allocuta maestast ita uoce miseriter.

'patria o mei creatrix, patria o mea genetrix, 50
ego quam miser relinquens, dominos ut erifugae
famuli solent, ad Idae tetuli nemora pedem,
ut aput niuem et ferarum gelida stabula forem,
et earum omnia adirem furibunda latibula,
ubinam aut quibus locis te positam, patria, reor? 55
cupit ipsa pupula ad te sibi derigere aciem,
rabie fera carens dum breue tempus animus est.
egone a mea remota haec ferar in nemora domo?
patria, bonis, amicis, genitoribus abero?
abero foro, palaestra, stadio et gyminasiis? 60
miser a miser, querendum est etiam atque etiam, anime.
quod enim genus figuraest, ego non quod obierim?
ego mulier, ego adolescens, ego ephebus, ego puer,
ego gymnasi fui flos, ego eram decus olei:
mihi ianuae frequentes, mihi limina tepida, 65
mihi floridis corollis redimita domus erat,

42 excitam *Lachmann*: excitum *V*   43 trepidantem *r*   eum
α: cùm *V*   pasitheo *V*: *corr.* ζ   45 ipsa *B. Guarinus*: ipse *V*
attis *G*, actis *R*, atris *O*   46 sineque is *O*, sineque his *X*   47 aestuante γ *et* rusum *Victorius*: estuanter usum *V*   retulit *V*: *corr. Calph.*
49 maestast ita uoce miseriter *Auantius*[3]: est ita uoce miseritus (al.
miseriter *Rmg*) maiestas (magestates *O*, maiestas al. maiestates *R*) *V*
52 tetuli *O*, retuli *X*   53 apud ε: caput *V* (capùd *R*)   stabilia
V: *corr. r* (stabilla *mg*)   54 earum omnia *multis suspectum*
55 patriam *O*   56 pupula η: popula *V*   ad te β: atte *V*
60 guminasiis *Ellis*: gummasiis *O*, ginnasiis *X* (gymn- *g*)   61 a]
ha *O*, ah *X* (*cf.* 64. 71)   62 figuraest *Lachmann*: figura est *V*
quid abierim *V*: *corr. Statius*   64 gimnasti *V*   sui *X*   oley *V*
66 corolis *Calph.*: circulis *V*

linquendum ubi esset orto mihi sole cubiculum.
ego nunc deum ministra et Cybeles famula ferar?
ego Maenas, ego mei pars, ego uir sterilis ero?
ego uiridis algida Idae niue amicta loca colam?   70
ego uitam agam sub altis Phrygiae columinibus,
ubi cerua siluicultrix, ubi aper nemoriuagus?
iam iam dolet quod egi, iam iamque paenitet.'
  roseis ut huic labellis sonitus ⟨citus⟩ abiit,
geminas deorum ad aures noua nuntia referens,   75
ibi iuncta iuga resoluens Cybele leonibus
laeuumque pecoris hostem stimulans ita loquitur:
'agedum', inquit 'age ferox ⟨i⟩, fac ut hunc furor
     ⟨agitet⟩,
fac uti furoris ictu reditum in nemora ferat,
mea libere nimis qui fugere imperia cupit.   80
age caede terga cauda, tua uerbera patere,
fac cuncta mugienti fremitu loca retonent,
rutilam ferox torosa ceruice quate iubam.'
ait haec minax Cybebe religatque iuga manu.
ferus ipse sese adhortans rapidum incitat animo,   85
uadit, fremit, refringit uirgulta pede uago.
at ubi umida albicantis loca litoris adiit,
teneramque uidit Attin prope marmora pelagi,
facit impetum. illa demens fugit in nemora fera;
ibi semper omne uitae spatium famula fuit.   90
   dea, magna dea, Cybebe, dea domina Dindymi,

67 liquendum *V*   sole ζ: solo *V*   68 nunc *Santen*: nec *V*
ferar γ: ferarum *V*   70 niue *Calph.*: nene *V*   71 columnibus *V*:
corr. θ   74 huic θ: hinc *V* (*fort. recte*) citus *add. Bentley*   abiit
η: adiit *V*   75 adauris *O*   76 ibi ζ: ubi *V*   77 pecoris *cod.
Vaticanus lat.* 1608: pectoris *V*   78 i *add. Scaliger*   face *ed.
Rom.* (*idem* 79 *et* 82)   agitet *add. ed. Cantabrigiensis anni mdccii*
79 uti *Lachmann*, ut hunc ζη: ut *V*   ictu *r*: ictum *V*   81 a
cede *G* (*al.* age cede *add. g*)   tergo *X*   ueruera *V* (uerum uera
legerunt OX): *corr. Calph.*   85 adhortans *Aldina altera*:
adortalis *O*, adhorta lis *X* (adorta lis *r*)   87 bumida *O*, humida
X   88 teneramque *Lachmann* (*cf.* 42, 45, 89; *an recte, dubitari
potest*): tenerumque *V*   actin *R*   marmorea pelago *V*:
corr. γ   89 facit *Calph.*: ficit *O*, fecit *X*   illa *Lachmann*: ille
V   90 omne *X*, esse *O*   91 dindimei *V* (-menei *mg*)

procul a mea tuos sit furor omnis, era, domo:
alios age incitatos, alios age rabidos.

64

PELIACO quondam prognatae uertice pinus
dicuntur liquidas Neptuni nasse per undas
Phasidos ad fluctus et fines Aeeteos,
cum lecti iuuenes, Argiuae robora pubis,
auratam optantes Colchis auertere pellem   5
ausi sunt uada salsa cita decurrere puppi,
caerula uerrentes abiegnis aequora palmis,
diua quibus retinens in summis urbibus arces
ipsa leui fecit uolitantem flamine currum,
pinea coniungens inflexae texta carinae.   10
illa rudem cursu prima imbuit Amphitriten;
quae simul ac rostro uentosum proscidit aequor
tortaque remigio spumis incanuit unda,
emersere freti candenti e gurgite uultus
aequoreae monstrum Nereides admirantes.   15
illa, atque ⟨haud⟩ alia, uiderunt luce marinas
mortales oculis nudato corpore Nymphas
nutricum tenus exstantes e gurgite cano.
tum Thetidis Peleus incensus fertur amore,
tum Thetis humanos non despexit hymenaeos,   20
tum Thetidi pater ipse iugandum Pelea sensit.

---

64. 1 *citat Marius Victorinus, ars gramm.* (*p.* 125 *K.*).

---

92 tuos *Ellis* (tuus *iam* δ): tuo *V*   93 rabidos θ: rapidos *V*
64. 1 pelliaco *V*   2 neptumni *rmg*   3 fasidicos *O*, fascidicos *X*: al. phasidos *add.* (*nisi fallor*) *rmg*   aeetheios *Parth.*: ceticos *O* (al. tetidicos *in margine*), oeticos *X*   4 pupis *O*, puppis *X*
7 uerentes *V*: corr. *rmg*   10 testa *X*   11 prima β: proram *O*, primam *X*   amphitritem *X* (al. amphitrionem *R*), aphitritem *O* (-te *O corr.*)   12 procidit *V*: corr. *Rmg*   13 totaque *V*: corr. *Auantius³*   incanuit *Aldina*: incanduit *V*   14 freti *Schrader*: feri *V*   16 atque haud *Bergk*, alia atque *Vahlen*: atque *X, om. O*   uidere *V*: corr. ζη   19 tum *X*, cum *O*   20 tum *m*: cum *V*   21 tum *Aldina*: cum *V*   sensit *V*: sanxit *Pontanus*

o nimis optato saeclorum tempore nati
heroes, saluete, deum genus! o bona matrum
progenies, saluete iter⟨um . . .   23b
uos ego saepe, meo uos carmine compellabo.
teque adeo eximie taedis felicibus aucte,   25
Thessaliae columen Peleu, cui Iuppiter ipse,
ipse suos diuum genitor concessit amores;
tene Thetis tenuit pulcerrima Nereine?
tene suam Tethys concessit ducere neptem,
Oceanusque, mari totum qui amplectitur orbem?   30
   quae simul optatae finito tempore luces
aduenere, domum conuentu tota frequentat
Thessalia, oppletur laetanti regia coetu:
dona ferunt prae se, declarant gaudia uultu.
deseritur Cieros, linquunt Pthiotica Tempe   35
Crannonisque domos ac moenia Larisaea;
Pharsalum coeunt, Pharsalia tecta frequentant.
rura colit nemo, mollescunt colla iuuencis,
non humilis curuis purgatur uinea rastris,
non glebam prono conuellit uomere taurus,   40
non falx attenuat frondatorum arboris umbram,
squalida desertis rubigo infertur aratris.
ipsius at sedes, quacumque opulenta recessit
regia, fulgenti splendent auro atque argento.
candet ebur soliis, collucent pocula mensae,   45
tota domus gaudet regali splendida gaza.
puluinar uero diuae geniale locatur

---

23 *Scholia Veronensia ad Verg. aen.* v. 80 Catullus: Saluete deum
gens o bona matrum progenies saluete iter . . . .

---

22 seclorum *r*: seculorum *V*   23 gens *Madvig*   matrum *scholia*
Vergiliana: mater *V* (al. matre *Rmg*)   23b om. *V*: *ex scholiis huc*
reuocauit Orioli   25 tedis *O*, thetis *X*   28 nereine *Haupt*:
nectine *V* (al. neptine al. neutumne *R*, al. neptine *mg*)   29 tethys
γ: thetis *V*   31 optate *ζ*: optato *V*   finite *O*   32 aduenere
ζη: adlenire *V*   35 Cieros *Meineke*, scyros *η*: siros *O*, syros, *X*
36 graumonisque *O*, graiunonisque *X*: *corr. Victorius*   moenia laris-
sea *θ*: nicenis alacrissea (-isea *X*) *V*   37 Pharsalum *Pontanus*:
farsaliam *V*   43 at *cod. Parisinus lat.* 8234: ad *V*

sedibus in mediis, Indo quod dente politum
tincta tegit roseo conchyli purpura fuco.

haec uestis priscis hominum uariata figuris   50
heroum mira uirtutes indicat arte.
namque fluentisono prospectans litore Diae
Thesea cedentem celeri cum classe tuetur
indomitos in corde gerens Ariadna furores,
necdum etiam sese quae uisit uisere credit,   55
utpote fallaci quae tum primum excita somno
desertam in sola miseram se cernat harena.
immemor at iuuenis fugiens pellit uada remis,
irrita uentosae linquens promissa procellae.
quem procul ex alga maestis Minois ocellis,   60
saxea ut effigies bacchantis, prospicit, eheu,
prospicit et magnis curarum fluctuat undis,
non flauo retinens subtilem uertice mitram,
non contecta leui uelatum pectus amictu,
non tereti strophio lactentis uincta papillas,   65
omnia quae toto delapsa e corpore passim
ipsius ante pedes fluctus salis alludebant.
sed neque tum mitrae neque tum fluitantis amictus
illa uicem curans toto ex te pectore, Theseu,
toto animo, tota pendebat perdita mente.   70
a misera, assiduis quam luctibus externauit
spinosas Erycina serens in pectore curas
illa tempestate, ferox quo ex tempore Theseus
egressus curuis e litoribus Piraei
attigit iniusti regis Gortynia templa.   75

65 *Isidorus, etym.* xix. 33. 3 (strophium) de quo ait Cinna 'strofio
lactantes cincta papillas'.   71–72 *citat sub uoce 'externauit'*
Nonius p. 154 *L.*

---

52 litora *R*   die ε: dia *OR,* dya *G*   54 adriana *V*: corr. η
55 quae uisit uisere *Vossius*: -que sui tui se *V*   56 tum *X,* tunc *O*
61 saxea *rmg*: saxa *V*   eheu *Bergk,* euoe *Aldina*: heue *V*   62 et
rmg: con *O, quid G et R latet*   64 contenta *O*   66 delapsa e ζη:
delapse *O,* delapso *G,* delapso e *R*   68 sed ζη, sic *Vahlen*: si *V*
tum *bis*] tamen *O*   69 te *om. O*   71 a] ha *O,* ah *X*   73 ferox
quo ex *Italos secutus Lachmann* (quo η): feroxque et *V*   75 cortinia
V: corr. *Pall.*   templa ε, 'alibi tecta *legitur' Parth.*: tempta *V*

    nam perhibent olim crudeli peste coactam
    Androgeoneae poenas exsoluere caedis
    electos iuuenes simul et decus innuptarum
    Cecropiam solitam esse dapem dare Minotauro.
    quis angusta malis cum moenia uexarentur,   80
    ipse suum Theseus pro caris corpus Athenis
    proicere optauit potius quam talia Cretam
    funera Cecropiae nec funera portarentur.
    atque ita naue leui nitens ac lenibus auris
    magnanimum ad Minoa uenit sedesque superbas.   85
    hunc simul ac cupido conspexit lumine uirgo
    regia, quam suauis exspirans castus odores
    lectulus in molli complexu matris alebat,
    quales Eurotae praecingunt flumina myrtus
    auraue distinctos educit uerna colores,   90
    non prius ex illo flagrantia declinauit
    lumina, quam cuncto concepit corpore flammam
    funditus atque imis exarsit tota medullis.
    heu misere exagitans immiti corde furores,
    sancte puer, curis hominum qui gaudia misces,   95
    quaeque regis Golgos quaeque Idalium frondosum,
    qualibus incensam iactastis mente puellam
    fluctibus, in flauo saepe hospite suspirantem!
    quantos illa tulit languenti corde timores!
    quanto saepe magis fulgore expalluit auri,   100
    cum saeuum cupiens contra contendere monstrum
    aut mortem appeteret Theseus aut praemia laudis!
    non ingrata tamen frustra munuscula diuis
    promittens tacito succepit uota labello.
    nam uelut in summo quatientem brachia Tauro   105

---

77 cum androgeanee (-ne *O*) *V*: -oneae η, cum *del. Calph.*   80 moe-
nia] incenia *O*   82 prohicere *O*, proiicere *X*   89 eurotae
1472: europe *V*   praecingunt *Baehrens*, progignunt θ: pergignunt *V*
mirtos *O*, mirtus *X* (al. -tos *R*)   96 quaeque (*1°*) β: quod neque
O, quique *X*   golgos *Hermolaus Barbarus teste Mureto, teste Statio
Petrus Bembus*: cholcos *O*, colchos *X*   100 quanto] quam tum
Faernus   102 oppeteret *X*   104 succepit *Statius* (subscepit
Laetus): succendit *V*   105 uelut] uult *O*

quercum aut conigeram sudanti cortice pinum
indomitus turbo contorquens flamine robur
eruit (illa procul radicitus exturbata
prona cadit, late quaeuis cumque obuia frangens),
sic domito saeuum prostrauit corpore Theseus   110
nequiquam uanis iactantem cornua uentis.
inde pedem sospes multa cum laude reflexit
errabunda regens tenui uestigia filo,
ne labyrintheis e flexibus egredientem
tecti frustraretur inobseruabilis error.   115

    sed quid ego a primo digressus carmine plura
commemorem, ut linquens genitoris filia uultum,
ut consanguineae complexum, ut denique matris,
quae misera in gnata deperdita laeta⟨batur⟩,
omnibus his Thesei dulcem praeoptarit amorem: 120
aut ut uecta rati spumosa ad litora Diae
⟨uenerit,⟩ aut ut eam deuinctam lumina somno
liquerit immemori discedens pectore coniunx?
saepe illam perhibent ardenti corde furentem
clarisonas imo fudisse e pectore uoces,   125
ac tum praeruptos tristem conscendere montes,
unde aciem ⟨in⟩ pelagi uastos protenderet aestus,
tum tremuli salis aduersas procurrere in undas
mollia nudatae tollentem tegmina surae,
atque haec extremis maestam dixisse querellis,   130
frigidulos udo singultus ore cientem:
'sicine me patriis auectam, perfide, ab aris,
perfide, deserto liquisti in litore, Theseu?

106 cornigeram *V*: *corr.* θ   sudanti *rmg*: fundanti *V*   109 late
quaeuis cumque *Ellis*: lateque cum eius *V*   obuia *O*, omnia al.
obuia *X*   114 laberinthis *O*, -theis *X*   116 a *r*: cum *V*
119 ignata *V* (ignata *R*)   laetabatur *Lachmann*: leta *V*   120 praeoptarit *Statius* (-ret *iam Laetus*, -uit θ): portaret *V*   121 ut *om.*
O   uecta *Rmg*: necta *V*   rati *Passerat*: ratis *V*   122 uenerit
add. *Lachmann*   ratis..., / aut ut eam placido *Laetus*   deuinctam
Laetus, deuictam η: deuincta *V*   123 inmemori *G* (al. nemori
add. g)   125 e *X*, ex *O*   126 tristem ζ: tristes *V*   127 in
add. ζη   protenderet *R*: pretenderet *V*   130 hoc *R* (*X?*)
132 patris *O*   auectam *rg* (al. auectam *m*): auertam *V*   133 in *om. O*

sicine discedens neglecto numine diuum
immemor a! deuota domum periuria portas?   135
nullane res potuit crudelis flectere mentis
consilium? tibi nulla fuit clementia praesto,
immite ut nostri uellet miserescere pectus?
at non haec quondam blanda promissa dedisti
uoce mihi, non haec miserae sperare iubebas,   140
sed conubia laeta, sed optatos hymenaeos,
quae cuncta aerii discerpunt irrita uenti.
nunc iam nulla uiro iuranti femina credat,
nulla uiri speret sermones esse fideles;
quis dum aliquid cupiens animus praegestit apisci,   145
nil metuunt iurare, nihil promittere parcunt:
sed simul ac cupidae mentis satiata libido est,
dicta nihil metuere, nihil periuria curant.
certe ego te in medio uersantem turbine leti
eripui, et potius germanum amittere creui,   150
quam tibi fallaci supremo in tempore dessem.
pro quo dilaceranda feris dabor alitibusque
praeda, neque iniacta tumulabor mortua terra.
quaenam te genuit sola sub rupe leaena,
quod mare conceptum spumantibus exspuit undis,   155
quae Syrtis, quae Scylla rapax, quae uasta Carybdis,
talia qui reddis pro dulci praemia uita?
si tibi non cordi fuerant conubia nostra,
saeua quod horrebas prisci praecepta parentis,
attamen in uestras potuisti ducere sedes,   160
quae tibi iucundo famularer serua labore,
candida permulcens liquidis uestigia lymphis,

134 discendens *G*   135 a] ha *O*, ah *X*   136 nullaue *V*:
corr. β   crudeles . . . mentes *V*: *corr. rmg*   138 mirescere *O*,
mitescere *X*: *corr. Calph.*   139 blanda *O*, nobis *X*   140 non
β: nec *V*   misere *V*: miseram *1472*   142 disserpunt *X*, dess- *O*
143 nunc *B. Guarinus*, hinc *Froehlich*: tum *V*   144 fidelis *O*
145 quis *V* (*supra scripto* pro quibus *X*): qui *r*   postgestit *V*: *corr.*
rmg   adipisci *V*: *corr. O et Rmg*   149 lecti *O*   153 praeda]
p'ea (postea) *O*   iniacta *Ellis* (iniecta *iam Calph.*): intacta *V*
156 sirtix *O*   scilla *O*, silla *X*   157 taliaque redis *O*   159 per-
emtis *O*   160 nostras *O*   *Post u.* 160 *collocat u.* 163 *O*

purpureaue tuum consternens ueste cubile.
sed quid ego ignaris nequiquam conquerar auris,
externata malo, quae nullis sensibus auctae   165
nec missas audire queunt nec reddere uoces?
ille autem prope iam mediis uersatur in undis,
nec quisquam apparet uacua mortalis in alga.
sic nimis insultans extremo tempore saeua
fors etiam nostris inuidit questibus auris.   170
Iuppiter omnipotens, utinam ne tempore primo
Cnosia Cecropiae tetigissent litora puppes,
indomito nec dira ferens stipendia tauro
perfidus in Cretam religasset nauita funem,
nec malus hic celans dulci crudelia forma   175
consilia in nostris requiesset sedibus hospes!
nam quo me referam? quali spe perdita nitor?
Idaeosne petam montes? at gurgite lato
discernens ponti truculentum diuidit aequor.
an patris auxilium sperem? quemne ipsa reliqui   180
respersum iuuenem fraterna caede secuta?
coniugis an fido consoler memet amore?
quine fugit lentos incuruans gurgite remos?
praeterea nullo colitur sola insula tecto,
nec patet egressus pelagi cingentibus undis.   185
nulla fugae ratio, nulla spes: omnia muta,
omnia sunt deserta, ostentant omnia letum.
non tamen ante mihi languescent lumina morte,
nec prius a fesso secedent corpore sensus,

171–2 *citat Macrobius, sat.* vi. i. 42.

164 sed *X*, si *O*   auris *rmg* (aureis *Baehrens*): aures *V*   165 extenuata *X*   aucte *V* (aucto al. -te *m*, al. -to *add. g*)   171 ne *V*:
non *Macrobius*   174 creta *O, fort. recte*   175 hic *X*, haec *O*
176 consilia in *η*: consilium (consc- *R*) *V*   nostris *om. O* ·   requiesset *η*: requisisset *V*   177 nitar *r*   178 Idaeosne *B. Guarinus
et Parth.*: idoneos (idoneos al. idmoneos *X*) ne *V*   at *Muretus*, ah
B. Guarinus: a *V*   179 ponti *O*, pontum *X*   ubi diuidit *V*: ubi
del. Auantius³   180 an patris *Rmg*: impatris *O*, in patris *G*
quem ne] quem uae *r*   182 consoles me manet *O*   183 quiue *X*
lentos *O*, uentos *X*   184 colitur *A. Palmer*: litus *V*   185 pater
R

quam iustam a diuis exposcam prodita multam   190
caelestumque fidem postrema comprecer hora.
quare facta uirum multantes uindice poena
Eumenides, quibus anguino redimita capillo
frons exspirantis praeportat pectoris iras,
huc huc aduentate, meas audite querellas,   195
quas ego, uae misera, extremis proferre medullis
cogor inops, ardens, amenti caeca furore.
quae quoniam uerae nascuntur pectore ab imo,
uos nolite pati nostrum uanescere luctum,
sed quali solam Theseus me mente reliquit,   200
tali mente, deae, funestet seque suosque.'
    has postquam maesto profudit pectore uoces,
supplicium saeuis exposcens anxia factis,
annuit inuicto caelestum numine rector;
quo motu tellus atque horrida contremuerunt   205
aequora concussitque micantia sidera mundus.
ipse autem caeca mentem caligine Theseus
consitus oblito dimisit pectore cuncta,
quae mandata prius constanti mente tenebat,
dulcia nec maesto sustollens signa parenti   210
sospitem Erectheum se ostendit uisere portum.
namque ferunt olim, classi cum moenia diuae
linquentem gnatum uentis concrederet Aegeus,
talia complexum iuueni mandata dedisse:
'gnate mihi longa iucundior unice uita,   215
gnate, ego quem in dubios cogor dimittere casus,
reddite in extrema nuper mihi fine senectae,
quandoquidem fortuna mea ac tua feruida uirtus
eripit inuito mihi te, cui languida nondum

190 muletam O, mulctam X   191 comprecer V: corr. ζη
192 mulctantes V   195 meas O, et meas X (corr. rmg)   198 uere
V   200 quali solam ζη (solam iam r): qualis sola V   201 fune-
stent r   204 inuito V: corr. α   205 quo motu Heyse:
quō (quomodo) tunc V   207 mentem θ, mentis η: mente V
211 Erechtheum Vossius: ereptum V   212 moenico V: corr. r
die r   213 cum crederet egens V: corr. r   215 longe Hoeufft
217 extremae r   219 cui O, quem X (cui rm, al. cui add. g)

lumina sunt gnati cara saturata figura, 220
non ego te gaudens laetanti pectore mittam,
nec te ferre sinam fortunae signa secundae,
sed primum multas expromam mente querellas,
canitiem terra atque infuso puluere foedans,
inde infecta uago suspendam lintea malo, 225
nostros ut luctus nostraeque incendia mentis
carbasus obscurata dicet ferrugine Hibera.
quod tibi si sancti concesserit incola Itoni,
quae nostrum genus ac sedes defendere Erecthei
annuit, ut tauri respergas sanguine dextram, 230
tum uero facito ut memori tibi condita corde
haec uigeant mandata, nec ulla oblitteret aetas;
ut simul ac nostros inuisent lumina collis,
funestam antennae deponant undique uestem,
candidaque intorti sustollant uela rudentes, 235
quam primum cernens ut laeta gaudia mente
agnoscam, cum te reducem aetas prospera sistet.'
haec mandata prius constanti mente tenentem
Thesea ceu pulsae uentorum flamine nubes
aereum niuei montis liquere cacumen. 240
at pater, ut summa prospectum ex arce petebat,
anxia in assiduos absumens lumina fletus,
cum primum infecti conspexit lintea ueli,
praecipitem sese scopulorum e uertice iecit,
amissum credens immiti Thesea fato. 245
sic funesta domus ingressus tecta paterna
morte ferox Theseus, qualem Minoidi luctum
obtulerat mente immemori, talem ipse recepit.

224 infulso *V*: *corr. rmg*   227 obscura *r*   228 Itoni *A.
Guarinus*: ithomi *O*, ythomi *X*   229 ac ζ: has *V*   Erechthei
Vossius: freti *V*   230 annuat *r*   231 tum *O*, tu *X*   232 ob-
liferet al. obliteret *mg*   233 ac ζ: hec *V*   234 antennae ne
ut uidetur V: *corr Rmg*   235 sustollant *rmg*: sustolant (subs- *G*)
V   237 aetas *V*: sors *A. Guarinus*   sistet *O*, sistens *G*, sistant *R*:
sistent *rmg*   239 ceu *rmg*: seu *V*   243 infecti *Sabellicus* (*teste
Auantio*) *et B. Guarinus*: inflati *V*   245 facto *O*   247 minoidi
ut uidetur r: minoida *V*

quae tum prospectans cedentem maesta carinam
multiplices animo uoluebat saucia curas.   250
   at parte ex alia florens uolitabat Iacchus
cum thiaso Satyrorum et Nysigenis Silenis,
te quaerens, Ariadna, tuoque incensus amore.

. . . .

quae tum alacres passim lymphata mente furebant
euhoe bacchantes, euhoe capita inflectentes.   255
harum pars tecta quatiebant cuspide thyrsos,
pars e diuolso iactabant membra iuuenco,
pars sese tortis serpentibus incingebant,
pars obscura cauis celebrabánt orgia cistis,
orgia quae frustra cupiunt audire profani;   260
plangebant aliae proceris tympana palmis,
aut tereti tenuis tinnitus aere ciebant;
multis raucisonos efflabant cornua bombos
barbaraque horribili stridebat tibia cantu.
   talibus amplifice uestis decorata figuris   265
puluinar complexa suo uelabat amictu.
quae postquam cupide spectando Thessala pubes
expleta est, sanctis coepit decedere diuis.
hic, qualis flatu placidum mare matutino
horrificans Zephyrus procliuas incitat undas,   270
Aurora exoriente uagi sub limina Solis,
quae tarde primum clementi flamine pulsae
procedunt leuiterque sonant plangore cachinni,
post uento crescente magis magis increbescunt,
purpureaque procul nantes ab luce refulgent: 275
sic tum uestibuli linquentes regia tecta

249 quae] quem *G1*   tum *r*: tamen *V*   prospectans *V* (prospectans al. aspectans *R*, aspectans al. prospectans *m*, aspectans *g*)
251 parte δ: pater *V*   252 cum] tum *O*   253 te *rmg*: et *V*
adriana *V*: corr. *η*   254 quae *Bergk, unum uersum excidisse
ratus*: qui *V*   255 euhoe . . . euhoe α: euche . . . euche *V* (euohe
rmg)   262 tintinitus *X* (*corr. rmg*)   263 multi *V*: corr. *Auantius³*
efflebant *V*: corr. β   267 thesalia *X* (*corr. rmg*)   269 hec *O*
270 procliuit *O1*   271 sub limina β: sublimia *V*   273 leuiterque
Or, leuiter *X*: leni θ   resonant *ηθ*   275 refulgens *V*: corr. *r*
276 tum β: tamen *O*, tamen al. tibi *X*   linquentis *V*: corr. *r*

ad se quisque uago passim pede discedebant.
quorum post abitum princeps e uertice Pelei
aduenit Chiron portans siluestria dona:
nam quoscumque ferunt campi, quos Thessala
    magnis   280
montibus ora creat, quos propter fluminis undas
aura parit flores tepidi fecunda Fauoni,
hos indistinctis plexos tulit ipse corollis,
quo permulsa domus iucundo risit odore.
confestim Penios adest, uiridantia Tempe,   285
Tempe, quae siluae cingunt super impendentes,
†Minosim linquens †doris celebranda choreis,
non uacuos: namque ille tulit radicitus altas
fagos ac recto proceras stipite laurus,
non sine nutanti platano lentaque sorore   290
flammati Phaethontis et aerea cupressu.
haec circum sedes late contexta locauit,
uestibulum ut molli uelatum fronde uireret.
post hunc consequitur sollerti corde Prometheus,
extenuata gerens ueteris uestigia poenae,   295
quam quondam silici restrictus membra catena
persoluit pendens e uerticibus praeruptis.
inde pater diuum sancta cum coniuge natisque
aduenit caelo, te solum, Phoebe, relinquens
unigenamque simul cultricem montibus Idri: 300

277 ad θ: at V (a r)   278 habitum X (corr. g)   280 quoscumque *ut uidetur* r: quodcumque V   campis V: *corr.* r   thesala X, thesalia O   282 aurea V: *corr. rmg*   parit g, perit V (*nisi fallor*): aperit *Housman*   283 corulis V, curulis al. corollis *Rmg*   284 quo *cod. Berolinensis anni mcccclxiii*, quis r: quod O, quot X   285 penies V (penios r, penies al. -os mg) adest ut V: *corr.* r   287 minosim V: Haemonisin *Heinsius, alii alia*   doris V; *locus multum uexatus*   288 non uacuos *Bergk* (-uus *iam B. Guarinus*): non accuos O, non acuos al. nonacrios (-as *Gr*) X   290 mutanti V: *corr. rmg*   sororum V: *corr.* r   291 flamati O, flamanti X   phetontis V   292 contesta V(*corr. R*)   293 uellatum V: *corr. rmg*   296 quam ζ: qua V   298 diui V: *corr. m*   natisque α: gnatisque V (gratisque m, al. gratis *add.* g)   300 ydri V (*uerum adhuc latere suspicor*)

Pelea nam tecum pariter soror aspernata est,
nec Thetidis taedas uoluit celebrare iugalis.

    qui postquam niueis flexerunt sedibus artus,
large multiplici constructae sunt dape mensae,
cum interea infirmo quatientes corpora motu   305
ueridicos Parcae coeperunt edere cantus.
his corpus tremulum complectens undique uestis
candida purpurea talos incinxerat ora,
at roseae niueo residebant uertice uittae,
aeternumque manus carpebant rite laborem.   310
laeua colum molli lana retinebat amictum,
dextera tum leuiter deducens fila supinis
formabat digitis, tum prono in pollice torquens
libratum tereti uersabat turbine fusum,
atque ita decerpens aequabat semper opus dens,   315
laneaque aridulis haerebant morsa labellis,
quae prius in leui fuerant exstantia filo:
ante pedes autem candentis mollia lanae
uellera uirgati custodibant calathisci.
haec tum clarisona pellentes uellera uoce   320
talia diuino fuderunt carmine fata,
carmine, perfidiae quod post nulla arguet aetas.

    o decus eximium magnis uirtutibus augens,
Emathiae tutamen, Opis carissime nato,
accipe, quod laeta tibi pandunt luce sorores,   325
ueridicum oraclum: sed uos, quae fata sequuntur,
    currite ducentes subtegmina, currite, fusi.
adueniet tibi iam portans optata maritis
Hesperus, adueniet fausto cum sidere coniunx,
quae tibi flexanimo mentem perfundat amore,   330

---

327 *citat Macrobius, sat.* vi. 1. 41.

301 palea *V* (*corr. G*)   307 his] hic *m*, al. hic *add. g*   uestis
Parth.: questus *V*   308 talos *B. Guarinus*: tuos *V*   intinxerat *OR*
309 roseae niueo '*alii*' *apud A. Guarinum*: roseo niuee (uinee *O*) *V*
311 collum *V*: *corr. rmg*   313 police *V*   319 custodiebant *X*
320 pellentes *V, uix recte*: uellentes *Fruterius*, pectentes *Statius*
324 tutum opus *O*, tutum opus al. tu tamen opis *X*: *expediuit Housman*
326 oraculum *V*   facta *O*   328 aptata *V*: *corr. rmg*   330 uersum om. *O*   flexo animo *X*   mentis p. amorem *X*: *corr. Muretus*

languidulosque paret tecum coniungere somnos,
leuia substernens robusto brachia collo.
    currite ducentes subtegmina, currite, fusi.
nulla domus tales umquam contexit amores,
nullus amor tali coniunxit foedere amantes,   335
qualis adest Thetidi, qualis concordia Peleo.
    currite ducentes subtegmina, currite, fusi.
nascetur uobis expers terroris Achilles,
hostibus haud tergo sed forti pectore notus,
qui persaepe uago uictor certamine cursus   340
flammea praeuertet celeris uestigia ceruae.
    currite ducentes subtegmina, currite, fusi.
non illi quisquam bello se conferet heros,
cum Phrygii Teucro manabunt sanguine ⟨campi,⟩
Troicaque obsidens longinquo moenia bello   345
periuri Pelopis uastabit tertius heres.
    currite ducentes subtegmina, currite, fusi.
illius egregias uirtutes claraque facta
saepe fatebuntur gnatorum in funere matres,
cum incultum cano soluent a uertice crinem,   350
putridaque infirmis uariabunt pectora palmis.
    currite ducentes subtegmina, currite, fusi.
namque uelut densas praecerpens messor aristas
sole sub ardenti flauentia demetit arua,
Troiugenum infesto prosternet corpora ferro.   355
    currite ducentes subtegmina, currite, fusi.
testis erit magnis uirtutibus unda Scamandri,
quae passim rapido diffunditur Hellesponto,

    331 sonos *V*: *corr.* β   332 leuia] uenia *O*   334 umquam
tales *V*: *corr. cod. Oxoniensis Laudianus anni mcccclx*   341 pre-
uertet β: peruertet *O*, preuertit *X*   344 teucro] teuero *ut uidetur*
G1   campi *Statius*, riui *Calph.*, trunci β: teuen *O*, tenen *G*, tenen *al.*
teuen *R*   347 (*et saepius*) sub tegmine *R*   350 *ita Baehrens*,
incuruo canos . . . crines *Ellis*   incultum] in ciuos *O* (in ciuum *O*
corr.), in ciuium *X*: in cinerem β   canos *V*   soleunt *O*   crimen
O, crines *X*   353 praecerpens *Statius*, prosternens η: precernens
V (*quid G1, latet*)   messor *O*, cultor *X*   *Post u.* 354 *uersum exci-*
disse censuit Vossius   355 prosternet *V* (prosternens *Rmg*) ferrum *O*   358 elesponto *V*

CARMEN 64

59

cuius iter caesis angustans corporum aceruis
alta tepefaciet permixta flumina caede.   360
   currite ducentes subtegmina, currite, fusi.
denique testis erit morti quoque reddita praeda,
cum teres excelso coaceruatum aggere bustum
excipiet niueos perculsae uirginis artus.
   currite ducentes subtegmina, currite, fusi.   365
nam simul ac fessis dederit fors copiam Achiuis
urbis Dardaniae Neptunia soluere uincla,
alta Polyxenia madefient caede sepulcra;
quae, uelut ancipiti succumbens uictima ferro,
proiciet truncum summisso poplite corpus.   370
   currite ducentes subtegmina, currite, fusi.
quare agite optatos animi coniungite amores.
accipiat coniunx felici foedere diuam,
dedatur cupido iam dudum nupta marito.
   currite ducentes subtegmina, currite, fusi.   375
non illam nutrix orienti luce reuisens
hesterno collum poterit circumdare filo,   377
anxia nec mater discordis maesta puellae   379
secubitu caros mittet sperare nepotes.   380
   currite ducentes subtegmina, currite, fusi.

talia praefantes quondam felicia Pelei
carmina diuino cecinerunt pectore Parcae.
praesentes namque ante domos inuisere castas
heroum, et sese mortali ostendere coetu,   385
caelicolae nondum spreta pietate solebant.
saepe pater diuum templo in fulgente reuisens,
annua cum festis uenissent sacra diebus,

359 cessis O   360 flumina V (lumina G): flumine al. lumina
uel flumina m, al. flumine add. g   364 percussae Parth.
366 ac ζ: hanc V   368 madefient η, mitescent ζ: madescent V
372 animi] añ (ante) O   277 esterno O, externo X   378 currite
ducentes subtegmina currite fusi seclusit Bergk   379–81 om.
O   381 currite (2º)] ducite X: corr. m   383 cecinerunt β (cf.
64. 16), cecinere e Baehrens: cecinere V (cernere O)   385 heroum
et Sigicellus apud Statium (et iam 1472), saepius et Calph.: nereus
V   Post u. 386 exhibuit V languidior tenera cui pedens (sic)
sicula beta (67. 21): eiecit Parth.   387 reuisens suspectum:
residens Baehrens   388 cum η: dum V   uenisset V: corr. η

conspexit terra centum procumbere tauros.
saepe uagus Liber Parnasi uertice summo 390
Thyiadas effusis euantis crinibus egit,
cum Delphi tota certatim ex urbe ruentes
acciperent laeti diuum fumantibus aris.
saepe in letifero belli certamine Mauors
aut rapidi Tritonis era aut Amarunsia uirgo 395
armatas hominum est praesens hortata cateruas.
sed postquam tellus scelere est imbuta nefando
iustitiamque omnes cupida de mente fugarunt,
perfudere manus fraterno sanguine fratres,
destitit extinctos gnatus lugere parentes, 400
optauit genitor primaeui funera nati,
liber ut innuptae poteretur flore nouercae,
ignaro mater substernens se impia nato
impia non uerita est diuos scelerare penates.
omnia fanda nefanda malo permixta furore 405
iustificam nobis mentem auertere deorum.
quare nec talis dignantur uisere coetus,
nec se contingi patiuntur lumine claro.

65

ETSI me assiduo confectum cura dolore
seuocat a doctis, Ortale, uirginibus,
nec potis est dulcis Musarum expromere fetus
mens animi, tantis fluctuat ipsa malis—
namque mei nuper Lethaeo gurgite fratris 5

389 terram *O*   procurrere (currus) γ   tauros *Italos secutus Lachmann*: currus *V*   391 thiadas *O*, thyadas *X*   ouantis *rmg*
392 certatum *V*: *corr.* α   tuentes *V*: *corr.* ζη   393 acciperet *V*:
corr. ζη   lacti *V* (lacti al. leti *R*, leti al. lacti *m*, leti *g*)   spumantibus η   394 mauros *G*   395 Amarunsia *Baehrens*, ramnusia
1472: ramunsia *O*, ranusia *X* (*cf.* 66. 71)   400 natos *X*   402 *uix sanum*, uti nuptae *Maehly*   potiretur *V*: *corr.* η   nouellae
Baehrens   404 penates *1472*: parentes *V*

65. 1 confectum *X* (al. defectum *R*), defectu *O*   2 seuocat ζη:
sed uacat *V*   3 dulcis musarum ζθ (dulces η): dulcissimus harum
V   fretus *O*: fletus ε   5 letheo θ, lethaeo in ·*Parth.*: loethi
O, lethei *X*   fratris] factis *O* (*cf.* 66. 22)

pallidulum manans alluit unda pedem,
Troia Rhoeteo quem subter litore tellus
    ereptum nostris obterit ex oculis.

.   .   .   .

numquam ego te, uita frater amabilior,   10
aspiciam posthac? at certe semper amabo,
    semper maesta tua carmina morte canam,
qualia sub densis ramorum concinit umbris
    Daulias, absumpti fata gemens Ityli.—
sed tamen in tantis maeroribus, Ortale, mitto   15
    haec expressa tibi carmina Battiadae,
ne tua dicta uagis nequiquam credita uentis
    effluxisse meo forte putes animo,
ut missum sponsi furtiuo munere malum
    procurrit casto uirginis e gremio,   20
quod miserae oblitae molli sub ueste locatum,
    dum aduentu matris prosilit, excutitur,
atque illud prono praeceps agitur decursu,
    huic manat tristi conscius ore rubor.

66

OMNIA qui magni dispexit lumina mundi,
    qui stellarum ortus comperit atque obitus,
flammeus ut rapidi solis nitor obscuretur,
    ut cedant certis sidera temporibus,
ut Triuiam furtim sub Latmia saxa relegans   5
    dulcis amor gyro deuocet aereo,

7 Tydia al. troya (troia R) X, Tidia ut uidetur O   retheo O,
rhetheo X   9 uersum om. V   11 at ζ: aut V   12 carmine
V: corr. γ   canam ζ: tegam V   14 Bauilla O, Baiula X (al.
Dauilas R, baiulas g)   assumpta O, as(s)umpti X   facta O
ithilei O, ythilei G, ithiley R   16 bactiade r: actiade V
   66. 1 despexit V: corr. Calph.   2 habitus V: corr. ε   4 cer-
tis] ceteris O   5 sub latmia Calph.: sublamina O, sublimia G,
sublimia al. sublamia uel sublimina (sublamina r) R   religans
V: corr. η   6 gyro 1472 (guro Ellis), cliuo ε: guioclero V

idem me ille Conon caelesti in lumine uidit
  e Beroniceo uertice caesariem
fulgentem clare, quam multis illa dearum
  leuia protendens brachia pollicita est,   10
qua rex tempestate nouo auctus hymenaeo
  uastatum finis iuerat Assyrios,
dulcia nocturnae portans uestigia rixae,
  quam de uirgineis gesserat exuuiis.
estne nouis nuptis odio Venus? anne parentum   15
  frustrantur falsis gaudia lacrimulis,
ubertim thalami quas intra limina fundunt?
  non, ita me diui, uera gemunt, iuerint.
id mea me multis docuit regina querellis
  inuisente nouo proelia torua uiro.   20
et tu non orbum luxti deserta cubile,
  sed fratris cari flebile discidium?
quam penitus maestas exedit cura medullas!
  ut tibi tunc toto pectore sollicitae
sensibus ereptis mens excidit! at ⟨te⟩ ego certe   25
  cognoram a parua uirgine magnanimam.
anne bonum oblita es facinus, quo regium adepta es
  coniugium, quod non fortior ausit alis?
sed tum maesta uirum mittens quae uerba locuta es!
  Iuppiter, ut tristi lumina saepe manu!   30
quis te mutauit tantus deus? an quod amantes
  non longe a caro corpore abesse uolunt?
atque ibi me cunctis pro dulci coniuge diuis

---

7 in lumine *Vossius* (lumine *iam* ζ), in culmine *Maehly*: numine *V*
8 ebore niceo *V*: corr. η   11 quare ex *V*: corr. *1473*   12 uastum *V*: corr. ζη   ierat *V*: corr. γ   15 anne θ: atque *V*
17 lumina *V*: corr. ζ   18 diui β: diu *V*   iuuerint *V*: corr. *1472*
21 et *O*, et al. at *X*   22 fratris] factis *O*   23 quam *Bentley*:
cum *V*   24 ibi *G*   tunc *O*, nunc al. tunc *X*   solicitet *V*: corr.
1473   25 te *add. Auantius³*   26 magnanima *V*: corr. ζη
27 quo *Auantius³*: quam *V*   adepta es *Calph.* (-ta's *Lachmann*):
adeptos *O*, adeptus *X*   28 quo (*ita* ζ) non fortius (*ita Iuntina*)
Muretus   ausit '*antiqui codices*' *teste Petro Nicetto apud Robor-*
tellum: aut sit *V*   29 cum *O*   32 adesse *G*   33 me
Colotius: pro *V*

non sine taurino sanguine pollicita es,
si reditum tetulisset. is haut in tempore longo   35
    captam Asiam Aegypti finibus addiderat.
quis ego pro factis caelesti reddita coetu
    pristina uota nouo munere dissoluo.
inuita, o regina, tuo de uertice cessi,
    inuita: adiuro teque tuumque caput,   40
digna ferat quod si quis inaniter adiurarit:
    sed qui se ferro postulet esse parem?
ille quoque euersus mons est, quem maximum in oris
    progenies Thiae clara superuehitur,
cum Medi peperere nouum mare, cumque iuuentus   45
    per medium classi barbara nauit Athon.
quid facient crines, cum ferro talia cedant?
    Iuppiter, ut Chalybon omne genus pereat,
et qui principio sub terra quaerere uenas
    institit ac ferri stringere duritiem!   50
abiunctae paulo ante comae mea fata sorores
    lugebant, cum se Memnonis Aethiopis
unigena impellens nutantibus aera pennis
    obtulit Arsinoes Locridos ales equos,
isque per aetherias me tollens auolat umbras   55
    et Veneris casto collocat in gremio.
ipsa suum Zephyritis eo famulum legarat,
    Graiia Canopitis incola litoribus.

34 taurino *om.* O   35 si] sed O, sed al. si X   haut *Statius*
(haud *iam Aldina*): aut V   41 ferat quod X, feratque O
adiuraret V: *corr. Aldina*   43 quem X, quae O   maximum
'*alii' apud A. Guarinum*: maxima V   44 Thiae *Vossius*: phitie
O, phytie X   45 cum *Rmg*: tum V   peperere η: propere V
cumque O, atque G, atque al. cumque R   48 Chalybon *Politianus*: celerum O, celitum G, celitum al. celorum R (al. celtum
add. r)   50 ferri (ita ζη) stringere·*Heyse*: ferris fringere (fingere
O) V   51 facta O   52 menonis ethyopis X   54 arsinoes
Og, asineos G, asineos al. arsinoes *Rm*   Locridos *Bentley*, Locricos
Statius: elocridicos V   alis V: *corr.* ζ   55 isque V: is quia,
al. -que *m*, al. quia *add. g*   aduolat X   56 collocat O,
aduolat X (al. collocat *Rmg*)   57 zyphiritis V   legerat X (al.
legarat *Rmg*)   58 Graiia *Baehrens* (graia *iam Lachmann*): gratia V
Canopitis *Statius*, canopieis *ed. Rom.*: canopicis (con- O) V

†hi dii uen ibi† uario ne solum in lumine caeli
    ex Ariadnaeis aurea temporibus   60
fixa corona foret, sed nos quoque fulgeremus
    deuotae flaui uerticis exuuiae,
uuidulam a fluctu cedentem ad templa deum me
    sidus in antiquis diua nouum posuit.
Virginis et saeui contingens namque Leonis   65
    lumina, Callisto iuncta Lycaoniae,
uertor in occasum, tardum dux ante Booten,
    qui uix sero alto mergitur Oceano.
sed quamquam me nocte premunt uestigia diuum,
    lux autem canae Tethyi restituit,   70
(pace tua fari hic liceat, Ramnusia uirgo,
    namque ego non ullo uera timore tegam,
nec si me infestis discerpent sidera dictis,
    condita quin ueri pectoris euoluam)
non his tam laetor rebus, quam me afore semper,   75
    afore me a dominae uertice discrucior,
quicum ego, dum uirgo quondam fuit omnibus expers
    unguentis, una uilia multa bibi.
nunc uos, optato quas iunxit lumine taeda,
    non prius unanimis corpora coniugibus   80
tradite nudantes reiecta ueste papillas,
    quam iucunda mihi munera libet onyx,

59 inde Venus *Postgate*, hic lumen *Mowat*; *locus multum uexatus*
lumine γ, limine θ: numine *V* (mumine *R*)   60 adrianeis *V*:
corr. η   61 uos *OG1*(*?*)   63 uuidulam *A. Guarinus* (-lum
iam η), umidulum ζ: uindulum *V* (uiridulum *rmg*)   fluctu *V*: fletu
Pall.   deum me ζ: decumme *V*   65 virgis *O*   66 Calli-
stoe iuncta Lycaoniae *Parth.*: calixto (calisto γ) iuxta licaonia *V*
69 quicquam *O*   70 autem *cod. Berolinensis anni mccclxiii*: aut
V   Tethyi *B. Guarinus*: theti *V*   restituem *V*: *corr. Lachmann*
71 pace *r*: parce *V*   ranumsia *O*, ranusia *X*   72 ullo *O*,
nullo *X*   73 si me θ: sine *V*   diserpent *V*   74 qui *V*
(qui al. quin *R*)   ueri *cod. Berol.* (uerei *Lachmann*): uere *V*,
fort. recte   euolue *V*: *corr. 1473*   75, 76 affore *V*   78 una
V: nuptae *Morel*   uilia *Lobel*: mil(l)ia *V*   79 quas *Calph.*:
quem *V* (quem al. quam *R*)   80 prius *B. Guarinus et Pall.*: post
V   uno animus *V*: *corr.* θ   81 retecta *V*: *corr.* η   82 quam
V: quin *Lachmann* (*seruato in u.* 80 post)

uester onyx, casto colitis quae iura cubili.
    sed quae se impuro dedit adulterio,
illius a mala dona leuis bibat irrita puluis: 85
    namque ego ab indignis praemia nulla peto.
sed magis, o nuptae, semper concordia uestras,
    semper amor sedes incolat assiduus.
tu uero, regina, tuens cum sidera diuam
    placabis festis luminibus Venerem,   90
unguinis expertem non siris esse tuam me,
    sed potius largis affice muneribus.
sidera corruerint utinam! coma regia fiam,
    proximus Hydrochoi fulgeret Oarion!

68

QVOD mihi fortuna casuque oppressus acerbo
    conscriptum hoc lacrimis mittis epistolium,
naufragum ut eiectum spumantibus aequoris undis
    subleuem et a mortis limine restituam,
quem neque sancta Venus molli requiescere somno   5
    desertum in lecto caelibe perpetitur,
nec ueterum dulci scriptorum carmine Musae
    oblectant, cum mens anxia peruigilat:
id gratum est mihi, me quoniam tibi dicis amicum,
    muneraque et Musarum hinc petis et Veneris.   10
sed tibi ne mea sint ignota incommoda, Mani,
    neu me odisse putes hospitis officium,
accipe, quis merser fortunae fluctibus ipse,

---

83 colitis] queritis *R*   85 leuis bibat dona *V*: *corr. 1472*
86 indignatis *O*, indigetis *G*, indigetis al. indignis al. indignatis *R*
87 nostras *V*: *corr. θ*   91 sanguinis *V*: *corr. Bentley*   siris *Lachmann* (siueris *iam Scaliger*): uestris *V*   tuam *Auantius*: tuum *V*
92 effice *V*: *corr. θ*   93 corruerint *Lachmann*, cur retinent? *Pontanus*: cur iterent *V*   94 id rochoi *V*: *corr. 1472*
   68. 1 quo *O*   2 hec *O*   mittit *X*   3 naufragium *V*: *corr. ζη*   6 disertum *G*   10 petit *G*   11 commoda *V*: *corr. γ*   Mani *Lachmann*, malli *α*, mi Alli *Schöll*: mali *V* (al. manli *R*)   12 seu *G*

ne amplius a misero dona beata petas.
tempore quo primum uestis mihi tradita pura est,   15
  iucundum cum aetas florida uer ageret,
multa satis lusi: non est dea nescia nostri,
  quae dulcem curis miscet amaritiem.
sed totum hoc studium luctu fraterna mihi mors
  abstulit. o misero frater adempte mihi,   20
tu mea tu moriens fregisti commoda, frater,
  tecum una tota est nostra sepulta domus,
omnia tecum una perierunt gaudia nostra,
  quae tuus in uita dulcis alebat amor.
cuius ego interitu tota de mente fugaui   25
  haec studia atque omnes delicias animi.
quare, quod scribis Veronae turpe Catullo
  esse, quod hic quisquis de meliore nota
frigida deserto tepefactet membra cubili,
  id, Mani, non est turpe, magis miserum est.   30
ignosces igitur si, quae mihi luctus ademit,
  haec tibi non tribuo munera, cum nequeo.
nam, quod scriptorum non magna est copia apud me,
  hoc fit, quod Romae uiuimus: illa domus,
illa mihi sedes, illic mea carpitur aetas;   35
  huc una ex multis capsula me sequitur.
quod cum ita sit, nolim statuas nos mente maligna
  id facere aut animo non satis ingenuo,
quod tibi non utriusque petenti copia posta est:
  ultro ego deferrem, copia siqua foret.   40

Non possum reticere, deae, qua me Allius in re
  iuuerit aut quantis iuuerit officiis,
ne fugiens saeclis obliuiscentibus aetas
  illius hoc caeca nocte tegat studium:

16 *uersum om. hinc* O, *post u.* 49 *iteratum in* V   27 catulle V :
corr. ζ   29 tepefactet *Bergk*, -faxit *Lachmann*, -fecit γ : tepefacit
V (*al.* -factat R)   30 Mani *Lachmann*, Malli *Calph.*, mi Alli
Schöll : mali V   37 noli O   38 ingenio V : *corr.* α   39 posta
V : praesto *Froehlich*, parta *Schwabe*   40 defferrem *1473* : differ-
rem V (differem G)   41 qua me Allius *Scaliger* : quam fallius V
42 inuenit . . . uiuerit O   43 ne *Calph.* : nec V   sedis V : *corr. 1472*

sed dicam uobis, uos porro dicite multis   45
  milibus et facite haec carta loquatur anus.

·   ·   ·   ·   ·   ·   ·   ·   ·   ·

  notescatque magis mortuus atque magis,
nec tenuem texens sublimis aranea telam
  in deserto Alli nomine opus faciat.   50
nam, mihi quam dederit duplex Amathusia curam,
  scitis, et in quo me torruerit genere,
cum tantum arderem quantum Trinacria rupes
  lymphaque in Oetaeis Malia Thermopylis,
maesta neque assiduo tabescere lumina fletu   55
  cessarent tristique imbre madere genae.
qualis in aerii perlucens uertice montis
  riuus muscoso prosilit e lapide,
qui cum de prona praeceps est ualle uolutus,
  per medium densi transit iter populi,   60
dulce uiatori lasso in sudore leuamen,
  cum grauis exustos aestus hiulcat agros,
ac, uelut in nigro iactatis turbine nautis
  lenius aspirans aura secunda uenit
iam prece Pollucis, iam Castoris implorata,   65
  tale fuit nobis Allius auxilium.
is clausum lato patefecit limite campum,
  isque domum nobis isque dedit dominae,
ad quam communes exerceremus amores.
  quo mea se molli candida diua pede   70
intulit et trito fulgentem in limine plantam

---

46 cerata *O*, certa *G*, certa al. carta *R*: cera *Statius*   47 *uersum
om. V* (deficit *in margine X*)   48 notescamque *G*   *Post u.* 49
exhibuit iocundum cometas florida ut ageret (*u.* 16) *V*: *del. 1473*
50 ali *X*   51 nam] non *G*   52 corruerit *V*: *corr. Turnebus*
54 cetheis *O*, eetheis *G*, oethis *R*   maulia *V*: *corr.* ζ   termopilis
O, -philis *G*, -phylis *R*   55 lumina θ: nummula *O*, numula *X*
56 cessarent θ: cessare ne *V*   59 ualde *V*: *corr.* ζη   61 dulce
Laetus: duce *V*   uiatorum *O*, uiatori *X* (al. -rum *R*)   lasso η:
basso *V*   leuamus *V*: *corr. Calph.*   63 ac] hec *O*, hic *X*   64 leuius
V: *corr.* β   65 implorate *V*: *corr.* η   66 allius *O* (uel manllius *in
margine*), manlius *X*: Manius *Lachmann*   67 classum *X*   68 dominae *Froehlich*: dominam *V*

innixa arguta constituit solea,
coniugis ut quondam flagrans aduenit amore
 Protesilaeam Laudamia domum
inceptam frustra, nondum cum sanguine sacro   75
 hostia caelestis pacificasset eros.
nil mihi tam ualde placeat, Ramnusia uirgo,
 quod temere inuitis suscipiatur eris.
quam ieiuna pium desideret ara cruorem,
 docta est amisso Laudamia uiro,   80
coniugis ante coacta noui dimittere collum,
 quam ueniens una atque altera rursus hiems
noctibus in longis auidum saturasset amorem,
 posset ut abrupto uiuere coniugio,
quod scibant Parcae non longo tempore abesse,   85
 si miles muros isset ad Iliacos.
nam tum Helenae raptu primores Argiuorum
 coeperat ad sese Troia ciere uiros,
Troia (nefas!) commune sepulcrum Asiae Europaeque,
 Troia uirum et uirtutum omnium acerba cinis,   90
quaene etiam nostro letum miserabile fratri
 attulit. ei misero frater adempte mihi,
ei misero fratri iucundum lumen ademptum,
 tecum una tota est nostra sepulta domus,
omnia tecum una perierunt gaudia nostra,   95
 quae tuus in uita dulcis alebat amor.
quem nunc tam longe non inter nota sepulcra
 nec prope cognatos compositum cineres

90 *Nonius p.* 291 *L.* (cinis) feminino aput Caesarem et Catullum et Caluum lectum est, quorum uaccillat auctoritas (*cf.* 101. 4).

73 amorem *V*: *corr.* ɼ   74 protesileam (-thes- *X*) laudomia *V*
75 incepta *V*: *corr. Turnebus*   77 rammusia *O*, ranusia *X*   79 desideret θ (defideret β): deficeret *V*   80 laudomia *V*   uirgo
V: *corr. rmg*   81 nouit *V* (nouit al. uouit *R*): *corr. Auantius*[3]
84 abrupto] abinnupto *O*   85 scirant *L. Mueller*, scibat *Lachmann*   abesse ζη: abisse *V*   87 cum *O*   91 quaene etiam
Heinsius: que uetet id *V*   frater *V* (frater al. fratri *R*)   92 hei
X   frateter *X*   93 hei *V*   iocundumque limine *O*   adeptum
V: *corr. a*   97 quem η: que *V*   98 cineris *V*

sed Troia obscena, Troia infelice sepultum
    detinet extremo terra aliena solo.   100
ad quam tum properans fertur ⟨lecta⟩ undique pubes
    Graeca penetralis deseruisse focos,
ne Paris abducta gauisus libera moecha
    otia pacato degeret in thalamo.
quo tibi tum casu, pulcerrima Laudamia,   105
    ereptum est uita dulcius atque anima
coniugium: tanto te absorbens uertice amoris
    aestus in abruptum detulerat barathrum,
quale ferunt Grai Pheneum prope Cyllenaeum
    siccare emulsa pingue palude solum,   110
quod quondam caesis montis fodisse medullis
    audit falsiparens Amphitryoniades,
tempore quo certa Stymphalia monstra sagitta
    perculit imperio deterioris eri,
pluribus ut caeli tereretur ianua diuis,   115
    Hebe nec longa uirginitate foret.
sed tuus altus amor barathro fuit altior illo,
    qui tamen indomitam ferre iugum docuit.
nam nec tam carum confecto aetate parenti
    una caput seri nata nepotis alit,   120
qui, cum diuitiis uix tandem inuentus auitis
    nomen testatas intulit in tabulas,
impia derisi gentilis gaudia tollens,
    suscitat a cano uolturium capiti;
nec tantum niueo gauisa est ulla columbo   125
    compar, quae multo dicitur improbius
oscula mordenti semper decerpere rostro,
    quam quae praecipue multiuola est mulier.

101 tuum *G*   lecta *add. Eldik* simul *1472, alii alia*   103 nec
V: *corr. G*   105 quod *V*: *corr.* ζ   cum *G*   laudomia *V*
109 peneum *V*: *corr. Auantius*   110 siccari *V* (sic- *O*): *corr.
Schrader*   112 audet *V*: *corr. Palmerius*   amphitrioniadis
(amphyt- *X*) *V*   114 pertulit *V*: *corr.* β   115 tereretur *R*,
terreretur *O*, treerretur *G*: terretur *rmg*   118 tamen *Heyse et*
indomitam *Statius*: tuum domitum *V*   119 tam *O*, causa *X*
(al. neque tam carum *R*)   124 scuscitata cano uoltarium *V*
128 quam quae *Auantius*[3], quantum *Calph.*: quamquam *V*

sed tu horum magnos uicisti sola furores,
    ut semel es flauo conciliata uiro.   130
aut nihil aut paulo cui tum concedere digna
    lux mea se nostrum contulit in gremium,
quam circumcursans hinc illinc saepe Cupido
    fulgebat crocina candidus in tunica.
quae tamen etsi uno non est contenta Catullo,   135
    rara uerecundae furta feremus erae,
ne nimium simus stultorum more molesti.
    saepe etiam Iuno, maxima caelicolum,
coniugis in culpa flagrantem concoquit iram,
    noscens omniuoli plurima furta Iouis.   140
atqui nec diuis homines componier aequum est,

   .   .   .   .

   .   .   .   .

    ingratum tremuli tolle parentis onus.
nec tamen illa mihi dextra deducta paterna
    fragrantem Assyrio uenit odore domum,
sed furtiua dedit mira munuscula nocte,   145
    ipsius ex ipso dempta uiri gremio.
quare illud satis est, si nobis is datur unis
    quem lapide illa dies candidiore notat.

hoc tibi, quod potui, confectum carmine munus
    pro multis, Alli, redditur officiis,   150
ne uestrum scabra tangat rubigine nomen
    haec atque illa dies atque alia atque alia.
huc addent diui quam plurima, quae Themis olim
    antiquis solita est munera ferre piis.
sitis felices et tu simul et tua uita,   155

129 tu horum η: tuorum V   130 es flauo ζη: efflauo O, eflauo X
131 tum *Auantius*[3]: tu V   139 concoquit iram *Lachmann*: coti-
diana (quot- X) V   140 furta ζ: facta V (*cf*. 23. 10)   141 atqui
θ, at quia δ: atque V   componier *Calph*.: componere V *Post
u*. 141 *lacunam indicauit Marcilius*   143 dextra θ: deastra
O, de astra X   144 flagrantem V   145 mira *uix recte* V:
rara *Haupt*   147 is] hiis O, his X   148 diem *1473, fort. recte*
149 quo *Muretus*   150 Alli *Scaliger*: aliis V   155 sitis ζη:
satis V   uita r: uice O, uite G, uirtute R

et domus ⟨ipsa⟩ in qua lusimus et domina,
et qui principio nobis †terram dedit aufert†,
　a quo sunt primo omnia nata bona,
et longe ante omnes mihi quae me carior ipso est,
　lux mea, qua uiua uiuere dulce mihi est.　　　160

70

Nvlli se dicit mulier mea nubere malle
　quam mihi, non si se Iuppiter ipse petat.
dicit: sed mulier cupido quod dicit amanti,
　in uento et rapida scribere oportet aqua.

72

Dicebas quondam solum te nosse Catullum,
　Lesbia, nec prae me uelle tenere Iouem.
dilexi tum te non tantum ut uulgus amicam,
　sed pater ut gnatos diligit et generos.
nunc te cognoui: quare etsi impensius uror,　　　5
　multo mi tamen es uilior et leuior.
qui potis est, inquis? quod amantem iniuria talis
　cogit amare magis, sed bene uelle minus.

73

Desine de quoquam quicquam bene uelle mereri
　aut aliquem fieri posse putare pium.
omnia sunt ingrata, nihil fecisse benigne
　⟨prodest,⟩ immo etiam taedet obestque magis;

72. 8 *citat Donatus in Terentium, Andr.* 718.

---

156 ipsa *add.* ζη, *post* qua *add.* nos *uel* olim *alii*　　　157 *locus
conclamatus*　　　158 bona ζ: bono *V*　　semina nata boni *Peiper*
159 qui *G*　　160 d. mihi est β, d. mihi ζ: mihi d. est *V*
72. 2 prae me *R*, prime *O*, per me *G*　　　6 mi tamen es *A.
Guarinus*: ita me nec *V*　　7 quod β: quam *V*
73. 1 quicquam ζ: quisquam *V*　　　4 prodest *add. Auantius*[3],
iuuerit *Baehrens*, iam iuuat *Munro*　　　obstetque *R* (stetque *r*)
magis *Aldina*: magisque magis *V*

ut mihi, quem nemo grauius nec acerbius urget   5
    quam modo qui me unum atque unicum amicum habuit.

75

Hvc est mens deducta tua mea, Lesbia, culpa
    atque ita se officio perdidit ipsa suo,
ut iam nec bene uelle queat tibi, si optima fias,
    nec desistere amare, omnia si facias.

76

Siqva recordanti benefacta priora uoluptas
    est homini, cum se cogitat esse pium,
nec sanctam uiolasse fidem, nec foedere nullo
    diuum ad fallendos numine abusum homines,
multa parata manent in longa aetate, Catulle,   5
    ex hoc ingrato gaudia amore tibi.
nam quaecumque homines bene cuiquam aut dicere possunt
    aut facere, haec a te dictaque factaque sunt.
omnia quae ingratae perierunt credita menti.
    quare iam te cur amplius excrucies?   10
quin tu animo offirmas atque istinc teque reducis
    et dis inuitis desinis esse miser?
difficile est longum subito deponere amorem,
    difficile est, uerum hoc qua lubet efficias:
una salus haec est, hoc est tibi peruincendum,   15
    hoc facias, siue id non pote siue pote.
o di, si uestrum est misereri, aut si quibus umquam
    extremam iam ipsa in morte tulistis opem,

5 quem *γ*: que *V*   6 habet *X* (habuit *in margine R*)
75. 3 uelle queat *Lachmann* (queam *θ*): uelleque tot *V*
76. 3 nullo *V* (*cf.* 48. 4): in ullo *θ*, *fort. recte*   5 manent *ζη*:
manentum *O*, manenti *X*   8 sint *O*   9 omniaque *V*   10 iam
te cur *ζη*: cur te iam *V*   11 quin *θ*: qui *V*   tu *r*: tui *V*
affirmas *R*   istinc teque *Heinsius*: instincteque *O*, -toque *X*
12 dis *γ*, deis *ε*: des *V*   13 amicum *R1*   14 hec *O*   quam
lubet *V*: corr. *ζ*   officias *O*   15 hoc *R*: hec *V*   16 hoc
R: hec *V*   faties *R*   17 miseri *O*   18 extremam *cod.*
Berol.: extremo *V* (-ma *r*)   ipsa in *Aldina*: ipsam *V*

me miserum aspicite et, si uitam puriter egi,
    eripite hanc pestem perniciemque mihi,   20
quae mihi subrepens imos ut torpor in artus
    expulit ex omni pectore laetitias.
non iam illud quaero, contra me ut diligat illa,
    aut, quod non potis est, esse pudica uelit:
ipse ualere opto et taetrum hunc deponere morbum. 25
    o di, reddite mi hoc pro pietate mea.

77

Rvfe mihi frustra ac nequiquam credite amice
    (frustra? immo magno cum pretio atque malo),
sicine subrepsti mi atque intestina perurens
    ei misero eripuisti omnia nostra bona?
eripuisti, heu heu nostrae crudele uenenum   5
    uitae, heu heu nostrae pestis amicitiae.

81

Nemone in tanto potuit populo esse, Iuuenti,
    bellus homo, quem tu diligere inciperes,
praeterquam iste tuus moribunda ab sede Pisauri
    hospes inaurata pallidior statua,
qui tibi nunc cordi est, quem tu praeponere nobis   5
    audes, et nescis quod facinus facias?

---

21 quae *Calph.*: seu *V*   torpor *η*: corpore *V*   22 delitias
R1   23 me ut *β*, ut me *ζ*: me ut me *V*   26 dei *V* (dii *R*)
mi *r*: michi *V*   pro pietate *m*: proprietate *V*
    77. 1 ruffe *V*: *corr. m*   amico *X*   3 surrepsti *Calph.*:
subrepti *O*, subrecti *X*   mei *V*   4 ei *Lachmann*, sic *ζ*: si *V*
(si al. mi *R*)   5 *et* 6 heu heu *r*: heu *V* (he heu *G*)   6 nostro
X   pestis *B. Guarinus*: pectus *V*
    81. 1 uiuenti *O*: *corr. 1472*   3 ab *V*: a *m*   pisanum *O*
5 qui *Calph.*: quid *V*   6 quod *ζη*: quid *V*

82

QVINTI, si tibi uis oculos debere Catullum
  aut aliud si quid carius est oculis,
eripere ei noli multo quod carius illi
  est oculis seu quid carius est oculis.

83

LESBIA mi praesente uiro mala plurima dicit:
  haec illi fatuo maxima laetitia est.
mule, nihil sentis? si nostri oblita taceret,
  sana esset: nunc quod gannit et obloquitur,
non solum meminit, sed, quae multo acrior est res,   5
  irata est. hoc est, uritur et loquitur.

84

CHOMMODA dicebat, si quando commoda uellet
  dicere, et insidias Arrius hinsidias,
et tum mirifice sperabat se esse locutum,
  cum quantum poterat dixerat hinsidias.
credo, sic mater, sic liber auunculus eius,   5
  sic maternus auus dixerat atque auia.
hoc misso in Syriam requierant omnibus aures;
  audibant eadem haec leniter et leuiter,
nec sibi postilla metuebant talia uerba,

---

83. 3 mulle *X*   4 sanna *O*, samia .*G*, samia al. sana *R*   6 hec
V: *corr. G*

84. 1 chommoda *Calph.*, chomoda *Pontanus*: commoda *V*   2 hinsidias *Politianus et Calph.*: insidias he (hee *O*) *V* (he *del. r*)   3, 4 *hic
collocauit Politianus, post u.* 10 *V*   4 hinsidias *Parth.*:
insidias *V*   5 liber *multis suspectum*   eius *η*: eius est *V*   7 hoc
ε: hec *O*, hic *G*, hic al. hec *R*   syriam *g*: syria *V* (sir- *O*)   8 audie-
bant *V*: *corr. η*

cum subito affertur nuntius horribilis, 10
Ionios fluctus, postquam illuc Arrius isset,
iam non Ionios esse sed Hionios.

85

Odi et amo. quare id faciam, fortasse requiris.
nescio, sed fieri sentio et excrucior.

86

Qvintia formosa est multis. mihi candida, longa,
recta est: haec ego sic singula confiteor.
totum illud formosa nego: nam nulla uenustas,
nulla in tam magno est corpore mica salis.
Lesbia formosa est, quae cum pulcerrima tota est, 5
tum omnibus una omnis surripuit Veneres.

87

Nvlla potest mulier tantum se dicere amatam
uere, quantum a me Lesbia amata mea est.
nulla fides ullo fuit umquam foedere tanta,
quanta in amore tuo ex parte reperta mea est.

---

86. 4 *Quintilianus, inst. orat.* vi. 3. 18 et Catullus, cum dicit 'nulla
est in corpore mica salis', non hoc dicit, nihil in corpore eius esse
ridiculum.

---

11 Arius *Calph.*: arcius *O*, artius *X*   esset *G*   21 hionios *θ*
et Politianus: ionios *V* (ionios . . . Ionios *X*)
85. 1 ama *R1*   2 sed] si *O*
86. 6 omnes *X*
87. 1 potest] pone *G*   2 est *V*: es *Scaliger*   3 umquam
in *Pall.*   tanto *V*: corr. ζη

92

Lᴇsʙɪᴀ mi dicit semper male nec tacet umquam
de me: Lesbia me dispeream nisi amat.
quo signo? quia sunt totidem mea: deprecor illam
assidue, uerum dispeream nisi amo.

93

Nɪʟ nimium studeo, Caesar, tibi uelle placere,
nec scire utrum sis albus an ater homo.

95

Zᴍʏʀɴᴀ mei Cinnae nonam post denique messem
quam coepta est nonamque edita post hiemem,
milia cum interea quingenta Hortensius uno

.   .   .   .

Zmyrna cauas Satrachi penitus mittetur ad undas,   5
Zmyrnam cana diu saecula peruoluent.
at Volusi annales Paduam morientur ad ipsam
et laxas scombris saepe dabunt tunicas.

92. 1–4 *Aulus Gellius* vii. 16. 2 (quispiam) cum esset uerbum 'deprecor' doctiuscule positum in Catulli carmine, quia id ignorabat,
frigidissimos uersus esse dicebat omnium quidem iudicio uenustissimos, quos subscripsi: 'Lesbia . . . amo'.
93. 2 *Quintilianus, inst. orat.* xi. 1. 38 negat se magni facere aliquis poetarum 'utrum Caesar ater an albus homo sit'.

92. 2–4 amat . . . nisi, om. *X*   3 mea *Vossius*: ea *O et traditus
Gelli textus*   4 uero *O*   amo al. amat *R*
93. 2 scire '*in uetustiori codice*' testatur *A. Guarinus*: si ore *V*
sis albus an ater *ex* '*probatissimis codicibus*' *Beroaldus*: si saluus an
alter *V*
95. 1 Zinirna *OG*   mensem *O*   5, 6 Zinirna, -am *V*
5 canas *V*: *corr.* ζη   6 peruoluit *V*: *corr. Calph.*

95*b*

PARVA mei mihi sint cordi monimenta . . .,
   at populus tumido gaudeat Antimacho.

96

SI quicquam mutis gratum acceptumue sepulcris
   accidere a nostro, Calue, dolore potest,
quo desiderio ueteres renouamus amores
   atque olim missas flemus amicitias,
certe non tanto mors immatura dolori est   5
   Quintiliae, quantum gaudet amore tuo.

100

CAELIVS Aufillenum et Quintius Aufillenam
   flos Veronensum depereunt iuuenum,
hic fratrem, ille sororem. hoc est, quod dicitur, illud
   fraternum uere dulce sodalicium.
cui faueam potius? Caeli, tibi: nam tua nobis   5
   perspecta ex igni est unica amicitia,
cum uesana meas torreret flamma medullas.
   sis felix, Caeli, sis in amore potens.

101

MVLTAS per gentes et multa per aequora uectus
   aduenio has miseras, frater, ad inferias,
ut te postremo donarem munere mortis

95*b*. *a praecedentibus seiunxit Statius, haud scio an recte*   1 sodalis *add.* Aldina, Catonis *Leo*, laboris ζη, *alii alia*   2 tumido
X, uel tu timido O   eutimacho V
   96. 1 et gratum V: *corr.* ε   3 que O   renouamur O
5 dolori β: dolor V   6 Quintilie *Rmg*: quintile V
   100. 1 Gellius O, Celius X   aufilenum, -nam V   2 tre-
ronensum O, ueronensum G, trenorensum al. ueronensum R   depereunt η: depereret V (al. -ant R)   6 perspecta ζ: perfecta V
ex igni *Schöll* (*sed* ex *uix recte*), egregie *Baehrens*: est igitur O, est
exigitur G, est igitur al. exigitur R

et mutam nequiquam alloquerer cinerem.
quandoquidem fortuna mihi tete abstulit ipsum, 5
heu miser indigne frater adempte mihi,
nunc tamen interea haec, prisco quae more parentum
tradita sunt tristi munere ad inferias,
accipe fraterno multum manantia fletu,
atque in perpetuum, frater, aue atque uale. 10

102

SI quicquam tacito commissum est fido ab amico,
cuius sit penitus nota fides animi,
meque esse inuenies illorum iure sacratum,
Corneli, et factum me esse puta Arpocratem.

103

AVT sodes mihi redde decem sestertia, Silo,
deinde esto quamuis saeuus et indomitus:
aut, si te nummi delectant, desine quaeso
leno esse atque idem saeuus et indomitus.

104

CREDIS me potuisse meae maledicere uitae,
ambobus mihi quae carior est oculis?
non potui, nec, si possem, tam perdite amarem:
sed tu cum Tappone omnia monstra facis.

101. 6 hei misero *Auantius*³ 7 hec *O*, hoc *X* priscoque *V*
8 tristis munera *Lachmann*
102. 1 amico *r*: antiquo *V*
103. 1 sextercia *V* 2 esto] est *O*, est o *X* 3 mīmi *O*, mi
mi *G*, mimi al. numi *R*
104. 3 si *om. O* perdita *O* amare *V*: *corr.* ʗ

105

MENTVLA conatur Pipleium scandere montem:
  Musae furcillis praecipitem eiciunt.

107

SI quicquam cupido optantique optigit umquam
  insperanti, hoc est gratum animo proprie.
quare hoc est gratum †nobis quoque† carius auro
  quod te restituis, Lesbia, mi cupido,
restituis cupido atque insperanti, ipsa refers te   5
  nobis. o lucem candidiore nota!
quis me uno uiuit felicior, aut magis †hac est
  †optandus uita dicere quis poterit?

108

SI, Comini, populi arbitrio tua cana senectus
  spurcata impuris moribus intereat,
non equidem dubito quin primum inimica bonorum
  lingua exsecta auido sit data uulturio,
effossos oculos uoret atro gutture coruus,   5
  intestina canes, cetera membra lupi.

109

IVCVNDVM, mea uita, mihi proponis amorem
  hunc nostrum inter nos perpetuumque fore.

105. 1 pipileium *V: corr. R*   scindere *V: corr. ζ*   2 furcilis
V: corr. R
  107. 1 quicquam *ε*, quoi quid *Ribbeck*: quid quid *O*, quicquid *X*
cupidoque *Aldina*   obtigit *X*   2 insperati *Heinsius*   3 nobis quoque *V*: nobisque est *Haupt*   5 inspiranti *O*   6 luce *V*:
corr. B. Guarinus   7 hac *O*, me *X*   hac res / optandas *Lachmann*.
  108. 1 sic homini *V: corr. B. Guarinus*   populari *V: corr. Statius*
(arbitrio populi *Calph.*)   4 execta *ζ*: exercta *O*, exerta *X*
  109. 1 amore *V: corr. ζη*

di magni, facite ut uere promittere possit,
   atque id sincere dicat et ex animo,
ut liceat nobis tota perducere uita   5
   aeternum hoc sanctae foedus amicitiae.

IIO

AVFILLENA, bonae semper laudantur amicae:
   accipiunt pretium, quae facere instituunt.
tu, quod promisti, mihi quod mentita inimica es,
   quod nec das et fers saepe, facis facinus.
aut facere ingenuae est, aut non promisse pudicae,   5
   Aufillena, fuit: sed data corripere
fraudando officiis plus quam meretricis auarae ⟨est⟩,
   quae sese toto corpore prostituit.

II3

CONSVLE Pompeio primum duo, Cinna, solebant
   Maeciliam: facto consule nunc iterum
manserunt duo, sed creuerunt milia in unum
   singula. fecundum semen adulterio.

II4

FIRMANO saltu non falso Mentula diues
   fertur, qui tot res in se habet egregias,

6 eterne *O*
110. 1 Auffilena *V*   2 quae] quia *O*   3 promisisti *V*:
corr. γ   4 et *B. Guarinus*: nec *V*   5 promisse *B. Guarinus
et Parth.*: promissa *V*   6 aut fillena *O*, auffilena *X*   7 officiis
Bergk, effectis *Ellis*, effecit *β*: efficit *V*   est *add. Calph.*   8 toto
γ, totam *Westphal*: tota *V*
     113. 2 Meciliam *G*: mecilia *V*   4 singulum *V*: *corr. 1472*
     114. 1 Firmano saltu *Aldina* (saltus *iam B. Guarinus*): firmanus
saluis *V*   mensula *V*: *corr. ε*

aucupium omne genus, piscis, prata, arua ferasque.
  nequiquam: fructus sumptibus exsuperat.
quare concedo sit diues, dum omnia desint.   5
  saltum laudemus, dum †modo ipse egeat.

115

MENTVLA habet instar triginta iugera prati,
  quadraginta arui: cetera sunt maria.
cur non diuitiis Croesum superare potis sit,
  uno qui in saltu tot bona possideat,
prata arua ingentes siluas saltusque paludesque   5
  usque ad Hyperboreos et mare ad Oceanum?
omnia magna haec sunt, tamen ipsest maximus ultro,
  non homo, sed uero mentula magna minax.

116

SAEPE tibi studioso animo uenante requirens
  carmina uti possem mittere Battiadae,
qui te lenirem nobis, neu conarere
  tela infesta ⟨meum⟩ mittere in usque caput,
hunc uideo mihi nunc frustra sumptum esse laborem, 5
  Gelli, nec nostras hic ualuisse preces.
contra nos tela ista tua euitabimus †amitha
  at fixus nostris tu dabis supplicium.

3 aucupium ζ, aucupia γ: aucupiam (an cupiam O) V   6 saltem X   dum modo V: dum tamen β, alii alia
  115. 1 instar (istar O) V: noster Auantius³, saltum Housman
3 potis sit ζ: potuisset V   4 bona Aldina: moda V   possi-
derat O   5 iugentis O   7 ipsest Froehlich (ipse est ζη): ipse
si V   ultro 1473: ultor V
  116. 1 requires V: corr. Auantius   2 batriade V: corr. Parth.
4 tela Muretus: telis (celis O) V   meum add. Muretus   mittere inusque codd. recentiores aliquot: mitteremusque V   6 hic
ζ: hinc V   7 euitamus ζ   amitha O, amicta X: amictu ε
8 at fixus ζ: affixus V

textui subiungit G, praescribit R:

Versus domini Beneuenuti de Campexanis de Vicencia
de resurrectione Catulli poete Veronensis.

Ad patriam uenio longis a finibus exul;
    causa mei reditus compatriota fuit,
scilicet a calamis tribuit cui Francia nomen
    quique notat turbae praetereuntis iter.
quo licet ingenio uestrum celebrate Catullum,
    cuius sub modio clausa papirus erat.

COMMENTARY

I

A DEDICATION to Catullus' fellow countryman and fellow poet, Cornelius Nepos. How much of the extant collection the dedication covered we have not the evidence to decide; see Appendix II.

The identification of Cornelius is assured by Ausonius, *Ecl.* i. 1 (p. 86 Peiper): '"cui dono lepidum nouum libellum?"/ Veronensis ait poeta quondam / inuentoque dedit statim Nepoti.' Cornelius Nepos came from one of the towns of Cisalpine Gaul (Pliny, *N.H.* iii. 127 calls him *Padi accola*), perhaps Ticinum (Pavia); at Rome he was an intimate friend of Cicero's (Gell. xv. 28. 1 'ut qui maxime amicus familiaris fuit'), and Macrobius ii. 1. 14 testifies to the existence of a separate collection of letters from Cicero to Nepos in at least two books. Besides his history (l. 5), now lost, and the biographical work of which the surviving collection of lives formed part, he had himself written light verse (Pliny, *Ep.* v. 3. 6).

Though his handling of it is highly individual, Catullus had Hellenistic precedent for the dedicatory poem: so Meleager prefixes to his anthology a complimentary dedication to Diocles (*A.P.* iv. 1)—Μοῦσα φίλα, τίνι τάνδε φέρεις πάγκαρπον ἀοιδάν; Martial's reminiscence (iii. 2) varies the formula: 'cuius uis fieri, libelle, munus? . . . Faustini fugis in sinum? sapisti.'

The Phalaecian hendecasyllable, the metre in which all but seventeen of the short poems 1–60 are written, is a lyric metre like the glyconic (which it resembles very closely) and the sapphic (which is also a hendecasyllable). It appears in early Greek lyric (Anacreon, fr. 33 D.) and sporadically in the lyrics of tragedy (e.g. Soph. *Phil.* 1140); it is the metre of the first two lines of the four-line Attic skolia (e.g. ἐν μύρτου κλαδὶ τὸ ξίφος φορήσω). Hellenistic poets used it both continuously (κατὰ στίχον)—so Phalaecus (whose name was given to it by ancient metricians because he was the first so to use it) in *A.P.* xiii. 6, Theoc. *Epig.* 22—and in an epodic line alternating with another metre—so Callim. *Epig.* 38 and 40 Pf. In Latin it was one of the lyric metres acclimatized by Laevius (fr. 32) and by Varro in his *Saturae*. In Greek practice the first two syllables may be – –, – ∪ or ∪ –, and Catullus retains that freedom; in Martial the spondee is invariable. In poems 55 and 58*b* hendecasyllables are varied with decasyllables.

1. **cui** : Catullus is likely to have used the form *quoi*, which
succeeds *quoiei* in inscriptions of the last century of the
Republic and was still normal in Quintilian's youth, though
its history had been forgotten (i. 7. 27 'illud nunc melius quod
"cui" tribus quas praeposui litteris enotamus, in quo pueris
nobis ad pinguem sane sonum "qu" et "oi" utebantur,
tantum ut ab illo "qui" distingueretur'). If he did, it is not
surprising that it has disappeared from the manuscript text,
as it has from the texts of other authors : even in Plautus it
has been modernized to *cui* when it was recognized and corrupted to *quo* or *qui* when it was not. (On traces of *quoi* in
Virgil see Norden on *Aen.* vi. 812.) The *qui* which is given
by *V* at 2. 3, 24. 5, and 67. 47 probably represents only
a learned 'improvement' (see W. G. Hale, *C.R.* xx [1906],
160) : but traces of *quoi* may be preserved at 17. 14, 71. 1,
107. 1. The grammarian Scaurus (*G.L.* 7. 28 K.) is probably
right in suggesting that the spelling of the dative with *c* was
introduced merely to avoid confusion with the nominative
after *-oi* had been reduced to *-i* : but inscriptions give little
evidence for the intermediate form *qui* which Ellis posits here
and Norden on *Aen.* vi. 812; see E. Kalinka, *Glotta*, xxx
(1943), 218–25.

   dono : probably a deliberative question, 'to whom am I to
give?' : the 'prospective' use of the indicative for the subjunctive in such questions is not uncommon (e.g. *quid ago?*;
cf. 63. 55 *reor*) and Ausonius' *inuento* (see introd.) suggests
that he took the words so. But the question which Catullus
asks himself may be simply 'to whom am I giving?'

   lepidum : 'charming' : for the colloquial use, as here, of
external appearance cf. Plaut. *Pseud.* 27 'lepidis litteris /
lepidis tabellis lepida conscriptis manu', *Epid.* 43 'forma
lepida . . . adulescentulam', ·222 'uestita aurata ornata ut
lepide ut concinne ut noue'.

2. **pumice expolitum** : pumice was used for giving a smooth
surface to the ends (*frontes*) of the rolled *uolumen* (which were
sometimes afterwards painted) before the *umbilicus* with its
cornua was inserted (see on 22. 7) : so Ov. *Tr.* i. 1. 11 'nec
fragili geminae poliantur pumice frontes'.

   arida : the manuscripts have *arido*, but Servius' comment
on *Aen.* xii. 587, 'masculino genere posuit . . . licet Catullus
dixerit feminino', points to his having had *arida* in his text
here. There are five other ancient testimonia for the line : all
of these agree with the manuscripts of Catullus in reading
arido, but two of them (Isidore, *Orig.* vi. 12. 3 and the Verona
Schol. on Virg. *Ecl.* 6. 1) are quoting the line for its subject-
matter and the others to illustrate metre. Ancient citations,

often made from memory, are not to be trusted for the form
of a word which is not the direct object of the citation, and
there is no reason to distrust Servius, especially since similar
variations of gender are found elsewhere—*finis* is feminine in
Catullus (64. 217), Lucretius, and Virgil (who also has the
masculine), *cinis* in Catullus (68. 90, 101, 4) and Calvus,
cortex in Lucretius and Virgil, *silex* in Virgil. [For a discussion of these feminines see Klotz in *Rh. Mus.* lxxx. 342 ff.:
Probus and Nonius, quoting *aer* and *lapis* feminine from
Ennius, ascribe the variation to the influence of corresponding
Greek words; and Klotz, not very convincingly, produces a
model for *pumex* feminine in κίσηρις.] For other evidence of
early corruption in the text see on 27. 4.

3. **Corneli, tibi :** cf. 100. 5 'cui faueam potius? Caeli, tibi'.

4. **aliquid putare :** cf. Cic. *Tusc.* v. 104 'quos singulos sicut
operarios barbarosque contemnas, eos aliquid putare esse
uniuersos', *Att.* iv. 2. 2 'si unquam in dicendo fuimus aliquid'.

   nugas : it is natural to refer *nugae* to the lighter forms of
verse, occasional pieces, and epigrams: so Martial uses it
several times (e.g. i. 113. 6, iv. 10. 4, v. 80. 3, xiii. 2. 4) of his
own work. Catullus might perhaps have described his long
poems conventionally as *lusus* (see on 50. 2) in contrast with
the massive work of Nepos, but he would not have thought
of them, even in modesty, as *nugae*.

5. **iam tum,** 'already in these days when . . .', implies that
Nepos' work had appeared a considerable time before these
words were written.

   unus Italorum : 'alone among Italians': the implied contrast is with Greece; cf. Prop. iii. 1. 3 'primus ego ingredior
puro de fonte sacerdos / Itala per Graios orgia ferre choros'.
Synopses of universal history had been written in Greek by
Apollodorus and others, and Nepos himself, according to
Gellius and Ausonius, used the Greek title *Chronica* for his
work; in Latin Varro and Atticus are known to have written
annales, but they may have dealt only with Roman history
and may have written after Nepos.

   Italorum : the first syllable is by nature short; the lengthening, though normal, is artificial and due to the necessity
of using *Italia* in hexameters (see Norden on *Aen.* vi. 61).
The *Ī* appears here first in Latin; 'Ἰταλία is already found in
Archestratus and in Callimachus.

6. **omne aeuum . . . explicare :** 'to unroll all the ages': cf. Val.
Max. i *praef.* 'quis omnis aeui gesta modico uoluminum
numero comprehenderit?' Cicero uses the same metaphor of

Atticus' history, *Brut.* 15 'ut explicatis ordinibus temporum uno in conspectu omnia uiderem'.

tribus . . . cartis : i.e. in three *uolumina. carta*, which is properly the sheet of papyrus, is extended to mean the series of sheets glued together to form the *uolumen*; cf. Mart. iv. 82. 7 'si nimis est legisse duos (libellos), tibi carta plicetur / altera' ('roll up one volume').

7. **laboriosis** : Gellius, not very acutely, quotes the same use from Calvus as if it were exceptional: ix. 12. 10 'C. Caluus in poematis "laboriosus" dicit non, ut uulgo dicitur, qui laborat sed in quo laboratur; durum, inquit, rus fugis et laboriosum'. In fact, while the adjective is not very common, the non-personal use is no rarer than the personal: e.g. Ter. *Heaut.* 807 'haec deambulatio/quam non laboriosa', Cic. *Leg.* iii. 19 'nihil laboriosius', Livy v. 19. 10 'operum longe maximum et laboriosissimum', Mart. xi. 6. 3 'uersu ludere non laborioso', x. 104. 13 'iucundos nec laboriosos secessus'.

8. **habe tibi** : 'It is yours, such as it is': *sibi habere* is a regular phrase of Roman law in reference to the disposal of property, but colloquially *tibi habe* often implies a certain indifference which is here in keeping with the self-disparagement of the following words: so Plaut. *Men.* 690 'tibi habe, aufer, utere', Cic. *Verr.* ii. 4. 18 'tibi habe canephoros, deorum simulacra restitue', Sen. *Ep.* 81. 32 'tibi habe quod accepisti, non repeto', Mart. ii. 48. 7 f. 'haec praesta mihi . . . et thermas tibi habe Neronianas' ('you can have them for all I care'). (There is often a contrast, expressed or implied, between what is casually given and what is retained: for examples see Munro on Lucr. iii. 135, Mayor on Juv. 5. 118.) The normal order is similarly inverted in Plaut. *Rud.* 1358 'si tuos est, habeas tibi'.

quidquid : for the depreciatory formula *quidquid hoc libelli* cf. Virg. *Aen.* i. 78 'quodcumque hoc regni'. The fuller form in Lucr. ii. 16 'hoc aeui quodcumque est' shows the construction of the words: the partitive genitive with *hoc* is itself depreciatory (so Cic. *Fam.* ii. 8. 3 'cum hoc ad te litterarum dedi'). The combination of two indefinite pronouns is paralleled, though not in the same formula, in Tac. *Ann.* xiv. 55 'quicquid illud et qualecumque tribuisset', and, without connective as here, in Pliny, *Ep.* viii. 22. 4 'quisquis ille qualiscumque sileatur'. Here *qualecumque* intensifies the disparaging effect of *quidquid*.

9. **qualecumque, quod, ⟨o⟩ patrona uirgo** : in *V* the line is one syllable short, and the old supplement ⟨o⟩ has been generally accepted. To the vulgate text it may be objected

(1) that the *o* of strong emotion (see on 46. 9) is not called for here (but cf. 36. 11); (2) that the abrupt address to a *uirgo* follows awkwardly on *tibi*, referring to Cornelius, in the previous line; (3) that the stop after *qualecumque* gives an enjambment which is extremely harsh in a poem where otherwise syntactical colon and metrical unit coincide. If the reading is right, the *patrona uirgo* must be the (or a) Muse, one of the *doctae uirgines* of 65. 2, who is the poet's *patrona* as in [Sulpicia] 11 ('precibus descende clientis et audi') the poet is Calliope's *cliens*; the characteristically Roman notion which represents the relation between divinity and worshipper as that of *clientela* appears in 34. 1. But even with the defining *patrona*, *uirgo* is curiously unexplicit. When Catullus begins a poem with an address to *deae* (68. 41), his meaning is obvious: *deae*, in that position, can only be the Muses. The poets sometimes address a singular Muse, but, when they do, they have a particular Muse in mind—Calliope, it may be, or Clio; but who is the Muse for a *libellus* of *nugae*? And there is something of a break in thought if Catullus bespeaks the patronage of the Muse for poems which he has just been taking pains, however ironically, to disparage and invites her to immortalize them.

Bergk's 'qualecumque quidem est, patroni ut ergo' ('so that for its patron's sake') both restores concinnity to the poem by removing the enjambment and gives it unity by removing the abrupt apostrophe; for the elision cf. 45. 8 *sinistra ut ante* (in an equally careful poem). The *libellus* will now have a *patronus* to speak for it—Cornelius himself. He, as Catullus has just said, is a figure in the world of letters and his name will ensure a future for the book in spite of its shortcomings. Catullus hopes for immortality, but not on his own merits; that is perhaps more like him than a somewhat inconsequent appeal to an indeterminate muse.

2

The *passer* of this poem and the next has shared the immortality of its mistress. No poems of Catullus were better known in antiquity—Martial has half a dozen direct references to them (i. 109. 1 his dog Issa *est passere nequior Catulli*; i. 7. 3 Stella's pet dove *uicit passerem Catulli*; iv. 14. 13, apologetically offering his own trifles to Silius, he says, with a fine indifference to chronology, 'sic forsan tener ausus est Catullus / magno mittere Passerem Maroni')—and none has had more imitators in modern literatures. That the *passer* was a common domestic pet in Italy we know: its name, like those of other pet animals, is a term of endearment (Plaut. *Asin.* 666 'dic me igitur passerculum, gallinam, coturnicem, / agnellum, haedillum', 693 'dic igitur med anaticulam, columbam uel catellum, / hirundinem, monerulam, passerculum putillum', *Cas.* 138 'meus pullus passer, mea columba, mi lepus': so Marcus Aurelius calls a little girl *passercula nostra*, Fronto iv. 6): the *passeres* are among the household animals that have to be looked after in a sudden removal, Apul. *Met.* viii. 15 'gerebamus infantulos et mulieres, gerebamus pullos, passeres, haedos, catellos'. Was it, then, our sparrow, as it has been for most of the translators and imitators of the poems? Our sparrow is, and no doubt was, as common in the Mediterranean as it is with us, and when Pliny speaks of the *passer*, it is *Passer domesticus* that he means. But it is not only notoriously dowdy and stiff-feathered but also 'the most intractable and least amiable of cage-birds' (D'Arcy Thompson, *Glossary of Greek Birds*[2], p. 270); it is practically untrainable and has none of the qualities of a pet. D'Arcy Thompson himself accepts the identification of Lesbia's *passer* with the blue rock-thrush, *Monticola solitarius*; that bird has borne the name of *passer* both in popular zoology (as *Passer solitarius*) and in common speech (as *passero* in Italy, *passera* being reserved for the sparrow, as *pascher* in the Tyrol); it is attractive in looks and easily tamed, and its friendly ways have made it a favourite pet in Italy.[1] The other pet bird of modern Italy is the goldfinch. That has its own Latin name of *carduelis* (in Petr. 46. 4 the boy who is *in aues morbosus* has three 'cardeles'), but the

---

[1] On the *passero* see Samuel Butler, *Alps and Sanctuaries of Piedmont* (London, 1881), p. 299: 'Nobody knows what a bird can do in the way of song until he has heard a *passero solitario*. . . . All other bird singing is loud, vulgar and unsympathetic in comparison. The bird itself is about as big as a starling, and is of a dull blue colour. It is easily tamed, and becomes very much attached to its master and mistress, but it is apt to die in confinement before very long. It fights all others of its own species; it is now a rare bird, and is doomed, I fear, ere long to extinction, to the regret of all who have had the pleasure of its acquaintance. The Italians are very fond of them, and Professor Vela told me they will even act like a house dog and set up a cry if any strangers come. The one I saw flew instantly at my finger when I put it near its cage, but I was not sure whether it did so in anger or play. I thought it liked being listened to, and as long as it chose to sing I was delighted to stay.' For modern discussions of the identity of the *passer* see Keller, *Antike Tierwelt* ii. 79, K. Dissel in *N. Jahrb.* xxiii (1909), 65, M. Schuster in *Wien. St.* xlvi (1927), 95

use of a derivative of *passer* in some of the Romance languages (Span. *pajaro*, Rum. *pásare*) as a general name suggests that *passer* itself may have been similarly extended in common usage to other small birds. The *passer saepiculae incantans* which a boy goes after in Apul. *Met.* viii. 20 is perhaps more likely to have been a finch than a sparrow.

1. meae puellae : Lesbia, as in 11. 15, 13. 11, 36. 2.

    deliciae : 'pet'; so *in deliciis habere* is to keep as a pet, Cic. *Div.* i. 76 'quam (simiam) rex Molossorum in deliciis habebat', Val. Max. i. 5. 3 'catellus quem puella in deliciis habuit'. The word can be applied to persons—Plaut. *Poen.* 365 'mea uoluptas, mea delicia', Cic. *Div.* i. 79 'amores ac deliciae tuae Roscius': the emperor Titus was called *deliciae generis humani*, 'the world's darling' (Suet. *Tit.* 1)—and even to things: Pliny writes of his native town to a correspondent 'Comum tuae meaeque deliciae' (*Ep.* i. 3. 1). For other uses of the word see on 50. 3.

2. quicum : *qui*, the instrumental case, common to all genders, of the pronominal *qui-* stem, which was displaced by *quo / qua*, the ablative of the alternative *quo-/ qua*-stem, survived in the combination *quicum*, which is normal in Cicero and even as late as Quintilian; for other uses of instrumental *qui* see on 116. 3 (relative) and 72. 7 (interrogative).

3. cui : see on 1. 1.

    primum digitum : 'finger-tip': similarly *Ciris* 212 'digitis primis' (tip-toe), Prop. ii. 26a. 11 'primas extollens gurgite palmas', Pliny, *N.H.* xi. 172 'prima lingua'.

4. incitare : 'provoke': so Stat. *Ach.* i. 170 'catulos apportat et incitat ungues'. The attitude is illustrated on a vase painting reproduced in Keller, *Antike Tierwelt*, ii. 71.

    morsus : of a bird in Cic. *Sen.* 51 'auium minorum morsus': cf. 68. 127 'mordenti rostro'.

5. desiderio meo : for the personal use cf. Cic. *Fam.* xiv. 2. 2 'hem mea lux, meum desiderium,' 4 'ualete, mea desideria', Petr. 139. 4 'tu desiderium meum, tu uoluptas mea', M. Ant. ap. Front. iv. 7. Phillimore's objection (*C.P.* v [1910], 217) that the use cannot be extended to oblique cases seems arbitrary. Literary examples of the use in the vocative are not many and examples in oblique cases might well be expected to be fewer: but Catullus himself provides a parallel at 104. 1 'meae maledicere uitae'.

    nitenti : cf. 61. 186 'ore floridulo nitens'.

7. solaciolum : the diminutive occurs only here and (with a false quantity) in an African sepulchral inscription, *Carm.*

Epig. 1288. 3 (*C.I.L.* viii. 7427) 'est autem uitae dulce
solaciolum', perhaps a reminiscence of this line.

7 ff. In spite of many attempts at solution, the difficulties of
these lines have not been satisfactorily solved. *V* read 'et
solaciolum sui doloris / credo ut cum grauis acquiescet ardor
tecum ludere sicut ipsa possem'. If that reading in l. 7
is right, *solaciolum* must be (*a*) a second object of *iocari*,
in sense epexegetic of *carum nescioquid*: the construction is
somewhat eased by Guarinus's *ut* for *et* (*carum nescioquid ut
solaciolum iocari*) but remains very awkward. It cannot be
taken as (*b*) a second subject of *lubet* (*iocari et solaciolum
lubet*): as Munro showed, *libet* is not used with a substantival
subject other than a pronoun or an expression of quantity.
Nor can it be, as Kroll suggests, (*c*) a second vocative
balancing *deliciae* ('darling of her gay hours and comfort of
her heartache'); that involves a use of *suus* for *eius* which it is
impossible to impute to Catullus on the strength of its occurrence in Cato (e.g. *Agr.* 37. 3). Garrod's neat *simul* for *sui*
would allow *solaciolum* to be taken as a vocative, and the
loose use of *simul* to mean 'also', not 'simultaneously', might
be supported by 55. 6; the vocatives would be far apart, but
the structure would be clear.

The only way of construing *V*'s *ut cum* in l. 8 is to take
ut . . . possem as optative: that leaves an intolerably weak
credo dangling from the previous line, its weakness emphasized by the surprising enjambment. With Guarinus's *ut
tum . . . acquiescat* and the punctuation of the Oxford text,
the lines yield reasonable sense if we assume that the lovers
are separated and that Catullus is equating his situation with
Lesbia's. The bird, he supposes (*credo*), must be comfort for
her *dolor* so that, when she plays with it, her *ardor* abates—
ardor, desire for the loved one, and *dolor*, pining at his
absence, are two ways of looking at the same emotion (cf.
50. 8 and 17)—and he wishes that he could find solace in the
same way. Alternatively, we may accept Baehrens's *credo
tum* (*ut cum* could easily have arisen from an adscript *ul* (i.e.
uel) *cum*) and retain *V*'s *acquiescet*, making *credo . . . acquiescet*
a separate sentence. But in either case the expression is
awkward and abrupt.

8. grauis acquiescat : both words are used of physical suffering:
cf. Celsus iii. 4. 14 'febris grauior', ii. 8. 23 'febris quieuit';
Pliny, *Ep.* iv. 21. 4 'magno tamen fomento dolor meus acquiescet'.

9. ipsa : 'your mistress': see on 3. 7.

2*b*

These three lines follow on poem 2 without a break in the manuscripts and various attempts have been made to provide a connexion. Ellis suggested taking *possem* in 9 as conditional (as he admits, *possim* would be expected) with *tam gratum est* as apodosis ('could I but play with you, it would be as welcome'), comparing such usages as Plaut. *Poen.* 921 'si eadem hic iterum iterem, inscitia est', Mart. ii. 63. 3 'luxuria est si tanti diues amares'. Housman proposed *passer* (vocative) for *possem* (taking *ludere* as subject of *tam gratum est*), Vossius *posse*. But the comparison is extremely inappropriate in the context and Palmer's argument (*Hermath.* iii. 302) that twice elsewhere Catullus uses a long and elaborate simile which is not apt in all its details does not convince one that Catullus could have said, 'I should like playing with Lesbia's bird as much as Atalanta liked the apple which meant the end of her maidenhood'. If the lines belong to this poem we must assume a considerable lacuna and we cannot guess what it contained. But it is more likely that their attachment to this poem is due to the same sort of accident which has attached to poems 14 and 51 lines which do not belong to them. Like the three lines of 14*b*, these lines do not fit anywhere else (attempts to combine them with 14*b* are quite unplausible) and it seems best to take them for the conclusion of a poem of which the rest has been lost.

11 ff. puellae pernici : the story of Atalanta, who challenged her suitors to a race and was beaten by Hippomenes (or Milanion), appears first in Hesiod; she is ποδώκης Ἀταλάντη in the *Eoeae*, fr. 21 Rz. The stratagem of dropping apples in her way, whether it is an original part of the story or an addition, is obviously connected with the familiar use of apples as love-tokens (see on 65. 19) and of μηλοβολία as a mode of flirting (cf. Virg. *Ecl.* 3. 64 and Gow's note on Theoc. 5. 88); it gave an opening for a characteristically Alexandrian refinement of the story which represented Atalanta as having fallen in love with her victor and welcoming defeat and which appears in Theoc. 3. 42 (so probably Philetas, fr. 18 Powell) and, with full psychological elaboration, in Ov. *Met.* x. 560–680.

12. aureolum : the diminutive is a lively word of popular speech, not (as some translators would suggest) a literary preciosity: Catullus' contemporary Varro uses it of a cock's neck-feathers, *collo uario aut aureolo* (and later Columella similarly of the bee, *apes ex aureolo uarias*). The legend did represent the apples of Hippomenes as being of gold (from the gardens of the Hesperides), but Catullus' adjective, like

Virgil's *aurea mala* (*Ecl.* 3. 71, 8. 52), probably refers merely
to the colour of ripeness. He uses it again, 61. 160, of the
bride's feet in her yellow slippers.

13. zonam soluit : cf. 61. 52–53 'tibi (Hymeni) uirgines / zonula
soluunt sinus', 67. 28 'zonam soluere uirgineam'.

    soluit : the trisyllabic value is not an artificial diaeresis
but the original (cf. Sommer, *Handbuch*, p. 131). Catullus
uses it again at 61. 53, 64, 66. 38, 74, and probably at 64.
297, 350: similarly *uolŭo*, 95. 6): elsewhere (36. 2, 64. 367,
67. 28) he has the disyllabic value, which appears already in
Ennius and Lucilius.

    diu ligatam : Priscian (i. 22) so quotes the line and is con-
firmed by the obvious imitation in *Carm. Epig.* 1504. 49
'zonulam ut soluas diu ligatam'. But *negatam* of *V*, besides
being the *lectio difficilior*, has some support from Claudian,
Fescenn. i. 38 (of Hippolyta) 'et seminudo pectore cingulum
forti negatum solueret Herculi'. The divergence may point
to early variation in the text of Catullus (see on 27. 4).

3

    This poem has something in common with a traditional type
of Greek elegiac epigram, the epitaph on an animal: book vii of
the *Greek Anthology* contains a number of examples (189–216)
of widely differing dates. Catullus may have had some of
these, or others like them, in mind (see on 11, 12), but the simple
emotion which turns the lament for the dead pet into a love-
lyric, and makes commonplace and colloquial language into
poetry, owes nothing to any predecessor. Nor do his successors
compete with him: Ovid's elegiacs on Corinna's parrot (*Am.*
ii. 6) and Martial's hendecasyllables on Publius' dog (i. 109) are
clever conceits, and Statius' hexameters (*Silv.* ii. 4) mourn
Atedius' parrot in an orgy of erudition. More natural in feeling
than any of these are the charming verses on the pet dog Myia,
by an unknown writer who remembered his Catullus better than
his grammar, which are found on an inscription of the second
century A.D. at Auch (*Carm. Epig.* 1512 Büch.):

> quam dulcis fuit ista, quam benigna
> quae cum uiueret in sinu iacebat
> somni conscia semper et cubilis.
> o factum male, Myia, quod peristi.
> latrares modo, si quis adcubaret
> riualis dominae, licentiosa.
> o factum male, Myia, quod peristi.

altum iam tenet insciam sepulcrum,
nec saeuire potes nec insilire,
nec blandis mihi morsibus renides.

[See Herrlinger, *Totenklage um Tiere*, Stuttgart, 1930.]

1. **Veneres Cupidinesque** : the phrase is repeated in 13. 12 and
borrowed twice by Martial. The *Cupidines* have generally
been identified with the Amores of later poetry, who first
appear in Propertius and Ovid; the multiplicity of Loves—
and indeed the reduction of *Ἔρως* himself to the familiar status
of the mischievous winged child attendant on Venus—is an
invention of Hellenistic romanticism. *Veneres* has been
variously explained—as due to assimilation to the following
plural (a usage for which a few examples can be cited, e.g.
Culex 351 'soles et sidera cuncta'), as meant to include the
Graces ('Venus and her following'), as an allusion to the
multiplicity of Venuses which Alexandrian mythology recognized (Callim., fr. 200a Pf. τὰς Ἀφροδίτας· ἡ θεὸς γὰρ οὐ μία, Cic.
N.D. iii. 59). None of these explanations is entirely convincing.
The analogy of Amores is probably misleading and *Cupidines*
(the plural occurs first here) as novel an expression as
Veneres. Venus and Cupido are the forces of love in the
world; with characteristic extravagance (and not without
thought for his metre ; it is sometimes too lightly assumed that
poets are above such considerations) Catullus has chosen to
turn both into indefinite plurals—all the powers of Charm
and Desire there are.

2. **quantum est** : the expression ('all the *homines uenusti* there
are') is colloquial, like the similar *quidquid est* (31. 14, 37. 4),
and Plautine (*Capt.* 836, *Poen.* 431, *Rud.* 706). See on 9. 10,
where Catullus uses the same form of words with a different
construction.

uenustiorum : *uenustus* is clearly one of the 'fashionable'
words of Catullus' society (see on 43. 8): he uses it of his
friends (13. 6), of his Lake Garda (31. 12), of a fellow poet's
work (35. 17), all objects which call out his emotion. But its
position here shows how real for him was its connexion with
Venus: it is 'endowed with *Venus*', and the emotion which it
conveys in his extravagant idiom is that of the lover.

5. **oculis suis** : cf. 104. 2 'quae carior est oculis', 14. 1 'ni te
plus oculis meis amarem,' 82. 2; Plaut. *M.G.* 984 'quae te
tam quam oculos amet'; Ter. *Ad.* 903 'pater qui te amat
plus quam hosce oculos'. Similarly in Greek: Callim. *Hymn*
3. 211 Ἀντίκλειαν ἴσον φαέεσσι φιλῆσαι, Moschus 4. 9 τὸν μὲν ἐγὼ
τίεσκον ἴσον φαέεσσιν ἐμοῖσιν.

6. mellitus : cf. 48. 1 'mellitos oculos tuos', 99. 1; Cic. *Att.* i.
18. 1 (of his son) 'mellitus Cicero': so in Petronius, Fronto,
and Apuleius.

6 f. suamque norat ipsam : these words are best taken together,
'his mistress': for the combination cf. *C.I.L.* vi. 15639 (a
freedman's epitaph on his mistress) 'Claudiae ... Gellius Zoilus
issae suae'. For the colloquial use of *ipse* and *ipsa* in this
sense cf. 2. 9, Plaut. *Cas.* 790 'ego eo quo me ipsa misit', *Aul.*
356 'si a foro ipsus redierit'. The vulgar superlative *ipsimus*
is similarly used (Petr. 63. 3 'ipsimi nostri delicatus', 76. 1
'cepi ipsimi cerebellum'); the dog Issa in Mart. i. 109 is Ipsa,
'Mistress'.

8. illius : the *-i-* of the pronominal genitive is invariably short
in Catullus with the one exception of 67. 23 *illīus*.

10. ad ... dominam : 'to greet his mistress': cf. 61. 212 'dulce
rideat ad patrem'.
   pipiabat : Columella (viii. 5. 14) uses the verb of chirping
chickens, Tertullian (*Monog.* 16) of infants.

11. The idea is found more than once in Greek epigram: *A.P.*
vii. 211. 3 (Tymnes, on a dog) νῦν δὲ τὸ κείνου / φθέγμα σιωπηραὶ
νυκτὸς ἔχουσιν ὁδοί, 203. 4 (Simmias, on a partridge) ᾤχεο γὰρ
πυμάταν εἰς Ἀχέροντος ὁδόν, 213. 6 (Archias, on a cicada) νῦν δέ σε
... Ἄιδος ἀπροϊδὴς ἀμφεκάλυψε μυχός.
   tenebricosum : 'gloomy': the word has no pathetic or
romantic associations in Catullus' contemporaries: Varro
uses it of a henhouse (*R.R.* iii. 9. 19), Cicero of a low tavern
(*Pis.* 18), of Vatinius' early career (*Vat.* 11), and in a translation of σκοτίη γνῶσις (*Ac.* ii. 73).

12. negant redire quemquam :   cf. Theoc. 17. 120 ἀέρι πᾳ
κέκρυπται ὅθεν πάλιν οὐκέτι νόστος, Philetas fr. 6 Powell ἄτραπον εἰς
Ἀίδαο / ἤνυσα τὴν οὔπω τις ἐναντίον ἦλθεν ὁδίτης.

13. at, marking an abrupt change of address: so often in imprecations, as in 27. 5, 28. 14; Plaut. *Most.* 38 'at te Iuppiter
dique omnes perdant', Virg. *Aen.* ii. 535, Hor. *Sat.* ii. 2. 40.
Cf. 14. 20, 36. 18.
   male ... malae : the *figura etymologica* (cf. 4. 6) in its many
forms is a regular feature of popular Latin: for this collocation cf. Plaut. *Aul.* 43 'mala malam aetatem exigas'.

14. Orci : a solemn word in the epic language of Ennius,
Lucretius, and Virgil: but its appearance in colloquial phrases
in Plautus (e.g. *Pseud.* 795 'Orcus recipere ad se hunc

noluit') and Petronius (45. 9 'habebit stigmam nec illam nisi
Orcus delebit'; cf. 46. 7) shows that it was not unknown in
popular speech.

bella : in the shorter poems Catullus uses *pulcer* only
twice, and both times for a particular reason—once in speaking of Lesbia (86. 5) and once probably to make a pun on her
brother's name (79. 1). Otherwise his word is the popular
bellus, an old word (a diminutive made from *bonus* before it
assumed its classical form) which in the Romance languages
has outlived its literary rival.

deuoratis : cf. Bion 1. 54 τὸ δὲ πᾶν καλὸν ἐς σε καταρρεῖ.

15. tam bellum : for the 'inverted consecutive' cf. 22. 17 'tam
gaudet in se', 65. 4.

16. *bonum factum male bonus ille passer* is the curious corruption offered by *V*. For the first half of the line the early correction *o factum male* is confirmed by the reminiscence in
Carm. Epigr. 1512 (quoted above) 'o factum male, Myia,
quod peristi'. For the phrase ('what a pity!', 'bad luck!')
cf. Cic. *Att.* xv. 1. 1 'o factum male de Alexione'. (Similarly
bene factum, 'good!', Plaut. *Most.* 643.) It is equally clear
that *bonus ille* conceals *miselle*: the diminutive seems to have
been regularly used in speaking of the dead (Tert. *Test. An.* 4
'cum alicuius defuncti recordaris, misellum uocas eum'; cf.
Petr. 65. 10 'Scissa lautum nouendiale seruo suo misello
faciebat', Apul. *Met.* viii. 1 'Charite . . . misella . . . manes
adiuit'). *o miselle* leaves a hiatus in the middle of the line.
Attempts to avoid it by substituting another exclamation for
the second *o* (*uae* Ellis, *io* Lachmann) lose the effect of the
repetition: the manuscript reading at 38. 2 shows hiatus at
the same point in the line, after an ejaculation as here.

18. turgiduli . . . ocelli : the 'affective' use of diminutives was a
native resource of Latin speech. The diminutive conveys an
emotional overtone—of affection and kindliness, it may be,
or familiarity or distress or amusement or contempt; it is the
counterpart in speech of a smile or a sigh or a shrug. The
speaker can reinforce the effect by doubling it—his *tener* can
become not only *tenellus* but *tenellulus*; and his adjective can
modify itself in sympathy with its noun—his *mulier exornata*
can become *muliercula exornatula* (Plaut. *Cist.* 306).[1] In the

---

[1] Those who are familiar with Northern Scots know the warmth
which that speech gains from its characteristic diminutives; its ability
to give a nuance of personal feeling even to the most casual and prosaic utterance by adding a diminutive suffix to almost any noun—
and on occasion doubling it—offers a close parallel to the Latin idiom.

common speech of high and low alike the idiom lasted as long
as Latin was spoken. Cicero's familiar letters are as full of
diminutives as Plautus' dialogue, and the Romance languages,
in which *auricula* and *lusciniola* have outlived *auris* and *lu-
scinia*, show that in the later vernacular the expressive form
had often superseded the basic one altogether. Catullus
makes free use of them nJt only in the personal poems which
mirror his own moods but also in high poetry (see on 64. 60),
where they serve to enhance that emotional colour which is
characteristic of his writing;[1] with him they express a whole
range of feelings—endearment (12. 17 *Veraniolum*), tender-
ness (17. 15 *tenellulo*, 61. 174 *brachiolum . . . puellulae*, 186 *ore
floridulo*, 64. 331 *languidulos . . . somnos*), pathos (2. 7 *solaciolum*, 30. 2 *dulcis amiculi*, 63. 35 *lassulae*, 64. 60 *ocellis*, 131
frigidulos, 65. 6 *pallidulum*), playfulness (10. 3 *scortillum*, 17.
3 *ponticuli*, 41. 3 *turpiculo*), scorn (25. 10 *manus mollicellas*).
After him they pass out of serious poetry. The severe taste
of the Augustan poets is chary of admitting these intimacies
of language; the adjectives disappear and only the more
conventional and colourless of the nouns survive.[2]

4

The subject is a sea-going yacht, built on the Black Sea,
which conveyed its master through Adriatic and Aegean,
reached a *limpidus lacus*, and is now in retirement, dedicated
to the Dioscuri, the sailor's patron deities. The poem has something in common with a regular Hellenistic type of literary
epigram, the ex-voto inscription written to accompany the
dedication to a god of the tools of a man's trade which have
served their day. Book vi of the Greek Anthology contains many
examples of the type: in several (e.g. vi. 69, 70) the object
dedicated is a ship. In the Greek epigrams the object is sometimes made to speak in its own person; a ship tells its story in
A.P. ix. 34 and 36, though these are not dedicatory but
'sepulchral' epigrams on burned ships. Here the conceit is a
little different: the lines are not spoken directly by the ship but
the speaker, whoever he is, is represented as quoting the ship's
account of itself.

[1] He was not the first thus to turn the diminutive to account;
Laevius, in those lyric experiments which foreshadow Catullus and
his contemporaries, had led the way with *hilarula* (fr. 22) and *manu
lasciuola ac tenellula* (fr. 4).

[2] For an analysis of Augustan practice see A. S. F. Gow in *C.Q.*
xxvi (1932), 150 ff.

The rare metre of the poem, pure iambic trimeter (as in
29), as well as some peculiarities of prosody (9, 18) and of
syntax (2), suggests that Catullus had Greek models in mind.[1]
The style is no less mannered than the metre: the compound
buxifer, the 'epic' words *impetus* and *trabs*, the artifice of
neque . . . nequisse and *negat . . . negare*, the anaphora of *tuo* in
16–17, the apostrophe in 13 and 27, the exploiting of the
romantic associations of place-names all show a high degree of
conscious elaboration combining elements of traditional technique with new effects.

Is the poem merely a literary fancy or is it to any extent
autobiographical? (*a*) The traditional view (accepted in its
simplest form by Ellis and with some variations by Munro and
Wilamowitz) is that the *erus* is Catullus himself, the *erus* of
Sirmio in poem 31, that the voyage described is his own journey
home from Bithynia (see poems 10 and 46), and that the *lacus*
is Benacus, the *lacus* which in poem 31 he greets on his return.
Catullus then sailed in the *phaselus* from Amastris in Paphlagonia (part of his province of Bithynia) or from another
Bithynian port through the Hellespont and the Aegean to the
Adriatic, and thence it made its way by the Po and the Mincio
to Sirmio on Benacus. The poem says nothing of the last part
of this journey. The objection that Catullus' own account of
his Bithynian adventure in poem 10 does not suggest that he
could have bought a yacht need not be taken very seriously.
One may fairly guess that in his references to his embarrassments there is a good deal of exaggeration—and even of convention: it is common form for the fashionable poet to be poor.[2]
senet in l. 26 may not be strictly consistent with a time so short
as that which, on the usually accepted chronology, elapsed
between Catullus' return from Bithynia and his death; the
yacht could hardly be said *senere* within two years of its voyage,
but the metaphor need not be pressed too hard—it has retired
from active life. More serious, perhaps, is the doubt whether a

[1] Though we have no pure iambics surviving in Greek: the hellenistic writers of *iambi* admit spondees.
[2] We remember what we know of his father's position and what
Catullus himself says of a villa at Sirmio (31), a house at Tibur (44),
and an establishment in Rome (68). And the poet's protestations of
his own poverty do not prevent him from making fun (conventionally
again, no doubt) of other people's (23, 33). As Svennung points out,
Tibullus' talk of his own *paupertas*, his *pauper ager*, his contempt of
diuitiae, might be taken at face value if his friend Horace did not say
di tibi diuitias dederunt. Catullus' account of his own finances is even
less to be taken literally.

vessel which could cross the Aegean, even hugging the shores in the way of ancient seamanship, would have found it easy to make the river-journey up to Lake Garda. But the Po was navigable as far as Turin in Pliny's time (*N.H.* iii. 123); the Mincio was a *flumen nauigerum* in the fifth century, when Theodoric, concerned to strengthen his fleet, instructed his praetorian prefect to clear the channel of fishermen's nets so that 'pateat amnis in nauium cursum' (Cassiod. *Variae* v. 17. 6), and may well have been navigable in Catullus' time.[1] The four-line epigram (fr. 11 Morel) in which Cinna speaks of bringing home a copy of Aratus, 'haec . . . / Prusiaca uexi munera nauicula', provokes pleasing fancies but no more. Cinna was probably with Catullus in Bithynia (see on 10. 30) but the fact that he returned on a Bithynian ship throws no light on what Catullus did, and, if the *phaselus* was Catullus', there is nothing to show that Cinna shared it.

(*b*) Baehrens was the first to bring into connexion with the poem the Berne scholium on Virgil, *Georg.* iv. 289 (p. 971 Hagen): 'phaselis: genus nauium pictarum sicus (? *sicut*) phasillus ille quem agiunt auctorem (? *aiunt auctores* ? *ait auctor*) esse nauium calaetarum (or *celaturum*: ? *celerrimum*) quem habuit hospes Serenus. Iunilius dicit.' (*Iunilius* represents the scholar—probably of the fifth century—Iunius Philargyrius of Milan.) Some reference to Catullus' poem clearly underlies this corrupt note, and Baehrens concludes that Serenus was the owner of the yacht, who took the voyage here described and had this dedicatory poem written for him by Catullus. Cichorius develops this suggestion, supposing that the *lacus* is the Bithynian Lake of Apollonia, accessible from the Propontis, and that the owner of the *phaselus* was one Serenus, a Bithynian friend and host of Catullus, who wrote the poem for him. These theories are far from plausible. If the text were certain, the name Serenus could not be dismissed as a mere invention: but it is hazardous to assume, in a scholium so corrupt, that the name is genuine and to build conjectures upon it.

(*c*) Others, more cautious, have taken the poem to be more or less fanciful. The poet may be imagining the life-story of an old ship, with his own journey in mind, or he may be telling, in a form suggested by Hellenistic epigram, the story of a ship, not his own, which had been brought home by the owner from

---

[1] Pliny speaks of the Clitumnus (*Ep.* viii. 8. 3) and the upper Tiber (v. 6. 12) as *nauium patiens*, the *naues* being rowed or punted upstream. Towing from the river bank (by men or by oxen) was also practised on rivers as on canals: cf. Prop. i. 14. 3–4, Dion. Hal. iii. 44 (Tiber), Auson. *Mos.* 41 (Moselle).

Bithynia to Italy. In any case the speaker is the poet himself, and there is nothing to support Wilamowitz's extravagant notion that the language and the rapid movement of the verse are meant to recall the 'patter' of a professional cicerone. And it seems clear that what was dedicated, or is represented as having been dedicated, is the ship itself (cf. Jachmann, *Gnomon*, i. 213); *ille quem uidetis* is inconsistent with the idea that it was some part of the ship (*acrostolium aut aplustre*, as Vossius suggested) which was dedicated and is being displayed.

The poem had the distinction of being made the object of a parody—the only parody of a whole poem which has survived from the classical period—in the tenth poem of the *Catalepton* which appears in the collection of juvenilia ascribed to Virgil. The parody, in which the poem is turned to fit the parvenu ex-muleteer 'Sabinus', follows very closely the language of the original, so closely as to justify a correction in the text of l. 2.

[For discussions of the poem see:

C. L. Smith, *Harvard Studies*, iii (1892), 75–89.
U. von Wilamowitz-Moellendorf, *Hellenistiche Dichtung*, ii. 295–8.
C. Cichorius, *Festschrift für O. Hirschfeld* (Berlin, 1903), 466 ff.
T. Birt, *Philol.* lxiii (1904), 453.
P. Sonnenburg, *Rhein. Mus.* lxxiii (1920), 129–36.
R. Holland, *Phil. Woch.* xlv (1925), 59–63.
H. Rubenbauer, *Bursians Jahresb.* ccxii (1927), 197.
L. A. Mackay, *Class. Phil.* xxv (1930), 77.
F. Zimmermann, *Festschrift für F. Poland* (= *Phil. Woch.* lii. 35/38, 1932), 175–86.
N. Terzaghi, *Stud. Ital. di Fil. Class.* N.S. xv (1938), 55 ff.
J. Svennung, *Opuscula Romana*, i (= Skrifter utgivna av Svenska Institutet i Rom, 4°, xviii: Lund 1954), 109–24.]

1. **phaselus** : The name, originally given, from a resemblance to a bean-pod (φάσηλος), to a light boat used in Egypt and made of papyrus or clay (Virg. *Georg.* iv. 287–9 'gens fortunata Canopi / accolit effuso stagnantem flumine Nilum / et circum pictis uehitur sua rura phaselis', Juv. 15. 127 'paruula fictilibus solitum dare uela phaselis / et breuibus pictae remis incumbere testae'), came to be used of pleasure-craft of a larger size: Nonius (857 L.) explains the word as *nauigium Campanum*, quoting from Varro 'alius domini delicias phaselon aptum(?) tonsilla litore mobilem in fluctum(?) soluit'; the word is used elsewhere in reference to cruising on the Campanian coast (Cic. *Att.* xiv. 16. 1, Mart. x. 30. 13) and a *phaselus* took Atticus from Campania to Epirus (Cic. *Att.*

i. 13. 1). When Propertius (iii. 21) is thinking of a journey to
Greece, it is on a *phaselus* that he imagines himself being
conveyed. The *phaselus* might be a ship of some burden: in
Sall. *Hist*. iii. 8 M. a *phaselus* is large enough for the transport
of a cohort, and Appian *B.C.* v. 95 speaks of φάσηλοι τριηριτικοί.

hospites : *Hospes* represents the common ὦ ξεῖνε of Greek
epigrams, especially sepulchral epigrams which address the
passer-by, in Cic. *Tusc*. i. 101 (translating Simonides), Varro,
Sat. 12. 8 Büch.: similarly Prop. iv. 1. 1, Sen. *Ep*. 21. 10 'cum
adieris eius (Epicuri) hortulos, erit inscriptum postibus
"hospes, hic bene manebis"'.

2. **ait fuisse nauium celerrimus** : the true reading, corrupted in
the manuscript tradition to the normal *celerrimum*, is restored from the parody in *Catalepton* 10, *ait fuisse mulio
celerrimus*, which guarantees the nominative. The nominative and infinitive after a verb of saying, where the infinitive
and the main verb have the same subject, is a rare construction in classical Latin. The one example in early Latin,
Plaut. *Asin*. 633–4 'uiginti minae . . . / quas . . . adulescens
. . . ipsi daturus dixit' has been generally suspected on the
ground that Plautus uses the normal Latin construction
many times and is unlikely to have abandoned it for a Graecism in a particular instance. (Norberg, *Syntaktische For-
schungen*, Uppsala, 1943, pp. 46–63 defends it as a native
idiom, noting the appearance of constructions of the type
promitto daturus in late Latin; Apul. *Met*. vii. 14. 3 'quoad
summos illi promitterent honores habituri mihi' perhaps
points in the same direction: see Löfstedt, *Syntactica*, ii. 429
n. 3.) Catullus' use of it, and the few later classical examples
(Hor. *Ep*. i. 7. 22 'uir bonus et sapiens dignis ait esse paratus',
Catal. 9. 24 'altera (puella) non fama dixerit esse prior', Ov.
Met. xiii. 141 'rettulit Aiax / esse Iouis pronepos'), must be
due to Greek influence. (Prop. ii. 9. 7 'uisura . . . quamuis
numquam speraret Ulixen' should perhaps be added: both
Norberg and Löfstedt confuse the issue by adducing the
quite different, and easier, construction of the nominative
and participle after a verb of perception.) Why these
authors should have resorted to the Greek use when they did
is an unsolved, and probably insoluble, question, but it may
have been made easier by the existence of superficially similar
constructions in Latin with other types of verb: cf. Cic.
T.D. ii. 60 'fortis esse didicisset', Ov. *Pont*. i. 5. 65
'consequor esse poeta', *A.A.* iii. 409 'emeruit contiguus poni',
Quint. x. 1. 97 'esse docti affectant', Ov. *Tr*. iv. 3. 51 'turpe
putas mihi nupta uideri', Lucan, ix. 1037 'tutumque putauit
iam bonus esse socer'. (See Wackernagel, *Vorlesungen*, i, p. 11.)

nauium celerrimus : in accordance with normal idiom the superlative follows the gender of the subject, not (as logic would require) that of the partitive genitive: similarly Cic. *T.D.* ii. 130 'Indus qui est omnium fluminum maximus', *Att.* iii. 7. 3 'id est maximum et miserrimum mearum omnium miseriarum', Gratius 50 'ne subeat uitiorum pessimus umor'. (See Kühner ii. 1. 34 and for a fuller discussion Reisig, *Lat. Synt.*² ii. 14.)

3. impetum trabis : *impetus* and *trabs* (or *trabes*) of a ship both belong to the vocabulary of early epic: Ennius 386 V. 'labitur uncta carina, uolat super impetus undas', 481 V 'impetus haud longe mediis regionibus restat'; cf. Virg. *Aen.* v. 219 of Mnestheus' ship 'illam fert impetus ipse uolantem'.

3 f. neque . . . nequisse : the double negative to express emphatically a positive idea already appears in Plautus (*Trin.* 1157 *haud nolo*) and clearly was felt to be a natural idiom in Latin (so Varro twice has *non inficiens*, although *inficiens* occurs nowhere else): it became a regular stylistic device in later verse. Cf. 8. 7 *nec . . . nolebat* and see Wackernagel, *Vorlesungen*, ii. 297–9.

4 f. palmulis . . . linteo : so Ovid, perhaps with this passage in mind, says of his ship, *Tr.* i. 10. 3–6 'siue opus est uelis, minimam bene currit ad auram, / siue opus est remo, remige carpit iter; / nec comites uolucri contenta est uincere cursu : / occupat egressas quamlibet ante rates'.

palmula, 'oar-blade', is found only here: Catullus has *palma* in 64. 7.

6 f. negat . . . negare : the 'figura etymologica', which in various forms is a favourite artifice of earlier Latin (e.g. Plaut. *Aul.* 181 *properare propero*), is used by Catullus for a new effect.

minacis : Sudden off-shore winds made the Adriatic a proverbially wicked sea : cf. Hor. *Od.* i. 33. 15 'fretis acrior Adriae', iii. 3. 5 'Auster dux inquieti turbidus Adriae', iii. 9. 22 'improbo iracundior Adria'. But see on 8 f. below.

7 ff. -ue . . . -que . . . -que . . . -ue : there is no need to read into the variation of particle any such precision as Munro suggests, regarding *-ue* as separating the three main sections of the voyage (Adriatic, Aegean and Propontis, Pontus—a singularly ill-balanced division) and *-que* as marking stages within them. For the alternation of *-ue* and *-que* see n. on 45. 6 and Löfstedt, *Komm. zur Per. Aeth.* 200.

8. Rhodum nobilem : 'famous' for its historical and cultural associations : similarly Rhodes is *clara* in Hor. *Od.* i. 7. 1, Mart. iv. 55. 6.

8 f. horridamque Thraciam Propontida : *Thraciam* must be an
adjective agreeing with *Propontida*, as Lachmann rightly
pointed out, though he was wrong in denying the existence
of *Thracia* as a noun beside the normal *Thrace* or *Thraca*:
Thracia is found in Varro's prose and in verse as early as Ov.
Met. vi. 435. To isolate *Propontida* in asyndeton and without
an epithet is to destroy the symmetry of the structure, in
which *horridamque Thraciam Propontida* corresponds to
trucemue Ponticum sinum. And while parts of Thrace deserved
the epithet *horridus*, the Thracian coast of the Hellespont
and Propontis, the only part of Thrace that the *phaselus*
would naturally see, was a fertile country dotted with settle-
ments: it is the sea which is *horrida*, as the sea behind is *trux*
and the sea in front is *minax*, and the epithets reflect the
normal attitude of a people who were no sailors and to whom
every sea was an enemy. Ellis's metrical objection to the
enjambment *Thraciam Propontida* is untenable: the enjambment is no more remarkable here than in 20–21 or 25–26.
J. A. K. Thomson (*C.R.* lxiv. 90) ingeniously proposes *Thracia*,
the ablative of *Thracias* (Θρᾳκίας), the NNW. wind which is
now, and no doubt was in Catullus' time, the prevailing storm-
wind of the Propontis. The name occurs elsewhere only in
technical contexts—Seneca (*N.Q.* v. 16. 6) writes it in Greek and
Pliny (*N.H.* ii. 120) uses the alternative form *thrascias*—
but the same is true of *Apheliotes*. It is not impossible
that Catullus used *Thracia* here as he used *Apheliotae* in
26. 3.

9. Propontidā trucemue : The metrical irregularity is repeated
in l. 18 *impotentiā freta* and (again in pure iambics) in 29. 4
ultimā Britannia. In normal Latin practice a short open
final syllable is not affected by two consonants beginning the
next word (so 4 *nequisse praeterire*, 8 *horridamque Thraciam*:
for the special case of *sc*, *sp*, *st* see on 17. 24, and for *gn* on
36. 13); i.e. the syllable remains open, the two consonants
being both attached to the following syllable. In Greek,
practice varies: in hexameters lengthening of such a syllable
is normal, even before a combination of mute and liquid: in
the verse of Attic drama lengthening is much restricted—
before mute and liquid it is rare in tragedy, unknown in
comedy, which cannot ignore the practice of ordinary speech.
The epic lengthening is occasionally imitated in Latin
(especially in Virgil) with *-que*; otherwise the only example
outside Catullus is Tib. i. 6. 34 'seruare, frustra clauis inest
foribus'. Catullus may have had precedent for his use in
Greek iambographers, who may well have followed epic
convention in this respect as they did in others.

10. **iste post phaselus** : 'the yacht to be': cf. Tib. iii. 1. 23 'haec tibi uir quondam, nunc frater, casta Neaera / mittit', Prop. ii. 28. 61 'redde etiam excubias diuae nunc, ante iuuencae', Livy xxiv. 32. 5 'ne proderent patriam tyranni ante satellitibus et tum corruptoribus exercitus'. The adjectival use of an adverb or adverbial phrase is no Graecism. Such phrases as *bis consul* and *paene insula* (and the common use of local ablatives to indicate a man's origin, as in Caes. *B.C.* i. 24. 4 *N. Magius Cremona*, Liv. i. 50. 3 *Turnus Herdonius ab Aricia*) show that it was a native idiom. It appears in Ennius (*ceteros tunc homines*) and thereafter in all periods and styles (e.g. Ter. *Ad.* 541 'a uilla mercennarium uidi, Cic. *Verr.* ii. 2. 156 'legatum et publice testem', Virg. *Aen.* i. 21 'populum late regem', Hor. *Ep.* i. 7. 75 'mane cliens', etc.). (On adverbial phrases with *a* and *ex* used adjectively see Munro on Lucr. ii. 51.)

11. **Cytorio in iugo** : the hills above the Paphlagonian seaport of Cytorus. The whole of the south coast of the Pontus was forested and provided wood for the local industries of ship-building (Hor. *Od.* i. 14. 11 *Pontica pinus*, i. 35. 7 *Bithyna carina*) and smelting.

12. **loquente . . . coma** : cf. Virg. *Ecl.* 8. 22 'Maenalus argutumque nemus pinosque loquentes / semper habet', Auson. *Epist.* 245. 14 'cumque suis tremulum loquitur coma pinea uentis', Corn. Seuer. fr. 10 Morel 'pinea frondosi coma murmurat Apennini'. So in Theoc. 1. 1 f. ἁδύ τι τὸ ψιθύρισμα καὶ ἁ πίτυς, αἰπόλε, τήνα / ἁ ποτὶ ταῖς παγαῖσι μελίσδεται.

13. **Amastris**, the capital of Paphlagonia (administered, as far as the Halys, as part of the province of Bithynia) and Cytorus were neighbouring ports on the Black Sea coast. The box-wood of Cytorus was famous: Virg. *Georg.* ii. 437 'iuuat undantem buxo spectare Cytorum', Plin. *N.H.* xvi. 71 'buxus Pyrenaeis ac Cytoriis montibus plurima', Strabo 544 πλείστη καὶ ἀρίστη πύξος φύεται κατὰ τὴν Ἀμαστριανὴν καὶ μάλιστα περὶ τὸ Κύτωρον. So πύξον εἰς Κύτωρον ἄγειν was 'carrying coals to Newcastle' (Eust. ad *Il.* i. 20).

buxifer : the compound occurs only here. The expressive compound was part of the early epic technique which classical verse abandoned (though Ovid found compounds in *-fer* and *-ger* metrically convenient): Catullus uses it freely in the longer poems, elsewhere only in poems of some elaboration (so 11. 6, 7) or to give a mock-solemn effect (36. 7, 58b. 3, 5).

The apostrophe (cf. 26–27, 64. 69, 253, 299) is a trick of later Greek poetry, first exploited for its emotional, subjective value but often in practice little more than a conventional piece of technique, commended by metrical convenience, which the Latin Alexandrians adopted and handed on to Virgil (cf. Gell. xiii. 27. 3, who admires *Aen.* iii. 119 'taurum Neptuno, taurum tibi, pulcher Apollo' as νεανικώτερος and *fucatior* than its straightforward Homeric original), Propertius, and Ovid. (See Norden on *Aen.* vi. 18.)

14 ff. tibi . . . tuo : Amastris and Cytorus are regarded as one unit.

14. cognitissima : the superlative is found only here: Ovid has the comparative twice (*Tr.* iv. 6. 28, *Met.* xiv. 15).

15. ultima ex origine : 'from her birth in the beginning': so Nepos *Att.* 1 'ab origine ultima', Virg. *Aen.* i. 372 'prima ab origine'; similarly 64. 217 'extrema fine', Hor. *Ep.* ii. 1. 12 'supremo fine'. The idea expressed by the noun is reinforced by an adjective of similar meaning: see on 46. 1.

17. imbuisse . . . in aequore : 'gave her oars their first lessons in your waters': the verb is figurative as in 64. 11 but the literal meaning 'dipped in your waters' (*imbuisse aequore*) may be hinted at.

18. impotentia : a vivid metaphor: the seas lack self-discipline, as in Horace the wind, *Od.* iii. 30. 3 'impotens Aquilo'. Catullus uses the adjective of himself (8. 9), of a sweetheart's love (35. 12). For the -*ā* see on 9 above.

19 f. laeua siue dextera uocaret : i.e. whether she were tacking to port or to starboard on a cross-wind or running before a following wind. For the omission of one *siue* cf. Hor. *Od.* i. 3. 16, *Sat.* ii. 5. 10, ii. 8. 16.

20 ff. Iuppiter is only here used with particular reference to wind: Catullus may have the Greek Ζεὺς οὔριος in mind.

　　secundus: often used of wind, perhaps retaining something of its original meaning as a verbal adjective from *sequor*.

　　utrumque . . . in pedem : i.e. the following wind falls square on the sail, making both the sheets (*pedes*) which braced its lower corners taut at the same length: so a ship driving before a stern-wind *pede labitur aequo* (Ov. *Fast.* iii. 565).

22. litoralibus deis : sea-deities like Glaucus, Panopea, and Melicertes (Virg. *Georg.* i. 437) or Palaemon (Stat. *Silv.* iii. 2. 39), or such major powers as Neptune, Venus, and the Dioscuri (68. 65), who had temples on the shore at which sailors paid the vows which they had made in time of storm: this self-sufficient vessel had had no need to appeal to them.

23. sibi : probably dative of agent, *a se* (rather than *pro se*, as Munro takes it). Catullus has the dative elsewhere with per-

fect participles (8. 5, 22. 4, 35. 18, 37. 13, 116. 5): cf. Prop.
ii. 9. 25 'haec mihi uota tuam propter suscepta salutem'.

a mari: Lachmann restores *marei*, the old form of the
ablative, from *amāret* of *V*.

23 f. mari nouissimo is taken by editors to mean 'remotest sea'
(i.e. the Pontus), but that meaning of *nouissimus* is doubtful.
In Ov. *Tr.* iii. 13. 27 'me terrarum pars paene nouissima
Pontus . . . habet' (quoted in support by Ellis and Kroll),
and in Tac. *Agr.* 10. 5, *Ann.* ii. 24. 4, Val. Flaccus v. 77, remote-
ness is indeed implied, but the meaning of *nouissimus* seems
to be 'latest', 'last to be reached': so the *nouissimum agmen*
of the Roman army and the *nouissima cauda* of Ov. *Met.* iii.
681 are the parts of the column and the tail to which one
comes last. In the present context *mare nouissimum* would
apply to the Adriatic rather than to the Pontus. *V*'s *nouissime* may perhaps be retained if the sentence can be translated 'never a vow had she made to the gods of the shore
when at the last' (or 'recently') she made her way up from
the sea to this clear lake', the historic perfect *esse facta* referring to a time preceding that of *ueniret*; the ambiguity
is all the more venial since the alternative of making *cum
ueniret* define the time of *esse facta* makes nonsense. The
early examples of *nouissime* all mean 'recently', but the other
meaning is found later: e.g. Sen. *Dial.* v. 5. 2 'primum . . . deinde
. . . nouissime'. The adverb came into use about Catullus'
time; Cicero avoided both it and *nouissimus* (Gell. x. 21), but
it is used by Sallust, Varro, and two of Cicero's correspondents.

24. limpidum: only here in verse: later poets prefer *liquidus*,
and *limpidus* appears elsewhere only in the most prosaic and
technical contexts (of clean water-supply in Vitruvius, of
unclouded wine in Columella). It may be a borrowing from
one of the other Italic languages: if so, it may be a doublet of
liquidus (Latin *-qu-* and Osc.-Umbr. *-p-* both representing an
original *-k^w-*); its connexion with *lumpa* (see on 64. 254) is
doubtful.

25. prius fuere: 'this is an old story': cf. Tib. ii. 5. 79 'haec
olim fuerant, sed tu iam . . .', iii. 5. 32 'siue erimus seu nos
fata fuisse uolent', Virg. *Aen.* ii. 325 'fuimus Troes, fuit
Ilium'.

26. senet: *seneo* is archaic: elsewhere in Pacuvius (275, 304 R.)
and Accius (612 R.).

27. The yacht dedicates herself to the Dioscuri as the pro-
tectors of seafarers: cf. 68. 65, Eurip. *Hel.* 1495, *Elect.* 1241,
Hor. *Od.* i. 12. 25, iv. 8. 31, Prop. i. 17. 18, Plin. *N.H.* ii. 101.

For the apostrophe see on 13 above. For the form of address to the brothers cf. Hor. *Epod.* 17. 42 f. 'Castor . . . fraterque magni Castoris', Prop. ii. 26. 9 'quae tum cum Castore fratri . . . excepi'. Castor is the predominant partner: their temple at Rome is called *aedes Castoris* for short (Cic. *Verr.* ii. 1. 129) and Statius goes so far as to conceal Pollux under the title of *alter Castor* (iv. 6. 15).

5

'Catulle est à la première page de son roman d'amour' (Benoist). The theme of the shortness of life to the lover goes back to Mimnermus: for expressions of it in the elegists see Tibullus i. 1. 69 f. 'interea, dum fata sinunt, iungamus amores; / iam ueniet tenebris mors adoperta caput', Propertius ii. 15. 23 f. dum nos fata sinunt, oculos satiemus amore: / nox tibi longa uenit nec reditura dies'.

1. **uiuamus** : for the emphatic sense, 'enjoy life', cf. Varro, *Sat.* fr. 87 Büch. 'properate uiuere puerae quas sinit aetatula ludere esse amare', *Copa* 38 'pone merum et talos; pereat qui crastina curat / mors aurem uellens "uiuite" ait, "uenio" ', *Carm. Epigr.* 190. 7 Büch. 'uiue dum uiuis', Cic. *Q.F.* iii. 1. 12 'sed quando uiuemus?', Hor. *Od.* iii. 29. 43.

2. **rumores senum seueriorum** : 'the gossip of puritan grey-beards'; cf. Prop. ii. 30. 13 'ista senes licet accusent conuiuia duri'.

3. **unius aestimemus assis** : there is a curious parallel in Sen. *Ep.* 123. 11 (the hedonist's advice) 'istos tristes et super-ciliosos alienae uitae censores, suae hostes, publicos paed-agogos assis ne feceris'.

5. **occidit lux** : observe here and in 7. 7 the effect of the break in the last foot caused by the rare monosyllabic ending. Such endings are to be distinguished from those in which an unemphatic monosyllable is combined with a preposition to form a disyllabic or trisyllabic word-group under one accent (10. 31 *ád-me*, 13. 1 *apúd-me*, 50. 20 *á-te*).

6. **perpetua una** : the phrase occurs again, in a very different context, in Cic. *Pis.* 33 'ut omnes . . . male precarentur, unam tibi illam uiam et perpetuam esse uellent'. For the idea cf. Hor. *Od.* i. 4. 15 ff., 28. 15, iv. 7. 13.

7. **basia** : *basium* (with *basio* and *basiatio*) occurs first in Catullus: after him it is common in Martial and Petronius but rare elsewhere (Phaedrus has it once, Juvenal twice, Fronto and Apuleius twice). Plautus and Terence use

sauium and *osculum*, Ovid only *osculum*. Its origin is obscure;
its form points to its being a non-Latin word (intervocalic *-s-*
normally indicates a loan-word unless the *-s-* is, as in *causa,
quaeso, usus, esum*, etc., a reduction of *-ss-*; so *casa, asinus,
fusus* are probably borrowings) and it is possible that
Catullus brought it (as Quintilian i. 5. 8 says he brought
ploxenum) from his native province. Its absence from
comedy makes it almost certain that it was not part of the
popular language before Catullus' time; but it must have
come into popular use later, for, while *sauium* and *osculum*
died with Latin, *basium* has survived into all the Romance
languages. The distinction made by the ancient grammarians
between the three words for 'kiss' (Don. ad Ter. *Eun.* 456
'oscula officiorum sunt, basia pudicorum affectuum, sauia
libidinum uel amorum': cf. Serv. ad *Aen.* i. 256) is not
borne out in usage: see Haupt, *Opusc.* ii. 106–9.

8. **mille altera :** 'a second thousand': so Virg. *Ecl.* 3. 71 'aurea
mala decem misi, cras altera mittam' ('a second ten').

9. **usque :** 'without a break'.

10. **milia multa :** cf. 16. 12 'milia multa basiorum', 61. 203
'multa milia ludi', 68. 45–46 'dicite multis / milibus'.

   fecerimus : for *facere* of making up a total cf. Juv. 14. 326
'fac tertia quadringenta' ('make a third four hundred'),
Nepos, *Epam.* 3. 6 'eam summam cum fecerat'. The quantity of the *-i-* of *-imus* (and *-itis*) was originally long in the
perfect subjunctive (an optative formation), short in the
future perfect indicative (a conjunctive formation), and this
distinction is maintained in Plautus. In later verse, for
metrical convenience, it is disregarded: *-ĭ-* in the fut. perf., first
found here in verse, is shown to have been Cicero's normal
pronunciation by his clausulae (Zielinski, *Philol.*, Supp. ix.
772).

11. **conturbabimus :** *conturbare*, 'to throw one's accounts into
confusion' (the object, presumably *rationes*, is always
omitted) is a technical term for fraudulent bankruptcy with
concealment of assets; Cic. *Att.* iv. 7. 1, *Q.F.* ii. 10. 5, *Planc.*
68, Mart. ix. 3. 5, Petr. 38. 16 'ne creditores illum conturbare
existimarent', *Digest* xv. 3. 16 'nummos uenditori non
soluerat, postea conturbauerat'. Since the verb in this sense
is elsewhere used without an object expressed, it is best taken
so here, *illa* being governed by *sciamus*. H. L. Levy (*A.J.P.*
lxii [1941], 222) sees in the alternation of *mille* and *centum*
a reference to the abacus. Catullus is keeping a tally, with
one pebble in the thousands column, then one in the hundreds,

and so on: they will shake the board and obliterate the
score. But the technical use of *conturbare* is too common
to be ignored, and he misses the point of it: they will cheat
the evil eye, as the bankrupt cheats his creditors, by faking
their books.

ne sciamus : not merely because 'pauca cupit qui numerare
potest' (Mart. vi. 34), but because to count one's blessings is
to invite Nemesis and the evil eye.

12. **inuidere** : here in its original use 'cast the evil eye on',
the equivalent of *fascinare* in 7. 12. Pliny uses the two words
together: *N.H.* xix. 50 statues of Satyrs are set up in gardens
'contra inuidentium effascinationes'. The common dative
construction has its origin in a personal 'dative of dis-
advantage' (*inuideo alicui aliquid*), the accusative being
normally suppressed. (See Wünsch in *Rhein. Mus.* lxix. 133.)

<h1 style="text-align:center">7</h1>

1 f. **basiationes . . . tuae** is most naturally taken as 'kisses of
you', i.e. 'on your lips'.

2. **satis superque** : 'enough and to spare': the expression is
commonplace (e.g. Cic. *Am.* 45 'satis superque esse sibi
suarum cuique rerum', Hor. *Epod.* i. 31 'satis superque me
benignitas tua ditauit', xvii. 19 'dedi satis superque poena-
rum tibi') but appears once in poetry of greater elevation,
Virg. *Aen.* ii. 642 'satis una superque uidimus excidia'.

3 ff. **harenae . . . sidera** : these illustrations of the innumerable
are combined again in 61. 199–201, as they are in Genesis
xxii. 17, in Plato, *Euthyd.* 294b, and often in later literature.
Here Catullus enlivens each of these literary commonplaces in
a characteristic way. To the first he brings that new gift of
doctrina to Latin poetry, the romantic use of the proper name,
exploiting the associations of a distant country and its
precious herb, a mysterious desert shrine, and the legendary
founder of that historic city which had produced his own
poetic master. The second he moulds to reflect the mood of
the poem: the countless stars are the kindly witnesses of his
love.

3. **Libyssae** : feminine of *Libys* (not, as L. & S. say, of *Libyssus*):
the adjective happens to occur in the same context in *A.P.*
xii. 145. 3 κἀπὸ Λιβύσσης / ψάμμου ἀριθμητὴν ἀρτιάσαι ψέκαδα.

4. **lasarpiciferis** : the plant commonly called *laserpicium* (or
lasar-) was the Greek σίλφιον, 'res fera et contumax et, si
coleretur, in deserta fugiens' (Pliny, *N.H.* xix. 38–45),

probably a variety of asafoetida. Its juice, 'magnificum in
usu medicamentisque', was given the name *laser*—a popular
misformation: *laserpicium* is itself *lac serpicium*, '*serpe*-
juice', *serpe* (or *sirpe*) being the Latin name of the plant,
probably an early borrowing from σίλφιον. (Plaut. *Rud.* 630
'sirpe et laserpicium' shows the original use.) It grew wild
on the fringe of the desert in inner Cyrenaica and was a
staple export of Cyrene so distinctive and profitable as to
appear as an emblem on its coinage: it was imported into
Rome by the state and on the outbreak of the Civil War
Caesar found 1,500 pounds of it in the treasury. By Pliny's
time it had died out in Cyrene and an inferior quality was
being imported from the East.

Cȳrenis : in Greek the name is always singular: in Latin
the plural is regularly used for the province (as it is here:
Ammonium is in the south-east of the territory, the town of
Cyrene itself in the north-west) but often also for the town.

The first vowel is long in Aristophanes and Apollonius,
short in Hesiod and Pindar; Callimachus has both quan-
tities. In Latin verse the long quantity is normal (Virgil,
Lucan, Statius, Silius): the short appears only here and in
Catalepton 9. 61. (See Marx in *Abh. d. Sächs. Akad.*, Ph.-Hist.
Kl. 38. 1.)

5. **oraclum Iouis :** the temple of Ammon, the Egyptian god
identified with Zeus and Jupiter, standing in the oasis of
Siwa in the Libyan desert (hence *aestuosi*) was the seat of an
oracle ('harenosum Libyci Iouis antrum' Prop. iv. 1. 103)
which was famous throughout the Greek world.

6. **Batti . . . sacrum sepulcrum :** Battus was the legendary
founder and first king of Cyrene (Herod. iv. 150-5): after his
death he was worshipped as a hero and his tomb stood
(Pind. *Pyth.* 5. 125) in the centre of his city. Callimachus, as
a native of Cyrene, claimed descent from Battus, and Catullus
gives him the patronymic *Battiades* (65. 16, 116. 2) which he
gave to himself.

7. **cum tacet nox :** see on 5. 5.

8. **uident amores :** Baehrens compares Stat. *Ach.* i. 643 'admo-
uet amplexus, uidit chorus omnis ab alto / astrorum', Juv.
viii. 149 'sed luna uidet, sed sidera testes / intendunt oculos',
Val. Flacc. viii. 50 'sidera . . . haec te meque uident'.

9. **te . . . basiare :** if *tuae* in l. 2 is 'of you', *basiare* is here constructed with two accusatives, a cognate internal accusative·
basia (cf. 61. 110-12, 63. 15) and a direct object *te*. The only
parallel in Latin is in Cato, *Agr.* 134. 2 'te . . . bonas preces
precor', but Moschus uses φιλεῖν in the same way, 3. 69

τὸ φίλημα / τὸ πρώαν τὸν Ἄδωνιν ἀποθνᾴσκοντα φίλησεν. If *tuae*
is 'from you', *te* must be taken as subject of *basiare* and the
whole phrase as subject of *satis est*—an awkward and unlikely construction.

10. **Catullo** : on Catullus' use of his own name see n. on 68. 135.

11. **curiosi** : 'busybodies': Plaut. *Stich*. 198, 'sed curiosi sunt
hic complures mali / alienas res qui curant studio maxumo',
shows how the adjective of *cura* acquired this uncomplimentary sense.

12. **mala ... lingua** : i.e. a tongue which utters curses or spells,
as in Virg. *Ecl*. 7. 28 'ne uati noceat mala lingua futuro'.

  fascinare : 'bewitch': the origin of the word and its relation to βασκαίνειν are uncertain. If it represents the root
which appears in *fa-ri*, φάσκειν, βάζειν, βάσκειν, its first
reference must have been to bewitching by spells, but it
is equally used of the operation of the evil eye (Virg. *Ecl*.
3. 103).

8

This soliloquy, one of the poems that Macaulay said he could
not read without tears,[1] is neither the record of some passing
attachment to an unknown *puella* nor an extravaganza on the
stock theme of the desperate lover. Here, as in 37. 12, the
puella amata quantum amabitur nulla must be Lesbia—the phrase
is echoed in two poems which speak of her by name (58. 2, 87. 1);
the emotion is the poet's own and the utter simplicity of the
words, only a hairsbreadth removed from conversational prose,
is a guarantee of their sincerity. Lesbia has turned away from
him and he is in despair. There is no suggestion that he has a
rival; he thinks of what has happened as a disaster for both of
them and pathetically turns from his own feelings to speak of
what he has meant to her and what she has lost. Those who
have found a difference of tone between the first part of the
poem and the second have misconceived the situation: Catullus'
appeal to himself to use his will is no more pathetic than his
reminder to Lesbia of the past.

The scazon or 'limping iambus' (ἴαμβος σκάζων or χωλίαμβος),
an iambic trimeter with a spondee in the sixth foot which gives
a check to the rhythm at the end of each line, was invented by
Hipponax in the 6th century B.C. for his satirical verses.
Like Hipponax himself, the hellenistic poets who took up the
metre—Callimachus (fr. 191 Pf.), Theocritus (*Epig*. 19),
Herodas in his mimes—permitted a spondee in the fifth foot

---

[1] Trevelyan, *Life of Macaulay*, ch. 14: the others were 38 and 76.

also: Catullus does not. Poems 22, 31, 39, 44, 59, and 60 are in the same metre.

1. **Catulle** : for the address to himself cf. 51. 13, 52, 76, 79: see on 68. 135.

   desinas ineptire: 'you must stop being silly'. The jussive subjunctive addressed to a definite person (cf. 32. 7, 76. 14, 16), less peremptory than the imperative, is common in comedy but rare elsewhere; the exx. cited from Cicero's letters are illusory (see Sjögren, *Eranos* xvi [1916], 10 f.) or doubtful. *ineptire* has the implication of misconceiving the situation, being blind to facts (in Cicero's phrase, 'quid postulet tempus non uidere': see on *ineptus*, 12. 4). So in Terence *ineptis* is a retort to one who (like Catullus' other self here) is unwilling to take the advice *actum ne agas* (*Ph.* 420) or one who makes an unrealistic proposal (*Ad.* 934).

2. **perisse perditum** : the same proverbial expression in Plautus, *Trin.* 1026 'quin tu quod periit perisse ducis ? '

3. **soles** : 'sunshine', the usual meaning of the plural: cf. Virg. *Georg.* i. 393 'ex imbri soles prospicere', ii. 332 'in nouos soles', Hor. *Od.* iv. 5. 8 'soles melius nitent', Ov. *Tr.* v. 8. 31 'si numeres anno soles et nubila toto'. *candidus* is 'bright' in both the literal and the figurative sense: Propertius has a striking use of the figurative sense, ii. 15. 1 'o me felicem, nox o mihi candida' (Horace has the converse, *Sat.* i. 9. 72 'huncine solem / tam nigrum surrexe mihi').

5. **nobis** : the illogical change of subject is natural enough: similarly Propertius has (ii. 8. 17–19) 'sic igitur prima moriere aetate, Properti? / sed morere, interitu gaudeat illa *tuo*. / exagitet *nostros* manes'.

6. **ibi** : temporal as in 63. 4, 48, 66. 33.

   iocosa : For the lover's *ioci* cf. Hor. *Ep.* i. 6. 65 'sine amore iocisque / nil est iucundum', Ov. *A.A.* iii. 580 'miscenda est laetis rara repulsa iocis'.

9. **nunc iam** : 'now it has come to this, that' is the force of the combination.

   impotens : 'undisciplined', 'lacking in self-control'; cf. 4. 18, 35. 12.

   noli : Avantius's supplement for the lacuna makes this line balance l. 7.

10. **quae fugit sectare** : cf. Theoc. 11. 75 τί τὸν φεύγοντα διώκεις;

    miser uiue : For the colloquial use of *uiuo* as an emphatic equivalent of *sum* cf. 10. 33 n. 'molesta uiuis': so in comedy, Plaut. *Men.* 908 'edepol ne ego homo uiuo miser'.

11. **perfer, obdura** : Ovid has *perfer et obdura* three times (*Am*. iii.
11. 7, *A.A*. ii. 178, *Tr*. v. 11. 7), Horace *persta atque obdura*
(*Sat*. ii. 5. 39).

13. **rogabit** : for *rogare* in this context cf. Ov. *Am*. i. 8. 43 'casta
est quam nemo rogauit', *A.A*. i. 711 'ut potiare, roga: tantum cupit illa rogari'.

14. **rogaberis nulla** : 'you are not wooed at all'. There is no
reason to suspect *nulla*: for this mainly colloquial use see on
17. 20. (Cic. has an example with a passive verb, as here,
Cat. i. 16 'misericordia quae tibi nulla debetur'.) Rossberg's
nullei (i.e. *nulli*), 'by no-one', introduces an irrelevant idea:
Catullus is concerned only with himself and Lesbia.

15. **scelesta** : 'unfortunate', as often in comedy: e.g. Plaut.
Cist. 685 'ilicet me infelicem et scelestam', *Most*. 563 'ne ego
sum miser, / scelestus, natus dis inimicis omnibus'. Both this
and the common meaning 'wicked' are derived from a
primitive religious use, 'accursed'; *scelus* is the taboo which
an offence brings upon the doer, putting him outside the pale
of his community. Plautus combines the two meanings in
Asin. 475 'age, inpudice, / sceleste, non audes mihi scelesto
subuenire'.

uae te : So Balthasar Venator for the *ne te* of *V*. The
accusative with *uae* is very rare; and Fröhlich's ingenious
quae te (*uae tibi*) *manet* is tempting; but Plaut. *Asin*. 481
uae te and Sen. *Apoc*. 4 *uae me* are enough to justify the
accusative here. No other suggested emendation of the
meaningless *ne te* is plausible. Postgate's *anenti* entirely
misses the point; there is nothing here of Horace's 'audiuere
di mea uota: fis anus' (*Od*. iv. 13. 1), no picture of the ageing
coquette (as in Prop. iii. 25. 11–16 or Ov. *A.A*. iii. 69): Catullus'
picture is of what life will be like for Lesbia now. Statius's
nullam . . . noctem brings in the same irrelevant notion.

tibi manet : 'is certain, reserved, for you': cf. 76. 5 'multa
parata manent . . . gaudia . . . tibi', Cic. *Phil*. ii. 11 'cuius tibi
fatum sicut C. Curioni manet'.

16. **bella** : see on 3. 14.

17. **cuius esse diceris?** i.e. she will not be spoken of as 'Catullus'
Lesbia' any more: cf. Prop. ii. 8. 6 'nec mea dicetur quae
modo dicta mea est', Ov. *Am*. iii. 12. 5 'quae modo dicta mea
est, quam coepi solus amare, / cum multis uereor ne sit
habenda mihi'.

19. **at tu** : As with *at* in 14 Catullus turns from himself to tell
Lesbia what she is doing, so here with *at* he breaks off that
thought and comes back to himself.

destinatus : 'be fixed and hold out': only here of a personal subject in the same sense as the normal *obstinatus*.

9

The Veranius who is here welcomed home from Spain appears in three other poems, 12, 28, and 47, in company with Fabullus: 12. 14–17 shows them in Spain together, perhaps at the time when that poem was written. In 28 and 47 they appear together in an unnamed province on the staff of one Piso at the time when Catullus was with Memmius in Bithynia, i.e. in 57–56 B.C.; and this Piso has been generally identified with L. Calpurnius Piso Caesoninus, who was proconsul of Macedonia from 57 to 55.

Finding difficulty in believing that the two served abroad together in different parts of the world, or arguing from 25. 7 that they must have been in Spain when Catullus was in Bithynia, some have tried to make their visit to Spain and their service with Piso coincide. Ellis, reviving the old theory that their Piso was Cn. Calpurnius Piso, an alleged accomplice of Catiline who was sent to Spain in 65 B.C. with the extraordinary office of *quaestor pro praetore*, involved himself (apart from other difficulties) in the hypothesis that Catullus was in Bithynia with Memmius not in his propraetorship but in an earlier special appointment for which there is no evidence. Kroll, accepting the identification with Caesoninus, suggests that Caesoninus may have been in Spain as propraetor: for that also there is no evidence, and, if he was there at all, he certainly was not there when Catullus was in Bithynia. It is just conceivable that the pair served together in Spain under some other Piso who cannot be identified: the *cognomen* was not uncommon, and we do not know the names of the governors of the Spains in 57. M. Pupius Piso, the consul of 61 B.C., who has been suggested most recently by Maas (*C.Q.* xxxvi [1942], 80) had already been proconsul in Spain in 69 and is not likely to have been found there again in 57.

But there is nothing unreasonable in supposing that two adventurous young men 'on the make'—for there is no question of official appointments—after returning from service with one governor in Spain got themselves attached to the *cohors* (see on 10. 10) of another and went on to seek their fortunes in Macedonia. (See R. Syme in *Classica et Mediaevalia*, xvii [1956], 129 ff.)

1 f. omnibus . . . trecentis : 'You who of all my friends are worth more in my eyes than a million': *antistans milibus trecentis* is loosely substituted for the superlative which *ex omnibus* leads one to expect. For the expression cf. Cic. *Att.*

ii. 5. 1 'Cato ille noster qui mihi unus est pro centum milibus',
Brut. 191 'Plato enim mihi unus instar est omnium'; for
trecenta milia of an indefinite large number cf. 48. 3, Hor.
Sat. ii. 3. 116 (*trecenti* alone is similarly used in 11. 18, 12. 10,
and often elsewhere). The alternative of taking *milibus trecentis* with *ex amicis*, 'who are worth more than a million of
all my friends', gives an absurd hyperbole and makes
omnibus otiose. Baehrens, reading *o* for *e*, takes *milibus
trecentis* in apposition to *omnibus amicis*, 'are worth more
than all my friends, the whole million of them', again a
pointless extravagance. Muretus's suggestion that *milibus*
means 'miles' ('who stand out among all my friends by more
than three hundred miles'; cf. Arist. *Clouds* 430 τῶν Ἑλλήνων
εἶναί με λέγειν ἑκατὸν σταδίοισιν ἄριστον) is ingenious but unnecessary.

3 ff. uenistine . . . uenisti: cf. Theoc. 12. 1 f. ἦλυθες, ὦ φίλε κοῦρε;
. . . ἦλυθες.

4. unanimos : 'loving': the word regularly refers to the sharing
of affection, not of opinions. So 30. 1 'unanimis sodalibus',
66. 80 'unanimis coniugibus', Virg. *Aen.* iv. 8 'unanimam
adloquitur male sana sororem', vii. 335 'unanimos armare
in proelia fratres'.

anumque matrem : *anus* can be used adjectivally of women
as *senex* is of men: Catullus twice uses it with non-personal
feminine nouns, 68. 46 *carta*, 78. 10 *fama*.

5. o mihi nuntii beati : following Lachmann on Lucr. v. 1006
Baehrens and Kroll take *nuntii beati* as an exclamatory
genitive. That construction is common in Greek (e.g. Arist.
Clouds 153 τῆς λεπτότητος τῶν φρενῶν) : in Latin it is very rare
and the only certain examples appear to be Plaut. *Most.* 912
'di immortales, mercimoni lepidi', *Truc.* 409 'o mercis malae',
Prop. iv. 7. 21 'foederis heu taciti'. Lucan ii. 45 'o miserae
sortis quod . . .' is wrongly added, e.g. by Löfstedt;
miserae sortis is adjectival and the phrase is equivalent
to *o (nos) miseros* or *o miseri*. (On the question whether the
use is a pure Grecism see Löfstedt, *Synt.* ii. 417–18.) But
as the genitive of *nuntius* in Catullus one would expect *nunti* :
in the genitive of nouns in -*io*- Catullus has a dozen examples of
the -*i* form, none of -*ii*, and the -*i* form is invariable not only
in Lucretius (with the possible exception of two quadrisyllables which would otherwise be unusable, v. 1006 *nauigii*,
vi. 743 *remigii*) but also in Horace and Virgil (with the one
exception of *Aen.* iii. 702 *fluuii*): as for prose, -*i* is regular in
Cicero and in republican inscriptions. On the other hand,
there is no objection to taking *nuntii* as nominative. The

exclamatory nominative, though it is not found elsewhere in Catullus and is in general much rarer than the accusative (which Catullus has three times: 26. 5 'o uentum horribilem', 56. 1 'o rem ridiculam', 107. 6 'o lucem candidiore nota'), is found a few times in republican Latin: e.g. Ter. *Ph.* 233 'o facinus audax! o Geta monitor', Cic. *Mil.* 94 'o frustra mihi suscepti labores', *Flacc.* 102 'o nonae illae Decembres'. And the plural (to which Kroll takes exception, holding that a 'poetic' plural is out of place in a poem of this kind) is not un- natural. It is reasonable to suppose that Catullus heard of Veranius' return from more than one informant: indeed his incredulity might suggest that it was only after repeated evidence that he believed the good news.

6. Hiberum: probably genitive plural of *Hiberus*, not of *Hiber*, which does not occur in the oblique cases. The archaic genitive in *-um* (the original form for the 2nd declension, which survived in regular use in a number of formal and official expressions, e.g. *nummum, iugerum, modium, socium, triumuirum, fabrum, liberum, deum*: cf. Cic. *Orat.* 155–6: the *-orum* form was introduced by analogy from the *-arum* of the 1st declension) is used elsewhere by Catullus only in the elaborate poems, in which it belongs to the epic tradition: *diuum* 64. 27, 134, 298, 387, 66. 69, 76. 4, *uirum* 64. 192, 68. 90, *cymbalum* 63. 21, *caelicolum* 68. 138, *Troiugenum* 64. 355). But the *-um* form is used even in prose with names of peoples: so Pliny has *Bructerum*, Livy has *Celtiberum* as well as *Celti- berorum*, and Caesar has *Santonum* beside *Santonos* and *-is*.

8. applicansque collum: 'drawing your neck towards me': cf. Petr. 24. 6 'uocatum ad se in osculum applicuit'. For the whole phrase cf. *Cons. ad Liuiam* 34 'collaque et os oculosque illius ore premam'. For a measure of ancient demonstrative- ness in affection see Cic. *Fam.* xvi. 27. 2, where Quintus Cicero writes 'ego uos a.d. iii kal. uidebo tuosque oculos, etiam si te ueniens in medio foro uidero, dissauiabor'—to his brother's amanuensis Tiro.

10. o quantum est hominum beatiorum: for the expression cf. 3. 2 'quantum est hominum uenustiorum'. Here, however, the words are not a vocative but are to be taken closely with those which follow, the whole *quantum* clause taking the place, as it were, of a partitive genitive and being equivalent to *omnium hominum beatiorum*, 'of all the happy men there are, who is happier than I?'; similarly in Hor. *Sat.* i. 6. 1 'Maecenas, Lydorum quicquid Etruscos / incoluit fines, nemo generosior est te', the *quicquid* clause is equivalent to *omnium Lydorum Etruscos fines incolentium*. In comedy *quantum est* is sometimes used without a dependent genitive (often reinforcing *omnes*): so Plaut. *Pseud.* 37 'at te di deaeque quantumst seruassint', Ter. *Ph.* 853 'omnium quantum est qui uiuont hominum homo ornatissume'. The construction here might be the same (Plaut. *Capt.* 836 'quantum est hominum optumorum optume' is similarly ambiguous): but the parallel of 3. 2 points to taking *hominum beatiorum* as depending on *quantum*, not on *quid*.

10

Written shortly after Catullus' return from Bithynia, probably in the spring of 56 B.C. (see Introduction, p. xii), a casual anecdote in racy dialogue, full of colloquialism and gay inconsequence.

The Varus of this poem is presumably the Varus who is addressed in 22: neither poem provides any data for identification. We know of two distinguished bearers of the name who were Catullus' contemporaries and fellow-countrymen. One is the jurist Alfenus Varus, who rose from humble origins at Cremona, if the scholiast on Hor. *Sat.* i. 3. 130 is to be credited, to a position of authority at the bar and an official career under Octavian; he was one of the commissioners who supervised the confiscation of lands in Cisalpine Gaul after Philippi and he attained the consulship, as *suffectus*, in 39 B.C. The other is Quintilius Varus, also a native of Cremona, the friend of Horace and Virgil, whose death in 24 B.C. Horace mourns in an ode (i. 24) addressed to Virgil. Either may have been a friend of Catullus when they were, like him, young Transpadanes making their way in Rome: but there is nothing to connect either with him except the fact that he addresses an Alfenus in poem 30.

1 f. ad suos amores uisum : for the personal use of the plural *amores*, 'beloved', cf. 15. 1, 21. 4, 40. 7 (*meos*), 6. 16 (*tuos*), 45. 1, 64. 27 (*suos*, as here), Cic. *Att.* ii. 19. 2 'Pompeius nostri amores', xvi. 6. 4 'Atticae deliciis et amoribus meis'. *uisere* (*ad*) is particularly used of sick-visiting: so Lucr. vi. 1238 'quicumque suos fugitabant uisere ad aegros', Ter. *Hec.* 188 f. 'aegram esse simulant mulierem: nostra ilico / it uisere ad illam', Ov. *Am.* ii. 2. 21 'ibit ad affectam quae non languebit amicam; / uisat', Tac. *Ann.* xv. 60 'prompsit missum se ad aegrotum Senecam ut uiseret', Petr. 101. 10 'officii causa uisere languentem', Apul. *Flor.* 23 'medici cum intrauerint ad aegrum ut uisant'. This, with the mention of *Serapis* in l. 26, suggests that Varus' *amica* is posing as an invalid.

3. repente : 'on the spot': Friedrich quotes a similar use of *subito* from Plautus, *Curc.* 481 'pone aedem Castoris ibi sunt subito quibus credas male'.

4. non . . . illepidum neque inuenustum : the same phrase again in 36. 17 of Lesbia's vow. *Venustus* (3. 2, 13. 6, 22. 2, 31. 12, 35. 17, 89. 2, 97. 9) and *lepidus* (6. 17, 36. 10, 78. 2) and their opposites are catchwords of Catullus' sophisticated society: see on 43. 8. For the double negative see on 4. 3 *neque . . . nequisse.*

5 f. incidere . . . sermones : cf. Pliny, *Ep.* iv. 22. 5 'incidit sermo de Catullo', Livy i. 57. 6 'incidit de uxoribus mentio'.

6 f. quid esset iam Bithynia : 'what was the news of Bithynia nowadays': cf. Cic. *Att.* xiv. 5. 3 'uelim scire quid aduentus Octavii, numqui concursus ad eum', iv. 11. 2 'perscribe ad me quid primus dies, quid secundus, quid censores, quid Appius'.

7. se haberet : so Cic. *Fam.* iv. 5. 6 'quem ad modum se prouincia habeat certiorem faciam'. Bithynia was still a young province: the original province had been acquired in 74, nominally by the bequest of King Nicomedes, but it was not under settled government until after the defeat of Mithridates in 64, when Pompey added Western Paphlagonia to it.

8. et quonam : Statius's *ecquonam* is very probable; cf. 28. 6 *ecquidnam.*

9. id quod erat : 'what was the truth': cf. Caes. *B.G.* iv. 32. 2 'Caesar id quod erat suspicatus aliquid noui a barbaris initum consili', Cic. *Fam.* iv. 6. 2 'existimabam, id quod erat, omnes me et industriae meae fructus et fortunae perdidisse', Livy xxx. 12. 11 'regem esse id quod erat rata'.

9 f. ipsis : 'the natives', as Gronovius explained it, comparing such expressions as Livy xxiv. 35. 1 'Helorum atque Herbesum dedentibus ipsis recepit': the reference back to Bithynia is obvious in spite of the intervening words. There is no inconsistency in *referret*, which need not imply leaving the province and may mean merely 'get as a result'. Löfstedt (*Beiträge*, p. 38), followed by Kroll, taking *ipsis* with *praetoribus*, explains *neque . . . nec* as a colloquial pleonasm: but, while irregularity in the use of negatives is characteristic of colloquial speech and examples of a pleonastic simple negative occur (e.g. Varro, *R.R.* iii. 2. 16 'quotus quisque est annus quo non uideas . . . collegia non epulari'), a pleonastic connective is another matter. It would be difficult to take the *nec* as repeating the *neque* even if these stood alone: the presence of a third *nec*, apparently coordinate with the other two, makes it even more difficult. If *ipsis* goes with *prae-toribus*, Westphal's *nunc* for *nec* is necessary.

The whole sentence is loosely put together as Catullus' indignation runs away with him; *praesertim quibus* refers to *cohorti* only and introduces two clauses of which the second is loosely attached to the first. And the illogicality is obvious—if there is nothing for the governor, he can hardly be blamed for the fact that his staff gets nothing; Catullus merely wishes to have a dig, whether seriously or not, at his *praetor*. Muretus's *(nec) quaestoribus* corrects the logic, and the corruption would be easily explained: but Catullus is not writing logically and the plural *praetoribus* is natural enough. Things are bad for natives, for successive governors and for their staffs: they are all the worse for the staff of this grudging governor.

10. **cohorti** : the *cohors praetoria* was originally the picked body of troops which acted as a commander-in-chief's personal bodyguard (according to Festus 249 L. it had been introduced by Scipio Africanus and its members received certain privileges) and the term continued to be used in that sense: so in *Fam.* xv. 4. 7 Cicero has learned that his *cohors praetoria* has annihilated an invading force of Parthian cavalry. But by Catullus' time the title had been extended to the unofficial entourage of personal friends which a provincial governor attached to himself (as Caesar in Gaul had with him men 'qui ex urbe amicitiae causa Caesarem secuti non magnum in re militari usum habebant', *B.G.* i. 39. 2), and Cicero uses it so in his letter of advice to his brother in Asia (*Q.F.* i. 1. 12), where he distinguishes between the governor's official subordinates and those 'quos aut ex domesticis conuictionibus aut ex necessariis apparitionibus tecum esse uoluisti, qui quasi ex cohorte praetoris appellari solent'. The republican *cohors praetoria* in this sense was the origin of the imperial institution of the emperor's *cohors amicorum* and the more intimate body of *comites Augusti* which played an important part in the administrative organization of the later empire. (See J. van Vliet, *De praetoria et amicorum cohortibus*, Utrecht, 1926.)

The system provided young men with a chance to see the world and perhaps to make some money: the *comites* were maintained at the public expense and there were ample opportunities for pickings under an unscrupulous, or even an easy-going, governor. Cicero enlarges on the enormities of Verres' *cohors*, but even a well-meaning governor like Cicero himself might have difficulty in controlling his *comites*: they resented, he says (*Att.* vii. 1. 6), his refusal to treat as a dividend the money which he had saved out of his allowance for administrative expenses but later (*Att.* vii. 3. 8) 'pulled themselves together' *admiratione integritatis meae*. Governors who had literary tastes, like Catullus' Memmius, used the *cohors* as a form of patronage for young men of letters: so Tibullus was to have been with the *cohors* of Messalla in the East (i. 3. 2) and Horace speaks of that which accompanied Tiberius to the East in 20 B.C. in terms which suggest a literary club rather than the staff of a commander on active service (*Ep.* i. 3. 6 'studiosa cohors': cf. i. 8, i. 9).

11. **caput unctius :** as for a celebration or a holiday: for the colloquial metaphor cf. Cic. *Verr.* ii. 2. 54 'ita palaestritas defendebat ut ab illis ipse unctior abiret' (with a play on the literal meaning of *unctus*): so *caput nitidum*, with similar play, Plaut. *Pseud.* 219 'num quoipiamst hodie tua tuorum opera conseruorum / nitidiusculum caput?'

13. **praetor:** C. Memmius, who was praetor in 58 B.C. and thereafter, probably in 57, went to Bithynia as governor, was a figure of some note in the literary world of his day whose sympathies were with the Alexandrian school. Ovid mentions him with Ticidas as a writer of amatory verse (*Tr.* ii. 433) and he appears in the company of several of the *neoterici* in Gell. xix. 9. 7: Cicero's description of his tastes (*Brut.* 247 'perfectus litteris sed graecis, fastidiosus sane latinarum') explains both his patronage of poets like Catullus and Cinna, who had turned from the old poetic tradition to the standards of Alexandria, and the interest in Epicureanism which led Lucretius to dedicate the *De Rerum Natura* to him. His private life was not without reproach; in politics he transferred his allegiance from Pompey, whose quaestor he had been, to Caesar (Suet. *Jul.* 73) but was denied the consulship, which he hoped thus to gain, by a conviction for *ambitus* in the wholesale scandal of the elections of 54 (Cic. *Q.F.* iii. 2. 3, 8. 3). Of his behaviour in his province we have no evidence apart from the complaints of Catullus here and in poem 28 (7 f. 'meum secutus / praetorem refero datum lucello') that his staff did not make as much as they hoped: there may have been two sides to the story.

15 f. **quod illic natum :** the 'local product' is the bearers, *ad lecticam homines* or *lecticarii*. But the *lectica octophorus* itself (cf. *octo* below) was particularly associated with Bithynia: Cic. *Verr.* ii. 5. 27 '(Verres) ut mos fuit Bithyniae regibus lectica octophoro ferebatur'. In the republican period the *lectica* was used by men only in the country or for travelling (so Cicero uses an *octophorus* at Baiae, *Q.F.* ii. 8. 2: cf. *Fam.*

iv. 12. 3, vii. 1. 5); women used it more freely and Julius Caesar had to place certain restrictions on their use of it (Suet. *Jul.* 43. 1).

16. **ad lecticam homines,** 'litter-men'; cf. Liv. xxxiv. 6. 13 'seruos ad remum': so often in titles of servants and officials on inscriptions, *C.I.L.* vii. 8877 'libertus ad libros', 3941 'Hilarus Liuiae ad argentum'.

17. **facerem**—'make myself out': cf. Plaut. *Asin.* 351 'facio facetum me atque magnificum uirum', Ter. *Ad.* 535 'facio te apud illum deum': Cic. *Flacc.* 46 'cum uerbis se locupletem faceret'. Similarly with *esse*, 97. 9 'se facit esse uenustum'.

unum . . . beatiorem—'particularly lucky'. The use of a qualifying *unus* ('uniquely') to intensify a superlative is common (e.g. Cic. *Brut.* 25 'rem unam esse omnium difficillimam'): here the idiom is extended to a comparative expression which approximates in sense to a superlative: cf. 58. 2 'quam Catullus unam / plus quam se atque suos amauit', Hor. *Epod.* xii. 4 ff. 'sagacius unus odoror . . . / quam canis'. For an illogical development of the idiom in negative and quasi-negative sentences see on **107. 7**.

18. **maligne :** 'things were not so short, did not go so stingily, with me'. For the colloquial idiom cf. 14. 10 'non est mi male, sed bene ac beate', 23. 5 'est pulcre tibi', 23. 15 'quare non tibi sit bene ac beate', 38. 1 'malest . . . tuo Catullo'.

20. **rectos :** 'straight', 'upstanding', of persons as in 86. 2: cf. Suet. *Jul.* 47 'seruitia rectiora', Juv. iii. 26 'recta senectus'.

21. **at :** introducing an aside: cf. Hor. *Sat.* i. 5. 60 f. 'at illi foeda cicatrix / saetosam laeui frontem turpauerat oris', Prop. iv. 4. 15.

neque hic neque illic : neither in Rome nor in Bithynia.

22. **grabati :** the truckle-bed of the poor (from κράβατ(τ)ος, an early borrowing; cf. 11. 6): so the farmer in *Moretum* 5 'membra leuat uili sensim demissa grabato'; Mart. xii. 32. 11 (of a beggar's flitting) 'ibat tripes grabatus et bipes mensa'. *fractum* intensifies the disparaging note.

23. **in collo . . . collocare :** the jingle is Plautine: *Asin.* 657 'hic istam colloca cruminam in collo plane', *Epid.* 360 'ipse in meo collo tuos pater cruminam collocauit'.

24. **hic :** 'thereupon'.

26. **commodă :** the shortened -*a* of the imperative may represent colloquial pronunciation. There is some evidence that the conditions which produced shortening in iambic words in speech (see on *mane*, 27) also produced shortening of the

final vowel of cretic words (see Lindsay, *Early Latin Verse*,
p. 40): so Plautus has *imperă* (*Mil.* 1031) and the ablatives
rusticā (*Pers.* 169), *candidā* (*Pseud.* 1262), *gratiā* (*Stich.* 327).

26 f. ad Serapim deferri : perhaps for a cure (see on 1). The
cult of Serapis (the usual Latin form for *Σάραπις*) had reached
Italy from Egypt by 105 B.C. when it is found in the seaport
colony of Puteoli (*C.I.L.* i. 577).

In the last century of the Republic successive attempts
were made—in 58 (Tert. *Apol.* 6), in 52 (Dio xl. 47. 3), and in
48 B.C. (Dio xlii. 26. 3)—to check the growth of Serapis-worship
and of other Oriental cults, especially that of Isis: it appears
to have been recognized formally for the first time in 43 B.C.
(Dio xlvii. 15. 3). Incubation was practised in the cult of Serapis,
as in that of Aesculapius with which it is associated (e.g. by
Cic. *de Div.* ii. 123 'an Aesculapius, an Serapis potest nobis
praescribere per somnum curationem, Neptunus gubernanti-
bus non potest ? '), and is satirized by Varro, *Eumenides*, fr.
12 Büch. 'hospes, quid miras nummo curare Serapim ? / quid ?
quasi non curet tanti item Aristoteles'.

For *ad Serapim* Ellis compares Ov. *Am.* ii. 2. 25 'fieri quid
possit ad Isin', 'at the temple of Isis': there is no need to
change to *ad Serapis* with the common ellipse of *aedes*.

27. manĕ : the manuscripts read *mane me inquit* (*-id O*): but
the sense clearly requires *mane* 'not so fast', 'just a moment',
not *mane me*, 'wait for me'. The shortening of the *-e*, which
is regular in comedy (e.g. Plaut. *Aul.* 655, *Asin.* 229, *Merc.*
474), represents the pronunciation of ordinary speech, in
which two syllables in one word, or one word-group, which
form an iambus may become a pyrrhic under the influence of the word-accent falling on the first of these syllables (or on the syllable following them): *modŏ, citŏ, sciŏ,
putŏ, ibĭ, mihĭ* beside *modō, sciō, ibī*, etc. represent the same
sort of variation as that between 'don't' and 'do not'. The
shortening is not due to the hiatus, since the *-e* might be
shortened in any position: *cavĕ* is similarly shortened in 50.
18, 19, 61. 145, *pută* in 102. 4, *uolŏ* in 17. 8, 23, 35. 5, *dabŏ*
in 13. 11, *homŏ* in 24. 7, 115. 8: see also on 61. 77 *vidĕn*. The
hiatus is itself in keeping with the casual, conversational style
of the poem, and such emendations as *minime* (*inquii*) (Pontanus), *meminei* (*inquio*) (Munro) are unnecessary.

  inquii : does not occur elsewhere, but its existence may be
taken to be implied by *inquisti*.

28. istud quod modo dixeram me habere : 'as for my saying I
had them': the *quod*-clause is best taken as adverbial like
the *quod scribis* of Cicero's letters (cf. 68. 27) or such

expressions as Plaut. *Truc.* 471 'ego quod mala sum matris
opera mala sum', Cic. *Att.* xii. 18 A. 2 'quod non aduocaui ad
obsignandum, primum mihi non uenit in mentem, deinde . . .',
Fin. i. 23 'quod securi percussit filium, priuasse se etiam
uidetur multis uoluptatibus', Phaedr. ii. 4. 8 'fodere terram
quod uides . . . aprum insidiosum, quercum uult euertere'.
Other examples are cited by Munro on Lucr. iv. 885, who
wrongly explains the construction by an impossible 'ellipse'.
The antecedent *istud* is not paralleled in this construction
elsewhere but serves to point the reference—'as for my
statement, to which you refer'; similarly *illud* in Ter. *Heaut.*
790 ff. 'illud quod tibi / dixi de argento quod ista debet
Bacchidi, / id nunc reddendumst illi'.

  dixeram : the use of the pluperfect is not illogical, as
Kroll suggests. Latin idiom often prefers the pluperfect,
to mark an action more precisely as occurring two stages
back, where modern languages are content to use the simple
past tense: so *dixeram* is 'I had said before you replied'. This
eminently logical idiom is common both in the dialogue of
comedy and in formal prose: later poets (especially the
elegiac poets) sometimes take advantage of it to substitute
the pluperfect for the perfect, where it is not so justified, for
metrical convenience. See on 64.158.

29. fugit me ratio : 'I made a mistake': so Plaut. *Amph.* 386
'fugit te ratio', *ad Herenn.* ii. 24 'qui se propter uinum aut
amorem aut iracundiam fugisse rationem dicet', ii. 40 'me
tum ratio fugit'. Fronto has (i. 2) 'me forsitan memoria
fugerit', 'I forgot'. For similar uses of *fugio* cf. (with an
infinitive) Cic. *Q.F.* ii. 10. 4 'fugerat me ad te scribere', (without a subject expressed) Cat. 12. 4.

29 f. The broken syntax of *meus sodalis—Cinna est Gaius— is*
may well represent the speaker's confused embarrassment,
and so may the inversion of *nomen* and *cognomen*, which,
though it is not impossible in verse in the republican period,
does not belong to common speech (Varro, *L.L.* v. 83 'Scaevola Quintus pontifex maximus' is exceptional in prose).
Munro punctuates *meus sodalis Cinna—est Gaius—is*, 'my
friend Cinna—Gaius Cinna, you know—it was he who', supposing that *est Gaius* is added to identify the particular
holder of a not uncommon name; but if Cinna was a common
name, the addition of the much commoner Gaius would not
be likely to assist identification. The emphatic use of *is*
to repeat the subject is a colloquialism frequent in comedy
and in Cicero's correspondence (see Hofmann, *Lat. Umgangs-
sprache*, 104–5): it is sometimes used even in more formal

writing to pick up the subject or object after a parenthesis
(e.g. Cic. *de Or.* ii. 125 'haec ipsa, quae nunc ad me delegare
uis, ea semper in te eximia fuerunt', *Off.* iii. 13 'illud quidem
honestum, quod proprie uereque dicitur, id in sapientibus
est solis'; for other exx. see Kühner ii. 1. 625). For the whole
expression cf. Cic. *Att.* ii. 3. 3 'nam fuit apud me Cornelius—
hunc dico Balbum, Caesaris familiarem—is affirmabat . . .'.

C. Helvius Cinna was probably a fellow-countryman of
Catullus from the neighbourhood of Brixia—the name Helvius
is found in inscriptions there and a fragment of his verse
(1 Morel 'at nunc me Genemana per salicta / bigis raeda rapit
citata nannis') suggests connexions with that region. He was a
poet of the neoteric school who reproduced the excesses of his
Alexandrian masters: besides his mannered and learned
epyllion on Smyrna (see on 95) and a *propempticon Pollionis*,
a geographical poem, prompted by a visit of Asinius Pollio
to Greece and the East in 56 B.C., which also needed a commentary, he wrote amatory verse and epigrams. This poem
of Catullus and an epigram of his own (fr. 11: see int. to 4)
suggest that he was in Bithynia along with Catullus. Later, if
the generally accepted identification is true, he embarked on
a political career on the side of Caesar: in 44 B.C. immediately
after the murder of Caesar one Helvius Cinna, a tribune who
had been working in Caesar's interest, was attacked and
killed by a mob which took him for a namesake, the praetor
L. Cornelius Cinna, who had been supporting the conspira-
tors. (Plut. *Brut.* 20. 8, *Caes.* 68. 2, Suet. *Jul.* 52. 3, 85. 1, Dio
xliv. 50. 4, Appian *B.C.* ii. 147, Val. Max. ix. 9. 2; the identification has been questioned on the doubtful ground that the
mention of Cinna in Virg. *Ecl.* 9. 35 shows him to have been
alive when that poem was written.)

32. tam bene quam mihi pararim : there is no need to suspect
the text and Statius's *paratis* is unnecessary. The ellipse of *si*,
which is regular after *tamquam*, is not surprising after *tam
bene quam*: Löfstedt, *Vermischte Studien*, 27, cites from later
Latin *Dig.* xli. 2. 44. 2 'non aliter amitti possessionem quam
(si) eam alius ingressus fuisset', *Carm. Epigr.* 208. 5 Eng-
ström, 'nihil pulchrius fuerat quam (si) coniugem in ante
misisset' (similarly Venant. Fort. xi. 6. 6–8 'uidet / te mihi
non aliis oculis animoque fuisse / quam (si) soror ex utero tu
Titiana fores'), and compares such ellipses as Cic. *Att.* ii. 21. 1
'tota (res publica) periit atque hoc est miserior quam reli-
quisti, quod . . . .' Munro's objection that, even if the ellipse
were possible, *parassem*, not *pararim*, would be required, is
untenable: the perfect subjunctive, far from being irregular,
is in fact normal in such comparative clauses: e.g. Cic. *Fam.*

xvi. 5. 1 'tam te diligit quam si uixerit tecum', *Phil*. vi. 10
'(Plancum) sic contemnit tamquam si illi aqua et igni inter-
dictum sit', Sall. *Jug*. 85. 19 'ita hos petunt quasi honeste
uixerint'.

33. **insulsa male ... uiuis :** for the colloquial use of *male* to reinforce a pejorative expression (Hofmann, *Lat. Umgangsp.*[2] 74;
Wölfflin, *Lat. u. Romanische Komparation*, 15) cf. Tib. (Sulp.)
iii. 16. 2 'male inepta' and the common expletive use with
verbs (*male odisse, male metuere*, etc.) in Plautus. The order
of the words is paralleled in Hor. *Sat*. i. 4. 66 'rauci male',
ii. 5. 45 'ualidus male' (where, however, *male* is differently
used to negative the adjective). For *uiuo* as an emphatic
substitute for *sum* in colloquial speech, cf., e.g., Plaut. *Trin*.
390 'lepidus uiuis', *Men*. 908 'ne ego homo uiuo miser',
Bacch. 614 'inamabilis illepidus uiuo', Cic. *Att*. iii. 5 'ego
uiuo miserrimus et maximo dolore conficior'.

11

For his final repudiation of Lesbia Catullus deliberately
returns to the form of poem 51, the lines translated from
Sappho, in Sappho's own metre, in which he had addressed her
in the early days of their love. The poem opens with three
stanzas of highly allusive romantic writing; in the fourth the
tone changes to cold realism. The catalogue of the lands of
adventure in the first three stanzas, and particularly the
reference to Gaul and Britain, point to a date not earlier than
55 B.C. Caesar crossed the Rhine in the summer of that year
and reached Britain in the autumn; in the spring Gabinius had
entered Egypt to restore Ptolemy to his throne; and in Novem-
ber Crassus set out on his ill-fated expedition to the tempting
East.

Furius and Aurelius, who are given this last message to
deliver, appear separately or together in six other poems (15,
16, 21, 23, 24, 26); in almost all of them the tone is abusive.
Furius has been identified with the poet Furius Bibaculus (see
on 26); to the identification of Aurelius we have no clue. Most
interpreters have concluded (the view is most strongly put by
Wilamowitz, *Hell. Dichtung*, ii. 307) that the stately opening is
ironical. Catullus chooses Furius and Aurelius to take his contemptuous message because he despises them also; perhaps they
had brought overtures from Lesbia to him and he prefaces his
rejection of these by denouncing her envoys and their grandiose
protestations of life-long devotion. The elaborate development
of the address to Furius and Aurelius is certainly meant to

contrast with the scathing simplicity of the message to Lesbia.
But if these lines are ironical, they are a very complicated kind
of irony, containing as they do what can only be a genuine
compliment to Caesar. Horace did not recognize irony in them,
if, as seems more than likely, he was thinking of them when he
wrote the opening of his Sapphic ode to Septimius (ii. 6),
Septimi, Gades aditure mecum. We do well to be cautious about
taking light-hearted abuse, however coarse and outrageous, at
its face value as evidence of animosity. Catullus' society is not
the only one in which convention has permitted friends to call
one another names and write scurrilous verses at one another's
expense.

1. **comites :** The *siue*-clauses have their apodosis in the verbal
notion implied in *comites.* Horace has this passage in mind
both in *Od.* ii. 6, where he applies the same test of friendship
('Septimi, Gades aditure mecum et / Cantabrum indoctum
iuga ferre nostra et / barbaras Syrtes, ubi Maura semper /
aestuat unda'), and in *Od.* iii. 4. 29–36, where the same motive
is turned to another use in a list of distant journeys on which
the Muses will be the poet's companions ('utcumque mecum
uos eritis, libens / insanientem nauita Bosporum / temptabo
. . . / uisam Britannos hospitibus feros / . . . uisam pharetratos
Gelonos / et Scythicum inuiolatus amnem'). Cf. *Epod.* 1.
11–14 'te uel per Alpium iuga / inhospitalem et Caucasum /
uel occidentis usque ad ultimum sinum / forti sequemur
pectore', Prop. i. 6. 1–4 'non ego nunc Hadriae uereor mare
noscere tecum, / Tulle . . . / cum quo Ripaeos possim conscendere montes / ulteriusque domos uadere Memnonias'.

2. **extremos . . . Indos :** 'the Indians at the end of the world':
the same phrase in Hor. *Ep.* i. 1. 45, 1. 6. 6.

3. **ut :** 'where', as in 17. 10. The local use is very rare, and the
Catullan instances are the only certain ones. In Plaut.
Amph. 241 'quisque ut steterat iacet' and *Bacch.* 815 'in
eopse adstas lapide ut praeco praedicat' *ut* can be given
its normal modal sense and Virg. *Aen.* v. 329 can be
similarly explained. The only other examples adduced are
from the two translators of Aratus, Cicero (*Arat.* 2), and
Germanicus (*Arat.* 233), who both use *ut* where their original
has ἧχι (Arat. *Phaen.* 231). Hence Löfstedt (*Synt.* ii. 415)
regards the use as a Graecism: but if the translators were
influenced by ἧχι, they might have been expected to represent it by the exactly corresponding *qua* rather than by *ut*,
and their use of *ut* may be the normal one.

longe resonante : cf. Virg. *Georg.* i. 358, 'resonantia longe
litora'. Hence Statius proposed *resonans* to avoid the double

epithet with *unda*: if change were needed, *Eoum* would be more likely, but it is not needed.

4. **tunditur unda :** note the effective adaptation of sound to sense, borrowed by Horace (see on 1 above).

5. **Hyrcanos :** the country of the Hyrcani lay along the southern shore of the Caspian (often called *mare Hyrcanum*), but Catullus' notions of the geography behind these fabulous oriental names are no more precise than those of other Latin poets.

   Arabas : the Greek form is the normal one in Latin for the accusative plural of *Arabs*.

   molles : the standing epithet for these peoples in Latin poetry, due to an assumption that those who produce luxuries are themselves luxurious; so Manil. iv. 654 f. 'in mollis Arabas terramque ferentem / delicias', Tib. ii. 2. 4 'tener Arabs', Virg. *Georg*. i. 57 'molles Sabaei'.

6. **Sagas :** the Sacae (Σάκαι) were a race of nomads on the northern borders of Persia, between the Caspian and Bactria. Manuscript evidence suggests that the name was regularly *Sagae* in Latin; the same substitution of *g* for Greek *k* is seen in such early borrowings as *Saguntum* (Ζάκυνθος), *gubernare* (κυβερνᾶν), *Agrigentum* (Ἀκράγαντα), *grabatus* (κράβατος).

   Parthos : at this time the Parthian kingdom, with its capital at Ecbatana, extended from the Euphrates to the Indus. As Crassus found to his cost, the Parthians were a warlike people, with a highly developed military technique, using mobile archers and heavily armoured cavalry in combination; for Parthian archers cf. Hor. *Od*. ii. 13. 17, Virg. *Georg*. iv. 313.

7. **septemgeminus :** Virgil repeats the epithet, *Aen*. vi. 800: so the Nile is ἑπτάρους in Aeschylus (fr. 300 N.) ἑπτάπορος in Moschus (2. 51).

   colorat : the verb normally means 'darken' and its use of bright colour (e.g. Ov. *Am*. ii. 5. 35 of the morning sky, Sen. *N.Q*. i. 5. 10 of the rainbow) is rare; so Col. vii. 8. 7 has *fumo coloratus*, Sen. *N.Q*. ii. 21. 2 *fuligine colorantur*, and *colorari* is regularly used of sunburn (e.g. Cic. *de Or*. ii. 60, Prop. iii. 13. 16, Sen. *Ep*. 86. 8, 108. 4).

8. **aequora Nilus :** 'the levels that are dyed by the seven streams of Nile'. The reference is to the alluvial deposit of the river: cf. Virg. *Georg*. iv. 291 'uiridem Aegyptum nigra fecundat harena', Cic. *N.D*. ii. 130 'Nilus . . . mollitos et oblimatos agros ad serendum relinquit'.

9. **gradietur :** 'marches'.

10. **uisens** : 'going to see': cf. Hor. *Od*. iii. 4. 33 quoted above.

monimenta : 'memorials'. For *monimentum* of what 'tells a story' and reminds (*monet*) those who see it of its associations cf. Prop. iii. 11. 61 'Curtius expletis statuit monumenta lacunis', iv. 6. 17 'Actia Iuleae pelagus monumenta carinae', Manil. i. 323 'Gnosia desertae . . . monumenta puellae'; so in Virgil of tokens which carry personal associations, *Aen*. iii. 486 'manuum . . . monimenta mearum', iv. 498 'nefandi . . . viri monimenta', v. 572 'monimentum et pignus amoris', xii. 945 'saevi monimenta doloris'.

magni must be seriously meant: *magnus*, like *praeclarus, egregius, unicus, bonus*, can be used ironically (cf. Cic. *Fam*. ii. 14, Ov. *Her*. 19. 90) but the tone of *Caesar magnus* is quite different from that of the mischievous *unice imperator* of 29. 11, 54. 7.

11. **Rhenum** : This is probably the first appearance of the Rhine in literature, and, to quote Friedrich's pained observation, it appears 'in French uniform'. Caesar reached it in his summer campaign of 55 B.C. and, thanks to his engineers, crossed it by a temporary bridge to make a short punitive expedition into Germany.

11 f. **horribile aequor ulti-mosque** : The manuscripts have *horribilesque ultimosque*, but the hiatus—as Bentley pointed out on Hor. *Od*. iii. 14. 11, there is no instance of a short final vowel in hiatus where there is no break in sense—and the coupling of two disparate epithets both point to corruption, but none of the many suggested remedies is entirely satisfactory. Bentley approved of *horribiles et* (*et* being postponed: see on 51. 11), but that leaves the awkwardly paired epithets. Haupt's *horribile aequor* is both palaeographically plausible and apt; Caesar had his troubles in the Channel (*B.G*. iv. 28), and any sea is *horribile* to a Latin poet, and while *aequor* properly refers to a smooth sea (Varro, *L.L*. vii. 23), it is often loosely used of a rough one (cf. 64. 179 *truculentum aequor*, 205 f.). The repetition *aequora–aequor* strikes a modern reader as awkward, but repetitions of this kind, which a careful writer of our day might try to avoid, are not uncommon even in the most finished Latin writing; even if *Aen*. x. 382–93 (where *discrimina* appears in two quite different senses) or iv. 406–14 'cogunt . . . cogis . . . cogitur' be disregarded as due to lack of revision, Virgil has such examples as *Ecl*. 6. 62–68 *amarae . . . amaro, Georg*. i. 69–74 *laetis . . . laetum*, 404–10 *liquido . . . liquidas*. (For accidental repetitions in Propertius see Shackleton Bailey, *Propertiana*, p. 9.) A more serious objection is that *aequor* might be

expected to have a particularizing epithet to match all the other items in the series. Palmer's *horribilesque uitro* (woad) *in* / *usque Britannos* perhaps deserves mention for its ingenuity; see Caes. *B.G.* v. 14. 3 'omnes uero se Britanni uitro inficiunt quod caeruleum efficit colorem atque hoc horridiores sunt in pugna aspectu' (cf. Prop. ii. 18. 23 'infectos Britannos', Ov. *Am.* ii. 16. 39 'uirides Britannos'). But *in* is uncalled for and, whatever is wrong in the text, *ultimos* agrees too well with the regular description of Britain in Latin poetry to be suspect; cf. 29. 4 'ultima Britannia', Hor. *Od.* i. 35. 29 'ultimos orbis Britannos', iv. 14. 47 'remotis Britannis', Virg. *Ecl.* i. 66 'toto diuisos orbe Britannos'.

14. caelitum : the solemn archaic word (cf. 61. 49, 190) is in keeping with the stately manner of the preceding lines.

 temptare : 'venture': cf. Hor. *Od.* iii. 4. 30 (quoted on 1 above), Virg. *Georg.* i. 207 'ostriferi fauces temptantur Abydi'.

16. non bona dicta : so Plaut. *Amph.* 25 'dictis bonis', 'kind words'.

17. uiuat ualeatque : 'let her live, and good luck to her': the formula (Hor. *Ep.* i. 6. 67, *Sat.* ii. 5. 110 'uiue uale') is here contemptuous; cf. Ter. *And.* 889 'ualeat uiuat cum illa'.

21. respectet: 'look to my love': there is no implication of looking back: cf. Lucr. v. 975 'taciti respectabant . . . dum . . .', Cic. *Planc.* 45 'ne par ab eis munus in sua petitione respectent'.

23. Virgil was perhaps remembering this simile of the 'flower on the edge of the meadow' when he wrote of the death of Euryalus (*Aen.* ix. 435), 'purpureus ueluti cum flos succisus aratro / languescit moriens'.

12

There is no reason to doubt the identification of 'your brother Pollio' (l. 6) with C. Asinius Pollio, the friend of Virgil and Horace, orator, critic, and historian. He was born in 76 B.C.; if we suppose that he was not more than 16 or 17 (l. 9, *puer*) when this poem was written, it will belong to Catullus' earlier years in Roman society before he went to Bithynia in 57. We have another indication of Pollio's connexion with Catullus' circle: Catullus' friend Cinna (see on 10. 29) made Pollio's journey to Greece the occasion for writing a *propempticon*. The family of the Asinii came from Teate in the country of the Marrucini and an ancestor of these brothers, probably their great-grandfather, Herius Asinius, had been the commander of the Marrucini in the Social War when

he was killed in 90 B.C. (Livy, *per.* 73). Their father, Cn.
Asinius, may have given one of his sons the *cognomen* 'Marru-
cinus' to commemorate the home of his ancestors, as Asinius
Pollio himself called his son Gallus because he was born in
Cisalpina; such common *cognomina* as Marsus and Sabinus have
their origin in family connexions of that kind. The suggestion
that Catullus puts the name in an emphatic position to emphasize the contrast between Asinius' behaviour and the simple
honesty of his Sabellian forbears is reading too much into an
inversion of the normal order of names which is not uncommon
in informal writing (Cicero in his letters often writes *cognomen*
before *nomen*): the metrical awkwardness of *Marrŭcine* is
reason enough. It may well be that Catullus is merely turning
a practical joke into an opportunity for saying 'Thank you' to
Veranius and Fabullus and paying a compliment to Pollio. He
uses a similar theme in poem 25, an ultimatum to the unknown
Thallus whom he accuses of stealing not only a Spanish handkerchief, one of the same set presumably, but his cloak (*pallium*)
as well.

1. **sinistra :** the left hand is *nata ad furta* (Ov. *Met.* xiii. 111),
   the hand for dirty work (cf. 47. 1) because its movements are
   less noticeable than those of the right.

2. **non belle uteris :** 'it isn't a nice use you make'. For *bellus*
   see on 3. 14. For the colloquial use of the adverb cf. Cic.
   Att. v. 17. 6 'Bruto nostro uelim dicas illum fecisse non belle
   qui aduentu meo discesserit', *Fam.* xvi. 9. 1 'bellissime
   nauigauimus', *Att.* v. 11. 7 'cum ego me non belle haberem'
   ('I wasn't feeling well'); like the corresponding English
   'pretty', it sometimes has a merely intensifying force, Cic.
   Att. vi. 1. 25 'sumus . . . belle curiosi'.

   in ioco atque uino : cf. 50. 6 'per iocum atque uinum': so
   the parrot in Pliny (*N.H.* x. 117) is 'in uino praecipue
   lasciua', 'particularly playful over the wine'.

3. **lintea :** linen handkerchiefs carried in the *sinus* and used for
   wiping the face (hence their technical name of *sudaria*) or
   at meals for wiping the hands. (The Romans, like everyone
   else before the introduction of table-forks in the fifteenth
   century, ate with their fingers.) Martial has two epigrams
   on dinner-thieves: the *luscus* (viii. 59) who uses his one eye
   to snap up the napkins (*mappae*) which the guests have
   brought with them, and Hermogenes (xii. 29) who never
   takes a *mappa* to a dinner but always takes one away and
   has such a passion for pocketing linen that the awnings
   in the theatre and the sails in the harbour are not safe
   from him. (The *mappae* which the host provides in Horace,

Sat. ii. 4. 81, *Ep.* i. 5. 22, may be table-mats or polishing-cloths.)

4. salsum : ' Do you think that's smart? You've got it wrong': see n. on 43. 8.

fugit : the subject is left unexpressed (as often with *fallit* in the same sense: e.g. Cic. *Att.* xiv. 12. 2 'nos nisi me fallit iacebimus'). At 10. 29 Catullus has the more explicit *fugit me ratio.*

inepte, of behaviour which is 'out of place'; cf. 39. 16. Cicero defines the idiomatic use (*in sermonis nostri consuetudine*) of the word (*de Or.* ii. 17): the *ineptus* is the man who 'quid tempus postulet non uidet aut plura loquitur aut se ostentat aut eorum quibuscum est uel dignitatis uel commodi rationem non habet'. The tiresome talkativeness of Greeks (*de Or.* ii. 18) and the electioneering patter which the candidate does not want his friends to hear (*de Or.* i. 111) are both *ineptiae,* 'in bad taste'.

5. quamuis sordida : 'as mean and common a thing as you like', (*tam*) *sordida quam uis.* For this, the original use of *quamuis,* from which its use as a concessive conjunction has developed, cf. Plaut. *Men.* 318 'quamuis ridiculus est ('he is as funny as you like') ubi uxor non adest', *Pseud.* 1175 'quamuis pernix hic homost', Varr. *R.R.* ii. 5. 1 'homo quamuis humanus ac iocosus', Cic. *Tusc.* iii. 73 'stultitiam accusare quamuis copiose licet'. The transition to its use as a conjunction is clearly seen in such a sentence as *quamuis sit magna, tamen eam uinces* 'let it be as large as you like: still you will overcome it'.

7 f. uel talento mutari : 'give as much as a talent to have your thefts undone', probably: for this use of *mutare* cf. Ter. *And.* 40, 'haud muto factum', Hor. *A.P.* 168 'commisisse cauet quae mox mutare laboret'. The ablative of price has suggested taking *mutari* in its commoner sense of 'be exchanged', i.e. redeemed, paid for. While *mutare* in reference to barter usually implies 'give in exchange', i.e. sell (e.g. Hor. *Od.* i. 29. 14 'libros Panaeti . . . mutare loricis', Virg. *Georg.* iii. 306 'magno uellera mutantur'), it can equally well imply 'take in exchange', i.e. buy (e.g. Hor. *Sat.* ii. 7.110 'puer uuam furtiua mutat strigili'): but it is difficult to see in what sense Pollio could be said to 'buy back' or 'redeem' his brother's *furta.*

talento : The reference to Greek currency is convenient since Latin has no single word for a large sum of money: so often in Horace (*Sat.* ii. 3. 226 'mille talenta', 7. 89 'quinque talenta', *Ep.* i. 6. 34).

8 f. leporum . . . ac facetiarum : the vulgate *disertus*

presents difficulty in the construction of the genitives.
These cannot be construed with *puer*, since the genitive
of description requires an accompanying epithet; *centum
puer artium* (Hor. *Od.* iv. 1. 15) or *omnium artium puerulus*
(Cic. *Rosc. Am.* 120) is Latin, but *puer artium* is not. The
alternative is to take *leporum ac facetiarum* closely with
disertus as defining genitives. This use of the genitive with
adjectives, which becomes increasingly common in Augustan
and post-Augustan Latin (e.g. *integer uitae, aeui maturus, seri
studiorum*) is already established as early as Laevius (fr. 12
Morel, *aegra sanitatis*). But in this use the limiting genitive
regularly conveys the sphere within which the quality expressed by the adjective is displayed, and it is doubtful
whether *disertus leporum* conforms to that pattern. The basic
implication of *disertus* is clarity and articulateness of speech,
either in enunciation—in Cic. *Fam.* ix. 19. 2 *diserti* are opposed
to *balbi*, those who have an impediment of speech—or in
expression: so *diserta explanatio* is a detailed exposition (*Ad
Her.* iv. 41), and the adverb *diserte* means 'explicitly', 'in so
many words' (e.g. Cic. *Verr.* ii. 3. 126, Livy xxi. 19. 3). The
disertus is the man who can express himself sharply and
clearly: he is to be distinguished from the *eloquens*, whose
gifts are of a higher order (for the contrast see Cic. *de Or.* i. 94),
and the suggestions of the word range from competent
public speaking on the one hand ('statuebam disertum', says
Cicero, 'qui posset satis acute et dilucide apud mediocres
homines ex communi quadam opinione hominum dicere') to
conversational glibness (Cic. *Cael.* 67 'ad uinum diserti') on
the other. *Lepores* and *facetiae* may very well contribute to
the quality of being *disertus*, but they do not limit it.

Passerat's correction *differtus* presents no grammatical
difficulty; it is not found with a genitive elsewhere, but
refertus is so used and the extension of the normal construction of *plenus* is entirely natural. The tone of the word in the
few places where it occurs is like that of the English 'chockfull': e.g. Caes. *B.C.* iii. 32. 4 (the province chockfull of tax-
collectors), Hor. *Sat.* i. 5. 4 (a township chockfull of bargees).
If Catullus used it here, it is a colloquial pleasantry—as we
might say 'cram-full of' or 'packed with wit'; but one may
wonder whether he would have thought that pleasantry
appropriate here.

For the combination *lepores ac facetiae* cf. 50. 7–8, Sall.
Cat. 25. 5 (of Sempronia) 'multae facetiae multusque lepos
inerat', Cic. *Brut.* 143 (of Crassus) 'cum grauitate iunctus
facetiarum et urbanitatis oratorius non scurrilis lepos', *Clu.*
141 'quo lepore et quibus facetiis praeditum'. *lepos* is a

general term, covering any sort of sparkle or grace in the spoken word. *facetiae*, a more urbane quality than *ridiculum* (fun) or *dicacitas* (witticism), is an ironic or whimsical humour, a sense of the absurdities and incongruities in people and things: so, for the public speaker, the field for *facetiae* is the telling of a story (Cic. *Or*. 87: compare Donatus' definition of *facetus* in his note on Ter. *Eun*. 427, *qui facit uerbis quod uult*; for a collection of instances see W. J. N. Rudd in *Mnem*. x [1957], 328 ff.).

10 f. aut . . . aut : for the idiom cf. 69. 9–10, 103. 1–3.

trecentos : 'a few hundred': of an indefinite large number as in 9. 2, 11. 18, and often elsewhere.

12. aestimatione : 'it isn't for its value that it concerns me': an early example of the concrete use ('value', not 'valuing') which is regular in legal Latin.

13. mnemosynum : 'a souvenir': the Greek word occurs only here in Latin: presumably it was (as 'souvenir' began by being) a colloquialism of the intelligentsia.

14. Saetaba : from Saetabis (the modern Jativa) in Tarraconensis, the centre of the Spanish linen industry, which had the reputation of producing the finest flax in Europe (Pliny, *N.H*. xix 9), 'telas Arabum spreuisse superba' (Silius iii. 374).

    ex Hiberis : the early correction is necessary (for the confusion of *-e* and *-is* cf. 14. 5, 44. 4). *Hiber* is not the Latin name for the river Ebro (which is always *Hiberus*) and, if it were, *ex Hibere* could only mean 'out of the Ebro'. *ex Hiberis*, 'from the country of the Hiberi', is confirmed by Martial, who twice ends a line with the words (iv. 55. 8, x. 65. 3).

15. miserunt mihi muneri : for *mappae* given as presents (at the Saturnalia) cf. Mart. iv. 88. 4, vii. 53. 4, x. 87. 6.

15 f. Fabullus et Veranius : for these two friends of Catullus and their service in Spain see on poem 9, which was written to welcome Veranius home.

17. Veraniolum : those editors who argue from the familiar diminutive that Veranius was the more intimate of the two friends, and those who inquire which of the two is the *sodalis* of l. 13, have failed to observe (1) that Fabullus' name is diminutive in form already and (2) that Catullus is writing in metre.

13

A playful invitation to dinner for Fabullus, who appears again, in company with his friend Veranius, in three poems

(12, 28, 47); see 9 int. One may imagine, if one chooses, that it was written to welcome Fabullus home from Spain, as poem 9 was written to welcome Veranius, and that Catullus makes play with his own impecuniousness in contrast to the fortune which he supposes Fabullus has brought back with him; it is as good a guess that it was written to please Lesbia. The invitation to a meal was no doubt a conventional type of occasional verse. We have a Greek example contemporary with Catullus in some lines by Philodemus to his patron Piso (*Anth. Pal.* xi. 44), an invitation to a party at which the company will be better than the meal, and two of Horace's odes—i. 20 and iv. 12—are formal pieces in the same genre; nearer in spirit and manner to Catullus is Horace's invitation to Torquatus (*Ep.* i. 5), although it is (or professes to be) a genuine invitation and is not, like Catullus' poem, sheer fun. If Catullus had a traditional type in mind, he has made something quite individual and untypical out of it.

1. mi Fabulle : so again in 28. 3; for the intimate *mi* (Cicero in his letters confines it to his family and his closest friends, like Atticus and Tiro) cf. 10. 25.

2. paucis . . . diebus : 'within a few days', 'one of these days'.

    si tibi di fauent : For the colloquial use of the present in the protasis of a conditional sentence referring to future time see on 55. 18.

4. non sine : more emphatic than *cum* here, perhaps, 'not forgetting' what is as important as the meal.

    candida puella : 'a pretty girl', as in 35. 8 (see note), Hor. *Epod.* 11. 27.

5. sale . . . cachinnis : 'wit and every sort of laughter'.

6. uenuste noster : cf. 14. 2 'iucundissime Calue', 50. 16 'iucunde': see on 3. 2, 43. 8.

8. plenus . . . aranearum : 'full of cobwebs': for the colloquial phrase cf. Afranius, fr. 412 R. 'tanne arcula tua plena est aranearum'.

9. contra : 'in return', 'on my side': cf. Ter. *Eun.* 355 'quod donum huic dono contra comparet', *Hec.* 583 f. 'tibi me certum est contra gratiam . . . referre', 76. 23 'contra me ut diligat illa', Virg. *Aen.* vii. 267 'uos contra regi mea nunc mandata referte'.

    meros amores : 'pure, unadulterated love': the plural makes the notion more concrete; see K. F. Smith on Tib. ii. 2. 11, who compares the English 'feelings'. Elsewhere in Catullus the plural has its personal force, 'loved one': see on 10. 1.

10. seu quid suauius : a favourite turn of phrase in Catullus: cf. 22. 12–13 'scurra / aut si quid hac re scitius uidebatur', 82. 1–2 oculos . . . / aut si quid carius est oculis'. For single *seu* equivalent to *aut* (*uel*) *si* cf. Ter. *And.* 190 'postulo siue aequom est te oro', Hor. *Sat.* ii. 1. 59 'Romae seu fors ita iusserit exsul', Tib. i. 6. 21 f. 'exibit quam saepe, time, seu uisere dicet / sacra bonae . . . deae'.

11. meae puellae : Lesbia, as in 2. 1, 3. 3, 11. 15, 36. 2.

12. Veneres Cupidinesque : see on 3. 1.

14. totum ut te faciant . . . nasum : 'make you all nose, entirely nose': for the idiomatic use of *totus* cf. Cic. *Fam.* vii. 33. 2 'me totum in litteras abdere', xi. 29. 2 'totum te ad amicitiam meam contulisti', *Att.* ix. 10. 3 'alia res nunc tota est', xiii. 21. 3 3 'est uerbum totum nauticum', and the corresponding use of *nullus* (8. 14 n., 17. 20).

14

C. Licinius Calvus, a little man, high-spirited and excitable (we have a vivid sketch of him from the elder Seneca, *Contr.* vii. 4. 7), was a member of an old and distinguished Roman family, son of the historian and orator Licinius Macer. He was Catullus' contemporary (slightly younger, probably; he was born in 82 B.C.) and his closest friend; this poem and poem 50 give a pleasant picture of their friendship. The names of the two are significantly coupled by their successors. So Ovid writes in his elegy on Tibullus (*Am.* iii. 9. 61–62) 'obuius huic (*sc.* Tibullo) uenias hedera iuuenilia cinctus / tempora cum Caluo, docte Catulle, tuo'; for Propertius also (ii. 25. 4, 34. 87 ff.) the two are inseparable, and for Horace (*Sat.* i. 10. 19) they represent the 'new' poets. As an orator, cultivating a precise 'Attic' severity of style, Calvus was outstanding, and his speeches were still being read in Tacitus' day (see on 53). The few fragments of his poetry show that it had the same range as Catullus' own—a narrative poem (on the story of Io) and epithalamia, in glyconics and in hexameters, on the one hand, satiric epigram (like Catullus, he attacked Caesar and Pompey) and elegy (see on 96) on the other. Cicero corresponded with him, and if that correspondence had survived it might have filled many gaps in our picture of the society in which they both moved; writing about him to Trebonius in 47 B.C. (*Fam.* xv. 21. 4), apparently after his death, Cicero says 'de ingenio eius ualde existimaui bene'—a tribute all the more striking as coming from one who was not in sympathy either with Calvus' literary tastes or with his way of life.

On the eve of the Saturnalia Calvus has sent Catullus a mischievous present in the form of a collection of bad verse—and
bad verse to them is verse which does not belong to their own
'modern' school. It is a *libellus* (l. 12) containing the work of a
number of poets (l. 5)—a selection made by Calvus himself for
the purpose, perhaps, rather than one which he found ready
made; we have no evidence for a published anthology in Latin
at this time, but such things may have existed. Catullus takes
his cue and uses his reply to pillory some of his 'old-fashioned'
contemporaries who do not write the new poetry. He returns
to the attack on Suffenus in 22; in 36 Volusius is another
victim.

1. plus oculis meis : cf. 3. 5, 82. 2, 104. 2.

2. iucundissime : see on 50. 16 *iucunde*.

 munere isto : 'for that present of yours'. The ablative
denoting external cause (as opposed to internal cause or
motive) is not common. The other instances in Catullus are
all of verbal nouns (65. 22 *aduentu matris*, 68. 25 *cuius interitu*, 68. 87 *Helenae raptu*), but Cicero has examples like
Phil. i. 30 'significarunt se beneficio nouo memoriam ueteris
doloris abiecisse', *Leg.* iii. 15 'regale ciuitatis genus . . . regis
uitiis repudiatum est'.

3. odio Vatiniano : 'with the hatred Vatinius bears you';
Vatinius had good reason to dislike Calvus, his determined
and effective enemy: see on 53. For the use of the adjective
see on 44. 10.

5. male perderes : for the colloquial intensifying *male*, which
is little more than an expletive, cf. Hor. *Sat.* ii. 1. 6 'peream
male si non optimum erat'; similarly with an adjective, 10.
33 'insulsa male'.

6. clienti : Catullus pretends to think that Calvus' present has
come to him as a gift from a grateful *cliens* for services
rendered, probably by way of advocacy. Assistance in court
was one of the services which a *patronus* might be called upon
to perform for his *clientes*: hence the use of *patronus* for
'advocate', but though *patronus* regularly has this specialized sense, the correlative *cliens* has not the restricted legal
sense of our 'client'.

 mala multa : cf. 28. 14 'at uobis mala multa di deaeque /
dent': Plautus has the opposite phrase, *Poen.* 208 'multa
tibi di dent bona'.

7. tantum . . . impiorum : 'this great collection of sinners': for
the construction cf. 5. 13 'tantum basiorum'. To think that
impiorum is meant to suggest by contrast the notion of the
pius uates is to take fun too seriously.

8. **repertum :** 'ingeniously devised', 'recherché', presumably, like *exquisitum*: but no parallel can be quoted for the use.

9. **dat :** 'is the donor': for the use of the present for a past action whose effect continues into the present, cf. Virg. *Aen.* ix. 266 'cratera antiquum quem dat Sidonia Dido', ix. 360 'ditissimus olim quae mittit dona . . . Caedicus'; similarly *Aen.* viii. 141 *generat*, 'is the father', *Georg.* i. 279 *creat*, *Aen.* x. 518 *educat*, Prop. iv. 4. 54 *nutrit*.

litterator : an elementary schoolmaster (γραμματιστής), teaching the three r's, as opposed to *litteratus* (γραμματικός), a teacher of literature; as Apuleius euphuistically puts it (*Flor.* 20), 'prima cratera [the first cup of knowledge] litteratoris ruditatem eximit, secunda grammatici doctrina instruit, tertia rhetoris eloquentia armat'. For the disparaging use cf. Suet. *de Gramm.* 4 (according to Cornelius Nepos *litterati* is the proper word for *poetarum interpretes*, but Messalla Corvinus called that distinguished teacher, Valerius Cato, a *litterator*). Sulla is unidentifiable.

10. **non est mi male,** 'I am not unhappy': for this colloquial use, cf. Plaut. *Most.* 52 'mihi benest et tibi malest', *Truc.* 745 'inuidere alii bene esse, tibi male esse, miseria est', and Martial's quip, x. 13. 10 'uis dicam male sit cur tibi, Cotta? bene est'. See also on 10. 18, 23. 5, 38. 1.

bene ac beate : The same phrase in 23. 15; cf. 37. 14 'boni beatique'. Cicero is fond of the combination: e.g. *Parad.* 15 'nihil est aliud bene et beate uiuere nisi honeste et recte uiuere'.

11. **dispereunt :** 'have not been wasted, gone for nothing': the simple *pereo* is so used, Plaut. *Truc.* 581 'haud perit quod illum tantum amo', Cic. *Att.* ii. 17. 1 'ne et opera et oleum . . . perierit', Ov. *Met.* i. 273 'longique perit labor irritus anni'.

12. **di magni :** again conversationally at 53. 5; in a solemn context at 109. 3.

sacrum : *sacer* is properly a ritual term used of an object set apart for a god and so in particular of a person 'made over' to a deity and 'outlawed' from human contacts: colloquially used, like our 'cursed', it is common in Plautus (e.g. *Poen.* 90, *Rud.* 158, *Bacch.* 784).

13. **scilicet :** ironical: 'and you sent it, of course, to your Catullus, so that . . . .'

14. **misti :** for the syncopated form in -*sti* for -*sisti* cf. 66. 21 *luxti*, 77. 3 *subrepsti*, 91. 9 *duxti*, 110. 3 *promisti*.

continuo : if *continuo* is the adverb, with its usual meaning of 'immediately', 'without more ado', which gives very good sense, *die optimo dierum* must be taken together with *Saturnalibus* in apposition. The hyperbaton may be defended by 44. 9, where the dislocation is much more violent, and by such appositional phrases as Virg. *Georg.* iv. 168 'ignauum fucos pecus'; see on 66. 18. The less likely alternative is to make *continuo* an adjective with *die* and take it to mean the day immediately succeeding the morning on which Catullus received his present. For that meaning there is no precise parallel: the nearest is Ovid's use of *continua die* (*Fasti* v. 734) for the day immediately succeeding a particular night and *continua nocte* (*Fasti* vi. 720) for the night immediately succeeding a particular day.

15. optimo dierum : the celebration of the Saturnalia proper fell on 17 December but the festivities continued on the following days (Cic. *Att.* xiii. 52. 1 'tertiis Saturnalibus') and under the early empire the popular celebrations extended over a good part of December. It was a season of merry-making and good humour and more than one of its customs have transferred themselves to the modern Christmas. Servants enjoyed liberties and might even be waited on by their masters; friends greeted one another with the wish '*bona Saturnalia!*'; and presents (*strenae*) were exchanged. Wax candles (*cerei*) and terracotta figures (*sigillaria*) were conventional gifts; Martial's Book xiv is a collection of couplets intended to accompany Saturnalia presents of all sorts, from a toothpick, a clothes-brush, and a handkerchief to a tame monkey and a copy of Catullus.

16. false does not seem appropriate, since Calvus has not broken his word, and *salse* is preferable: cf. 12. 4 'hoc salsum esse putas', Hor. *Sat.* i. 9. 65 'male salsus/ridens dissimulare' (both of mischievous joking).

sic abibit : 'it will not come off like that for you': cf. Ter. *And.* 175 'mirabar hoc si sic abiret', Cic. *Fin.* v. 7 'hoc fortasse non poterit sic abire', *Att.* xiv. 1. 1 'non posse istaec sic abire'.

17. si luxerit : for this use of *si* where no real uncertainty is implied cf. Hor. *Ep.* i. 7. 10 'quod si bruma niues Albanis illinet agris, / ad mare descendet uates tuus', Virg. *Aen.* v. 64 'si nona diem mortalibus almum / Aurora extulerit ... prima ... ponam certamina'. There is a similar use in a phrase of conventional politeness which is not uncommon in Cicero: e.g. *Acad.* ii. 20 'adgrediar igitur si pauca ante quasi de fama mea dixero', *Off.* ii. 22 'quemadmodum sit utendum eo dicemus si prius iis de rebus quae uirtuti propiores sunt dixerimus', *Phil.* xiv. 6 'ad litteras ueniam si pauca ante quae ad ipsas litteras pertineant dixero'. Both uses are expressions of diffidence or caution, dictated in the one case by piety (*si* being equivalent to 'when, God willing'), in the other by good manners (*si* being equivalent to 'when, with your permission'), which have become formal.

librariorum: Cicero uses *librarius* of clerks or copyists, skilled slaves in the service of Atticus (e.g. *Att*. xii. 40. 1 'misi librum ad Muscam ut tuis librariis daret') or of himself (e.g. *Att*. viii. 13. 1 'lippitudinis meae signum tibi sit librari manus'). Here the word clearly refers to booksellers in ordinary trade maintaining copyists to provide their wares. We have hardly any information from Catullus' time about the book-trade in Rome: all our evidence comes from the Augustan period and the early empire. But Cicero speaks (*Phil*. ii. 21) of a *taberna libraria* in or near the Forum, a booth with stairs leading to an upper story. Catullus has to wait till morning because the shops would be closed on the day of the Saturnalia.

18. scrinia were cylindrical wooden boxes (*scrinia curua* in Ov. *Tr*. i. 1. 106) used for holding *uolumina*, placed upright on their ends, whether books (Hor. *Ep*. ii. 1. 113 'calamum et chartas et scrinia posco') or letters or other documents (Sall. *Cat*. 46. 6, Plin. *Ep*. x. 65. 3, Suet. *Nero* 47. 2).

Caesios, Aquinos: generalizing plurals, 'the like of Caesius and Aquinus'. The change to the singular in *Suffenum* is a mere matter of metrical convenience (Persius does the same thing for the same reason, iii. 79 'non ego curo/esse quod Arcesilas aerumnosique Solones'); there is no need either to suppose that Suffenus is being given special prominence or to take *Suffenum* as genitive plural. For Suffenus see on poem 22; Caesius is unknown. It is tempting to identify Aquinus with the poet whom Cicero mentions in *Tusc*. v. 63: 'adhuc neminem cognoui poetam (et mihi fuit cum Aquinio amicitia) qui sibi non optimus uideretur'. Catullus' contempt means no more than that Aquinus was a poet of the old school (see on 22); but if Cicero is speaking of the same man, old-fashionedness was not his only fault.

19. omnia . . . uenena: for *omnia* summing up a series cf. Plaut. *Men*. 1158 'uenibunt serui supellex fundi aedes omnia', Lucil. 1113 'armamenta tamen malum uela omnia seruo', Juv. 10. 78 'qui dabat olim / imperium fasces legiones omnia'.

21. hinc . . . ualete abite: the two verbs form a single expression, 'get away with my blessing from here': for the use of *ualete* (like Greek χαίρετε) see Servius on *Aen*. xi. 97: 'hinc ortum est

ut etiam maledicti significationem interdum "uale" obtineat,
ut Terentius "ualeant qui inter nos discidium uolunt", hoc
est ita a nobis discedant ut numquam ad nostrum reuer-
tantur aspectum'.

22. malum pedem : for the expletive *malum* cf. 44. 7 'malam
tussim', 21 'malum librum'. There is a play on two meanings of *pes* : for *pes*, 'metre', cf. Ov. *Ibis* 43 f. 'prima quidem
coepto committam proelia uersu, / non soleant quamuis hoc
pede [i.e. elegiac metre] bella geri', *Tr.* i. 1. 16 'contingam
certe quo licet illa pede'. It is true, as Verrall pointed out in
a lively paper (*Studies in Greek and Latin Scholarship*, 249 ff.),
that this line is given a rhythm unparalleled in Catullus by
the succession of two iambic words (producing a violent
conflict between ictus and word-accent in the middle of the
line) and the elision, but his suggestion that it is deliberately
so written to exemplify the bad metre of the *pessimi poetae* is
more ingenious than plausible.

23. saecli incommoda : 'nuisances of our times': for *saeclum*
see on 43. 8.

14*b*

These lines are attached in the manuscripts to poem 14, to
which they clearly do not belong, and there is no context elsewhere into which they fit. If we suppose that they are the
opening of a poem which Catullus left unfinished, we must also
suppose that an editor collecting his work was so unintelligently
conscientious as to include a scrap which is not even a complete
sentence. It is easier to believe that they are a fragment of a
poem, addressed perhaps to the poet's readers (though it is
idle to conjecture its content or its purpose), of which the rest
has been lost; the three lines attached to poem 2 (*2b*) and the
last strophe of poem 51 seem to be relics of the same kind of
accident. The apologetic modesty of *si qui forte* and *non horre-*
bitis is matched by the ironic self-depreciation of *ineptiae*. In
Martial (xi. 1. 14) and Pliny (*Ep.* iv. 14.8, ix. 25. 1) that description
has become conventional for light verse. In Catullus it is to be
interpreted in the light of his use of *ineptus* (see on 8. 1 and 12. 4;
cf. 39. 16); he chooses to regard his verses as a tiresome aberra-
tion, as something which he ought to know better than to do.

17

On a fellow townsman who does not look after his young wife
as he should. Catullus would have him pitched over the old

bridge of a town that wants, and badly needs, a new one, to
see if that may bring him to his senses. Like 67 and 100 the.
poem belongs to the provincial side of Catullus' life and the
allusions to local scenes, personalities, and scandals may well
have been as obscure to a Roman reader as they are to us. Even
the place cannot be identified; the references of lines 1 and 6
are lost on us and in Catullus' waterlogged province many a
stream must have had its pools and backwaters. By *municeps
meus* Catullus must mean a fellow-Veronese, but it does not
follow that the town he is addressing is not Verona, and
Kroll's objection that *municeps meus* must distinguish the
colonia from Verona is untenable. *A priori*, Verona is the likeliest setting; but though Tacitus makes Verona a *colonia* in
A.D. 69 (*Hist.* iii. 8), we do not know when or how it became one,
and Pliny's omission of it from his list of the *coloniae* of his
own province (*N.H.* iii. 130) makes its status doubtful. Guarinus and Murétus identified the *colonia* with the modern
Cologna Veneta, a small town about 20 miles east of Verona
which not only seems to preserve the name but actually offers
a Ponte di Catullo, the site of a bridge over the Guá, now
diverted; but there is no evidence for the existence of a *colonia*
there in Catullus' day and 'Ponte di Catullo' may be no more
than a *jeu d'esprit* or the fanciful invention of civic pride.

The lively abandon of the poem is matched by the rollicking
Priapean metre, a simple lyric system in which a glyconic is
followed by a pherecratean. As in Catullus' longer glyconic
systems (three glyconics followed by a pherecratean in 34, four
glyconics followed by a pherecratean in 61), synaphea is observed; elision is permitted between glyconic and pherecratean,
but not syllaba anceps or hiatus. The combination occurs
sporadically in Greek lyric and tragedy (e.g. Pind. *Ol.* 1. 1,
Aesch. *Agam.* 407–8, Soph. *O.T.* 1187): it was written continuously by Anacreon (fr. 69 D. ἠρίστησα μὲν ἰτρίου λεπτοῦ μικρὸν
ἀποκλάς κ.τ.λ.). In hellenistic times the use of it for hymns to Priapus gave it its technical name. In Latin, apart from this poem, it
is represented only by two fragments of Catullus from a Priapus
poem or poems, one of the Priapus poems included in the
Appendix Virgiliana, and four lines of Maecenas (fr. 4 Morel).

1. **ludere :** i.e. hold a religious festival with its associated
   merrymaking and dancing.

   ponte . . . longo : The long bridge of l. 1—Pons Longus may
   have been its actual name—is the 'miserable bridge'
   ponticulus, of l. 3.

2. **salire paratum habes :** *habere aliquid paratum* with a noun
   object (*iter, exercitum, consilium, classem,* etc.) is a very
   common use in which the verb and the participle have

each its normal function ('have an army in readiness'). Here
the noun is replaced by an infinitive: 'have dancing in readiness, all set'. The nearest parallel seems to be Tac. *Ann.* xi. 1. 2
'turbare nationes promptum haberet', 'found it easy to'. (For
a discussion of these phrases and of the later development of
habere as an auxiliary verb see P. Thielmann in *A.L.L.* ii.
391–3.)

inepta : 'ill-fitting', the opposite of *aptus* in its literal sense
of 'well-fitted' (in which it is opposed to *solutus*, 'loose', in
Cic. *Orat.* 228); the word is not so used elsewhere.

3. axulis : *ac sulcis* of the manuscripts may point to the old
spelling *acsuleis* (cf. 46. 3). *axis* is a technical term for a
board or plank (Fest. Paul. 3 L. 'tabula sectilis axis appella-
tur'; Colum. vi. 30. 2 'stabula roboreis axibus constrata',
'stalls floored with oak boards'): the diminutive does not
occur elsewhere. *assula*, a diminutive of *assis*, apparently a
by-form of *axis*, is found but refers to something smaller,
'shavings' or 'chips' of wood (Fest. Paul. 75 L., Plaut. *Merc.*
130) or marble (Vitruvius vii. 6. 6).

rediuiuis : *rediuiuus* is a builder's term for second-hand
material used over again: Cic. *Verr.* ii. 1. 147 'columnam effi-
cere ab integro nouam nullo lapide rediuiuo', Vitruvius vii.
1. 3 'rediuiuus rudus' ('old rubble'). The word is probably
cognate with *reduuiae*, but popular etymology connected it
with *redeo* and *uiuo*, and in ecclesiastical Latin it is common in
the sense 'restored to life'.

4. supinus eat : means no more than 'fall flat' and does not
imply turning a somersault: cf. Prop. iv. 8. 44 (a table col-
lapses) 'reccidit inque suos mensa supina pedes'.

caua in palude : 'in the surrounding, engulfing, swamp':
a not uncommon use of *cauus* to describe not a permanent
attribute (like our 'hollow') but a relation. Ovid has the
same phrase, *Met.* vi. 371 'tota caua submergere membra
palude'; cf. the Virgilian 'nube caua amicti' (*Aen.* i. 516), 'caua
umbra' (ii. 360, on which Heyne rightly comments 'quatenus
ipsi ea circumdantur'), 'cauis exspectant turribus hostem'
(ix. 46, 'the sheltering towers': so Prop. iv. 10. 13 'ante
cauas . . . turres'). So in 64. 259 'obscura cauis celebrabant
orgia cistis', the point of *cauis* is not merely that the caskets
are hollow (since caskets are never anything else) but that
they conceal the mystic emblems inside.

5. sic : 'on this one condition'. *sic* anticipates the condition
attached to the wish: the condition is expressed by the
following imperative. So Virg. *Ecl.* 9. 30 'sic tua Cyrneas
fugiant examina taxos, / . . . incipe', Hor. *Od.* i. 3. 1 ff. 'sic

te diua potens Cypri . . . regat . . ., reddas', Ov. *Met*. viii. 857
'sic sit tibi piscis in unda / credulus . . ., / dic ubi sit'. Sometimes the order is reversed and the imperative comes first, as
in Tib. ii. 5. 121 'annue: sic tibi sint intonsi, Phoebe, capilli',
or in Martial's reminiscence of this passage, vii. 93. 7 f. 'sed iam
parce mihi nec abutere, Narnia, Quinto: / perpetuo liceat sic
tibi ponte frui'. For a similar use of *sic* in asseveration see
45. 13–16.

6. Salisubsali : if this word is a genitive, *Salisubsalus* (or *-ius*)
must be taken to be either the title of a god in whose honour
cult-dances were performed or the name of dancers who performed them. Its form has suggested a connexion with Salii,
the 'leaping priests', associated particularly with Mars, who
are found not only at Rome but at other places in Italy,
Verona among them. But the title is otherwise unknown:
for the line which Guarinus cited and explicitly ascribed to
the *Armorum Iudicium* of Pacuvius, 'pro imperio nostro
Salisubsulus si excubet', is not to be found in any ancient
author. (Its origin is a mystery; it is hard to see why a
forger should have produced a line which is not only unmetrical but also inexplicable.) Statius proposed *Salisubsilis*
as a dative of the agent, referring to the dancers. (Birt's
fantastic suggestion that *sali subsili*—two imperatives—is
a ritual cry placed in loose apposition to *sacra* is perhaps
worth mentioning as a curiosity: he attempts to support it
by the entirely different *recuso euge tuum* of Pers. i. 49 and
does not explain why the ritual cry should be in the singular.)

7. maximi . . . risus : a descriptive genitive, 'this highly entertaining favour'; it is less natural to take *munus* in its special
sense of 'public exhibition', as Ellis and Kroll do.

8. municipem meum : 'a fellow-townsman of mine': so *ciuis
meus, tribulis meus*, in Gk. δημότης ἐμός, πολίτης ἐμός. Strictly
the word *municeps* should refer to a member of a *municipium*,
but it is used also of members of a *colonia* in default of a
corresponding term: cf. Sen. *Suas*. 6. 27 'municipem nostrum'
(of Corduba), Pliny, *Ep*. i. 19. 1 'municeps tu meus (of Comum)
et condiscipulus', Sen. *Apoc*. 6. 1 'Lugduni natus est, Marci
municipem uides'.

uolŏ : see on 10. 27.

9. per caputque pedesque : 'head over heels': the phrase is not
found elsewhere, but compare Livy, *per*. xxii 'ab equo . . .
per caput deuolutus', 'head first'.

10. uerum . . . ut : '*and* (let it be) where'. For this corrective or
defining use cf. Ter. *Heaut*. 598 'dicam, uerum ut aliud ex

alio incidit'. A similar use of *sed* is more common: e.g.
Plaut. *Cas.* 692 'etiamne habet Casina gladium?—habet, sed
duos' ('yes, in fact two'); Mart. i. 117. 7 'scalis habito
tribus sed altis' ('three stairs up, and high ones'); for other
examples see Mayor on Juv. 5. 147.

   totius : with one exception (67. 23 *illīus*) the pronominal
genitive always has -*ī*- in Catullus: he has seven instances of
illīus, three of *ipsīus*, and one of *alterīus*, *ullīus*, and *unīus*.

   ut : 'where': see on 11. 3.

12. homō : with the original quantity, as in 81. 2 (*bellus homo*);
homŏ with iambic shortening (see on 10. 27) at 24. 7 (*homo
bellus*) and 115. 8.

   pueri instar : 'he has not as much sense as a child'. *instar*,
the relic of an obsolete noun (hence the following genitive), in
classical Latin has always a quantitative reference, either
literal (of size or amount: e.g. Virg. *Aen.* ii. 15 'instar montis
equum', 'a horse as large as a mountain') or metaphorical
(Cic. *Pis.* 52 'unus ille dies mihi immortalitatis instar fuit',
'was as good as immortality', *Brut.* 191 'Plato mihi unus
instar est omnium', Livy xxxviii. 7. 5 'armati instar muni-
menti erant, 'were as good as a rampart'). For a full analysis of the usages of the word see Nettleship, *Contributions to
Latin Lexicography*, pp. 487–9.

13. tremula : here not of the shakiness of old age (as in 61.
154, 68. 142) but of the movement of rocking or dandling.
Nemesianus has a pleasant description of Silenus playing
nursemaid to the infant Bacchus (3. 28 ff.): 'aut gremio fouet
aut resupinis sustinet ulnis,/euocat aut risum digito motuque
quietem / allicit [i.e. rocks him to sleep] aut tremulis quassat
crepitacula palmis' (shakes his rattle for him).

14. cui cum : most editors have followed Scaliger in reading
quoi: Catullus probably wrote *quoi* always (see on 1. 1) but
the *cui iocum* of *V* does not seem to be strong enough ground
in itself for restoring it here.

15. et puella : for the emphatic repetition with *et* cf. Cic. *Fam.*
ii. 7. 4, 'a tribuno plebis et a Curione tribuno', *Sest.* 54 'gener
et Piso gener', *Sull.* 18 'ueniebat ad me et saepe ueniebat',
Verr. ii. 3. 65 'sterni triclinia et in foro sterni iubebat', ii. 5. 121
'errabas, Verres, et uehementer errabas', *Leg. Man.* 10 'de
Lucullo dicam alio loco et ita dicam ut . . .'.

   tenellulo : the double diminutive might well have been
ascribed to Catullus' invention, but *manu tenellula* happens
to have survived in a fragment of Laevius (fr. 4 Morel).

delicatior : 'more skittish', the word conveys the notion of the capricious, wilful behaviour of a spoiled person or animal: see on 50. 3 'ut conuenerat esse delicatos'. So Augustus said (Macr. ii. 5. 4) 'duas se habere filias delicatas quas necesse haberet ferre', 'two spoiled daughters that he had to put up with'—Rome and Julia.

17. ludere : 'lets her flirt as she pleases'.

uni : the adjectival form of the genitive is quoted by Priscian from the comic poet Titinius, and Cato has the feminine dative *unae*. But instances of pronominal adjectives following the adjectival in preference to the normal pronominal declension are not confined either to archaic or to informal use: they occasionally appear, without obvious explanation, in formal prose (Caesar has *toto*, *B.G.* vii. 89. 5) and verse (Propertius has *nullae curae* (dat.) i. 20. 35, *toto orbi* iii. 11. 57). (See Kühner[2] i. 622 sqq., Neue[4] ii. 518 sqq.)

18 f. alnus . . . securi : the elaborate Homeric simile of the felled poplar (*Il.* iv. 482–7) to which editors refer, has nothing in common with the vivid local colour of Catullus' image, in which the proper name calls up a picture of the forest-jungle of the wet Ligurian highlands, and the lively metaphor of *suppernata*.

19. suppernata: 'hamstrung by a Ligurian axe': cf. Fest. 396. 22 L. 'suppernati dicuntur quibus femina sunt succisa in modum suillarum pernarum'.

20. nulla sit : 'as if it did not exist at all'. This use of *nullus* as an emphatic negative is found both with *sum* and with other verbs: cf. (*a*) Cic. *Acad.* ii. 22 'cernere ea potest quae aut nulla sunt aut internosci a falsis non possunt', *Off.* iii. 104 'non ad iram deorum, quae nulla est, sed ad iustitiam et ad fidem pertinet', Ov. *Met.* ix. 735 'uellem nulla forem', Liv. xxxii. 35. 2 'Philippus nullus usquam'; (*b*), 8. 14 'cum rogaberis nulla', Plaut. *Asin.* 408 'is nullus uenit', Ter. *Eun.* 216 'etsi nullus moneas', Cic. *Rosc. Am.* 128 'haec bona in tabulas publicas nulla redierunt'. See Löfstedt, *Synt.* ii. 370, Hofmann, *Lat. Umgangssp.* 80; as Munro notes on Lucr. i. 377, the idiom is parallel to the common 'adverbial' or 'predicative' uses of *omnis* and *totus* (cf. 13. 14).

21. talis iste meus stupor : 'my dim-witted friend of whom I am telling you is just like that'. For the use of the abstract noun of a person, compare the common *scelus*, *odium*, *pestis*; for the colloquial *meus* cf. Phaedr. v. 7. 32 'homo meus se in pulpito . . . prosternit', Petr. 62. 13 'miles meus', Mart. v.

54. 1 'extemporalis factus est meus rhetor'. But *iste meus*
is a very surprising combination and Passerat's ingenious
merus, 'unadulterated dullness' (cf. 13. 9 *meos V* for *meros*) is
probably right.

22. **qui sit :** cf. Plaut. *Capt.* 560 'quin suom ipse interdum
ignorat nomen neque scit qui siet', *Aul.* 714 f. 'quo eam
aut ubi sim aut qui sim / nequeo cum animo certum in-
uestigare'. *qui* is the normal form in this collocation
(again in 78b. 4 'qui sis fama loquetur anus'), presumably for
reasons of euphony (so before *se*, 66. 42) : see on 61. 46.

24. **si pote :** 'on the chance that he can': *pote* is personal; see
on 45. 5.

potē stolidum : for the lengthening, cf. 63. 53 *gelidā
stabula*, 64. 186 *nullā spes*, 44. 18 *nefariā scripta*: there may
be another instance at 67. 32 *supposita speculae.* (22. 12 *modo
scurra* is doubtful since *modō* may have its original quantity.)
Elsewhere lengthening of a final syllable containing an open
short vowel before a combination of *s* and another consonant is
extremely rare; in elegiac verse there is only one instance
(Tib. i. 5. 28 *segete spicas*), in Augustan hexameters two
(Grattius 142 *generosa stirpibus*, 259 *uulpina species*). Allowing
a syllable to remain short in the same position, as Catullus
does at 64. 357, *unda Scamandri*, is almost as rare: see note on
that line. In general the poets clearly avoid the collocation
altogether.

excitare : 'shake up his lethargy': similarly with *torporem*
Plin. *N.H.* xix. 155, *inertiam* Quint. *Decl.* 374, *somnos*
Claud. xv. 447. By an idiom common both in Latin and
in Greek the subject is represented as doing what is in fact
done to him: see on 64. 305.

25. **supinum :** 'spineless', 'phlegmatic'; for the metaphorical
use cf. Quint. x. 2. 17 'otiosi et supini', xi. 3. 3 'supini
securique' ('languid and indifferent'): Mart. vi. 42. 22 has
the curious phrase *aure supina* 'with listless ear'.

26. **soleam :** the Romans did not use shoes nailed to the hoof:
the *solea* was a slipper of leather with metal on the sole (so
ferrea here: Nero had silver plates on his mules' shoes, Suet.
Nero 30, and Poppaea carried ostentation even farther with
gold, Pliny, *N.H.* xxxiii. 140), drawn over the animal's foot
on the road to assist it when the going was difficult.

22

Of Suffenus, apart from this poem and a passing mention in
a list of bad poets in 14. 19, we know nothing at all: even the
name does not occur elsewhere (though Sufenās is known as
a cognomen), but there is no reason to suppose that it is not a
real name. His verses, says Catullus, unlike the man himself,
are dull, insensitive, and 'provincial', that is, unfashion-
able; that condemnation may well mean merely that like
Volusius, on whom the same kind of judgement is passed in
36. 19–20, he was a poet of the old school, an unadventurous
follower of the staid Ennian tradition who ignored the new
idiom which Catullus and his friends were giving to Latin poetry.
The opening address to Varus which disguises literary criticism
as a letter to a friend is a piece of hellenistic technique (see Kroll,
Studien zur Verständnis der römischen Literatur, 231–3); he is
presumably the Varus of poem 10, whether he is one of Catullus'
known fellow countrymen of that name, Alfenus Varus the jurist
or Quintilius Varus the critic, or someone unknown.

1. **probe :** for the colloquial use cf. Ter. *Heaut.* 180 'hunc
Menedemum nostin?—probe', Cic. *de Or.* iii. 194 'Antipater
quem tu probe meministi,' *Fam.* ii. 12. 2 'quod cum probe
scirem'. The weakening of the adverb is like that of English
'properly'; compare such uses as Plaut. *Most.* 102 'aedes . . .
factae probe', *Men.* 465 'hanc (pallam) hodie probe/lepideque
concinnatam referam', where it refers to good, honest work
or dealing, with such as *Amph.* 975 'errant probe', *M.G.* 1397
'uide ut . . . sit acutus . . . culter probe', *Trin.* 896 'ludam
hominem probe', Ter. *Heaut.* 1020 'tui similis est probe'.

2. **uenustus :** cf. 3. 2, 13. 6: perhaps the most difficult word to
analyse of all Catullus' social vocabulary, implying the charm
in speech and behaviour which comes of taste and breeding.
   dicax et urbanus : words for wit and humour in Latin are
so loosely used that they are very difficult to define; Cicero,
for example, at one point makes *dicacitas* and *cauillatio* sub-
divisions of *facetiae* (*de Or.* ii. 218); *facetiae* and *dicacitas* are
combined in *de Or.* ii. 221 ('hominibus facetis et dicacibus': cf.
Cael. 67), but distinguished in *Or.* 90 ('Demosthenes non tam
dicax fuit quam facetus: est autem illud acrioris ingeni, hoc
maioris artis'). But *dicacitas* is usually pointed witticism,
the gift of saying clever things (*dicta*), particularly at other
people's expense: cf. Quint. vi. 3. 21 'dicacitas . . . proprie
significat sermonem cum risu aliquos incessentem'. *urbanitas*
(see on 39. 8) is the sophistication in speech and manners

which distinguishes the cultivated member of a city society from the *rusticus*.

3. **idemque** : 'and at the same time', with a neat suggestion of the inconsistency which is to be pointed out; cf. 14 and 15 below.

longe plurimos : 'far more lines than anyone else'.

4. **aut . . . aut** : 'thousands, it may be ten or it may be more', makes *mille* the unit of measurement of Suffenus' production.

5. **sic ut fit** : 'in the ordinary way'.

in palimpseston : *Palimpsestus* (παλίμψηστος) refers to used writing material which has been cleaned to take fresh writing, usually parchment, though papyrus could also be reused; Trebatius wrote a letter to Cicero on used *carta*, i.e. papyrus (see below). *In palimpsesto* has caused difficulty, since the normal usage for 'write up in' is *referre in* with the accusative: so, for example, Cic. *Phil.* viii. 28 'sententias uestras in codicillos et omnia uerba referebat', *Rosc. Com.* 1 'ut mea causa falsum ('a forgery') in codicem referret' (at *Rosc. Com.* 5 the manuscript reading 'in codice' must be corrected to agree). Hence Lachmann substituted the Greek accusative *palimpseston* (following the suggestion of Marcilius, who wrote it in Greek characters), though accusatives in -*on* very rarely appear before the Augustan poets, and Catullus himself, when he uses a Greek second-declension neuter (*mnemosynum* 12. 13, *epistolium* 68. 2), latinizes the termination, as Cicero does with *macrocollum*, *chirographum*, and *embolium*. In fact the word is very rare in literature, either Greek or Latin. In Greek there are only two occurrences of it, both in Plutarch, *Mor.* 779c (βιβλίον παλίμψηστον) and 504d (παλίμψηστα), and both figurative. The only other instance in Latin is practically contemporary with this poem: acknowledging a letter from Trebatius in 53 B.C. Cicero writes (*Fam.* vii. 18. 2) 'quod in palimpsesto (*sc.* scribis), laudo equidem parsimoniam'. *In palimpsesto* may have been so much of a set phrase (perhaps even the only phrase in which the word was used) that Catullus found it natural to use it even with *referre*.

6. **cartae** are the material (χάρται, masculine in Greek), *libri* the rolls (*uolumina*) into which it was made up.

regiae clearly is a technical term for high-grade paper. Pliny (*N.H.* xiii. 74, the *locus classicus* for the papyrus trade) says that the best quality produced in Egypt, originally called *hieratica* from its use for priestly records, was renamed *Augusta* in compliment to the Emperor; Suetonius (*ap.* Isid. *Orig.* vi. 10. 2) gives the name of the best large-sized papyrus as *Augustea regia*. Hero of Alexandria speaks of χάρται βασιλικοί; perhaps the name *regia* displaced *hieratica* in Egypt and was an intermediate stage between that and *Augusta*.

7. **noui umbilici** : the *umbilicus* was the stick of wood or ivory round which the *uolumen* was rolled (so Hor. *Epod.* 14. 7 f. 'iambos ad umbilicum adducere', Mart. iv. 89. 2 'peruenimus usque ad umbilicos', of finishing the writing of a book) with projecting knobs or bosses (*cornua*), sometimes painted or decorated, at its ends. The plural *umbilici*, when used of a single *uolumen*, refers to the bosses; so Martial says to his book (iii. 2. 9) 'pictis luxurieris umbilicis' (cf. i. 66. 11 '(liber) umbilicis cultus', v. 6. 15 'nigris pagina creuit umbilicis') and Statius speaks of his as (*Silv.* iv. 9. 8) 'binis decoratus umbilicis'.

lora rubra membranae : the *membrana* was the parchment wrapper which might be put round a papyrus roll for protection and ornament; it was often stained red: cf. Mart. iii. 2. 10 (addressing his book) 'te purpura delicata uelet', x. 93. 4 'carmina purpurea ... modo culta toga' ('a red jacket'). With the manuscript reading *membranae* must be taken as genitive, 'the red *lora* of the wrapper'; if it were nominative it would need an epithet like the other items in the list. Avantius meant his *membrana* to be taken with *derecta plumbo*, but these words do not provide a suitable epithet, since the cover would not normally need ruling, and are more naturally attached to *omnia*.

lora does not occur elsewhere as a term of book-production. It is easiest to suppose that *lora* are vellum or leather strings for tying up the roll. No literary *volumen* so secured has survived, but there are examples of documentary rolls tied up with strips of papyrus (see the illustration in Schubart, *Das Buch* ii, p. 55); in editions de luxe like Suffenus' the strings might well be red to match the wrapper. The alternative is to refer *lora* to the title-tabs, for which the ordinary name is *index*, strips of parchment attached to the end of the roll and bearing the title of the contents. The *index* which has survived in its place on the Oxyrhynchus papyrus 1091 of Bacchylides is not very ornamental, being a strip of palimpsest parchment, but there are literary references to more conspicuous *indices* on which the title was written in red: so in Mart. iii. 2. 11 'cocco rubeat superbus index' and in Ov. *Tr.* i. 1. 7 (whose book is to be denied the usual ornamentation) 'nec titulus minio, nec cedro carta notetur'.

8. **derecta ... aequata** : 'the whole thing ruled with lead and smoothed down with pumice'.

plumbo ... pumice: *plumbum* is the small circular lead plate which was used, with a ruler, for marking out lines to guide the writer's hand: both instruments appear in a series of Greek epigrams in which draughtsmen dedicate the tools of their trade (*A.P.* vi. 62. 1 κυκλοτερῆ μόλιβον σελίδων σημάντορα πλευρῆς, 65. 1–2 τὸν τροχοέντα μόλιβδον ὃς ἀτραπὸν οἶδε χαράσσειν/ὀρθὰ παραξύων ἰθυτενῆ κανόνα, 66. 3 κανόνα τροχαλοῖο κυβερνήτηρα μολίβδου). *pumex* was used for rubbing down the rough edges of the papyrus and giving an even surface to the ends (*frontes*) of the rolled *uolumen*: cf. I. 2 'arida modo pumice expolitum', Prop. iii. 1. 8 'exactus tenui pumice uersus eat', Ov. *Tr.* i. 1. 11 'nec fragili geminae poliantur pumice frontes [Ovid's book is to be in mourning], / hirsutus sparsis ut uideare comis'.

9. **haec cum legas tu :** 'when one reads these things'. The subjunctive of the indefinite second person is not uncommon in temporal clauses of this kind: so Lucr. v. 100 'ut fit ubi insolitam rem adportes auribus', Sall. *Iug.* 31. 28 'bonus tantum modo segnior fit ubi neglegas', Cic. *Or.* 225 'plurimum ualet maximeque eis locis cum argua aut refellas', Sen. *Ep.* 75. 4 'qui et cum uideas illum et cum audias idem est'. But the addition of *tu* when the second person is being used indefinitely is very rare: in Cic. *Tusc.* i. 91 'uirtutis quam necessario gloria, etiam si tu id non agas, consequatur', it is emphatic ('even if one is not aiming at that oneself'); here, as in 23. 22, it looks like a metrical stopgap.

.   **bellus :** of one who knows and observes the usages of polite society (cf. 24. 7, 81. 2); Cic. *Fam.* vii. 16. 2 'sed mehercules extra iocum ('joking apart') homo bellus est', *Att.* i. 1. 4 'durius accipere hoc mihi uisus est quam homines belli solent' ('took this rather more rudely than nice people usually do'). For a lively description of the *bellus homo*, the society man, of a century later see Martial iii. 63.

10. **unus caprimulgus aut fossor,** 'any ordinary' farm-labourer: for this use of *unus* cf. Cic. *de Or.* i. 132 'sicut unus paterfamilias his de rebus loquor' ('like an ordinary citizen'), *Att.* ix. 10. 2 'me una haec res torquet quod non . . . Pompeium tamquam unus manipularis secutus sim' ('like an ordinary soldier'). While in its use to strengthen a superlative *unus* emphasizes uniqueness, in this idiom it has just the opposite implication, 'one among many'.

11. **abhorret ac mutat :** it is difficult to determine the precise sense of *abhorret*. Munro cites two instances of the absolute use of the verb in which it means 'be out of place, incongruous', Cic. *de Or.* ii. 85 'sin plane abhorrebit et erit absurdus', Livy xxx. 44. 6 'uestrae istae absurdae atque

abhorrentes lacrimae'; to these may be added Livy xxvii.
37. 13 'carmen . . . illa tempestate forsitan laudabile
. . . nunc abhorrens et inconditum si referatur'. The idea
here may be similar, but it is perhaps likelier that *a se* is to be
understood: 'he is so unlike himself', 'so disappointing'.

mutat : the intransitive use is not uncommon: cf. Cic.
Orat. 59 'ergo ille princeps (our consummate orator) uariabit
et mutabit', Livy ix. 12. 3 'animi mutauerant'.

12. **hoc quid putemus esse** : 'what are we to make of this?'
A letter of Pliny's has several reminiscences of this poem:
Ep. iv. 25. 3 'quid hunc putamus domi facere qui in tanta re
tam serio tempore tam scurriliter ludit, qui denique in senatu
dicax et urbanus est?'

modō : the second vowel of the adverb is normally shortened and Catullus always has *modŏ* elsewhere (on the 'law of
iambic shortening' which operates in such words, see on
10. 27), but Plautus not infrequently uses *modō*, and Lucretius also uses both quantities. Similarly Catullus has both
homŏ (24. 7, 115. 8) and *homō* (17. 12, 81. 2). It is not necessary to suppose that the length is due to the following *sc-*(see
on 17. 24).

scurra has not yet acquired the implication of professional
buffoonery which it came to have later. In Plautus 'urbani
adsidui ciues quos scurras uocant' (*Trin.* 202) are city-bred
'wits', dandies and gossips who 'falson an vero laudent,
culpent quem uelint / non flocci faciunt dum illud quod
lubeat sciant': so in *Most.* 15 one slave taunts another 'tu
urbanus uero scurra, deliciae popli, / rus mihi tu obiectas?' A
scurra might do very well for himself, but for all his *urbanitas*
respectable society looked askance at him: cf. Cic. *Har. Resp.*
42, 'scurrarum locupletium libidines', *Quinct.* 55 'uetus est
de scurra multo facilius .diuitem quam patrem familias fieri
posse', Hor. *Ep.* i. 15. 27 'urbanus coepit haberi, / scurra uagus
non qui certum praesepe teneret'.

13. **aut si quid** : for the characteristic turn of phrase cf. 13. 10
23. 13, 42. 14, 82. 2.

hac re scitius : *V*'s *tristius* is obviously corrupt. Both the
old correction *tritius* and Munro's *tersius* (he actually proposed the alleged archaic form *tertius*) are palaeographically
plausible but neither seems appropriate here. *tersus* when
used metaphorically elsewhere refers to neatness of style or
nicety of judgement; *tritus* means either 'commonplace'
or 'practised' (*tritae aures* Cic. *Fam.* ix. 16. 4, *tritae manus*
Vitr. ii. 1. 6). Müller's *scitius* suits the context better and
scitus is a word of common speech (e.g. Ter. *And.* 486 'scitus
puer', Plaut. *Merc.* 755 'satis scitum filum mulieris'). But

the corruption may extend further: *hac re*, referring to *scurra*, may be accepted as a colloquialism (though there is no exact parallel: in Sen. *Ep.* 47. 13 'nihil hac re humilius', *hac re* refers to a whole preceding sentence), but one might expect the *est* which Catullus does not omit elsewhere in such phrases.

14. infaceto . . . infacetior: another favourite turn of Catullus: cf. 27. 4, 39. 16, 99. 2, and 14. For *infacetus* see on 43. 8. *rus* is the concentration of *rusticitas*: cf. 36. 19 (of another uninspired poet) 'pleni ruris et inficetiarum'.

idem: as often, points a contrast—of two attributes which inconsistently, and so surprisingly, exist in the same person (so, for example, Hor. *Sat.* ii. 7. 23 'laudas / fortunam et mores antiquae plebis et idem, / si quis ad illa deus subito te agat, usque recuses'): our corresponding idiom 'at the same time' has the same implication. But there is careless writing in the repetition of *idem* in l. 15: 'the man who seemed a wit is at the same time a dullard at poetry and at the same time nothing makes him so happy'.

15. attigit: 'turns his hand to poetry'; cf. Nepos, *Att.* 18. 5 'attigit poeticen', Cic. *Or.* 41 'omnibus qui unquam orationes attigerunt'.

16. beatus: cf. Hor. *Ep.* ii. 2. 107 (again of self-satisfied poets) 'gaudent scribentes et se uenerantur et ultro, / si taceas, laudant quicquid scripsere beati', Cic. *Mur.* 26 'praetor interea ne pulcrum se ac beatum putaret ['in case he might feel too pleased with himself'] atque aliquid ipse sua sponte loqueretur, ei quoque carmen compositum est'.

17. gaudet in se: 'is delighted with himself': so Prop. ii. 4. 18 'gaudeat in puero'. For *in aliquo* used of the object of emotion see on 64. 98.

18. nimirum: 'the fact is', offering an explanation (often, but not here, an ironical one).

idem . . . fallimur: 'we make the same mistake': for the internal accusative cf. Hor. *A.P.* 354 *peccat idem*.

19. in aliqua re . . . Suffenum: 'a Suffenus in something': the descriptive use of a proper name in the singular is not common, but cf. Vell. ii. 18 (of Mithridates) 'consiliis dux, miles manu, odio in Romanos Hannibal', Juv. 14. 41 'Catilinam / quocumque in populo uideas'. For *quisquam . . . aliqua* see on 73. 1 f., 76. 7.

21. manticae quod in tergo est: 'the part of the knapsack that is on our back'. The reference is to the fable of Aesop which represented man as carrying two knapsacks, one slung in

front holding his neighbours' faults, the other slung behind
holding his own; in Phaedrus' version (iv. 10), ' peras imposuit
Iuppiter nobis duas: / propriis repletam uitiis post tergum
dedit, / alienis ante pectus suspendit grauem'. Horace refers
to the same fable, *Sat.* ii. 3. 299 'respicere ignoto discet
pendentia tergo'; Persius has a variation, 4. 24 'sed praece-
denti spectatur mantica tergo', 'what we see is the bag on
the back of the man in front of us'.

23

The Furius whose financial difficulties are the occasion for
this extravagant ribaldry appears again in 26 and by implication in 24: presumably he is also the messenger who in 11 is
charged with conveying a final repudiation to Lesbia. He is
homo bellus, moving in fashionable society (or at least having
pretensions in that direction); he needs money; he is accused of
'cutting out' Catullus with Juventius; he is (or has been) in
Lesbia's circle. Knowing nothing more about him than that,
we cannot say whether Catullus' language represents the good-
natured mischief of friendship or the expression of pique or
snobbery; nor do we know how much of this ironical picture of
the blessings of poverty was suggested by the Greek iambographers. Identifying this Furius with the one Furius we know
of who might fit, the poet Furius Bibaculus, is a pleasant
speculation. (See on 26.)

1. **neque seruus est neque arca :** This poem and the next would
   gain point if this phrase was deprecatingly or jokingly used
   by Furius himself of his own straits (as Catullus says 'plenus
   sacculus est aranearum' of his, 13. 8) and was recognizable
   as a quotation from him. Catullus then takes up the phrase
   here, embroiders it with *nec cimex*, etc. and indeed builds
   the whole poem on it, and in 24 uses it (repeating it emphatically three times) as a description in which his readers
   would recognize Furius.

2. **nec cimex neque araneus :** He has not even the humblest
   animal companions of human poverty.

3. **nouerca :** a proverbially uncongenial member of a household:
   Virg. *Ecl.* iii. 33 'est mihi namque domi pater, est iniusta
   nouerca', Hor. *Epod.* 5. 9 'quid ut nouerca me intueris?'

4. **silicem comesse :** because they are hungry enough for any
   diet or because flint would be no harder than the bread
   they eat?

5. **est pulcre :** 'you have a fine time', as in Hor. *Sat.* ii. 8. 18 'quis cenantibus una/. . . pulcre fuerit tibi nosse laboro', Cic. *N.D.* i. 114 'propone ante oculos deum nihil aliud in omni aeternitate nisi "mihi pulcre est " et "ego beatus sum " cogitantem'. For the colloquial use cf. l. 15 'sit bene ac beate', 14. 10 'est mi male'.

6. **lignea :** 'wiry', 'stringy': cf. Lucr. iv. 1161 (of a thin girl) 'neruosa et lignea'.

7. **nec mirum :** cf. 57. 3, 62. 14, 69. 7.

   nam : Catullus has *nam* in the second place again at 37. 11 and 64. 301, *namque* in the second at 64. 384 and in the fifth at 66. 65. The postponing of connective particles, which becomes a regular metrical device in later verse (for Virgil see Norden, *Aeneid vi*, pp. 402–4; for the elegists, Platnauer, *Latin Elegiac Verse*, pp. 93–96) first appears in Catullus: it was probably suggested by the practice of Hellenistic poets with καί, ἀλλά, and οὐδέ. Catullus postpones *atque* at 64. 93, *nec* or *neque* at 64. 173, 210, 379, 68. 55, 116, *at* at 64. 43, 58, *sed* at 51. 9, 63. 102: he has no example of postponed *et*.

8. **pulcre concoquitis :** 'you have fine digestions'.

   nihil timetis : having nothing to lose, you are not afraid that your house will go on fire (*incendia*) or fall down with a crash (*graues ruinas*) or that your nearest and dearest will murder you for your money (*impia . . . ueneni*). Propertius perhaps had these lines in mind when he wrote, ii. 27. 9–10, 'praeterea [you need not fear] domibus flammam domibusque ruinas / neu subeant labris pocula nigra tuis'.

9. **incendia . . . ruinas :** both everyday risks in Rome: cf. Sen. *Contr.* ii. 1. 11 'tanta altitudo aedificiorum est tantaeque uiarum angustiae ut neque aduersus ignem praesidium neque ex ruinis ullam in partem effugium sit', Sen. *Ben.* iv. 6. 2 'ingens tibi domicilium sine ullo incendii aut ruinae metu struxit', *Dial.* vii. 26. 2 'uos domus formosa, tamquam nec ardere nec ruere possit, obstupefacit', Juv. 3. 190 ff.

10. **facta impia :** Haupt's *furta* is mistaken. The corruption would have been an easy one (though not quite so easy here, where *furta* is readily intelligible, as at 68. 140, where it has a special sense) and thieves are one of the worries of the man of property (Hor. *Sat.* i. 1. 77 'formidare malos fures, incendia . . .'). But *impia* is too strong an epithet for *furta* and the general phrase 'unnatural acts' is unobjectionable. The following *doli ueneni* are one example of these *impia facta*: Horace's 'parentis . . . si quis impia manu / senile guttur fregerit' (*Epod.* 3. 1) would be another.

11. casus . . . periculorum : 'occurrences of dangers': cf. Cic. *Fam.* vi. 4. 3 'ad omnes casus subitorum periculorum magis obiecti sumus', v. 16. 5 'ferre immoderatius casum incommodorum tuorum', Caes. *B.G.* iii. 13. 7 'quarum rerum omnium nostris nauibus casus erat extimescendus'.

12. atqui here 'caps' the negatives with a further positive fact.

sicciora cornu : 'as dry as a bone', in our idiom (see on 35. 18): for *cornu* in this connexion cf. Pliny, *N.H.* xxxi. 102 'cornea uidemus corpora piscatorum' (with exposure to sun and salt), Petr. 43. 7 'corneolus fuit, aetatem bene ferebat'. The *siccum corpus*, which is free from noxious humours, is healthy (so Cicero says, *Sen.* 34, of the nonagenarian Massinissa 'audire te arbitror . . . summam esse in eo corporis siccitatem': for the opposite, cf. Livy xxxiv. 47. 5 'mollia et fluida corpora Gallorum), and *siccitas* is secured by temperate living: Cic. *T.D.* v. 99 'adde siccitatem quae consequitur hanc continentiam in uictu'.

13. aut siquid magis aridum est : a favourite turn of Catullus: cf. 13. 10, 22. 13, 42. 14, 82. 2.

15. quare non tibi sit : 'why shouldn't you be comfortable ? ', 'of course you are comfortable': cf. 89. 4 'quare is desinat esse macer ? '.

bene ac beate : cf. 14. 10: here the mischievous irony of *beate* is repeated in 24 and 27, *beata . . . beatus*.

16 f. sudor . . . pituita nasi : compare Varro *ap.* Non. 634 L. 'Persae propter exercitationes puerilis modicas eam sunt consecuti corporis siccitatem ut neque spuerent neque emungerentur'.

19. salillo : the polished salt-cellar which was a feature even of a simple table: Hor. *Od.* ii. 16. 13 'cui paternum / splendet in mensa tenui salinum', Persius iii. 25 'rure paterno / est tibi far modicum, purum et sine labe salinum'.

22. tu : for the rare addition of the unemphatic pronoun to a subjunctive of the indefinite second person cf. 22. 9 'haec cum legas tu'. In l. 24 (as in 24. 9) the *tu* is definite: this emphatic use of *tu* with an imperative is common.

23. non umquam : an emphatic colloquialism for *nunquam*: cf. Plaut. *Merc.* 288.

posses should probably be corrected to the normal *possis*: the 'mixed condition' of 6. 2 'ni sint illepidae atque inelegantes, uelles dicere' is not parallel.

25. nec : for the very natural use of *nec* for *aut* after *noli* (as if *ne spreueris* had been written) cf. Plaut. *Poen.* 1129 'mirari noli neque me contemplarier', Cic. *Fam.* xii. 30. 1 'noli impudens esse nec mihi molestiam exhibere': similarly it is sometimes used after *nescire* (e.g. Cic. *Tusc.* v. 116) and *negare* (e.g. Cic. *Ac.* ii. 79).

26. precari : a strong word for a request for an accommodation, implying an urgent appeal.

24

The Juventii were an old and distinguished Roman family, originally from Tusculum (Cic. *Planc.* 19); the name is also found at Verona. Where and how this Juventius came to be known to Catullus there is nothing to show. Catullus expresses his own feelings for him in 48 and 99, his jealousy of other admirers here and in 81.

1. flosculus : cf. 100. 2 *flos Veronensum*, 63. 64 *gymnasi flos*.

2. horum : 'those that we know' i.e. the present generation of them.

2–3. quot . . . annis : cf. 49. 2 and the passages there quoted: here the formula is mere affectionate exuberance.

4. Midae : the first appearance in Latin literature of Midas and his golden touch: but the proverbial use of the name is old in Greek (Tyrtaeus 9. 6 D. πλουτοίη δὲ Μίδεω ... μάλιον, Plato, *Rep.* 408b οὐδ' εἰ Μίδου πλουσιώτεροι εἶεν).

5. isti . . . arca : the *iste* who has 'neither servant nor cashbox' ·is identified from 23. 1 as Furius; see notes on that poem.

6. sic : 'like that', 'as you are doing'.

7. qui? : 'how?' For the old instrumental form see on 72. 7; for its elliptical use in dialogue cf. Plaut. *Bacch.* 53 *qui, amabo?, Merc.* 404 *qui uero?*

 homo bellus : for the social connotation of the phrase see on 22. 9.

9. abice eleuaque : 'minimize that as much as you like': both verbs are technical terms of rhetoric: for *abicere* opposed to *augere* ('enhance') cf. Cic. *Or.* 127 'augendis rebus et contra abiciendis nihil est quod non perficere possit oratio', *de Or.* iii. 104.

 quam lubet (*quamlibet*) normally accompanies an adjective, rarely a verb as here and in Phaed. i. 25. 6.

26

These lines are merely a vehicle for a verbal joke on the two meanings of *oppositus*, 'facing' and 'pledged'. If *nostra* is read in l. 1, Catullus is making fun of his own embarrassments, as he

does in 10 and 13: if *uestra*, the *uillula* is Furius' family home
and Furius is being teased, as he is in 23 ('Furi, cui neque seruus
est neque arca / nec cimex neque araneus neque ignis'), about
being hard up. In either case the enumeration of the cardinal
points is serving only to build up the joke in the last lines. Some
commentators have supposed that Furius wants to borrow
money (as he does in 23) and is being told that Catullus is in no
position to lend; others that Furius boasted of the situation of
his villa and that Catullus is deflating him with a reminder that
though his house is not exposed to the elements, it is exposed to
a mortgage. In fact we have no clue to the background of the
poem beyond the conventional poverty of poets.

Furius appears again in 11, where with Aurelius he is given
a last message to Lesbia, and in two pieces of abusive banter
(16, 23). We know something, though not very much, of one
Furius who may well be the person whom Catullus is addressing
—the poet Furius Bibaculus, a Northerner from Cremona, who
certainly was associated with the *noui poetae*. Two hendeca-
syllabic epigrams of his (fr. 1, 2 Morel) are concerned with the
famous *grammaticus* Valerius Cato, who was born about 100–90
B.C. and from whose teaching and example the new movement
received inspiration (Suet. *Gramm.* 11), and Tacitus mentions
him with Catullus as having written verses lampooning 'the
Caesars', which Julius and Octavian were generous enough to
ignore (*Ann.* iv. 34. 8). From his references to Cato, which are
those of a devoted pupil to an ageing teacher, and from the clear
implication in Tacitus that he attacked Octavian, it seems
that the date which Jerome gives for his birth, 103 B.C., is at
least twenty years too early and must be ascribed to some confusion, perhaps with another poet named Furius. The evidence
points to his having been a contemporary of Catullus and a
poet of the same school.

1. **Austri :** for the cardinal points of the wind-rose Catullus
   uses two Latin names, *Auster* for the South wind and
   Fauonius for the West, and two Greek, *Boreas* for the North
   and *Apheliotes* for the East. *Apheliotes* (like its native
   equivalent *Subsolanus*) is elsewhere confined to technical
   writing: in poetry *Eurus* (properly SE.) takes its place.
   In Attic the word was written ἀπηλιώτης, the unaspirated
   Ionic form having been adopted from Ionic-speaking sea-
   men, but the aspirated form may have become current by
   Catullus' time.

2. **opposita :** for the local sense, 'facing', cf. Cic. *Off.* ii. 14
   'moles oppositas fluctibus'; for the financial, 'pledged',
   'mortgaged' (the full phrase is *pignori opponere*), Ter. *Ph.* 661

'ager oppositus pignori ob / decem minas est', Juv. 11. 18
'lancibus oppositis' ('having pawned his plate').

4. **milia quindecim et ducentos** : the mortgage is not large, to
judge from the little we know about rents: 30,000 sesterces
was a possible rent for a good town house and Caelius rented
a flat in an *insula* for 10,000 (Cic. *Cael.* 17). But one need
not expect from Catullus an accurate statement of his
finances, or of other people's, and this number neatly fills
the line.

5. **horribilem atque pestilentem** : an unhealthy wind, like the
sirocco in Hor. *Od.* iii. 23. 5, 'nec pestilentem sentiat
Africum / fecunda uitis', and one that makes you shiver.

27

These 'lines written at a drinking party' have their counterparts in Greek in two fragments of Anacreon: 43 D. ἄγε δὴ φέρ'
ἡμίν, ὦ παῖ, / κελέβην ὅκως ἄμυστιν / προπίω, τὰ μὲν δέκ' ἐγχέας / ὕδατος,
τὰ πέντε δ' οἴνου, / κυάθους ὡς ἀνυβρίστως / ἀνὰ δηὖτε βασσαρήσω, and
27 D. φέρ' ὕδωρ, φέρ' οἶνον, ὦ παῖ, / φέρε δ' ἀνθεμόεντας ἡμῖν / στεφάνους
ἔνεικον ὡς δὴ / πρὸς Ἔρωτα πυκταλίζω.

1. **uetuli** : 'good old Falernian': the familiar endearing diminutive (which Martial takes over, i. 18. 1, viii. 77. 5, xi. 26.
3) seems to have been regular in this connexion; so in the
proverbial recipe for mead which Macrobius gives (vii. 12. 9),
'mulsum quod probe temperes miscendum esse nouo Hymettio
et uetulo Falerno'.

2. **inger** : the shortened imperative, apparently analogous to
fer and its compounds, occurs only here and we have no
clue to its associations. The existence of a shortened infinitive *biber*, which Charisius cites from the comic poet Titinius
(fr. 78 *date illi biber*) and the historian Fannius (fr. 2 *iubebat
biber dari*), and which in late Latin gave rise to a declinable
substantive *biber*, is probably no more than a coincidence.
Ellis rightly points out that the verb, when used of liquids,
generally implies pouring in quantity.

  amariores : possibly 'of a drier vintage': some Falernians
were made drier than others—Athenaeus i. 26c distinguishes
two sorts, αὐστηρός and γλυκάζων, Pliny *N.H.* xiv. 63 three,
austerum, dulce, tenue—and the *amaritudo* of old wine might
itself be palatable; cf. Sen. *Ep.* 63. 5 'in uino nimis ueteri
ipsa nos amaritudo delectat'. More probably, as the following lines suggest, 'mixed with less water'. The phrase will
then have the same meaning as the Homeric ζωρότερον κέραιε

(*Il.* ix. 203) and the similar phrases of comedy: cf. the fragment of dialogue from Diphilus (58 K.), ἔγχεον σὺ δὴ πιεῖν. / εὐζωρότε-ρόν γε νὴ Δί’, ὦ παῖ, δός· τὸ γὰρ / ὑδαρὲς ἅπαν τοῦτ’ ἐστὶ τῇ ψυχῇ κακόν.

3. **lex . . . magistrae :** a drinking-party was presided over by an *arbiter* or *magister* chosen, it might be, by a throw of the dice (Hor. *Od.* ii. 7. 25), who prescribed the amount and strength of the wine to be drunk: for these *leges* cf. Cic. *Verr.* ii. 5. 28 'qui populi Romani legibus numquam paruisset, illis legibus quae in poculis ponebantur obtemperabat', Hor. *Sat.* ii. 6. 68 'siccat inaequales calices conuiua solutus / legibus insanis'. Here Postumia appears to be acting as president: her name suggests not a counterpart of the Damalis and Glycera who share Horace's *conuiuia* but a Roman lady of position. Clodia herself, according to Cicero, attended 'uirorum alienissimorum conuiuia' (*Cael.* 49), and Postumia may have been an equally unconventional matron: but the identification of her with the wife of Ser. Sulpicius Rufus, consul in 51 B.C., whom scandal connected with Caesar but who in Cicero appears as a wife of blameless reputation, is no more than a guess.

4. **ebrioso acino ebriosioris :** *V*'s *ebriose acino* points clearly to *ebrioso acino* as the true reading and there would have been no reason to doubt that but for the quotation of the poem by Gellius (vi. 20. 6). The text of Gellius has been corrupted, both in the quotation and in his comment on it, but with Haupt's corrections his comment shows that he himself reads (1) *ebria acina* and that he knows of two variant readings, (2) *ebriosa acina* and (3) *ebrioso acino*. He prefers (1) on the ground of the peculiar *suauitas* produced by the *concentus* of the two *a*'s in hiatus, which he supposes Catullus to have contrived in imitation of similar effects in Homer; (2) and (3) he ascribes to *corrupta exemplaria*. His preference for *ebria* is clearly misguided: for (*a*) there is no similar example of hiatus in Catullus' hendecasyllabics and the reason which he gives for this one is fanciful; (*b*) the repetition of the adjective is so much in Catullus' manner—cf. 22. 14 *infaceto infacetior*, 39. 16 *inepto ineptior*, 99. 2 *dulci dulcius*, 14 *tristi tristius*—as to be certain here.

As for *acina*, Gellius thinks that Catullus used the feminine instead of the normal neuter form to secure the collision of *a*'s. If he used it, it cannot have been for that reason, but it is unlikely that he did use it. The masculine *acinus* is well attested as an alternative to the neuter form, but the feminine is not found till long after Catullus' time (it appears in late medical writers and in glossaries), and the grammarian Nonius (284 L.), who probably compiled his dictionary in the fourth century, notes the variation between masculine and neuter but does not mention the feminine. There are a number of nouns which show both neuter and feminine forms: the neuter plural originated in a collective feminine singular (the 'heteroclite' declension of some masculine nouns which have a neuter plural form—e.g. *locus* / *loca*—is a relic of this collective function, and *acinum* itself is probably a back-formation from an old collective plural *acina*, 'cluster', corresponding to the masculine singular *acinus* 'grape'), and the process was later reversed in some nouns, in which a neuter plural gave rise to a new feminine singular—e.g. *ostium* / *Ostia*, *rapum* / *rapa*, *spicum* / *spica*. (See Sommer, *Handb. d. lat. Laut- u. Formenlehre*, 334; H. Zimmermann, *Glotta* xiii [1924], 224.) In late Latin this development became very common, as the transformation of Latin neuters into feminines in the romance languages shows. It is most likely that *acina* is a popular by-form and that in both words Gellius, with poor critical judgement, a perverse taste for abnormality, and a fanciful thesis to maintain, preferred the corrupt to the genuine. The value of his note is in the evidence it gives for early variation in the text of Catullus; see on 1. 2, 2*b*. 13.

5. **at uos** : cf. 3. 13.

6. **pernicies** : so Martial speaks of 'murdering' good Falernian by mixing it with an inferior Vatican vintage: 'scelus est iugulare Falernum' (i. 18. 5).

6 f. **ad seueros migrate** : 'find a new home with puritans'.

7. **Thyonianus** : Bacchus is called *Thyoneus* (Hor. *Od.* i. 17. 23, Ov. *Met.* iv. 13) from Thyone, another name of his mother Semele (*Hom. Hymn* i. 21), and *Thyonius* is a possible alternative form (cf. the doublets Μελάνθευς—Μελάνθιος). *Thyonianus* (which Ausonius apparently misunderstood as a name for Bacchus himself, p. 207 Peiper) seems to be made from *Thyonius* by the addition of the suffix common in Roman names of wines, 'the unadulterated vintage of Thyonius'. Normally these names are neuter, agreeing with *uinum* (*Formianum*, *Albanum*, etc.); if this explanation is right, *Thyonianus* presumably takes its gender from οἶνος like *Tmolius* and *Phanaeus* in Virg. *Georg.* ii. 98.

29

This attack on Mamurra and on his patrons Caesar and Pompey, an iambic lampoon in the tradition of Archilochus (see on l. 1), is dated approximately by the reference to Caesar's invasion of Britain: it was probably written soon after the first reconnaissance in the autumn of 55 B.C., when talk of fortunes to be made from British plunder was in the air and a second expedition was in prospect.

Mamurra came of a well-to-do equestrian family from Formiae in South Latium, the place which Horace (who knew this poem: see on 6–7) calls *urbs Mamurrarum* (*Sat.* i. 5. 37). After serving with Pompey in the Mithridatic War he attached himself to Caesar; he was with Caesar in Spain in 61 B.C. and he served as *praefectus fabrum* (though Caesar himself does not mention him) in the Gallic campaigns. He appears again in 41, 43, and 57 and under a nickname in 94, 105, 114, and 115. For Catullus he is a pretentious upstart who has made a fortune with the connivance of Pompey and Caesar and has run through it. We know from Cicero's more sober evidence (*Att.* vii. 7. 6) that the wealth he had acquired was something of a scandal, and the appointments of his town house on the Caelian set a new standard in luxury which gave colour to such charges: Pliny (*N.H.* xxxvi. 48) quotes Cornelius Nepos' contemporary account of it and adds 'quem (*sc.* Mamurram), ut res est, domus ipsa clarius quam Catullus dixit habere quicquid habuisset comata Gallia'. But the position which he occupied as chief engineer to Caesar, who chose his officers carefully, in operations on the scale of the Gallic campaigns shows that there was more to him than that, and the accusations of feathering his own nest would come better from one who did not abuse other provincial commanders, as Catullus does (10. 9–10, 28. 1), for denying their subordinates opportunities of doing the same thing. One may suspect that the reasons for Catullus' vendetta are personal and that Mamurra offended not so much by his morals or his politics as by cutting a figure in society in Rome and in Cisalpine Gaul, where Caesar had his winter quarters; in poems 41 and 43 a provincial belle who is his *amica* serves for an indirect attack on him as his indulgent superiors do here. We know from Suetonius that this poem and the even more scurrilous and impudent 57 got under Caesar's skin, though he later accepted an apology: *Jul.* 73 'Catullum, a quo sibi uersiculis de Mamurra perpetua stigmata imposita non dissimulauerat, satis facientem eadem die adhibuit cenae'. That the poem was well known is shown both by Horace's reminiscences of it and by the quotation of the last line in a scurrilous epigram which has survived in the *Catalepton* ascribed to Virgil (6. 5 'ut ille uersus usque-quaque pertinet, / "gener socerque perdidistis omnia"'); Quintilian quotes it (ix. 4. 141) to illustrate the use of iambics for *aspera et maledica*.

The metre is pure iambic trimeter, as in poem 4, without substitution, but see on lines 3, 20, 23.

1. **uidere :** the editors compare Theog. 58 τίς κεν ταῦτ' ἀνέχοιτ' ἐσορῶν; and the line may well be a 'motto' borrowed from a Greek original (perhaps Archilochus himself), serving to place the poem in the tradition of the iambographers. (On this literary device see Fraenkel, *Horace*, p. 159².)

   quis potest pati : for the formula of indignation cf. Laberius fr. 108 R. 'hominem me denegare quis posset pati?', Caes. *B.G.* i. 43. 8 'quod ad amicitiam populi Romani attulissent id eis eripi quis pati posset?' Similarly 42. 5 'si pati potestis'.

2. **aleo :** a vulgar synonym of *aleator*, one of a series of popular forms in *-o* denoting immoderate proclivities: others are *gulo, ganeo, helluo, lustro, edo, bibo.*

3. **Mamurram :** the first vowel is properly long, and is so treated by Horace (*Sat.* i. 5. 37), and Martial (ix. 59. 1, x. 4. 11): Catullus either arbitrarily shortens it (such liberties with proper names are sometimes taken even in serious verse: so Horace has both *Prŏserpina* and *Prōserpina, Ŏrion* and *Ōrion, Diana* and *Dīana*) or regards an intractable proper name as excusing a break in the series of iambi.

   comata was used as an unofficial term for the Transalpine province of Gaul, where the natives wore their hair long, as *togata* was used for the Cisalpine province, where Roman dress had established itself; Caesar does not use it but Cicero puts it into the mouth of Antony, *Phil.* viii. 27 'Galliam, inquit, togatam remitto, comatam postulo'.

4. **uncti :** 'rich', used first of food and then more generally, as in 22 below. But Faernus's correction is far from certain and Statius's *ante* is possible.

   ultima Britannia : for the lengthening of the final syllable see on 4. 9. For *ultimus* as a stock epithet of Britain (cf. 12 below) see on 11. 12. If rumour had represented the island as an Eldorado, reports from Caesar's second expedition in 54 disproved it: in July 54 Cicero writes to Trebatius, who was then with Caesar in Britain (*Fam.* vii. 7. 1) 'in Britannia nihil esse audio neque auri neque argenti' and to Atticus (*Att.* iv. 17. 6) 'etiam illud iam cognitum est nec argenti scrupulum esse ullum in illa insula neque ullam spem praedae nisi ex mancipiis'.

5. **Romule :** i.e. Caesar: with similar irony Cicero is called *Romulus Arpinas* in the pseudo-Sallustian Invective against Cicero (4. 7) and Sulla *scaeuus iste Romulus* in a fragment of Sallust's *Histories* (i. 4. 45 M.).

6. **superbus et superfluens :** 'overbearing and over-flush'.

7. **perambulabit :** 'strolls', nonchalant and assured. Horace has

three reminiscences of these lines in the *Epodes*: 4. 5 'licet superbus ambules pecunia', 17. 41 'perambulabis astra', 5. 69 'indormit unctis omnium cubilibus'.

8. columbus aut Adoneus : the white dove and Adonis are both Venus' pets: cf. Alexis, fr. 214 K. λευκὸς Ἀφροδίτης εἰμὶ γὰρ περιστερός. Plautus has the archaic latinization *Adoneus*, *Men.* 144.

10. The triad of abusive epithets repeated from line 2 and here applied to Caesar is a commonplace of conventional vituperation: Cicero, when he speaks of Antony, has the same catalogue, *Phil.* iii. 35 'libidinosis, petulantibus, impuris, impudicis, aleatoribus, ebriis seruire', xiii. 24 'in lustris popinis alea uino tempus aetatis omne consumpsisses'. Caesar may have deserved the first and third: he did not deserve the second, for in eating and drinking he was notoriously moderate.

11. eone nomine . . . ut : 'was it on this account . . .?', equivalent to *ideo* or *ob eam causam*.

   imperator unice : the ironical address to Caesar is repeated in the corrupt and fragmentary poem 54.

13. uestra : the plural, as in *fouetis* (21), refers to Caesar and Pompey, though Pompey is not explicitly addressed until l. 24.

14. ducenties : stands, with the regular ellipse, for *ducenties centena milia sestertium*, 'twenty million sesterces'.

   comesset : *comedere* is often colloquially used of the spendthrift: e.g. Plaut. *Pseud.* 1107 'comedunt quod habent', Cic. *Phil.* xi. 37 'beneficia Caesaris comederunt', Hor. *Ep.* i. 15. 40 'non hercule miror . . . si qui comedunt bona', Mart. v. 70. 5 'quanta est gula centies comesse'. See on 22 *deuorare*.

15. quid est alid sinistra liberalitas? : 'what is perverse generosity but this?': English idiom reverses the comparison, 'what is this but perverse generosity?'. So e.g. Cic. *Phil.* x. 5 'quid est aliud librarium Bruti laudare, non Brutum?', 'what is this but paying a compliment to B.'s secretary, not to B.?', i. 22 'quid est aliud hortari adulescentes ut turbulenti, ut seditiosi, ut perniciosi ciues uelint esse?'

   sinistra liberalitas : cf. Pliny, vii. 28. 3 *sinistra diligentia*, 'perverse precision'. Catullus turns to Caesar's discredit what was spoken of as one of his virtues: at this very same time Cicero, writing to Trebatius, who is going to serve with Caesar, tells him that he will have *imperatorem liberalissimum* (*Fam.* vii. 7. 2) and says 'cum . . . hominis liberalitatem in-

credibilem et singularem fidem nossem, sic ei te commendaui
et tradidi ut grauissime diligentissimeque potui' (*Fam.* vii.
17. 2).

alid : the by-forms *alis* (66. 28), *alid* for *alius, aliud* (perhaps formed on the analogy of *is, quis*) seem to have had a
short literary life. Lucretius uses *alid* several times and the
dative *ali* once; *alis* is cited only from Sallust.

16. **expatrauit** : 'hasn't he finished off enough?' The verb
occurs only here.

17. **lancinata** : the rare verb does not appear again till Sen.
Ep. 32. 2 'diducimus illam (*sc.* uitam) in particulas et lan-
cinamus': but Sallust has *lacero* in the same sense, *Cat.* 14.
2 'quicumque impudicus . . . bona patria lacerauerat'.

18. **praeda Pontica** : the loot acquired by Pompey and his army
in the campaign against Mithridates of Pontus in 64–63 B.C.

19. **Hibera** : the mention of the Tagus (the modern Tejo) makes
it clear that the reference is to the campaign which Caesar
conducted in Lusitania as propraetor of Hispania Ulterior
in 61 B.C.: for the wealth which it brought to him and his
troops cf. Plut. *Caes.* 12 ἀπηλλάγη τῆς ἐπαρχίας αὐτός τε πλούσιος
γεγονὼς καὶ τοὺς στρατιώτας ὠφεληκὼς ἀπὸ τῶν στρατειῶν. The gold
deposits in the Tagus (cf. Ov. *Am.* i. 15. 34 'cedat et auriferi
ripa benigna Tagi') were a spectacular side-line in the mineral
wealth of the Iberian peninsula; the mines there were the
main source of Rome's gold supply for centuries.

quam scit : i.e. of which the Tagus could tell a story:
similarly in a solemn context Virgil has (*Aen.* xi. 259) 'scit
triste Mineruae / sidus et Euboicae cautes' (the rocky coast of
Euboea could give an eye-witness account of the shipwreck
of the Greek fleet); the same type of personification is not
uncommon with *conscius* (e.g. Prop. i. 12. 2, ii. 13. 42), and
with *testis* (see note on 64. 357).

20. **nunc Galliae timetur et Britanniae** : so corrected the line
gives good sense, 'now fears are felt for G. and B.', but *nunc*,
an early correction for *V*'s *hunc*, making the one certain
spondee in the poem, can hardly stand. No plausible alternative has been offered.

21. **malum** : 'why the devil do you coddle *him*?': the expletive
interjection *malum* strengthens an indignant question or
exclamation in comedy and in Cicero's less formal style;
e.g. *Phil.* i. 15 'quae malum est ista uoluntaria seruitus?'
Verr. ii. 2. 43 'quae malum ista fuit amentia?', *Off.* ii. 53 'quae
te malum ratio in istam spem induxit?'

22. **deuorare** : a stronger equivalent of *comedere* (l. 14): cf. Cic.

Phil. ii. 67 'non modo patrimonium . . . sed urbes et regna celeriter tanta nequitia deuorare potuisset', Ps.-Cic. *Inu. in Sall.* 20 'patrimonio non comeso sed deuorato'.

23. eone nomine : see on 11.

opulentissime is the meaningless reading of the manuscripts; the easy change to *opulentissimi*, 'wealthiest men in Rome', would give good sense but would break the series of iambi. *o piissimei* (Haupt: his *orbis*, to be taken with *omnia*, is indefensible) introduces a not very relevant point and a doubtful form: if Cicero in 43 B.C. could make fun of Antony for using the superlative, 'quod uerbum nullum in lingua latina est' (*Phil.* xiii. 43), it is at any rate doubtful whether Catullus used it. *o potissimei* (Müller), 'most important men in Rome' is more attractive: cf. Plaut. *Men.* 359 'hinc ultro fit, ut meret, potissumus nostrae domi ut sit' ('counts for most in our house').

24. socer generque : to secure his hold on Pompey Caesar had married his daughter Julia to him as his fourth wife, breaking an existing betrothal, in 59 B.C. The relationship between the rivals clearly was a byword and becomes a cliché in later literature: so Virg. *Aen.* vi. 830–1 'aggeribus socer Alpinis atque arce Menoeci / descendens, gener aduersis instructus eois', Lucan i. 290 'socerum depellere regno / decretum genero est', iv. 802 'gener atque socer bello contendere iussi', x. 417 'non in soceri generique fauorem / discedunt populi', Mart. ix. 70. 3 'cum gener atque socer diris concurreret armis'.

perdidistis omnia : Catullus is echoing, perhaps, a phrase of the opposition: cf. Cic. *Att.* ii. 21. 1 'iracundiam atque intemperantiam illorum [Caesar and Pompey] sumus experti qui Catoni irati omnia perdiderunt', i. 16. 5 'ita fortes tamen fuerunt ut summo proposito periculo uel perire maluerint quam perdere omnia', xiv. 1. 1 'quid quaeris? perisse omnia aiebat'.

30

These reproaches, plaintive rather than angry, addressed to a friend who has broken his word—Catullus' conception of *amicitia* as a *foedus*, a contract, which others regard more lightly than himself, appears again and again both in relation to his friends and in relation to Lesbia: cf. 76. 3, 87. 3, 109. 6— are conveyed in terms so general as to give no clue to their occasion. We do not even know who the offender was. He may have been Catullus' fellow countryman P.(?) Alfenus Varus, who rose from humble origins at Cremona to be a distinguished jurist, served as one of the three commissioners who supervised

the confiscations of land in his native province in 41 B.C., and
was the first Cisalpine to hold the consulship (Porph. ad Hor.
Sat. i. 3. 130; Donatus, *Vita Verg.* 19; Gellius vii. 5. 1; *Digest*
i. 2. 2. 44). If so, the Varus of poems 10 and 22 may be the
same person.

The stiffness of the language, as compared with that of the
other personal poems, and the awkward contortion of line 12,
may be due in part to the difficulties of an exacting metre, the
greater asclepiadean. Sappho and Alcaeus had written in it
and it was used for Athenian skolia (e.g. that quoted in Arist.
Wasps 1239, Ἀδμήτου λόγον, ὦταῖρε, μαθὼν τοὺς ἀγαθοὺς φίλει). We
have nothing in it from the Alexandrian epigrammatist Asclepi-
ades from whom it received its name, but we have examples of
its Alexandrian use from Callimachus (fr. 400 Pf.) and Theocritus (28 and 30). The basis, which is free in Greek, is always
spondaic in Catullus, as it is in Horace's asclepiadeans (*Od.* i. 11
and 18, iv. 10); but Catullus knows nothing of the restriction
which in Horace makes the end of both the first and the second
choriamb coincide with the end of a word.

1. **immemor :** as often, implies not mere forgetfulness but indifference or treachery: cf. 64. 58, 123, **248.**
   unanimis : see on 9. 4. The dative with *falsus* is not found
   again till Seneca (*Medea* 654 'omnibus uerax, sibi falsus uni').

3. **iam :** 'is it come to this, that you do not hesitate . . . ?'

4. **nec . . . placent :** the reflection is Homeric: *Od.* xiv. 83.
   caelicolis : a solemn epic word, as in 64. 386, **68.** 138.

4 f. **nec . . . quae :** both connexions are difficult. Munro was
certainly wrong in explaining *nec* as equivalent to simple *non*.
nec was used as a simple negative in early Latin: that use
appears in the Twelve Tables (e.g. *cui suus heres nec escit*, i.e.
non erit) and it survives in a series of compounds (*necopinatus,
neglego, negotium*) and in a few fixed formulae—*neque satis
factum* (twice in Cato), *nec recte* (common in Plautus), *nec
bene* (Virg. *Ecl.* 9. 6 *nec uertat bene*), *nec di sinant* (Plin. *Ep.*
ii. 2. 3), and the legal phrases *res nec mancipi, furtum nec
manifestum* and *nec oboediens* (Cic. *Leg.* iii. 6). (For a full
account of these uses see Löfstedt, *Syntactica*, i². **338.**) But in
literary Latin it is confined to these survivals, in all of which
nec negatives a single word or phrase. The emendations *num*
(Schwabe) and *nunc* (Baehrens) are unconvincing. If the
text is sound, *nec* can only be taken as the weak connective
which is often found strengthened by *enim, uero,* or *tamen* and
sometimes appears by itself, usually in elliptical phrases of the
type of *nec mirum, neque iniuria, neque invitus,* but also in
independent sentences in which it has the function, so to

speak, of a negative *autem*; but that use seems hardly possible after a question.

quae cannot refer to *facta impia*: there is no evidence that *facta impia neglegere* could mean 'heedlessly commit unnatural acts'. If it is right, it must be taken to refer generally to the idea conveyed in the preceding line—the displeasure of heaven at *impia facta*; but in that case there is no obvious explanation of the plural. Hence Guarinus and Auantius suggested *quos* (referring to *caelicolis*: 'you pay no heed to the gods'), Munro *quom* (making *me* the object of *neglegis* and punctuating with a comma after *malis*).

In view of the double difficulty Ellis may be right in thinking that between 3 and 4 two lines have been lost which contained another *nec*, corresponding to that in 4, and a plural antecedent for *quae*.

7. **certe tute iubebas :** '*you* kept telling me, you know': for *certe* introducing a reminder which justifies a grievance cf. 64. 149, Virg. *Aen.* i. 234.

animam tradere : 'to surrender my soul': cf. Plaut. *Asin.* 141 'amans ego animum meum isti dedi'.

tuta omnia: for the phrase cf. Virg. *Aen.* i. 583 'omnia tuta uides', iv. 298 'omnia tuta timens', Prop. ii. 19. 16 'omnia ab externo sint modo tuta uiro', Ov. *F.* v. 134 'quod (lares) praestant oculis omnia tuta suis'.

9. **idem** emphasizes the contrast: see on 22. 14.

retrahis te, 'you back away'; cf. Hor. *Ep.* i. 18. 58 'ne te retrahas et inexcusabilis absis'.

10. **uentos . . . sinis :** the cliché in various forms has a long history in Greek: cf. Homer, *Od.* viii. 408, Eur. *Tro.* 419, Apoll. i. 1334, Theoc. 22. 168, 29. 35. Catullus uses it again of broken promises in 64. 59, 142, 65. 17: for other examples in Latin cf. Virg. *Aen.* ix. 312 (of idle prayers) 'aurae / omnia discerpunt et nubibus irrita donant', Lygd. 6. 27 'uenti temeraria uota / aeriae et nubes diripienda ferant', *Culex* 380, 383.

11. **at :** for *at* emphasizing the apodosis of a conditional sentence cf. 64. 158–60, Virg. *Aen.* i. 543 'si genus humanum et mortalia temnitis arma, / at sperate deos memores fandi atque nefandi'.

Fides : the cult of Fides was very old-established in Rome, where Numa was its legendary founder: whatever the original meaning of the cult, Fides was in later times the presiding spirit of good faith, the quality that makes men keep their word. So it is here, as it is in Cicero (*Off.* iii. 104 'qui ius iurandum uiolat, is Fidem uiolat') and in Virgil (*Aen.* i. 292) and Horace (*Od.* i. 35. 21, *C.S.* 57), for whom Fides presides over the new age of Augustus.

12. The order is *quae faciet ut te paeniteat facti tui*: for the position of *faciet* see on 44. 9, 66. 18.

<h1 style="text-align:center">31</h1>

After his Bithynian adventure, in 56 B.C., Catullus comes home to Sirmio—a long, thin, rocky promontory running out into Benacus (Lago di Garda) and connected by a narrow isthmus with the southern shore. As Sirmione it still keeps its old name—and Tennyson and Carducci have made that name more familiar, perhaps, in modern times than Sirmio was to Roman readers—but Tennyson's 'Roman ruin', the so-called *grotte di Catullo*, which stands at its tip, is not that of Catullus' villa, though it may be on the same site. One may guess that the villa at Sirmio was a family possession; Verona is only some twenty miles away.

1. paene insularum : adverb and noun constitute a single notion: the phrase occurs several times in Livy (e.g. xxv. 11. 1 'mari quo in paene insulae modum pars maior circumluitur', xxxi. 40. 1 'oppidum . . . in paene insula situm'). *paene* is occasionally used to modify other nouns: e.g. Caes. *B.G.* vi. 36. 2 'illius patientiam paene obsessionem appellabant', 'practically a siege', Cic. *ad Brut.* i. 18. 3 'pro adulescentulo et paene puero', 'practically a child', Ov. *Pont.* iv. 12. 20 'paene mihi puero cognite paene puer'.

insularumque : 'gem of all the peninsulas—and all the islands, for that matter', enhancing the compliment.

2. ocelle : Cicero uses the colloquialism in a similar context, *Att.* xvi. 6. 2 'cur ocellos Italiae, uillulas meas, non uideo?' Compare the personal use of *ocelle* as a term of endearment, 50. 19. Editors quote Pindar *Ol.* 2. 12 Σικελίας ὀφθαλμός (of Syracuse), Eur. *Phoen.* 802 Ἀρτέμιδος χιονοτρόφαν ὄμμα Κιθαιρών, but in these and similar Greek phrases the metaphor, though it no doubt has the same origin as the Latin idiom, is more conscious and literary.

2 f. liquentibus . . . uasto : 'on sheets of clear water or on the wide sea'. *liquentibus*: cf. 64. 2 'liquidas Neptuni . . . undas'. *uastus* expresses more than mere size and conveys the sense of emptiness or desolation (its original meaning) or the implication of awesomeness derived from it; see on 64. 156.

3. uterque Neptunus : 'both Neptunes' is most naturally taken in relation with the words which immediately precede:

uterque Neptunus is 'Neptune in either capacity', i.e. as god of seas and as god of inland waters, just as in Mart. *Spect.* 13. 5 *numen utriusque Dianae* is Diana of childbirth and Diana of the chase (similarly *A.P.* ix. 268. 2 ἀμφοτέρην Ἄρτεμιν), and in Ov. *Met.* i. 338 'sub utroque iacentia Phoebo' or Rutil. ii. 28 'qua fert atque refert Phoebus uterque diem' *uterque Phoebus* is the sun in his rising and in his setting. Munro, following Statius, refers *uterque Neptunus* to the two seas which wash Italy, the *mare superum* and the *mare inferum*. That restriction to Italian tidal waters seems pointless in the context: Sirmio is not in either sea, and Catullus—returning, be it remembered, from a region richer in island beauty than Italy—must mean that Sirmio is a gem among islands, not among Italian ones. Schulze interprets 'the Eastern and the Western seas', adducing Virg. *Aen.* vii. 100 'qua sol utrumque recurrens / aspicit oceanum', Ov. *Met.* xv. 830 'gentes ab utroque iacentes / oceano', Virg. *Georg.* iii. 33 'utroque ab litore gentes', Prop. iii. 9. 53 'currus utroque ab litore ouantes'. But *uterque oceanus* is the ocean bounding the world at either extreme, and *utrumque litus*, however loosely Virgil and Propertius may be using it, implies the same notion; Catullus is concerned with waters in the world, not beyond it or on its fringe, and there is nothing to suggest that *uterque Neptunus* could represent an antithesis between the Eastern and the Western Mediterranean.

4. quam . . . libenter quamque laetus : the loose coordination of adverb and adjective can be paralleled not only from comedy (Plaut. *Men.* 1073 'si quid stulte dixi atque imprudens tibi', *Bacch.* 474 'Pistoclerum falso atque insontem arguis') but even from more formal writing (e.g. Cic. *T.D.* v. 5 'tibi nos . . . penitus totosque tradimus').

   inuiso : here 'look upon', as in 64. 233; the more usual sense is 'go to see', 'visit'.

5. uix mi ipse credens : cf. Plaut. *Rud.* 245 f. 'ut uix mihi / credo ego hoc, te tenere', *Amph.* 416 'egomet mihi non credo quom illaec autumare illum audio'. So the returning Eurybates greets his home in Sen. *Agam.* 392 f., 'delubra et aras caelitum et patrios lares / post longa fessus spatia uix credens mihi / supplex adoro.'

   Thuniam atque Bithunos : the Thyni and the Bithyni (Catullus may well have used the forms in -*u*- here, though *y* to represent Greek *v* was coming into general use in his time; if so, he wrote *Bithunia* at 10. 7, *Thunos* at 25. 7, and probably *Ludiae* in l. 13 below and *Surias* at 45. 22) were two related tribes, of Thracian origin, who settled in the region of Asia Minor across the Propontis to which the name of

Bithynia was generally given. The name of the Thyni passed out of ordinary use, though it provided a metrically convenient alternative: Catullus himself uses it so at 25. 7 (similarly Hor. *Od*. iii. 7. 3). Here perhaps Catullus is whimsically using the high-sounding phrase to express his pleasure at leaving 'the whole place' behind.

7. **o** here and in 12, as usual, expresses strong emotion.

   solutis . . . curis : 'than the loosing of one's cares': the common idiomatic use of the participial phrase to express an abstract idea.

8 f. **peregrino labore :** 'the hardships of foreign travel': *peregrino* and *nostrum* are placed in emphatic opposition.

11. **hoc est . . . tantis :** 'this is something that by itself is' (or 'here is the one thing that is') 'recompense for our pains'. Cicero uses the phrase somewhat differently, *Att*. ii. 5. 1 'Cato ille noster qui mihi unus est pro centum milibus', 'is as good as a million by himself'.

12. **salue, o uenusta :** no line of Catullus has been more distorted by translators than this. Their 'Hail' is for us an archaism and 'lovely' has for us lost its connexion with love. One must remember that *salue* is the Roman's everyday word of greeting, and that *uenustus* is still for Catullus the adjective of *Venus* (cf. 3. 2 n.).

   gaude : verbs of emotion like *gaudere* often imply the expression, and not merely the feeling, of the emotion: for *gaudere* cf. Hor. *Ep*. i. 8. 15 'si dicet recte, primum gaudere memento', 'express your pleasure': so *dolere* (Hor. *A.P*. 95), *mirari* (Prop. iv. 6. 59).

13. **uosque :** the early editors' correction of the unmetrical *uos quoque* of the manuscripts. Kroll takes *uosque* as an example of the supposed use of *-que* for *quoque* with pronouns, 'you too': but that use is extremely dubious and the evidence for it inadequate (see on 102.3). On the other hand if *-que* is given its normal coordinating function, as it is by Ellis (who compares Prop. iii. 21. 15 'Romanae turres et uos ualeatis, amici, / qualiscumque mihi tuque puella, uale'), the displacement of it (*gaudete uosque* for *uosque gaudete*) is without parallel in Catullus. Bergk's *gaudente* neatly removes the difficulty and gives a smooth construction ('salue, o uenusta Sirmio, atque ero gaude / gaudente, uosque, o L. l. undae, / ridete quidquid . . .'): the repetition *gaude gaudente* is not less in Catullus' manner than *gaude, gaudete*.

   Lydiae : so the early editors for *lidie* of the manuscripts. The waves of Benacus are 'Lydian' because (1), as Livy (v. 33) and Tacitus (*Ann*. iv. 55) knew, the Etruscans had estab-

lished themselves in the Po basin—probably in the sixth
century—and maintained their supremacy there until they
were dislodged by the invasion of the Gauls in the fourth
century, and (2), whether or not the Etruscans were of
Lydian origin (the tradition that they migrated from Lydia,
first found in Herodotus, i. 94, is not supported by archaeo-
logical evidence: see M. Pallottino, *The Etruscans*, Eng.
trans. [1955] pp. 53 ff.), they certainly were believed to be
Lydian. Both traditions are used by Catullus' fellow countryman Virgil: Mantua possesses *Tusco de sanguine uires* (*Aen.*
x. 203; cf. viii. 479), and the Tiber, rising in Etruria, is
Lydius Thybris (*Aen.* ii. 781). Editors have objected to a
'learned allusion' as being out of keeping with the simple
sincerity of this poem, and a series of adjectives (*ludiae,
lucidae, uiuidae, incitae, uuidae*) has been suggested to replace
Lydiae. But 'learned allusion' begs the question. Catullus
had learned from Alexandria, as Virgil learned, the romantic,
associative value of the proper name, and that is part of his
doctrina: but *Lydiae* is no piece of imported pedantry but the
embodiment of a living tradition. Catullus is sincere, but he
is a poet: it is not less sincere to call the waves 'Lydian', and
so vividly bring to the reader's mind the history of the place
as well as its beauty, than to call them 'bright' or 'wet'.

14. **quidquid est domi cachinnorum :** the *quidquid*-clause (for
this favourite idiom of Catullus cf. 3. 2 n., 9. 10, 37. 4) takes
the place of an internal accusative with *ridete* (cf. Cic. *Fam.*
vii. 25. 1 *rideamus γέλωτα σαρδάνιον*). The noisy laughter of the
breaking waves is not a fresh metaphor but belongs to the
stock of poetry: Accius had used it in tragedy (fr. 573 R. 'stagna
sonantibus excita saxis . . . crepitu clangente cachinnant')
and Catullus himself has it in the mannered style in 64. 273
'leuiterque sonant plangore cachinni'. But the combination
with *ridere* (itself a visual metaphor applied elsewhere to
water: cf. Aesch. *P.V.* 90 *ποντίων κυμάτων ἀνήριθμον γέλασμα*,
Lucr. ii. 559 'ridet placidi pellacia ponti', v. 1005 'ridentibus
undis': see on 64. 284) perhaps gives it new vigour.

    est domi : not 'at my home' (Ellis) but 'of your own', 'at
your command', 'in stock', a not uncommon idiomatic use:
cf. Plaut. *Rud.* 292 'quicquid est domi, id sat est habendum',
Persa 45 'si id domi esset mihi iam pollicerer', *M.G.*1154
'domi esse ad eam rem uideo siluai satis', Cic. *Att.* x. 14. 2
'id quidem domi est', Sen. *Ben.* iii. 3. 1 'quicquid est domi
uile est'. Similarly *domi habere* Plaut. *M.G.* 194, Ter. *Ad.* 413;
domi nasci, Cic. *Acad.* ii. 80, Seneca, *Ep.* 23. 3; *domo experiri*,
Plaut. *Amph.* 637; *domo doctus* 'from personal experience',
Merc. 355; *Truc.* 454; *domi coniecturam facio*, *Cas.* 224.

[For a full list of examples see Sonnenschein in *C.R.* xii. 360, Bonnet in *C.R.* xiii. 35.]

34

A hymn addressed to Diana by a choir of boys and girls. There is no evidence, either internal or external, to suggest that it was written for some particular occasion, and, like Horace's short hymn to Apollo and Diana (*Od.* i. 21), which it may have suggested, it was probably written to be read, not to be sung. Glyconics had been used for hymns in Greek (we have the opening of a glyconic hymn to Artemis herself by Anacreon, fr. 1 D.), but the whole colour of Catullus' poem is Roman and it obviously is not a translation. On the other hand, in its structure it follows the traditional lines of the hymn-style (see on 7, 13 ff., 21–22, 23) and Catullus may have had a Greek poem in mind. A prooemium in the first stanza is followed by the invocation of the goddess, with the recital of her ancestry: the third enumerates the spheres of concern of Diana as a goddess of the country and the fourth three of her particular manifestations; the fifth takes up one of these aspects and relates it to the petitioners, and the last contains the prayer that the goddess will continue her favours towards them.

In primitive Italian belief Diana was a spirit of the wild and the woods: at Aricia, where her most celebrated cult was shared by the surrounding Latin towns, her title of Nemorensis recalled her origins. Like Silvanus, she had been 'reclaimed' and 'brought into friendly and useful relations' with the farmer's life (Warde Fowler, *Roman Festivals*, 201). But the Diana of this poem, and the Diana of Latin literature generally, is for the most part Artemis and the powers associated or identified with her—Ilithyia, Hecate, Selene. While the Italian Diana probably had a particular association with childbirth (see on 12), she was not a chthonic deity, like Hecate, or a moon-goddess. But long before this time Diana had become inextricably fused with Artemis; at the first lectisternium in 398(9?) B.C. (Livy v. 13. 6) she is already Artemis, appearing in ritual association with the other members of the Greek triad, Apollo and Leto, naturalized under her Latin name of Latona. The conflation with Artemis involved identification with Hecate and Selene, and Diana is *diua triformis* for Horace (*Od.* iii. 22. 4), *tria uirginis ora Dianae* for Virgil (*Aen.* iv. 511).

For the metre of the poem, a four-line system of three glyconics and a pherecratean, see introd. to 61. As in 61, synaphea is observed within the stanza: elision occurs between lines twice (11, 22) and there is no syllaba anceps. In the first foot, which is free, the proportion of spondees to trochees is much higher than in 61 and the rhythm is correspondingly slower and more sedate. An iambic base occurs twice (perhaps four times: see on 1).

1. **Dianae** : the -*i*- is originally long, but is usually shortened in dactylic verse. Virgil has *Dī*- once, *Dĭ*- nine times: Horace in the *Carmen Saeculare* uses both quantities. Here the quantity cannot be determined; Catullus may have begun all four lines in his first stanza with an iamb.

    in fide : A characteristically Roman notion: the phrase regularly described the relation between the client and the patron who 'guarantees' him protection: cf. Ter. *Eun.* 886 'ego me tuae commendo et committo fidei, / te mihi patronam capio', Cic. *Rosc. Am.* 83 'quaere in cuius fide sint et clientela', *Planc.* 97 'cum omnia illa municipia quae sunt a Vibone ad Brundisium in fide mea essent'. On this and similar uses see Fraenkel in *Rh. Mus.* lxxi (1916), 193 ff.

2. **integri** : with both *pueri* and *puellae* (cf. 61. 36 'integrae uirgines'): to be taken as the equivalent of Horace's 'castis cum pueris ignara puella mariti' (*Ep.* ii. 1. 132) rather than as representing the *patrimi et matrimi*, 'having both parents alive' (Gk. ἀμφιθαλεῖς) which was a necessary qualification for persons taking part in some religious acts.

5. **Latonia** : the first appearance in extant literature of the adjective whose convenient prosody commended it to dactylic poets as an alternative to Diana.

    maximi magna : cf. Hor. *Od.* i. 16. 1 matre pulcra filia pulcrior, Virg. *Aen.* vii. 656 satus Hercule pulcro / pulcer Auentinus.

7. **quam** : the relative clause is a typical feature of the recital of the deity's γοναί in the hymn: *Hom. H.* 4. 3 ἄγγελον ἀθανάτων ἐριούνιον ὃν τέκε Μαῖα, Alcaeus 308 L.-P. χαῖρε Κυλλάνας ὁ μέδεις . . . τὸν κορυφαῖσιν †αὔγαῖς† Μαῖα γέννατο.

8. **deposiuit** : the verb is used elsewhere of birth only in Phaedrus (i. 18. 5 of human birth, i. 19. 4 of a litter of puppies). *posiui* is the regularly formed original perfect: when *pono* was no longer recognized as a compound of *sino*, the apparently anomalous *posiui* was supplanted by a new perfect *posui* formed on the analogy of those apparently similar verbs, like *geno* and *gemo*, in which a supine in -*itum* corresponded to a perfect in -*ui*. *posiui* is regular in Plautus and Terence (though it has often been 'modernized' in the manuscripts, as it has been in the manuscripts of Catullus here) and in Cato; apart from two dubious instances (*posi-*

uerunt in Cic. *T.D.* v. 83 and *opposierit* in a letter from
Plancus, *ad Fam.* x. 9. 3) it has disappeared from later prose.
But it survives in formal contexts in inscriptions down to the
early empire, and the formal manner of this poem justifies the
use of the archaism here: elsewhere Catullus has the current
posui three times.

oliuam : the tree which assisted the sacred birth on Delos
is an olive in the Delian Hymn but a palm in the Homeric
Hymn to Apollo (117) and in Theognis (5). Other versions
combine the variants and sometimes introduce the laurel as
well: so Euripides, *Ion* 919–20, *Hec.* 458–60, Call. *Hymn* 4.
210 and 262. The tourist in later times was shown the
authentic palm on Delos (Pliny, *N.H.* xvi. 240): but Ephesus
could offer an equally authentic olive in support of its claim
to be the real birthplace (Tac. *Ann.* iii. 61).

9 ff. montium . . . siluarum . . . saltuum . . . amnium : the
descriptions are commonplaces for Artemis–Diana: Hom.
Od. vi. 102 οἴη δ' Ἄρτεμις εἶσι κατ' οὔρεος ἰοχέαιρα; *Hom. Hymn*
5. 18 τῇ ἅδε τόξα καὶ οὔρεσι θῆρας ἐναίρειν/. . . ἄλσεά τε σκιόεντα; Hor.
Od. i. 21. 5 'laetam fluuiis et nemorum coma', iii. 22. 1 'montium custos nemorumque uirgo', *Carm. Saec.* 1 'siluarum
potens', Virg. *Aen.* xi. 557 'nemorum cultrix'. A *saltus* is
wild, rough country with wood or scrub, grazed by hardy
beasts and hunted for game; for ancient definitions see Fest.
392 L. (quoting the jurist Aelius) 'saltus est ubi siluae et
pastiones sunt', Varro, *L.L.* v. 36.

13 ff. tu . . . tu . . . tu : on this formula of the hymn-style see
Norden, *Agnostos Theos*, 150 ff.; Lucretius uses a similar
pattern in the invocation to Venus in the opening lines of
book i.

Diana had her own association with childbirth: references
to it in Ovid (*Fast.* iii. 269–70) and Propertius (ii. 32. 9–10)
are confirmed by votive offerings found in her precinct at
Aricia. But her identification with Iuno Lucina was assisted
by the conflation of her with Artemis, who in the same function had early absorbed the birth-goddess Ilithyia: so Horace
makes Ilithyia and Lucina alternative titles for the invocation of Diana (*Carm. Saec.* 14–15). *Triuia* represents Τριοδῖτις,
an epithet of the chthonic goddess Hecate, whose concern
with the underworld is reflected in her worship at the cross-
roads and her association with sorcery and who came to be
identified with Artemis (cf. Eur. *Phoen.* 108 παῖ Λατοῦς Ἑκάτα).
Luna as a manifestation of Diana is also due to the influence of
Greek belief, in which the moon-goddess was closely associated or identified with Artemis–Hecate.

14 f. dicta . . . es : 'thou hast received the name'; a more formal expression than *diceris*.

15. potens : the adjective is particularly associated with magical powers: Ov. *Her.* 12. 168 'Hecates sacra potentis', Virg. *Aen.* vi. 247 'Hecaten caeloque Ereboque potentem', Val. Flacc. vi. 440 '(Medea) nocturnis qua nulla potentior aris'.

    notho : 'spurious', because not her own but got from the sun, as Parmenides already knew (fr. 14 D.-K. νυκτιφαὲς περὶ γαῖαν ἀλώμενον, ἀλλότριον φῶς). Lucretius has the same phrase, v. 575 'luna . . siue notho fertur loca lumine lustrans / siue suam proprio iactat de corpore lucem'.

17 f. cursu . . . menstruo metiens iter annuum : 'measuring in thy monthly progress thy journey through the year': the etymology which is implied here and explicitly stated by Cicero (*N.D.* ii. 69 'lunae cursibus qui, quia mensa spatia conficiunt, menses nominantur') has more truth in it than most ancient etymologies. *mensis* and μήν, like their English cognates *month* and *moon*, are formed from the root which is also seen in *metior, mensus*.

19. frugibus . . . exples : for Diana–Luna as giver of fertility cf. Hor. *Od.* iv. 6. 37–40 'canentes / rite crescentem face Noctilucam, / prosperam frugum celeremque pronos / uoluere menses'; Seneca has a more scientific theory, *Ben.* iv. 23. 1 'num dubium est quin hoc humani generis domicilium circuitus solis et lunae uicibus suis temperet, quin alterius calore alantur corpora, . . . alterius tepore efficaci et penetrabili regatur maturitas frugum?'

21 f. quocumque . . . nomine : the formula is a literary adaptation recalling a conventional feature of primitive prayer. To ensure the efficacy of his prayer, the petitioner must see that he invokes his spirit by that one of its names which applies to the particular function in which its help is needed; accordingly, after reciting such titles as he knows, he insures himself against the risk of having failed to include the essential one by adding an 'escape clause' to cover any omissions. So an old prayer quoted by Macrobius (iii. 9. 10) runs 'Dis pater Veiouis Manes siue quo alio nomine fas est nominare'; another quoted by Servius (ad *Aen.* ii. 351) 'Iuppiter optime maxime siue quo alio nomine te appellari uolueris'. Compare the prayer in Apuleius, *Met.* xi. 2: 'regina caeli, siue tu Ceres alma . . . seu tu caelestis Venus . . . seu Phoebi soror . . . seu nocturnis ululatibus horrenda Proserpina'. Horace makes a similar literary use of the liturgical formula in *Carm. Saec.* 15

'siue tu Lucina probas uocari / seu Genitalis': he turns it to
a very different purpose in the opening stanzas of *Od.* iii. 21,
where, as Norden observed (*Agnostos Theos*, 144 ff.), suggestions of this and other formulae of liturgical style are
applied, almost by way of parody, in addressing the wine-jar
nata mecum consule Manlio. The usage has its counterpart in
Greek (cf. Plato, *Cratylus* 400e ἐν ταῖς εὐχαῖς νόμος ἐστὶν ἡμῖν εὔχεσθαι
οἵτινές τε καὶ ὁπόθεν (οἱ θεοὶ) χαίρουσιν ὀνομαζόμενοι), and in the first
chorus of the *Agamemnon* (160 ff. Ζεύς, ὅστις ποτ᾽ ἐστίν, εἰ τόδ᾽
αὐτῷ φίλον κεκλημένῳ, τοῦτό νιν προσεννέπω: see Fraenkel ad loc.)
Aeschylus uses the primitive form of words to convey his
religious conviction.

22. sancta : 'be hallowed'. The vocative *sancte* or *sancta*, either
by itself or with a name, is common in the language of prayer
(so 64. 95 *sancte puer*), but to take *sancta* as vocative here involves two difficulties. *sis quocumque tibi placet nomine* should
mean 'possess any name' (cf. Plaut. *Capt.* 590 'neque . . .
ullus seruos istoc nomine est', *Men.* 1122 'uno nomine ambo
eratis')—a pointless adjuration, since Diana possesses all her
names already: it does not mean 'be addressed (on this particular occasion) by any name'. And even if the latter meaning
were possible, the connexion between this clause and the following would not naturally be expressed by -*que*. The meaning
must be 'receive our homage—under any name—and help
us': so Tibullus, ii. 6. 31, putting himself as a *cliens* under
the *fides* of his mistress's dead sister, who is to speak for him,
says of her 'illa mihi sancta est'.

23. antique ut solita es corresponds to the common εἴ ποτε
formula of a prayer: Kroll quotes Sappho, fr. 1. 5 L.-P, τυίδ᾽
ἔλθ᾽, αἴ ποτα κἀτέρωτα,/ τὰς ἐμὰς αὔδας ἀίοισα πήλοι / ἔκλυες, Hom. *Il.*
v. 116f. εἴ ποτέ μοι καὶ πατρὶ φίλα φρονέουσα παρέστης . . ., νῦν αὖτ᾽ἐμὲ
φίλαι, Ἀθήνη, Soph. *O.T.* 165 f. εἴ ποτε καὶ προτέρας ἄτας ὕπερ ὀρνυ-
μένας πόλει/ἠνύσατ᾽ ἐκτοπίαν φλόγα πήματος, ἔλθετε καὶ νῦν. *antique*
has been suspected, since in its few other classical occurrences it is equivalent to *antiquo more*, 'in the manner of
long ago', and not to *antiquitus*, as it must be taken to be
here. The early correction *Ancique*, 'the race of Romulus and
Ancus', which commended itself to Scaliger and to Niebuhr,
does not fit the context: Ancus typifies the early kings in
Hor. *Od.* iv. 7. 15 'ubi decidimus / quo pater Aeneas, quo
diues Tullus et Ancus' and *Ep.* i. 6. 27 'ire tamen restat
Numa quo deuenit et Ancus', but here clearly the whole
emphasis must be on the eponymous founder of the race and
the relevant Horatian parallel is not these lines but *Carm.
Saec.* 47 'Romulae genti date remque prolemque'. *antique*
in this sense may well be a conventional archaism (as *deposiuit*

and *sospites* are, and as *bonae fruges* may be) fitting the manner of the poem.

24. sospites : the verb belongs to solemn liturgical language: So Enn. *sc.* 295 V. 'regnumque nostrum ut sospitent superstitentque', Plaut. *Aul.* 546 'di . . . istuc sospitent quod nunc habes', Livy i. 16. 3 'pacem precibus exposcunt uti (Romulus) uolens propitius suam semper sospitet progeniem'. *bona ope* occurs again in a similar archaic formula in 67. 2 'teque bona Iuppiter auctet ope'.

35

An invitation to a fellow poet, Caecilius, to come to Verona from Comum. The poem cannot be earlier than 59 B.C.: for it was in that year that Comum received the name of Nouum Comum when under the Lex Vatinia Caesar resettled it with 5,000 colonists (Appian, *B.C.* ii. 26; Suet. *Jul.* 28). Of Caecilius we know nothing beyond the little that we learn from this poem—that he had made Cybele the subject of a poem; it is a pleasing fancy to see in him an ancestor of the younger Pliny, who was a Caecilius by birth and the son of a magistrate and benefactor of Comum.

1. poetae tenero : i.e. a poet of love; so in Ovid *teneri uersus* (*A.A.* ii. 273) are love-poetry, *teneri modi* (*Am.* ii. 1. 4) elegiacs, and Catullus himself is *tener Catullus* for Martial (vii. 14. 3, xii. 44. 5).

   sodali : Caecilius is an intimate friend, as Cinna (10. 29) and Veranius and Fabullus (12. 13, 47. 6) are or as Alfenus (30. 1) has been.

3. relinquens : cf. 63. 51, 64. 287, 299, Prop. iv. 6. 27 'Phoebus linquens . . . Delon / adstitit Augusti puppim super'. There is no impropriety in the use of the present participle, for *relinquens* is not 'departing from' but 'leaving behind', 'forsaking': Virg. *Aen.* vii. 7 'tendit iter uelis portumque relinquit', viii. 125 'progressi subeunt luco fluuiumque relinquunt' are not cases of hysteron proteron.

4. Comi : Comum, at the end of the south-western arm of the *lacus Larius*, which in modern times has taken its name, had been a settlement of the Gallic tribe of the Insubres when Marcellus subdued the territory in 186 B.C. It was one of the many Cisalpine communities which Pompeius Strabo. had reorganized in 89, but it had suffered from the raiding of Alpine tribes and needed replenishment thirty years later.

Larium litus : Ellis compares Ov. *F.* vi. 765 *Trasimena litora* and Prop. i. 11. 30 *Baiae aquae* (using a name as an adjective without adding an adjectival termination is a mannerism of Propertius); but it is possible that *Larius* is always an adjective.

5. uolŏ : see on 10. 27.

amici sui meique has generally been taken to be a playful way of referring to the writer himself (of the same sort as *noster*, 'our friend' used by the speaker of himself in Plaut. *Rud.* 1245 and Hor. *Sat.* ii. 6. 48); if it is, there is no knowing, and little use in guessing, what kind of *cogitationes* he wishes to impart. That they are criticisms of Caecilius' work is unlikely, in view of the terms in which Caecilius' poem is introduced eight lines later; more probably, perhaps, the phrase might be a modest description of something Catullus himself had written. But while the playful periphrasis seems possible, there is no parallel to it, and *amici sui meique* may have its literal meaning and refer to a common friend: the type of expression is not uncommon in Cicero's letters, e.g. *Att.* viii. 15*a*. 3 'Balbi mei tuique aduentu', iv. 2. 5 'Varronis tui nostrique'.

7. si sapiet : 'if he is wise, he will eat up the road'. For the colloquial phrase cf. Plaut. *Bacch.* 1001–2 'non dabis, si sapies; uerum si das maxume, / ne ille alium gerulum quaerat, si sapiet, sibi', Ter. *Ad.* 565 'continebit si sapiet manus'. *si sapit* would also be possible: see on 55. 18. The metaphor of *uorare* (cf. Shakespeare, *Henry IV* 2. 1. 1. 47 'He seem'd in running to devour the way') does not occur elsewhere.

8. candida : like Fabullus' *puella* in 13. 4. Strictly the word refers to complexion, but it is often more generally used for good looks. The use of *candidus* as a general term for beauty, the frequency of cliché-metaphors of roses and lilies, snow and milk (see on 61. 187), the convention which makes heroines (even the Phoenician Dido) blonde (cf. 64. 63), and the suggestions (e.g. Virg. *Ecl.* 2. 15–18) that dark beauty needs some apology, all raise interesting questions about pigmentation in ancient Rome.

10. roget morari : the infinitive after *rogare* is very rare; Catullus has the normal construction at 13. 13.

11. Statius notes the fortuitous coincidence with (Cic.) *Fam.* x. 33. 1 'si quidem quae nuntiantur ulla ex parte uera sunt'.

12. deperit : with a direct object, 'is desperately in love with', as often in comedy; so in 100. 2; the simple *perire* is similarly used in 45. 5.

impotente : 'uncontrolled': see on 4. 18; cf. Plin. *Ep*. ii. 2. 1
'amor iniquus interdum, impotens saepe'. For the ablative
in *-e* see on 43. 4.

13 f. quo tempore . . . ex eo : 'from the time when': for the
placing of the relative clause first, a relic of the origin of the
relative clause in an indefinite or interrogative sentence which
is common in early Latin, see Kroll in *Glotta*, iii (1912), 7 ff.

legit : 'since she read'; there is no reason why the *puella*
should not be the subject and no need to make Caecilius
read his poem to her.

incohatam . . . Dindymi dominam : a poem on Cybele which
he has begun. *incohatam* probably means merely 'begun but
not yet finished', as it does in Cic. *Arch*. 28 (of a poem by
Archias on Cicero's own doings) 'quas res nos gessimus . . .
attigit hic uersibus et incohauit, quibus auditis . . . hunc ad
perficiendum hortatus sum'. For the idiom which substitutes
the subject of the poem for the poem itself cf. Juv. 1. 6
'scriptus et in tergo necdum finitus Orestes'.

14. Dindymi : cf. 63. 13 and 91; the mountain-range of Dindymus (or -um) rose above Pessinus in Phrygia, a centre of the
worship of Cybele from which her cult was brought to Rome.
See intr. to poem 63.

misellae : of the victim of love as in 45. 21.

15. medullam : see on 45. 16.

16 f. Sapphica . . . musa : i.e. *Sapphus musa*, 'Sappho's poetry'
or 'Sappho as a poetess', as Ovid has *Callimachi musa*
(*A.A.* iii. 329–30 'sit tibi Callimachi, sit Coi nota poetae, /
sit quoque uinosi Teia musa senis'), and *Turrani musa*
(*Pont*. iv. 16. 29). There is no need to see an allusion to the
notion of Sappho as the tenth Muse which appears several
times in the Greek Anthology (e.g. vii. 14, ix. 506). Caecilius'
puella is *doctior*, has more poetry in her, than Sappho: from
Catullus' time onwards *doctus* is almost a technical term for
poetic ability. So for Catullus himself the Muses are *doctae
uirgines* (65. 2), for Horace *doctae frontes* are the brows of
poets (*Od*. i. 1. 29), and in the eyes of Propertius not the
least of Cynthia's charms is that she is *docta puella* (i. 7. 11).
The extravagant compliment is a little less absurdly extravagant if we remember that Latin often uses a comparative,
'more . . . than', where our idiom is content with 'as . . .
as': so *candidior niue, splendidior uitro, blandius Orpheo*.
Martial clearly has Catullus' phrase in mind when he com-
pliments the poetess Sulpicia: 'hac condiscipula uel hac
magistra / esses doctior et pudica, Sappho' (x. 35. 15).

36

Lesbia is represented as having made a vow to Venus and Cupid that if Catullus came back to her and stopped writing abusive verses (like poem 37, perhaps) about her, she would burn, by way of sacrifice, the pick of the poems of the worst poet in the world, by which she meant his. Catullus takes up the words and puts another meaning on them. Clearly the worst poet in the world is Volusius: so his *Annals* go to the flames and Lesbia's vow is paid for her. The obvious improbability of the story does not matter; for the story is not to be taken seriously. The point of the poem is in the line which begins and ends it. A reconciliation with Lesbia there may well have been, and Catullus may have been in the same mood of exhilaration that poem 107 reflects. Anyhow, he sees a neat way of scoring a hit at Volusius, the representative here and in 95 of the old tradition of historical epic and of all that Catullus and the new poets found repugnant, and fires his shot under cover of a love-poem.

1. **Annales Volusi :** following a suggestion of Muretus, Haupt and others identified Volusius with the Tanusius who is cited by Suetonius (*Iul.* 9) and Plutarch (*Caes.* 22) as an authority for events of the years 56 and 55 B.C. and who appears in Sen. *Ep.* 93. 11, as a type of long-winded writing. Speaking of the short life of the philosopher Metronax, Seneca says that a short book may be more worth while than a long one: 'et paucorum uersuum liber est et quidem laudandus atque utilis; annales Tanusii scis quam ponderosi sint et quid uocentur. hoc est uita quorundam longa, et quod Tanusii sequitur annales'. *quid uocentur*, it is argued, is '*cacata carta*': Seneca and Catullus must be speaking of the same person and Catullus must be thinly disguising his name. But (1) Seneca is not talking about poetry (*uersus* means a line of prose as well as a line of verse) and the other references to Tanusius' historical work point to its having been in prose. (2) It is not Catullus' practice to disguise the names of those whom he attacks: if he could attack Caesar and Pompey, not to mention humbler persons, by name, he would not have resorted to a pseudonym for a poetaster. And (3) if, for some unknown reason, he had chosen to do so and, following the familiar practice first pointed out by Bentley on Hor. *Od.* ii. 12. 13, to half-conceal Tanusius' name under another of the same metrical value, he would hardly have chosen for that purpose a genuine and respectable *gentilicium*. If, as seems very likely, Seneca's *quid uocentur* is a reference to the *cacata carta* of this poem, the natural explanation is that the

similarity of name had tempted someone wickedly to apply to Tanusius what Catullus had said of Volusius.

2. mea puella : Lesbia, as in 2. 1, 3. 3, 17, 11. 15, 13. 11.

3. sanctae Veneri : cf. 68. 5 *sancta Venus*, 64. 95 *sancte puer* (of Cupid).

4. restitutus : cf. 107. 4 *te restituis*. Notice the 'hissing' alliteration on *s* in this and the following lines.

5. uibrare iambos : 'hurl my savage lampoons'. *iambus* here as in 40. 2, 54. 6, refers to the content of the verses, not to their metre. *uibrare* is literally used of the shaking of a weapon as it is launched, Ov. *Met.* viii. 374 'uibrata per auras / hastarum tremulo quatiebant spicula motu', Virg. *Aen.* viii. 524 'uibratus ab aethere fulgor'; in the metaphorical use *uibrare* is elsewhere intransitive, Cic. *Brut.* 326 'oratio incitata et uibrans' ('quivering'), Quint. x. 1. 60 (of Archilochus' *iambi*) 'cum ualidae tum breues uibrantesque sententiae'.

6. electissima parodies the common formula of a genuine vow: cf. Eurip. *I.T.* 20 (of Agamemnon's vow) ὅ τι γὰρ ἐνιαυτὸς τέκοι / κάλλιστον ηὔξω φωσφόρῳ θύσειν θεᾷ.

7. tardipedi deo : Vulcan: the periphrasis has a mock-solemn effect: so Hephaestus is χαλαίπους in Nicander, *Ther.* 458 and δύσπους (probably) in Callim. fr. 228. 63 Pf.

daturam : cf. 42. 4 'negat reddituram'. The omission of the reflexive subject in oratio obliqua, when it is unemphatic, is common in comedy (e.g. Plaut. *Pseud.* 565 'neque sim facturus quod facturum dixeram', Ter. *And.* 401 'pollicitus sum suscepturum') and occasionally found in prose (e.g. Cic. *Rosc. Am.* 59; see Madvig on *Fin.* v. 31) and in serious verse (e.g. Virg. *Aen.* ii. 432, iv. 383).

infelicibus ... lignis : a technical term of ritual. '(arbores) infelices existimantur damnataeque religione quae neque seruntur nec fructum ferunt' (Pliny, *N.H.* xvi. 108): they are *inferorum deorum ... in tutela* and ritual prescribes their use for the burning of *prodigia* or *monstra* (Macr. iii. 20. 3): similarly primitive law condemned a criminal to hanging *arbori infelici* (Cic. *Rab. Perd.* 13). The offending poems are to be treated as *monstra*. But the phrase is often used with a more general sinister implication: so in Cic. *Mil.* 33 Clodius' body, hastily burned on an improvised pyre, is *infelicissimis lignis semiustilatum*.

10. 'and the naughty girl realized that this vow of hers was a pretty piece of fun.'

iocose lepide : the asyndeton cannot be regarded as impossible. Scaliger neatly proposed *ioco se*, but the repetition of *se* at so short an interval is unlikely: Riese's *iocosis* would refer to Venus and Cupid.

11. nunc : the time for payment has come. The solemn recital of Venus' cult-titles in a series of relative clauses parodies the formal hymn style: compare the serious use of the style in poem 34. The *o* (see on 46. 9) emphasizes the solemnity of the address.

caeruleo creata ponto refers to the mythical birth of Aphrodite from the sea-foam, from which the Greeks, rightly or wrongly, derived her name.

12 ff. Idalium (cf. 61. 17, 64. 96), **Amathus** (cf. 68. 51 *Amathusia*), and **Golgi** (64. 96), all in Cyprus, were old and famous sites of the worship of Aphrodite: cf. Theoc. 15. 100 δέσποιν' ἃ Γολγώς τε καὶ ᾿Ιδάλιον ἐφίλησας.

Urios has not been explained, and the epithet (*apertus* is regular in geographical descriptions of an 'open', exposed terrain) gives no help towards identifying it. Strabo mentions a Urion on the Apulian coast (vi. 284) and a Uria, an inland town between Tarentum and Brundisium (vi. 282), but neither was a place of any importance and neither has any known connexion with Venus. Of the emendations proposed the least unlikely is Bergk's *Chutros*: Chytri was a place in Venus' island of Cyprus.

13. Ancona : Ancon (the Greek form which Catullus uses here) or Ancona (the Latin) was a town on the Adriatic coast in Picenum, an old Greek colony which celebrated its cult of Venus by using her head on its coinage: cf. Juv. 4. 40 'domum Veneris quam Dorica sustinet Ancon'.

Cnidumque : Cnidus, on the coast of Caria, in SW. Asia Minor, had three temples of Venus, one of which contained the famous statue by Praxiteles: for the reeds which it exported cf. Pliny, *N.H.* xvi. 157. The manuscripts have *Gnidum*, but that Catullus used the spelling *Cnidum*, and not the later form, is shown by the -*ĕ* before it. There is no evidence that a syllable could be left short before initial *gn*-: see Housman in *C.Q.* xxii (1928), 1–9.

15. Durrachium : on the Illyrian coast opposite Brundisium, was an important centre of trade and traffic as the eastern terminus of the short sea passage between Italy and Greece. So it is the 'inn' or 'roadhouse' of the Adriatic: similarly Strabo (xii. 577) calls Apamea in Phrygia τῶν ἀπὸ τῆς ᾿Ιταλίας καὶ τῆς ῾Ελλάδος κοινὸν ὑποδοχεῖον. The cult of Venus, which is mentioned only here, is not surprising in a large seaport.

Hadriae : *Hadria* is a borrowing from Greek (Ἀδρίας *sc.* κόλπος: the Greeks gave the sea its name from the old Greek

settlement of (H)adria in the Po delta) which appears first
here and provides a convenient alternative to *Hadriaticum*
(*mare*) (4. 6).

16. **acceptum face redditumque :** 'enter as received and duly
paid': *acceptum facere* (e.g. Gaius, *Inst.* iii. 171 'id quod
debeatur . . . mulier . . . acceptum facere non potest') and
acceptum (*re*)*ferre* are technical phrases of law and commerce
for making a credit entry. (Similarly *expensum ferre* is to
make a debit entry: on these and other terms of accounting
see G. E. M. de Ste Croix, 'Greek and Roman Accounting' in
Littleton and Yamey, *Studies in the History of Accounting*
(London, 1956), pp. 44–47.)

   face : the original form of the imperative, common in
comedy (though in Plautus the shortened form is already the
commoner), is here used for metrical convenience: it should
perhaps be restored in 63. 82 (and in 78 and 79).

17. **illepidum . . . inuenustum :** cf. 10. 4.

18. **at uos interea :** cf. 14. 21.

19. **pleni ruris et inficetiarum :** see on 22. 14 *infaceto rure.*

20. The first line repeated rounds off the poem as in 16, 52, 57.

38

A message written in physical illness, it may be, or, more
probably perhaps, in mental distress. In his depression
Catullus seeks the comfort of poetry from a fellow poet, as
Allius (68. 1–4) seeks it from him. That is characteristic: for
him and his friends their poetry was an integral part of life, and
doctrina was not mere external accomplishment but an attitude
colouring all their thought. In this crisis of emotion Catullus
thinks of Simonides as in another (51) he turned to Sappho.

The person addressed can be identified with reasonable certainty. Q. Cornificius was quaestor in 48 (and so probably was
somewhat younger than Catullus), when he conducted a successful campaign for Caesar in Illyricum. In 46 he went to the
East, probably as governor of Cilicia, and for the next three
years we have a series of intimate letters from Cicero to him
(*Fam.* xii. 17–30). After Caesar's death, when he was proconsul
in Africa Vetus, he declared for the Senate and, encouraged by
Cicero, held his province for the Senatorial cause. He refused
to surrender it to the nominee of the triumvirs and found himself involved in fighting with his neighbour in Africa Noua; in
41 he was killed when his troops deserted him. We know where
his literary sympathies lay both from Ovid, who mentions him

with Catullus, Caluus, and Cinna (*Tr*. ii. 435–6) and from the meagre fragments that we possess of his work, hendecasyllabics and a hexameter poem on Glaucus. An able officer of Caesar's, the husband of Catiline's widow (Cic. *Fam*. viii. 7. 2), a brother poet of Catullus, a critic of oratory whom Cicero found congenial, he reminds us at once how small Catullus' world was and how little we know of it.

1. **malest :** for this colloquial use of the adverb cf. 14. 10. It is common in comedy and in Cicero's letters of 'feeling ill': e.g. Plaut. *Amph*. 1058 'animo malest: aquam uelim', *Cist*. 59 'excrucior: male mihist'; similarly Cic. *Fam*. xvi. 5. 1 'cum meliuscule tibi esset' ('you were feeling a little better'). For the similar use of *male sit* in imprecations, cf. 3. 13, Cic. *Att*. xv. 15. 1 'L. Antonio male sit si quidem Buthrotiis molestus est!'

2. **me hercule, et :** of the corrections proposed to remove the hiatus, *et est l.* (Sillig) is the most attractive. Phaedrus, the only other writer to use *mehercule* in verse, (v. 5. 22) makes it trisyllabic as Catullus does here: in comedy the normal form is *mĕhercle*.

   laboriose : for *laboriosus* of illness cf. Cic. *Phil*. xi. 8 'dolores Trebonius pertulit magnos: multi ex morbi grauitate maiores, quos tamen non miseros sed laboriosos solemus dicere'. *labor* (cf. 50. 14) and *laborare* are regularly used of both mental and physical suffering; e.g. Cic. *Fam*. vii. 26. 1 'cum ex intestinis laborarem', ix. 23 'quod ex pedibus laborares'.

3. **magis magis :** cf. 64. 274, Virg. *Georg*. iv. 311: at 68. 48 Catullus uses *magis atque magis*.

4. **allocutione :** 'words of sympathy': so *adloquium*, Hor. *Epod*. 13. 18, Livy ix. 6. 8. The verb *adloqui* often has this implication; cf. Varro, *L.L*. vi. 57 'adlocutum mulieres ire aiunt cum eunt ad aliquam locutum consolandi causa', Val. Max. ii. 7. 6 'urbs incerta gratulandi prius an adloquendi officio fungeretur', Sen. *Ep*. 98. 9 'in ea epistula qua sororem amisso . . . filio adloquitur'.

6. **sic meos amores :** if *amores* is personal (as it generally is in Catullus when it is accompanied by a possessive adjective: see on 10. 1), it must refer to Cornificius and be subject of an exclamatory infinitive understood, 'that my dear friend should behave so.' To take it as object, 'that you should treat my beloved so', is clearly inappropriate here: if Cornificius had injured Catullus in relation to Lesbia (or some other person), Catullus would not be asking for his sympathy. But *amores* may be impersonal (for the plural

cf. 13. 9) and the words a question, 'is this how you treat my affection?'

7. **paulum quid lubet allocutionis :** 'any scrap of sympathy you like, something sadder than Simonides' tears': again there is an ellipse of a verbal notion ('send me' or the like) and *paulum quid lubet* is like *paulum nescioquid* (Cic. *Rosc. Am.* 115), *paulum aliquid* (*De Or.* i. 95). For similar ellipses in conversational style cf. Cic. *Att.* x. 16. 6 'et litterarum aliquid interea (mitte)', *Fam.* xvi. 24 'de publicis omnia mihi certa (scribes)'. To take *paulum quid* as subject of *lubet* is grammatically just possible (*libet* with a pronoun—generally *id* or *quod*—as subject is not uncommon in Plautus and Terence and is occasionally found later), but gives a much weaker sense 'I have a fancy for some scrap of sympathy'.

8. **Simonideis :** the lyric dirges (θρῆνοι) of Simonides of Ceos (556–467 B.C.)—the *Cea nenia* of Horace, *Od.* ii. 1. 38—were famous and his simple pathos (τὸ οἰκτίζεσθαι μὴ μεγαλοπρεπῶς ἀλλὰ παθητικῶς, Dionysius of Halicarnassus, *de Imit.* ii. 2. 6) was especially admired by ancient critics: so Quintilian says of him (x. 1. 64) 'praecipua eius in commouenda miseratione uirtus ut quidam in hac eum parte omnibus eius operis [i.e. lyric poetry] auctoribus praeferant'.

39

The reason for this scurrilous attack appears from 37. 17-20; Egnatius, the bearded, long-haired dandy from Spain, is one of Lesbia's lovers. He bears a good Italian name and presumably came of a Roman or Italian family settled in Spain: it suits Catullus to make him a Spanish savage. The Egnatius from whose poem *de rerum natura* Macrobius (vi. 5. 2 and 12) quotes a few lines may have been a contemporary of Catullus:[1] but we know nothing about him.

2. **renidet usque quaque :** 'beams wherever he goes'.

2 f. **rei . . . subsellium :** cf. Cael. ap. Cic. *Fam.* viii. 8. 1 'at ego inuocatus ad subsellia rei occurro'. The wooden benches occupied by the defendant and his supporters and those occupied by the prosecution (Cic. *Rosc. Am.* 17 'accusatorum subsellia') faced each other across the floor of the court

---

[1] In the longer fragment—

> roscida noctiuagis astris labentibus Phoebe
> pulsa loco cessit concedens lucibus altis—

the ecthlipsis of final -*s* suggests at any rate that Egnatius, if he was a contemporary of Catullus, was not a neoteric (see on 116. 8).

(Sen. *Contr.* vii. 4. 7); to have practice both as defending and
as prosecuting counsel is 'in utrisque subselliis uersari'
(Cic. *Fam.* xiii. 10. 2). So *subsellia* is used for 'the courts':
Cic. *Brut.* 289 'subsellia grandiorem et pleniorem uocem
desiderant', *de Orat.* i. 264 'is qui habitaret in subselliis'
('a man who lived in the courts'). Quintilian (vi. 1. 38) has
a word on the client who defeats his advocate's pathetic
effects by smiling in the wrong place (*intempestiue renidentes*).

4. **lugetur :** 'there is mourning'; for the impersonal passive cf.
Ter. *And.* 129 'in ignem impositast: fletur'.

6. **quidquid est :** 'whatever is happening, wherever he is'.

7. **hunc habet morbum :** 'it is a disease with him': cf. Sen.
de Clem. ii. 6. 4 'scias morbum esse, non hilaritatem, semper
adridere ridentibus'. Similarly *morbus* is used of Verres'
weakness for *objets d'art* (Cic. *Verr.* ii. 4. 1), of a weakness for
talking (Cato ap. Gell. i. 15. 9), for writing (Sen. *Ep.* 79. 4),
for asking silly questions (Sen. *Dial.* x. 13. 2): in Petronius
46. 3 Echion's young son is *in aues morbosus*, 'mad on birds'.
The expression recalls the Plautine *hunc habet morem* (*Capt.*
233, *Curc.* 377, *Men.* 338, 573); perhaps Catullus' phrase is a
distortion of that common idiom.

8. **urbanum :** in l. 10 below *urbanus* has its local sense, 'from
the city' (of Rome): here, as in 22. 2, it is a term of social
convention, 'well-bred'. The semantic development of the
word is not easy to trace in detail. Sometimes Cicero seems
to be using it of an indigenous, traditional type of wit: so in
Fam. ix. 15. 2 'Romani ueteres et urbani sales' is contrasted
with Attic wit ('salsiores quam illi Atticorum') and para-
phrased as 'antiqua et uernacula festiuitas'. But elsewhere
in Cicero the emphasis is not on indigenousness but on mod-
ernity—so in *Cael.* 33 'seuere et grauiter et prisce agere' is
contrasted with 'remisse et leniter et urbane (agere)'—or on
'good taste': so in *Off.* i. 104 a *genus iocandi* which is *illiberale,
petulans, flagitiosum, obscenum* is opposed to one which is
elegans, urbanum, ingeniosum, facetum (cf. *Cael.* 6 '[contu-
melia] si petulantius iactatur, conuicium, si facetius, urbanitas nominatur'). And when Cicero, writing to Appius Claudius
in 51 B.C. (*Fam.* iii. 8. 3), describes his own use of the word
as a 'modern' one—'te hominem non solum sapientem uerum
etiam, ut nunc loquimur, urbanum'—it is perhaps this use
to which he is referring.

After criticizing two definitions of *urbanitas* as inadequate,
Quintilian (vi. 3. 107) makes a painstaking attempt to define
it himself as it is applied to the spoken word. It cannot be
precisely defined: for it covers the complex of qualities which

belongs to the self-conscious sophistication of a privileged society. When Brutus asks for a definition of *urbanitatis color* (*Brut.* 171), Cicero replies that it is a *je ne sais quoi* ('nescio: tantum esse quendam scio') which the Roman speaker has and provincials, even the best of them, have not, a *sapor uernaculus* detectable not only in vocabulary but also in pronunciation and in a quality of wit. Like ἀστειότης, *urbanitas* is often restricted to verbal wit, but it can be seen in what is not said as well as in what is said: irony, *dissimulatio*, is *urbana* (*de Or.* ii. 269). And the spoken word is only one of the media in which *urbanitas* shows itself; it is seen in behaviour too, in the *savoir faire* which Egnatius so conspicuously lacks, in the ease and assurance, the *frons urbana* (Hor. *Ep.* i. 9. 11), which shows up the awkward shyness, *pudor subrusticus* (Cic. *Fam.* v. 12. 1), of less accomplished people.

9. monendum : either *te est* (Spengel) or *est te* (Maehly) is necessary; the latter brings the pronouns into idiomatic juxtaposition; cf., e.g., Cic. *pro Sulla* 23 'sed tamen te a me pro magnis causis monendum esse etiam atque etiam puto'.

The impersonal use of the gerundival periphrastic tense in which the gerundive governs a direct object is not properly described as an archaism. It is as rare in early Latin as it is in classical prose and verse: Plautus has only one example of it (*Trin.* 869 'agitandumst uigilias') against many examples of the normal personal construction (e.g. *Cas.* 475 'aures sunt adhibendae'). The impersonal use is common only in Catullus' contemporaries Lucretius (who has nine instances: e.g. i. 381 'motu priuandum est corpora', ii. 1129 'manus dandum est') and Varro, and in the jurists. Cicero has the construction twice (*Scaur.* 13 'obliuiscendum uobis putatis . . . scelera', *de Sen.* 6 'uiam quam nobis quoque ingrediundum sit'), Virgil once (*Aen.* xi. 230 'pacem . . . petendum', perhaps a Lucretian reminiscence).

10. urbanus : 'a man from Rome'.

11. pinguis Vmber aut obesus Etruscus : *obesus Etruscus* accords with Virgil's *pinguis Tyrrhenus* (*Georg.* ii. 193) and with representations of Etruscans in art. But *V*'s *parcus Umber* is surprising on two counts. (1) One would expect an adjective denoting some physical characteristic, like the other epithets in the list, *obesus, ater, dentatus*: and *parcus* has no such meaning. (2) 'Thrifty Umbrian' is at variance with what is said of the habits and way of life of Umbrians elsewhere: they are *pingues* in Persius (3. 74), and Athenaeus (xii. 526) quotes the historian Theopompus as saying τὸ τῶν Ὀμβρικῶν

ἔθνος . . . ἐπιεικῶς εἶναι ἁβροδίαιτον παραπλησίως τε βιοτεύειν τοῖς
Λυδοῖς χώραν τε ἔχειν ἀγαθὴν ὅθεν προελθεῖν εἰς εὐδαιμονίαν. Of the two
passages which Ellis cites in support of *parcus* as 'a habitual
epithet of the race', Mart. xii. 81. 2 and Silius viii. 450 ff., the
first is absurdly irrelevant: Martial writes *Umber* . . . *pauper*,
but *Umber* is a man's name. The other is concerned not
with the abstemiousness of Umbrians but with their soldierly
qualities: Silius calls them not *parci* but *haud parci Martem
coluisse*, 'warlike'. But none of the proposals for correct-
ing *parcus* into a less inappropriate adjective is at all convincing: *porcus* (Scaliger) is out of place among the adjectival
epithets; *fartus* (Venator) could hardly have the meaning
required without an ablative or *pastus* (Voss) without an
object.

While the manuscripts of Catullus agree in reading *parcus*,
the indirect tradition points to *pinguis*. The Liber Glossarum
(*Glossaria Latina*, ed. Lindsay, i, p. 443; *C.G.L.* v. 233) has a
gloss 'pinguis: crassus, nam obesus plus est quam pinguis:
Catullus ait aut pinguis ubera aut obesus et grossus'. The
quotation from Catullus is clearly this line and the reading
pinguis is guaranteed by the fact that it is just for the
distinction between *pinguis* and *obesus* that the line is cited.
But if Catullus wrote *pinguis*, of which Persius' phrase might
well be a reminiscence, it is difficult to account for the corruption except on the hypothesis suggested (not very
seriously) by Lindsay (*C.R.* xxxiii, 1919, 105), that *parcus*
was a deliberate correction by an indignant Umbrian reader.

12. **Lanuuinus :** from Lanuvium, a town in the west of Latium;
we hear nothing from any other source of dark complexions
there or of fine sets of teeth to be set off by them.

13. **aut Transpadanus :** 'or a Transpadane, to lay a finger on
my own people': see introduction, p. x.

14. **puriter lauit :** 'washes with clean water' (Fest. 293 L. 'pure
lautum: aqua pura lauatum'). Catullus has *puriter* again in
76. 19: in early Latin the suffix *-iter* was freely used to form
adverbs from adjectives of the second declension as well as
from those of the third, and relics of that freedom survive in
Caesar and Cicero, who both use *firmiter* and *largiter*.

lauit : The first declension form of the verb was originally
intransitive, the third declension form transitive, but that
distinction has already broken down in Plautus, and in him
the first declension form is the commoner. In prose Varro
and Sallust use *lauere*, but not Caesar or Cicero: later verse
shows a few isolated instances like Virg. *Georg.* iii. 221, Hor.
Od. iii. 12. 2, *Sat.* i. 5. 24. Why Catullus should have used it

in this poem (where, unlike the old-fashioned *puriter*, it offers no metrical convenience), we can only guess. It has been suggested, not very convincingly, that the old-fashioned words *lauit* and *puriter* fit the sarcastic flavour of the poem: the same has been said of *monendum est te*, though it is hard to see why an idiom which is used casually in Varro's prose should have any such nuance in Catullus. Perhaps *puriter lauit* is an echo of a religious formula.

16. risu . . . nulla est : the commentators quote Menander's line (*monost.* 88) γέλως ἄκαιρος ἐν βροτοῖς δεινὸν κακόν. For the characteristic turn of phrase cf. 22. 14 'infaceto . . . infacetior rure', 27. 4 'ebrioso acino ebriosioris', 99. 2 'dulci dulcius ambrosia', 14 'tristi tristius elleboro'. For *ineptus*, 'in bad taste', 'out of place', see on 8. 1, 12. 4.

17. nunc : 'as it is'.

Celtiber : the Celtiberi (the nominative singular occurs only here and in Mart. x. 20. 1) were the hardy people of north central Spain, a mixed race due to invasion of Celtic territory by Iberians; the conquest of them by Rome had been a long and difficult operation extending over most of sixty years, from the outbreak of revolt in 195 B.C. to the final breaking of their resistance by the destruction of Numantia in 133.

Celtiberia in terra : in Livy, who particularly affects it, this periphrasis seems to have an air of formality: a good example is xxv. 7. 4 'neu (quis miles) in Italiam reportaretur donec hostis in terra Italia esset'.

19. russam : *russus* is rare in literature; Ennius uses it of a cock's throat (and *russescere* of leaves), Lucretius of a theatre-awning, Martial of a mask; its non-literary currency is shown by the use of it for one of the party colours in the circus-races under the Empire (Juv. 7. 114) and by its survival in Italian *rosso* and French *roux*.

defricare : Apuleius, quoting the line (*Apol.* 6) substitutes *pumicare*, no doubt by a slip of memory.

20. uester : while *nos* and *noster* are freely substituted for *ego* and *meus* (see on 107. 3–4), *uos* is never equivalent to *tu* in classical Latin, and *uester*, where it does not refer directly to a plural subject, generally has an obvious plural implication: so, for example, 64. 160 'uestras sedes' ('of you and your kin') Virg. *Aen.* i. 140 'uestras, Eure, domos' (of you and your brothers), x. 188 'crimen, Amor, uestrum' (of you and your mother Venus), Prop. iii. 15. 44 'uestra ira' (of you women), Ov. *Her.* 1. 75 'uestra libido' (of you men). But there is a residue of cases in which the plural reference is far

from obvious and in which *uester* looks like the equivalent of
tuus. That it should be so would be *a priori* doubly surprising, since (1) one would expect the use of *uester* to correspond exactly to that of *uos*, and (2) if *uester* could be a
substitute for *tuus*, one would expect to find it substituted
not a few times only but, like *noster* for *meus*, many times,
and it is natural to suspect that in these cases a plurality
was vaguely present to the writer's mind. Three of them
are in Catullus. In 68. 151 a dim plural reference for *uestrum* can be found—*uestrum nomen* is the name which Allius
shares with his family and the immortalizing of his name
will mean the immortalizing of theirs—though that reference is not relevant in the context. In the present passage
it can be argued that *uester*, though strictly inconsistent
with the following *te*, is loosely used because Egnatius is
represented as typical of his race, i.e. that the words are an
illogical way of saying 'the more polished your teeth (like
those of your fellow countrymen) are'. But in 99. 6, *uestrae
saeuitiae*, the plural reference is more shadowy still: not more
than one person has been mentioned or even implied, and if
uester is not merely *tuus* the thought which justifies it must
be 'your *saeuitia* (for you, like others of your kind, are
saeuus)'. Even more awkward is Ov. *Am.* ii. 16. 24 'uestros,
curva Malea, sinus', where, if a plurality is implied, it is
certainly not a plurality of promontories, and *uestros* has to
be interpreted as something like 'of you and your inhabitants'.
But if *uester* was interchangeable with *tuus*, it is almost incredible that Ovid resorted to this expedient only once; it is
easier to believe that the usage is due to a looseness of
thought. (See Housman in *C.Q.* iii [1909], 244 ff.; Postgate
in *Hermathena*, xviii [1919], 91 ff.)

40

The rival in love who is here attacked is unknown, and the
cognomen Rauidus, while it is not in itself remarkable—it
would be one of a large class of names derived from personal
colouring; *rauus* is 'grey-eyed'—is not found elsewhere.
  'Omnino huic simile illud ex epodis Archilochi' said Scaliger,
citing frag. 88 Diehl:

πάτερ Λυκάμβα, ποῖον ἐφράσω τόδε;
τίς σὰς παρήειρε φρένας
ἧς τὸ πρὶν ἠρήρεισθα; νῦν δὲ δὴ πολὺς
ἀστοῖσι φαίνεαι γέλως,

the opening lines of the epode in which Archilochus attacked his father-in-law Lycambes; the gist of some later lines can be recovered from the paraphrase given by Lucian (*Pseudolog.* 1), καὶ σὺ δή, ὦ κακόδαιμον ἄνθρωπε, τί βουλόμενος ποιητὴν λάλον παροξύνεις ἐπὶ σεαυτὸν αἰτίας ζητοῦντα καὶ ὑποθέσεις τοῖς ἰάμβοις; Similarity in one or two phrases there certainly is (τίς σὰς παρήειρε φρένας—*quaenam te mala mens agit*: ἀστοῖσι φαίνεαι γέλως—*peruenias in ora uulgi*) and the poem may have been in Catullus' mind (see also on l. 3), but these phrases belong to the stock-in-trade of invective and Catullus' words might well have been written without suggestion from Archilochus.

1. **mala mens :** 'infatuation': cf. 15. 14 'quod si te mala mens furorque uecors / in tantam impulerit, sceleste, culpam'; Tib. ii. 5. 104 'ferus ille . . . plorabit sobrius idem / et se iurabit mente fuisse mala'; Sen. *Ben.* iii. 27. 2 'cum malam mentem habuisse se pridie iurasset'. Similarly *bona mens*, 'sanity': Sen. *Ben.* ii. 14. 3 'cum ad mentem bonam redierit'; Ov. *Fast.* iv. 366 'qui bibit inde furit; procul hinc discedite, quis est / cura bonae mentis'.

   Rauide : elision of a hypermetric syllable into the first syllable of the following line is unparalleled in hendeca-syllabics and most improbable here. If the text is sound, *Rauide* must be treated as a dissyllable, *Raude*: for evidence of such syncopation, under the influence of the accent on the first syllable, in common speech see Plaut. *Bacch.* 276 (a pun on *audi* and *auidi*), Cic. *de Div.* ii. 84 (Crassus, embarking at Brundisium for the East in 55 B.C., hears a fig-seller's street-cry of *Cauneas*—i.e. *Cauneas ficos uendo*—and takes it as a warning, *caue ne eas*).

2. **agit praecipitem :** for the metaphorical use cf. Cic. *Verr.* ii. 1. 7 (of Verres infatuated by his own criminal career) 'agunt eum praecipitem poenae ciuium Romanorum'.

   iambos : 'lampoons', as in 36. 5 'truces uibrare iambos', 54. 6 'irascere iterum meis iambis', without reference to the metrical form which gave its name to the genre.

3. **quis deus :** for the pronoun see on 61. 46.

   non bene aduocatus : perhaps 'invoked in an evil hour, to ill purpose', i.e. better left uninvoked (cf. Prop. iv. 6. 43 'quam [patriam] nisi defendes, murorum Romulus augur / ire Palatinas non bene uidit aues', i.e. it would be better if Rome had never been founded); more probably 'invoked amiss', i.e. invoked under a wrong or inadequate formula and so offended with the petitioner: on the importance in primitive belief of using the right formula see on 34. 21 f. A fragment of Archilochus, 45 Diehl, τίς ἄρα δαίμων καὶ τέου χολούμενος; which may belong to the same epode as the lines quoted above, bears some resemblance to Catullus' expression here. But the formula is an old one (cf. Homer, *Il.* xvii. 469 Αὐτόμεδον, τίς τοί νυ θεῶν νηκερδέα βουλὴν / ἐν στήθεσσιν ἔθηκε καὶ ἐξέλετο φρένας ἐσθλάς;) and Catullus gives an original turn to it.

5. **an ut . . . :** 'Or is it really that you want to be talked about?', with an ellipse of *hoc fecisti* or the like.

peruenias in ora : the plural is regular in this and similar phrases, even in prose: so Livy ii. 36. 3 'timor uicit ne in ora hominum pro ludibrio abierit'; for the same phrase used of favourable notoriety cf. Hor. *Ep.* i. 3. 9 'Romana breui uenturus in ora', Prop. iii. 9. 32 'uenies tu quoque in ora uirum'. With *esse* and *uersari*, on the other hand, the singular is always used: Cic. *Verr.* ii. 1. 121 'istius nequitiam et iniquitatem tum in ore uulgi atque in communibus prouerbiis esse uersatam', *Tusc.* i. 116 'Harmodius in ore est'. Ovid combines the two idioms, *Trist.* iii. 14. 23 '[opus meum] nunc incorrectum populi peruenit in ora, / in populi quicquam si tamen ore meum est'.

6. **quid uis? :** 'what are you after?', like the common *quid tibi uis?*, Hor. *Sat.* ii. 6. 29, Prop. i. 5. 3, Cic. *de Or.* ii. 269.

qualubet : 'no matter how': cf. 76. 14.

notus : cf. Cic. *Cael.* 31 'cum Clodia, muliere non solum nobili uerum etiam nota'.

7. **meos amores :** see on 10. 1.

8. **cum longa . . . poena :** cf. 77. 2 'magno cum pretio atque malo', Plaut. *Bacch.* 503 'illud hercle cum malo fecit suo', Caes. *B.G.* i. 10. 2 'id . . . intellegebat magno cum periculo prouinciae futurum'.

41

This poem and 43 presumably belong to Catullus' life in Verona (43. 6); in both the *puella* seems to be serving as material for an indirect attack on one of his aversions, Mamurra.

1. **Ameana :** the manuscripts agree on these letters, but the name, if it is a name, has not been convincingly explained. That Catullus used a 'rustic' form *Ameana* for *Ammiana* is not at all likely; if he did, we have no idea what 'Ammius' girl' (cf. 44. 10) means. A local adjective seems more probable: hence Haupt's *Ametina* (Ametinum was a township in Latium), but it is merely a guess.

2. **tota milia . . . decem :** *tota* emphasizes the amount: 'ten whole thousand', 'all of 10,000 sesterces'.

3. **turpiculo naso :** cf. 43. 1: the original physical sense of *turpis*, 'ugly', maintained itself beside the later moral sense.

4. **decoctoris** : *decoquere*, properly used of melting down metal, was a colourful colloquialism (like *comedere*, 29. 14 n.) for getting through one's money which became a technical term for bankruptcy: so Cicero speaks of the *rustici decoctores* who attached themselves to Catiline (*Cat.* ii. 5) and asks Antony 'tenesne memoria praetextatum te decoxisse?' ('you were a bankrupt while you were still a boy', *Phil.* ii. 44).

Formiani : the 'bankrupt of Formiae' must be Mamurra, the 'macula Formiana' of 57. 4; see introduction to poem 29.

5 f. **propinqui . . . conuocate** : the person and property of an insane man (*furiosus*) came under the charge of his next-of-kin (*agnati*); failing such, by early law it came under that of the members of his *gens* (*gentiles*), later under that of a *curator* appointed by the praetor. That procedure lies behind such turns of speech as Varro, *R.R.* i. 2. 8 (of a man who takes to farming without the prospect of profit) 'mente est captus et ad agnatos et gentiles est deducendus' and Hor. *Ep.* i. 1. 101 ff. 'insanire putas sollemnia me neque rides / nec medici credis nec curatoris egere / a praetore dati'. But it did not apply to women, since an adult woman, even if she were *sui iuris*, was at least formally under the charge of a *tutor legitimus*, and here there need be no technical point: when, with her looks, she asks for that amount of money, the girl has obviously gone off her head and her relatives had better be looking after her.

7 f. **rogare . . . imaginosum** : Fröhlich's correction is certain: 'she never asks the reflecting bronze'— i.e. the mirror; ancient mirrors were commonly polished bronze—'what she is like'. *imaginosus* is not found elsewhere but the fanciful phrase rings true. Those editors who read with Schwabe 'nec rogate qualis est: solet esse imaginosa' intended the words to mean 'don't ask what is the matter with her; she is a chronic sufferer from delusions': *imagines* is used medically of delusions (Celsus iii. 18. 3, 19), but *qualis sit* cannot be equivalent to *quo morbo laboret*.

42

Catullus' writing-tablets are in the hands of a young woman who refuses to give them back, and he summons an army of hendecasyllables to demand them. Calling her uncomplimentary names louder and louder has no effect: so he reverses his tactics and sees whether he can disconcert her by calling her complimentary names instead.

1. **adeste** : he calls hendecasyllables to his aid as the proper

metre for abuse: so he warns a thief who has stolen his napkin, 12. 10 'aut hendecasyllabos trecentos / exspecta aut mihi linteum remitte'.

quot . . . estis omnes : the reinforcing of *quot* by *quotquot* and the emphatic repetition of *omnes* emphasizes the idea of 'all the hendecasyllables in the world'.

3. **iocum :** for the personal use cf. Prop. ii. 24. 16 'fallaci dominae iam pudet esse iocum', Petr. 57. 4 'spero me sic uiuere ut nemini iocus sim'.

4. **nostra :** the correction is almost certain: if *uestra* is retained, the tablets are represented as belonging to the hendeca-syllables because they are used for writing verses on (see below).

    reddituram : for the omission of the reflexive see on 36. 7.

5. **pugillaria,** called *codicilli* below and *tabellae* in 50. 2, were wax-coated wooden tablets, with a rim to prevent rubbing, hinged together in pairs or sets by straps at the side, and used for writing which was not meant to be permanent. In 50. 2 the *tabellae* are the 'notebook' which Catullus uses to scribble verses down as they occur to him; here the use may be the same and the tablets may have been stolen or picked up when he dropped them. But they were also used for letters, particularly for hasty notes, the answer to which might be sent back on them by the recipient. So Cicero sends a question to Balbus and gets the information he wants by return (*Fam.* vi. 18. 1 'quaesiui a Balbo per codicillos quid esset in lege: rescripsit . . .'); Ovid proposes an assignation to a lady and gets her refusal (*Am.* i. 12. 1 'tristes rediere tabellae: / infelix hodie littera posse negat'). Catullus per-haps has sent a proposal of the same kind and the recipient, instead of replying, has kept the tablets.

    The name *pugillaria* refers to the size of the tablets (*pugillus* is a handful, what can be held in the *pugnus*) as *codicilli* refers to their shape (*codex* is a wooden block). The normal form is *pugillares*: the grammarian Charisius (p. 97 K.) says that Catullus used the neuter 'saepius . . . in hendecasyllabis', but in our text the word occurs only here; elsewhere it is cited from Laberius and used by the archaizing Gellius.

    si pati potestis : though it is not found elsewhere, is clearly a current formula of indignation unrelated to the structure of the sentence, like the common indignant *si dis placet*, 'just imagine', 'if you please' (e.g. Plaut. *Capt.* 454, Ter. *Ad.* 476, Cic. *Rosc. Am.* 102, Livy vi. 40. 7: Catullus' *si placet Dionae*, 56. 6, seems to be a variation of it).

6. reflagitemus : *flagito* implies loud and importunate demand: the compound occurs only here.

8. turpe : the neuter accusative used adverbially: so 51. 5 *dulce*, 61. 7 *suaue*.

   incedere : the *meretrix* betrays herself by her carriage (*incessus*). So Cicero says with reference to Clodia, *Cael*. 49, 'si denique ita sese gerat non incessu solum sed ornatu atque comitatu . . . ut non solum meretrix sed etiam proterua meretrix procaxque uideatur'; on the other hand the matron Claudia is described in her epitaph (*C.I.L*. i². 1211) as 'sermone lepido tum autem incessu commodo'. For the importance attached by the Romans to *incessus* as an index of character cf. Sen. *Ep*. 52. 12 'argumentum morum ex minimis quoque licet capere: impudicum et incessus ostendit', 66. 5 (among things to be reckoned as *bona*) 'modestus incessus et compositus et probus uultus et conueniens prudenti uiro gestus'.

   mimice : her laugh is like that of a *mima*, a vulgar comedienne. The *mimus* (the same word is used for the entertainment and the actor in it) was a popular farce originally imported from Magna Graecia and largely consisting of extempore impersonation and gesticulation; it acquired more literary and dramatic form in the hands of Laberius and Publilius in Catullus' own time, but mimicry and buffoonery seem to have remained its characteristic ingredients. Women, who were excluded from 'regular' drama, acted in the mime. (See Beare, *The Roman Stage*, 141 ff.)

9. catuli . . . Gallicani : *Gallicanus* properly refers to the old provinces of Cisalpina and Narbonensis: so the *saltus Gallicanus* of Cic. *Quinct*. 79 is in Narbonensis and the *legiones Gallicanae* of Cic. *Cat*. ii. 5 are those of Cisalpina. 'Gallic' breeds of dogs are spoken of by the writers on hunting (Arrian *Cyneg*. 3. 1, Grattius 155 ff.) and mentioned by Ovid (*Met*. i. 533) and Martial (iii. 47), but there is nothing to connect them with Cisalpina in particular. *Catella Gallicana*, the title of one of Martial's couplets to accompany presents (xiv. 198), probably comes from Catullus.

13. o lutum : for this term of abuse cf. Plaut. *Persa* 406 'o lutum lenonium', Cic. *Pis*. 62 'o tenebrae, o lutum, o sordes'.

14. potes : so the manuscripts, but Catullus may well have written *potest*, a variation on the formula 'aut si quid -ius est', which is one of his favourite turns; cf. 13. 10 n., 22. 13, 23. 13, 82. 2.

   perditius : the comparative occurs elsewhere only in Cicero's letters (*Att*. xi. 18. 2, xiv. 1. 1, *Q.F*. iii. 9. 1).

15. non . . . tamen hoc : what we have been doing is not enough after all (*tamen*).

16. quod si non aliud potest : 'so if nothing else is possible': for the ellipse of *fieri* see on 72. 7. The sense is: 'if we cannot make her give up the tablets, let us at least make her blush'.

17. ferreo : a picturesque alternative for *os durum* (Ter. *Eun.* 806); we use another metal and say 'brazen'. So Cic. *Pis.* 63 'os tuum ferreum'; Suetonius records a witticism by the orator Licinius Crassus on Cn. Domitius Ahenobarbus (*Nero* 2.2) 'non esse mirandum quod aeneam barbam haberet cui os ferreum, cor plumbeum esset'.

  canis : the type of shamelessness as early as Homer (*Il.* viii. 423 κύον ἀδεές, iii. 180 κυνῶπις): cf. Ter. *Eun.* 803 *ain uero canis?* Here *canis* suggests the fourfold alliteration on *r*, the *littera canina* which sounds like a dog's snarl (Lucilius 2 M. '(r littera) inritata canes [archaic nom. sing.] quam homo quam planius dicit', Persius i. 109).

  exprimamus : 'let us wring a blush': Seneca has the same phrase, *Ep.* 11. 7 'ruborem sibi exprimere non possunt'.

21 f. 'But we are making no progress; she isn't worrying. You must change our plan and method, if you can make some progress that way'. For the present indicative in the *si*-clause cf. Plaut. *Men.* 417 'adsentabor quicquid dicet mulieri / si possum hospitium nancisci' ('I shall agree with anything she says if in that way I can get entertainment'), 1048 'ibo intro si possum exorare'; with *possum* the idiom is entirely logical: the possibility is present, though the realization of it is future.

24. pudica et proba : Horace's ironical 'tu pudica tu proba / perambulabis astra sidus aureum' (*Epod.* 17. 40), in a similar ironical palinode, is perhaps a reminiscence of Catullus, but the alliterative phrase was probably conventional: cf. Afranius, fr. 116 R. 'proba et pudica quod sum consulo et parco mihi'.

43

See on 41, which is addressed to the same *puella*: here the shortcomings of this local belle are shown up even more devastatingly than those of the Quintia of poem 86.

2. nec bello pede, &c.: the attributes listed in this ruthless catalogue are those whose opposites—small feet, dark eyes, long fingers—the elegists also admire: Ov. *Am.* iii. 3. 7 'pes erat exiguus: pedis est aptissima forma', Prop. ii. 2. 5 'fulua coma est longaeque manus', ii. 12. 23 'caput et digitos et lumina nigra puellae'.

4. **nec sane . . . lingua :** 'and a tongue, to tell the truth, that is not very refined': the lack of refinement may have been either in her speech or in the things she said. For *sane* cf. 10. 4.

nec . . . nimis : 'not very': so 93. 1 *nil nimium,* 'not very much'. The original use of *nimis* as an intensifying adverb equivalent to *ualde* and the corresponding use of *nimius* are common in comedy: Catullus uses *nimis* so at 56. 4 *nimis iocosa,* 64. 22 *nimis optato* (probably also at 60. 5, 64. 169), *nimius* at 63. 17, 36. This use in positive sentences does not appear after Catullus, but the use with a negative, as here, is found both in informal and in formal prose: cf. Cic. *Fam.* xii. 30. 7 'non nimium probo quod scribis', *de Or.* i. 133 'ea dicis non nimis deesse nobis', Caesar *B.G.* vii. 36. 6 'praesidio . . . non nimis firmo'.

elegante : for the use of the ablative in -*e* as a metrically convenient substitute for the normal form in -*i* cf. 35. 12 *impotente,* 63. 7 *recente,* 68. 99 *infelice;* so Lucretius has *pernice* (ii. 635, but *pernici* v. 559), Virgil *impare* (*Ecl.* 8. 75), Ovid *reduce* (*Her.* 8. 103).

5. **decoctoris . . . Formiani :** see on 41. 4.

6. **ten :** the suppression of unstressed final -*ĕ* early became standard in many words (e.g. *quin, hunc, nec* and *ac* as doublets of *neque* and *atque,* imperatives such as *dic* and *fac,* neuter nominatives such as *lac, animal, exemplar*); in colloquial idiom it is common in forms with the suffix -*ne*: *men, tun, ten, ain* (for *aisne*), *satin* (for *satisne*), *uiden* (for *uidesne,* with consequent shortening of the -*en*: see on 61. 77).

prouincia must be Catullus' own province of Gallia Cisalpina—'the province' to its inhabitants. The title ceased to be applicable in Cisalpina after the extension of Roman citizenship to it in 49 B.C.; it remained applicable in its neighbour Narbonensis, which is 'Provence' to this day. That 'the province' should gossip about Mamurra's *amica* is natural enough; Caesar wintered with his troops in Cisalpina during the Gallic campaigns and Mamurra was no doubt a familiar figure there.

bellam : see on 3. 14.

8. **o saeclum . . . infacetum :** 'what a world! so stupid! so dull!' *saeculum,* originally 'a race of creatures' (the usual meaning in Lucretius: e.g. ii. 995 'saecla ferarum', 503 'aurea . . . pauonum . . . saecla', v. 866 'bucera saecla'), came to have the specialized sense of 'a human generation'; in that temporal sense it acquired quite early a social or

moral implication (like our 'the times') derived from its context, as it is here and in such passages as Plaut. *Trin.* 283
'noui ego hoc saeculum moribus quibus siet', Ter. *Ad.* 304
'hocine saeclum! o scelera!', Cic. *Phil.* ix. 13 'maiorum continentiam diligebat, huius saeculi insolentiam uituperabat',
Cael. 48 'abhorret non modo ab huius saeculi licentia uerum
etiam a maiorum consuetudine', *Cons. ad Liuiam* 45 'tenuisse
animum contra sua saecula rectum'. Hence in later usage
saeculum by itself comes to mean 'the fashion', 'the spirit of
the times': so Sen. *Contr.* ii. 1. 18 'tum paupertas erat saeculi',
Mart. ix. 27. 9 'cum theatris saeculoque rixaris', Tac. *Germ.*
19. 3 'nec corrumpere et corrumpi saeculum uocatur'.

  infacetum : *facetus* (12. 9, 50. 8) and *infacetus* (22. 14, 36.
19), *salsus* (12. 4, 14. 16) and *insulsus* (10. 33, 17. 12, 37. 6),
uenustus (3. 2, 13. 6, 22. 2, 31. 12, 35. 17, 97. 9) and *inuenustus*
(10. 4, 12. 5, 36. 17), *elegans* (13. 10, 39. 8) and *inelegans*
(6. 2), *urbanus* (22. 2, 39. 8) and *rusticus* (34. 19) are the
clichés which, though their nuances must elude us, reflect the
attitudes and values of Catullus' society, a society which puts
a premium on attractiveness (*uenustas*), discrimination (*elegantia*), piquancy (*sal*), metropolitanism (*urbanitas*), and has
only scorn for the dull, the insensitive, the clumsy and the
provincial. (See on 12. 8, 39. 8.) The *facetus* has a sense of
humour, alert to the incongruities of things, and *facetiae* is
distinguished from *dicacitas*, the gift of saying smart things
(Cic. *Or.* 87, 89); the *infacetus* is the 'dreary' person who
takes things seriously.

44

Catullus gets an invitation from Sestius, who writes bad
speeches but gives good dinners: he knows that he is expected
to read Sestius' latest speech (of which the author has perhaps
given him a copy), but he is tempted and takes the risk. The
speech is so 'frigid' that it gave him a cold, he says, and he had
to go to the country, missing the dinner, to nurse himself.

  The piece is merely a vehicle for the pun on *frigus*. *Frigidus*
and *frigere* are (like ψυχρός, ψυχρότης) technical terms of literary
criticism for the bad taste which shows itself in bombast,
affectation, or preciosity (see Arist. *Rhet.* iii. 1–3, with Cope's
notes), and the joke in various forms has a long history—
Aristoph. *Ach.* 140 (a play by Theognis at Athens is enough to
account for the freezing of rivers in Thrace), Machon ap.
Athen. 579E (some plays of Diphilus dropped in wine to cool
it), Caelius ap. Cic. *Fam.* viii. 9. 5 ('Calidius . . . in accusatione
satis frigidus'), Mart. iii. 25 (the rhetor Sabineius will cool the

hottest bath), Plut. *Alex*. 3. 3. Catullus is here at his most
unelaborate: the three *dum*-clauses within six lines, the quasi-
expletive *malus*, the resumptive *sed*, are the informalities of
conversation thrown into metrical form; the old-fashioned
autumant and *recepso* may, like the formal *grates*, be pieces of
mock-solemnity, but Ronconi (*Studi Catulliani*, 203), who
attempts to analyse the language of the poem, underestimates
the factor of metrical convenience.

Sestius is certainly the P. Sestius who is known to us from
Cicero. As quaestor in 63 he had helped Cicero against Catiline
and Cicero defended him in 56 on a charge of *uis*, when as
tribune in 57 he had fallen foul of Clodius, and again four years
later on a charge of *ambitus*; he was one of Cicero's advisers
at Rome during his exile (*Q. Fr*. i. 4. 2) and worked vigorously for his recall (*Att*. iii. 20. 3).Cicero was alive to the faults of
his style. In 51 B.C. (*Fam*. vii. 32. 1) he is indignant at the
news that other people's epigrams, 'even Sestius'' ('omnia
omnium dicta, in his etiam Sestiana'), are being imputed to
himself, though they are patently not up to his standard: in
49 B.C. he regrets that the writing of an important letter from
Pompey to Caesar has been entrusted to Sestius (*Att*. vii. 17. 2
'accusaui mecum ipse Pompeium, qui cum scriptor luculentus
esset, tantas res atque eas, quae in omnium manus uenturae
essent, Sestio nostro scribendas dederit. itaque nihil unquam
legi scriptum σηστιωδέστερον ').

1. **funde** : the jurist Florentinus (*Digest* l. 16. 211) defines the
word: *ager cum aedificio fundus dicitur*; hence *tua uilla* below.

   seu Sabine seu Tiburs : an easy attraction from *seu Sabinus
   (es) seu Tiburs*: with the ellipse of the verb, *seu* is naturally
   felt as a particle and not a conjunction. The attraction
   from nominative into vocative in the predicate of which edd.
   cite examples here (e.g. Tib. i. 7. 53) is a more artificial construction.

2 **ff.** Catullus' country house, like Horace's (Suet. *uit. Hor*.
   p. 298 R. 'uixit plurimum in secessu ruris sui Sabini aut
   Tiburtini'), was beyond Tibur in the direction of the *ager
   Sabinus*, on the fringe of which the old Latin town of Tibur
   lay. The fertility of the district and its proverbial salubrity
   (Hor. *Od*. i. 18. 2 'mite solum Tiburis', ii. 6. 5–20) made
   Tibur and its neighbourhood a resort where many Romans
   of wealth and position had country-houses (for a description
   of one of them see Statius, *Silu*. i. 3). Catullus can take
   advantage of his proximity to Tibur to give himself a
   'fashionable address' but this pretension can be pricked: 'a
   place in the Sabine country' has no aristocratic associations,
   and suggests farming and simple, even primitive, ways of life.

2. **autumant** : 'assert': the verb is not uncommon in early Latin
(Plautus has 30 examples, Pacuuius 6) but had passed out of
regular use by this time: here and in Hor. *Sat.* ii. 3. 45 its
effect seems to be mock-solemnity. For Quintilian (viii. 3. 24)
it is *tragicum* and one of the words to which 'dignitatem dat
antiquitas'. Like some other archaisms it was revived in
post-classical prose; for its later history see A. Ernout in
Latomus, i (1937), 75–79.

4. **quouis . . . pignore . . . contendunt** : 'are ready to maintain
with any stake': Phaedrus has the phrase in a similar antithesis (iv. 21. 3) 'quicquid putabit esse dignum memoria, /
Aesopi dicet; si quid minus adriserit, / a me contendet fictum
quouis pignore': cf. Gell. v. 4. 2 'librarius in quoduis pignus
uocabat si in una uspiam littera delictum esset', Cic. *Fam.*
vii. 32. 2 'ut sacramento [a solemnly deposited stake] con-
tendas mea non esse'.

5. **sed** : resumptive after the parenthesis, as often in Cicero:
see Kühn.–Steg. ii. 2. 76.

6. **fui libenter** : the same colloquial idiom occurs in similar
contexts in Cicero's letters : *Att.* xii. 3. 1 'Tusculanum, ubi
ceteroquin sum libenter', xvi. 6. 1 'Veliae . . . ubi quidem
fui sane libenter apud Talnam nostrum', xvi. 7. 1 'erat uilla
Valeri nostri ut familiariter essem et libenter', xvi. 14. 2 '(in
Tusculano) ero libentius'. Similarly *Att.* xiii. 52. 1 (Caesar
as a guest) 'fuit periucunde', 'he thoroughly enjoyed himself', *pro Rege Deiot.* 19 'cum in conuiuio comiter et iucunde
fuisses'.

   suburbana : it may not be genuine Tibur, but it is not in
the wilds.

7. **malam . . . expuli tussim** : 'I got rid of a nasty cough': cf.
Hor. *Ep.* ii. 2. 137 'expulit elleboro morbum bilemque
meraco'.

8 f. **dedit** : the principal verb is inserted into the middle of the
subordinate clause. The similar involution at 66. 18 'non,
ita me diui, uera gemunt, iuerint' occurs in a highly artificial poem and Catullus had Hellenistic precedent for it (see
note on that line). Such a violent dislocation is more surprising in this informal poem, which otherwise closely follows the
idiom of prose, and the very similar hyperbaton in Horace's
informal writing, *Sat.* ii. 3. 211 'Aiax dum immeritos occidit
desipit agnos' (cf. i. 5. 72 paene macros arsit dum turdos
uersat in igni', ii. 1. 60 'quisquis erit uitae scribam color'), suggests that both Catullus and Horace may have had in mind
an effect which eludes us.

10. Sestianus: as in Cicero's *dicta Sestiana* (*Fam.* vii. 32. 1; see
above), the adjective has no 'generic' meaning but merely
takes the place of a genitive: so *odio Vatiniano* 14. 3. This
use is already found with personal adjectives in early Latin
(Plaut. *Mil.* 1413 *Venerium nepotulum*, Lucil. 606 M. *uim
Volcaniam*; cf. such regular phrases as *flamen Dialis*) and the
substitution of an adjective for a genitive is not uncommon
in classical prose (see Kühn.–Steg. ii. 1. 209–13). Archaic
Greek shows a similar idiom, which the tragedians adopted
and the Hellenistic poets made a mannerism; in classical
Latin verse imitation of Greek practice encourages the extension of what was a native idiom (cf. 61. **223**, 64. 368). See
Wackernagel, *Vorlesungen*, ii. 70 ff., *Kleine Schriften* ii.
1346 ff., Löfstedt, *Syntactica*, i². 107 ff., *Peregr. Aeth.* 76 ff.
R. S. Radford, 'The Suffixes *-anus* and *-inus*', *Studies in
Honor of B. L. Gildersleeve* (Baltimore, 1912), pp. 95 ff., limits
the use unduly: it is true that the possessive adjective is often
used of commercial and legal relations, but that 'the genitive
alone can represent the individual in voluntary personal and
social relations' is clearly disproved.

dum uolo : 'in my desire to dine with S.' Here, and in *dum
appeto* above, *dum* has its temporal meaning—*dum appeto,
dum uolo* are equivalent to *appetenti, uolens*—but a causal
connexion is implicit. This use, in which the subject (or the
logical subject) of the main clause and of the *dum*-clause is
the same, is common in classical prose, both with present and
with perfect in the *dum*-clause (e.g. Cic. *Cael.* 17 'dum illi
placere uultis, ad tempus eius mendacium uestrum accom-
modauistis', *Fin.* ii. 43 'dum in una uirtute sic omnia esse
uoluerunt, uirtutem ipsam . . . sustulerunt', *Off.* ii. 29 'in has
clades incidimus dum metui quam cari esse et diligi malu-
mus'; similarly with *cupio, studeo, uereor*); from it developed
the use of *dum* as a causal conjunction in later Latin.

11. petitorem : probably 'as a candidate for office' as in Hor.
Od. iii. 1. 11 'descendat in campum petitor': Cicero uses only
candidatus in this sense, though he has *competitor*, but
Macrobius iii. 14. 7 quotes *petitor* from a speech of Scipio
Africanus Minor and it is so used in the *de Petitione Consulatus*
ascribed to Quintus Cicero. In that case Sestius' speech was
presumably designed to secure the disqualification of Antius
on the ground of illegal practices; so in 64 B.C. Cicero delivered a speech against his fellow candidates Antonius and
Catiline. The other technical meaning of *petitor*, 'plaintiff'
(in a private suit), is possible but less likely: the words sound
like the exact title of the speech.

Antium : Antius cannot be identified. One C. Antius

Restio appears on coins of 49–45 B.C. and appears to have
been the author of a short-lived sumptuary law mentioned
by Macrobius iii. 17. 13 and Gellius ii. 24. 13.

12. ueneni might by itself refer to the virulence of Sestius'
speech, as in Hor. *Sat.* i. 7. 1 'Rupili pus atque uenenum',
Mart. vii. 72. 13 'atro carmina quae madent ueneno'. But
the combination with *pestilentia* and the context suggest that
it is his 'poisonous' style that is in Catullus' mind: cf. 14. 19
omnia uenena.

13. hic : 'thereupon': cf. 10. 24.
    grauedo is our 'cold'. Celsus describes the all too familiar
symptoms: iv. 5. 2 'nares claudit, uocem obtundit, tussim
siccam mouet . . . haec autem et breuia et, si neglecta sunt,
longa esse consuerunt'.
    frequens and **quassare** are medical terms: cf. Celsus iv.
11. 2 'frequens tussis sanguinem quoque extundit'; Suet.
Aug. 81 '(temptabatur) austrinis tempestatibus grauedine,
quare quassato corpore neque frigora neque aestus tolerabat':
Macrob. vii. 15. 9 'tussim nimis asperam et alias quassationes'.

15. recuraui : in this sense again in Apul. *Met.* vi. 25 'plagas
recurantibus', viii. 18 'corpora laniata recurare'.
    otio et urtica : Celsus so prescribes: iv. 5. 8 'in grauedine
primo die quiescere'; iv. 10. 4 'utilis in omni tussi est . . .
cibus interdum mollis, ut malua et urtica'.

16 f. grates ago : the archaic and formal *grates*, associated with
thanksgiving to the gods, has a humorous solemnity.

17. es ulta : he is now addressing the *uilla*; the transition is
natural enough in a piece as informal as this and Muretus's
ultu', i.e. *ultus*, with the ecthlipsis of final *s* which Catullus
has only once elsewhere (see on 116. 8), is unnecessary.

18 f. nec deprecor . . . quin : 'I offer no plea to prevent . . . .'
    nefaria scripta : on the short syllable lengthened . before
scr- see on 17. 24.

19. recepso : the archaic future in *-so* is in origin the conjunctive of an *s*-aorist; like the corresponding optative form in
-sim it is already obsolescent in Plautus. The *-so*-future,
which emphasized the result of an action, tended to be
equated with the future perfect (as here) and the two are
used as alternatives by Plautus (fr. 74 L. 'peribo si non
fecero; si faxo, uapulabo'). *recepso* is found only here: *capso*
and *occepso* occur in Plautus and *accepso* in Pacuvius. For
other archaic *s*-aorist forms see 66. 18, 91.

20. non mi sed ipsi Sestio : a παρὰ προσδοκίαν of a type common
in comedy.

21. tunc uocat me, cum : 'who invites me only when I have read his nasty book' for the emphatic *tunc* cf. Cic. *de Or.* ii. 260 'aut frigida sunt aut tum salsa cum aliud est exspectatum', Mart. ii. 79. 1 (a reminiscence of this passage) 'inuitas tunc me cum scis, Nasica, uocatum', vii. 67. 11 'fas sibi tunc putat reuerti / cum coloephia sedecim comedit'.

legi : Lachmann's correction is necessary. The earlier editors followed Auantius in reading *legit* for *legi* in l. 12, supposing that Sestius invited only those who had submitted to a recitation of his speech: but (1) the change of subject in *dum volo . . . legit* is doubtful latinity and (2) *recepso* is most naturally taken as implying that Catullus had had the speech in his hands.

45

Beneath the airy lightness of this love-idyll is an unmistakably deliberate symmetry of construction. Two groups of seven lines, the declarations of the lovers, are followed each by the two-line refrain; then a pair of carefully balanced couplets is enclosed between two others. The scheme is $7+2: 7+2: 2+(2+2)+2$. And while the particular effects which Latin poets sought to obtain by alliteration and the principles on which they applied it may elude us, the use of it here as a piece of formal technique is obvious: Septimius' alliteration of six p's is balanced by Acme's five m's and the pattern of vowels in ll. 14–16 is not accidental.

How much the poem and its pattern may owe to some Hellenistic model we cannot guess. The refrain, which in its simple exclamatory form goes back to Greek tragic lyric, appears as a structural element in the Alexandrian bucolic poets, who may have taken it up from some popular verse-forms; Catullus' use of it here may have been suggested by something in Hellenistic lyric or epigram. But while the care for form is Alexandrian, Catullus pursues it in his own Italian way, as the peculiarly Italian use of alliteration and assonance shows. Whatever lies behind it, the poem is not a mere exercise; its characters, whoever they were, are real persons, and the delicacy and gaiety of the piece are Catullus' own.

1. Acmen Septimius : the juxtaposition, as Ellis points out, sets the note of reciprocity which runs through the poem. We cannot identify either of the persons. Septimius—or Septumius, the older form which Catullus may well have used; the change in the spelling of this vowel was occurring in his time (cf. Quint. i. 7. 21)—is a common *gentilicium*; the only Septimius of suitable date of whom we know anything

is the P. Septimius who was Varro's quaestor and to whom
Varro addressed books ii–iv of his *De Lingua Latina*, and he
is not likely to have been Catullus' friend unless Varro held
the praetorship unusually late. The name Acme, not uncommon in inscriptions, points to a Greek freedwoman.

suos amores : cf. 10. 1.

3. perdite : 'desperately': cf. 104. 3 'tam perdite amarem'; an
expression of common speech, as in Ter. *Heaut.* 97 'amare
coepit perdite', *Ph.* 82.

porro, 'on and on' (so probably in 68. 45), of indefinite
future time, as often in early Latin: cf. Cato, fr. 29 'me
sollicitum et exercitum habitum esse atque porro fore',
Afranius 359 R. 'sinunt di et porro passuros scio', Plaut. *Mil.*
1091 'iam ex sermone hoc gubernabunt doctius porro',
Ter. *Hec.* 764 'fac eadem ut sis porro'. Later it more
often indicates immediate succession, but the indefinite use
is occasionally found: e.g. Livy x. 8. 9 'aeque adhuc
prosperum plebeium ac patricium fuit porroque erit', xl. 36. 1
'diuinare posse quid in animo Celtiberi haberent aut porro
habituri essent'.

5. quantum qui pote : the construction is *quantum is amat qui
potest plurimum perire* (i.e. *amare*). The expression of the
thought is no more logical than a lover's protestation ought
to be, but other similar ellipses help to suggest how it arises:
cf. Cic. *Fam.* v. 2. 6 'tam sum amicus rei publicae quam qui
maxime', xiii. 22. 2 'huic commendationi meae tantum tri-
bueris quantum cui tribuisti plurimum', and the common
quantum potest ('as quickly as possible') of comedy.

pote : in early Latin *potis* and its doublet *pote* (in origin
probably a neuter form corresponding to the masc.-fem.
potis) are both used indifferently with personal and with
non-personal subjects: so, for example, Ennius, *Ann.* 174 V.
'quis potis ingentis oras euoluere belli', 403 'nec pote quisquam . . . corpus discerpere ferro', Plaut. *Amph.* 693 'qui
istuc potis est?', *Curc.* 269 'locus non praeberi potis est',
Truc. 317 'ego illum . . . spero immutari pote', Ter. *Heaut.*
321 'neque ferri potis es', *Ph.* 535 'hic si pote fuisset exora-
rier'. In Catullus *pote* has a personal subject here and at
17. 24, 67. 11, a non-personal at 76. 16, 98. 1 (in all these cases
the copula, *est* or *sit*, is omitted); *potis* is personal at 65. 3,
76. 24, 115. 3, non-personal at 72 .7. *potis* goes out of regular
use after Varro (who, like Plautus, uses it with a plural subject, *R.R.* ii. 2. 1 'quid pastores potis sint'), though Virgil
twice revives it (*Aen.* ix. 796, xi. 148) as an archaism. *pote*
occurs not only in informal prose of the Ciceronian period

(e.g. Varro, *R.R.* i. 15, *B. Afr.* 54. 4, Cic. *Att.* xiii. 38. 1, *Brut.* 172 'hospes, non pote minoris' [sc. *uēnire*: an *anicula* is speaking]), but also occasionally in later verse as a metrically convenient substitute for *potest* (e.g. Prop. ii. 1. 46, iii. 7. 10, Pers. i. 56, Mart. ix. 15. 2); it reappears among the archaisms of Fronto and Apuleius. It also survives in *utpote*, a phrase ('as may well be') which has become little more than a particle.

perire : 'love to desperation', *perdite amare*, an emphatic colloquialism like the commoner *deperire* (35. 12, 100. 2).

6 f. solus . . . leoni : Statius cites Semonides, fr. 12 D. οὐκ ἄν τις οὕτω δασκίοις ἐν οὔρεσιν | ἀνὴρ λέοντ' ἔδεισεν οὐδὲ πάρδαλιν | μοῦνος στενυγρῇ συμπεσὼν ἐν ἀτραπῷ.

Libya Indiaque : Latin idiom often prefers *que* or *et* where English normally uses 'or' in cases where either the copulative or the disjunctive may be logically justified, though they represent different points of view. The variation can be most easily seen in numeral expressions (*bis terque*, 'twice and in fact three times', *bis terue* 'twice or for that matter three times') and in 'corrective' phrases (Cic. *Verr.* ii. 3. 11 'magna atque adeo maxima', *ad Q. Fr.* ii. 13. 1 'magna uel potius maxima'); such pairs as Tac. *Ann.* i. 9 'uita eius uarie extollebatur arguebaturue' and *Ann.* i. 25 'diuersis animorum motibus pauebant terrebantque', Pliny, *N.H.* ii. 229 'fons eodem quo Nilus modo ac pariter cum eo decrescit augeturue', and (a few lines later) 'pariter cum aestu maris crescunt minuunturque' show how readily interchangeable the two usages are. The fact that they can be used indifferently in such cases, and in many others in which two ideas can be associated equally well in either way (e.g. 68. 54), leads to (*a*) the extension of *et* (and *que*) to cases in which it is more difficult to explain logically, like the present case, (*b*) the correspondingly unlogical use of *uel* (and *aut*), especially in interrogative clauses, where logic requires a copulative, and (*c*) the combination of the two forms of expression. For other examples of (*a*) cf. Lucr. v. 984 'fugiebant saxea tecta / spumigeri suis aduentu ualidique leonis', Virg. *Georg.* iii. 121 (the charger) 'patriam Epirum referat fortisque Mycenas', *Aen.* x. 708 'aper multos Vesulus quem pinifer annos / defendit multosque palus Laurentia' (V. is in the Alps, L. on the coast of Latium); for (*b*) Virg. *Aen.* vi. 769 'pariter pietate uel armis / egregius', ii. 74 'hortamur fari quo sanguine cretus / quidue ferat', Livy vii. 14. 1 'quaenam haec res sit aut quo acta more percontatur': for (*c*) Cat. 4. 7–9, Lucr. iii. 551 'manus atque oculus naresue seorsum / secreta ab nobis nequeunt sentire', Virg. *Aen.* vi. 608–14 'quibus . . . aut qui

... quique ... quique'. On these uses see Löfstedt, *Synt.*[2] ii. 348, *Peregr. Aeth.* 200.

7. **caesio** : 'green-eyed': so in Hom. *Il.* xx. 172 the lion γλαυκιόων ἰθὺς φέρεται; cf. Plin. *N.H.* viii. 54 '(leonum) omnis uis constat in oculis'. Elsewhere *caesius* is used only of persons (in Cic. *N.D.* i. 83 'caesios oculos Mineruae' translates γλαυκῶπις; in Lucr. iv. 1161 the *caesia puella* is a Pallas in her lover's sight), but Donatus on Ter. *Hec.* 440 ('magnus, rubicundus, crispus, crassus, caesius') explains it as 'felis oculos habens'.

8 f. Clearly Amor answers each lover's protestations in turn with a favouring sign. There can be no question of a transition from an unfavourable attitude to a favourable one or of a previous omen given before the poem opens. The picture is whole and complete and it is a picture of perfect felicity. Clearly, too, 8–9 and 17–18 are identical and are to be construed in the same way; to punctuate in one place *sinistra ut ante, dextra* and in the other *sinistra, ut ante dextra*, breaking the clearly marked coincidence of grammatical colon and metrical unit, is impossible.

What then is the point of *sinistra* and *dextra*? The facts about relevant ancient beliefs are these:

(*a*) For both Greeks and Romans any sneeze might be a favourable sign, especially in love: so Hom. *Od.* xvii. 541, Xen. *Anab.* iii. 2. 9, Theoc. 7. 96, Prop. ii. 3. 24 'candidus argutum sternuit omen Amor', Ov. *Her.* 19. 152 'sternuit [of a sputtering lamp] et nobis prospera signa dedit'. (For a full collection of instances see A. S. Pease in *C.P.* vi [1911], 429–43.)

(*b*) For the Greeks a sneeze on the right was a particularly lucky sign: Plut. *Them.* 13. There is some evidence that a sneeze on the left was unlucky; Plut. *de gen. Socr.* 11, which explains Socrates' δαιμόνιον in terms of sneezes, a sneeze on the right being encouraging, one on the left restraining, cannot be taken seriously (since the δαιμόνιον, as we know from Plato and Xenophon, was always negative), but it points to some such belief, and in Diog. Laert. vi. 48 a sneeze on the left disconcerts a δεισιδαίμων.

(*c*) In Roman divination the left was the lucky side (Cic. *de Div.* ii. 82: a favourable omen might be called *sinistrum* even if it occurred on the right), but the Romans took over the Greek belief which made the right the lucky side and inconsistently combined it with their native tradition: so while *dexter* never means 'unlucky', *laeuus* and *sinister* may imply either good luck (*Aen.* ii. 693 'intonuit laeuum', Phaedr. iii. 18. 12 'laeua omina'; Plaut. *Pseud.* 762 (aui sinistera, auspicio liquido atque ex sententia') or bad (*Aen.* x. 275 'laeuo contristat lumine caelum'; Ov. *Her.* 13. 49 'a nobis omen remouete sinistrum').

The most plausible explanation is that of the early editors that *sinistra ut ante dextra* is equivalent to *primum dextra, deinde sinistra*; Amor, hovering round the lovers (cf. 68. 134), sneezes both on the left and on the right after each lover's protestation, so making his approval unmistakable since (as Servius on *Aen.* ii. 691 observes) two omens are better than one. H. J. Rose makes the point (*Harvard Studies*, xlvii [1936], 1–2) that in the position in which they are depicted what is on Acme's right is on Septimius' left and vice versa and, since she is a Greek and he an Italian, their lucky sides are right and left respectively, so that, whichever side Love stands on, the omen he gives can be construed as favourable to one or other; but in view of the confusion in Latin usage it seems doubtful whether that conceit would have been readily appreciated by Catullus' readers.

9. **sternuit approbationem :** Propertius repeats the internal limiting accusative after *sternuere* with a variation, ii. 3. 24 'candidus argutum sternuit omen Amor'.

10. **at** turns the reader's eye to the other side of the picture.

leuiter reflectens : she is lying with her head on his breast (*in gremio*; like Venus in Ov. *Met.* x. 556 'inque sinu iuuenis posita ceruice reclinis'), and tilts her head back to look at him.

11. **ebrios :** the 'intoxication' of love, as in Anacreon 17 D. μεθύων ἔρωτι which editors compare, is not in point here. Love has gone to the eyes, not to the head: they are *ebrii* because they have drunk love and are swimming, 'natantes et quadam uoluptate suffusi' (Quint. xi. 3. 76).

12. **illo purpureo ore :** 'those rosy lips of hers', may perhaps be a reminiscence of Simonides 44 D. πορφυρέου ἀπὸ στόματος ἱεῖσα φωνὰν παρθένος. In any case *purpureus* probably conveys something more than mere redness both here and in Hor. *Od.* iii. 3. 12 'purpureo bibit ore nectar', though Bentley's comment on the latter passage, 'nihil aliud est purpureo ore quam pulchro et formoso', simplifies overmuch. In poetry, though *purpureus* sometimes clearly connotes a definite colour (as with *pannus* in Hor. *A.P.* 15, *aulaea* in Virg. *Georg.* iii. 25, *pudor* in Ov. *Am.* ii. 5. 34), it often expresses the idea of radiance or sheen without any reference to colour. Swans (Hor. *Od.* iv. 1. 10), snow (*Eleg. in Maec.* 1. 62), salt (Val. Flacc. iii. 422) are none of them red or anything like it, but all may be sparkling; similarly the word expresses the sparkle of the eyes (Val. Flacc. iii. 179), the effulgence of Love's wings (Ov. *R.A.* 701), of Love himself (Ov. *Am.* ii. 1.

38), of spring flowers (*Dirae* 21), of spring (Virg. *Ecl.* 9. 40), of youth (Virg. *Aen.* i. 591). [For an attempt to classify the uses of the word see J. André, *Les termes de couleur dans la langue latine*, 93 ff.] Apuleius repeats Catullus' phrase (*Apol.* 9) 'proque rosis [redde] oris sauia purpurei'.

illo: far from being, as Kroll suggests, merely articular, the pronoun enhances the vividness of the picture, directing the reader's eye (see on 64. 288). Observe the effect of the series of broad vowels 'illo *purpureo* ore suauiata', contrasting with the *e*'s and *i*'s of the next line.

13. mea uita : so 109. 1 (to Lesbia); Cic. *Fam.* xiv. 2. 3, 4. 1 (to Terentia).

Septimille : an endearing familiar diminutive, like *Atticilla, Chrestilla, Maronilla* in Martial.

13 ff. sic . . . ut : in this common formula of protestation the wish or prayer introduced by *sic* (or *ita*) is the guarantee of the statement introduced by *ut* : so, e.g., Ov. *Met.* viii. 866 'sic has deus aequoris artes / adiuuet ut nemo iamdudum litore in isto / constitit', Prop. i. 18. 11 'sic mihi te referas leuis ut non altera nostro / limine formosos intulit ulla pedes', Cic. *Att.* v. 15. 2 'ita uiuam ut maximos sumptus facio'. English normally reverses the construction: 'as I hope we may serve to the end the one master (i.e. Amor) whom we now own (*huic*), the passion that burns in me is far fiercer than yours'. For a similar use of *sic* with a following imperative see on 17. 5.

15. maior acriorque : 'fiercer than yours', not 'than it was before': the lovers protest against each other, like the pair in Sen. *Contr.* ii. 2. 2 'assiduae contentiones erant: "ego magis amo": "immo ego": "sine te uiuere non possum": "immo ego sine te".'

16. in medullis : cf. 35. 15 'ignes interiorem edunt medullam', 64. 93 'imis exarsit tota medullis', 66. 23 'exedit cura medullas'; the lodging of emotion in the innermost part of the bodily frame, *ossa* and *medullae*, is a commonplace. It is unnecessary to explain *mollibus* as 'melting under the heat of passion'. The *medullae* are *molles* here, as in Virg. *Aen.* iv. 66 'est mollis flamma medullas', because they are a woman's: so they are *tenerae* in Ov. *Am.* iii. 10. 27 'tenerae flammam rapuere medullae'.

20. mutuis animis : in *Fam.* v. 2. 3 Cicero coldly analyses the expression, which his correspondent (Q. Metellus Celer, Clodia's husband) had used in writing to him: 'quod ita scribis pro mutuo inter nos animo, quid tu existimes esse in amicitia mutuum nescio; equidem hoc arbitror, cum par uoluntas accipitur et redditur'.

amant amantur : for the idiom cf. Tac. *Ann.* vi. 35 'ut conserta acie corporibus et pulsu armorum pellerent pellerentur'. Phaedrus has the same asyndeton (ii. 2. 2 *ament amentur*) but without the reciprocal sense.

21. **misellus :** of love-sickness again at 35. 14.

22. **Syrias Britanniasque :** 'any Syria or Britain': names of romantic adventure, the fabulous East and the mysterious end of the world. The choice of them suggests a date in 55 B.C. when the expedition of Crassus to the East and that of Caesar to Britain were in the air and no doubt in the thoughts of enterprising young men who hoped to make their fortunes. The 'generalizing' plural is less common with names of places than with names of persons; but cf. Cic. *Att.* viii. 16. 2 'nescio quas eius Lucerias horrent', *Fam.* vii. 11. 2 'una mehercule collocutio nostra pluris erit quam omnes Samarobriuae', Prop. ii. 16. 10 'alias nauiget Illyrias'.

23. **in :** the use of *in* with a personal object ('in relation to', 'over') is especially common with reference to love: see on 64. 98 *in flauo hospite suspirantem*.

24. **facit delicias :** 'takes her pleasure' (cf. 74. 2); see on 50. 3. The more usual meaning of the phrase is 'trifle, tease' (e.g. Plaut. *Men.* 381, *Poen.* 280).

26. **auspicatiorem :** i.e. 'ab auspiciis melioribus profectam': the rare comparative appears first here and again in Pliny, *N.H.* xiii. 118.

46

These gay lines, written on leaving Bithynia, probably in the spring of 56 B.C. (see Introduction, p. xii), have their complement in poem 31, in which Catullus greets Sirmio on his return. Here, with the prospect of the homeward journey before him, he is at his most exuberant: witness the repeated *iam*, the excited self-address, the emotional leave-taking.

1. **egelidos :** 'from which the chill has passed off': so Ov. *Am.* ii. 11. 10 'et gelidum Borean egelidumque Notum', Colum. x. 282 'nunc uer egelidum, nunc est mollissimus annus': in technical prose, Celsus iv. 18. 3 'aqua neque ea ipsa frigida sed potius egelida danda est', iv. 25. 2 'potio . . . egelida et frigidae propior', Pliny, *N.H.* xxxi. 4 '(aquae) alibi frigidae, alibi calidae, . . . alibi tepidae egelidaeque'. The other sense of 'intensely cold' appears first in Virgil, *Aen.* viii. 610 'in ualle reducta / ut procul egelido (so Seruius, who explains the word) secretum flumine uidit' (the river is *gelidum* in 597) and later in Manilius v. 131 'egelido polo'. Ausonius has

both uses—280. 97 (Peiper) 'egelidae ut tepeant hiemes', 193. 85 'egelido ab Istro'.

tepores : for the concrete use of the plural, 'warm weather', cf. Livy ii. 5. 3 'mediis caloribus', v. 6. 4 'ut . . . non aestus, non frigora pati possint', Cic. *Att.* x. 18. 1 'mirificae tranquillitates'. By a common Latin idiom the idea expressed by the noun is reinforced by an adjective of the same or similar meaning: *egelidi tepores* is like *muta silentia* (Ov. *Met.* vii. 184), *mora tarda* (63. 19), *laeta gaudia* (64. 236), *extrema fine* (64. 217), *primum initium* (Lucr. i. 383).

2. caeli . . . aequinoctialis : the gales attending the spring equinox, which kept Cicero from leaving Italy in May, 49 B.C.: *Att.* x. 17. 3 'nunc quidem aequinoctium nos moratur quod ualde perturbatum erat'.

3. Zephyri : the west winds of spring are a commonplace: Hor. *Od.* i. 4. 1 'soluitur acris hiems grata uice ueris et Fauoni', Pliny, *N.H.* ii. 122 '(ueris) in principio Fauonii hibernum molliunt caelum', xviii. 337 'Fauonius . . . uer incohat aperitque terras tenui frigore saluber'.

aureis : the old spelling, given here by *V*, may well be what Catullus always wrote; in 64. 164 *aures* in *V* points to the same form. See on 17. 3.

4. Phrygii . . . campi : the lowlands of Western Bithynia (the *Bithyni campi* of 31. 5) in which Nicaea lay. While the name Phrygia is generally used of Greater Phrygia, bordering Bithynia on the south and extending over central Asia Minor, it covers also Lesser Phrygia (Φρυγία ἡ μικρά) which stretched from the western parts of Bithynia along the coast as far as the Troad.

5. Nicaea : one of the two chief cities of Bithynia, founded by Antigonus on the site of an earlier Greek colony. It lay on an inland plain on lake Ascania: *uber* and *aestuosae* are both confirmed by Strabo's description (xii. 565) περίκειται κύκλῳ πεδίον μέγα καὶ σφόδρα εὔδαιμον, οὐ πάνυ δὲ ὑγιεινὸν τοῦ θέρους. Its more northerly rival Nicomedia was the seat of the governor and of provincial administration.

6. claras Asiae . . . urbes : *clarus* suggests the sightseeing tour, a favourite word in the Baedeker-style of Mela and Pliny: so Hor. *Od.* i. 7. 1 'laudabunt alii claram Rhodon aut Mitylenen / aut Epheson', Ov. *Trist.* i. 2. 77 'nec peto quas quondam petii studiosus Athenas, / oppida non Asiae, non loca uisa prius, / non ut Alexandri claram delatus ad urbem / delicias uideam, Nile iocose, tuas.'

7. praetrepidans : 'a-flutter with anticipation' (cf. 64. 145 *praegestit*): in composition with verbs *prae-* has its local or temporal sense, though with adjectives it may be merely intensive (as it is in *praetrepidus*). The verb, perhaps a coinage of Catullus, appears again after five centuries in Paulinus of Périgueux.

uagari : see on 64. 271.

9. o is not the normal accompaniment of a vocative, as ὦ is in classical Greek usage, but both in colloquial and in literary Latin has an emotional content, and marks sentimental (as here), pathetic, or impassioned address. It is significant that, as K. F. Smith (on Tib. i. 4. 9) points out, *o* is never used with a vocative by the unimpassioned Tibullus, often by the passionate Propertius.

comitum ... coetus : his fellow members of the propraetor's *cohors* or unofficial entourage (see on 10. 10): Catullus is addressing them as his own *comites*, but they were sometimes spoken of in non-technical language as the governor's *comites* (28. 1 *Pisonis comites*: hence the later title of the *comites Augusti*, who developed into an elaborate official hierarchy).

10. longe : with *profectos*: *proficisci* is to make a journey with an objective and does not refer exclusively to the start of a journey; so it can be used with an accusative of extent, Cic. *Acad.* ii. 100 'si ... ex hoc loco proficiscatur Puteolos stadia triginta'. For the use of *longe* cf. Cic. *Verr.* ii. 2. 65 'longe mihi obuiam processerunt'. The use of the preposition with *domo* (as with names of towns) after *longe* is normal.

11. diuersae uarie : *diuersus* and *uarius*, which are used together elsewhere (e.g. Cic. *Leg. Man.* 28, *de Or.* i. 262, iii. 61), are not here synonyms. *Diuersus* emphasizes differences between two or more things, *uarius* differences within a whole; the roads go in all directions and each is diversified.

47

The Piso of this poem has already appeared, with Veranius and Fabullus, in 28, which shows that they were serving together in his entourage as Catullus served in that of Memmius in Bithynia, and about the same time. The coincidence favours the identification (see on 9) with L. Calpurnius Piso Caesoninus, the father of Caesar's wife Calpurnia, who went to Macedonia as proconsul in 57 B.C. and of whose proceedings in that province Cicero gives a highly coloured account in the scathing and often scurrilous attack which he delivered against him after his recall in 55. His connexion with Caesar would not have commended him to Catullus.

1. **Porcius** and **Socration** are unknown. Porcius can hardly
be the Cato addressed in 56, who is evidently a member
of Catullus' circle. Suggested identifications—e.g. with a
Porcius who was employed in Gaul by Fonteius in 76–
73 B.C. (Statius) or with M. Porcius Cato, tribune in 56 B.C.
(Kroll)—have nothing to support them. As for Socration,
the pairing with Porcius perhaps suggests that the name is
genuine and not a nickname. The appearance of a Greek is not
unexpected: Cicero makes much play with Piso's fondness
for Greek society (*Pis.* 22 'iacebat in suorum Graecorum
fetore atque uino'; 67 (at one of P.'s dinner-parties) 'Graeci
stipati quini in lectulis, saepe plures, ipse solus'). The name
Σωκρατίων is rare, but Galen mentions a physician so called
(xii. 835 K.) and in Latin it appears in Dacia on two
2nd-century A.D. inscriptions (*C.I.L.* iii, p. 948). Friedrich
suggested that Σωκράτιον, the 'imitation Socrates', represents
Philodemus, the Epicurean philosopher-poet of Gadara who
was an intimate of Piso (see Allen and De Lacy, 'The Patrons
of Philodemus', *C.P.* xxxiv [1939], 59–65). The fact that
Cicero, in the course of his invective against Piso and his
Epicureanism, speaks of Philodemus with some respect (*Pis.*
68–70 'homo, uere ut dicam, humanus . . . facilis et ualde
uenustus . . . non philosophia solum sed etiam ceteris studiis
. . . perpolitus'), and in *Fin.* ii. 119, writing more soberly,
calls him a *familiaris* of his own, does not in itself make the
identification impossible, especially as we do not know how
seriously Catullus' abuse is to be taken: association with Piso
and the profession of poverty (Philodemus seems to have
been a genuine practising Epicurean) might well be all that
lay behind it. But our evidence for personal relations in the
society of Catullus is so fragmentary and so tendentious that
such an identification is precarious.

duae, as Ellis points out, is not otiose but emphasizes the
confederacy of the pair.

sinistrae : they are not the governor's 'hands' only (Cic.
Verr. ii. 2. 27 'comites illi tui delecti manus erant tuae', Tac.
Agr. 15. 2) and they are not his 'right hands', as Maecenas is
Caesar's (*Eleg. in Maec.* i. 13 'tu Caesaris almi dextera'), or
as young Quintus Cicero is Antony's (Cic. *Att.* xiv. 20. 5
'Antoni dextella'). They do his thieving for him, the left
hand's work: so Plaut. *Pers.* 226 'ubi illa altera est furtifica
laeua?', Ov. *Met.* xiii. 111 'natae ad furta sinistrae'. Cf. 12. 1.

2. **scabies famesque mundi** is most naturally taken to mean
'itching greed whose object is the *mundus*'. The phrase seems
to be formed on the analogy of such abusive phrases, in which
an abstract noun followed by an objective genitive is applied

to a person, as Plaut. *Pseud.* 364 'permities adulescentum',
Ter. *Eun.* 79 'nostri fundi calamitas', Cic. *Rab. Perd.* 2
'pestem et perniciem ciuitatis', Hor. *Ep.* i. 15. 31 'pernicies et
tempestas barathrumque macelli'; for *scabies* cf. Hor. *Ep.* i.
12. 14 'tantam scabiem et contagia lucri', Mart. v. 60. 11 'nos
hac a scabie (sc. detrectandi) tenemus ungues'.

Down to the time of Catullus *mundus* refers either to the
universe as a whole or in particular to the heavens (see
Bücheler, *Kl. Schriften,* i. 628 ff.), and Catullus himself
twice uses the word elsewhere, both times of the firmament—
64, 206 'concussit micantia sidera mundus', 66. 1 'omnia qui
magni dispexit lumina mundi'. It is first found in reference
to the human world in Horace (*Sat.* i. 3. 112 'tempora si
fastosque uelis euoluere mundi') and Propertius (iv. 6. 19
'huc mundi coiere manus', 37 'mundi seruator'), both of
whom use it also in its earlier sense. Here the word cannot
bear the earlier sense—the exaggeration would be too extravagant to have any point. If the text is sound, one must
assume that the word was already current, colloquially perhaps, in the later sense. None of the suggested emendations is
convincing. There is nothing to connect any known owners
of the proper name Mindius or Mundus (Statius) or Munius
(Ellis) with this context. *nummi* (Baehrens) gives good sense
(cf. Juv. 14. 139 'crescit amor nummi') but the corruption is
unlikely. Bücheler's *mundae* is a little more plausible as an
example of the colloquial idiom found in Petr. 41 'mundum
frigus habuimus' (surprisingly like the colloquial Eng. 'tidy')
than (what he himself preferred) as an oxymoron like Mart.
iii. 58. 45 (of an elegant but poor estate) 'famem mundam',
'genteel starvation': but Catullus' point is just that Porcius
and Socration are not starving, or likely to starve.

4. **Priapus** : i.e. *homo libidinosus*; Piso, whose *libidines* are
faithfully dealt with by Cicero. (For examples of similar
uses of proper names see van Wageningen in *Mnem.* xl
[1912], 153 ff.)

5. **uos** : 'You have grand, expensive, banquets at all hours, do
you, while my friends are angling for invitations at the
street-corner?' The point lies in the contrast between the
two notions; English idiom makes it by subordinating one
to the other, Latin and Greek by setting them side by side,
Latin in asyndeton, Greek with μὲν . . . δέ.

lauta sumptuose : here at least they were unlike their
patron as Cicero chooses to represent him: *Pis.* 67 'nihil
apud hunc lautum, nihil elegans, nihil exquisitum—laudabo
inimicum—ne magno opere quidem quicquam praeter libidines sumptuosum'.

6. **de die** : 'in the day-time', not 'in broad daylight': dining in
daylight was in itself no more reprehensible then than it is
now. The regular dinner-time was not before the ninth
hour, after the working day was finished: to dine earlier was
a sign of high living; *conuiuia tempestiua* (Cic. *Att.* ix. 1. 3) are
'smart' parties. So Ter. *Ad.* 965 'apparare de die conuiuium',
Livy xxiii. 8 'epulari coeperunt de die'. *de die* implies taking
time off the normal day, as *de nocte* taking time off the normal
night, Hor. *Ep.* i. 2. 32 'ut iugulent hominem surgunt de
nocte latrones', Cic. *Mur.* 22 'uigilas tu de nocte ut tuis con-
sultoribus respondeas'. Sometimes the phrases are strengthened as in Hor. *Sat.* ii. 8. 3 'de medio potare die', Caesar,
B.G. vii. 45. 1 'mittit complures equitum turmas eo de media
nocte'. Similarly Cic. *Q.F.* ii. 1. 3, 'fac ut considerate dili-
genterque nauiges de mense Decembri', 'before December
is over'.

7. **quaerunt . . . uocationes** : 'angle for invitations', like the
parasites of Plautus or Alciphron. *uocare* in this sense is
regular (so 44. 21): *uocatio* is not elsewhere so used but the
concrete use of nouns in -*tio* (e.g. *cogitatio, ambulatio, uenatio*)
is well established by Catullus' time. Under the Empire
uocator is a slave whose business is to issue invitations (Sen.
de Ira iii. 37. 4, Pliny, *N.H.* xxxv. 89, Mart. vii. 86. 11,
Suet. *Cal.* 39).

49

The occasion of this address to Cicero has been the subject of
much fruitless speculation. Schwabe, accepting the identification of Catullus' Lesbia with the famous Clodia and of his
Caelius with M. Caelius Rufus (see pp. xv–xvi), took the poem
to be an acknowledgement of Cicero's services in defending
Caelius Rufus in 56 B.C. and exposing Clodia, who had engineered
the charge against him: Baehrens refined on this idea with the
suggestion that Catullus' particular cause for gratitude was that
his own name had been kept out of the proceedings. It seems
poor psychology to suppose that Catullus would have gone out of
his way to thank Cicero for defending his rival or that, though
he could abuse Lesbia's morals himself, as he had a right to do
(even in poem 11 she is still *mea puella*), he would have thanked
an advocate for vilifying her professionally. Westphal found
an earlier occasion about 62 B.C., supposing that Cicero, who
was visiting Clodia at that time (Plut. *Cic.* 29, Cic. *Fam.* v. 2. 6),
during the absence of her husband Metellus Celer in Gaul, had
introduced Catullus to her circle. Kroll suggests that Catullus

may be acknowledging a copy of one of Cicero's speeches, perhaps the *In Vatinium* of 56 B.C.

These theories, some wilder than others, are only guess-work, and guesses can be multiplied. Cicero and Catullus were moving in the same society and they had friends in common (Cornelius Nepos, for example, was intimate with both), but nothing whatever is known of the relations between them. In default of this knowledge, it is useless to build hypotheses.

Irony can be read into the poem, and some have taken it so. It has been suggested that the formality of the address is malicious, that Catullus means to call Cicero *optimus* just as little as he means to call himself *pessimus* and that *optimus omnium patronus* itself may contain a double entendre ('best of all advocates' and 'best advocate for all and sundry'), that the critic who spoke slightingly of the νεώτεροι could not be genuinely admired by one of them. Thus B. Schmidt (*Rh. Mus.* lxix. 273), following Wölfflin, takes the poem to be an ironical rejoinder to a disparagement of Catullus' poetry by Cicero, who in 54 by his successful defence of Vatinius (whom he had attacked two years before) against a prosecution by Catullus' friend Calvus had, he suggests, both offended Catullus and laid himself open to the charge of indiscriminate advocacy. To each of these points there is a reply: a formal address from a young poet to a distinguished public figure may be not inappropriate; even if *pessimus omnium* is mock modesty, it does not follow that *optimus omnium* is mock praise, and the use of the phrase *omnium patronus* of Cicero in a letter (*Fam.* vi. 7. 4) by Caecina, who means no disparagement by it, is a mere coincidence; and, though Cicero's own taste in poetry was for the old tradition which he admired in Ennius and himself continued and he was no doubt out of sympathy with the literary standards of the new poets, there is nothing to suggest any personal animosity, and both his references to the new school (*Tusc.* iii. 45, *Att.* vii. 2) were made some time after Catullus' death. The poem may be meant to be taken at face value, as a genuine expression of admiration and gratitude. If there is irony in it, it lies, as Havelock (*The Lyric Genius of Catullus*, p. 110) suggests, in the 'deprecating humour' with which Catullus looks not only at himself but at other people also: without being sarcastic, Catullus may have his tongue in his cheek.

1. **Romuli nepotum**: a solemn quasi-heroic phrase: so 58. 5 *magnanimi Remi nepotes*, in an ironical context. Pascal sees a sarcastic reference to Cicero's provincial origin: Cicero was no *Romuli nepos*, but, as Sallust makes Catiline say of him (31. 7), *inquilinus ciuis*. But the sarcasm would have the less point since Cicero himself, far from concealing his Italian

birth, made capital out of it, and it would come ill from one whose origin was even more provincial.

2 f. quot sunt . . . annis : the same turn, with slight variations, in 21. 2–3 and 24. 2–3; the formula is used by Plautus with mock-solemn extravagance (*Persa* 777 'qui sunt qui erunt quique fuerunt quique futuri sunt posthac', *Bacch.* 1087) and by Cicero (*post Red. ad Quir.* 16 'Cn. Pompeius uir omnium qui sunt fuerunt erunt uirtute sapientia gloria princeps', *Fam.* xi. 21. 1 'nequissimo omnium qui sunt qui fuerunt qui futuri sunt').

2. Marce Tulli : the formal address by *praenomen* and *nomen* does not belong to common usage. It was the ceremonial style of address in the Senate (Cic. *Att.* vii. 3. 5 'quid fiet cum erit dictum "dic, M. Tulli"?', vii. 7. 7), a survival from the time when the *cognomen* was not officially used (it seems to have come into use in official documents in the Sullan period): similarly Cicero uses it in the solemn words to himself put into the mouth of the country (*Cat.* i. 27 'si omnis res publica sic loquatur "M. Tulli, quid agis?"') or his client (*Mil.* 94 'ubi denique tua illa, M. Tulli, quae plurimis fuit auxilio uox et defensio?'), and Pliny opens his eloquent apostrophe to Cicero, 'facundiae Latiarumque litterarum parens' (*N.H.* vii. 116), with the question 'sed quo te, M. Tulli, piaculo taceam?'

7. quanto tu optimus omnium patronus : *patronus* (*Or*) is required to balance *poeta*. *patronum* (*GR*), which Ellis accepts (as gen. plur.), is due to accidental assimilation and spoils the point of the poem; *R*'s *omniums* presumably arose from the misinsertion of a suprascript *s* added to correct *patronum*.

50

A glimpse of the *novi poetae* at play; Catullus has spent an evening in gay improvisation with the lively little Calvus (see on 14 and 53), longs for another meeting, and demands it with characteristic extravagance. There is artifice in the form, of course. The lines are 'To Calvus', but Calvus did not need to be told what he had been doing the night before; Catullus is writing for other readers.

1. hesterno . . . die : the periphrasis for *heri* is probably not so 'formal' (Ellis) as it sounds to us; it appears in the very informal conversation of Petronius' characters (131. 2, 139. 5).

    otiosi : 'having nothing to do'; cf. 10. 2.

2. lusimus : 'we amused ourselves': so *ludebat* below. From this way of speaking comes the regular, and almost technical, use of *ludere* and *lusus* for the writing of the lighter forms of verse: cf. 68. 17 'multa satis lusi', Virg. *Ecl.* 6. 1, *Georg.* iv. 565 (of pastoral), Pliny, *Ep.* vii. 9. 9. See Wagenvoort, *Studies in Roman Literature*, pp. 30 ff., who points out that the term is relative; *lusus* may refer to trifling verse as opposed to serious poetry, to 'slight' poetry as opposed to epic and tragedy, or even to any poetry as opposed to active life.

in meis tabellis : a pair (or set: Martial speaks of sets of three and five leaves, xiv. 6. 1, 4. 2) of waxed wooden tablets, with a raised rim to prevent rubbing, hinged together at one side, which Catullus carried with him as a notebook, the *pugillaria* of 42. 5 (so called because they could be held in the closed hand) and the *codicilli* of 42. 11. (See C. H. Roberts in *Proc. of the Brit. Acad.* xl, p. 170.) Editors have made much of the fact that Calvus' tablets are not mentioned: but even if the meeting was (as one would guess from the poem) in Calvus' house, why should Catullus' notebook not have been passed to and fro between the two partners in the game as ideas occurred to them?

3. **conuenerat esse delicatos :** 'we had agreed to be naughty'. The basic notion of *deliciae* seems to have been 'allurement' and its simplest use is perhaps to be seen in the meaning 'pet', 'darling' (cf. 2. 1 'deliciae meae puellae' and phrases there quoted). The relation between *deliciae* and *delicatus*, 'pampered' (e.g. Plaut. *Men.* 119 'nimium ego te habui delicatam', 'I have spoiled you', Sen. *Ep.* 55. 9 'praesentia nos delicatos facit': see on 17. 15) is obscure and it may well be that the words have entirely different origins; in any case, whether because of a real connexion or because of a fortuitous similarity, *delicatus* was treated as the adjective corresponding to the noun *deliciae*. Between them the words come to cover the whole range of uninhibited behaviour from wilfulness (Varro, *L.L.* ix. 10 'si quis puerorum per delicias pedes male ponere . . . coeperit'), caprice (Cic. *Fin.* i. 5 'fastidii delicatissimi'), egoism (Sen. *Ep.* 104. 3 'qui perseuerabit mori, delicatus est'), airs (Cic. *Att.* i. 17. 9 ecce aliae deliciae equitum uix ferendae'), fads and affectations (Cic. *Or.* 39 'Herodotus Thucydidesque longissime a talibus deliciis . . . afuerunt', Quint. i. 11. 6 'illas circa s litteram delicias'), dandyism (Quint. ix. 4. 113 'equorum cursum delicati minutis passibus frangunt'), to irresponsible pleasure-seeking, frivolity, dissipation, and sensuality (Cic. *Am.* 52 'homines deliciis diffluentes', Prop. ii. 15. 2 'lectule deliciis facte beate meis'). Cicero uses the words as a moralist castigating the moral irresponsibility of the bohemian society of his day

('libidinosa et delicata iuuentus', *Att.* i. 19. 8); Catullus and Calvus speak the language of the society he is castigating. In *Cael.* 44 Cicero quotes the word *deliciae* with obvious distaste as a fashionable euphemism for the amours of Clodia's set—'amores et deliciae quae uocantur'; for Catullus there is nothing to be ashamed of in *deliciae*—in poem 45 his Acme 'in Septimio delicias facit'. So with *delicatus*: Cicero makes capital of *delicatissimi uersus* written in Piso's Epicurean circle which he cannot quote (*Pis.* 70); for Catullus and Calvus *delicati uersus* are something of which they make no secret—irresponsible naughtiness is life to them.

5. illoc : the deictic suffix *-c(e)*, which survives in classical usage only in the declension of *hic* and in certain demonstrative forms used as adverbs (*illuc, illinc, illic,* &c.) is in earlier Latin attached to any demonstrative form.

6. reddens mutua : 'giving and taking': cf. Ov. *Met.* viii. 717 'mutua . . . reddebant dicta'.

    per iocum atque uinum, 'over our fun and our wine': cf. 12. 2 'in ioco atque uino'.

7. atque : 'and then', 'and so', continuing a rapid, vivid narrative, as often in comedy.

    lepore . . . facetiisque : 'brilliance and humour': the same combination again in 12. 8–9. On *facetiae* see note on 12. 8.

8. incensus : there is no suggestion in *incensus* or in *dolor* (17) that Catullus was out of temper or angry. The words are those which represent a lover's emotions—desire and heartache (the *ardor* and *dolor* of 2. 7–8); extravagantly, no doubt, but not insincerely, Catullus finds in these an analogy to his own feelings for the object of his admiration.

11. toto . . . lecto : cf. Prop. ii. 22b. 47 'quanta illum toto uersant suspiria lecto', i. 14. 21 '(Venus non timet) miserum toto iuuenem uersare cubili', Juv. 13. 218 'toto uersata toro iam membra quiescunt'.

    indomitus : 'uncontrollable': cf. 64. 54 'indomitos furores'; Catullus slightly changes the phrase to avoid an awkward succession of ablatives. *furor* is a strong word (it is the technical term for mental derangement): Catullus is having a 'nervous breakdown'.

13. simul essem : 'be with you', a colloquial phrase: cf. 21. 5 'simul es', Hor. *Ep.* i. 10. 50 'excepto quod non simul esses cetera laetus', Cic. *Fam.* ix. 1. 2 'dum simul simus'.

14. labore : 'my suffering': for *labor* used of mental distress cf. Plaut. *Curc.* 219 'ualetudo decrescit, accrescit labor', *Pseud.* 695 'scis amorem, scis laborem, scis egestatem meam'. So 38. 2 *laboriose*.

15. **iacebant**: the imperfect after *postquam*, when the verb indicates not an event but a state of things, is uncommon but regular: e.g. Cic. *Quinct.* 70 'postquam qui tibi erant amici non poterant uincere, ut amici tibi essent qui uincebant effecisti'; *Att.* iii. 19. 1 'postea quam omnis actio huius anni confecta nobis uidebatur, in Asiam ire nolui'; Caes. *B.C.* iii. 60. 5.

    semimortua: the adjective occurs first here and not again till Apuleius.

16. **iucunde**: so 14. 2 'iucundissime Calue': the *iucundus* is one whose company gives pleasure: cf. Hor. *Sat.* i. 3. 93 'ob hanc rem . . . minus hoc iucundus amicus / sit mihi', i. 5. 44 'nil ego contulerim iucundo sanus amico'.

18. **cauĕ**: cf. 61. 145. For the 'iambic shortening' see on 10. 27; the -*ĕ* is regular in comedy and frequent in Horace and the elegiac poets.

    preces: 'my petition' continues the exaggeration of the earlier lines.

19. **despuas**: only here in this sense, but *respuo* is often so used.

    ocelle: 'apple of my eye': the familiar endearment is common in comedy. Cf. 3. 5 and 31. 2.

20. **reposcat**: 'claims retribution' for the pride which refuses a suppliant.

    a te: see on 5. 5.

21. **est uemens dea**: perhaps suggested by the line of Antimachus quoted by Strabo xii. 588 ἔστι δέ τις Νέμεσις μεγάλη θεός. The formal second imperative *caueto* enhances the effect of mock solemnity.

51

The original of this poem is an ode of Sappho of which four strophes have been preserved in quotation by the author of the treatise περὶ ὕψους (c. 10): for the Greek text see p. 407. Sappho describes, with extraordinary intensity and objectivity, her own physical reactions at the sight of a girl whom she loves talking with a man—whether her husband, as Wilamowitz thought (*Sappho und Simonides*, pp. 58, 75), or, as D. L. Page argues (*Sappho and Alcaeus*, pp. 26 ff.), some other. Following the Greek closely, with a few slight expansions and omissions, Catullus turns it to describe the sensations which the presence of his Lesbia excites in him. The particular κῆνος ὤνηρ of Sappho is replaced by a general *ille*, and Catullus is not contrasting himself with someone more fortunate but finding expression for his own rapture. Clearly the poem belongs to the early days when his Lesbia, with her beauty, her gifts, her emancipation, had carried him away. With the *doctrina*, the sensitiveness to a literary past, which colours all his thought, he makes words written five centuries before in Lesbos the channel of his own emotions and gives the object of his adoration a name which is charged with association and which places her, and his passion, in the tradition of the poetry of love.

The fourth strophe brings a sudden and violent change of thought. It is an abrupt moralizing soliloquy, corresponding to nothing in Sappho's poem and completely different in tone from what precedes it. Attempts to relate it to the rest of the poem are unplausible special pleading: Friedrich's suggestion that the strophe was added long after the rest was written, though incredible, is perhaps more sensible than Kroll's idea that by this addition Catullus contrived to avoid offering Lesbia a mere translation. The three strophes which he has closely translated were not the whole of Sappho's poem; we possess a fourth, and it was not the last. It is possible that he translated no more; it is hardly conceivable that to his version of so famous a poem, in which he had made Sappho's words his own, he should have appended a self-admonitory quatrain which threw cold water on his passion with the virtuous opening 'Your trouble, Catullus, is not having anything to do'. It is far more easy to believe that some accident, such as has happened elsewhere in the text of Catullus, and has left the fragments 2*b* and 14*b* attached to poems to which they do not belong, has at this point removed, along with the end of the version of Sappho (if he did translate more), the beginning of an original poem.

[For discussion of Sappho's poem and the relation of Catullus' to it see A. Goldbacher, *W.S.* xxix (1907), 110 ff.; N. Vulič, *W.S.* xxxii (1910), 316 ff.; W. Kranz, *Hermes* lxv (1930), 236 f.; B. Snell, *Hermes* lxvi (1931), 71 ff.; O. Immisch, *Sitz. Akad. Heidelb.*, 1933–4, 10; C. M. Bowra, *Greek Lyric Poetry*[2], 185 ff.; F. Tietze, *Rh. Mus.* lxxxviii (1939), 346 ff., E. Bickel, *Rh. Mus.* lxxxix (1940), 194 ff.; R. Lattimore, *C.P.* xxxix (1944), 184 ff.]

1. Ille mi : the 'effective antithesis' which Snell sees in these words is an illusion: the attachment of an unemphatic pronoun as enclitic to an emphatic one is normal Latin idiom.

par . . . deo : there is no reason to suppose that Catullus means anything different from what his original meant by the cliché ἴσος θέοισιν; to enjoy Lesbia's presence is superhuman bliss. In l. 2 Catullus enhances the idea and adds the characteristically Roman conventional formula of caution *si fas est*; cf., for example, Ov. *Tr.* v. 3. 27 'me quoque, si fas

est exemplis ire deorum, / ferrea sors uitae difficilisque pre-
mit', and a similar formula in the epigram of Lutatius
Catulus quoted by Cic. *N.D.* i. 79 'pace mihi liceat, caelestes,
dicere uestra: / mortalis uisust pulchrior esse deo'.

3. aduersus : 'opposite': Sappho has ἐνάντιος, but *aduersus* is
more likely to be preposition or adverb than adjective. The
addition of *identidem* generalizes what is a particular situation in Sappho's poem.

5. dulce ridentem : Horace borrows the phrase, *Od.* i. 22. 23,
adding the *dulce loquentem* which Catullus has omitted from
Sappho. (For another reminiscence of Catullus in Horace's
sapphics see on 11. 1.)

    quod : with general reference to the preceding words.

    misero : of the lover's passion, like *misellus* 35. 14, 45. 21.

6. eripit sensus : cf. 66. 25 'sensibus ereptis'.

8. The sense of the missing adonic is clear. The *uocis* which
appears in most of the suggested supplements (*uocis in ore*
Doering, *uocis amanti* Meissner, *gutture uocis* Westphal) is
likely enough, though their authors probably wrongly supposed that it corresponded exactly to φώνας in Sappho. *nihil
uocis* is good Latin, but οὐδὲν φωνῆς is not Greek, and Sappho
wrote φώναισ', the aorist infinitive of φωνέω (or φώννημι): cf.
Theoc. 2. 108 οὐδέ τι φωνῆσαι δυνάμαν. Friedrich's supplement
Lesbia, uocis has the merit of accounting for the loss of the
line.

9 ff. Lucretius describes the symptoms of fear in similar
language, iii. 152 ff. 'ubi uementi magis est commota metu
mens, / consentire animam totam per membra uidemus, /
sudoresque ita palloremque exsistere toto / corpore et infringi
linguam uocemque aboriri, / caligare oculos, sonere auris,
succidere artus'.

9. torpet : 'is paralysed': cf. Ov. *Her.* 11. 82 'torpuerat gelido
lingua retenta metu'.

9 f. tenuis . . . flamma : Sappho's λέπτον πῦρ, a subtle fire which
penetrates into the whole body (*sub artus*).

11. gemina : if the text is sound, *gemina* must be taken as a
very bold transferred epithet ('a double night covers my
eyes'), a piece of sophistication which seems suspiciously out
of place in a poem whose language is otherwise so simple.
The objection made to Spengel's *gemina et*, that postponement of *et* is not found elsewhere in Catullus and is rare before
Virgil (see Haupt, *Opusc.* i. 115 ff.) can hardly be maintained
in view of the postponed *sed*, a much rarer phenomenon, two
lines above; but, if the text is to be changed, Schrader's *geminae*

is preferable as not only giving a phrase which Catullus himself uses elsewhere (for *geminae aures* see on 63. 75) but also improving the metre by breaking the monotonous repetition of a pause after the fifth syllable of the line. But it may be that Catullus has allowed a reminiscence of an Alexandrian conceit to intrude on Sappho.

13–16. Horace has this stanza in mind in the opening lines of *Od*. ii. 16 with their thrice-repeated *otium*.

13. molestum est : cf. Hor. *Ep*. i. 1. 108 'pituita molesta est', 'a cold bothers you', Cic. *Fam*. vii. 26. 1 'δυσεντερικὰ πάθη sibi molesta esse', *Cael*. 43 'amores et hae deliciae . . . quae firmiore animo praeditis molestae non solent esse'.

For the thought cf. Ov. *R.A*. 139 ff. 'otia si tollas, periere Cupidinis arcus. / . . . qui finem quaeris amori / —cedit amor rebus—res age: tutus eris'.

14. exsultas . . . gestis : both verbs primarily refer to physical restlessness and both imply riotous emotion: Cicero similarly combines them, *Tusc*. iv. 13 'cum inaniter et effuse animus exsultat, tum illa laetitia gestiens uel nimia dici potest quam ita definiunt: sine ratione animi elationem', v. 16 'inani laetitia exsultans et temere ('irrationally') gestiens'. In Livy vi. 36. 1 the townspeople of Velitrae break out because they are *otio gestientes*.

15. beatas : 'wealthy': cf. 61. 149–50 'domus beata', Hor. *Od*. iii. 29. 11 'omitte mirari beatae / fumum et opes strepitumque Romae'.

16. urbes : on Hellenistic moralizing about the effects of *otium* on the life of a community see Fraenkel, *Horace*, 212–13.

52

This outburst of disgust at the good fortune of the triumvirs' protegés probably belongs to one of the last years of Catullus' life, 55 or 54 B.C.

The reference in l. 3 is not to Vatinius' consulship—he actually held the consulship only for a short time, as *suffectus*, at the end of 47 B.C.—but to his arrogant anticipation of it. When he was quaestor in 63 he was already talking about the consulship (Cic. *Vat*. 6), and even the two consulships (*Vat*. 11), which would come to him. As tribune in 59 he had worked for Caesar and Pompey and had sponsored the legislation which gave Caesar his extraordinary command in Gaul and recognized Pompey's settlement in the East. In the next years his

fortunes were chequered (see on 53), but with the restoration of
the coalition between Caesar and Pompey in 56 he had reason
to expect a reward for his services. He may have appeared on
the *paginulae futurorum consulum* (Cic. *Att.* iv. 8*a*. 2) which the
triumvirs then drew up at their meeting at Luca; and he had an
immediate encouragement for his hopes when he became praetor
for 55, after a scandalous election engineered by his patrons,
since a praetorship carried some presumption of a consulship to
follow. 'Homo natus et ad risum et ad odium', Seneca calls
him (*Dial.* ii. 17. 3), but he was a man of ability, energy, and
humour who could disconcert his enemies by laughing at himself. When we read Cicero's abuse of him, it is worth remembering that in 47 he outfought the Pompeians and saved the
situation for Caesar in Illyricum (*Bell. Alex.* 43), that it was he
who called Cicero 'our consular comedian' (*consularis scurra*,
Macr. ii. 1. 12), and that in 54 Cicero was defending him to
oblige Caesar.

Who the Nonius of l. 2 was is not certain. We have an
accidental glimpse of him again in Pliny (*N.H.* xxxvii. 81), who
says that a son of his ('filius strumae Nonii eius quem Catullus
poeta in sella curuli uisum indigne tulit') found himself pro-
scribed in 43, when Antony cast eyes on an opal in his possession,
but managed to escape with his treasure; unfortunately Pliny
gives no *cognomen*. We have no record of a Nonius in any of the
magistracies (curule aedileship, censorship, praetorship, and
consulship) which entitled their holders to the *sella curulis*, but
we know of two Nonii who were persons of some prominence in
these years. L. Nonius Asprenas appears on Caesar's staff in
the Spanish and African campaigns and had probably been
praetor when he acted *pro consule* in Africa in 46, but his earlier
career is unknown. More likely, perhaps, is Pompey's supporter
M. Nonius Sufenas. As a tribune in 56 he worked in the interests
of the triumvirs (Cic. *Att.* iv. 15. 4) and he was probably an ex-
praetor when he served in a province in 50–51 (Cic. *Att.* vi. 1.
13); his tribunician services may have been rewarded at the
first opportunity, two years later, with a curule aedileship of 54.

So in 55 or 54 Catullus may have seen one parvenu oppor-
tunist, Vatinius, made even more confident of his consulship than
before and another, Sufenas, elected to his first curule office.

1. **quid est?** 'What's all this, Catullus? Why don't you die and
   have done with it?' For the impatient question, followed by
   another question or an exclamation, cf. Plaut. *Rud.* 676 'quid
   est? quid illaec oratiost?', *Capt.* 578 'quid est? ut scelestus
   nunc iste te ludos facit', Cic. *de Or.* ii. 59 '"quid est," inquit
   "Catule?" Caesar; "ubi sunt qui Antonium graece negant
   scire?"'

2. **struma**: Cicero taunts Vatinius with the same deformity, *Vat.* 4, 10, 39: cf. *Sest.* 135, *Att.* ii. 9. 2.

3. **peierat**: i.e. Vatinius confirmed his statements with the pledge *sic consul fiam ut . . .*, swearing by his dearest ambition, as Trajan used the formula *sic pontibus Istrum et Euphratem superem* and Julian *sic sub iugum mittam Persas* (Amm. Marc. xxiv. 3. 9). Catullus neatly makes two hits in one phrase: Vatinius has the impudence to pledge his word by his consulship—and his word is not worth much anyhow.

53

A versified anecdote of a compliment paid to his friend Calvus (see introd. to poem 14). It was for his speeches against Vatinius that Calvus was remembered in the time of Tacitus when, unlike the rest of his work, they were still read by every student of oratory: *Dial.* 21. 2 'in omnium studiosorum manibus uersantur accusationes quae in Vatinium inscribuntur, ac praecipue secunda ex his oratio: est enim uerbis ornata et sententiis, auribus iudicum accommodata'. There were at least three of them (as Tacitus' *secunda* shows), but the chronology of them cannot be established with certainty. The first recorded prosecution of Vatinius was in 58, the year after his fateful tribunate, when he was charged under the Lex Licinia Iunia but escaped by the efforts of Clodius and the *populares*, who broke up the court: the prosecutor is not mentioned, but may well have been Calvus. He first prosecuted Vatinius when he was not much more than 22 years old (Tac. *Dial.* 34. 7), and in 58, if Pliny's date for his birth (*N.H.* vii. 165) is right, he was 23 or 24. Cicero's speech *in Vatinium* of March 56 B.C. belongs not to a prosecution of Vatinius but to the trial of Sestius, whom Cicero successfully defended: Vatinius was a witness against Sestius whom Cicero was concerned to discredit. Calvus was also appearing for Sestius: he was then known as an old enemy of Vatinius and there was some talk of his launching an attack on Vatinius himself (Cic. *ad Q.F.* ii. 4. 1); but apart from the Scholia Bobiensia on *Vat.* 10 (145 Stangl), whose account of the matter is confused, there is no evidence that there was a prosecution, and Vatinius' holding of the praetorship of 55 suggests that there was not. In 54 B.C., when Vatinius, after his praetorship, was charged with illegal electioneering practices, Cicero (under pressure from the triumvirs) was defending him. Again we do not know who prosecuted (we have not Cicero's speech, which would have told us), but it was probably Calvus. Even if Calvus did prosecute Vatinius in 56, it is

unlikely (as H. Comfort points out, *C.P.* xxx [1935], 74) that
Catullus would have heard him; for Calvus would hardly have
ventured to attack Vatinius after the Conference of Luca in
April and Catullus, if he left Bithynia in the spring of 56, is not
likely to have been back in Rome before it. So the poem seems
to belong either to 58 B.C., before Catullus left for Bithynia, or
to 54, probably the last year of his life.

The remark which is the point of the lines comes from the
corona, the crowd of bystanders which gathered round a court
(any court was better than none: as Quintilian says, xii. 10. 74,
'nulli non agentium parata uulgi corona est') and, far from
maintaining the decorum of a modern court-audience, freely
expressed its interest in the proceedings by applause or interruption. How much its presence meant to an advocate is shown
by the confession which Cicero puts into the mouth of Brutus
(*Brut.* 192)—'in eis etiam causis in quibus omnis res nobis cum
iudicibus est, non cum populo, tamen si a corona relictus sim
non queam dicere': compare the vivid picture of the scene at a
'big trial' in *Brut.* 290 'cum surgat is qui dicturus sit, significe-
tur a corona silentium, deinde crebrae adsensiones, multae
admirationes'.

Calvus himself was a protagonist of the revolt against the
ample, elaborate, and emotional manner represented by Cicero,
and in a more extreme form by Hortensius, in favour of the
plain, unpretentious style—the 'Attic' style, as its exponents
liked to call it, though Cicero insists that it is a distortion of the
range and variety of Attic oratory. In Cicero's prejudiced
judgement he was too meticulous and precise; the cultivated
listener saw the quality of his style, but the man in the street
merely gulped it down without appreciating its flavour (*Brut.*
283, 'eius oratio nimis religiosa et attenta doctis audientibus
erat illustris; a multitudine autem et foro, cui nata eloquentia
est, deuorabatur'). No doubt Calvus knew that the grand
manner was not for him. Seneca (*Contr.* vii. 4. 7) portrays him
as a little man (*paruolus statura*: cf. Ov. *Tr.* ii. 431 *exigui Calui*),
animated and vivacious (*uiolentus actor et concitatus*): his
excitement would even carry him across the court till he
ended up by speaking from the wrong side. His assets were
verve and speed, and Cicero's disparaging remarks about the
ineffectiveness of the 'Atticists' (*Brut.* 289 'cum isti Attici
dicunt, non modo a corona, quod est ipsum miserabile, sed
etiam ab aduocatis relinquuntur'), if they were true at all
were not true of Calvus. That he could secure his effects,
though they were not Cicero's, is shown by this anecdote and
by Seneca's story that, while Calvus was speaking (perhaps on
the same occasion), Vatinius himself jumped up and protested

'rogo uos, iudices: num si iste disertus est, ideo me damnari
oportet?'

2. mirifice : cf. 71. 4, 84. 3: the colloquially emphatic variation
on *mire* is common in Cicero's letters.

Vatiniana : 'had set out the charges against Vatinius': for
the adjective cf. 14. 3 and see on 44. 10 (*Sestianus*).

4. manus tollens : for the gesture of astonishment or admiration
cf. Cic. *Acad.* ii. 63 'Hortensius autem uehementer admirans,
quod quidem perpetuo Lucullo loquente fecerat, ut etiam
manus saepe tolleret . . .', *Fam.* vii. 5. 2.

5. di magni : cf. 14. 12.

salaputium : the manuscripts have *salapantium*: *salaput-*
(*t*)*ium* is preserved in the manuscripts of Seneca, *Contr.* vii. 4.
7, who quotes the phrase. Seneca explains the remark as referring to Calvus' small stature, but the meaning and origin of
the word are obscure. It is found nowhere else, but *Salaputis*
occurs as a proper name in an African inscription of the reign
of Commodus, *C.I.L.* viii. 10570 'cura(m) agente C. Iulio
⟨Pel⟩ope Salaputi mag(istro)'. *-putium* may be connected
with *putus*, a vulgar word for *puer*. (See W. Goldberger in
Glotta xviii [1930], 54. The quantity of the *u* is doubtful: the
diminutive *putillus* has *ŭ*, but Romance derivatives point to
a form with *ū*.) The other suggestions which have been put
forward—Thielmann's *salapittium* (*A.L.L.* iv. 601), which he
explains as a diminutive of *salapitta*, a vulgar form of *sal-
picta*, i.e. σαλπίγκτης, and Garrod's proposal (*C.Q.* viii. 48) to
retain *salapantium* as a diminutive from a hybrid *salapanta*,
equivalent to *halapanta*, a variant recorded by Festus for
halophanta (ἀλοφάντης), which Plautus uses along with *syco-
phanta*—are far from plausible. (For other discussions of the
word see Bickel in *Rh. Mus.* xcvi [1953], 94, V. Pisani in
Rh. Mus. xcvi [1953], 181, J. Whatmough in *Ogam* v [1953],
65, who explains the word as Celtic.)

55

The occasion of this *jeu d'esprit* is Catullus' fruitless search
for the elusive Camerius through the resorts where a young man
might be seeking pleasure. It must belong to his last years: for
the Porticus Pompei (l. 6) was not built till 55 B.C. Here
Catullus ventures on a metrical experiment, varying normal
Phalaecian hendecasyllables with decasyllables in which a
spondee is substituted for the dactyl. The variation does not
follow a regular pattern; apart from the doubtful line 9 there
are twelve decasyllables to nine normal lines.

Attempts have been made to find a place in this poem for the ten lines (58*b*) which in the manuscripts are attached to poem 58. The Aldine added them at the end; Guarinus inserted them after l. 12, the Roman edition of 1475 (followed by Lachmann, Haupt, and Postgate) after l. 13, Fröhlich (followed by Schwabe and Ellis) after l. 14. The subject of the two pieces is clearly the same and they share the same metrical novelty. But 55 is a lively, playful poem, simple in structure and recalling the easy, casual style of poem 10, while 58*a* is a mannered and self-conscious piece of mock-solemnity, loaded with allusion and clumsy to the point of obscurity.

There is obvious corruption in lines 9–11 and the strange latinity of l. 11 suggests that more than the end of that line has been lost.

1. si forte non molestum est : for the conventional phrase of politeness, 'if you don't mind', cf. Plaut. *Rud.* 120 'nisi molestum est, paucis percontarier / uolo ego ex te', Ter. *Ad.* 806 'ausculta paucis nisi molestum est', Cic. *Phil.* ii. 41 'uelim mihi dicas nisi molestum est'.

2. tenebrae : 'your lair'; the word has something of the suggestion of disreputableness which *tenebricosus* has in Cic. *Pis.* 18, *Prov. Cons.* 8.

3. quaesiuimus : *V*'s *quaesiuimus in* is a syllable too long. If *quaesiuimus* is retained, it is best to transpose *in* to follow *te*; Scaliger deleted *in* as a dittography (of *m-*), leaving *campo minore* as a local ablative, but it is very unlikely that the preposition was omitted in the first of four parallel cola. Birt's *quaesimus in* is ingenious, but the evidence for syncopation in the first person plural of perfects in -*ui* is very doubtful. The only possible instances are *suemus* Lucr. i. 60, 301, iv. 369, *consuemus* Prop. i. 7. 5, *enarramus* Ter. *Ad.* 365, *flemus* Prop. ii. 7. 2, *narramus* Prop. ii. 15. 3, *mutamus* Prop. ii. 15. 9, and none of these is certain. (These syncopations are to be distinguished from the common shortened forms produced by haplology in -*s*- perfects: see on 14. 14 *misti*.)

Campo . . . minore : presumably *minor* distinguishes this *campus* from the Campus Martius (regularly called *campus* without an adjective), but the name is not found elsewhere. It may be the ἄλλο πεδίον, furnished with porticoes and temples, which Strabo mentions (v. 236) as adjoining the Campus Martius; it is less likely to be the more distant Campus Martialis, a space on the Mons Caelius where the Equirria were held when the Campus Martius was flooded (Fest. 117. 25 L.).

4. Circo : the Circus Maximus in the hollow between Palatine and Aventine.

tě in : cf. 97. 1 'non ita me dĭ ament'. That shortening of
unaccented long monosyllables in hiatus was a feature of
ordinary speech is shown by Plautus and Terence where such
scansions as *sĭ amas, mě amat, sě habent, quĭ amant, tŭ homo*
are regular (see Lindsay, *Early Latin Verse*, 226) : elsewhere
there are a few instances, e.g. Lucr. ii. 617 *quĭ in oras*, iv.
1061 *sĭ abest*, v. 74 *quĭ in orbi*, Virg. *Ecl.* 8. 108 *an quĭ amant*,
Aen. vi. 507 *tě amice*, Hor. *Sat.* i. 9. 38 *si mě amas*.

omnibus libellis : *libelli* has generally been taken to mean
'bookshops' here and in Mart. v. 20. 8 (a list of the resorts of
a leisured life in Rome) 'gestatio ("promenade"), fabulae,
libelli, / campus, porticus, umbra, Virgo, thermae'. τὰ βιβλία
'the book-market', is vouched for by Pollux (ix. 97), and
though that phrase does not occur in extant literature,
similar uses are not uncommon in Greek (e.g. Ar. *Wasps* 789
ἐν τοῖς ἰχθύσι, *Eccl.* 303 ἐν τοῖς στεφανώμασιν, Eupolis fr. 304
περιῆλθον εἰς τὰ σκόροδα καὶ τὰ κρόμμυα, Lysias 23. 6 ἐλθόντα εἰς
τὸν χλωρὸν τυρόν, Theophr. *Char.* 11. 4 προσελθὼν πρὸς τὰ κάρυα ἢ
τὰ μύρτα). There were bookshops in or near the Forum in
Catullus' time ; cf. 14. 17 f. and Cic. *Phil.* ii. 21, where Antony
takes refuge in a *taberna libraria*. (The *codices librariorum*
which were seized to make a pyre there for Clodius (Ascon.
in Mil. p. 33 Clark) were probably official documents.) But
(i) there is no evidence, apart from these two passages of
Catullus and Martial, that a similar idiom existed in Latin ;
(ii) even if it did, *omnibus* would still be surprising : while τὰ
βιβλία meant the place where books were sold, there is nothing
to suggest that πάντα τὰ βιβλία could mean 'all the bookshops'.
The other meaning which has been suggested for *libelli*,
'placards' or 'public notices', is authenticated (e.g. of sale
notices, Cic. *Quinct.* 27 'libellos deicit', Sen. *Ben.* iv. 12. 3
'suspensum amici bonis libellum'; of a notice of lost
property, Apul. *Met.* vi. 7) : but *in libellis* in this sense
would be an anomalous item in the list Campus, Circus,
Capitol.

5. templo . . . sacrato : the temple of Jupiter on the Capitoline
hill, which had been dedicated after rebuilding in 69 B.C.
For *sacrato* equivalent to *sacro* cf. Tib. i. 2. 84 *sacratis
liminibus*.

6. Magni . . . ambulatione : the *porticus Pompei*, an open
columned court, planted with trees and hung with tapestries
on the walls (Prop. ii. 32. 11), which was attached to the
theatre built in the Campus Martius by Cn. Pompeius Magnus
and dedicated in 55 B.C.—a popular rendezvous for young
men looking for female society ; cf. Ov. *A.A.* i. 67 'tu modo

Pompeia lentus spatiare sub umbra', iii. 387 'at licet et prodest Pompeias ire per umbras', Prop. iv. 8. 75.

    simul : 'as well', 'besides', obviously not 'at the same
time'; the loose use is presumably colloquial.

7. **femellas** : the diminutive is found only here.

    prendi : 'accosted', 'button-holed'; cf. Ter. *And*. 353
'tuus pater modo me prendit: ait . . .', Cic. *Att*. xii. 13. 2,
Fam. (Caelius) viii. 11. 2; the 'frequentative' *prensare* is common in the same sense.

8. **uultu uidi tamen sereno** : 'but in spite of my suspicions
(*tamen*) I saw them without a cloud on their faces' (i.e., presumably, with expressions of innocence): the opposite of
Martial's *nubila fronte* (ii. 11. 1).

9. **auelte** is certainly corrupt and Munro's defence of *a uel te*,
with *uel* modifying *sic* ('ah, even so I continued to demand
you'), is a counsel of despair: even if the hyperbaton were
possible, the interjection *a* would be quite pointless here.
None of the proposed corrections (*auelli sinite* Avantius,
auertistis, saepe Riese) is convincing. *uel te* looks like an
adscript variant which has found its way into the text;
Mr. G. W. Williams suggests that the text may have read
iratus sic with the adverb noted as a variant for the adjective.
ipse has been suspected, since there is no other speaker with
whom Catullus can be contrasting himself; but it may be an
example of the use of the pronoun, without any implication
of contrast, to give lively emphasis to a statement (like 'actually'; *ultro* is similarly used: cf. 115. 7); cf. Shackleton
Bailey, *Propertiana* p. 257 and instances there cited.

10. **Camerium** : the ellipse of an imperative (here *da, cedo*, or
the like) is common in familiar language. The first syllable
of *Camerius* is short (cf. 58*b*. 7); we must assume either that
the name is here pronounced as a trisyllable with consonantal
i (*Cămērium*: cf. 62. 57) or (less probably) that to accommodate it Catullus has allowed himself the unique liberty of
substituting a tribrach in the first foot. In either case there
is a break in the otherwise continuous series of initial spondees.
There is a similar anomaly due to a metrically awkward name
at 29. 3 where, in a poem otherwise written in pure iambics,
one spondee is allowed to accommodate the intractable
Māmurra.

11. **nudum reduc . . .** : none of the supplements which have
been proposed is satisfactory. *nudum reducta pectus* (Ellis)
could only mean 'with her chest drawn back' or 'with a
hollow in her chest'. *nudum sinum reducens* (Auantius) or
recludens (Riese) ignores the meaning of *sinus*: since *sinus*

refers primarily to the covering garment, *sinus nudus* is an impossible phrase. '*nudum reclude pectus*' (Friedrich) is possible as the start of the *femella*'s impertinent answer if *reclude* can here mean 'uncover': elsewhere *recludere pectus* means 'open the breast' (e.g. Virg. *Aen.* x. 601 'pectus mucrone recludit', Hor. *Epod.* 17. 71 'ense pectus . . . recludere', Sen. *Tro.* 1001 'reclude ferro pectus') and that meaning (which Friedrich intends) is too absurd here. The corruption may extend further: for the beginning of the line is suspicious. Catullus uses forms of *inquam* introducing direct speech nine times elsewhere, always in the normal position, inserted in the quotation. Since there are isolated instances of *inquit* preceding a quotation in Seneca (*Ep.* 122. 13) and Apuleius (*Met.* vi. 13), the exceptional position cannot be regarded as impossible here; if it is right, one can only guess that Catullus resorted to it for convenience, perhaps to secure the neat coincidence of sense-unit and line which is maintained through most of the poem.

12. en : *em* ('there!', an exclamation *aliquid offerentis*, originally the imperative of *emo*, 'take') is not impossible; hiatus after *em* is normal (Lindsay, *Early Latin Verse*, 243). But the fact that in this poem (apart from the exceptional l. 10) the first foot is regularly spondaic confirms *en*.

13. iam : i.e. after the trouble you have been giving me.

   Herculei : the *-i* (*-ei*) and *-is* forms of the genitive were both current in Catullus' time (Varro, *L.L.* viii. 26): on the question whether Cicero used only *Herculi* (and similarly *Aristoteli, Pericli, Praxiteli*, &c.) or varied between *Herculi* and *Herculis* see Madvig on *Fin.* i. 14. For the proverbial use of the labours of Hercules cf. Plaut. *Persa* 1 f. 'qui amans egens ingressus est princeps in amoris uias / superauit aerumnis is suis aerumnas Herculi', Cic. *Acad.* ii. 108 'credo Clitomacho ita scribenti, Herculi quendam laborem exanclatum a Carneade'.

   labos : the original form of the nominative retains its long final vowel, while in the later form *labor* (formed by analogy from the oblique cases, in which *-r-* was the regular development of *-s-* between vowels) it is shortened on the analogy of other types of substantive (e.g. nouns of agent in *-tor*). Later poets occasionally find that *labōs* suits them (e.g. Virg. *Aen.* vi. 277): in Catullus' time it may have been still current, as was *honos*, which Cicero regularly uses.

14. tanto te in fastu : the manuscript reading *te in* gives good sense 'it's a labour of Hercules to put up with you now: you withhold yourself in such a high and mighty way'), *tanto . . .*

negas being an 'inverted consecutive' of a common type, like
22. 11 'tantum abhorret', 17 'tam gaudet': the modal use of
in is unusual, but cf. Plaut. *Bacch.* 1014 'in stultitia si
deliqui', Lucr. iii. 295 'effervescit in ira', 826 'inque metu
male habet'. Muretus's *ten*, which makes the line a question
('are you withholding yourself?'), is not without difficulty in
the attaching of the interrogative particle to an unemphatic
pronoun.

15. **sis futurus**, 'where you will be found to be': so Cic. *Fam.*
vi. 2. 3 'tu uelim scribas ad me quid agas et ubi futurus sis'.
For this use of the future compare such expressions as Plaut.
Pseud. 677 'profecto hoc sic erit' ('you will find it is so'),
Asin. 734 'hic inerunt uiginti minae' ('you will find there
are 20 minae in this purse').

17. **tenent . . . tenes**: for similar accidental repetitions cf. 37.
3–5 'putatis . . . vobis . . . licere . . . putare', 67. 5–7 'ferunt
. . . feraris'.

18 f. **tenes . . . proicies**: this use of the present in the protasis
of a conditional sentence in future time is not uncommon in
comedy and in Cicero's letters where the verb in the protasis
refers to the immediate future, especially in threats or
admonitions: so Plaut. *Rud.* 1391 'si sapis, . . . tacebis'
(Plautus also uses *si sapies*; see on 35. 7), *Merc.* 510 'bona si
esse uis, bene erit tibi', Cic. *Fam.* v. 12. 9 'haec . . ., si recipis
causam nostram, uitabimus', xvi. i. 2 'si statim nauigas, nos
Leucade consequēre', Brutus *ap.* Cic. *ad Br.* i. 13. 1 'hoc si a
te impetro, nihil profecto dubitabis pro iis suscipere'. The
same use (especially with *nisi*) is occasionally found in more
formal writing: Cic. *Phil.* vii. 19 'si bellum omittimus, pace
numquam fruemur', *Acad.* ii. 93 'erunt (molesti) nisi cauetis',
Tib. i. 8. 77 'te poena manet ni desinis esse superba'.

19. 'you will fling away all the joys of love' (for *fructus amoris*
cf. Prop. iii. 20. 30).

20. **gaudet Venus**: the opposite of this (as editors since
Muretus have pointed out) is a more common sentiment
(e.g. Prop. ii. 25. 29 'tu tamen interea, quamuis te diligat
illa, / in tacito cohibe gaudia clausa sinu'), but Catullus is
saying what suits the occasion, not discussing the psychology
of love.

    loquella: Lachmann's canon (enunciated in his note on
Lucr. iii. 1015) that in the republican period this termination
(representing an earlier *-esla*) is written *-ella* when the preceding syllable is short, *-ela* when it is long (so *cautela*,
suadela) is borne out by inscriptions.

21. palatum : of speech (not, as usual, of taste) as in Hor. *Sat.*
ii. 3. 274 'balba feris annoso uerba palato', Ov. *Am.* ii. 6. 47
(of a talking parrot) 'nec tamen ignauo stupuerunt uerba
palato'.

22. uestri sim particeps amoris : *uestri sis* of *V* clearly does
not give relevant sense. If *uestri sim* (Scaliger, following
Avantius) is read, *uestri* will refer to Camerius and his girl
and Catullus must be taken to mean 'I don't mind your
keeping your love a secret from other people so long as I
share it' or 'so long as I know about it': for *particeps*, 'privy
to', cf. Cic. *Fam.* x. 12. 2 'feci continuo omnes participes
meae uoluptatis'. But it is not easy to supply the 'from
other people' which is necessary to the sense, and *nostri
sis* may be right: 'so long as you are not detaching yourself
from my love'.

58

In this poem, as in poem 11, Catullus' disillusionment is
complete. The repetition of Lesbia's name, the reference to
himself in the third person, the declaration of his own devotion,
are sentimental dwelling on the past; the poem ends, as 11 does,
with a sudden turn to the cold realism of ugly words. It is
reasonable to think that the Caelius to whom Catullus turns is
the Caelius of poem 100 who had befriended him in his love—
presumably for Lesbia. Whether he is Marcus Caelius Rufus,
who, if Lesbia is the famous Clodia, had been another of her
victims and perhaps ousted Catullus only to share his fate
(see on 77), is another question; see introd., pp. xv f.

1. nostra : i.e. *mea*, as in 43. 7: on Catullus' use of *noster* see on
107. 3.

2. unam : for *unus* ('uniquely') strengthening a comparative
see on 10. 17.

3. plus quam se : cf. Cic. *T.D.* iii. 72 'quasi fieri ullo modo
possit, quod in amatorio sermone dici solet, ut quisquam
plus alterum diligat quam se'.

4. quadriuiis et angiportis : 'the street-corners and the alleys':
angiportus is a connecting lane between or behind houses.
(See J. André, 'Les noms romains du chemin et de la rue',
R.É.L. xxviii [1950], 124 ff.)

5. magnanimi Remi nepotes : the quasi-epic grandiose phrase
(like *Romuli nepotes* in 49. 1) is ironical and the irony is
enhanced by the contrast with the offensive verb; the heirs

of Rome's greatness are the associates of Lesbia's degradation.

58ᵇ

The subject of this piece is the same as that of 55 and it
shares the same metrical novelty (though here the proportion
of decasyllables is much smaller), but its style is markedly
different (see on 55). The syntax of the lines is obscure. (1) If
the manuscript order is retained, ll. 3 and 4 must be taken to
be loosely attached, without syntactical connexion, to the
preceding lines: 'not (even if I were) Ladas or Perseus or
Rhesus' team'. With Muretus's transposition of l. 3 to follow
l. 1, the construction is *non si fingar custos ille Cretum, non
(si fingar) Ladas Perseusue, non si Pegaseo ferar uolatu, non (si
ferar uolatu) Rhesi bigae* and the ellipses are still difficult.
(2) Besides, whatever is to be made of ll. 1–4, these lines do not
in any case fit the rest of the poem. *Non si* demands some such
apodosis as *sine lassitudine te reperirem*, 'even if I had the speed
of some mythical creature, I should not be equal to the search
for you' (for examples of the idiom see on 70. 2); the apodosis
essem defessus leaves the anticipatory *non* meaningless. Paral-
lels can be found for the shift from *fingar . . . ferar* in the protasis
to *essem* in the apodosis, but it is hard to suppose that the parenthesis of ll. 5–7 made Catullus forget a *non* which he had repeated
four times. (3) Lines 5–7 are grammatical in themselves, as a
parenthetical afterthought, if *quos* is taken as final, 'add to
these all feathered creatures, and find me the speed of the winds,
to bestow them on me yoked in a team'. If, on the other hand,
as Lachmann proposed, *quos dicares* is taken as a concessive
protasis without introductory conjunction (of the type of Cic.
Off. iii. 75 'dares hanc uim M. Crasso, in foro saltaret'), or if,
as Postgate suggested, a concessive conjunction is supplied
by the insertion of *ut* after *mihi* '(even if you were to bestow
these on me, I should be weary'), ll. 5–10 can be made to form
a grammatical unity, but at the cost of leaving ll. 1–4 without
any construction at all.

Either the lines are a roughly versified draft of phrases which
Catullus meant to work up into a poem (the awkward combination *niueae citaeque* in l. 4 and the otiose *mihi* in l. 10 might be
taken as further signs of hasty writing) or else a beginning,
containing a negative sentence on which the *non si* clauses
depended, has been lost.

1. non . . . si : see on 70. 2. Propertius has a curiously similar
catalogue, ii. 30. 1–6 'quo fugis, a demens? nulla est fuga.

tu licet usque / ad Tanaim fugias, usque sequetur amor. / non si Pegaseo uecteris in aere dorso, / nec tibi si Persei mouerit ala pedes, / uel si te sectae rapiant talaribus aurae, / nil tibi Mercurii proderit alta uia'.

fingar : 'if I were made into the shape of': for the use of the verb the editors cite *Paneg. Mess.* 206 (of transmigration) 'mutata figura / seu me finget equum rigidos percurrere campos / doctum seu . . . .' But the use of it here is presumably suggested by the fact that the *custos* was *fictus*, a bronze figure.

custos . . . ille Cretum : the 'sentinel of Crete' is Talos, the bronze giant made for King Minos by Hephaestus. He ran round the island three times a day, repelling strangers and destroying any who landed; for an account of him and of the effect of Medea's spells on him see Apoll. iv. 1638–88.

2. **Ladas** : the Spartan victor in the long-race at Olympia who died in the moment of success (Paus. iii. 21. 1) and whose name became proverbial for speed (*ad Her.* iv. 4, Juv. 13. 97, Mart. x. 100. 5).

   pinnipes : the compound occurs only here; Perseus was given winged sandals by the nymphs when he set out to find the Gorgons.

3. **Pegaseo** : for Pegasus as a proverbial type of speed cf. Cic. *Quinct.* 80 'o hominem fortunatum qui eiusmodi nuntios seu potius Pegasos habeat', Sen. *Tro.* 385 'aetas Pegaseo corripiet gradu'.

4. **Rhesi . . . bigae** : the Thracian King Rhesus, Hecuba's brother, came to assist Priam at Troy with his team of white horses, λευκότεροι χιόνος, θείειν δ' ἀνέμοισιν ὁμοῖοι (*Il.* x. 437); on the night of his arrival Odysseus and Diomede raided his quarters, captured the horses, and killed their master. White horses were credited with superior speed (Virgil borrows the Homeric description of Rhesus' team for the horses of his Turnus, *Aen.* xii. 84); hence the proverbial phrases of Plaut. *Asin.* 279 'numquam edepol quadrigis albis (occasionem) indipiscet postea', Hor. *Sat.* i. 7. 7 'adeo sermonis amari, / Sisennas Barros ut equis praecurreret albis'.

   bigae : if ll. 2 and 3 are transposed, *bigae* must be genitive singular. Properly *bigae*, a two-horse team, is *plurale tantum*, being an adjective (from earlier *biiugae*) agreeing with *equae* understood: Varro explicitly says (*L.L.* x. 24) 'non dicitur una biga . . . sed unae bigae', and the singular is not found elsewhere before Statius. Hence Muretus himself proposed *niueis citisque bigis*. But Varro used the equally dubious singular *quadriga* in verse (Gell. xix. 8. 17) and that is good enough authority for *biga* in Catullus.

5. **plumipedas uolatilesque :** 'add to these the feather-footed, flying creatures': *plumipeda* (for the form cf. *decempeda*, 'ten-foot rod': Varro may have used *remipedas* of ducks, *Sat.* fr. 489. 1 Büch.) is another ἅπαξ εἰρήμενον.

7. **iunctos :** 'harnessed in a team', is more probable than *uinctos*, which must be explained as an allusion to the Homeric Aeolus who ἀνέμων κατέδησε κέλευθα and gave them to Odysseus in a bag (*Od.* x. 17 ff.).

   dicares : 'bestow', 'make over', of a solemn gift: cf. Virg. *Aen.* i. 73 'conubio iungam stabili propriamque dicabo'.

8 ff. **defessus . . . quaeritando :** Plautus has the same phrase in one of the passages in which he makes comic use of the search for an elusive friend, *Amph.* 1009 ff.

   omnibus medullis . . . languoribus : 'I should be weary in all my bones and worn away with repeated fatigue'. For *medullae* in this connexion cf. Plaut. *Stich.* 340 'at ego perii quoi medullas lassitudo perbibit'; for *languor*, Ter. *Heaut.* 807 'me haec deambulatio quam . . . ad languorem dedit'.

60

A *cri de cœur* in scazons: as in 104, there is no clue to the occasion and nothing to show to whom it was addressed, whether to false friend, like 30 or 77, or to fickle lover.

1 ff. **leaena . . . procreauit :** the commonplace in various forms has a long history going back to Homer, *Il.* xvi. 33 (Patroclus to Achilles) νηλεές, οὐκ ἄρα σοί γε πατὴρ ἦν ἱππότα Πηλεὺς / οὐδὲ Θέτις μήτηρ, γλαυκὴ δέ σε τίκτε θάλασσα / πέτραι τ' ἠλίβατοι: Catullus uses it again in Ariadne's address to Theseus, 64. 154-6 'quaenam te genuit sola sub rupe leaena, / quod mare conceptum spumantibus exspuit undis, / quae Syrtis, quae Scylla rapax, quae uasta Carybdis ?' For other developments of it see Virg. *Aen.* iv. 366 'duris genuit te cautibus horrens / Caucasus Hyrcanaeque admorunt ubera tigres', Ov. *Met.* viii. 120 'non genetrix Europa tibi est sed inhospita Syrtis / Armeniae tigres austroque agitata Carybdis'.

1. **Libystinis :** a rare variation on the adjective, presumably a Hellenistic invention. Its appearances in extant Greek are later than this: in Latin it occurs elsewhere only in the Sicilian cult-title Apollo Libystinus in Macr. i. 17. 24.

2. **latrans . . . parte :** out of the six-headed creature of Homer (*Od.* xii. 85) later literature developed the familiar picture of Scylla the monstrous mermaid, woman above the waist and barking dogs below, which appears again in Lucr. v. 892

'rabidis canibus succinctas semimarinis / corporibus Scyllas',
Virg. *Ecl.* 6. 75 'candida succinctam latrantibus inguina
monstris'.

4. **in nouissimo casu** : Varro (*L.L.* vi. 59) speaks of *nouissimus* in the sense of *extremus* as a novelty which in his own
day some of the older generation refused to recognize: the
use does not appear again until Tacitus, who is partial to it
(e.g. *Ann.* vi. 50. 8 'nouissima exspectabat', xii. 33. 2 'nouissimum casum experitur', xv. 44. 8).

5. **contemptam haberes** : 'regard with indifference': the effect
of the periphrasis, expressing permanent state, is to emphasize the deliberateness of the act: so in comedy, Plaut. *Bacch.*
572 'neque tu me habebis falso suspectum', *Cas.* 189 'uir me
habet pessimis despicatam modis', Ter. *Eun.* 384 'nostram
adulescentiam / habent despicatam'. In classical prose it is
confined to a few regular phrases (*compertum, cognitum,
exploratum habere*).

61

The marriage-song appears in Homer; it is a feature of the
wedding on Achilles' Shield (*Il.* xviii. 493) and recurs in the
same phrase (πολὺς δ' ὑμέναιος ὀρώρει) in the fuller description in
the Hesiodic *Shield* (273–9). There the ὑμέναιος is the processional song; but the word is also used more generally to include
the songs which accompanied the wedding-feast and the
ἐπιθαλάμιος (ὕμνος)—or ἐπιθαλάμιον (μέλος)—which belonged to the
final stage of the ceremony.[1] Alcman wrote marriage-songs
famous enough to justify the description ὑμνητὴρ ὑμεναίων
which Leonidas of Tarentum gives him (*A.P.* vii. 19), but the
primacy belonged to Sappho, and the fragments of her hymenaeals, some lyric, some in hexameters, which were collected
into one book, probably the ninth, by her Alexandrian editors,[2]
are the only surviving examples of the form from earlier Greek
literature. In Attic literature the genre is reflected in drama—
in Eur. *Troades* (307–40) and *Phaethon* (fr. 781 N.) and, by way
of burlesque, in Arist. *Birds* (1725 ff.) and *Peace* (1333 ff.).
Philoxenus and Telestes wrote dithyrambs, to which the title
ὑμέναιος is given, but the fragments of them are too meagre to
show how they handled the theme. As an independent literary

---

[1] In Latin only the neuter form *epithalamium* is used. For a full
discussion of the usage of ὑμέναιος and ἐπιθαλάμιος see R. Muth,
Wiener Studien lxvii (1954), 5–45.

[2] See Page, *Sappho and Alcaeus*, 112, 119–22.

form the hymenaeal came to life again in the Alexandrian age, but of Alexandrian hymenaeals only Theocritus 18 survives; it represents a literary development of the form, a song for the marriage of legendary characters. In Latin two of Catullus' contemporaries, Ticidas and Caluus, wrote lyric hymenaeals (from each of them we have a single glyconic fragment), and Caluus seems to have written an epithalamium in hexameters also.

Catullus' poem is clearly not a hymn to be sung on the actual occasion of the marriage which provides its theme. There is no ground for distributing the lines between two choruses, one of girls and one of boys, or for assigning the successive parts of the poem to successive stances, and attempts to synchronize the lines with the stages of the ceremony are quite unconvincing. It is a fantasy in which the traditional topics of the genre and Hellenistic formulae are combined with a vivid and colourful representation of some of the main features of a Roman wedding. The poet himself is the speaker throughout, acting as leader of an imaginary chorus and master of ceremonies, compère, as it were, and commentator on the scenes as they succeed one another before him, and as a poet he selects from his material; nothing is said of the marriage-feast, which both in Greece and in Rome was a regular part of the ceremony, and we hear nothing of some of the characteristic features of Roman practice—the sacrifices, the peculiarities of the bride's dress, the ritual acts performed by the bride at the door of her new home and by the bridegroom as soon as she entered it. The device of quasi-dramatic presentation by the mouth of the poet may have gone back to Sappho herself. Whether it did or not, Catullus could have found precedent for his method in Alexandrian poetry: Callimachus employs a similar technique in some of the *Hymns*.

What particular use Catullus made of his Greek predecessors in this poem the meagre remains of Greek lyric do not help us to guess.[1] But that he closely followed the traditional lines of the genre we know; for the λόγος ἐπιθαλάμιος of later Greek rhetoric took over much of its content from the poetic epithalamium, and the Greek rhetoricians of the third, fourth, and fifth centuries A.D. provide precepts for composing it, analyses of the topics appropriate to it, and specimens of it. The praises of Hymenaeus as *boni coniugator amoris*, the picture of the blessings of marriage for the family and the race, the adjurations to bride and bridegroom, the encomium of the bride-

---

[1] The only considerable fragments of Sappho's lyric hymenaeals are frr. (L.-P.) 110a and 111 (badinage of door-keeper and bridegroom), 112 and 115 (the bridegroom's good fortune and his looks).

groom's virtues and the bride's beauty (and even the floral comparisons), the prayer for children—everything in fact in Catullus' poem which is not specifically Roman appears among the set themes of epideictic rhetoric.[1]

The bridegroom is a Manlius Torquatus; his bride is called both Junia (16) and Aurunculeia (82). Of the bridegroom's distinguished family the known person who best fits the occasion is L. Manlius Torquatus, a slightly older contemporary of Catullus who was praetor in 49 B.C. and was killed on service in Africa with the Pompeian forces in 47. He appears as one of the interlocutors, the champion of Epicureanism, in Cicero's *De Finibus*—in a letter to Atticus (xiii. 5. 1) Cicero calls the first book 'Torquatus' from his part in it—and both there and in his tribute to his memory in the *Brutus* Cicero bears witness to his distinction as scholar and speaker.[2] To the identity of the bride we have no clue. Even her names are puzzling. If she was a Junia (as the manuscripts agree in calling her),[3] her possession of a second *gentilicium*, Aurunculeia, is surprising. It is best explained by the assumption that she was an Aurunculeia by birth who had passed by adoption into the *gens* Junia. It is less likely that Junia was her father's *gens*, Aurunculeia her mother's; for though the metronymic style is not uncommon under the Empire (e.g. Julia Agrippina), there is no evidence for its use among free-born women in the republican period.[4]

The invocation of Hymenaeus (1–45) and the encomium of him (46–75) both closely follow the traditional formulae of the hymn style, but Hymenaeus himself wears a Roman dress and his function is not merely that of the spirit of the wedding but that of the presiding genius of married life, the Γάμος of the λόγος ἐπιθαλάμιος.[5] In 76–113 the scene is in front of the bride's home, where the crowd is waiting for the *deductio* to begin; the

[1] See A. L. Wheeler, 'Tradition in the Epithalamium', *A.J.P.* li. 205 ff.: the sources are the Τέχνη ῥητορική of Ps.-Dionysius, the treatise of Menander περὶ ἐπιδεικτικῶν (3rd cent.), the orations of Himerius, Choricius, Aphthonius, and Libanius, and Gregory Nazianzen.

[2] *Brut.* 265 'erant in eo plurimae litterae nec eae uulgares sed interiores quaedam et reconditae; diuina memoria, summa uerborum et grauitas et elegantia; atque haec omnia uitae decorabat dignitas et integritas'.

[3] Or a Vinia: that less common gentile name might well have been corrupted into the common Iunia.

[4] R. Syme's suggestion that *Iunia* conceals *Vibia*, a known Oscan *praenomen*, would give the bride connexions with Central Italy.

[5] Γάμος was addressed in Philoxenus' dithyrambic hymenaeal: Γάμε, θεῶν λαμπρότατε (fr. 9 B.) is the only surviving fragment.

hesitant bride is reassured by praise of her beauty. At 114 the bride appears, and to the jubilant *io Hymen* refrain the procession moves on its way to the bridegroom's house, with the traditional Roman accompaniments of the throwing of nuts and the ribald *versus Fescennini*, here sublimated, as it were, into the poet's homily to bridegroom and bride. At 174 the bride has reached her new home and passes to the *thalamus*: the poem closes with the *epithalamium* in the strict sense, the address to the wedded pair and the prayer for their happiness.

The poem is written in strophes of four glyconics and a pherecratean, a system used by Anacreon (fr. 2 D.), and no doubt by others. In his handling of the metre Catullus follows Greek precedent. As in Anacreon, synaphea is observed—i.e. the stanza is regarded as a metrical unity: hiatus and *syllaba anceps* do not occur within the strophe (elision occurs between lines at 115, 135, 140, 184, 227) and a word may be divided between two lines (82, perhaps 46).[1] The basis, as in Greek practice, is free, but the great preponderance of trochees over spondees in the first foot gives the rhythm of the poem its lightness and speed.[2]

The ritual cry which Catullus uses as a refrain appears in various arrangements in Euripides (*Phaethon* fr. 781 N. ὑμὴν ὑμήν, *Tro.* 314 ὑμὴν ὢ ὑμέναι' ἄναξ, 331 ὑμὴν ὢ ὑμέναι' ὑμήν), Aristophanes (*Birds* 1743 ὑμὴν ὢ ὑμέναι' ὢ, *Peace* 1332 ὑμὴν ὑμέναι' ὢ), Theocritus 18. 58 (ὑμὴν ὢ ὑμέναιε) and Plautus (*Cas.* 800, 809 *hymen hymenaee o hymen*). ὑμήν (whatever its etymology) was originally an interjection, and the personified Hymen does not begin his long career till Ovid (*Her.* 6. 44 'sertis tempora uinctus Hymen'): ὑμέναι' ὢ was a lengthened form of the cry (perhaps due, as Maas suggests, to rhythmical considerations) from which first the name of the marriage-song and later, when it had come to be interpreted as a vocative, the name of the god or demi-god Hymenaeus, arose.[3] Fifteen stanzas end with the ritual cry as refrain (four with repeated *o*, eleven with *io*), and there are three other adonic refrains—*comparavier ausit* (three times), *concubine, nuces da* (twice), and *prodeas, noua nupta* (three times).

[1] The manuscripts show breach of synaphea at two places, 184–5 (hiatus) and 216 (*syllaba anceps*). It is highly unlikely that a rule which is otherwise observed throughout the poem (the more noticeably since at the end of stanzas hiatus and *syllaba anceps* are frequent) should be broken twice: see notes on these lines.

[2] Horace in his glyconics does not observe synaphea and makes the basis rigidly spondaic.

[3] On the origin and development of the cry see P. Maas. *Philol.* lxvi (1907), 590 ff., lxix (1910), 447.

2. cultor : 'dweller'. The noun is not common in this sense, but Plautus has *caeli cultor* of Jupiter (*Amph.* 1065) and Virgil *cultor nemorum* of Aristaeus (*Georg.* i. 14); cf. 64. 300 *cultricem*, 63. 72 *siluicultrix*.

    Vraniae genus : Hymenaeus appears in mythology late: there is no trace of him in Homer. Later he is a young demigod, son of Apollo and a Muse; so first in Pind. fr. 139 Snell, where Linus, Ialemus, and he are sons of Muses who died young. His Muse-mother is variously named—Calliope in Sch. Pind. *Pyth.* 4. 313, Clio in Apollodorus, Terpsichore in Alciphron:: she seems to have been Urania in Callimachus (fr. 2a. 42 Pf.).

    genus : cf. 64. 23 *deum genus*.

3. rapis : there is no need to see reference here to the marriage by violence or capture, the *raptus* which left (or was believed to have left) traces in the Roman marriage ceremony: cf. 62. 21 *auellere*.

4 f. For the refrain see introd., p. 238. The quantity of the first vowel in *hymen* (as of that in ὑμήν) is variable. Catullus uses the short quantity in this poem, the long (which seems to have been an invention of Hellenistic poetry to make the use of the refrain in hexameters possible) in 62; Ovid also uses both quantities.

    The second line cannot be established with certainty from the confusion of the manuscript reading (which repeats the first), but *o hymen hymenaee*, with trochaic first foot, seems preferable to *hymen o hymenaee*.

6 ff. cinge . . . soccum : Hymen is dressed like the bride herself, with the *flammeum* and the yellow shoes: she too wore a chaplet of flowers under her veil (Paul. Fest. 56 L. 'corollam noua nupta de floribus uerbenis herbisque a se lectis sub amiculo ferebat'). He is similarly represented in [Ovid], *Her.* 21. 165–8 (Hymenaeus will not grace Cydippe's forced marrage): 'proicit ipse sua deductas fronte coronas, / spissaque de nitidis tergit amoma comis; / et pudet in tristi laetum consurgere turba, / quique erat in palla, transit in ora rubor'.

7. amaraci : the fragrant red marjoram, *origanum majorana*, an African relative of thyme and mint: cf. Virg. *Aen.* i. 693 'mollis amaracus illum / floribus et dulci adspirans complectitur umbra', Col. x. 296 'odoratas praetexit amaracus umbras'.

8. flammeum : the bride's veil of orange-yellow, taking its name from its colour, which covered the bride from head to foot but left her face exposed: the word for the wearing of it, *nubere*, gave its name to the whole ceremony, *nuptiae*.

9 f. niueo . . . luteum : on the picturesque use of colour-contrast (within a limited range and often amounting to little or nothing more than conventional cliché) in Latin poetry see J. André, *Étude sur les termes de couleur dans la langue latine* (Paris, 1949), pp. 345–51, who classifies the examples of the device. See also 187, 64. 309.

10. luteum . . . soccum : the loose shoe which women wore: for the bride it is orange-yellow like the veil (cf. 160 *aureolos pedes*). *luteum*, which is regularly used of the bridal colour (cf. Plin. *N.H.* xxi. 46 'lutei uideo honorem antiquissimum, in nuptialibus flammeis totum feminis concessum'; Lucan ii. 361 'lutea demissos uelarunt flammea uultus') is a reddish yellow (or yellowish red): Gellius (ii. 26. 8) classes it among the reds and Nemesianus (*Cyn.* 319) writes *rubescere luto*.

13. tinnula : the high-pitched voice of a boy or a woman: cf. Pomponius, fr. 57 R. 'uocem deducas oportet ut uideantur mulieris / uerba.—iube modo adferatur munus: ego uocem dabo / tenuem et tinnulam'.

15. pineam . . . taedam : the pine-torch at the marriage ceremony is a familiar symbol (*Aen.* vii. 397, Ov. *Fast.* ii. 558, &c.: hence the use of *taedae* for *nuptiae*, first in Catullus— 64. 25, 302—and thereafter common); Hymenaeus is represented as carrying it in a fresco from the house of Meleager at Pompeii (Daremberg–Saglio iii. 335). But a special feature of the Roman marriage was the torch of whitethorn; the bride was escorted (Fest. 282 L.) by three *pueri praetextati patrimi et matrimi*, one of whom walked in front carrying *facem ex spina alba* while the other two walked on either side of her. Hence Parthenius proposed, unnecessarily, to read *spineam* here.

16. On Junia and Manlius see introd., p. 237.

17 ff. The bride's beauty is compared to that of Venus when she appeared before Paris.

    Idalium : see on 36. 12.

    iudicem : so Horace calls him 'fatalis incestusque iudex', *Od.* iii. 3. 19.

19. bona cum bona : for similar emphatic repetition of the same word in different forms (*traductio*) cf. 44 *bonae . . . boni*, 179 f. *bonae . . . bene*, 195–7 *bona . . . bonum*.

20. alite : the taking of auspices was a regular part of Roman marriage ritual, but by this time it was a mere formality (Cic. *de Diu.* i. 28 'nihil fere quondam maioris rei nisi auspicato ne priuatim quidem gerebatur, quod etiamnunc nuptiarum auspices declarant qui re omissa nomen tantum tenent') and though the presence of the *auspex* was essential to a proper marriage (Cic. *Clu.* 14), he had become merely a witness to the marriage settlement. The reference here is no more particular than in Horace's 'mala ducis aui domum' (*Od.* i. 15. 5) or Ovid's 'hac aue coniuncti Procne Tereusque' (*Met.* vi. 433).

21. The comparison with flowers is one of the rhetorical commonplaces of the marriage-hymn: cf. Rohde, *Griech. Roman²*, pp. 161–4. The connexion of the myrtle with Venus gives it special point here; the same comparison is used for Ariadne in 64. 89. Ancient taste admits trees and shrubs in such comparisons more freely than ours: so Nausicaa is like a palm-tree in Homer (*Od.* vi. 163), Helen like a cypress in Theocritus (18. 30).

22. Asia : elsewhere *Āsius* refers to the coastal region of Lydia at the mouth of the Maeander, the Ἄσιος λείμων of *Il.* ii. 461, the *Āsia prata*, *Āsia palus* of Virg. *Georg.* i. 383, *Aen.* vii. 701. (Cf. Serv. ad *G.* i. 383 'de palude Asia a longa est; nam de prouincia corripit a'.) Here the reference is probably the same: for the myrtle thrives in a marshy habitat and may well be associated with the Cayster here as with the Eurotas in 64. 89. In the wider reference 'de prouincia', though *Asis* has *ā* in Ovid, following Alexandrian precedent, the adjective *Asius* and the noun *Asia* always have *ă*: so in Catullus 46. 6, 66. 36, 68. 89.

23 ff. quos . . . nutriunt : 'which the wood-nymphs feed with dew-drops to be their plaything'; the phrase was perhaps suggested by παίγνιον or ἄθυρμα. Sappho wrote of the gardens of the Nymphs (Demetr. *de Eloc.* 132); for a treatment of the garden-motif in lyric poetry see H. Fränkel in *Gött. Nachrichten*, 1924, 2, p. 67.

24. roscido : the *rosido* of the manuscripts is an impossible form. Catullus used the usual adjective *roscido*; the much rarer (though more regularly formed) *roridus* appears first in Propertius.

25. nutriunt umore : the substitution of spondee for dactyl in the pherecratean is without parallel in Catullus' glyconics in this poem or in poem 34. The similar substitution in the second foot of the hendecasyllabics of poem 55 is not analogous: for that poem is a metrical experiment in which 'spondaic' lines are more or less evenly distributed among 'dactylic', whereas here the spondee is an isolated exception, and its effect seems to be out of harmony with the lightness

of movement which is characteristic of the metre. (In one
of his glyconic odes, *Oedipus* 882–914, Seneca substitutes
spondee for dactyl in this position in 20 lines out of 32; in
the three others, *H.F.* 875–94, *H.O.* 1031–1130, *Thy.* 336–43,
he does not repeat the experiment.) Maehly's *nutriuntur
honore* neatly restores the dactyl with the archaic deponent
form (used by Virgil in *Georg.* ii. 425); but there is no reason
to suspect *roscido umore* (Pliny has the same phrase, *N.H.*
ix. 38 'roscido, ut creditur, umore uiuentes') and Wilamowitz
(*Hell. Dicht.* ii. 280, n. 1) may be right in explaining the
irregular spondee as due to misunderstanding of apparent
analogies in Greek glyconics: in Anacreon's συρίγγων κοϊλώτερα
(fr. 11 D.) the dactylic second foot looked like a spondee.

26. aditum ferens : cf. 43 *aditum ferat*, 63. 47 *reditum tetulit*,
79 *reditum ferat*, 66. 35 *reditum tetulisset* ; the solemn periphrasis
is revived by Apuleius.

27. perge linquere : 'set about leaving'; the phrase 'throws
more circumstance into the act' (Ellis).

27 f. Thespiae rupis : Helicon, at the foot of which Thespiae
lay; Hymenaeus shares the home of the Muses. Helicon was
not in Aonia, but that old name of the region round Thebes
and the Ismenus provides Latin verse with a convenient
synonym, used first here and often by later poets, for
Boeot(i)us; cf. Virg. *Ecl.* 10. 12 'Aonie Aganippe', *Georg.* iii.
11 'Aonio rediens deducam uertice Musas'.

29. nympha : the fountain is personified as its immanent
nymph: the spring feeds the river Tecmessus and she is
Tecmessus' daughter.

30. frigerans : though *refrigero* is in common use from Cato
onwards, the simple verb occurs only here in classical Latin;
its next appearance is in the fifth-century medical treatise of
Caelius Aurelianus.

31. domum dominam : the bride is about to become the *domina*
of her husband's *domus*: *domus* and *dominus* or *domina* are
often thus placed in emphatic correlation: so Cic. *Fin.* i. 58
'neque . . . beata esse potest . . . in discordia dominorum
domus', *Phil.* xiii. 19 'cum . . . minaretur dominis, notaret
domos', Ov. *Tr.* iii. 1. 58 'isdem sub dominis aspiciare
domus', Petr. 76. 'dominus in domo factus sum'. The correlatives appear together again at 68. 68 'isque domum nobis
isque dedit dominam (?)', where text and interpretation are
uncertain.

32. coniugis cupidam noui : *cupidam* is most naturally taken
with *dominam*: 'summon the mistress to her new home,
filled with desire for her husband' (and so overcoming her

hesitation: cf. 81), 'binding her heart with love's ivy'.
Wilamowitz (*Hell. Dicht.* ii. 285), following Bonnet, punctuates after *uoca* and takes *cupidam* with *mentem*, 'binding the
bridegroom's impassioned heart': but the action of *reuinciens*
is then entirely unrelated to that of *uoca* and this seems a
dubious use of the participle.

34. tenax hedera : 'a common simile applied in an uncommon
way' (Ellis). Usually it is the lover that is the clinging ivy
(Hor. *Od.* i. 36. 20 'Damalis . . . lasciuis hederis ambitiosior',
Epod. 15. 5): here it is love.

36. integrae : cf. 34. 2. **par dies :** i.e. the day of their own
marriage.

38. in modum : 'in tune': the same 'modal' use of *in* is seen in
in numerum (Virg. *Ecl.* 6. 27, &c.), *in orbem, in ordinem, in
versum*.

42. citarier : Catullus has the archaic infinitive four times again
in this poem (65, 70, 75 *compararier*, 68 *nitier*), probably also
at 68. 141.

44. bonae Veneris : 'hoc dicit quia est et mala Venus' (Landi).

45. coniugator : the noun occurs only here: Cicero uses the verb
(*Off.* i. 58).

46. quis deus : cf. 40. 3 'quis deus', 66. 31 'quis te mutauit
tantus deus ?', 62, 20 and 26. As Löfstedt points out (*Synt.* ii.
83), the distinction often drawn between *quis* as the substantival and *qui* as the adjectival form of the interrogative
pronoun is without foundation: in many authors *quis* is the
more frequent form in both uses and the evidence suggests
that *qui* was a development from *quis* due to the nature of the
following sound and that in both uses *quis* was the more
literary form. Throughout Latin literature *quis deus*, not *qui
deus*, is the normal expression; from the classical period
Löfstedt cites 22 examples of *quis* against only one of *qui*.
In the indefinite the same preference is clear: *si quis deus* is
normal and there seems to be only one certain instance of
si qui deus. On the other hand, *(scire) qui sim (sis, sit)* is
universally preferred to *quis sim*; see on 17. 22.

46 f. magis est ama-/tis petendus amantibus : Bergk's transposition (for inversion of order in the manuscripts see 1. 8,
23. 13; 30. 8) neatly restores the metre, but the reading is not
as convincing as it looks at first sight: for *amant amantur* and
similar phrases quoted in support (see on 45. 20), in which
reciprocity is expressed by active and passive in asyndeton,
are not strictly parallel to this, and the use of *amatis* to take
the place of a present participle is dubious. An adjective—

perhaps *anxiis*, suggested by Haupt—may have been assimilated to the following *amantibus*.

51. tremulus : of the shakiness of age, as in 68. 142 (cf. 61. 154, 64. 307).

    suis : 'on behalf of his children': cf. Plaut. *Amph.* 1061 'deos sibi inuocat'.

53. soluunt : for the prosody see on 2*b*. 13.

55. captat : 'strains to catch' the sound of the approaching procession. **nouos maritus:** 'the bridegroom'; cf. Ter. *Ad.* 938 'ego nouos maritus anno demum quinto et sexagesimo / fiam ?' so 66. 20 'nouo ... uiro'; similarly *noua nupta*, 'bride', in 91.

56. fero : of the *ardor uiolentus* of love, as Ellis says. There is no need to accept his further suggestion that the word contains a reference to the survivals of primitive marriage by violence. *a gremio* may contain a suggestion of the token removal of the bride from the arms (*e gremio*) of her mother or her next-of-kin which seems to have been the first act of the marriage ceremony (Fest. 364 L.), and *in manus* may carry a reminiscence of the old formula of marriage *in manum*. But *a gremio* is a natural phrase, which does not need that explanation, and the principle of marriage *in manum* was obsolescent or obsolete in Catullus' time, when the wife did not normally pass into the legal *manus* of her husband but remained in the *potestas* of her father or, if he was not alive, was *sui iuris*.

61. The three following stanzas present successively the blessings of marriage in the relation of man and woman, in the family, and in society. Ellis appositely cites Cic. *Off.* i. 54 'prima societas in ipso coniugio est, proxima in liberis, deinde una domus, communia omnia: id autem est principium urbis et quasi seminarium rei publicae'.

67. liberos dare : cf. 205 *liberos date*. *dare* does not occur in prose in this connexion, but the use of it here and elsewhere in verse suggests an old formula: so Virg. *Aen.* i. 274 'geminam partu dabit Ilia prolem', Ov. *Her.* 6. 122 'pignora Lucina bina fauente dedi', Hor. *Od.* iii. 6. 47 'mox daturos / progeniem uitiosiorem', Tib. ii. 5. 91 'fetus matrona dabit'.

    It is true that children born without *iustae nuptiae* were legally not *liberi* (Gaius i. 64), but the contrast here implied is not between *spurii* and *legitimi* but between children and childlessness. 'C. will eben nicht als Statistiker sondern als Hochzeitsdichter verstanden sein' (Riese).

68. stirpe nitier : the metaphor of the family as prop or stay is common: cf. Cic. *Cael.* 79 'qui hoc ... filio nititur': similarly

fulcire, Prop. iv. 11. 69 'serie fulcite genus', Plin. *Ep*. iv. 21. 3
'nunc unus . . . domum pluribus adminiculis paulo ante
fundatam fulcit ac sustinet', Sen. *Contr*. ii. 1. 7 'non tibi per
multos fulta liberos domus est'.

72. praesides : the sense of 'defender', which is normal in
praesidium, is rare in *praeses* : but cf. Cic. *Sest*. 137 'senatum
rei publicae custodem praesidem propugnatorem', Livy vi.
16. 2 'uestrum (i.e. deorum) militem ac praesidem', xxiii. 48.
7 'praesides prouinciarum exercitus'.

77. adest : that is, she has left the women's quarters and is in
the hall of her house, ready to join the procession, though she
is still shyly hesitating inside. There is no need to change to
ades, which anyhow is too peremptory a command for this
context; contrast the respectful *prodeas* of ll. 87–113.

77 f. uiden ut . . . quatiunt : cf. 62. 8 'uiden ut perniciter exsiluere'. The quasi-parenthetical use of *uiden* (= *uidesne*)
with an exclamatory phrase (like *voici* or *voilà*) is a regular
colloquial idiom (e.g. Plaut. *Curc*. 311 'uiden ut expalluit',
Most. 1172 'uiden ut astat furcifer'), which seems to have
been adopted by the *neoterici* : in classical poetry it is confined
to Catullus and Virgil.[1] Both use *uiden*, the colloquial origin
of which is revealed by the 'iambic shortening' (see on 10. 27)
of the second syllable (*Aen*. vi. 779 'uiden ut geminae stant
uertice cristae'), and both have the similar use of *aspic(it)e*
(62. 12 'aspicite ut . . . requirunt', *Ecl*. 5. 6 'aspice ut antrum /
siluestris raris sparsit labrusca racemis', 4. 52, *Aen*. vi. 855,
viii. 190); Virgil has also the variant *nonne uides* (*Georg*. i. 56).
In 94 below *uiden?* is similarly used without *ut*, which has
been wrongly inserted in the manuscripts to conform to this
line.

78. quatiunt comas : the torches are being swung to fan the
flame: cf. Prop. i. 3. 10 'et quaterent sera nocte facem pueri',
Plin. *Ep*. iv. 9. 11 'ut ignem faces assidua concussione custo-
diunt'. The metaphor is as old as Aeschylus (*P.V.* 1044
πυρὸς ἀμφήκης βόστρυχος) : cf. Sen. *Oed*. 309 'ignis . . . summam
in auras fusus explicuit comam'.

79. The general sense of the missing lines is clear: there is a
last-minute conflict in the bride's mind between her restraining *pudor* on the one hand and the promptings of love (or of
the waiting crowd's cries?) on the other, and she is tempted
to listen (*magis audiens*) to the voice of *pudor*: the next
words reassure her. Since the subjunctive *tardet* may well
have been governed by the construction of the missing lines,

[1] Tibullus has *uiden ut* once (ii. 1. 25), but with the subjunctive.

there is no need to assume that Catullus used an intransitive *tardeo* which, unlike the analogous *lenteo*, is nowhere found.

79. ingenuus pudor : the delicacy of feeling which comes from birth and breeding; cf. Sen. *Dial.* ii. 15. 1, Plin. *N.H. praef.* 21 (for a list of instances from later literature see D. R. Shackleton Bailey, *Propertiana*, p. 112). Similarly Cic. *de Or.* ii. 10 'pudore a dicendo et timiditate ingenua quadam refugisti'.

80. audiens : 'listening to' i.e. paying attention to: cf. Cic. *Fam.* ii. 7. 1 'numquam labere si te audies', *Fin.* i. 42 'si Epicurum audire uoluerint', Virg. *Georg.* i. 514 'neque audit currus habenas'.

84 ff. ne qua . . . uenientem : 'that any woman more beautiful has ever seen the bright day coming from ocean': a variation on the commoner formula of, e.g., Eur. *Hec.* 635 τὰν καλλίσταν ὁ χρυσοφαὴς Ἅλιος αὐγάζει. A more homely assurance is given to a bride in a *togata* of Titinius (fr. 106 R.), 'accede ad sponsum audacter: uirgo nulla est talis Setiae'.

87. uario : 'many-coloured': a favourite word in Latin poetry, with its fondness for suggestions of bright colour-contrast (see on 10 and 187): cf. Virg. *Aen.* iv. 202 'uariis florentia limina sertis', vi. 708 'floribus insidunt uariis', *Ecl.* 9. 40 'uarios hic flumina circum / fundit humus flores', Tib. i. 7. 45.

88–89. diuitis . . . hyacinthinus : there may be a verbal echo of two Homeric phrases, *Od.* vi. 231 οὔλας ἧκε κόμας ὑακινθίνῳ ἄνθει ὁμοίας and *Il.* xi. 68 ἀνδρὸς μάκαρος κατ' ἄρουραν. *diuitis* is not otiose; for the flower-garden is the privilege of means. Sappho (fr. 105 (c) L.-P.) had compared the unwanted girl, perhaps, to the wild ὑάκινθος trampled underfoot (see p. 254): Grimal's suggestion (*Les jardins romains*, p. 401) that Catullus' words are a deliberate inversion of that figure is fanciful, but he has some good remarks on the 'topiary' quality of Catullus' references to flowers.

89. hyacinthinus : the first appearance of the *hyacinthus* in Latin. What plant the Romans—and the Greeks—meant by the name, and whether they always meant the same one, cannot be said with certainty. But all the plants with which *hyacinthus* has been identified (martagon, larkspur, cornflag) *stant*, i.e. rise erect on tall stems.

91. noua nupta : the ordinary term for 'bride'; cf. 66. 15, Ter. *Ad.* 751. Similarly *nouus maritus* in 55.

92 f. si iam uidetur : *iam* adds a touch of impatience to the normal polite formula.

94 f. uiden . . . comas : see on 77.

97. leuis : of fickleness in love: so Prop. ii. 24. 18 'tam te formosam non pudet esse leuem'.

    in mala : For the use of *in*, 'over', of the object of interest or affection, see on 64. 98. With *deditus* the only other classical examples are in Lucr. iii. 647 'in pugnae studio quod dedita mens est', iv. 815 'quibus est in rebus deditus ipse'.

102. lenta : see on 64. 183.

    adsitas : 'planted beside them', a technical term of viticulture: Cato 32. 3 'arbores facito ut bene maritae sint uitesque uti satis multae adserantur', Varro, *R.R.* i. 16. 6 'uitis adsita ad holus facere solet'.

103. implicat : Catullus varies the usual metaphor (so commonplace that it appears even in the technical prose of Cato and Columella: see on 62. 54 'ulmo coniuncta marito'), which makes the tree husband the vine.

107. o cubile : a fragment of a glyconic epithalamium of Ticidas (see Introd., p. xix) has a similar apostrophe: 'felix lectule talibus / sole amoribus'.

108. candido : i.e. of ivory.

110 ff. gaudia, quae . . . gaudeat : 'what pleasures for him to enjoy in the night or in the daytime': for the cognate accusative cf. Ter. *And.* 964 'hunc scio mea solide solum gauisurum gaudia', Cael. ap. Cic. *Fam.* viii. 2. 1 'ut suum gaudium gauderemus'.

    uaga nocte : 'ranging', not 'fleeting', as some translations have it; the proper reference of *vagus* is to range of movement, not to speed: see on 64. 271. Night is thought of as ranging the sky in her chariot, as in Enn. *scaen.* 112 V. '(Nox) quae caua caeli / signitenentibus conficis bigis', Virg. *Aen.* v. 721 'Nox atra polum bigis subuecta tenebat', viii. 407 'medio iam noctis abactae / curriculo'.

    medio die : cf. Ov. *Am.* i. 5. 1, 26.

117. io Hymen Hymenaee io : if the text is sound, *io* must be monosyllabic, as it is in Martial xi. 2. 5 (in another ritual cry) 'clamant ecce mei "io Saturnalia" uersus', and probably in a fragment of trochaic dialogue from an *Atellana* (Ribbeck, p. 332) 'io bucco!—quis me iubilat?—uicinus tuus antiquus'.

120. Fescennina iocatio : the singing of ribald extempore lines was a regular accompaniment of the Roman marriage ceremony. (Seneca anachronistically makes a chorus of Corinthians refer to it, *Medea* 107, 113.) Of the two ancient derivations (Fest. p. 76 L.) of their name of *uersus Fescennini*, one (offered also by Servius on *Aen.* vii. 695), from the Faliscan town of Fescennium, may be mere popular etymology; the other, from *fascinum*, the evil eye, may be true. For the custom represents a familiar form of primitive superstition, the attempt, at moments of human happiness, to cheat the power of the evil eye, of *inuidia* (see on 5. 12), by 'taking down' the fórtunate person. The abusive lines sung by the troops at a victorious general's triumph were of the same sort and had the same purpose: in Pliny's striking phrase (*N.H.* xxviii. 39), they were addressed to 'Fortuna gloriae carnifex'. At weddings the tradition lasted into the late Empire; Claudian writes literary *Fescennina* on the marriage of Honorius and Ausonius' hymenaeal cento has its Fescennine passage (p. 216 Peiper).

121. nuces : walnuts were scattered among the crowd during the singing of the *Fescennini*: cf. Plin. *N.H.* xv. 86 'nuces iuglandes nuptialium Fescenninorum comites'. Virgil's 'sparge, marite, nuces' (*Ecl.* 8. 31) may mean either that the bridegroom throws them himself or that he has them thrown; here they are scattered by the *concubinus*. The ancient explanations of the custom cannot be taken seriously: Festus can only offer the vague suggestion 'ut nouae nuptae intranti domum noui mariti secundum fiat auspicium', and Servius the fantastic one 'quod proiectae in terram tripudium solistimum faciunt'.

Nuts were used as playthings in children's games—Hor. *Sat.* ii. 3. 171, Suet. *Aug.* 83 '(Augustus) modo talis aut ocellatis nucibusque ludebat cum pueris minutis'—and *nuces ponere* or *relinquere* is to put away childish things (Mart. xiv. 185. 2 'ne nucibus positis "arma uirumque" legas', Pers. 1. 10 'nucibus facimus quaecumque relictis'). Hence the point of 125–6; the pampered favourite now has to grow up.

122 f. desertum . . . amorem : 'realizing from what he hears that his master's love for him is forsaken'.

127. Talasio or **Talassio** was a ritual cry at the *deductio*, of unknown origin. The ancients knew two accounts of it, an historical one explaining it as the dative of a proper noun and connecting it with the rape of the Sabine women (Livy i. 9, Plut. *Q.R.* 31, *Rom.* 15), and an etymological one connecting it with τάλαρος, and interpreting it as an indication that the bride was passing to the duty of *lanificium* in her husband's house (Varro ap. Fest. 478 L.). Whatever its origin, a marriage-god was made out of it—Talas(s)ius (or Talassus, Mart. xii. 42. 4), a Roman counterpart of Hymenaeus. Here *Talasio* must be dative: 'your master now chooses to take Talasius as his master'.

129. sordebant . . . uilicae : the pampered and privileged city-bred *delicatus* thought himself too good for the homely bailiffs' wives on the country estate: cf. Virg. *Ecl.* 2. 44 'sordent tibi munera nostra', Plin. *N.H.* xxxv. 88 '(Protagenes) sordebat suis', 'was not good enough for his own countrymen'.

130. hodie atque heri : 'the other day'. The phrase occurs only here in this form but Plautus has *hodie aut heri* (*Most.* 953) and *heri aut hodie* (*St.* 152) in the same sense.

132. tondet : now his long hair is on the point of being cut off by the barber; cf. Hor. *Od.* iv. 10. 2 cum . . . / . . quae nunc humeris inuolitant deciderint comae', Stat. *Silv.* iii. 4 (on the dedication of the *capilli* of the Emperor's favourite Earinus). The *cinerarius* is properly the hair-dresser, so called because his curling-irons were heated *in cinere* (Varro, *L.L.* v. 129) or because he used powder as a hair-dye: now he is to cut off the boy's hair instead of curling it. Martial, with these lines in mind, makes the bride see to it herself: xi. 78. 3 'flammea texuntur sponsae: iam uirgo paratur: / tondebit pueros iam noua nupta tuos'.

134 ff. male . . . abstinere : 'have difficulty in keeping off': cf. Virg. *Geo.* i. 360 'a curuis male temperat unda carinis', Ov. *Am.* i. 14. 51 'lacrimas male continet'.

139. licent : a pronominal subject with *licet* is not uncommon (e.g. Cic. *Cael.* 48—with a similar reference—'quando denique fuit ut quod licet non liceret?'), but the plural is rare before the silver age: Ov. *Met.* x. 329 'felices quibus ista licent', Sen. *Contr.* ix. 25. 17 'quaedam quae licent tempore et loco mutato non licent' seem to be the earliest examples.

145 f. ne neges, ni . . . eat : *nē* and *ni* (reduced from earlier *nei*, formed from *ně* and deictic *-i*) were originally simple negative particles without subordinating function. Relics of their original use survive in (*a*) *nē . . . quidem, nēquaquam, nēquiquam*, and the combinations *ut ne, dum ne, quomodo ne*, &c., (*b*) *nimirum, quidni*. Both became subordinating conjunctions and they were differentiated in function. *ni* has already acquired its specialized use in conditional clauses in the Twelve Tables: in Plautus it is interchangeable with *nisi*, which later supplanted it except in certain fixed phrases (such as *quod ni ita sit*) and in poetic diction, in which it provided a convenient alternative. But sporadic traces survive of the earlier use of *ni* in final clauses, in which later convention required *ne*. It occurs twice in Lucretius (iii. 286, 734, where *niue* corresponds to a preceding *ne*), twice in Virgil (*Aen.* vi. 353, attested by Rufinianus, iii. 686, attested by Donatus and

Servius) and once in Propertius (ii. 7. 3). Catullus has final *ni* only here, where it may be due to desire to avoid having two *ne*-clauses depending on the same verb; he has final *ne* ten times.

149 f. potens et beata : both adjectives refer to material prosperity: for *potens* cf. Ter. *Eun.* 353 'quis is est tam potens cum tanto munere hoc ? ', Phaedrus i. 24. 1 'inops potentem dum uult imitari perit'; for *beata* 51. 15 'beatas urbes', Hor. *Od.* iii. 7. 3 'Thyna merce beatum', *Ep.* i. 2. 44 'beata uxor'.

152. The refrain interrupts a sentence here only.

155. anilitas is not found elsewhere: but *puerilitas* and *iuuenilitas* are both used by Varro.

156. adnuit : the shaking head looks like a continuous 'Yes': Ovid makes a similar point, *Her.* 19. 45 'adnuit illa fere non nostra quod oscula curet / sed mouet obrepens somnus anile caput '.

159 f. transfer . . . limen . . . pedes : the double accusative occurs with *transferre* elsewhere only in *Bell. Alex.* 60. 5 ('castra Baetim transfert') but is common with *traicere* and *traducere*.

160. aureolos : see on 2*b*. 12.

161. forem : the singular is not uncommon in Plautus and is found in prose: Cic. *Tusc.* v. 59 'cum forem cubiculi clauserat', Livy vi. 34. 6 'forem uirga percuteret'.

   rasilem : may refer to the polished wood—or metal (cf. *rasilis fibula* Ov. *Met.* viii. 318, *rasile argentum* Vell. ii. 56. 2) —of the door itself; more probably *foris* is being used of the doorway and *rasilis* refers to its worn threshold, the *tritum limen* of 68. 71.

   The bride has now reached her new home. There by custom she was lifted over the threshold by her attendants, whether that rite was a formal relic of marriage by capture and the abduction of an unwilling bride (an explanation given among others by Plutarch, *Q.R.* 29; for reasons against believing that it is the true one see H. J. Rose, *Plutarch's Roman Questions*, pp. 103 ff.) or was intended to avoid the possibility of stumbling and consequent bad luck. *Transfer* is not inconsistent with her being lifted across, but perhaps she steps across unaided circumspectly as the bride is enjoined to do in Plautus, *Cas.* 815: 'sensim supera limen tolle pedes, mea noua nupta; / sospes iter incipe hoc '.

164. The bridegroom, awaiting the bride's arrival, is seen through the doorway. *accubare* is normally used of reclining at table, but that can hardly be implied here; the marriage feast was held in the bride's home before the *deductio* began. Nor can *torus* be the marriage-couch; as ll. 184–5 show, it

was in an inner room. Pasquali (*Stud. It.* i [1920], 5 ff.) thinks
that the *torus* is the *lectus genialis* which stood in the *atrium*
of the Roman house; but in classical times at any rate it was
not meant for occupation by a human wedded pair but was
a symbolic sacred object tenanted by the *genius* and the *juno*
of the pair. [The *lect(ul)us aduersus* (facing the door) seems
to have been the solemn seat of the *materfamilias* (Ascon. in
Mil. p. 38 K., Laberius ap. Gell. xvi. 9. 4), but the identification of it with the *lectus genialis* is doubtful.] It may be best
to suppose that the bridegroom is merely pictured as lying on
a couch, while he waits for the bride's procession to arrive, as
his modern counterpart would sit on a chair. By Roman
custom he would admit her formally to share his home (*aqua
et igni accipere*) on her arrival: that ceremony Catullus
passes over. *unus* in the sense of 'unaccompanied' can perhaps be supported by Lucan v. 806, 'uiduo tum primum
frigida lecto / atque insueta quies uni, nudumque marito /
non haerente latus' but Statius' *intus* is probable.

166. **totus immineat :** 'he is entirely intent on you': for *im-
    minere* of mental direction cf. *Culex* 90 f. 'huc imminet, omnis /
    dirigit huc sensus', Ov. *Met.* i. 146 'imminet exitio uir co-
    niugis'.

169. **non minus ac :** the illogical use of *ac* after a comparative,
    by analogy from its use after *similis, alius, aeque, secus*, is
    rare except in Horace, who favours it.

170. **uritur :** *uri* is common of the lover's passion (cf. 83. 6
    uritur, Virg. *Aen.* iv. 68, Hor. *Od.* i. 13. 9, &c.): but this use
    with *flamma*, not the person or the thing heated, as the sub-
    ject, is unparalleled.

171. **penite :** the adverb *penitus* (a formation from *penus*
    parallel to *funditus, medullitus, radicitus*) has already become
    an adjective in Plautus (e.g. *Asin.* 41 'ex penitis faucibus',
    Pers. 541 'ex Arabia penitissima', *Cist.* 63 'pectore penitis-
    simo'), and the use was later revived by the archaizers (e.g.
    Apul. *Met.* xi. 6 'penita mente conditum'). The secondary
    adverbial formation *penite* occurs only here.

174. The bride's escort leaves her at the door of the bride-
    chamber. There is no difficulty in the singular *praetextate*:
    the command is addressed to each of her supporting *prae-
    textati*, one on either side, at the same time, and there is no
    need to suppose that on the threshold they had handed her
    over to the torchbearer.

179 f. **uos ... feminae :** addressed to the *pronubae*, the *matronae
    uniuirae* (Fest. 282 L., Serv. ad *Aen.* iv. 166) who prepared
    the bride.

senibus . . . cognitae bene : long and happily mated to one
husband. For *cognitae* in this sense cf. Prop. ii. 29. 33 'sat
erit mihi cognitus unus'.

bonae . . . bene : cf. 19 n., 44, 195–7.

181. collocate : the technical term, as Donatus notes on Ter.
Eun. 593 'deinde eam in lecto conlocarunt'.

184. The bridegroom is summoned from the *atrium* to join the
bride; the *epithalamium* proper, addressed to the wedded pair,
follows.

185. tibi est : Bentley's transposition removes the hiatus: for
inversion in the manuscripts cf. 46.

187. parthenice : presumably the white camomile which Pliny
(*N.H.* xxi. 176) calls *parthenium*; the poppy is *luteum*, i.e. red
(see on 10). Virgil similarly describes a white-and-red complexion, *Aen.* xii. 67–69 'Indum sanguineo ueluti uiolauerit
ostro / si quis ebur, aut mixta rubent ubi lilia multa / alba
rosa, tales uirgo dabat ore colores': cf. [Tib.] iii. 4. 30 ff. 'color
in niueo corpore purpureus, / ut iuueni primum uirgo deducta
marito / inficitur teneras ore rubente genas, / et cum contexunt
amarantis alba puellae / lilia et autumno candida mala
rubent', Prop. ii. 3. 11 ff. 'ut Maeotica nix minio si certet
Hibero / utque rosae puro lacte natant folia'. The cliché is
a favourite one in Latin verse; a long list of examples from
Ennius to Claudian is given by H. Blümner, *Philol.* xlviii
(1889), pp. 157–8. For other examples of colour contrast see
10 and 64. 308–9.

189. at : turning to the bridegroom: *at* marks another transition at 225.

189 f. ita me iuuent caelites : cf. 66. 18 'ita me diui · .. iuerint';
97. 1 'ita me di ament'.

193. ne remorare : the same archaism at 62. 59, 67. 18.

196 f. palam quod cupis cupis : for the juxtaposition cf. Plaut.
Epid. 196 'age si quid agis', Lucr. iv. 723 'quae ueniunt,
ueniant'.

199 f. puleuris . . . siderum : cf. 7. 3–8.

201. subducat : either jussive ('let him first reckon up the
number of the sands') or potential ('the man who wants to
count your pleasures would sooner count the sands').

203. multa milia ludi : cf. 16. 12 'milia multa basiorum': the
sing. *ludi* is used collectively. For *ludus* in this context cf.
Livy xxvi. 50. 5 'si frui liceret ludo aetatis praesertim in
recto et legitimo amore et non res publica animum nostrum
occupasset'.

204. ludite ut lubet : cf. 17. 17.

208. ingenerari : 'but be constantly inbred from the same source'—i.e. without resort to adoption.

209 ff. paruulus ... similis patri : Virgil remembered these lines and repeated *paruulus* with a new pathos in Dido's words, *Aen.* iv. 328–9, 'si quis mihi paruulus aula / luderet Aeneas qui te tamen ore referret, / non equidem omnino capta ac deserta uiderer'.

uolŏ : see on 10. 27.

212. rideat ad patrem : 'smile to greet his father': cf. Virg. *Ecl.* 4. 60 'incipe, parue puer, risu cognoscere matrem'. For the use of *ad* cf. 3. 10, Ov. *Met.* iii. 245 'ad nomen caput ille refert'.

213. semihiante : the compound appears first in Catullus (as do *semimortuus* 50. 15, *semirasus* 59. 5, *semilautus* 54. 2) and not again till Apuleius, who repeats the phrase (*Flor.* 2. 15 *semihiantibus labellis*). For the prosody (‿◡‿, the first *i* having consonantal value) cf. Virg. *Aen.* viii. 194 *semihominis Caci*, poet. *ap.* Gell. xix. 11. 4 *semihiulco sauio*.

215 f. insciis ... omnibus : *V*'s *insciens* has been defended but the only sense it can give ('may he be readily recognized, though he is unconscious of it, by everyone') is quite pointless. *insciis* must mean 'those who do not know the facts (of his relationship)', not 'who do not know him'. *omnibus / et* breaks the rule of synaphea elsewhere invariable in this poem and Dawes's transposition of *insciis* and *omnibus* or Pleitner's *obuiis* (for the corruption cf. 64. 109) should be accepted.

217 f. pudicitiam ... ore : i.e. his resemblance to his father will prove his mother's faithfulness: for the idea cf. Hor. *Od.* iv. 5. 23 'laudantur simili prole puerperae', Mart. vi. 27. 3 (a reminiscence of this passage) 'est tibi, quae patria signatur imagine uoltus, / testis maternae nata pudicitiae'. [In Ov. *Tr.* iv. 5. 31, *Pont.* ii. 8. 32, the reference is to moral resemblance: a son's virtues show him to be his father's son.]

219. talis : 'may he have a good name inherited from a good mother to establish his descent, like the matchless reputation derived from his mother that rests on Telemachus'. The comparison is awkwardly expressed, but the point is clear; the good name which he owes to his mother will prove him his mother's son.

223. Penelopeo : the personal adjective (see on 44. 10, 64. 368) emphatically closes the stanza. For the orthography of the adjective see on 68. 109.

227. munere : for the erotic sense cf. Petr. 87. 8 'et non plane iam molestum erat munus'; similarly *officium*, Prop. ii. 22. 24, ii. 25. 39, Ov. *Am.* iii. 7. 24.

228. exercete : 'give play to': cf. Phaedr. *App.* 10. 4 'exercebat feruidam adulescentiam', Calp. Sic. 5. 11 'gnauam exercere iuuentam'.

62

This marriage-poem, unlike poem 61, has no reference to a particular occasion; it is not even tied to a particular locality. It is a fanciful composite picture in which Greek and Roman motifs are combined.

The time is evening, the traditional time for weddings both in Greece and at Rome. The scene of the opening lines is that of a Greek wedding, with a feast, the θοίνη γαμική, in the bride's father's house, men and women sitting apart. The separate tables suggest the motif of competition between two choirs which provides the pattern of the poem. But the bride is not present at the feast with the wedding-party, as Greek custom prescribed (Lucian, *Conv.* 8, Athen. xiv. 644d): she comes to join them later (4 *iam ueniet uirgo*), as she joined the procession at a Roman wedding for the *deductio* to her new home.

The young men see the evening star first and rise to be ready to greet the bride (1–4); the girls take their cue and rise to face them (6–9); then the men set the stage for the competition in eight lines of playful self-admonition. The amoebaean contest begins at l. 20. Five lines addressed to the evening star by the girls (20–25) are answered by five, closely parallel in structure, from the men (26–31). The symmetry of the second pair of stanzas is mutilated; only the first of the girls' lines is preserved and the beginning of the men's is lost. The third pair again correspond very closely in structure—the men take up the girls' words and ingeniously turn them in mischievous parody—but not exactly in length: unless a line has been lost, as Spengel suggested, after 41, the girls have nine lines (39–47), the men ten (49–58). Regarding themselves as the winners, the men take the last word and proceed to address their homily (59–65) to the bride, who has appeared during the singing. The hymenaeal refrain serves to make the pattern clear, marking off each section from the next: the manuscripts omit it after 58, probably rightly, since there is no change of speaker and with *et tu* the men go straight from their triumphant conclusion to point the moral for the bride.

Echoes of Sappho have been detected in the poem: l. 32 has been related to one of the hymenaeal fragments (104 L.–P.) Ἕσπερε, πάντα φέρων ὅσα φαίνολις ἐσκέδασ᾽ Αὔως, and the metaphor

of the garden-flower (39 ff.) to another (105 (c) L.–P., οἴαν τὰν
ὐάκινθον ἐν ὤρεσι ποίμενες ἄνδρες / πόσσι καταστείβοισι, χάμαι δέ τε
πόρφυρον ἄνθος . . .. But these resemblances are far from striking.
The poem owes much to Greek poetry: the careful symmetry,[1]
the calculated repetitions[2] and the formal use of the refrain show
how much Catullus had learned from it.[3] But the spirit of the
poem is original and the humour and vivacity[4] are his own.
  [For a study of the poem see E. Fraenkel, *J.R.S.* xlv (1955),
1 ff.]

1. Vesper : the evening star, in earlier Latin *Vesperugo*;
  Catullus is the first to use this name, presumably on the
  analogy of the Greek Ἕσπερος (l. 20 *Hesperus*).

  Olympo, 'in the heavens', a local ablative like *caelo* in l. 20.
  For *Olympus* in this sense cf. Virg. *Ecl.* 6. 86 'inuito processit
  Vesper Olympo', *Georg.* i. 450 '(sol) emenso cum iam decedit
  Olympo', iii. 223 'reboant siluaeque et longus Olympus';
  Ὄλυμπος is already so used in Soph. *Ajax* 1389 Ὀλύμπου τοῦδ'
  ('these heavens that we see') ὁ πρεσβεύων πατήρ.

2. uix tandem : for the emphatic use of *uix* strengthening
  tandem (implying that the event takes so long to happen that
  it comes near to not happening at all) cf. 68. 121, Plaut.
  Most. 727 'uix tandem percepi super his rebus nostris te
  loqui', Ter. *And.* 470 'ah / uix tandem sensi stolidus', Cic.
  Fam. iii. 9. 1 'uix tandem legi litteras'; similarly 66. 68
  uix sero. Like other forceful idioms of ordinary speech (e.g.
  nec non, satis superque, aspice ut) it is taken up by Virgil (e.g.
  Aen. ii. 128, iii. 309).

  tollit : cf. Ov. *F.* iv. 944 '(Eos) sustulit immenso ter iubar
  orbe suum'.

4. iam ueniet uirgo : i.e. she will leave her father's house and
  join the procession as she is summoned to do in 61. 92–96.

  hymenaeus : the processional marriage-song: see introduction to 61.

  dicetŭr : for the lengthening see on 64. 20.

5. For the refrain see on 61: here it is adapted to form a

---

[1] 20–24)(26–30, 42–47)(53–58.
[2] Epanalepsis in 8–9 'exsiluere . . . exsiluere', 21–22 'complexu
auellere matris, / complexu matris . . . auellere', 60–61 'pater . . .
ipse, / ipse pater'; anaphora in 3–4, 18, 28, 42, 44, 50, 53, 55.
[3] The frequency of the characteristically Greek rhythm produced
by the trochaic caesura in the third foot (9, 13, 16, 60, 61) is noticeable.
[4] Observe the conversational flavour of the sprightly opening lines,
with *nimirum, sic certest, uiden ut, non temere, nec mirum.*

hexameter, with a variation of quantity in *Hymen—Hyme-naee*, as in Theoc. 18. 58 'Υμὴν ὦ 'Υμέναιε, γάμῳ ἐπὶ τῷδε χαρείης.

7. **Oetaeos . . . ignes** : the epithet has no local significance here; Oeta is conventionally associated with the rising of the evening star: cf. Virg. *Ecl.* 8. 30 'sparge, marite, nuces: tibi deserit Hesperus Oetam' (on which Servius says that there was a cult of Hesperus on Mount Oeta and that he was represented on Locrian coinage), *Culex* 203 'piger aurata procedit Vesper ab Oeta': so of the morning star, *Ciris* 350, Stat. *Silv.* v. 4. 8.

Noctifer : formed on the analogy of *Lucifer*; perhaps a coinage of Catullus.

8. **sic certest** : 'Yes, that is what it is': cf. 80. 7.

uiden ut . . . exsiluere : on the indicative in this stereotyped idiomatic formula (note that the singular *uiden* is used although it is addressed to a number of persons) and in the similar formula *aspic(it)e ut*, see on 61. 77.

9. **non temere** : 'not for nothing': cf. Ter. *Heaut.* 620 'nescioquid tristis est: non temere est', Hor. *Ep.* ii. 1. 120 'uatis auarus / non temere est animus' ('it takes something to make the poet a miser'), Livy i. 59. 6 'quicquid sit, haud temere esse rentur'.

uincere : Guarinus's conjecture is necessary. Even if the use of *uisere* were possible, which is very doubtful (in the instances adduced in support—Virg. *Aen.* iv. 490 'mugire uidebis / sub pedibus terram', Hor. *Sat.* ii. 8. 77 'uideres stridere. . . susurros', Prop. ii. 16. 49 'uidistis toto sonitus percurrere caelo'—the verb does not mean 'look at', as it would have to mean here, but only 'see'), it is inappropriate; the young women here, like the young men in 11, are not concerned with admiring their rivals, but with beating them.

11. **parata** : 'we have no easy victory ready made': for *paratus* in this sense (corresponding to ἕτοιμος) cf. Petr. 15. 9 'nec uictoria mi placet parata', Pliny, *Pan.* 88. 4 'paratum id quidem et in medio positum'.

12. **aspicite . . . requirunt** : see on 8 above and on 61. 77.

meditata requirunt, 'they are searching in their minds (*secum*) for what they have learned': for *meditata*, 'rehearsed', 'studied', cf. Pliny, *Ep.* i. 16. 2 'siue meditata siue subita proferret', Tac. *Ann.* xiii. 3 'nec in Claudio, quoties meditata dissereret, elegantiam requireres', Stat. *Silv.* ii. 1. 74 'compositosque sales meditataque uerba locutus', Suet. *Aug.* 84 'meditata et composita oratio'.

14. **nec mirum . . . quae** : i.e. *nec mirum est eas non frustra meditari quae*, &c. For the indicative in a causal clause of this

type see on 64. 157; in 21 and 27 below Catullus has the normal subjunctive.

15. nos : 'whereas we': as often, a strong contrast is marked by asyndeton.

    alio ... diuisimus aures : probably 'we have let our minds and our ears go in different directions' (i.e. we have been listening without thinking) rather than 'we have let both our ears and our minds be distracted'. In either case *animos conuertite* is contrasted, 'turn your minds to business'.

16. amat uictoria curam : there is a reminiscence of this half-line in Virg. *Ecl.* 3. 59 'alternis dicetis: amant alterna camenae', and in *Ciris* 55 'nam uerum fateamur: amat Poly-hymnia uerum'. *cura* is the 'pains' implied in *meditata*.

20. The amoebean contest begins with the girls' address to the evening star.

    quis ... ignis : see on 61. 46.

21. possis : 'have the heart to', 'can bear to': cf. 68. 41, 104. 1,

24. quid ... urbe : for this comparison cf. Prop. iv. 8. 54 'spectaclum capta nec minus urbe fuit', Ov. *Tr.* i. 3. 26 'haec facies Troiae cum caperetur erat', *Met.* xii. 225 'captaeque erat urbis imago'.

27. desponsa ... conubia : Vesper brings to accomplishment the marriage already (*ante*) pledged at the *sponsio* or *pactio nuptialis* (*pepigere*)—in early law a contract legally enforce-able, later a less formal engagement—when the future hus-band and the bride's father (*uiri* and *parentes* are generalizing plurals: the bride's mother was not concerned) exchange undertakings, the one promising to give his daughter, the other to marry her.

    conubia : see on 57 below.

28. pepigere ... pepigerunt : for the variation cf. Virg. *Ecl.* 10. 13–15 *fleuere ... fleuerunt*.

29. iunxere has as its object the means by which union is effected; cf. Cic. *de Or.* i. 37 'Sabinorum conubia coniunxisse': similarly 63. 76 'iuncta iuga', 78. 3 'iungit amores'.

    extulit : cf. Virg. *Aen.* viii. 591 '(Lucifer) extulit os sacrum caelo'.

30. optatius : see on 64. 22.

32. The missing stanza of the girls no doubt enlarged on the idea of Hesperus as a thief: the young men reply that he is, as Eous, a thief-catcher.

33. custodia : 'the watch(men)', to whom the rising of Hesperus gives the signal to be on the alert: there is no need to look for any particular reference in *custodia*—*custodes* of private property were common enough.

34. idem, as often, emphasizes identity in difference: cf. 43, 22. 15 and Cinna, fr. 8 (quoted below).

saepe, like 'many a time', often emphasizes the regular repetition of an action rather than its frequency: cf. Lucr. iv: 34 'in somnis cum saepe figuras / contuimur miras', Virg. *Georg.* i. 354 f. 'quid saepe uidentes / agricolae propius stabulis armenta tenerent', i. 451 f. 'saepe uidemus / ipsius (*sc.* solis) in uultu uarios errare colores', *Aen.* i. 148 'ueluti magno in populo cum saepe coorta est / seditio'.

35. Eous is Schrader's certain correction; *eosdem* here is as unidiomatic as *idem* in l. 34 and αὐτοί in Call. fr. 291 Pf. (quoted below) are idiomatic. That the evening star and the morning star are the same, i.e. that the planet Venus is visible sometimes in the morning and sometimes in the evening, was already known in the fifth century B.C., and the fancy of later poets played on the notion of their identity with varied ingenuity: for other forms of the conceit cf. Callim. fr. 291 Pf. αὐτοὶ μὲν φιλέουσ', αὐτοὶ δέ τε πεφρίκασιν· / Ἑσπέριον φιλέουσιν, ἀτὰρ στυγέουσιν Ἐῷον (imitated in reverse in *Ciris* 351–2 'quem pauidae alternis fugitant optantque puellae: / Hesperium uitant, optant ardescere Eoum'), Plato, *A.P.* vii. 670 ἀστὴρ πρὶν μὲν ἔλαμπες ἐνὶ ζωοῖσιν Ἐῷος, / νῦν δὲ θανὼν λάμπεις Ἕσπερος ἐν φθιμένοις, Meleager, *A.P.* xii. 114 Ἠοῦς ἄγγελε, χαῖρε, Φαεσφόρε, καὶ ταχὺς ἔλθοις / Ἕσπερος ἦν ἀπάγεις λάθριος αὖθις ἄγων, Cinna, fr. 8 (from his *Zmyrna*) 'te matutinus flentem conspexit Eous / et flentem paulo uidit post Hesperus idem'. The implication in Cinna, and probably in Catullus, that the evening star of one day is the morning star of the next, is a poetic fiction.

36. ficto ... questu : cf. 66. 16 *falsis lacrimulis*.

37. quid tum : 'what if they *do* abuse you when they are secretly longing for you?': cf. Virg. *Ecl.* 10. 38 'quid tum, si fuscus Amyntas?' ('what about it, if A. is swarthy?'), Grattius 525 'quid tum, si turpia colla?'.

39 ff. In the traditional epic style the simile is interrupted by a change of subject (42: so also in the corresponding 53): cf. 64. 108–9, Virg. *Aen.* iv. 441 ff.

nascitur : 'grows' as in Virg. *Ecl.* 3. 92 'qui legitis flores et humi nascentia fraga', 106 'dic quibus in terris inscripti nomina regum / nascantur flores', Cic. *de Diu.* ii. 135 'dicere quo illa (radicula) loci nasceretur'.

hortis : the plural, as usual, of a pleasure-garden; the singular is generally used of a kitchen- or market-garden.

40. conuolsus : cf. 64. 40 'glebam conuellit uomere taurus'.

41. mulcent : 'stroke', of a caressing touch (cf. 64. 162, 284); the wind's caress is a common conceit: e.g. Prop. iv. 7. 60 'mulcet ubi Elysias aura beata rosas', Ov. *Met.* i. 108 'mulcebant Zephyri natos sine semine flores', *Fasti* v. 161 'frigidus Argestes summas mulcebit aristas'. So in Drayton 'the west winde stroakes the violet leaves'.

educat : brings to maturity: cf. 50, Tib. i. 1. 13 'quodcumque mihi pomum nouus educat annus', Ov. *ex P.* i. 3. 51 'non ager . . . dulces educat uuas'.

42. optauere : cf. 55 *coluere*: Catullus is the first Latin writer to use the 'gnomic' perfect, probably suggested by the similar Greek use of the aorist. This line and the balancing 44 are imitated by Ov. *Met.* iii. 353–5 'multi illum iuuenes, multae cupiere puellae / . . . nulli illum iuuenes, nullae tetigere puellae'; cf. also Virg. *Aen.* xi. 581 f. 'multae illam . . . / optauere'.

43. tenui carptus . . . ungui : cf. Prop. i. 20. 39 'decerpens tenero pueriliter ungui', Ov. *Her.* 4. 30 'tenui primam deligere ungue rosam'.

45. dum . . . dum : 'as long as . . . so long', repeated in the balancing line 56. Quintilian's quotation (ix. 3. 16) makes *dum . . . dum* certain (though by a slip of memory he has *innupta* for *intacta*); his comment is 'prius dum significat quoad, sequens usque eo', and there is no reason to doubt that explanation. The normal use of *dum* as a subordinating conjunction is a development from its original use as a temporal particle ('for a time', or the like); vestiges of that original use survive in a few instances of *dum . . . dum* equivalent to *modo . . . modo* or *nunc . . . nunc* (Plaut. *Merc.* 348–9, Afranius, fr. 372R., Accius, fr. 395R.), in the compounds *interdum, nondum, uixdum, dudum,* and in the enclitic use of *dum* with imperatives (*agedum, circumspicedum*). The paratactic use of *dum . . . dum* here, parallel to the common uses of *tum . . . tum* (which has degenerated into a connective formula) and *simul . . . simul,* may be presumed to be a genuine archaism—Ribbeck was probably right in restoring it in Plaut. *Truc.* 232 'dum habeat, dum amet : ubi nil habeat, alium quaestum coepiat', where the manuscripts have 'dum . . . tum'—but Catullus may have been influenced by similar paratactic uses in Greek, such as that of τόφρα μὲν . . . τόφρα δέ in Callimachus (*Hymn* 4. 39–40).

49. uidua . . . uitis : *marita* and *maritare* are vivid terms of the

countryman for the 'marrying up' of the vine and its supporting tree (Cato 32 'arbores facito ut bene maritae sint',
Columella xi. 2. 79 'per hos dies . . . ulmi quoque uitibus recte
maritantur'). The poets take up the image of the wedded
pair (though both members are grammatically feminine),
either of which is *uidua* without the other: so Hor. *Od.* iv.
5. 30 'uitem uiduas ducit ad arbores', *Epod.* 2. 9 'adulta
uitium propagine / altas maritat populos'. Similarly the
plane-tree is *caelebs* because on account of its thick foliage it
cannot be used for supporting vines, Hor. *Od.* ii. 15. 4.

52. iam iam contingit : 'all but touches (is on the point of
touching) its topmost shoot with its root': for *iam iam* see
on 63. 73.

53. iuuenci : the farmer's oxen share in the cultivation of the
vineyard by breaking up the soil round the roots with the
plough: Virg. *Georg.* ii. 356 'ipsa / flectere luctantis inter
uineta iuuencos'.

54. marito : see on 49 above. Catullus may have made *ulmus*
masculine, but it is feminine even in this context elsewhere
(so Quint. viii. 3. 8 *maritam ulmum*) and T's *marita*, agreeing
with *eadem*, may well be right.

57. conubium : at l. 27 and at 64. 141, 158, Catullus has
conūbia. If the *-u-* was invariably long, *conubium* here (and in
Stat. *Theb.* i. 69, the only other occurrence of the accusative
singular) must be a trisyllable, the *-i-* being given consonantal
value—a licence (not uncommon in Virgil but otherwise rare)
of which the only instance in Catullus is the doubtful
Camerium at 55. 10. It is more likely, as Munro argued on
Lucr. iii. 776, that the quantity of the vowel was variable
and the poet's choice between *-ŭ-* and *-ū-* a matter of convenience; Wackernagel is probably right in holding (*Festschrift für P. Kretschmer* [1926], 289 ff. = *Kleine Schriften*, ii
1280 ff.) that *conūbium* was the original form and *-nub-* an
alternative 'literary' prosody for a word which in the general
sense of 'marriage' (as opposed to its stricter technical sense)
is practically confined to hexameter verse.

58. cara . . . parenti : the *uirgo* has the affection of a husband,
as she had not before: she ceases to be an encumbrance to
her father, as she was before. For the attitude implied in
inuisa cf. Menander, fr. 18 K. χαλεπόν γε θυγάτηρ πῆμα καὶ
δυσδιάθετον, 60 θυγάτηρ κτῆμ' ἔστιν ἐργῶδες πατρί.

59. et tu : the bride is brought into relation with what has just
been said; for *et* thus marking the turn from a general truth
to a particular application cf. Virg. *Ecl.* 10. 69 'omnia uincit
amor: et nos cedamus amori': so in Greek οὕτω καὶ σύ.

ne pugna : for this archaic usage cf. 61. 193 *ne remorare*, 67. 18 *ne dubita*.

60. cui : i.e. *ei* (or *cum eo*) *cui* : for the omission of the antecedent see on 110. 2.

63. pātrist : for the rare lengthening cf. *sācro* (7. 6, 64. 388, 68. 75), *cūpressu* (64. 291).

64. pugnare duobus : the dative with *pugnare* is a poetic usage (cf. Virg. *Aen.* iv. 38, Prop. i. 10. 21). The phrase may be proverbial: cf. Plato, *Phaedo* 89c πρὸς δύο λέγεται οὐδ' ὁ Ἡρακλῆς οἱός τ' εἶναι, *Laws* 919b ὀρθὸν μὲν δὴ πάλαι τε εἰρημένον ὡς πρὸς δύο μάχεσθαι καὶ ἐναντία χαλεπόν.

65. iura is general here, without technical implication: the bride's mother had no legal *iura* over her daughter.

63

The ecstatic cult of the Anatolian nature-goddess Cybele, the Great Mother, had its origins in Phrygia and was especially associated with the mountains of Dindymus and Ida. By Pindar's time (*Pyth.* 3. 78, fr. 80 Sn.) it was familiar in Greece, where Cybele was sometimes identified with the Cretan mother-goddess Rhea (Eur. *Bacch.* 59; cf. Ov. *Fasti* iv. 201 ff.) and sometimes with Demeter (Eur. *Hel.* 1301 ff.). Attis, in origin another vegetation god, appears in a variety of legends (Paus. vii. 17. 9, Diod. iii. 58, 59) as her Phrygian lover: the story of his death and resurrection was enacted in her ritual and his name was given to her high priests. The worship of the Magna Mater was the first of the oriental cults to reach Rome. According to tradition it was brought there in 204 B.C., at a critical moment in the second Punic War when, in obedience to the Sibylline books, a sacred stone, said to represent the *mater Idaea*, was obtained from Attalus, king of Pergamus, and placed in a temple on the Palatine (Livy xxix. 14. 10 ff.; Ov. *Fasti* iv. 247 ff.). The annual festival of the Megalesia on 4 April was established in her honour, but the cult was kept under strict supervision; its priests, the *galli*, were still orientals in Catullus' time and citizens were not allowed to take part in it (Dion. Hal. ii. 19. 4–5). [A convenient account of the worship of the Magna Mater and related cults is to be found in E. O. James, *The Cult of the Mother Goddess* (London, 1959), pp. 161 ff.]

The story of Attis had been told by the Alexandrian poet Hermesianax (Paus. vii. 17. 9), apparently in elegiacs, and the myth may well have been handled by others. But Catullus' Attis bears no resemblance to the Attis of myth and ritual. He

is not a Phrygian at all, but a Greek—a youth who has been
moved by a sudden urge to cross the seas and abandon himself
to Cybele in a devotion of which, when he comes to his senses,
he repents in vain—and the contrast between civilization and
savage nature, between the humanism of the Greek city-state
and the excesses of oriental fanaticism, is at the heart of the
poem. Its spirit is so Greek (see especially on 60) that it seems
certain that Catullus was translating or adapting a Greek
original which gave this turn to the Attis motif. What that
original was we cannot guess. The metrician Hephaestion
(12. 3), illustrating the metre, quotes two galliambic lines—

> Γάλλαι, μητρὸς ὀρείης φιλόθυρσοι δρομάδες,
> αἷς ἔντεα παταγεῖται καὶ χάλκεα κρόταλα,

and it has been suggested that these come from Catullus'
source.[1] There is an obvious general resemblance to Attis' call
to his companions in ll. 12–25 of Catullus' poem and a particular coincidence in the use of the feminine Γάλλαι; on the other
hand the metre, having no anaclasis, differs markedly from the
Catullan galliambic (see below).

Whatever its origin, there is no need to connect the poem
with Catullus' short stay in Asia Minor. The cult of Cybele was
familiar in Rome. The imagination of Lucretius was struck by
the procession of begging dervishes conveying the image of the
turret-crowned goddess through the streets to the sound of their
wild outlandish music (ii. 610 ff.); Varro cynically described the
ritual in one of his satires, the *Eumenides*. The poem on the
Magna Mater by Catullus' friend Caecilius (see poem 35) reflects
the same interest, and the giving of a Latin form to a Greek
poem which handled the theme in a strikingly original way was
a natural choice for Catullus.

Some of the features of the narrative technique are those
which appear in the hexameter narrative poem 64 (see introduction to that poem)—the use of words from the old 'epic'
vocabulary (e.g. *ratis, pelagus, sonipes, stabula, marmora*), the
use of anaphora (9, 20, 21–25, 63–64) and epanalepsis (9, 13, 50,
55, 61, 78), alliteration and assonance (e.g. 9–10, 16, 22, 24–25,
28–30, 91). Some are dictated by the requirements of the
metre, a peculiarly exacting one in Latin in which the runs of
short syllables which it demands do not readily present themselves; hence the resort to archaic or unusual forms (9 *typanum*,
47 *tetulit*, 60 *gyminasiis*, 71 *columinibus*), 'poetic' plurals

---

[1] Choeroboscus, commenting on Hephaestion, adds the information that Callimachus wrote galliambics, but there is no proof that
the lines which Hephaestion quotes are by Callimachus.

(1 *maria*, 7 *sola*, 75 *nuntia*, 84 *iuga*) and unique compounds
(23 *hederigerae*, 34 *properipedem*, 51 *erifugae*, 72 *nemoriuagus*)
and the repetition of words—*ferus* (40, 57, 85, 89), *uagus* (4, 13,
25, 86), *animus* (4, 18, 38, 61, 85), *loca* (3, 14, 70, 82, 87),
nemora (12, 20, 32, 52, 58, 79, 89, with *nemori-* 72, all at the
same point in the line), *adiit* (3, 30, 54, 87)—and phrases—
itaque ut (6, 35), *quiete molli* (38, 44), *-antibus oculis* (39, 48),
citus abiit (42, 74). But the technical ingenuity is combined
with intense imaginative vigour and sensitiveness and the
distinctive character of the metre gives the effect of tumultuous
and breathless speed.[1]

The galliambic metre owed its name to its connexion with
the cult of Cybele, but how or when it was developed we do not
know. In Greek the two lines quoted above are the only
galliambics we possess. In Latin Varro had used it at an
appropriate point in his *Eumenides*, which was written in a
medley of metres,[2] and Maecenas was to use it in the same context.[3] The basis of the metre is a line of four ionics a minore,
the last catalectic, with diaeresis after the second; resolution
in both halves and, in the Latin form, anaclasis (in Catullus
regular in the first half, rare in the second: see 73, 76) produce
its peculiarly agitated movement.

2. **Phrygium . . . nemus**: the forests of Ida in the Troad, as
appears from l. 30. The Troad, the north-west corner of Asia
Minor, was inhabited by Phrygians in prehistoric times,
though later invasions drove them inland and the boundaries
of the region called Phrygia in the historical period lay far to
the east and south of it: the Trojans are *Phryges* in Virgil
(*Aen.* ii. 191, ix. 599) and Ida is *Phrygia* (*Georg.* iv. 41).

3. **deae**: i.e. Cybele.

4. **ibi**: 'thereupon', as in 48.
   furenti rabie: cf. 38 *rabidus furor*.

[1] The effect is reinforced by the accumulation, in the first half of
the poem, of words conveying the idea of movement: *celer, citatus,
uagus, citus, rapidus, agite, ite, uolitare, trepidare, properare, iacere,
quatere*.

[2] fr. 131 Büch. Phrygius per ossa cornus liquida canit anima.
   fr. 132   tibi tympanon inani sonitu matris deum
                    tonimus ⟨chorus⟩ tibi nos, tibi nunc semiuiri
                    teretem comam uolantem iactant tibi famuli.
                                                        (galli *codd.*)

[3] fr. 5 Morel   ades, inquit, o Cybebe, fera montium dea,
                  ades et sonante typano quate flexibile caput.
   fr. 6   latus horreat flagello, comitum chorus ululet.

uagus animis : for the plural cf. Virg. *Aen.* viii. 228 *furens animis*. But *animi* may be right: the limiting genitive is common with adjectives—*aeger animi, ferox animi, infelix animi*.

6. **itaque** : 'and then', as in 35: see on 64. 84.

   sine uiro : cf. Ov. *Fasti* iv. 242 *signa uiri*, Lucan x. 134 *exsecta uirum*.

7. **terrae sola** : so Ennius *Ann.* 455 V. *sola terrarum*, Lucr. ii. 592 *sola terrae*: the same 'poetic' plural again in 40 *sola dura*.

8. **leue typanum** : the doublets τύμπανον and τύπανον exist together in Greek; Catullus uses the commoner *tympanum* below in 29. The τύπανον, a hoop with a sheet of hide stretched over it (hence 10 *terga tauri*), was especially associated with Cybele-worship: cf. Eur. *Hel.* 1346 τύπανα βυρσοτενῆ, *Bacch.* 124 βυρσότονον κύκλωμα. The same alliteration on *t* appears in the same context in Lucr. ii. 618 'tympana tenta tonant palmis', Varro, fr. 132, and Maecenas, fr. 5 (quoted above).

   citata : from this point onwards the change of gender to the feminine marks the change in Attis' state. Hence feminines have been substituted, probably rightly, for the masculine forms which the manuscripts give at 42, 45, and 89. At 51 the masculine *miser* (which Fröhlich proposed to change to *misera*) may stand as referring to Attis' past, and perhaps as stressing, in contrast with *furibunda* in 54, if that is singular, the contrast between his past and his present state. In 78 and 80 the masculines may be taken as marking Cybele's recognition of his rebellion and return to his old self; if they are right, the masculine in 88 may be right also.

9. **Cybebe** : Catullus uses the alternative forms *Cybēbe* and *Cybēle* as the metre demands: both Κυβήβη and Κυβέλη are used in Greek.

   initia is applied elsewhere to the initiation ceremonies of mystery-cults (Varro, *R.R.* iii. 1. 5 'initia uocantur potissimum ea quae Cereri fiunt sacra': so Cic. *Leg.* ii. 36 of the Eleusinian rites). Here it is transferred to the instruments or objects of worship: similarly *orgia* (Prop. iii. 3. 28 f. 'pendebantque cauis tympana pumicibus, / orgia Musarum', Virg. *Aen.* vii. 403 'capite orgia mecum', Sen. *H.O.* 594 'orgia ... condita cistis': so perhaps 64. 259), *mysteria* (Ov. *A.A.* ii. 609 'condita si non sunt Veneris mysteria cistis').

11. **tremebunda** : i.e. quivering with ecstatic frenzy.

    comitibus : Attis' companions are taken for granted, with the usual compression of Hellenistic narrative (see p. 274): who they were is not said, nor what happened to them.

12. **Gallae** : the name of the devotees of Cybele, Γάλλοι (the

feminine is found only in the anonymous fragment quoted on
p. 262 above), is of unknown origin; the ancient derivation
from the Phrygian river Γάλλος is unlikely.

13. Dindymenae: cf. 35. 14 *Dindymi dominam*: so in Greek μητὴρ
Διυδυμήνη (Herod. i. 80). The mountain of Dindymus lay in
eastern Phrygia.

    uaga pecora : Cybele's 'roving sheep': so Ovid, *Ibis* 455,
calls the priests *pecus magnae parentis*.

14. The hypermetric *celeri* which the manuscripts give at the
end of this line is perhaps a misplaced marginal correction of
the unmetrical *celere* in l. 1.

15. sectam meam exsecutae : i.e. *me secutae*: the cognate accusative occurs only here with *exsequi*, but is not uncommon with
sequi (accompanied, as a cognate accusative normally is, by
a defining adjective or genitive) as an archaism preserved
in formal or solemn language: Cic. *Sest.* 97 'sunt principes
publici consili, sunt qui eorum sectam sequuntur', *Rab. Perd.*
22 'cuius sectam sequi, cuius imperio parere potissimum
uelles', Livy xxix. 27. 2, xxxvi. 1. 5.

    mihi here, like *sibi* in 56, is a metrical stopgap.

16. truculentaque pelagi : this use of the neuter plural adjective
with a partitive genitive is a favourite device in Lucretius,
who has *pelagi seuera* (v. 35), *ponti profunda* (v. 417), *caerula
caeli* (vi. 96), as well as more striking instances like *strata
uiarum* (iv. 415) and even *prima uirorum* (i. 86); similarly
Virgil has *pelagi alta* (*Aen.* ix. 81). Catullus does not use the
idiom elsewhere, but there is no reason to suspect it here,
and Victorius's *pelage* (the Greek plural, which Lucretius
uses twice) is unnecessary.

    truculenta : for the 'bullying' sea cf. 64. 179 *truculentum
aequor*, Hor. *Od.* i. 3. 10 *truci pelago*: the adjective reflects the
normal Roman feeling for the sea (cf. 4. 9).

17. nimio : i.e. *maximo*, as in 36: see on 43. 4.

18. erae . . . animum : they are to gladden Cybele's heart by
their frenzy. Avantius's *erae* is certain (according to Servius
on *Aen.* iii. 113 *era* was a regular title of Cybele); Lachmann's
aere is metrically wrong since it makes the first half of the
line consist of two unresolved ionics (cf. 54).

19. mora tarda : for the adjective repeating the sense of the
noun see on 46. 1.

21. cymbalum : i.e. *cymbalorum*: for Catullus' use of the archaic
genitive plural in *-um* see on 9. 6.

22. curuo : the Phrygian *tibia* (see on 64. 264) had a curved,
horn-shaped lower end: so Virg. *Aen.* xi. 737 'curua . . . tibia
Bacchi', Tib. ii. 1. 86 'obstrepit et Phrygio tibia curua sono'.

23. Maenades . . . hederigerae : the Maenads, the ivy-wreathed wands (*thyrsi*), and the *thiasus* (28) properly belong to the worship of Dionysus, but the two ecstatic Asiatic cults had been identified long before Catullus: compare with these lines the description of Bacchus and his followers in 64. 251 ff. (especially *uolitabat* 251, *capita inflectentes* 255).

24. sacra sancta . . . agitant : 'celebrate their inviolable rites': for *agitare* in this sense cf. Ter. *Heaut.* 733 'Dionysia agitat', Virg. *Georg.* iv. 533 'choros . . . agitabat', Cic. *Verr.* ii. 2. 51 'dies festos agitare'.

ululatibus : the yells (ὀλολυγμός: both words are normally used of women's cries) of the ecstatic worshippers are conveyed in the *a*'s and *u*'s of the line.

25. uolitare : see on 64. 251.

26. celerare : Lucretius has this rare intransitive use, i. 387 *celerantibus auris*.

tripudiis : Catullus transfers to Cybele worship a term of Roman liturgy: *tripudia* are the wild dances of primitive ritual which survived in the dances of the Salii and the Fratres Aruales.

27. simul : 'as soon as': so in 31. The two sentences are parallel: 'simul Attis haec cecinit, thiasus ululat, adit Idam chorus; simul Attis uadit dux, ducem Gallae sequuntur'.

30. uiridem . . . Idam : cf. Virg. *Aen.* v. 252 *frondosa . . . Ida*; Homer, *Il.* xxi. 449 Ἴδης . . . ὑληέσσης, Theoc. 17. 9 Ἴδαν ἐς πολύδενδρον.

31. animam agens : 'gasping': here without the usual implication 'at one's last gasp', which the phrase has, e.g., in Cic. *Fam.* viii. 13. 2 'Hortensius cum has litteras scripsi animam agebat', and in Seneca's epigram (*Ep.* 101. 12) 'est tanti habere animam ut agam?'

32. comitata tympano : for this use of an impersonal accompaniment cf. *Moretum* 83 'comitatus merce macelli': Juvenal similarly uses the active, 1. 89 'neque enim loculis comitantibus itur'.

33. indomita : 'unbroken', as in 68. 118: the original use of *domare* is that of breaking in animals.

35. lassulae : for the 'sympathetic' diminutive see on 64. 60.

36. nimio : see on 17.

e labore : 'after their exertion': for this common use of *e*, cf. Caesar, *B.C.* ii. 14. 1 'ex diutino labore quieti se dedisset'.

sine Cerere : without food: because they are too exhausted to eat.

37. piger ... operit : 'a lazy slumber covered their eyes with a drooping swoon'. *labare* is often used of sinking or swooning with such subjects as *membra* or *oculi*: here the swoon, *languor*, is itself made the subject. The similar transference of *piger* from the patient to the cause is not uncommon: cf. Lucr. v. 746 'bruma niues adfert pigrumque rigorem / reddit', Tib. i. 2. 29 'pigra frigora'.

39. oris aurei : a genitive of description with *sol*, corresponding to a compound adjective in Greek, 'the golden-visaged sun': the sun is χρυσοφαής in Eur. *Hec.* 636.

40. lustrauit : 'surveyed', probably: for *lustrare* of a gaze which moves from point to point cf. Virg. *Aen.* ii. 564, viii. 153. Lucretius (v. 693, 1437) and Virgil (*Aen.* iv. 6, 607, vii. 148) use the same solemn word (primarily a term of ritual applied to purificatory ceremonies, often processional) in similar contexts of the Sun or the Dawn traversing the world: the use may go back to Ennius.

    aethera album : cf. Caesar, *B.C.* i. 68. 1 'albente caelo', Virg., *Aen.* iv. 586 'primam albescere lucem / uidit'.

41. sonipedibus : this descriptive compound, in which later poetry finds a useful alternative to *equus*, had already been used by Lucilius and Accius.

    uegetis : 'fresh', after their night's rest.

43. Pasithea is in Homer (*Il.* xiv. 267 ff.) one of the Graces, who (in return for a favour) is promised in marriage to Sleep by Hera; her only later appearance is in an epigram by Antipater on a musician (*A.P.* ix. 517. 5f.), ἀφυπνώσαι κεν ἀκούων / αὐτὸς Πασιθέης Ὕπνος ἐν ἀγκαλίσιν. This piece of far-fetched mythological erudition points to an Alexandrian source.

    trepidante ... sinu : 'fluttering' with excitement: cf. Ov. *A.A.* iii. 722 'pulsantur trepidi corde micante sinus'.

44. ita : for the continuative use see on 64. 84.

    de : 'after', like the common *e* in l. 36: the nearest parallel is Plaut. *Most.* 697 'non bonust somnus de prandio': cf. Lucr. v. 651 'ubi de longo cursu sol ultima caeli / impulit'.

45. recoluit : for *recolere*, 'go over' (in mind), cf. Cic. *Phil.* xiii. 45 'quae si tecum ipse recolueris', Ov. *Her.* 5. 113.

46. liquida mente : with unclouded mind; cf. the colloquial *liquido animo* in Plaut. *Epid.* 643 'animo liquido et tranquillo es' (imperative), *Pseud.* 232 'nihil curassis: liquido es animo'.

    ubique : i.e. *et ubi*.

47. rusum : the spelling (normal in Lucretius) with *-rs-* reduced to *-s-* (through the intermediate stage of *-ss-*: cf. *gessi* from *ger-si*) represents a pronunciation which survived in popular use (so Ital. *dosso*, Fr. *dos* from *dorsum*).

tetulit : the archaic reduplicated perfect form, regular in comedy, is used by Catullus again in l. 52 and 66. 35 and by Lucretius (vi. 672). For *reditum ferre* (repeated in l. 79) compare *aditum ferre* in 61. 26, 43.

48. **uasta** : see on 64. 156.

49. **miseriter** is used by Ennius and Lucretius: for the forma-tion of an adverb in *-ter* from an *o*-stem, compare *puriter* (39. 14 n., 76. 19).

50. **mei** : the objective genitive is justified by the fact that the verbal notion is more clearly felt in *creatrix* than in *genetrix*.

51. **relinquens** : see on 35. 3.

53. **gelida stabula** : for the prosody see on 64. 357. Virgil re-peats the use (probably derived from earlier poetry) in *stabula alta ferarum* (*Aen.* vi. 179, x. 723).

54. **et earum omnia adirem** : *V*'s reading is suspect on metrical grounds, since it makes the first half of the line consist of two unresolved ionics (cf. 18), and also on linguistic, since *omnia* could only be a weak stopgap and the genitives of *is* are very rare in serious verse except in Lucretius (see Axelson, *Un-poetische Wörter*, p. 72). No plausible correction has been proposed: Avantius's *et earum ad omnia irem* and Postgate's *et earum ut omnia adirem* remove the first objection only and leave the weak *earum* in an emphatic position.

furibunda : probably feminine singular as in 31: see on 8.

55. **quibus locis** : Ellis cites Nepos, *Dat.* 4 'quaerit quibus locis sit Aspis'; the expression is vaguer than *quo loco*.

reor : the periphrastic expression is of a not uncommon type; cf. Cic. *Rosc. Am.* 153 'uidete . . . quem in locum rem publicam peruenturam putetis', Plaut. *Curc.* 1 'quo ted hoc noctis dicam proficisci foras ?', Hor. *Ep.* i. 4. 2 'quid nunc te dicam facere in regione Pedana ?'

56. **derigere aciem** : 'direct its vision': cf. 64. 127 'aciem . . . protenderet'.

sibi : a stopgap like *mihi* in l. 15.

58. **remota**: best taken with *ego*.

59. **genitoribus** : 'parents' as in Lucr. ii. 615 'ingrati genitoribus sunt inuenti': so in Greek, Apoll. iv. 361 πάτρην τε κλέα τε μεγάρων αὐτούς τε τοκῆας / νοσφισάμην. For other similar uses see on 72. 4.

60. **foro . . . gyminasiis** : the market-place, the wrestling-ground, the running-track, and the sport-school, the resorts of young manhood in the Greek city. Three of the terms are

Greek words—σταδιον, παλαίστρα, γυμνάσιον—for which Latin has no equivalents. *forum* represents ἀγορά, though the *forum* had not the associations of the ἀγορά as a meeting-ground for leisured conversation and discussion; the normal associations of *forum*, to the Roman the centre of business and public life, are entirely different.

gyminasiis : the old five-syllable form, preserved by the manuscripts in Varro, *R.R.* i. 55. 4 and rightly restored here by Ellis for *gymnasiis*, which gives an unresolved ionic in the third foot, shows the euphonic vowel which Latin inserted between two consonants in early borrowings from Greek: so *mina* from μνᾶ, which survived in regular use, and the Plautine forms *drachuma* from δραχμή, *techina* from τέχνη, *Alcumena* from Ἀλκμήνη. Catullus may be presumed to have written the word *guminasiis* (see on 31. 5).

63. adulescens . . . puer : the four 'ages' are enumerated in descending order. The term ἔφηβος was technically applied at Athens and in other Greek cities to youths of 18–20 spending two years under state supervision in military training or public duty: here as in Ter. *And.* 51, *Eun.* 824, it is used generally. *ego mulier* is awkward, since *sum* must be understood with these words while *fui* is understood in the other clauses: the repetition of *ego* makes it impossible to take *mulier* as appositional ('I the *mulier* was *adulescens*', &c.).

64. gymnasi : the later form can stand here, but presumably Catullus wrote *guminasi*: see on 60.

flos : cf. 24. 1, 100. 2.

decus olei : the oil with which the wrestler rubbed himself is put by a common type of metonomy for the wrestling-ground: so we might describe a boxer as 'the pride of the gloves'.

65. frequentes . . . tepida : his door was thronged with admirers who made the threshold warm by spending the night on it: cf. Prop. i. 16. 22 'turpis et in tepido limine somnus erit', Hor. *Od.* iii. 10. 19 f.

66. corollis : cf. Lucr. iv. 1177–8 'lacrimans exclusus amator limina saepe / floribus et sertis operit'; Prop. i. 16. 7 (the door speaks) 'mihi non desunt turpes pendere corollae'.

67. esset : the subjunctive in an indefinite clause is occasionally found in republican Latin with *cum* and *si* (see on 84. 1): with *ubi* it is rare before the silver period, but cf. Hor. *Od.* iii. 6. 41 'sol ubi montium mutaret umbras'. Plaut. *Bacch.* 431 'ubi reuenisses domum' is not parallel, since the words occur in a hypothetical sentence.

68. deum ministra : for the generalizing plural cf. 75.

ferar : 'be called', 'reckoned' as in 114. 2 (without infinitive, as here cf. Hor. *Od.* ii. 19, 27) rather than 'go ranging' as in l. 58.

71. **columinibus :** here 'peaks', the sense usually carried by the syncopated form *culmen*.

73. **iam iamque :** *-que* does not connect the second *iam iam* with the first: *iam iam*, an emphatic *iam* (cf. Cic. *de Or.* iii. 90 'iam iam intellego quid dicas', Virg. *Aen.* ii. 701 'iam iam nulla mora est', xii. 676 'iam iam fata, soror, superant'), is repeated in the form *iam iamque* (cf. Cic. *Att.* xvi. 9 'iam iamque uideo bellum', Virg. *Aen.* xii. 940 'et iam iamque magis cunctantem flectere sermo / coeperat'). The implication, often conveyed by *iam iam* or *iam iamque*, of an action so imminent that it seems to have happened already (e.g. Cic. *Att.* vii. 20. 1 'illum ruere nuntiant et iam iamque adesse', Virg. *Aen.* ii. 530 'insequitur iam iamque manu tenet', viii. 708 'ipsa uidebatur . . . uela dare et laxos iam iamque immittere funis': so *iam iam* at 62. 52) is not present here.

74. **citus :** Bentley's supplement (cf. 30, 42: the loss of *citus* after *sonitus* is readily explained) is likelier than Lachmann's addition of *celer* (from the otiose *celer* which the manuscripts have at l. 14) at the end of the line.

75. **geminas deorum ad aures :** instances of *geminus* applied to the ears, eyes, or hands, without any obvious special force, are to be found in verse (e.g. Virg. *Aen.* vi. 788 'huc geminas nunc flecte acies', *Culex* 150 'geminas auium uox obstrepit auris', Ov. *Met.* x. 116 'nitebant / auribus e geminis circum caua tempora bacae', Varro Atac. fr. 3 Morel 'geminis capiens tellurem Oeaxida palmis') and *geminas deae ad aures* would not be a surprising phrase. The plural *deorum* makes the phrase more difficult and the difficulty is not lessened by the use of the plural where only one deity, Cybele, is in question. But Catullus has another novel use of *geminus*, if the manuscript reading is sound, at 51. 11.

noua nuntia : 'surprising tidings': the neuter form is found elsewhere only in Lucr. iv. 704 and Varro, *L.L.* vi. 86.

76. **ibi :** 'thereupon' as in 4, 48.

iuncta iuga : *iungo* may have its object not, as usual, the things joined but the means by which junction is effected: *iugum iungere* is like the common *pontem iungere*: cf. 62. 29.

leonibus : both in literature and in art Cybele is represented as riding in a car drawn by lions: so Soph. *Phil.* 400 ἰὼ μάκαιρα ταυροκτόνων λεόντων ἔφεδρε, Lucr. ii. 600 'hanc ueteres Graium docti cecinere poetae / sedibus in curru biiugos agitare leones', Virg. *Aen.* iii. 113 'iuncti currum . . . subiere leones'.

77. **laeuum pecoris hostem** : *pecoris hostis* perhaps represents a
Greek compound like ταυροκτόνος (Soph. *Phil.* 394, quoted on
76) or ταυροφόνος, but *laeuum* is unexplained. The particularizing of one member of the team perhaps adds a little to the
vividness of the picture, but *saeuum* is tempting.

81. **caede terga cauda** : cf. Hom. *Il.* xx. 170 f. οὐρῇ δὲ πλευράς
τε καὶ ἰσχία ἀμφοτέρωθεν | μαστίεται ἑὲ δ᾽ αὐτὸν ἐποτρύνει μαχέσασθαι,
Pliny, *N.H.* viii. 49 'leonum animi index cauda. . . . immota
ergo placido, clemens blandienti, quod rarum est; crebrior
enim iracundia, cuius in principio terra uerberatur, incre-
mento terga ceu quodam incitamento flagellantur'.

82. **retonent** : the compound occurs only here.

83. **torosa** : cf. Virg. *Aen.* xii. 6 (of a lion) 'gaudetque comantis |
excutiens ceruice toros'.

   ceruice: the singular is regular in poetry both before and
after Catullus (apart from a few exx. of *cervicibus*): the
plural is invariable in comedy and in prose up to the time
of Cicero: see Maas in *A.L.L.* xii. 501 f.

84. **religat** : 'unties', repeating *resoluens* (76).

85. **ferus** : 'the beast': for the substantival use of the masculine
cf. Virg. *Aen.* ii. 51, vii. 489, and *saeuum* in 64. 110.

   sese adhortans : Homer's ἑὲ αὐτὸν ἐποτρύνει (see on 81 above).
rapidum is proleptic, 'rouses himself to fury' (cf. 66. 3);
animo, presumably to be taken with *incitat* ('in his heart')
looks like a stopgap.

.87. **albicantis** : white, probably, not with sand but with the
foam or the sparkle of waves; unlike 'shore', *litus* can refer
to the edge of the sea as well as to the edge of the land; cf.
Virg. *Aen.* vi. 362, Lucan viii. 698, Ov. *Met.* xv. 53.

88. **marmora pelagi** : the metaphor from the radiance of
marble, borrowed from Greek (Hom. *Il.* xiv. 273 ἅλα μαρμαρέην),
belongs to the conventional epic vocabulary: so Ennius has
'mare marmore flauo '(*Ann.* 384 V.), Lucretius 'canos candenti
marmore fluctus' (ii. 767), Virgil 'lento luctantur marmore
tonsae' (*Aen.* vii. 28).

89. **fera** : for the adjective applied to inanimate natural
objects cf. Varro, *R.R.* i. 7. 7 'in locis feris (arbores) plura
ferunt', Virg. *Ecl.* 5. 28 'feri montes', Hor. *Sat.* ii. 6. 92 'feris
siluis'.

91 ff. The personal prayer concluding the narrative, or inserted in it (as at 68. 77–78), corresponds to Alexandrian
technique: cf. Callim. *Hymn* 3. 136 f. πότνια, τῶν εἴη μὲν ἐμοὶ
φίλος ὅστις ἀληθής, / εἴην δ᾽ αὐτός, ἄνασσα, μέλοι δέ μοι αἰὲν ἀοιδή, 6.
116 f. Δάματερ, μὴ τῆνος ἐμὶν φίλος ὅς τοι ἀπεχθὴς / εἴη μηδ᾽ ὁμότοιχος.

64

The Marriage of Peleus and Thetis, to give the poem its usual modern title, represents Catullus' own experiment in the form which he admired in the *Zmyrna* of his friend Cinna (see on 95); it is a narrative poem in the 'new' style, strongly influenced by Alexandrian technique. That it is a translation of a Greek original, like poem 66, there is no reason to suppose. Two lines can be related to lines by Alexandrian poets which happen to have been preserved in isolation—one, probably by Euphorion, may have suggested l. 30; the other, perhaps by Callimachus, clearly lies behind l. 111; l. 102 looks like a reminiscence of Apollonius, and the resemblances to Nonnus in 139 ff. and 160 ff. suggest that Catullus had in mind the same Alexandrian source on which Nonnus was drawing about four centuries later. He certainly was not confined to one hellenistic source.

The narrative poem which the Alexandrians developed in their reaction against the more spacious forms of poetry[1] is distinguished from epic not only by its smaller scale, achieved by deliberate selection of episodes, but also by the subjective, sentimental, and romantic handling of its theme. The poet passes rapidly over the familiar incidents of his story, or omits them altogether, to enlarge on those parts of it which lend themselves to colourful description of detail or the portrayal of human emotion; he relieves his narrative with personal turns of phrase—exclamations, apostrophes, or questions—and courts the interest of the cultivated reader by giving a novel twist to his story or embellishing it with conceits of language. Little has survived of the large volume of narrative poetry which Alexandria produced. Callimachus' *Hecale* (a hexameter poem on an episode in the story of Theseus) and his *Aitia* (a series of

---

[1] The quasi-technical term *epyllion*, 'miniature epic', which is frequently used by modern scholars to describe this and similar poems in Latin and their Alexandrian prototypes, has no ancient authority; it was first used by Haupt, in a lecture on this poem, in 1855 (*Opuscula*, pp. 67 ff.). ἐπύλλιον is only once applied to a work of literature—by Athenaeus (ii. 65a), who uses it of a poem ascribed to Homer; *epyllium* is not found in Latin before Ausonius, who uses it twice (pp. 335, 360 Peiper) as a general term for short poems. The term has a certain convenience, but it is misleading in so far as it obscures the fact that the technique of story-telling was essentially the same in 'miniature epics' (like Callimachus' *Hecale*) and in narrative elegies (like his *Aitia*) or in the narrative parts of hymns (like his hymn on the Bath of Pallas).

elegiac poems on the legendary origins of local rites) are represented by fragments, few of them of any considerable length;
of the work of Euphorion and others we have even less. The
only examples of this kind of narrative poetry which have
survived entire are three poems in the Theocritean corpus,
Hylas (13), *The Infant Heracles* (24), and *Heracles the Lion-
killer* (25), the first two of which are certainly by Theocritus
himself, and the *Europa* (*Id.* 2) of Moschus. The Italian
neoterici brought the style into Latin; besides Cinna's *Zmyrna*,
we know of an *Io* by Calvus and a *Glaucus* by Cornificius. There
are examples of the same technique in the pseudo-Virgilian
Ciris, in the Aristaeus episode of Virgil's fourth *Georgic* (315–
558), and in Ovid's *Metamorphoses*, a series of ingeniously connected narratives, and the essentials of the same pattern
appear in some of the narrative elegies of Propertius (especially
i. 20, iv. 5).

Catullus' poem contains a story within a story. More than
half (ll. 50–267) is occupied by the tale of the desertion of
Ariadne; the pretext for its introduction is a description of the
scene embroidered on the bridal couch of Peleus and Thetis.
Similarly in Callimachus' *Hecale* the tale of Erichthonius seems
to have been woven into the adventure of Theseus which was
the theme of the poem, and in the fourth *Georgic* the tale of
Orpheus and Eurydice is inserted into the story of Aristaeus.
The particular form of digression which Catullus employs, the
detailed description of a work of art, goes back to Homer's
description of the shield of Achilles (*Il.* xviii. 478 ff.) and was
favoured by Hellenistic poets;[1] so Apollonius describes at
length the embroidery on Jason's mantle (i. 721–67), Theocritus
the carving on his goat-herd's bowl (1. 29–55), Moschus the
design on Europa's golden flower-basket (2. 44–61). In Catullus
the disproportion is very much more marked. The description
of the coverlet serves to introduce a long narrative which has no
obvious connexion with the original theme, and that narrative
in turn contains a further digression (76–115), a recapitulation
of the story of Theseus' visit to Crete. Returning to the
marriage-scene, Catullus makes the song of the Parcae a means
of extending his narrative into the future with a prediction of
the doings of Achilles (338–70), and the song itself leads on to
yet another digression, the moralizing epilogue on human degeneracy (384–408) with which the poem abruptly ends.

The word 'digression' is misleading in so far as it suggests

[1] On this form of digression (ἔκφρασις) see Friedländer, *Joannes
von Gaza*, 11 ff. Catullus may well have been thinking of a particular
representation of the Ariadne story in art: the theme was a common
one.

casual composition. Catullus' 'digression' is deliberate, a part
of the structure of the poem. Why he chose to construct it as
he did we cannot profess to know. It has been argued that the
Peleus and Thetis narrative is a frame for the story of Ariadne
which is Catullus' main concern, that a connexion between the
two stories is to be found in the contrast between happy
marriage and unhappy love, that the key to the poem is the
moral reflection of the topical epilogue, in relation to which the
choice of stories portraying the union of god and man has a
symbolic significance. The last of these views gives a plausible
account of the genesis of the poem, taken, as we have to take it,
in isolation; whether that was the pattern that Catullus intended we cannot say without a fuller knowledge of its hellenistic background.

Both in the handling of his story and in his language Catullus
shows some of the characteristic features of Alexandrian technique. He selects what gives an opening for realistic description
or for the sentimental analysis of emotion. Peleus falls in love
with Thetis when he is in the Argo, outward bound for the end
of the world, and she is among her Nereid sisters; there is a
gap between that romantic encounter and a wedding in Thessaly, described in a series of pictures full of colour and movement, of the palace, of the streaming crowds of sightseers, of
the guests—Chiron with a present of flowers, Peneus with
greenery, and the Fates, weird figures in white and red, biting
the threads of their wool between their aged lips. Within the
digression, the familiar story of the thread that guided Theseus
to safety is only glanced at in passing, and there is room for
other pictures—of Ariadne on the shore, of Bacchus' outlandish
following; the thoughts of the forsaken Ariadne are pursued for
some seventy lines and Aegeus' parting from his son for twenty-
five. And Catullus writes for a sophisticated reader who is
equipped to seize on hints and expand allusions. Jupiter's
renunciation of Thetis receives a brief mention (27) and Prometheus appears as a wedding-guest (294); but nothing is said
of the reason for Jupiter's change of mind or of the part which
Prometheus played in it. The reader's attention is caught by
a reference to Apollo's absence from the wedding (299); that
variation of the story, which occurs in no other version of it
that we have, is stressed by way of challenge to the common
account; what lies behind his absence the reader must explain
for himself.

As for form, Catullus takes from Alexandria the enlivening
devices of exclamation (22, 71, 94), apostrophe (69, 299), and
interjected question (28, 116), the learned allusion (228 *sancti
incola Itoni*, 290 *sorore flammati Phaethontis*, 324 *Opis nato*),

the romantic, evocative use of the proper name (89 *Eurotae*, 105 *Tauro*), and the tricks of emphasis and arrangement which the Alexandrians exploited for their emotional value, anaphora (24 *uos . . . uos*, 19–21 *tum . . . tum . . . tum*, 39–41, 63–65, 69–70, 96, 136–48, 186–7, 328–9, 387–94) and epanalepsis (26–27 *Iuppiter ipse, / ipse . . ., / ipse . . .*, 61–62 *prospicit, eheu, / prospicit,* 132–3 *perfide ab aris, / perfide,* 259–60 *orgia cistis, / orgia,* 285–6 *uiridantia Tempe, / Tempe . . .*). The characteristic Alexandrian metrical mannerism of the spondaic hexameter is repeated thirty times, at one point (78–80) in three consecutive lines. But these Alexandrian artifices are imposed on the traditional style of the Latin hexameter as it had come down from Ennius, and the slow, ponderous, and sometimes awkward dignity of what had been an adventurous experiment in Ennius' day but was now two centuries old contrasts sharply with the preciosity and bravura of the new technique. The traditional epic vocabulary, with nouns like *pubes* (4), *uada* (6), *flamen* (9), *tempestas* (73), *templa* (75), *pelagus* (127), and compounds like *fluentisonus* (52), *clarisonus* (125) and *raucisonus* (263), *amplifice* (265) and *iustificus* (406), is blended with Greek borrowings like *gaza* (46), *calathiscus* (319), and *chorea* (287) and uncompromising Greek forms like *Phasidos* (3), *Pelea* (21), and *Minoidi* (247). To the same 'Ennian' tradition belong the long rambling periods (e.g. 1–10, 60–67), the prosaic connexions (some of them common in Lucretius: 56 *utpote quae*, 198 *quae quoniam*, 218 *quandoquidem*, 278 *quorum post abitum*), the loosely attached participial phrases (5–10 *optàntes . . . uerrentes . . . coniungens*: cf. 54, 63, 101, 203, 238), the alliterations[1] (a native ornament of style in Italy), the end-stopped lines and the absence of internal pauses.[2] In two respects Catullus develops purely Latin devices, which owed nothing directly to Greek precedent and which were to become an accepted part of the technique of hexameter verse. The first is the 'bracketed' structure in which a line is enclosed between a noun and its adjective (27 lines are of this pattern: e.g. 54 *indomitos . . . furores*, 125 *clarisonas . . . uoces*, 265 *talibus . . . figuris*). The second is the parallel or chiastic arrangement of two nouns and their adjectives within the line; 58 lines (that is, one line in seven) show one or other of the possible forms of such arrangement:[3] e.g. 7 *caerula uerrentes abiegnis aequora*

---

[1] e.g. 68 (6 *t*'s), 92 (4 *c*'s), 159 (4 *p*'s), 258 (6 *s*'s), 282 (3 *f*'s), 293 (3 *u*'s); the purpose of a particular consonantal alliteration often cannot be detected, but the effect of vowel-assonance in echoing in the sense is sometimes very obvious, as it is in 155 and in 261–4.

[2] Only 55 lines have an internal pause: contrast Virgil's practice.

[3] At 63–65 three consecutive lines are thus constructed on three different patterns (abAB, abBA, aAbB). Virgil used the device

palmis, 39 *non humilis curuis purgatur uinea rastris*, 42 *squalida desertis rubigo infertur aratris*, 46 *tota domus gaudet regali splendida gaza*.[1]

The coincidences of language between this poem and Lucretius cannot be taken to prove that either poet was borrowing from the other, and there is no need to inquire whether Catullus could have known Lucretius' work, the posthumous publication of which was not before 54 B.C., probably the year of Catullus' own death: such phrases as *luce refulgent* (275), *pectore ab imo* (198), *uasta Carybdis* (156) come from a common poetic stock. (For other examples see 209, 261–4.) With Virgil the case is very different; clearly this poem of Catullus was in his mind and, whether in deliberate borrowing or in unconscious reminiscence, he freely uses its phrases.[2]

[For discussions of poem 64 see W. Reitzenstein in *Hermes*, xxxv (1900), 73 ff.; G. Pasquali in *Stud. It. di Fil. Class.* i (1920), i ff.; D. Comparetti in *Atene e Roma* i (1920), 14 ff.; G. Ramain in *Rev. de Ph.* xlvi (1922), 135 ff.; A. Morpurgo in *Riv. di Fil.* lv (1927), 331 ff.; G. Perrotta in *Athenaeum* ix (1931), 400 f.; C. Murley in *Trans. Am. Phil. Ass.* lxviii (1937), 305 ff.; R. Waltz in *Rev. des Ét. Lat.* xxiii (1945), 92 ff.; J. P. Boucher in *Rev. des Ét. Lat.* xxxiv (1956), 190 ff.; F. Klingner, *Catulls Peleus-Epos*, Sitzungsb. Bayer. Akad. d. Wiss., 1956.]

1 f. **quondam . . . dicuntur** : *quondam*, like *olim* in 76, sets the scene in the romantic legendary past; *dicuntur* emphasizes at the outset the traditional source of the story. So *fertur* (19), *perhibent* (76, 124), *ferunt* (212): the Alexandrian scholarpoet stresses his dependence on tradition, though the tradition he follows may be an unusual one: cf. Call. fr. 612 Pf. ἀμάρτυρον οὐδὲν ἀείδω, *Hymn* 5. 56 μῦθος δ' οὐκ ἐμός, ἀλλ' ἑτέρων. On this literary convention, which Virgil and Propertius maintain, see Norden, *Aeneid vi*, p. 123.

prognatae : an old-fashioned, stately word which appears in the epitaphs of the Scipios (*C.I.L.* i². 7 'Cornelius Lucius Scipio Barbatus Gnaiuod patre prognatus') and in Ennius, and which Plautus uses in formal or solemn contexts (e.g. *Amph.* 365, *Capt.* 170); it survived (like our 'issue') in legal language.

much more sparingly—in the *Aeneid* in one line in forty-three: see Norden, *Aeneid vi*, pp. 394 ff.

[1] In his use of diminutives, a pure latinism, Catullus was not followed: see on l. 60.

[2] For unmistakable instances see 115, 141, 156, 327; there are other verbal echoes which were probably unconscious, e.g. 404 'impia non uerita est diuos scelerare penates'—*Aen.* vi. 612–13 'quique arma secuti / impia nec ueriti dominorum fallere dextras . . .'

2. **liquidas** : cf. 162: a stock epithet of the epic style (cf. Virg. *Aen.* v. 859 'liquidas proiecit in undas').

nasse : cf. 4. 3 *natantis trabis*, and for a similar use of the voyagers themselves 66. 46.

Phasidos ad fluctus : 'to the waters of Phasis', the river of Colchis which flowed from a source in the Caucasus into the Black Sea, 'and the lands of Aeetes', the king of Colchis in whose lands the golden fleece was to be found.

Phasidos : in earlier Latin verse Greek names are normally given Latin inflexions; such exceptions as *Hectora* in Ennius are few. Catullus uses Greek terminations freely. In this poem he has: 1st decl.—acc. sing. *Amphitriten* (11); 2nd decl. —nom. sing. *Scyros* (? *Cieros*) (35), *Penios* (285); 3rd decl.— acc. sing. *Pelea* (21, 301), *Thesea* (53, 239), *Minoa* (85); voc. sing. *Peleu* (26), *Theseu* (69, 133); gen. sing. *Phasidos* (3) [but Latin *Thetidis* (19, 302)]; dat. sing. *Minoidi* (247) [but Latin *Thetidī* (21, 336)], *Pelei* (382) [but *Peleo* (336)]; nom. plur. *Nereides* (15), *Eumenides* (193) [so *heroes* (23)]; acc. plur. *Thyiadas* (391). [To these forms a Greek dative plural may fall to be added in 287.] Elsewhere he has *Cycladas* (4. 7), *Arabas* (11. 5), *Acmen* (45. 21), *Cybeles* and *Cybebes* (63. 12, 20, 35, 68), *Attin* (63. 88), *Athon* (66. 46), *Locridos Arsinoes* (66. 54), *Callisto* (dat., 66. 66), *Booten* (66. 67), *Tethyi* (66. 70), *Hydrochoi* (dat. ?, 66. 94) and (almost certainly) *Chalybon* (gen. plur., 66. 48). For the genitive of names ending in -*eus* he uses only the Latin termination: *Thesei* (120), *Erechthei* (229), *Pelei* (278), -*ei* becoming one syllable by synizesis.

fines : the plural is masculine here and in 66. 12: the singular is feminine in 217. The same variation is found with *cinis*: masculine plural at 68. 98, feminine singular at 68. 90.

Aeeteos : hexameters with a spondee in the fifth foot (σπονδειάζοντες) are not infrequent in Homer: the Alexandrians, always ready to cultivate the novel and the unobvious, took up this rhythm and made a mannerism of it (in Callimachus one in every eleven hexameters is a σπονδειάζων, in Aratus one in every six) and their Italian followers took over the affectation. Writing to Atticus about his voyage to Greece (*Att.* vii. 2. 1), Cicero writes 'flauit ab Epiro lenissimus Onchesmites' (a wind) and adds 'You can pass that off as your own and see what one of the modern poets will give you for it' ('hunc σπονδειάζοντα si cui uoles τῶν νεωτέρων pro tuo uendito'). In this poem Catullus has 30 σπονδειάζοντες; he admits the σπονδειάζων in elegiacs also (as Callimachus does not) and has four in each of poems 66 and 68 and one in each of 65, 76, 100, and 116. In eleven lines the spondaic ending consists of a Greek proper name and the rhythm is clearly being cultivated

for its own sake, but there are others (as there are in the
Alexandrians) in which it seems to be used to echo the sense
in sound: so in 15 it may convey the gaze of wonder, in 91
the lingering look of love, in 98 its sighs, in 67 and 274 the
continuous movement of the waves, in 277 the slow dispersal
of the crowd, in 297 the lingering torture of Prometheus: for
other examples see 78, 269, 286. Virgil continues the use
of the spondaic ending, usually as an echo of Greek rhythm
(e.g. *Aen.* iii. 74 'Nereidum matri et Neptuno Aegaeo'),
sometimes with an obvious adaptation of sound to sense (e.g.
Georg. iii. 276 'saxa per et scopulos et depressas conualles'),
but is much more sparing with it: in over 12,000 hexameters
he has 33 σπονδειάζοντες, little more than Catullus has in the
408 lines of this poem. After Virgil the rhythm goes out of
use. In a σπονδειάζων the fourth foot is normally a dactyl;
Catullus has a spondee only in this line and in l. 44.

On the orthography of the adjective see on 68. 109.

4. lecti iuuenes, Argiuae robora pubis : cf. Virg. *Aen.* viii. 518
'robora pubis lecta'. For the archaic *pubes* ('man-power') cf.
267 'Thessala pubes', 68. 101. The phrase represents the
λεκτοὶ ἡρώων and φέριστον ἡρώων of Apollonius.

5 ff. optantes . . . uerrentes: Catullus uses this prosaic participial
construction again and again in this poem (cf. 54, 63, 72, 101:
there are 32 examples in the narrative of ll. 1–131): Virgil
prefers paratactic structure with finite verbs. (See Norden,
Aeneid vi, p. 380.)

5. auertere is used especially of carrying off spoil: cf. Virg. *Aen.*
i. 472 'auertit equos in castra', viii. 208 'quattuor a stabulis
tauros auertit', Caes. *B.C.* iii. 59. 4 'praedam omnem domum
auertebant'.

6. uada salsa : another epic phrase which Virgil repeats, *Aen.*
v. 158 'sulcant uada salsa carina'.

   decurrere : cf. Virg. *Aen.* v. 212 'prona petit maria et
pelago decurrit aperto', and, for the accusative, *Aen.* iii. 191
'uastumque caua trabe currimus aequor'.

7. uerrentes : cf. Enn. *Ann.* 384 V. 'uerrunt extemplo placidum
mare marmore flauo', Virg. *Aen.* vi. 320 'remis uada liuida
uerrunt', iii. 208 'torquent spumas et caerula uerrunt'.

   abiegnis . . . palmis : cf. 4. 4 *palmula*.

8. quibus refers back to *iuuenes* (4).

   diua . . . retinens . . . arces : i.e. Athena in her function of
πολιοῦχος or πολιάς, worshipped on the acropolis of Athens. For
retinens 'occupying' cf. Lucr. iv. 412 'terrarum milia multa /
quae uariae retinent gentes'.

9. ipsa : Catullus makes no reference to Argus, the shipwright who built the Argo under Athena's guidance (Apoll. i. 18–19, 111–12).

currum : the word is applied to a ship only here, but ὄχος and ὄχημα are so used in Greek (Aesch. *Supp*. 33 ὄχῳ ταχυήρει, Soph. *Tr*. 656 πολύκωπον ὄχημα ναός).

10. **texta carinae** : 'fitting the pine timbers to the curved keel': the transference of *texo* from weaving to carpentry (in which ribs and crossbeams correspond to the criss-crossing warp and weft) is old and regular: Enn. *trag*. 66 V. 'mari magno classis cita texitur' (and, of a shipyard, *Ann*. 477 V. 'campus habet textrinum nauibus longis'), Virg. *Aen*. xi. 326 'Italo texamus robore nauis', Ov. *Tr*. i. 4. 9 'pinea texta sonant pulsu', *Fasti* i. 506 'pinea . . . ter pede texta ferit' (of deck planks): so of the wooden horse, Virg. *Aen*. ii. 112 'trabibus contextus acernis', 186 'roboribus textis'.

11. **prima . . . Amphitriten** : 'it was Argo which first handselled the untried Amphitrite with sailing', i.e. introduced the sea to the new experience of being sailed over: for the sense cf. Ov. *Am*. ii. 11. 1 'prima malas docuit, mirantibus aequoris undis, / Peliaco pinus uertice caesa uias': for *imbuit* cf. 4. 17, Val. Fl. i. 69 'ignaras Cereris qui uomere terras / imbuit'. *primam . . . Amphitritem* of *GR* gives no sense: Baehrens, reading *proram . . . Amphitrite*, translates 'she (Athena) first handselled with sea water (*Amphitrite*) Argo's prow untried in voyaging', but *rudem cursu* is an unparalleled phrase and the innocence of the sea is more in point than the inexperience of the ship.

Amphitrite : the use of the name of this Nereid, wife of Poseidon, by metonymy for the sea appears first here: no doubt Catullus found it in hellenistic poetry.

12. **uentosum . . . aequor** : cf. Virg. *Aen*. vi. 335 'uentosa per aequora uectos', *Georg*. 1. 206.

proscidit : 'first ploughed the windy seas': *proscindere* is a technical form for a first ploughing (Varro, *R.R*. i. 29. 2 'terram cum primum arant, proscindere appellant', Lucr. v. 209, Virg. *Georg*. i. 97).

13. **torta** : 'the water churned by the oars grew white with foam': cf. Virg. *Aen*. iii. 207 'nautae / adnixi torquent spumas'.

incanuit : most editors accept the Aldine's correction for *incanduit*, believing that Catullus would not have written *candenti* immediately after *incanduit*. Both *canesco* (cf. 18 *gurgite cano*, Homer's πολίη ἅλς) and *candeo*, *candesco* can be used in this context: Lucretius has both in ii. 766 'ut mare, cum magni commorunt aequora uenti, / uertitur in canos candenti marmore fluctus'.

14. freti : Schrader's necessary correction of *V*'s *feri*: even if the apposition *Nereides, feri uultus*, were possible, the adjective is clearly unsuitable. *emersere* is transitive, governing *uultus*, 'lifted their faces' (cf. *Dirae* 56 'monstra . . . emersere furenti corpora ponto', Manil. v. 198 'ex undis . . . sese emersit in astra'). The author of the *Octavia* may have had this in mind when he wrote (706) 'talis emersam freto / spumante Peleus coniugem accepit Thetim'.

    gurgite: see on 65. 5.

15. monstrum, 'apparition': unlike the English 'monster' in modern use, *monstrum* has no implication of size. It is a word of religious language (*mon(e)strum* from the stem of *moneo*), first applied to an object which conveys a portent, as in Virg. *Aen.* iii. 59 *monstra deum*, then extended to other 'uncanny' things. In Horace, *Od.* i. 37. 21 Cleopatra is *fatale monstrum*; Virgil uses the word of the Trojan horse (*Aen.* ii. 245), of Io's gadfly (*Georg.* iii. 152), and (with mock solemnity) of the pests of the stack-yard (*Georg.* i. 185).

    Nereidĕs : the Greek nominative plural; see on 3.

    The spondaic ending perhaps represents the lingering looks of surprise.

16. illa atque ⟨haud⟩ alia : Bergk's correction is the most likely ('on that day and no other'), although this appearance of the Nereids escorting a ship is by no means unparalleled in poetry: cf. Soph. *O.C.* 716–19 ἁ δ' εὐήρετμος . . . πλάτα / θρώσκει, τῶν ἑκατομπόδων / Νηρῄδων ἀκόλουθος, Eur. *El.* 433 κλειναὶ νᾶες . . . πέμπουσαι χόρους μετὰ Νηρῄδων Vahlen's *illa, alia atque alia*, which goes to the opposite extreme ('on that day and other succeeding days'), is pointless and obscure; 68. 152, *haec atque illa dies atque alia atque alia*, which suggested it, is neither.

17. oculis regularly adds emphasis to *uidere*: e.g. Ter. *Hec.* 863 'numquam ante hunc diem meis oculis eam uideram'.

18. nutricum tenus : the use of the genitive with the preposition *tenus* (explained by the fact that *tenus* was originally a noun) is not uncommon with plural substantives, even in prose where there is no question of metrical convenience (so Virg. *Georg.* iii. 53 *crurum tenus*, Cic. *Arat.* 83 *lumborum tenus*, Quint. xii. 2. 17 *aurium tenus*, Cael. *ap.* Cic. *Fam.* viii. 1. 2 *Cumarum tenus*): with singular substantives the ablative is normal. The use of *nutrices* for *papillae* is unparalleled and seems to have been suggested by the similar use of τίτθη.

19. Peleus : with the characteristic compression of the style, Catullus does not mention that Peleus was on board the Argo. This romantic story of love at first sight between the mermaid and the mortal is found only here. In the usual form of the legend, as it is told by Apollonius (i. 558), Peleus is already the husband of Thetis and the father of Achilles when he goes with the Argo: in Valerius Flaccus (i. 130) the wedding scene appears on the Argo's décor and (i. 255 ff.) little Achilles is brought to see his father off. As for the courtship, in Homer (*Il.* xviii. 433) Thetis marries Peleus οὐκ ἐθέλουσα and in Ovid's version (*Met.* xi. 221) Peleus, instructed by Jupiter to marry Thetis, has to overcome a series of Protean metamorphoses before he can secure her.

19 ff. The anaphora of *tum* (cf. 39–41, 63–65), an Alexandrian mannerism, is accompanied by another in the repetition of the name in different cases: for the first cf. Call. *Hymn* 4. 70–72 φεῦγε μὲν Ἀρκαδίη, φεῦγεν δ' ὅρος ἱερὸν Αὔγης / Παρθένιον, φεῦγεν δ' ὁ γέρων μετόπισθε Φενειός, / φεῦγε δ' ὅλη Πελοπηίς . . .; for the second, *Hymn* 2. 44 ff. (Φοίβῳ . . . Φοίβου . . . Φοῖβον).

19. Thetidis . . . Thetidī : see on 3.

20. despexīt hymenaeos : Catullus has this irregular lengthening in the fifth foot before the Greek word *hymenaeus* again at 62. 4 dicetur hymenaeus, 66. 11 auctus hymenaeo, clearly echoing a Greek rhythm (see Norden, *Aeneid vi*, p. 451); Virgil takes over the mannerism, *Aen.* x. 720 *profugus hymenaeos*, vii. 398 *canit hymenaeos*, and has similar examples of lengthening before *hyacinthus* (*Ecl.* 6. 53, *Georg.* iv. 137, *Aen.* xi. 69).

21. pater ipse : i.e. Jupiter (*ipse diuum genitor* in 27): so Virg. *Georg.* i. 121, 328, *Aen.* ii. 617.

  sensit : 'judged': Pontanus's *sanxit* is unnecessary: for this use of *sentire* cf. Hor. *C.S.* 73.

22. The apostrophe belongs to the hymn-style: cf. Call. *Hymn* 1. 91–94 χαῖρε μέγα Κρονίδη πανυπέρτατε . . . χαῖρε πάτερ, χαῖρ' αὖθι.

  nimis : 'very': see on 43. 4.

  optato : cf. 31, 141, 328, 62. 30, 66. 79, all in contexts relating to love and marriage: so Virg. *Aen.* viii. 405 *optatos amplexus*, xi. 270 *coniugium optatum*, Prop. i. 14. 9.

  saeclorum tempore : for the periphrasis cf. Prop. i. 4. 7 'formosi temporis aetas', Tib. i. 8. 47 'primi temporis aetas'.

23. The manuscripts have the meaningless *o bona mater*: the quotation in the Verona scholia on *Aen.* v. 80 corrects the last word to *matrum* and adds half of the following line. Munro's *iterumque iterumque bonarum* and Peerlkamp's *iterum salvete bonarum* are equally possible supplements. For *bona matrum bonarum progenies* cf. 34. 5 'maximi / magna progenies Iouis': for *iterum* cf. Virg. *Aen.* v. 80 'salue sancte parens, iterum saluete recepti / nequiquam cineres animaeque umbraeque paternae' (so αὖθι in Callim. quoted on 22 above).

deum genus : cf. 61. 2 'Uraniae genus', Virg. *Aen.* vi. 792 'Augustus Caesar, diui genus': Catullus' phrase may have been suggested by Hesiod, *W.D.* 159 ἀνδρῶν ἡρώων θεῖον γένος.

24. saepe . . . compellabo : the promise is not fulfilled, but it is a regular formula of the hymn-style from the Homeric hymns onwards: cf. *Hom. Hymn* 3. 546 αὐτὰρ ἐγὼ καὶ σεῖο καὶ ἄλλης μνήσομ' ἀοιδῆς (so in several other hymns), Theoc. 1. 144 χαίρετε πολλάκι, Μοῖσαι, / χαίρετ'· ἐγὼ δ' ὕμμιν καὶ ἐς ὕστερον ἅδιον ᾀσῶ, 17. 135 χαῖρε, ἄναξ Πτολεμαῖε, σέθεν δ' ἐγὼ ἴσα καὶ ἄλλων / μνάσομαι ἡμιθέων.

25. teque adeo : *adeo*, as often, marks a climax: cf. Virg. *Ecl.* 4. 11 'teque adeo decus hoc aeui, te consule, inibit', *Georg.* i. 24 'tuque adeo' (addressed to Augustus at the end of a series of divinities).

eximie . . . aucte, 'blessed beyond others': cf. 66. 11 'nouo auctus hymenaeo'.

taedis, i.e. *nuptiis,* as in 302: Catullus is the first to use this metonymy, which becomes regular in later verse.

Thessaliae columen : for the metaphor cf. Plaut. *Cas.* 536 'senati columen', Cic. *Verr.* ii. 3. 176 'columen familiae', Hor. *Od.* ii. 17. 4 'Maecenas mearum / grande decus columenque rerum': so, in Greek, Hector is Τροίας κίων, Pind. *Ol.* 2. 82.

26 f. ipse, / ipse : epanalepsis is a favourite device in this poem (as it is in Lucretius), sometimes as here (and in 321) emphatic, sometimes pathetic (61, 132, 403) or picturesque (259, 285). The device goes back to Homer (e.g. *Od.* i. 23, *Il.* ii. 849) and was cultivated by the Alexandrians (e.g. Call. *Hymn* 1. 33, 4. 118, Theoc. 9. 2).

27. suos . . . amores : for the personal use see on 10. 1. Jupiter's waiving of his claim in favour of a mortal was prompted by the prophetic warning of Prometheus (Aesch. *P.V.* 911 ff.)—or Themis (Pind. *Isth.* 8. 32 ff.)—that a son born to Thetis would be greater than his father.

28. Nereine : Haupt's correction of *nectine* is the most probable. *Nereine* does not occur elsewhere except in the late Greek poets Oppian and Quintus Smyrnaeus, but they no doubt had hellenistic precedent for it: the normal Latin form is *Nerine* (Virg. *Ecl.* 7. 37). Ellis's *Neptunine* is an illegitimate hybrid: the Greek suffix *-ine* is not uncommon in Latin but only attached to Greek names (*Aeetine, Euenine*).

tene Thetis tenuit : the question is a hellenistic device: so, e.g., Call. *Hymn* 3. 113. For *tenuit* cf. 45. 2, 72. 2.

29. neptem : Oceanus and Tethys are the parents of Doris, mother of the Nereids.

30. The line may have been suggested by the line ascribed to Euphorion (fr. 122 Powell) ὠκεανός, τῷ πᾶσα περίρρυτος ἐνδέδεται χθών.

31. quae . . . luces: i.e. the marriage-day (the 'poetic' plural is here, more clearly than anywhere else in Catullus, a metrical expedient): the relative forms a loose connexion with the idea of the preceding lines.

finito tempore : 'at the appointed time': for *tempus finire* cf. Livy xxxix. 17. 2 'diem certam se finituros', xlv. 12. 7 'die finita'.

33. laetanti : used adjectivally again in 221.

35. Cieros : the manuscript readings point to *Scyros*, but Scyros, an island lying out in the Aegean east of Euboea, seems out of place in this Thessalian list. The only possible explanation of its appearance here would be that Catullus, who shared the inaccuracy in matters of foreign geography to which all Latin poetry is prone (see Kroll, *Studien z. Verständnis d. röm. Literatur*, 293 ff.: cf. 324), was misled by the connexion of Scyros with the later episode in the story of Thetis and Achilles. (Achilles was concealed in Scyros by his mother in a vain attempt to prevent his going to the Trojan War.) Meineke's *Cieros*, the name of an old town in Thessaliotis (Strabo ix. 435) saves Catullus' geography: the mention of so obscure a place among the well-known names of these lines would be a piece of hellenistic erudition.

Pthiotica Tempe : Tempe, the valley of the Peneus between Olympus and Ossa (see on 285) is in the very north of Thessaly, far from Phthiotis, the southerly region of the country, but Catullus had precedent for his confusion in Callimachus (*Hymn* 4. 112 Πηνειὲ Φθιῶτα, τί νῦν ἀνέμοισιν ἐρίζεις;). For the spelling, cf. 211 *Erectheum*; Greek double aspirates were not preserved in Latin transliteration.

36. Crannon and Laris(s)a were the two chief towns of Central Thessaly, lying north of Pharsalus.

37. Pharsalum : *Pharsaliam* is not impossible. Repetition of a word with change of quantity (*Pharsăliam . . . Pharsālia*) is an Alexandrian mannerism (e.g. Theoc. 6. 19 τὰ μὴ κᾱλὰ κᾱλὰ πέφανται, 18. 51 Κύπρις δὲ θεὰ Κύπρις, Call. *Hymn* 4. 204 πέρᾱ πέρᾱ εἰς ἐμέ; cf. 62. 5), and, while there is no authority for the quantity *Pharsălia*, it might be supported by such novelties as Ovid's *Leucŏsia* and *Crimīsen* (Λευκωσία and Κριμῖσα are the only forms known in Greek). Alternatively it would be possible to suppose that the -a- keeps its length and that the word as scanned is a trisyllable, *i* being treated as a consonant. But *Pharsalia* is nowhere else found for *Pharsalus* as the name of

the town, whereas the combination with Crannon and
Larissa, the absence of a preposition, and perhaps the verb
coeunt, point to the name of a town here.

38. mollescunt : i.e. the skin hardened by the yoke grows soft
again: here and in 42 the commonplace description of the
deserted countryside (cf. Tib. ii. 1. 5–7, Ov. *F.* i. 665–6) is
pursued with extravagant hyperbole.

39. humilis . . . uinea : these are vines growing low and not
trained on trees (*humilis* is Varro's technical term, opposed to
sublimis, *R.R.* i. 8. 1): the soil round them is hoed to loosen it
and clear it of weeds (Colum. iv. 4. 3).

40. prono . . . uomere, 'no ox tears up the clods with deep-driven
share': cf. Virg. *Georg.* ii. 356 'presso exercere solum sub
uomere'. The slow rhythm of the four spondees conveys the
impression of effort, of the ox toiling along the furrow (for
a similar effect cf. Virg. *Georg.* iv. 174, of the blacksmith
Cyclopes, 'illi inter sese magna ui bracchia tollunt') : Catullus
uses the same metrical device in 130 and 202, where it
represents Ariadne's slow and halting cries.

41. frondatorum : the pruners thin the foliage which is keeping
off the sunlight (Virg. *Georg.* i. 156 'ruris opaci / falce premes
umbras', Colum. v. 6. 17) and at the same time get leaves for
fodder.

42. squalida : 'a scaly rust spreads over the abandoned ploughs'.

43. at turns the reader's eye to the other side of the picture:
cf. 58, 251. For the postponement of *at* see on 23. 7.

 ipsius : i.e. the master, Peleus himself: cf. Virg. *Ecl.* 3. 3
'ipse Neaeram / dum fouet', Ter. *And.* 360 'ipsus tristis': see
on 3. 7, and cf. 114. 6, 115. 7.

 quacumque . . . recessit : 'as far as the sumptuous palace
stretched back': *recessit* conveys the idea of a vista of a
series of rooms or courts: cf. Pliny, *Ep.* ii. 17. 21 'contra
parietem medium zotheca recedit'.

45. soliis . . . mensae : dative: 'the thrones have white ivory,
the table glittering cups': so Virg. *Aen.* vi. 603 'lucent
genialibus altis / aurea fulcra toris'.

46. gaudet : 'is gay': only here in this use, but there are similar
uses of *ridere* (Hor. *Od.* iv. 11. 6 'ridet argento domus') and
γελᾶν (Hom. *Il.* xix. 362 γέλασσε δὲ πᾶσα περὶ χθὼν / χαλκοῦ ὑπὸ στεροπῆς).

 gaza : first here and in Lucr. ii. 37, a Persian word borrowed
from Greek.

47. puluinar . . . geniale : Catullus thinks in Roman terms of the
lectus genialis which stood in the *atrium* at and after a

Roman wedding: for a hero and a goddess the *lectus* becomes
a *puluinar*, the seat provided ceremonially at a *lectisternium*
for the gods, represented by their images.

48. **Indo . . . dente** : i.e. ivory: for the construction cf. Virg.
Aen. v. 663 'pictas abiete puppis', xi. 890 'duros obice postes'.
The couch is inlaid with ivory (cf. 61. 108) and covered with
a purple cloth (for the white–red contrast cf. 309, 61. 9 f. n.,
187): cf. Varro, *Sat.* 447 Büch. 'in eborato lecto ac purpureo
peristromate', Hor.*Sat.* ii. 6. 102 'rubro ubi cocco / tincta super
lectos canderet uestis eburnos', Suet. *Jul.* 84 'lectus eburnus
auro ac purpura stratus'.

49. **conchyli purpura fuco** : 'covered by a purple cloth steeped
in the red dye of the conchylium'. Strictly *purpura* and
conchylium apply to animal colouring matter, the product
of the molluscs of these names (for an account of them and
of the technical processes see Pliny, *N.H.* ix. 125–38), *fucus*
to a vegetable colouring, the product of archil (the source of
litmus in modern times): technically the latter was used as
a base for the former (Plin. *N.H.* xxvi. 103 'fucus marinus
conchyliis substernitur'). But they are regularly identified in
Latin poetry as they are here. *Purpura* (πορφύρα) is first the
shell-fish itself, then the colour of the dye produced from it
(Virg. *Georg.* iv. 275 'uiolae sublucet purpura nigrae') or (as
here and in Prop. iv. 3. 51) the cloth dyed with it.

50–266. The description of the coverlet, portraying the story
of Ariadne.

50. **uariata** : for *uariare* of embroidery cf. Val. Flacc. iii. 12
'uestes / quas . . . picto . . . uariauerat auro'; so of painting,
Prop. ii. 6. 33 'istis olim uariabant tecta figuris'. See on
uario 61. 87.

51. **uirtutes** : 'deeds of prowess': cf. 348, 357, 68. 90, Virg. *Aen.*
i. 565–6 'quis Troiae nesciat urbem / uirtutesque uirosque?'

52. **fluentisono** : the compound occurs only here: cf. 125, 320
clarisonus, 263 *raucisonus*.

   Diae : the name is already in Homer's account of Ariadne
(*Od.* xi. 321), where Dia is an island on which Ariadne was
killed by Artemis on her way from Crete to Athens. By
Alexandrian times it had been identified with Naxos: Callim.
fr. 601 Pf. ἐν Δίῃ· τὸ γὰρ ἔσκε παλαίτερον οὔνομα Νάξῳ.

53. **cum classe** : *classis* is not in itself a plural notion and can
refer to an expedition consisting of one ship (Hor. *Od.* iii. 11.
48, Virg. *Aen.* vi. 334 with Servius' note), but *puppes* in 172
seems to imply that Theseus had more than one.

54. **furores** : of the passion of love as in 94, 124, 50. 11 (*in-*

domitus furore), 68. 129; cf. Virg. *Aen*. i. 658 ff. 'ut . . . Cupido furentem / incendat reginam atque ossibus implicet ignem', iv. 101 'ardet amans Dido traxitque per ossa furorem'.

55. **uisit uisere :** Voss's palmary emendation : as at 211 *uisere* provides a convenient metrical alternative to *uidere*.

56. **utpote . . . quae :** 'no wonder, since she . . .': cf. 67. 43; *utpote qui* is a prosaic construction found elsewhere in verse only in Horace's satiric hexameters.

57. **sola :** 'deserted' as in 154, 184: so Virg. *Aen*. xi. 545 'solorum nemorum', 569 'solis montibus'.

58. **immemor** is again applied to Theseus in 123, 135, 248. In one version of the story Theseus was represented as having been visited with amnesia by Dionysus (schol. on Theoc. 2. 48). But *immemor* regularly implies not mere absent-mindedness but indifference to one's obligations, ingratitude, or treachery (cf. 30. 1).

    at : see on 43.

    pellit uada remis : note the rare cadence produced by the strong caesura in the fifth foot, which extends the conflict between ictus and word accent to that foot, in which they normally coincide. (On Virgil's use of it see Norden, *Aeneid vi*, p. 446.) The unusual cadence and the series of dactyls may perhaps represent the splashing of the oars, as Kroll suggests.

60. **ex alga :** from the seaweed at the edge of the shore: cf. 168.

    ocellis : for the diminutive, an intimacy of common speech conveying an emotional overtone, see n. on 3. 18. In admitting it to high poetry Catullus makes it a means of enhancing the sentimental, romantic treatment of the theme: of nouns he has also *lectulus* (88), *munusculum* (103), *labellum* (104), of adjectives *frigidulus* (131), *aridulus* (316), *languidulus* (331). The author of the *Ciris*, writing in the same manner, has *labellum* (496) and *frigidulus* (251, 348). But the innovation had a short life: in the narrative verse of the Augustans and their successors it is abandoned (see A. S. F. Gow, *C.Q.* xxvi [1932], 150 ff.).

61. **bacchantis :** Ariadne is wild as a maenad but silent and motionless.

    prospicit : see on 26 f.: the pathetic repetition makes Bergk's *eheu* certain.

62. **fluctuat :** for the metaphor cf. Virg. *Aen*. viii. 19 'magno curarum fluctuat aestu', Lucr. vi. 34 'uoluere curarum tristes in pectore fluctus'.

63. flauo : cf. 98, 66. 62, 68. 130. Fair hair conventionally belongs to the heroes and heroines of legend, even to *Sidonia Dido* (Virg. *Aen.* iv. 590: for a list of references see Pease's note there).

mitram : the *mitra* was a cap or bonnet with strings under the chin (*redimicula*, Virg. *Aen.* ix. 616) associated with the East and particularly with Lydia. *subtilem* has its literal sense of 'fine-woven'.

64–65. contecta . . . pectus, . . . uincta papillas : this poetic idiom probably had a native origin in the use of a verb in the middle voice (expressing an action done in relation to the agent himself) with a direct object. Traces of a transitive middle survive in a few expressions such as Hor. *Sat.* ii. 7. 38 'nasum nidore supinor', *A.P.* 302 'purgor bilem', and a middle form has persisted in the participles of a few verbs whose sense is essentially middle (*gauisus, pransus, cenatus*). In *contecta pectus, vincta papillas,* and similar phrases the object is a part of the agent's own body: so Ennius 400 V. 'succincti corda machaeris',Virg. *Ecl.* 6. 68'crinis ornatus', 7. 32 'suras euincta cothurno', *Georg.* iv. 337 'caesariem effusae' (where the verb plainly cannot be passive), *Aen.* iv. 518 'exuta pedem', xi. 877 'percussae pectora'. (In others the object is something external to the agent: so Virg. *Aen.* ii. 510 'inutile ferrum cingitur', 392 'galeam . . . induitur'.) But Catullus' *restrictus membra* (296) or Virgil's *percussa mentem* (*Georg.* iv. 357) cannot be explained thus: the participial 'middle' idiom seems to have become confused with a much wider poetic use taken over from Greek, that of the accusative 'of respect' with verbs, active or passive, and adjectives.

uelatum repeats the idea contained in *contecta*: similarly in Tib. i. 6. 67 'quamuis non uitta ligatos / impediat crines', *ligatos* repeats the idea in *impediat.*

65. tereti : see on 314.

66 f. quae . . . alludebant : the verb is used of the sea again in Cic. *N.D.* ii. 100 'mare terram appetens litoribus adludit', Ov. *Met.* iv. 342, Stat. *Theb.* ix. 336: Val. Flacc. vi. 665 repeats the transitive use.

67. ipsius : their mistress's feet: *ipse*, as often, marks the central figure of the picture.

68. sed neque tum . . . neque tum : the same anaphora (cf. 19–21) in *Ciris* 116.

68 f. mitrae . . . uicem curans : 'not troubling on account of . . .': the editors quote Cic. *Att.* viii. 2. 2 'quoius ego uicem doleo',

Fam. xii. 23. 3 'tuam uicem saepe doleo', Livy xliv. 3. 5
'sollicito consuli . . . eorum uicem'.

69. ex te . . . Theseu : the apostrophe was developed by
hellenistic poetry as a device to give a subjective, personal
quality to the narrative, and thence was adopted by the
neoterici: thereafter it becomes a regular part of the technique of Latin verse (Norden, *Aeneid vi*, pp. 122, 126). Cf.
253, 299: see also on 4. 13.

69 f. pectore . . . animo . . . mente : no distinction is to be
drawn; the words reinforce one another.

71. externauit : *externare* and *consternare* are both compounds of
an intensive verb in *-are* corresponding to *sternere* as, for
example, *(pro)fligare* corresponds to *(af)fligere*: but the
Romans themselves probably connected it *externare* with
externus and explained it as 'put beside oneself'.

   a misera : for the exclamation cf. Calvus, fr. 9 M. 'a uirgo
infelix: herbis pasceris amaris'.

72. Erycina : Venus, who had an old-established cult, with a
famous temple, on Mount Eryx in west Sicily: the cult was
familiar in Rome and a temple of Venus Erycina was built
there in 181 B.C.

   serens : 'planting': the verb is not confined to sowing seed;
cf. Hor. *Od.* i. 18. 1 'nullam, Vare, sacra uite prius seueris
arborem', Cic. *Rep.* iii. 16 'Transalpinas gentis oleam et
uitem serere non sinimus'. For the metaphor cf. Soph. *Ajax*
1005 ὅσας ἀνίας μοι κατασπείρας φθίνεις.

   curas : of the sorrows of love: cf. 68. 18, 51.

73. illa tempestate . . . quo ex tempore : for *tempestas*, 'time',
cf. 66. 11 *qua tempestate*: by Cicero's day it was a poetical
archaism which he was prepared to allow occasionally in
prose (*de Or.* iii. 153; he uses it himself in *de Div.* i. 75);
Sallust and Livy both favour it. The repetition of *tempestate*
by its synonym *tempore* in the relative clause is a simple
instance of the idiom discussed on 96. 3 (*dolore . . . desiderio*);
but we should expect *illa ex tempestate . . . quo tempore*, 'from
the time at which' (cf. 35. 13 *quo tempore . . . ex eo*).

74. curuis . . . litoribus : an epic phrase: cf. Accius fr. 570 R.
curuum litus. Piraeus was the harbour of Athens.

75. iniusti : so Minos is ὀλοόφρων in Homer, *Od.* xi. 322, ἄγριος
καὶ χαλεπὸς καὶ ἄδικος in [Plato], *Minos* 318d.

   Gortynia : Minos' capital was at Cnossus (*Od.* xix. 178),
not at Gortyn, and no stress is to be put on the adjective:
Catullus finds *Gortynia* a convenient adjective for 'Cretan',
as Virgil does in *Aen.* xi. 773 *spicula . . . Gortynia*.

templa : from its original meaning of a space ritually marked out, in the sky or on the ground, for purposes of augury, *templum* comes to be used on the one hand of any sacred enclosure or building (of a palace, as here, in Ennius, *Andromache* 92 V. 'o Priami domus, / saeptum altisono cardine templum') and on the other generally of a region, abode, or seat (66. 63 'templa deum'; so in Plaut. *M.G.* 413 'mein locis Neptuniis templisque turbulentis / seruauit', and often in Lucretius, e.g. i. 120 'Acherusia templa', v. 1436 'mundi templum', v. 948 'siluestria templa Nympharum').

76. perhibent : see on l. 1.

77. Androgeoneae . . . caedis : 'the murder of Androgeon': for the use of the adjective see on 368. Minos' son Androgeon (Prop. ii. 1. 62 uses the same Latin form: only Ἀνδρογέως is found in Greek) met his death while he was on a visit to Attica: Minos held the Athenians responsible, attacked their city, and imposed his terms on them: for the story cf. Virg. *Aen.* vi. 20 ff. (a description of Daedalus' carvings on the temple of Apollo at Cumae) 'in foribus letum Androgeo, tum pendere poenas / Cecropidae iussi—miserum—septena quotannis / corpora natorum: stat ductis sortibus urna'.

78. electos : need not refer to the choosing of the victims by lot (see Virgil quoted above): cf. 4 *lecti iuuenes*, 36. 6 *electissima*.

79 f. Three consecutive σπονδειάζοντες (see on l. 3) occur in Latin only here: but Catullus had hellenistic precedent (e.g. Theoc. 13. 42–44, Call. *H.* 3. 222–4, Apoll. iv. 1191–3, Aratus 953–5, Euphorion, fr. 34 Powell).

79. Cecropiam : again in 83, 172: a convenient equivalent for Athens or Attica (from its legendary King Cecrops) which hellenistic poets had discovered (e.g. Call. *Hymn* 3. 227, 4. 315, Apoll. i. 95).

dapem : *daps* (Catullus has the rare singular again in 304) is a solemn, religious word, originally used of a sacrificial meal.

80. angusta : the συνοικισμός of Attica credited to Theseus was still to come: Athens was still small and the sacrifice of its youth was the more felt.

82. proicere optauit : 'chose to sacrifice': cf. Virg. *Aen.* vi. 435 'lucemque perosi / proicere animas'.

potius quam . . . portarentur : for the construction cf. Plaut. *Aul.* 11 'inopemque optauit potius eum relinquere / quam eum thesaurum commonstraret', Ter. *And.* 797 'sese inhoneste optauit parere hic diuitias / potius quam in patria honeste pauper uiueret', Cic. *Tusc.* ii. 52 'perpessus est omnia potius quam conscios delendae tyrannidis indicaret', Nepos

Eum. 11. 4 'cur non in proelio cecidisti potius quam in potestatem inimici uenires?'

83. **funera . . . nec funera** : 'living corpses': the phrase is constructed on the model of such Greek expressions as γάμος ἄγαμος, πόλις ἄπολις, χάρις ἄχαρις, δῶρα ἄδωρα. Cicero ventures on *insepulta sepultura* (*Phil.* 1. 5, of Caesar's funeral, which was no funeral) and quotes *innuptis nuptiis* (γάμοις ἀγάμοις) from a tragic poet (*de Or.* iii. 219), but Latin does not lend itself to the formation of such negative compounds. For *nec* in the sense of *nec tamen* ('corpses and yet not corpses') cf. Ov. *Met.* viii. 231 'pater infelix nec iam pater', *Carm. Epig.* 428. 6 'nunc umbra nec umbra'. The same notion is otherwise expressed by Manilius, v. 549 (of Andromeda) 'uirginis et uiuae rapitur sine funere funus', and Apul. *Met.* iv. 34 (of Psyche) 'uiuum producitur funus'. For *funus* = νεκρός cf. Virg. *Aen.* ix. 491 'lacerum funus'; in prose Varro, *R.R.* i. 4. 5 '(cum) omnes domus repletae essent aegrotis ac funeribus'.

84. **ita** : 'that being so' refers back to the circumstances just described, in this case Theseus' decision ('in pursuance of that purpose'): but *atque ita* (cf. 315: similarly *itaque* in 63. 6, 35), like καὶ οὕτως, is often simply a continuative formula equivalent to our 'and then' (cf. Hor. *Sat.* i. 3. 101, Ov. *Her.* 18. 115).

naue . . . nitens : cf. Prop. iv. 6. 63 'illa petit Nilum cymba male nixa fugaci'.

85. **magnanimum** : a conventional epic epithet, representing μεγάθυμος.

86. **cupido . . . lumine** : 'eyes', as *lumina* in 92, 233; for the singular cf. Virg. *Aen.* ii. 754 'uestigia . . . lumine lustro', Ov. *Her.* 16. 37 'ante tuos animo uidi quam lumine uultus'. As Kroll points out, love at first sight is *de rigueur* in hellenistic poetry: cf. Theoc. 2. 82 ὡς ἴδον, ὡς ἐμάνην, Apoll. iii. 286 ff., *Ciris* 130 'ni Scylla nouo correpta furore / . . . o nimium cupidis Minoa inhiasset ocellis', Prop. iv. 4. 21 ff. 'obstupuit regis facie et regalibus armis / interque oblitas excidit urna manus'.

87. **odores** : so in Homer, *Od.* iv. 121 Helen has a θάλαμος θυώδης.

88. **alebat** : she grows up in the women's quarters, in the inner part of the house, under the charge of her mother, Pasiphae.

89. **quales . . . myrtus** : the conventional comparison (see on 61. 21) is enlivened, in a characteristically Alexandrian way, by the particularity of a proper name, *Eurotas*, as it is by *Asia* in 61. 22. Cf. 105.

praecingunt : Baehrens's correction for V's *pergignunt*: but *progignunt* (cf. 1 *prognatae*) is perhaps more likely.

90. distinctos : i.e. differentiated, with much the same sense as *uario* in 61. 87: for the plural *colores* used of the gay colours of flowers cf. Virg. *Georg.* iv. 306 'ante nouis rubeant quam prata coloribus', Prop. i. 2. 9 'aspice quos summittat humus formosa colores', Tib. i. 4. 29 'quam cito purpureos deperdit terra colores', *Culex* 70 'florida cum tellus gemmantis picta per herbas / uere notat dulci distincta coloribus arua', Val. Flacc. vi. 492 'lilia per uarios lucent uelut alba colores'.

91. declinauit : cf. Ov. *Met.* vii. 86–88 'in uultu ueluti tum denique uiso / lumina fixa tenet . . . nec se declinat ab illo'.

92. concepit corpore flammam : the fire of love is thought of as physical: cf. Virg. *Aen.* vii. 356 'in toto percepit pectore flammam' (with a similar alliteration), iv. 101 'ardet amans Dido traxitque per ossa furorem', viii. 389 f. 'accepit solitam flammam notusque medullas / intrauit calor et labefacta per ossa cucurrit'.

93. medullis : see on 45. 16.

    atque : for the postponement of the connective see on 23. 7.

94 f. heu . . . sancte puer : for the apostrophe cf. Apoll. iv. 445 σχέτλι' Ἔρως, μέγα πῆμα, μέγα στύγος ἀνθρώποισιν, / ἐκ σέθεν οὐλόμεναί τ' ἔριδες στοναχαί τε γόοι τε.

94. furores : see on 54.

95. sancte puer : see on 34. 22, 36. 3: cf. Tib. ii. 1. 81 (to Amor) 'sancte, ueni dapibus festis sed pone sagittas'.

    misces : cf. 68. 18 'quae dulcem curis miscet amaritiem'.

96. Golgos . . . Idalium : see on 36. 12: the line looks as if it were suggested by Theoc. 15. 100 δέσποιν' ἃ Γόλγως τε καὶ Ἰδάλιον ἐφίλησας.

98. in flauo . . . hospite : for *flauus* cf. 63. For *in* ('over') used of a personal object of emotion, cf. 119, 22. 17, 45. 23, 61. 97, Ter. *Eun.* 567 'in hac commotus sum', Hor. *Od.* i. 17. 19 'laborantes in uno / Penelopen uitreamque Circen', Prop. i. 13. 7 'perditus in quadam tardis pallescere curis / incipis', Ov. *A.A.* i. 732 'pallidus in lenta Naide Daphnis erat', *Am.* i. 9. 33 'ardet in abducta Briseide magnus Achilles', *Met.* vii. 21 'quid in hospite, regia uirgo, / ureris?'

99. languenti : 'fainting'; see on 219.

100. fulgore expalluit auri : see on 81. 4.

    quanto : if the manuscript reading is right, *quanto* must be taken as ablative of measure of comparison with *magis*, 'how much more'. But Faernus's *quam tum* (*quam* with *saepe*, 'how often') may be right: the corruption would be easily explained by assimilation to the preceding line.

101. monstrum : i.e. the Minotaur: see on 15.

102. praemia laudis : i.e. reward consisting in glory: Cicero has
the same phrase *Mil.* 81 'id fateri ex quo etiam praemia
laudis essent petenda'; so *Tusc.* i. 34 'mercedem gloriae'.
The line is a reminiscence of Apoll. iv. 205 ἠὲ κατηφείην ἢ καὶ
μέγα κῦδος ἀρέσθαι.

   appeteret is clearly required: for *mortem appetere* of a
voluntary death cf. Sen. *Ep.* 24. 23, Suet. *Nero* 2. 3.

103. non ingrata tamen : in spite of her fears (*tamen*) the gifts
she promised were not without return or promised ineffectually. *frustra* reinforces *ingrata* as *nequiquam* reinforces
uanis in 111; cf. Virg. *Aen.* ii. 101 'sed quid ego haec autem
nequiquam ingrata reuoluo ?'. For *ingrata* see on 73. 3.

103 f. munuscula . . . labello : see on 60.

104. succepit uota : the manuscripts read *succendit*; *uota
succendere* is an improbable phrase for making a burnt offering which has been vowed, and in any case a reference to
the promise, not to the discharge of it, is needed here.
Statius's *succepit* is probable: Ovid has 'uota publica suscipi-
mus' *Met.* vii. 450, and the archaic form of the compound is
preserved several times elsewhere (though always with the
literal sense, 'take up'): e.g. Virg. *Aen.* vi. 248 'cruorem /
succipiunt pateris', Prop. iv. 9. 36 'caua succepto flumine
palma'. The early correction *suspendit* would mean 'let her
prayers hang irresolute', 'left them half spoken' (cf. Lucr. v.
1069 'suspensis dentibus' of a dog's teeth half closed in play,
Quint. x. 7. 22 'suspensa ac velut dubitans oratio'), reinforced by *tacito*—a neat phrase but palaeographically less
likely.

105–11. The simile of the falling tree has its prototype in
Homer (e.g. *Il.* v. 560 ff., xiii. 389 ff.) and in Apollonius
(iii. 967 ff., iv. 1680 ff., quoted on 108): here as in 89 Catullus
uses the Alexandrian device of particularity to add colour
and life to the image: the falling tree is on the summit of
Taurus, the great massif which closes the central plateau of
Asia Minor on the south. On Horace's use of the same device
see Heinze on *Od.* i. 1. 14.

105. brachia : cf. ˌVirg. *Georg.* ii. 296 'late ramos et brachia
tendens': but the word is in ordinary use as a technical term
of forestry.

106. conigeram : *coniger* occurs only here, but Virgil has *conifer*,
Aen. iii. 680.

   sudanti cortice : of resin here, as of amber in Virg. *Ecl.*
8. 54 'pinguia corticibus sudent electra myricae'.

107. indomitus turbo : 'ungovernable'; the whirlwind has no
control over itself.

contorquens . . . robur : 'wrenching the trunk': cf. Virg. *Georg.* i. 481 (of the Po) 'insano contorquens uortice siluas'. For *robur* cf. *Aen.* iv. 441 (in another tree simile) 'annoso ualidam cum robore quercum', *Georg.* ii. 64 'solido de robore myrtus'.

108. eruit : the pause after the first foot perhaps represents the sudden 'give'.

illa procul, &c. : the change of subject is regular in the epic simile, e.g. Apoll. iv. 1682 ff.:

> ἀλλ' ὥς τίς τ' ἐν ὄρεσσι πελωρίη ὑψόθι πεύκη,
> τήν τε θοοῖς πελέκεσσιν ἔθ' ἡμιπλῆγα λιπόντες
> ὑλοτόμοι δρυμοῖο κατήλυθον· ἡ δ' ὑπὸ νυκτὶ
> ῥιπῇσιν μὲν πρῶτα τινάσσεται, ὕστερον αὖτε
> πρυμνόθεν (*radicitus*) ἐξαγεῖσα κατήριπεν· ὡς ὅ γε κ.τ.λ.

exturbata : a strong word, 'flung out roots and all'.

procul need not imply a great distance, as is clearly shown by such Virgilian instances as *Ecl.* vi. 16 'serta procul ('to one side') tantum capiti delapsa iacebant', *Georg.* iv. 424 'ipsa procul nebulis obscura resistit', *Aen.* vi. 651 'arma procul currusque uirum miratur inanis'.

109. quaeuis cumque : *V*'s *lateque cum eius* is unmetrical and meaningless. Ellis's *quaeuiscumque* is weak and pedestrian (the only parallel forms are *cuiusuiscumque* in Lucr. iii. 388 and *quouiscumque* in Mart. xiv. 1. 13), but nothing more plausible has been proposed. Lachmann's *late qua est impetus obuia* and Munro's *lateque comeis obit obuia* are both unattractive.

110. saeuum : 'laid low the savage creature': for the unusual substantival use cf. 63. 85 *ferus*. Perhaps, like the next line, it comes from a Greek original and represents τὸν ἄγριον.

111. 'tossing his horns ineffectually to the insubstantial breezes': a translation of the line quoted by Cic. *Att.* viii. 5. 1, perhaps from Callimachus' *Hecale*, πολλὰ μάτην κεράεσσιν ἐς ἠέρα θυμήναντα. For *uanis* cf. Lucan iv. 726 'caput uanas serpentis in auras / effusae'.

113. regens : 'guiding': cf. Virg. *Aen.* vi. 30 (of Daedalus in the labyrinth) 'caeca regens filo uestigia'.

115. tecti . . . error : 'the untraceable maze of the building (i.e. the labyrinth) baffle him'; for *inobseruabilis* cf. Virg. *Aen.* ix. 392 'uestigia retro / obseruata legit'. The rhythm of the line, with its two polysyllables and the weak caesura in the third foot, is clearly intended to echo the sense. Virgil has the phrase in mind twice, *Aen.* vi. 27 'hic labor ille domus et inextricabilis error', *Aen.* v. 588–91 'fertur labyrinthus . . . / mille uiis habuisse dolum qua signa sequendi / falleret indeprensus et irremeabilis error'.

116. **sed quid ego** : the poet interrupts himself to justify his
παράλειψις, passing rapidly over a part of his story: so Apoll.
i. 648 ἀλλὰ τί μύθους / Αἰθαλίδεω χρειώ με διηνεκέως ἀγορεύειν;
The digression from the *primum carmen* began at 76 with the
story of Theseus' coming to Crete: he now returns to the
deserted Ariadne in Naxos.

117. **ut**, 'how'.
   genitoris filia : the juxtaposition emphasizes the unnatural-
ness of her act: Kroll quotes Cic. *Deiot.* 2 'qui nepos auum
in capitis discrimen adduxerit'.

118. **consanguineae . . . matris** : Minos and Pasiphae had four
daughters: the reference is presumably to Phaedra, the best
known of Ariadne's three sisters; in the famous picture by
Polygnotus at Delphi described by Pausanias (x. 29. 3) she
was represented along with Ariadne.

119. **deperdita** : the participle of *deperire* in the idiomatic sense
'love to distraction' (35. 12, 100. 2): for *in* applied to the
object of affection see on 98.

120. **praeoptarit** : with synizesis of the first two syllables, as in
comedy (e.g. Plaut. *Trin.* 648, Ter. *Hec.* 532): the verb does
not occur in later verse (in which *prae* in composition is
shortened before a following vowel).

121. **Diae** : see on 52.

122. **deuinctam lumina** : see on 64.
   eam : the forms of *is* are rare in verse after Lucretius (see
Axelson, *Unpoetische Wörter*, 70): Catullus has *eum* 63. 43,
earum 63. 54 (if the text is sound), *ei* 82. 3, *eius* 84. 5.

123. **immemori** : see on 58.

124. **perhibent** : see on 1.
   ardenti corde furentem : for *furentem* see on 54: for *ardenti*
cf. 197, Virg. *Aen.* iv. 101 'ardet amans Dido'.

125. **clarisonas** : Catullus has the compound again in 320,
Cicero in *Arat.* 280 'e clarisonis auris Aquilonis'.

126 ff. **conscendere . . . procurrere** : the present infinitives represent the imperfect of oratio recta.

127. **aciem . . . protenderet** : 'stretch her gaze over the swell
of the ocean'; cf. 63. 56 'cupit ipsa pupula ad te sibi derigere
aciem', Cic. *Acad.* ii. 80 'intendi acies longius non potest'.
   uastus : see on 156.

129. **tegmina surae** : i.e. her chiton (*nudatae* is proleptic): cf.
Apoll. iii. 874 ἂν δὲ χιτῶνας / λεπταλέους λευκῆς ἐπιγουνίδος ἄχρις
ἄειρον.

130. extremis : because she is *moribunda*: cf. 188, Prop. iii. 7. 55 'flens tamen extremis dedit haec mandata querellis'.

131. udo . . . ore : ablative of attendant circumstance, 'with tear-stained face'.

frigidulos : for the diminutive see on 60.

132-201. Ariadne's lament. She begins with reproaches against Theseus (132-63): then surveys her own desperate situation (164-87): and ends with a prayer to heaven for vengeance (188-201).

The first part is reminiscent of Medea's lament in Euripides (*Medea* 165 ff., 670 ff.) and in Apollonius (iv. 355 ff.); in its turn it has been used by Virgil (*Aen.* iv. 305 ff.) and Ovid (*Heroides* 10, *Fasti* iii. 459 ff.).

132. sicine : in an indignant, disillusioned question—'you have left me like this, have you?'—as often in comedy: see on 77. 3.

patriis : i.e. the altars of her ancestral gods, as in Virg. *Aen.* xi. 269 'inuidisse deos patriis ut redditus aris / coniugium optatum et pulchram Calydona uiderem'.

134. neglecto numine diuum : 'indifferent to the will of the gods', by whom he had sworn.

135. portas : he carries a freight of broken promises: there is a curious parallel in Demosthenes, *de Falsa Leg.* 220 ὑμεῖς τὴν ἄραν καὶ τὴν ἐπιορκίαν οἴκαδε ἐσηνέγκατε.

deuota : 'under curse': *deuouere* is to make over to the gods of the underworld: cf. Hor. *Od.* iii. 4. 27 'deuota arbos', *Epod.* xvi. 9 'deuoti sanguinis aetas'.

138. uellet miserescere : 'was prepared to pity', 'felt like pitying'.

139. at non haec : the same formula in Nonnus xlvii. 368-9 (spoken by Ariadne), οὐ τάδε μοι κατέλεξεν ἐμὸν μίτον εἰσέτι πάλλων, / οὐ τάδε μοι κατέλεξε παρ' ἡμετέρῳ λαβυρίνθῳ, indicates that Catullus' words had the same Alexandrian original behind them (cf. 160).

blanda : since the anaphora *non haec . . . non haec* requires that *mihi* belong to the first clause, *nobis* is not wanted. On the other hand *uoce* needs an epithet in this context and *blanda uoce* is a familiar combination (Ennius 50 V. *blanda uoce uocabam*, Ov. *A.A.* i. 703, Virg. *Aen.* i. 670 *blandis uocibus*).

140. miserae : the dative after *iubere* is a doubtful construction for which Cic. *Att.* ix. 13. 2 'hae mihi litterae Dolabellae iubent ad pristinas cogitationes reuerti', provides insufficient support, since there *mihi* can be taken as an ethic dative ('I find Dolabella's letters telling me . . .'); the earliest certain examples are in Tacitus. *misere sperare* might be supported by *misere cupere* ('desire desperately') but hardly suits this context, and the old correction *miseram* may well be right, the corruption being due to assimilating *miseram* to *mihi*.

sperare iubebas : cf. Virg. *Georg.* iv. 325 (the disappointed Aristaeus) 'quid me caelum sperare iubebas?'

141. conubia ... hymenaeos : cf. Virg. *Aen.* iv. 316 'per conubia nostra, per inceptos hymenaeos': Catullus has the plural *conubia* (perhaps suggested by the common γάμοι, λέκτρα) again in 158, 62. 27.

142. irrita : 'tear them into nothingness': for the proleptic use cf. 30. 10 *irrita ferre*, Virg. *Aen.* ix. 313 'aurae / ... omnia discerpunt et nubibus irrita donant'.

143. nunc iam : see on 8. 9. Ovid borrows this line for his Ariadne (addressing Dionysus, who she thinks has deserted her, not Theseus), *Fasti* iii. 473 ff. 'dicebam, memini, "periure et perfide Theseu": / ille abiit; eadem crimina Bacchus habet: / nunc quoque "nulla uiro" clamabo "femina credat"'.

145. quis : the antecedent is to be understood out of the singular *uiro*. For the dative cf. 193, 203, 263, 307, 63. 37.

praegestit : the prefix is intensive as in *praetrepidat*, 46. 7.

apisci : the simple verb, normal in comedy, was displaced in later usage by the compound *adipisci* but survives as a mannered archaism as late as Tacitus: cf. 150 *creui*.

146. nil metuunt iurare : 'there is no oath they scruple to take, no promise they forbear to make'.

148. metuere : the change from *metuunt* (146) to *metuere* and the combination of the gnomic perfect *metuere* (see on 62. 42) with the present *curant* are awkward and *dicta metuere* is a surprising phrase: Czwalina's *meminere* removes both difficulties.

149. certe : see on 30. 7.

in medio ... turbine leti : for the metaphorical use of *turbo* cf. Ov. *Met.* vii. 614 'attonitus tanto miserarum turbine rerum', Sil. ix. 287 'fati tam saeuo in turbine'.

This intensive use of *medius* is common in poetry (see Vahlen, *Opusc. Acad.*, ii. 540): so Virg. *Aen.* vi. 339 'mediis effusus in undis', 342 'medio sub aequore mersit', iv. 620 'media inhumatus harena', vii. 372 'mediae Mycenae', Prop. i. 11. 1 'mediis cessantem ... Baiis', iv. 2. 40 'medio puluere ferre rosam', Juv. 3. 80 'mediis sed natus Athenis' ('a thorough Athenian'); in non-spatial contexts, Virg. *Ecl.* 10. 65 'frigoribus mediis', *Aen.* ii. 533 'in media iam morte tenetur', *Georg.* i. 230 'ad medias sementem extende pruinas' ('right into the frosts'); similarly in prose *medius* is idiomatically applied to what is essential or genuine, as opposed to what is marginal, Cic. *Or.* 11 'ingressionem e media philosophia repetitam' ('genuine philosophy'), *Tusc.* iii. 70 'in media stultitia haerere', *Leg.* ii. 53 'hoc e medio est iure ciuili' ('essential law'), *Off.* i. 63 'quae sunt ex media laude iustitiae'.

150. germanum is not strictly true: the Minotaur was her half-brother, the unnatural offspring of Pasiphae and the bull.

   creui : 'decided': the old use of the simple verb (cf. Lucil. 122 M. 'praesidium castris educere creuit'), later supplanted by *decerno*, survived in legal language (e.g. Cic. *Leg.* iii. 6 'quodcumque senatus creuerit agunto'). Cf. 145 *apisci*.

151. quam . . . dessem : see on 82.

   supremo in tempore : for *tempus* of a critical point of time cf. 169 'extremo tempore', Hor. *Od.* ii. 7. 1 'o saepe mecum tempus in ultimum / deducte'.

152. feris . . . alitibusque : cf. Hom. *Il.* i. 4 αὐτοὺς δὲ ἑλώρια τεῦχε κύνεσσι / οἰωνοῖσί τε πᾶσι, Soph. *Ant.* 29 ἄκλαυστον ἄταφον οἰωνοῖς γλυκὺν / θησαυρὸν εἰσορῶσι πρὸς χάριν βορᾶς. Ovid characteristically makes his Ariadne enumerate the likely fauna: *Her.* 10. 83 ff. 'iam iam uenturos aut hac aut suspicor illac / qui lanient auido uiscera dente lupos; / forsitan et fuluos tellus alat ista leones; / quis scit an et saeuam tigrida Dia ferat?'

153. iniacta : for the unreduced vowel cf. 43. 8 *insapiens*.

   iniacta . . . terra : without burial—or at least the token burial of the scattering of earth—the spirit has no rest.

154–6. For the conceit see on 60. 1: to the lioness and the monstrous legendary whirlpools, types of heartless cruelty, the Syrtes, the dreaded shallows off the African coast, are added here as they are in Ov. *Met.* viii. 120.

154. sola sub rupe : so Virg. *Ecl.* 10. 14; cf. 57, 184.

156. uasta Carybdis : Lucretius has the same phrase (i. 722) and Virgil uses the whole line, *Aen.* vii. 302 'quid Syrtes aut Scylla mihi, quid uasta Charybdis / profuit?' The basic implication of *uastus* (a cognate of *uacuus* and *uanus*) is the emptiness or desolation which repels or appals the beholder. It is a favourite word with Virgil, who uses it in a great variety of contexts, always charged with an emotional suggestion of awe or horror: so of the sea, *Aen.* i. 118 'rari nantes in gurgite uasto', iii. 191 'uastum aequor', iii. 421 'uastos fluctus', vi. 296 'uasta uoragine'; of beasts, viii. 295 'uastum leonem'; of sounds, i. 245 'uasto cum murmure montis', x. 716 'uasto clamore lacessunt'. Similarly in common speech *uastus* expresses a repellent uncouthness without any suggestion of

size: so *uastus homo* (Cic. *de Or.* i. 117), *uasta littera* (Cic. *Or.* 153, of the repulsive sound of *x*), *uasta oratio* (*ad Her.* iv. 18).

157. qui reddis : the indicative in a relative clause of this type is the original usage; in Plautus indicative and subjunctive are interchangeable (*Men.* 309 'insanit hic quidem qui ipse male dicit sibi', but 312 'tu . . . non sanus satis . . . qui nunc ipsus male dicas tibi') and the indicative is the commoner; even Cicero sometimes chooses to use an indicative attributive clause instead of emphasizing the causal relation with the subjunctive (*Att.* xiii. 29. 3 'o te ferreum qui illius periculis non moueris', but *Att.* x. 10. 1 'me caecum qui haec antea non uiderim'; *Acad.* i. 18 'sumne sanus qui haec uos doceo?': see Madvig on *de Fin.* i. 43). Catullus uses the indicative construction again at 62. 14; at 62. 21 and 27 he has the subjunctive.

158. fuerant : the appearance of the pluperfect where the imperfect might be expected can often be explained by the fact that it expresses a remote past state not in relation to the present but in relation to an intermediate event or state which is implied: e.g. Ter. *Hec.* 648 'si dudum fuerat ambiguum hoc mihi, nunc non est' ('if it had been doubtful before I learned better'), Virg. *Aen.* v. 397 'si mihi quae quondam fuerat . . . foret illa iuuentus' ('which I had had before I grew old'), Prop. i. 12. 11 'non sum ego qui fueram' ('the man I had been before Cynthia left me'), Ov. *Am. epig.* 1 'qui modo Nasonis fueramus quinque libelli, / tres sumus' ('who had been five before two were removed'). But in many cases, as here, such precision of thought cannot be read into it: the pluperfect encroached on the imperfect in colloquial speech, and poets (especially Propertius and Ovid) found its metrical convenience tempting.

159. prisci : 'old-fashioned', with the implication of severity: cf. Hor. *Od.* iii. 21. 11 'prisci Catonis', *Copa* 34 'pereat cui sunt prisca supercilia'.

160 ff. attamen . . . cubile : the turn is as old as Euripides: fr. 132 N.² (Andromeda) ἄγου δέ μ', ὦ ξέν', εἴτε πρόσπολον θέλεις / εἴτ' ἄλοχον εἴτε δμωίδα. The resemblance in phrasing to Nonnus' version of Ariadne's lament (xlvii. 390 ff.) suggests that Catullus and he were using the same hellenistic source (cf. 139):

> δέξο με σῶν λεχέων θαλαμηπόλον, ἢν ἐθελήσῃς·
> καὶ στορέσω σοι λέκτρα μετὰ Κρήτην Μαραθῶνι
> οἷά τε ληισθεῖσα· καὶ ὀλβίστῃ σέο νύμφῃ

64. 156–74

τλήσομαι ὡς θεράπαινα πολύκροτον ἴστον ὑφαίνειν
καὶ φθονεροῖς ὤμοισιν ἀήθεα κάλπιν ἀείρειν
καὶ γλυκερῷ Θησῆι φέρειν ἐπιδόρπιον ὕδωρ.

160. attamen : for the use of *at* in apodosis cf. 30. 11.

uestras : i.e. the home of your family: see on 39. 20.

161. quae : the antecedent is *me* understood with *ducere*.

162. permulcens ... lymphis : cf. Pacuvius, fr. 244 R. (Euryclea speaks to the disguised Ulysses) 'cedo tuum pedem mi lymphis flauis fuluum ut puluerem / manibus isdem quibus Ulixi saepe permulsi abluam'. For *permulceo* cf. 284.

uestigia : 'feet': first here in this use in which later poets find a convenient synonym for *pedes*: e.g. Virg. *Aen.* v. 566 'uestigia primi / alba pedis frontemque ostentans ... albam'.

lymphis : see on 254 *lymphata*.

164. sed quid ego : Ariadne breaks off her vain reproaches with the same formula with which the poet interrupts himself at 116.

165. externata : see on 71.

nullis sensibus auctae : 'endowed with no feelings': cf. Lucr. iii. 630 'sic animas intro duxerunt sensibus auctas'.

166. audire ... reddere : 'can neither hear words uttered nor give them in reply': cf. Virg. *Aen.* i. 409 'ueras audire et reddere uoces', vi. 689.

169. nimis : see on 43. 4.

insultans ... saeua fors : cf. Hor. *Od.* iii. 29. 49 'Fortuna saeuo laeta negotio et / ludum insolentem ludere pertinax'.

extremo tempore : see on 151.

170. etiam with *inuidit* : 'even grudges my plaint a hearing'.

171. utinam ne ... : cf. Ennius, *Medea* 246 V. 'utinam ne in nemore Pelio securibus / caesa accedisset abiegna ad terram trabes / neue inde nauis incohandi exordium / coepisset', &c., a passage itself suggested by the opening lines of Euripides' *Medea*, εἴθ' ὤφελ' Ἄργους μὴ διαπτάσθαι σκάφος, κτλ. Virgil varies the·motif, *Aen.* iv. 657–8 'heu nimium felix si litora tantum / numquam Dardaniae tetigissent nostra carinae'.

172. Gnosia : Minos' palace was indeed at Cnossus, but the adjective is no doubt used here, as often elsewhere (e.g. Virg. *Georg.* i. 222), as equivalent to 'Cretan': so *Gortynia* 75.

173. dira ... stipendia : 'the grim tribute', i.e. the human tribute paid to the Minotaur (75 ff.): *stipendia* implies a regular payment.

173. nec : for the postponement see on 23. 7.

174. in Cretam religasset must mean 'unmoored his ship for the

voyage to Crete': but while *religare* can mean 'untie' (as in
63. 84 *religat iuga*), with *funem, nauem*, and the like as object
it is so regular in the sense of 'tie up' that Catullus is unlikely to have used it otherwise here and *O*'s *Creta* should
probably be preferred, 'tied up his cable in Crete': cf. Ov.
Met. xiv. 248 'Circaeo religata in litore pinu', xiii. 439 'litore
Threicio classem religarat Atrides'.

177. nam : the connexion is 'I wish he had never come here:
for he has left me in a desperate plight'. Ariadne's analysis
of her dilemma recalls Medea's in Euripides (502 ff.) :

> νῦν ποῖ τράπωμαι; πότερα πρὸς πατρὸς δόμους
> οὕς σοι προδοῦσα καὶ πάτραν ἀφικόμην;
> ἢ πρὸς ταλαίνας Πελιάδας; καλῶς γ' ἂν οὖν
> δέξαιντό μ' οἴκοις ὧν πατέρα κατέκτανον.

178. Idaeos : the mountains of her native Crete (Call. *Hymn* 1.
51 Ἰδαίοις ἐν ὄρεσσι), where Mount Ida (*mons Idaeus* in Virg.
Aen. iii. 105) dominates the island. Lachmann's *Idomeneus*,
based on the variant *idmoneos* in *GR*, not only involves an
anachronism, since Idomeneus was Ariadne's nephew, son
of her brother Deucalion, but introduces a genitive termination which exists in Greek (Ἰδομενεῦς, Hom. *Il.* xiii. 424) but
is unknown in Latin.

178 f. at . . . aequor : *V*'s *a . . . ubi* gives no satisfactory sense;
at, as often, introduces the speaker's own objection.

179. discernens . . . diuidit : for the combination of synonyms
cf. 221 'gaudens laetanti pectore', 313 f. 'torquens . . . uersabat'.

  truculentum : cf. 63. 16 *truculenta pelagi*.

180. an . . . reliqui? : 'or am I to hope for help from my father?
The father that I left of my own free will?' The relative
clause is put as a question (so *quine* 183), as often in the
dialogue of comedy: e.g. Ter. *Ph.* 921–3 illud mihi / argentum
rursum iube rescribi, Phormio. / — quodne ego descripsi
porro illis quibus debui?' ('you mean the money I paid out?').
quaene in 68. 91 represents a different and less straightforward
use: see on that line.

181. caede : 'blood': for the concrete sense cf. 360, 368.

182. consoler : Ariadne's rhetoric is better than her logic when
she speaks of finding comfort in a husband's love for a husband's desertion.

183. lentos : the basic meaning of *lentus* seems to be 'yielding
under pressure': so, as one or other half of that definition is
emphasized, it means on the one hand (1) 'flexible', 'pliant'
(so of the vine, 61. 102, of the poplar, 64. 290), and on the

other (2) 'sticky', 'tough', 'viscous' (and metaphorically
'slow', 'phlegmatic'). That the meaning here is (1), *lentos*
repeating the notion of *incuruans*, is shown by Virg. *Aen*. iii.
384 'Trinacria lentandus ("must be made *lentus*", i.e. bent)
remus in unda'.

184. nullo colitur . . . tecto : 'is inhabited by no dwelling': so
Ovid's Ariadne says (*Her*. 10. 59) 'uacat insula cultu'. With
the manuscript reading *nullo litus sola insula tecto* the construction must be *litus nullo tecto, sola insula*: the interlaced
structure of two appositional phrases is a very common
device of later poetry (e.g. Virg. *Ecl*. 9. 9 'ueteres iam fracta
cacumina fagos', Ov. *Met*. xiii. 598 'da precor huic aliquem
solacia mortis honorem', Hor. *Epod*. 14. 7 'inceptos, olim
promissum carmen, iambos', Prop. ii. 3. 14 'non oculi,
geminae, sidera nostra, faces'), but Catullus does not use it
elsewhere and the loose ablative of description *nullo tecto*,
'a shore without dwellings' (which would not be surprising
in Propertius) is unlikely in Catullus. For *sola* cf. 57, 154.

186. nullā spes : see on 357.
   omnia muta . . . letum : cf. Prop. iv. 3. 53 'omnia surda
tacent', Virg. *Aen*. i. 91 'praesentemque uiris intentant
omnia mortem'.

190. multam : properly a legal fine or forfeit: a prosaic word,
not elsewhere used in elevated verse: cf. *multantes* 192.

191. fidem : 'protection': cf. 34. 1.

192–3. Ariadne appeals to the Furies, in Homer the punishers
of perjury: *Il*. xix. 259 Ἐρινύες αἵ θ' ὑπὸ γαῖαν / ἀνθρώπους τίνυνται
ὅτις κ' ἐπίορκον ὀμόσσῃ.

192. uindice : here first used adjectivally: again in Ov. *Met*. i.
230 *uindice flamma*. Note the threefold repetition of the
same idea in *multantes uindice poena*.

193. anguino . . . capillo : in literature as in art the Furies are
depicted with snakes for hair (or with snakes entwined in
their hair): Pausanias (i. 28. 6) says that Aeschylus was the
first so to represent them (*Cho*. 1049 πεπλεκτανημέναι πυκνοῖς
δράκουσι): cf. Virg. *Georg*. iv. 482 'caeruleosque implexae
crinibus angues / Eumenides', Tib. i. 3. 69 'Tisiphoneque
impexa feros pro crinibus angues'.

194. exspirantis : with *iras*: 'whose brows wreathed with snaky
hair display the blast of wrath from their hearts'.
   praeportat : in the sense of *prae se fert*; elsewhere only in
Catullus' contemporaries Lucretius (ii. 621 'telaque prae-
portant uiolenti signa furoris') and Cicero (*Arat*. 430 'prae se /
scorpius infestus praeportans flebile acumen').

195. huc huc : for the summons to the goddesses cf. 61. 8.

196. uae, usually accompanied by a dative (though in 8. 15 Catullus uses it with an accusative), is here used absolutely as in Ov. *Am.* iii. 6. 101 'uae demens narrabam', Hor. *Od.* i. 13. 3 'uae meum tumet iecur', Virg. *Ecl.* 9. 28.

    extremis . . . medullis : cf. 93 'imis medullis', 198 'pectore ab imo': for *extremus* in this context cf. Ov. *Her.* 4. 70 'acer in extremis ossibus haesit amor'.

197. cogor : i.e. by destiny; this use of the verb is a mannerism in Propertius (e.g. i. 1. 8, i. 7. 8, i. 12. 14, i. 16. 13 'grauibus cogor deflere querellis').

    furore : see on 54.

198. quae quoniam : a favourite connective formula in Lucretius (e.g. i. 21).

    pectore ab imo : Lucretius has the same verse ending in iii. 57.

200. quali . . . mente : i.e. *immemori*: Ariadne's curse is fulfilled in 207 ff., though the Eumenides are there forgotten and it is Jupiter himself who answers her prayer.

202–48. The story of the return of Theseus and the fulfilment of Ariadne's curse.

204. inuicto . . . numine : as *inuicto* shows, *numine* has here its normal sense of 'divine power' or 'will', but in combination with *adnuit* it has perhaps some suggestion of its original meaning of 'nod', which is found in literature only in Lucretius (ii. 632 'quatientes numine cristas'; cf. iv. 179). Livy vii. 30. 20 'annuite, patres conscripti, nutum numenque uestrum inuictum Campanis' suggests that the phrase belongs to an old prayer formula.

204 f. numine . . . quo motu : for the antecedent repeated in the relative clause by a synonym or a word of similar sense see on 96. 3.

205–7. The idea goes back to Homer *Il.* i. 528 ἦ καὶ κυανέῃσιν ἐπ' ὀφρύσι νεῦσε Κρονίων / . . . μέγαν δ' ἐλέλιξεν "Ολυμπον; Virgil repeats it in *Aen.* ix. 106 'adnuit et totum nutu tremefecit Olympum'.

205 f. horrida . . . aequora : 'ruffled': so Hor. *Od.* iii. 24. 40.

206. concussit . . . sidera mundus : i.e. 'concussa sunt sidera mundi': for the idiom see on 305.

    mundus : the firmament as in 66. 1: see on 47. 2. For the expression of these lines cf. Ov. *Met.* viii. 780 '(Ceres) adnuit his capitisque sui pulcherrima motu / concussit grauidis oneratos messibus agros', Stat. *Theb.* vii. 3 'concussitque caput motu quo celsa laborant sidera', Claud. *R.P.* iii. 66 'dixit et horrendo concussit sidera motu'.

207. caeca ... caligine : cf. 68. 44 *caeca nocte*: Lucretius (iii. 304, iv. 456) and Virgil (*Aen.* iii. 203, viii. 253) have the same phrase.

208. consitus : literally 'sown' or 'planted with': for the metaphorical use ('fitted' or 'covered with') cf. Plaut. *Men.* 756 'consitus sum senectute', Lucr. ii. 211 'sol lumine conserit arua': *obsitus* is common in the same use (Virg. *Aen.* viii. 307 'obsitus aeuo', Ter. *Eun.* 236 'pannis annisque obsitum').

209. mandata ... tenebat : cf. Lucr. ii. 582 'memori mandatum mente tenere'. The words are picked up in 232 (*mandata*) and 238 (*mandata ... tenentem*).

210. dulcia ... sustollens signa : 'hoisting the welcome signal', i.e. the white sail.

    nec : for the position of the connective see on 23. 7.

211. Erectheum ... portum : the harbour of Athens, from its king Erechtheus, in legend Aegeus' great-grandfather. For the spelling cf. 35 *Pthiotica*.

212. ferunt : see on 1.

    diuae : i.e. Athena, the tutelary goddess of Athens.

    classi : for the ablative cf. 66. 45 'iuuentus / per medium classi barbara nauit Athon'; Catullus has the normal *classe* in l. 53.

213. concrederet: an old compound, common in Plautus but otherwise rare.

215. iucundior ... uita : cf. 65. 10 'uita frater amabilior', 68. 106 'uita dulcius atque anima / coniugium': similarly Virg. *Aen.* v. 724 'nate mihi uita quondam, dum uita manebat, / care magis', Cic. *Sull.* 88 'huic puero qui est ei uita sua multo carior', *Fam.* xiv. 7. 1 'Tulliolam quae nobis nostra uita dulcior est'. Hoefft's *longe* is tempting, but Catullus' fondness for the balancing of two nouns and their adjectives within the line (see intr., p. 275 ; 66.38 n.) confirms *longa*, even if it is little more than a stopgap.

217. reddite : Theseus was taken to Troezen in infancy by his mother Aethra and brought up there by her father King Pittheus: on reaching manhood he came to Athens and was recognized by his father.

    extrema ... fine: for the strengthening of a noun by an adjective of the same meaning cf. Hor. *Ep.* ii. 1. 12 *supremo fine* and see on 46. 1. For the gender see on 3.

219. languida : 'swooning eyes': so 188 'languescent lumina morte'. Catullus is fond of the sentimental associations of these words (cf. 99 *languenti corde*, 331 *languidulos somnos*).

221. gaudens laetanti pectore : for the pleonasm cf. 103, 179, 192, 313–14.

225. infecta : 'dyed', usually with an accompanying ablative, but cf. Prop. iii. 18. 23 *infectos Britannos*.

uago : not 'swaying' but 'journeying': see on 271.

226. luctus . . . incendia : cf. Virg. *Aen.* ix. 500 *incendentem luctus*.

227. obscurata : i.e. *infecta*.

ferrugine : *ferrugo* is a puzzling word. In ordinary technical language (Plin. *N.H.* xxiii. 151) *ferrugo* is 'iron-rust', corresponding in meaning as in form to *aerugo*, 'vert de gris', and *ferrugineus sapor* (*N.H.* xxxi. 12) is an iron taste in water. But when *ferrugo* and *ferrugineus* are used with reference to colour they clearly do not describe, as one might expect, the colour of rust. Servius on *Aen.* ix. 582 defines the colour as *uicinus purpurae subnigrae*, and a dark purple suits all but one of the passages in which the words are used. Virgil uses them of the hyacinth (*Georg.* iv. 183), of the sun's light in eclipse (*Georg.* i. 467 'caput obscura nitidum ferrugine texit'), of Charon's boat (*Aen.* vi. 303; it is *caerulea* in 410), of a cloak (*Aen.* ix. 582 'pictus acu chlamydem et ferrugine clarus Hibera', xi. 772 'peregrina ferrugine clarus et ostro'): in Ov. *Met.* v. 404 Dis has 'obscura tinctas ferrugine habenas': in Tib. i. 4. 43 *picea ferrugo* is applied to a stormy sky. In Plaut. *M.G.* 1178–9 a character disguising himself as a sailor is advised 'palliolum habeas ferrugineum; nam is colos thalassicus est': that might well be purple, but in Ov. *Met.* xiii. 960 'uiridem ferrugine barbam / caesariemque' the sea-god's hair was sea-green.

Hibera : the (*H*)*iberia* with which *ferrugo* is connected here—and in *Aen.* xi. 582 (quoted above)—is probably Spain (which produced linen and also dyes) rather than the legendary Iberia of Hor. *Epod.* 5. 21, near the country of the Chalybes (so Servius on *Aen.* xi. 582).

dicet appears to be used with the sense of *indicet*, 'show', 'declare': the only parallel is Lucilius 108 'sicubi ad auris / fama tuam pugnam clarans (? praeclaram?) adlata dicasset'. For the archaic use of a simple verb normally replaced by a compound cf. 145 *apisci*, 150 *creui*.

228. quod tibi si : 'but if . . .': for the insertion of the enclitic pronoun cf. Sen. *Dial.* vi. 16. 3 'quod tibi si uis exempla referri . . . .'

incola Itoni : Athena; Itonus (or Iton, Hom. *Il.* ii. 696)

was a town in Phthiotis (Paus. i. 13. 2)—or in Boeotia (Paus.
ix. 34. 1)—with a famous sanctuary of Athena; she is *'Ιτωνία* in
Bacchylides (fr. 15 Sn.), *'Ιτωνίς* in Apollonius (i. 551), *'Ιτωνίας* in
Callimachus (*Hymn* 6. 74). The cult of Athena Itonias was
to be found even in Athens, but to make a king of Athens,
the chief seat of the goddess, use this description of her is an
absurd piece of Alexandrian erudition: for similar learned
periphrases cf. 290, 324).

229 f. defendere . . . annuit : 'wills the defending of' (by herself), 'vouchsafes to defend': *annuo* is used again with an
infinitive in Virg. *Aen.* xi. 19, but somewhat differently, in
the sense of 'permit', 'ubi primum uellere signa / adnuerint
superi', 'will the tearing up of the standards (by us)'. (In
Livy xxviii. 17. 8 'amicitiam se Romanorum accipere annuit'
the meaning is 'indicated by nodding'.)

231. facito ut : cf. Virg. *Aen.* xii. 438 'facito . . . sis memor':
the emphatic periphrasis is common in prose (e.g. Cic. *Flacc.*
57 'facite ut recordemini'). The second imperative in -*ito*,
expressing a command the fulfilment of which is contingent,
has its usual note of solemn injunction.

233 f. ut . . . deponant : the *ut*-clause is epexegetic of *haec* in 232.
lumina, 'your eyes'.

234. antennae does not imply that Theseus had more than one
ship; the plural is used of a single yard: cf. Ov. *Met.* xi. 483
'antennis totum subnectite uelum'.

235. intorti : i.e. made of plaited rushes: cf. Virg. *Aen.* iv. 575
'tortos incidere funis'.

237. aetas normally means a period of time (as in 232, 322,
68. 43 'fugiens aetas'): here it seems to be equivalent to
tempus.

reducem . . . sistet : cf. Virg. *Aen.* ii. 620 'tutum patrio te
limine sistam': the phrase belongs to formal religious
language: so Livy xxix. 27. 3 (a general's prayer to the gods
for his troops) 'uos precor . . . uti . . . saluos incolumesque . . .
mecum domos reduces sistatis', Suet. *Aug.* 28 'ita mihi
saluam ac sospitem rem publicam sistere in sua sede liceat'.

238 f. The construction is *haec mandata Thesea prius constanti
mente (ea) tenentem liquere ceu nubes montis cacumen (linquunt).*

The vivid simile of the cloud lifting from the hilltop was
perhaps suggested by *Iliad* v. 552 ff. νεφέλῃσιν ἐοικότες ἅς τε
Κρονίων / νηνεμίης ἔστησεν ἐπ' ἀκροπόλοισιν ὄρεσσιν / ἀτρέμας, ὄφρ'
εὕδῃσι μένος Βορέαο καὶ ἄλλων / ζαχρηῶν ἀνέμων, οἵ τε νέφεα σκιόεντα /
πνοιῇσιν λιγυρῇσι διασκιδνᾶσιν ἀέντες.

239. ceu belongs to the old epic style.

240. niuei : a favourite word of Catullus: cf. 303, 309, 364, 58b. 4, 61. 9, 68. 125.

241. ex arce : i.e. from the Acropolis of Athens.

  prospectum . . . petebat : cf. Virg. *Aen.* i. 180 'omnem prospectum late pelago petit'.

242. absumens : using up, wasting, his eyes on weeping: the construction with *in* of the object on which resources are spent is common with *consumo*.

243. infecti is unnecessary after 235 and *V*'s *inflati* need not be changed: it adds a picturesque touch—the bellying of the sail lets Aegeus see its colour all too clearly.

246 f. funesta . . . paterna morte : 'in mourning for his father's death', looks back to *funestet* in 201.

246. domus . . . tecta : for the periphrasis cf. 276 *uestibuli tecta*.

247. Minoidi : the Greek dative form is rare in Latin: Catullus has *Tethyi* 66. 70; elsewhere it occurs only in Statius, who has *Iasoni*, *Doridi*, *Palladi*. For other Greek forms see on 3.

249. prospectans takes the reader back to 52 and 60.

250. saucia curas : both as often of the sorrows of love: cf. Enn. *Medea* 254 V. 'amore saeuo saucia', Virg. *Aen.* iv. 1 '(Dido) iam dudum saucia cura'.

250–64. The story of Ariadne resumed with the arrival of Dionysus.

251. at parte ex alia : *at* turns the reader's eye to another scene on the embroidered picture.

  florens : fresh ¡and vigorous: Dionysus–Iacchus is always represented as a youthful god; so Arist. *Frogs* 395 τὸν ὡραῖον θεὸν παρακαλεῖτε, Ov. *Met.* iv. 17 f. 'tibi enim inconsumpta iuuenta est, / tu puer aeternus, tu formosissimus alto / conspiceris caelo', Tib. i. 4. 37 'solis aeterna est Phoebo Bacchoque iuuentas'.

  uolitabat : cf. 63. 25. The verb has often a suggestion of bustling, swaggering, or flaunting: cf. Virg. *Aen.* xii. 126 'mediis in milibus ipsi / ductores auro uolitant ostroque superbi', Cic. *Phil.* xi. 6 '(Antonius) tota Asia uagatur, uolitat ut rex' *de Domo* 49 'cum tu florens ac potens per medium forum . . . uolitares'.

  Iacchus is properly a minor deity—in origin probably the personification of a ritual cry, like Hymenaeus—associated with Demeter and Persephone in the Eleusinian mysteries, but already in Greek literature he has come to be identified with Bacchus, a cult title of Dionysus.

252. Nysigenis : Nysa, the place with which the origins of of Dionysus and his cult were connected in legend, was variously placed: Homer (*Il.* vi. 133) puts it in Thrace, later literature in Arabia or Ethiopia or India. The satyrs and *sileni*, spirits of wild nature, male counterparts of the Nymphs, came to be associated with Dionysus and his wild train: in literature and in art from Hellenistic times the satyrs are represented as youthful, the *sileni* (or Silenus) as old.

253. te . . . Ariadna : see on 69.

tuo . . . amore : 'love for you', as in 87. 4.

254. quae tum : *V*'s *qui tum* cannot be right, since *harum* in 256 requires a preceding feminine. With Bergk's *quae tum* we must assume the loss of a line (or more) introducing the maenads and containing the antecedent of *quae*. If *bacchantes* could be taken substantivally as equivalent to *Maenades*, it would be easy to read either (with Baehrens) *quicum* (i.e. *quibuscum*) or (as Dr. Skutsch has suggested to me) *cui tum* (referring to *Iacchus*: for the dative—'in whose honour', 'at whose bidding'—cf. Virg. *Aen.* vii. 390 f. 'mollis tibi sumere thyrsos, / te lustrare choro, sacrum tibi pascere crinem', Stat. *Theb.* vii. 679 'utinam ipse ueniret / cui furis', Claudian *IV Cons. Hon.* 604 f. 'dubitassent orgia Bacchi / cui furerent'), but there is no evidence for such a substantival use.

lymphata mente : *lymphatus*, 'maddened', is a coinage made on the analogy of *laruatus* (possessed by *laruae*, ghosts), to render νυμφόληπτος, which represents the popular Greek belief that the anger of the nymphs caused madness. *lympha*, originally *lumpa*, an Italic word for 'water', probably owed its spelling to a mistaken etymology which connected it with νύμφη. *lymphatus* is already used in the context of Bacchic worship in Pacuvius, fr. 422 R. 'lymphata aut Bacchi sacris commota': cf. Hor. *Od.* i. 37. 14 'mentem lymphatam Mareotico'.

255–60. The acts and attributes described in these lines are the usual accompaniments of Bacchic worship in literature and art—the Bacchic cry of εὐοῖ, the thyrsus, the σπαραγμός, the oriental music of tambourines, horns, and αὐλοί: for other descriptions see Virg. *Aen.* iv. 300 ff., vii. 385 ff. All of course have their prototypes in Euripides' *Bacchae*: 25 θύρσον . . . κίσσινον βέλος, 697 καταστίκτους δορὰς / ὄφεσι κατεζώσαντο, 739 ἄλλαι δὲ δαμάλας διεφόρουν σπαράγμασι.

255. euhoe : the ejaculation stands outside the construction as in Soph. *Tr.* 218 ἰδού μ' ἀναταράσσει εὐοῖ μ' ὁ κισσός: so Virg. *Aen.* vii. 389 'euoe, Bacche, fremens'.

256. tecta . . . cuspide : wreathed with vine-leaves (Virg. *Aen.* vii. 396, Ov. *Met.* iii. 667) or ivy and topped with a pine-cone (Virg. *Ecl.* 5. 31).

259. orgia : 'secret rites' (ὄργια): the word is especially connected with the mysteries and with Bacchic worship: cf.
Virg. *Georg.* iv. 521 'inter sacra deum nocturnique orgia
Bacchi', *Aen.* iv. 302 'audito stimulant trieterica Baccho /
orgia'. The *cista* was a cylindrical basket, originally made of
wickerwork, later more elaborate, in which the cult-objects
were kept (cf. Ov. *A.A.* ii. 609 'condita . . . Veneris mysteria
cistis', Tib. 1. 7. 48 'leuis occultis conscia cista sacris'), and
orgia may be used of these objects themselves, as in Sen.
H.O. 594 'nos Cadmeis orgia ferre / tecum solitae condita
cistis'.

   cauis is not a mere stopgap; for *cauus* often emphasizes not
so much the hollowness of an object as the fact that it surrounds, conceals, or protects something within it, expressing
not a permanent attribute but a relation: so Virg. *Aen.* i. 516
'nube caua speculantur amicti' (a cloud that surrounds them),
ii. 360 'nox atra caua circumuolat umbra', Prop. iii. 14. 12
'cauo protegit aere caput' (the protection of a helmet), iv.
10. 13 'cauas turris' (towers holding men), Ov. *Tr.* iv. 8. 17
'in caua ducuntur quassae naualia puppes' (the shelter of
the dock)'. See on 17. 4.

260. quae . . . profani : cf. *Hom. Hymn* 2. 476 καὶ ἐπέφραδεν ὄργια
πᾶσιν / σεμνὰ τά τ' οὔ πως ἔστι παρεξίμεν οὔτε πυθέσθαι, Eur. *Bacch.*
471–2 (Pentheus) τὰ δ' ὄργι' ἐστὶ τίν' ἰδέαν ἔχοντά σοι; (Dion.)
ἄρρητ' ἀβακχεύτοισιν εἰδέναι βροτῶν.

   profani : the uninitiated: so Virg. *Aen.* vi. 258 'procul,
o procul este, profani', Hor. *Od.* iii. 1. 1 'odi profanum uulgus
et arceo'.

261–4. Note the adaptation of sound to sense throughout this
description of the oriental (*barbara,* 264) music which roused
the ecstasy of the worshippers—the alliteration of *p* and *t* in
261–2, the *o* and *u* sounds of 263 and the contrasting *i*'s of
264. The same four instruments—tambourine, cymbals,
horn, and *tibia*—appear with the same alliterative effects in
Lucretius' description of Cybele-worship, ii. 618 ff.:

   tympana tenta tonant palmis et cymbala circum
   concaua rauciusonoque minantur cornua cantu
   et Phrygio stimulat numero caua tibia mentis.

261. proceris : i.e. with long fingers outstretched to beat the
tambourine.

262. tereti . . . aere : i.e. the cymbal, a bronze half-sphere, the
aera rotunda Cybebes of Prop. iv. 7. 61. For *teres* see on 314.
   tinnitus . . . ciebant : cf. Virg. *Georg.* iv. 64 'tinnitusque cie
et matris quate cymbala circum'.

263. multis : 'many had horns blaring out their hoarse boom':
for the dative cf. 307 *his*.

raucisonos ... bombos : cf. Virg. *Aen.* vii. 615 'aereaque
assensu conspirant cornua rauco', Pers. i. 99 'torua Mimal-
loneis implerunt cornua bombis', Lucr. iv. 545 'tuba de-
presso grauiter sub murmure mugit / et reboat raucum retro
cita (?) barbara bombum'.

Cymbals and horns are primarily associated in art with
Cybele worship (cf. Hor. *Od.* i. 18. 13 'saeua tene cum Bere-
cyntio / cornu tympana', Ov. *F.* iv. 181, 'inflexo Berecynthia
tibia cornu'), but the orgiastic cults tend to be assimilated
to each other and the syncretism is already seen in Eur.
Bacchae 120 ff. Conversely in the *Attis* (63. 23–30) terms
associated with Bacchic worship (*Maenades hederigerae,
thiasus*) are transferred to that of Cybele.

264. barbara ... tibia : 'the outlandish pipe screamed with its
frightening note', i.e. Asiatic, as in 63. 22: so in Hor. *Epod.*
9. 6 *barbarum carmen* is opposed to *Dorium*.

The *tibia* (αὐλός) bore no resemblance to the modern flute
except in being a wind-instrument. Unlike the flute (but like
the oboe or the clarinet) it was played through a reed which
was held (as in these modern instruments) between the lips
or (especially in its oriental varieties) within the mouth.

265–302. The description of the marriage ceremony and the
guests is resumed.

265. amplifice does not appear again before the artificial
language of Fronto: it is an 'enhanced' epic form like
iustifica (406), *regifice* (Enn. *Sc.* 96 V.), *largifica* (Lucr. ii. 627).

266. complexa ... amictu : 'clasped and clothed the couch with
its covering'.

267 f. spectando ... expleta est : cf. Hom. *Od.* iv. 47 αὐτὰρ ἐπεὶ τάρ-
πησαν ὁρώμενοι ὀφθαλμοῖσιν, Virg. *Aen.* viii. 265 'nequeunt expleri
corda tuendo'.

267. Thessala pubes : cf. 4, 68. 101: *pubes*, properly a formal
collective term for the adult male population (cf. the parody
of a formal announcement in Plaut. *Ps.* 126 'pube praesenti
in contione') provides a convenient poetical alternative to
populus: in prose it is little used except in Livy, where it has
an archaic ring.

268. decedere : 'give place'; the verb implies respectfulness:
cf. Hor. *Ep.* ii. 2. 213 *decede peritis*.

269. hic : 'thereupon': the departing crowd of sightseers is compared to the waves stirred by a morning breeze from the west,
moving slowly at first, then faster and faster as the wind rises.

The simile goes back to Hom. *Il.* iv. 422 ff. (of the columns going forward to battle):

> ὡς δ' ὅτ' ἐν αἰγιαλῷ πολυηχέι κῦμα θαλάσσης
> ὄρνυτ' ἐπασσύτερον Ζεφύρου ὕπο κινήσαντος·
> πόντῳ μέν τε πρῶτα κορύσσεται, αὐτὰρ ἔπειτα
> χέρσῳ ῥηγνύμενον μεγάλα βρέμει . . . .

270. horrificans : 'ruffling' (cf. 205 *horrida*): so Hom. *Il.* vii. 63 (of Greeks and Trojans marching to battle) οἵη δὲ Ζεφύροιο ἐχεύατο πόντον ἔπι φρὶξ / ὀρνυμένοιο νέον.

procliuas : 'tumbling forwards': cf. Lucr. vi. 728 (of a stream running downhill) 'procliuis item fiat minus impetus undis'.

271. aurora . . . Solis : 'when the dawn is rising towards the threshold of the journeying Sun'; cf. Hom. *Od.* xxiv. 12 'Ηελίοιο πύλαι, Virg. *Aen.* vi. 255 'primi sub limina Solis et ortus'.

uagi : *uagus* is a favourite word of Catullus: 225 'uago malo', 277 'uago pede', 340 'uago certamine cursus', 61. 110 'uaga nocte', 63. 4 'uagus animi', 13 'uaga pecora', 25 'uaga cohors', 31 'uaga uadit' 86 'pede uago'. Here, as often, *uagus* is 'always on the move': the idea conveyed is restlessness rather than unsteadiness or uncertainty: so of a heavenly body which is not wandering but far-travelling in Laevius (?), fr. 32 M. 'hac qua sol uagus igneas habenas / immittit', *Paneg. Mess.* 76 'uagi sileantur pascua solis', of the shifting sea in Tib. ii. 6 3 'uaga aequora', ii. 3. 39 'uago ponto', of the restless travelling merchant (who is quite certain where he is going) in Tib. i. 3. 39 'uagus nauita', Hor. *A.P.* 117 'uagus mercator'. So *uagari* in 46. 7 is 'get abroad': as Henry says on *Aen.* v. 560, it excludes 'the idea of not knowing where one is included in "wander", of fickleness included in "rove", of eccentricity and going beyond bounds included in "ramble", of indolence and idleness included in "saunter"'.

273. leuiter : 'softly': of a low sound as in 84. 8, Virg. *Ecl.* 1. 55 'saepe leui somnum suadebit inire susurro', Prop. i. 3. 43 'leuiter mecum deserta querebar', ii. 32. 15 'leuiter lymphis tota crepitantibus urbe', Ov. *Her.* 3. 80 'et leuiter dicas "haec quoque nostra fuit" ', Cic. *Sull.* 31 'ea quae leuiter dixerat uobis probare uolebat, eos autem qui circum iudicium stabant audire nolebat'. (For a discussion of this and other meanings see Löfstedt, *Coniectanea* (1950), 73 ff.) Seneca borrows this phrase from Catullus, *Agam.* 680 'licet alcyones Ceyca suum / fluctu leuiter plangente sonent'.

cachinni : for the bubbling laughter of the waves cf. Accius fr. 573 R. 'stagna sonantibus excita saxis . . . crepitu

plangente cachinnant': so καχλάζω in Theocritus (6. 12
καχλάζοντος ἐπ' αἰγιαλοῖο) and Apollonius (ii. 570 καχλάζοντος
κύματος). See on 31. 14. *Cachinni* is nominative, subject of a
clause parenthetically inserted: the subject *quae* is resumed
in 274.

274. magis magis : cf. 38. 3, Virg. *Georg.* iv. 311 'magis magis
aera carpunt'; at 68. 48 Catullus has the commoner *magis
atque magis*.

275. ab luce refulgent : 'sparkle with the light': for *ab* 'as a
result of' cf. 66. 63 'uuidulam a fluctu', 'wet with the wave',
Virg. *Georg.* i. 234 'torrida semper ab igni', Ov. *Met.* i. 66
'madescit ab Austro' (Ovid is very fond of the use), Prop.
iii 2. 23 'nomen ab aeuo / excidet' ('with time'). The idiom
is not common in prose, but Cicero uses it in a context very
like this, *Acad.* ii. 105 'mare illud quod nunc Fauonio nascente
purpureum uidetur idem huic nostro uidebitur, nec tamen
assentietur, quia nobismet ipsis modo caeruleum uidebatur,
mane rauum, quodque nunc, qua a sole collucet, albescit et
uibrat'. (Similarly *N.D.* ii. 92 'conflagrare ab ardoribus'.)

  purpurea : cf. Cic. *Acad.* ii. 105 quoted above and see on
45. 12.

  nantes : for waves 'floating' cf. Enn. *Ann.* 596 V. 'fluctus-
que natantes': so Virgil uses *praenatare* (*Aen.* vi. 705),
Horace *innare* (*Od.* iii. 17. 7) of a river.

276. uestibuli . . . tecta : cf. 246 *domus tecta*.

277. ad se : 'to their homes': so Plaut. *M.G.* 525 'transcurrito
ad uos': Cic. *Att.* xvi. 10. 1 'ueni ad me in Sinuessanum', *Rep.*
iii. 40 'cum uenerat ad se in Sabinos'.

  uago . . . pede : see on 271: there is no implication that they
did not know where they were going, but they went far
and wide.

  discedebant : the σπονδειάζων (see on l. 3) perhaps conveys
the idea of slow and unwilling movement.

278. princeps : 'leading the way': Chiron the centaur, a local
god of the hills, comes first as a friendly neighbour from his
cave on Pelion (Πηλίου ἐκ κορυφῆς, *Il.* xvi. 144): in one form of
the legend (Pind. *Nem.* 3. 97) Chiron gives Thetis to Peleus.
In Homer he brings an ash spear as his gift: here, with a
characteristically Alexandrian touch, he brings flowers.

280 f. Thessala . . . ora : 'the region of Thessaly' (cf. 66. 43):
fluminis : i.e. the Peneus (285).

282. aura . . . Fauoni : cf. Call. *Hymn* 2. 80 σεῖο δὲ βωμοὶ / ἄνθεα
μὲν φορέουσιν ἐν εἴαρι τόσσα περ ὧραι / ποικίλ' ἀγινεῦσι Ζεφύρου
πνείοντος ἐέρσην.

283. indistinctis : 'twined in unsorted wreaths': Chiron's present is an unsophisticated one.

284. quo . . . odore : 'and with that scent'.

permulsa : 'caressed', of a soothing touch, as in 162; so Cic. *Arat.* 184 'Aram quam flatu permulcet spiritus Austri'. See on 62. 41 'mulcent aurae'.

risit : the metaphor goes back to Hom. *Il.* xix. 362 γέλασσε δὲ πᾶσα περὶ χθὼν / χαλκοῦ ὑπὸ στεροπῆς; for Catullus' use cf. *Hom. Hymn.* 2. 13 κῷζ' ἥδιστ' ὀδμή, πᾶς δ' οὐρανὸς εὐρὺς ὕπερθεν / γαῖά τε πᾶσ' ἐγέλασσε καὶ ἁλμυρὸν οἶδμα θαλάσσης. Compare *gaudet* in 46.

285. Penios : Πηνειός, the eponymous god of the river: for the Greek termination cf. 35 *Cieros*.

Tempe : the fertile valley between Olympus and Ossa through which the Peneus winds to the sea. Its beauty was so famous that the word becomes a common noun: Virg. *Georg.* ii. 469, 'frigida tempe', Cic. *Att.* iv. 15. 5 'Reatini me ad sua τέμπη duxerunt'.

285 f. uiridantia . . . siluae . . . inpendentes : Pliny's description repeats Catullus' adjective: *N.H.* iv. 31 'in eo cursu Tempe uocant ("in that stretch is what they call T.") . . . ultra uisum hominis attollentibus se dextra laeuaque conuexis iugis, intus silua late uiridante: hac labitur Penius uitreus calculo, amoenus circa ripas gramine, canorus auium concentu'; cf. Ov. *Met.* i. 568 'est nemus Haemoniae praerupta quod undique claudit / silua: uocant Tempe, per quae Peneus ab imo / effusus Pindo spumosis uoluitur undis'.

287. linquens : see on 35. 3.

Minosim . . . doris celebranda choreis : *Minosim* looks as if it represented a Greek dative plural; the most likely of those which have been suggested is Heinsius's *Haemonisin*, 'Thessalian women' (Ovid has *Haemonis, Her.* 13. 2). *doris* has not been satisfactorily explained or emended. The adjectival form *Dorus* for *Dorius* or *Doricus* is not found elsewhere and the reference of the adjective is not clear: a reference to the martial Dorian music is clearly not in place and Baehrens's suggestion that it might refer to the dress of the dancers, wearing the Dorian chiton, is only a guess. Statius's *doctis* is weak: Madvig's *duris* is ill-judged: *durae choreae* would be clod-hopping dancers, as they are in Ov. *Fast.* iii. 537 ('ducunt posito duras cratere choreas': cf. Lucr. v. 1401 'membra mouentes / duriter').

celebranda : to be filled, made *celebria*: cf. *Aen.* iii. 280 'Actiaque Iliacis celebramus litora ludis'.

288. uacuos : 'empty-handed': cf. Juv. 10. 22 'cantabit uacuus coram latrone uiator'; *inanis* is similarly used (e.g. Plaut. *Amph.* 330, Prop. iv. 5. 47).

ille is not 'unbetont wie *il portait*', as Kroll says, but deictic, drawing the reader's attention to the figure: 'there he was, with trees in his hands'. For this 'pictorial' use of *ille* cf. Prop. i. 1. 12 'nam modo Partheniis amens errabat in antris, / ibat et hirsutas ille uidere feras', iv. 2. 45 'nec flos ullus hiat pratis quin ille decenter / impositus fronti langueat ante meae'. So in Virgilian similes: *Aen.* x. 707 'ac uelut ille canum morsu de montibus altis / actus aper', xii. 4 ff. 'Poenorum qualis in aruis / saucius ille graui uenantum uulnere pectus / tum demum mouet arma leo'.

radicitus 'root and all': cf. Virg. *Georg.* i. 20 'teneram ab radice ferens cupressum'.

289. recto . . . stipite : 'straight-stemmed'; the ablative of description takes the place of a compound adjective (cf. 294), a device of which Virgil makes much effective use.

290. nutanti : 'waving': cf. Enn. *Ann.* 490 V. 'capitibus nutantis pinos rectosque cupressos', Virg. *Aen.* ix. 681 f. 'quercus . . . sublimi uertice nutant'.

sorore : i.e. the poplar; when Phaethon, driving his father the Sun's chariot, met his fiery death, his mourning sisters were turned into poplars shedding tears of amber: see Ov. *Met.* ii. 340 ff.

lenta : 'supple': see on 183.

291. cūpressu : the lengthening of the first syllable in this word is found only here: cf. 151 *sŭpremo*.

292. late contexta : i.e. wherever one looked (*late*) there was a screen of foliage.

294. sollerti corde : the ablatival phrase corresponds to the Greek compound adjectives πολύμητις, ποικιλόβουλος which are applied to Prometheus as inventor of the arts: *cor*, as usual, is the seat of the intelligence, not the emotions (cf. Lucr. v. 1106 'ingenio praestare et corde uigere'). Prometheus' appearance here is an allusion to the story that after his release from his punishment Prometheus sealed his reconciliation with Zeus by warning him of the fatal consequences of the marriage with Thetis which he contemplated, since her offspring was destined to be greater than his father (Aesch. *P.V.* 768).

295. extenuata . . . uestigia : the faint scars left by his punishment; cf. Ov. *Am.* iii. 8. 19 'cicatrices, ueteris uestigia pugnae'. Similar uses of *extenuare* are common in medical writers: e.g. Pliny, *N.H.* xxxii. 24 (of a medicinal substance) 'cicatrices extenuat'.

296. silici . . . catena : the construction is awkward, but not impossible: for *silici restrictus* cf. Cic. *Tusc.* ii. 23 (translated from Aeschylus) 'aspicite religatum asperis uinctumque saxis', Man. v. 551 'astrinxere pedes scopulis'.

297. persoluit : probably quadrisyllabic: see on 2*b*. 13. For the spondaic ending, see on 3.

298. natisque : the only hypermetric hexameter (in which the final syllable is elided into the following line) in Catullus' longer poems; he has another in elegiacs (if the text is sound) at 115. 5. There are isolated examples in Lucilius and Lucretius, but the device is rare before Virgil, who makes considerable use of it (mostly with *-que*) and exploits its dramatic effect. (For a striking example see *Aen.* iv. 629, where Dido's final speech ends with hypermetric *-que*.) In Greek the earliest example is in an elegiac epigram of Callimachus (*Ep.* 41. 1 Pf. οὐκ οἶδ' / εἰ); Catullus and Virgil may have taken it from Hellenistic practice—and the Alexandrians, with their taste for the unusual, may have derived it from some Homeric lines in which they took the ending Ζῆν to be Ζῆνα with elision—but there is no example in extant Alexandrian hexameter poems.

299. Phoebe : for the apostrophe see on 69. In the accounts of Homer (*Il.* xxiv. 63) and Pindar (*Nem.* 5. 41) Apollo is present at the wedding; in Aeschylus (fr. 450, quoted by Plato, *Rep.* 383b) Thetis accuses him of treachery—he had sung at her wedding of the blessings in store for her and then had killed her son. Catullus is following another version in which the death of Achilles at Apollo's hands (directly or through Paris) has coloured the earlier part of the story and Apollo's enmity is acknowledged from the beginning.

    caelo is most naturally taken with *aduenit*, 'from heaven': so *Aen.* vi. 190 'columbae / ipsa sub ora uiri caelo uenere uolantes'.

300. unigenam : 'sister': so in 66. 53 *unigena* translates Callimachus' γνωτός. The usual meaning of *unigena* is 'only begotten', μονογένης, but while μονογένης is a regular epithet of Hecate (as the only child of Perseus and Asterie) and might well be transferred to Artemis, with whom Hecate is often identified (see on 34. 13), it could hardly be applied to Artemis here when her brother has been mentioned in the preceding line.

    cultricem montibus Idri : Catullus himself provides the only parallel to the construction, 66. 58 'Canopitis incola litoribus'; for *cultrix* cf. 61. 1-2 'collis o Heliconii / cultor'.

    Idri : if the reading *Idri* is right, Idrus must be presumed

to be the eponymous founder (on coins and inscriptions his
name appears as Idrieus) of the town of Idrias in Caria, a
region associated with Hecate-worship, which according to
Stephanus of Byzantium had its own cult of Hecate and got
the name of Hecatesia from it.

301. nam : for the postponement of *nam* see on 23. 7.

303. niueis : i.e. ivory (l. 45).

flexerunt . . . artus : for the phrase cf. Soph. *O.C.* 19 κῶλα
κάμψον τοῦδ᾽ ἐπ᾽ ἀξέστου πέτρου. In accordance with the practice
of the heroic age, the gods do not lie on couches but sit at
meals: cf. Athen. i. 17f καθέζονται ἐν τοῖς συνδείπνοις οἱ ἥρωες,
οὐ κατακέκλινται.

304. constructae . . . mensae : cf. Cic. *Tusc.* v. 62 'mensae
conquisitissimis epulis exstruebantur', Ov. *Met.* xi. 120
'mensas posuere ministri / exstructas dapibus'.

305. cum interea : here simply temporal as in Lucr. iv. 1205
(where also the words begin the line), without the adversative or concessive implication which the phrase has in 95. 3
and usually elsewhere.

quatientes corpora : by a not uncommon idiom the subject
is represented as performing an action in which he is actually
the patient; cf. 17. 24 'si pote . . . excitare ueternum', 206
'concussit micantia sidera mundus' (the sky had its stars
dashed together), 68. 122 'nomen . . . intulit in tabulas' (had
his name entered), Lucr. v. 415 'constiterunt imbres et flumina uim minuerunt', vi. 645 'complebant pectora (i.e. their
own hearts) cura', Prop. iv. 3. 27 'diceris et macie uultum
tenuasse' (your face has been thinned), ii. 19. 25 'formosa suo
Clitumnus flumina luco / integit' (has its waters sheltered by
its woods).

307. his : dative of 'advantage': 'they had a white robe
wrapping their ankles': cf. 263 *multis*.

tremulum : of age as in 61. 51, 161, 68. 154.

308. candida purpurea : in Plato, *Rep.* 617c, the Fates are
λευχειμονοῦσαι, στέμματα ἐπὶ τῶν κεφαλῶν ἔχουσαι; here the colour-
contrast of white and red which is a favourite cliché of Latin
verse (see on 61. 10 and 187) is added to both their accoutre-
ments: their white robes have a red edge and the ribbons on
their white hair are red.

309. at : turns the reader's eye from foot to head.

roseae niueo : Guarinus's correction for *roseo niueae* is
necessary. *roseo uertice* would mean either that they rivalled
the unique 'purple lock' of Scylla's father Nisus (*roseus
crinis*, *Ciris* 122) or that they had garlands of roses (? cf.

myrtea coma, [Tib.] iii. 4. 28), an unlikely adornment for these aged ladies. For the contrasting·red ribbon cf. Prop. iv. 9. 52 'puniceo canas stamine uincta comas', *Ciris* 511 'purpureas flauo retinentem uertice uittas'.

310. carpebant . . . laborem: 'pursued their task of spinning', an extension from such phrases as Virg. *Georg.* iv. 335 'uellera carpebant', i. 390 'carpentes pensa', in which *carpere* refers to the action here described in 312 (*deducens fila*).

311. colum : usually feminine: here masculine as in Prop. iv. 1. 72, 9. 48, Ov. *A. A.* i. 702.

311 ff. laeua . . . fusum : the left hand held the spindle in its wrapping of soft wool (i.e. with the *globus* of wool on it): the right alternately (1) held palm upwards (*supinis digitis*) towards the distaff nimbly drew down the fibres and shaped them into thread, and (2) turned palm downwards (*prono pollice*) twirled on the thumb the spindle (to a notch in the top of which the fibre was attached) poised on its rounded whorl. For (1) cf. Tib. i. 3. 86 'deducat plena stamina longa colu', Ov. *Met.* iv. 36 'leui deducens pollice filum': for (2) Ov. *Met.* vi. 22 leui teretem uersabat pollice fusum', Tib. ii. 1. 64 'fusus et apposito pollice uersat opus'.

314. turbine : *turbo* is the disk or 'flywheel' on the lower end of the spindle, serving to steady its motion and also to tauten the thread by its weight. When the spindle approached the ground with the lengthening of the twisted yarn, the length of formed yarn was wound up on it, as on a bobbin, and the process started again.

tereti : *teres*, of a smooth, rounded surface: so it is applied to *brachiolum* (61. 174), *strophium* (64. 65), *bustum* (64. 363). Ovid uses it of the *fusus* itself (*Met.* vi. 22).

315. atque ita : 'and then', like καὶ οὕτως, 'that being done': see on 84.

decerpens : i.e. all the time (*semper*) they cleaned the fibre by picking off with their teeth the tufts that made it uneven: cf. *Eleg. in Maec.* i. 73 f. 'torsisti pollice fusos, / lenisti morsu leuia fila parum'.

dens : the abnormal rhythm produced by the stressed monosyllable at the end of the line, conveying the snap of the broken thread, and the sentimentalizing diminutives (see on 60) of the next line, 'their poor old dry lips', give life to the picture. The only other instance in Catullus of a stressed final monosyllable is at 68. 19 where again its effect, enhanced by the pause after the first word of the pentameter, is unmistakable.

316. morsa : the substantival use is found only here, but Cicero uses *mansa* similarly, *de Or.* ii. 162.

319. uellera : the masses of crude wool (*rudis lana* in Ov. *Met.* vi. 19) awaiting spinning.

uirgati : probably here 'made of *uirgae*', plaited twigs of osier (cf. Virg. *Georg.* ii. 241 'spisso uimine qualos', Ov. *F.* iv. 435 'lento calathos e uimine textos') : elsewhere the word has always the derived sense of 'striped'.

calathisci : the Greek diminutive form (καλάθισκος) is found only here and in Petronius, but Virgil, Ovid, and Propertius have *calathus*.

custodibant : for the form cf. 68. 85 *scibant*, 84. 8 *audibant*.

320. haec : nominative plural feminine : the form with deictic -*c* is regular in comedy; the evidence for its survival in Cicero (e.g. at *Sest.* 5) and in Virgil (e.g. at *Aen.* vi. 852) is dubious.

pellentes uellera : if *pellentes* is right, it presumably means striking the masses of wool to loosen the fibres, but the phrase is unparalleled and improbable. *uellentes uellera* (Fruterius) would be a deliberate *figura etymologica* : the Romans themselves connected the two words (Varro, *L.L.* v. 54)—and, as it happened, were right in doing so (that *lana* was cognate with them, as it probably is, they naturally did not guess). Statius's *pectentes* is ingenious, but out of place : *pectere* refers to the preliminary operation of carding which prepares the wool for the spinner.

321. fuderunt . . . fata : 'uttered words of destiny' : an epic phrase (cf. Lucr. v. 110 'fundere fata') in which *fata*, 'oracular speech', preserves its connexion with *fari*; cf. Virg. *Aen.* vi. 45 'poscere fata' ('seek an oracle'), i. 382 'data fata secutus', Cic. *Cat.* iii. 9 'ex fatis Sibyllinis'.

diuino : 'prophetic', 'inspired', as in 383 : so Enn. *Ann.* 19 V. 'diuinum pectus habere', Virg. *Aen.* iii. 373 'canit diuino ex ore sacerdos' : cf. the substantival use of *diuinus*, 'soothsayer' (e.g. Hor. *Sat.* i. 6. 114).

323–81. In the older versions of the legend (e.g. in Eur. *I.A.* 1040 ff.) the Muses sang the marriage-song in honour of Peleus and Thetis. By transferring it to the Fates the poet finds opportunity for carrying his story on into the future with a prediction of the doings of Achilles. The first twelve lines and the last seven are devoted to celebrating the bridal pair and the occasion in an adaptation of traditional form; Achilles is the theme of the twenty-seven lines between. The song is punctuated by a refrain, a device borrowed from

Alexandrian poetry. As in the first and second idylls of
Theocritus, the refrain occurs at irregular intervals, marking
the ends of sentences of five, four, or three lines; Bergk
rightly deleted the refrain at 378, where it interrupts a
sentence.

323. o decus ... augens : 'enhancing your rare glory by deeds of
prowess': *decus* is either the inherited distinction of Peleus'
race—a characteristically Roman notion: cf. *C.I.L.* i². 15
(elogium of Scipio) 'uirtutes generis mieis moribus accumu-
laui', Nepos, *Timoth.* 1. 1 'a patre acceptam gloriam multis
auxit uirtutibus', Ov. *Pont.* 1. 8. 17 'ille memor magni generis
uirtute quod auget'—or perhaps his own physical beauty
(cf. Virg. *Aen.* vii. 473 'decus egregium formae').

324. Housman's repunctuation of this line on which, in the
form *Emathiae tutamen opis, carissime* (or *clarissime*) *nato*,
editors had exercised their ingenuity for centuries, is the
most spectacular contribution of modern scholarship to the
interpretation of Catullus.

   Emathiae tutamen : cf. 26 'Thessaliae columen Peleu':
Emathia is properly the name of a part of Macedonia, but
Virgil, Ovid, and Lucan all follow Catullus in making it a
synonym for Thessaly. (For geographical inaccuracy in
Catullus see on 35.)

   Opis carissime nato represents the Homeric διφίλης: Homer
does not actually use that epithet of Peleus, but he calls him
(*Il.* xxiv. 61) Πηλέι ὃς περὶ κῆρι φίλος γένετ᾽ ἀθανάτοισιν. The
Italian goddess Ops came to serve as the Italian counterpart
of Rhea, wife of Cronos and mother of Zeus: so the child of
Ops is Jupiter here as in Plaut. *Persa* 252 'Ioui opulento
incluto Ope nato', *M.G.* 1082 'Iuppiter ex Ope natust'. The
'learned' periphrasis is in the Alexandrian manner: cf. 228,
290, 346, 395.

326 f. sed uos . . . fusi : on its first occurrence the refrain is
linked with the previous line. The construction is *currite
fusi ducentes subtegmina quae fata sequuntur*: i.e. destiny
answers to, corresponds to, the spinning of the Fates. The
yarn which the spindles draw as they run is called by anticipation *subtegmina*, properly the threads forming the weft on
the loom, on which they are woven across the threads of the
warp, *stamina*: so Horace has *certo subtemine* of the fateful
spinning of the Fates. (On the forms *subtegmen* and *subtemen*
see Nettleship, *Contr. to Lat. Lex.* p. 590.) It might equally
well be called *stamina* and Ovid calls it so, *Met.* iv. 34 'ducunt lanas aut stamina pollice uersant'. Virgil echoes the
line in *Ecl.* 4. 46 'talia saecla, suis dixerunt, currite, fusis'.

328. adueniet : as in the opening lines of 62 the Evening Star, the *faustum sidus*, brings the wedded pair together.

330. flexanimo : 'to flood your heart with soul-charming love': *flexanimus* is here *animum flectens* (θελξίφρων) as in Pacuvius 177 R. 'o flexanima atque omnium regina rerum oratio': cf. Virg. *Georg.* iv. 516 'nulla Venus, non ulli animum flexere hymenaei'. Elsewhere the compound is used passively, *cui animus flectitur*: Pacuv. 422 R. 'flexanima tamquam lymphata aut Bacchi sacris commota'.

335 f. nullus amor . . . qualis concordia : cf. 66. 87-88.

336. Peleo : for the synizesis cf. Virg. *Aen.* ix. 716 *Typhoeo*: the Latin form of the dative is used here but the Greek in 382.

340. uago . . . certamine : 'the far-ranging race': see on 271.

341. flammea . . . uestigia : cf. Virg. *Aen.* xi. 718 'uirgo pernicibus ignea plantis / transit equum cursu'. Achilles is ποδώκης or πόδας ὠκύς in Homer: for his exploits in the hunt see Pind. *Nem.* 3. 86.

343. non illi : so Homer makes Achilles say of himself (*Il.* xviii. 105) τοῖος ἐὼν οἷος οὔτις Ἀχαιῶν χαλκοχιτώνων / ἐν πολέμῳ. The following lines sum up the whole course of the Trojan War, though Achilles did not live to see the last stage of it and the destruction (*uastabit* 346) of Troy. Catullus combines three adjectives for 'Trojan', *Phrygii, Teucro, Troica*.

345. longinquo . . . bello : *longinquus* can be used as equivalent to *longus* in the temporal sense, though not in the spatial: so Enn. *Ann.* 413V. *longinqua aetas*, Cic. *Fin.* ii. 94 *longinquus dolor*, Caes. *B.G.* v. 29. 7 *longinqua obsidione*. (On the usage of the word see Nettleship in *J. of Phil.* xx [1892] 176.)

346. periuri : Pelops bribed Oenomaus' charioteer Myrtilus to help him to win a chariot race and thereby secure marriage with his daughter Hippodamia: after his victory he murdered Myrtilus and so brought a curse on his house.

Pelopis . . . tertius heres is certainly Agamemnon but the implied genealogy is doubtful. The normal usage of *tertius heres* would exclude Pelops himself from the reckoning: so in Ov. *Met.* xiii. 28 'ab Ioue tertius Aiax' represents the line Jupiter–Aeacus–Telamon–Ajax. Catullus may be following either the Homeric version of the succession in the kingship of Argos (*Il.* ii. 105 ff.)—Pelops: his son Atreus: his second son Thyestes: Atreus' son Agamemnon—or the variant legends which introduced Plisthenes into the genealogy as son of Atreus and father of Agamemnon.

350. incultum . . . soluent : Baehrens's conjecture is plausible; they leave their hair loose and uncombed in token of mourning :

cf. Virg. *Aen.* xi. 35 'maestum Iliades crinem de more solu-
tae', Ov. *F.* iv. 854 'maestas Acca soluta comas', *F.* iii. 470
'incultis . . . comis'. Ellis meant his *incuruo* (*uertice*) to
mean 'with bowed head' but the phrases which he cites in
support, *curua anus* and the like, are obviously not parallel
and it is doubtful whether *incuruo uertice* could refer to anything but a physical deformity like that of Homer's Thersites,
φοξὸς ἔην κεφαλήν (*Il.* ii. 219).

351. uariabunt : they will leave discoloured marks on their
withered breasts: for *uarius* of weals cf. Plaut. *M.G.* 216
'uarius uirgis', *Poen.* 26.

353. praecerpens messor : the simile of the reaper was perhaps
suggested by Hom. *Il.* xi. 67 ff. οἱ δ' ὥς τ' ἀμητῆρες ἐνάντιοι
ἀλλήλοισιν | ὄγμον ἐλαύνωσιν ἀνδρὸς μάκαρος κατ' ἄρουραν | πυρῶν ἢ
κριθῶν, τὰ δὲ δράγματα ταρφέα πίπτει, | ὣς Τρῶες καὶ Ἀχαιοὶ ἐπ'
ἀλλήλοισι θορόντες | δῄουν. Notice how the particularity of *sole
sub ardenti* and the colour of *flauentia* give vividness to the
picture.

355. Troiugenum : *Troiugena* (also in Lucr.) and *Graiugena* (in
Pacuvius and Lucr.) are words of the old epic style modelled
on Greek compounds in -γένης. The genitive plural form in
-*um* properly belonged to the second declension only (see on
9. 6), but is extended in verse to masculine nouns of the first:
so 68. 138 *caelicolum*.

357. testis erit : these lines are based on *Il.* xxi. 17 ff.: Accius
has similar phrases in his *Epinausimachia*, fr. 322 R. 'Sca-
mandriam undam salso sanctam obtexi sanguine / atque
aceruos alta in amni corpore expleui hostico'. For the
device of calling on the scene of a hero's exploits to witness
to them cf. Enn. ap. Cic. *de Or.* iii. 167 (on Scipio) 'testes
sunt campi magni', Hor. *Od.* iv. 4. 38 'quid debeas, o Roma,
Neronibus, / testis Metaurum flumen', Tib. i. 7. 11 'testis
Arar Rhodanusque celer magnusque Garumna', Prop. iv.
7. 21. For a similar personification see on 29. 19.

unda Scamandri : the treatment of a final syllable containing a short open vowel before the combination of *s* and
another consonant seems to have presented a problem to
Latin poets. Of a syllable left short in that position, as here,
there are few examples. Apart from cases involving *smarag-
dus* and *Zacynthus* which, like *Scamander*, cannot otherwise
be used in dactylic verse, there are ten in Lucretius, five in
Propertius, and one in Virgil (*Aen.* xi. 309, where the syllable
is followed by a strong pause). Lengthening a syllable in that
position is almost as rare: Catullus has *nullā spes* at 186 and
probably *suppositā speculae* at 67. 32 (besides *potē stolidum*

in priapeans at 17. 24 and *gelidā stabula* in galliambics at
63. 53): elsewhere there are three examples, one in Tibullus
(i. 5. 28 *segetē spicas*) and two in Grattius (142, 259).

359. caesis is awkward before *caede* but correction to *celsis* is
uncalled for.

360. tepēfaciet: so 90. 6 *liquēfaciens*, but 68. 29 *tepĕfactet* (if
that reading is right) 64. 368 *madēfient*. In ordinary speech
the original -*ē*- in these compounds (and in *calefacio* and
patefacio) was reduced to -*ĕ*- by the operation of iambic
shortening (see on 10. 27). The poets sometimes find it convenient to preserve it: so Ovid has *liquēfaciunt* as well as
liquĕfiunt.

   permixta . . . caede: no doubt an epic phrase: Lucretius has
it twice.

362. denique: the final testimony paid to Achilles' *uirtutes*
after his death when, on the fall of Troy, the Greeks at the
command of his ghost sacrificed Priam's daughter Polyxena
to be his bride in the other world.

   reddita: 'duly paid'. For *morti* cf. Ov. *Met.* ii. 340 'lugent
et inania morti / munera dant lacrimas': similarly 101. 3
'munere mortis'.

363. bustum: the mounded (*teres*; see on 314) barrow.

366. fessis: cf. Hor. *Od.* ii. 4. 11 'tradidit fessis leuiora tolli /
Pergama Graecis'.

367. soluere: for the infinitive after *copiam dare* cf. Virg. *Aen.*
ix. 484 'nec te . . . / adfari extremum miserae data copia
matri'.

   Neptunia . . . uincla: i.e. the walls built for Laomedon by
Poseidon; the use of *soluere* is perhaps suggested by Homer's
Τροίης ἱερὰ κρήδεμνα λύωμεν (*Il.* xvi. 100).

368. Polyxenia: the use of an adjective in place of a genitive
(cf. *Neptunia* above) is an old idiom which the poets found
metrically convenient: so in this poem Catullus has 77
Androgeoneae, elsewhere 61. 223 *Penelopeo*, 66. 8 *Beroniceo*,
66. 60 *Ariadnaeis*, 68. 74 *Protesilaeam*. See on 44. 10 *Sestianus*.

369. quae: the antecedent (Polyxena) is contained in the
adjective *Polyxenia*: so often in prose, e.g. Cic. *Brut.* 112
'senatoriam sententiam cuius (i.e. senatus) erat ille princeps'.
Cf. 66. 83.

370. summisso poplite: so in Ov. *Met.* xiii. 477 (describing the
same scene) 'defecto poplite labens'.
   proiciet: 'lets her body fall forward'.

371–80. The Fates end their song with two stanzas which are more in keeping with the outspoken badinage of a Roman wedding (cf. 61. 97 ff., 144 ff.) than with the heroic age.

372. optatos : the word is a favourite with Catullus in this connexion: cf. 31, 141, 328, 62. 30, 66. 79.

coniungite amores : similarly of reciprocal affection 78. 3 'iungit amores', Tib. i. 1. 69 'interea, dum fata sinunt, iungamus amores', Ov. *Tr.* ii. 536. *animi* perhaps serves to stress the notion of wholeheartedness and sincerity.

374. dedatur : cf. 61. 58 *dedis*.

iam dudum is best attached to *dedatur* with the implication of 'immediately', a not uncommon use in jussive phrases: cf. Virg. *Aen.* ii. 103 'iamdudum sumite poenas', Ov. *A.A.* i. 317 'iamdudum de grege duci / iussit', ii. 457 'candida iamdudum cingantur colla lacertis', *Met.* xiii. 457 'utere iamdudum generoso sanguine', Sen. *Ep.* 75. 7 'iamdudum gaude', 84. 11 'relinque ista iamdudum'.

377. hesterno . . . filo : i.e. *filo quo heri collum circumdedit*: the belief is referred to in Nemesianus 2. 10.

379. discordis : i.e. estranged from her husband.

380. secubitu : cf. 61. 101.

382. praefantes : *praefari* is a technical term for uttering either a formula which is to be repeated by others (so Livy v. 41. 3 'pontifice maximo carmen praefante') or, as here, a formula preliminary to a solemn ritual act, in this case the marriage.

Pelei : the Greek dative form: in 336 Catullus used the Latin *Peleo*.

383. diuino : see on 321.

384–407: taking up a suggestion from Homer (*Od.* vii. 201 ff. (Alcinous to Odysseus) αἰεὶ γὰρ τὸ πάρος γε θεοὶ φαίνονται ἐναργεῖς / ἡμῖν εὖτ' ἔρδωμεν ἀγακλείτας ἑκατόμβας / δαίνυνταί τε παρ' ἄμμι καθήμενοι ἔνθα περ ἡμεῖς), the poet justifies his marvellous tale to his reader and passes into a moralizing epilogue which reflects the general ancient belief in the degeneracy of mankind and the decline from a primitive Golden Age.

Hesiod's account of human degeneration (*Works and Days,* 174 ff.) is echoed in Aratus, *Phaen.* 100 ff., and Catullus may have had some similar hellenistic source in mind. Virgil is clearly thinking of this poem in the fourth *Eclogue* where (a) the refrain of the Fates' song is verbally echoed (46 'talia saecla, suis dixerunt, currite, fusis'), (b) Achilles, in Catullus the consummation of the heroic age, is to be reborn in the new golden age, and (c) the child is to see the gods face to face when Justice returns to earth, as men did before she fled (15 'ille deum uitam accipiet diuisque uidebit / permixtos heroas et ipse uidebitur illis'). The reminiscence of Catullus is unmistakable; whether Catullus meant his whole poem to have a symbolic significance and chose to tell the story of Peleus and Thetis to point the moral which the *envoi* makes explicit is another question.

384. namque : for the postponement see on 23. 7.

praesentes : in bodily shape, Homer's ἐναργεῖς.

ante : adverbial, 'in former days', τὸ πάρος in Homer.

385. coetu : again in 66. 37: the dative form in *-u* is common in Lucretius and in Virgil.

386. nondum spreta : i.e. when *pietas* (see on 76. 2) was not ignored as it has been in later days.

387. reuisens : 'paying his regular visit', but the construction is harsh: Baehrens's *residens* derives some support from Hom. Hymn 2. 27 (Ζεὺς) νόσφιν / ἧστο θεῶν ἀπάνευθε πολυλλίστῳ ἐνὶ νηῷ.

388. uenissent : 'came round': cf. Ov. *Am.* iii. 10. 1 'annua uenerunt Cerealis tempora sacri'.

390. uagus : see on 271. Liber, that is, Dionysus (the Italian wine-god early took over the mythology of his Greek counterpart), is represented as he is in Eur. fr. 752 N.² (*Hypsipyle*) Διόνυσος ὃς θύρσοισι καὶ νεβρῶν δοραῖς / καθαπτὸς ἐν πεύκαισι Παρνασὸν κάτα / πηδᾷ χορεύων παρθένοις σὺν Δελφίσιν. The name *Thyiades* (Θυιάδες)—applicable, like *Maenades*, to any female devotees of orgiastic rites—was particularly attached to the Delphian women who followed Dionysus: cf. Paus. x. 32. 7.

391. euantis : the verb, formed (like εὐάζειν) from the maenad cry (cf. 255), appears first here.

392. Delphi : here the citizens, not the city.

394. Mauors : the archaic form of *Mars* belongs to the epic style; so probably does the phrase *belli certamine*; cf. Lucr. i. 475, v. 1296 *certamina belli*.

395. Tritonis era represents Athena's Homeric title Τριτογένεια, which ancient mythographers derived from a lake Triton or a river of that name (*rapidi* shows that Catullus has a river in mind) variously placed in Libya, Boeotia, and Thessaly.

Amarunsia uirgo : the early and obvious correction of the *ramunsia* or *ranusia* of the manuscripts is *Ramnusia*, the title which Catullus himself uses in 66. 71 and 68. 77 for Nemesis. But while the intervention of Ares and Athena in the fighting of mortals is familiar from Homer, (*Il.* iv. 439 ὦρσε δὲ τοὺς μὲν Ἄρης, τοὺς δὲ γλαυκῶπις Ἀθήνη: cf. v. 447, 676, xx. 33 and 39), the appearance of Nemesis in this

connexion is quite inexplicable. Baehrens's *Amarunsia* is
certain (apart from the matter of spelling): it is a cult-title
of Artemis derived from Amarynthus (Ἀμάρυνθος) in Euboea
(Paus. i. 31. 4 writes Ἀμαρυσία: Livy has the alternative form
Amarynthis, xxxv. 38. 3), and Artemis is with the other major
deities in *Il.* xx. 39. Wilamowitz's attempt (*Antigonos von
Karystos*, 11) to find justification for calling either Artemis or
Aphrodite *R(h)amnusia* is curiously misguided: *R(h)amnusia*
here would have to mean what it means in the two other
places where Catullus uses it.

399–404. The verbs emphatically placed at the beginning of
three successive lines, the repeated *natus . . . nati . . . nato*,
the balanced *fraterno . . . fratres*, the reiterated *impia*, all
serve to heighten the enormity of human sin.

399. fratres : so in similar contexts Lucretius writes (iii. 72)
'crudeles gaudent in tristi funere fratris' and Virgil (*Georg.*
ii. 510) 'gaudent perfusi sanguine fratrum'.

401. primaeui : cf. Virg. *Aen.* vii. 162 'primaeuo flore iuuentus'.

402. liber . . . nouercae : the text as it stands has to be taken
to mean 'desired his son's death so that without hindrance
he might possess himself of a virgin who would be a stepmother': one must suppose that the father is marrying a
young second wife and wants to get rid of a grown-up son
who threatens to disturb his felicity. But *innuptae nouercae*
seems impossibly compressed and *innuptae* is pointless—his
intended bride is presumably *innupta* and it is only when she
becomes *nupta* that she can be *nouerca*: Maehly's *uti nuptae*
'possess himself of a bride as a stepmother' is the only
plausible correction that has been proposed. Wilamowitz's
suggestion that *in-* is prepositional, not negative, and that
innupta represents ἐπιγαμηθεῖσα 'brought in as a new wife',
cannot be taken seriously: there is no evidence that *innupta*
could bear that sense and a reader familiar with the ordinary
usage of the word—a common word which Catullus himself
uses at l. 78—could not be expected to recognize it.

404. penates : *V* read *parentes. di parentes*, or *di parentum*, are the
spirits of dead ancestors whose goodwill their descendants
seek with propitiatory offerings (*parentatio*). A letter of Cor-
nelia, mother of the Gracchi, quoted by Nepos (fr. 16 Peter)
has 'ubi mortua ero, parentabis mihi et inuocabis deum
parentem', and dedicatory inscriptions have *dis parentibus
sacrum* and the like (e.g. *C.I.L.* vi. 29852*a*: a series from
Verona, *C.I.L.* v. 3283–90, has the variant *diis parentibus
augustis*). But while the *di parentes* are offended by injuries
done to parents by their children (Festus 260 L. quotes an

old law, 'si parentem puer uerberit . . . puer diuis parentum
sacer esto'), the mother's sin here described is not an offence
against them. The old correction *penates* is probably right:
it is the life of the family, and the *penates* who preside over
it, that she outrages.

405. omnia fanda nefanda : cf. Ov. *Met.* vi. 585 'fasque nefasque / confusura ruit', Sen. *Dial.* iv. 9. 2 'uelut signo dato
ad fas nefasque miscendum coorti sunt'.

406. iustificam : the adjective occurs only here but is one of a
class of poetic compounds characteristic of the archaic style:
so Ennius has *regificus* for *regius*, Lucretius *largificus* for
largus. Cf. *amplifice* 265.

407. talis brings the reader back, somewhat prosaically, to the
theme of the poem.

408. contingi . . . lumine claro : probably (1) 'be touched by the
bright light of day' and so be visible to men, rather than
(2) 'be reached by bright (human) eyes': for the latter meaning Kroll compares Lucr. iv. 824 'lumina . . . oculorum clara
creata / prospicere ut possimus'.

65

There is little doubt that the (H)ortalus to whom this poem
is addressed and the Hortensius of poem 95 are to be identified
with Catullus' older contemporary Q. Hortensius Hortalus,
Cicero's Asianist rival in the courts and a poet whose tastes
seem to have been those of the new school (see on 95. 3). The
poem is a letter, written shortly after the death of Catullus'
brother, conveying, in reply to a request from Hortensius, a
translation from Callimachus, poem 66. It consists of a single
long sentence of 24 lines, broken by a parenthesis of ten lines
(5–14) on his brother's death and his own sorrow, but the
structure is more compact than that of the similar letter,
68. 1–40; the long period is effectively rounded off, and the
sombreness relieved, by the charmingly vivid and unexpected
simile of the last lines.

1. confectum : cf. Cic. *Att.* iii. 5 'maximo dolore conficior'.

2. doctis . . . uirginibus : the Muses, the *doctae sorores* of [Tib.]
iii. 4. 45, Ov. *Tr.* ii. 13, *Met.* v. 255; for the implications of
doctus see on 35. 16 f.

   uirginibus : in the ending of the pentameter Catullus
maintains the freedom of the Greek elegiac poets. In this
poem he has one word of five syllables, 3 of four, 4 of three,
and 4 of two; in the accompanying poem 66 he has 24 words

of four syllables, 9 of three, and 12 of two. In poem 68 and 76
the proportion of disyllables is higher: 68 has 38 disyllables
against 26 words of three syllables, 13 of four, 2 of five, and
1 of seven; 76 has 8 disyllables against 1 monosyllable, 1 trisyllable, and 3 quadrisyllables.

3. potis est : see on 45. 5.

    fetus, 'births of the Muses', perhaps, but the fact that
English has no equivalent for *fetus*, which can be used of any
new life, plant as well as animal, makes it difficult to convey
the metaphor. The *fetus* are *dulces* because they are *carmina*,
and *carmina* are *dulcia* to the lover of poetry. In *expromere*
the metaphor is that of bringing out from a store; cf. 64. 223.

4. mens animi : 'the thought of my mind'; this old-fashioned
phrase for the intellectual faculty appears in Plautus (*Cist.*
210) and several times in Lucretius (e.g. iii. 615, iv. 758).

    ipsa : i.e. it has such troubles *of its own* that it is not free to
turn elsewhere.

5. Lethaeo gurgite : the stream of Lethe is one of the rivers of
the underworld: cf. Virg. *Aen.* vi. 714 'Lethaei ad fluminis
undam / securos latices et longa obliuia potant'. *gurges* (a
cognate of *uorare*) is properly used of an engulfing body of
water, which swallows or sweeps away, but the poets often
use it more generally (see Henry, *Aeneidea*, i, pp. 368 ff.).
Catullus applies it to the sea four times in poem 64 (14, 18,
178, 183).

6. pallidulum : the ghost is *pallidus* (or *pallens*, Virg. *Aen.* iv.
26: cf. Hor. *Od.* i. 4. 13 *pallida Mors*) as having lost its natural
colour: see on 81. 4. For the diminutive see on 64. 60.

7. Troia... tellus : 'on whom the soil of Troy lies heavy beneath
the shore of Rhoeteum': for Catullus' brother's death at
Troy cf. 68. 91, 99. Rhoeteum was a promontory in the
Troad; Virgil repeats the phrase *Rhoeteo litore*, *Aen.* vi. 505.
For *obterit* cf. Lucr. iii. 893 'urgeriue superne obtritum
pondere terrae'.

10. uita ... amabilior : see on 64. 215.

12. tua ... morte : perhaps to be taken with *canam* (for this
ablative of 'external' cause see on 14. 2) rather than with
maesta.

14. Daulias ... Ityli : the simile of the nightingale's lament is
Homeric: *Od.* xix. 518 ff. ὡς δ' ὅτε Πανδαρέου κούρη, χλωρηὶς
ἀηδών, / καλὸν ἀείδησιν ἔαρος νέον ἱσταμένοιο / δενδρέων ἐν πετάλοισι
καθεζομένη πυκινοῖσιν (*densis ramorum umbris*), / ἥ τε θαμὰ τρωπῶσα
χέει πολυηχέα φωνήν, / παῖδ' ὀλοφυρομένη, Ἴτυλον φίλον, ὅν ποτε χάλκῳ /
κτεῖνε δι' ἀφραδίας, κοῦρον Ζήθοιο ἄνακτος. In the post-Homeric

version of the story Procne is daughter of king Pandion of Athens and wife of the Thracian Tereus and avenges her husband's violence to her sister Philomela by killing her own son Itys; when Tereus pursues the sisters, the gods intervene and turn Procne (or, in the Latin versions, Philomela) into a nightingale and her sister into a swallow (Ov. *Met.* vi. 442 ff.). Though Catullus uses the Homeric name Itylus in preference to the later Itys, *Daulias* (*auis*), 'the Daulian bird', implies the later version; Tereus was king of Daulia in Phocis (cf. Thuc. ii. 29. 3).

absumpti: cf. Prop. iii. 10. 10 'increpet absumptum nec sua mater Ityn'.

15. sed tamen introduces the apodosis after *etsi* (l. 1): so after *licet*, Cic. *Fam.* xiii. 27. 1.

16. expressa: 'translated': the usual technical term, a metaphor from the imprinting of a seal or the modelling of a statue; cf. Ter. *Ad.* 11 'uerbum de uerbo expressum extulit', Cic. *Fin.* i. 4 'fabellas latinas ad uerbum expressas', fr. 16 Morel 'conuersum expressumque latina voce Menandrum'.

carmina: the plural need not imply that more than one poem accompanied the letter.

Battiadae: Callimachus, who uses the name for himself in *Epigr.* 35 Pf.; his father's name was Battus, but the patronymic recalled the legendary King Battus, founder of his native city of Cyrene (cf. 7. 6), from whom he claimed descent.

17. credita uentis: 'committed to the roving winds': cf. 30. 9, 64. 59. For the pathetic *nequiquam* cf. 64. 164, 101. 4; for *uagis* see on 64. 271.

18. effluxisse: cf. Cic. *Verr.* ii. 4. 57 'quod totum effluxerat' ('which had entirely slipped my mind'), *Fam.* vii. 14. 1 'dabo operam ut istuc ueniam antequam plane ex animo tuo effluo'.

19. missum . . . malum: cf. Prop. i. 3. 24 'furtiua cauis poma dabam manibus'. For the apple as a love-token see Theoc. 5. 88 (with Gow's note).

furtiuo munere: for the ablative cf. 101. 8.

sponsi: the situation suggests that *sponsus* is used, by anticipation, of the lover: cf. Hor. *Ep.* i. 2. 28 *sponsi Penelopae*.

20. gremio: cf. 66. 56 'casto collocat in gremio'.

22. aduentu: for the ablative see on 14. 2; the poor girl (*miserae*) jumps up at her mother's appearance.

23. The distinctive rhythm, with spondees in all the feet except the fourth, is clearly meant to echo the sense, whether it represents the girl's bewilderment or the slow roll of the apple, and *atque* emphasizes the sudden and unexpected conclusion; the alliterative combination of adjectives recurs at 68. 59. Virgil has borrowed the words and their effect, *Georg.* i. 203 'atque illum in praeceps prono rapit alueus amni'.

24. conscius . . . rubor : 'the blush of guilt'; for the transferred epithet cf. 68. 61.

66

The Greek text of the poem of Callimachus of which this is a translation was unknown, apart from a few meagre citations, until two papyri, the first published by G. Vitelli in 1929,[1] the second by E. Lobel in 1952,[2] made it possible to restore some twenty-five lines with more or less certainty. The poem was probably written in 246 or early in 245 B.C., shortly after its occasion, and later attached by Callimachus himself to the fourth book of his *Aitia* with the addition of some lines (represented by 79–88 in Catullus' version) dealing with the origin or αἴτιον of a wedding custom.[3]

On his accession to the throne of Egypt in 247 B.C. Ptolemy III (Euergetes) married his second cousin Berenice (B in the stemma below), daughter of the king of Cyrene. Shortly after the marriage he set out on an invasion of Syria (see on l. 12) and his queen vowed a lock of her hair for his safe return. He returned in triumph; the vow was paid and the lock dedicated, apparently in a Pantheon at Alexandria. From there it disappeared, and the astronomer Conon turned his professional skill to courtly use by finding it—in the sky, as a cluster of stars between Virgo and the Bear. Callimachus took up Conon's ingenious compliment, enlarged on it and added new conceits of his own; putting his poem into the mouth of the lock itself, he made it tell the story of its translation and proclaim, from its new home in the heavens, its devotion to the queen and its longing to be restored to her head.

The piece is gallant court-poetry, characteristically Alexandrian in its parade of allusion, drawn from astronomy, history, and mythology, in its compressed and selective handling of incident, in its playful and arch sentimentality, and in its interest in the psychology of love. For the most part Catullus' version follows the Greek closely, even reproducing its structure

---

[1] P.S.I. 1092, *Studi Ital. di Fil. Class.* vii. 1 ff.

[2] P. Oxy. 2258, *The Oxyrhynchus Papyri*, xx. 69 ff.

[3] See Pfeiffer, *Callimachus*, vol. ii, p. xl.

and rhythm (see especially ll. 47–48, 51–54, 75–76), though he
sometimes contracts (l. 45) or expands (l. 62) and once at any
rate (ll. 77–78) fails (as our text stands) to bring out an essential
point in the Greek.

The surviving fragments of the Greek text are printed (with
the omission of some lines of which only a few letters remain) in
the appendix, p. 407. For a full text with critical apparatus and
commentary see Pfeiffer, *Callimachus*, vol. i, pp. 112 ff.; for a
tentative reconstruction of the missing lines, E. A. Barber in
Greek Poetry and Life (Oxford, 1936), pp. 343 ff.

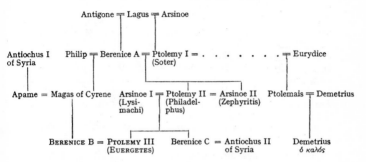

1. **dispexit** : 'sighted', i.e. saw clearly and distinctly.

   lumina mundi : the constellations; in Virg. *Georg.* i. 5
   clarissima mundi lumina are the sun and moon. *mundus*, the
   firmament, as in 64. 206.

3. **ut** : 'how': this clause and the two which follow are objects
   of *comperit*, parallel to the nouns *ortus atque obitus*.

   rapidi : 'the devouring sun', as in Virg. *Georg.* i. 92 'rapidi
   potentia solis', *Ecl.* 2. 10 'rapido aestu'.

   obscuretur : for the spondaic ending see on 64. 3.

5 f. **Triuiam . . . aereo** : 'how Love calls the Moon down secretly
   from her heavenly orbit and banishes her to the rocks of
   Latmus': a romantic periphrasis for the occultation of the
   Moon. When she is invisible in the sky, she is visiting the
   mortal Endymion in the cave where he lies asleep on Mount
   Latmus in Caria.

5. **Triuiam** : for the identification of Hecate, one of whose cult-
   titles Triuia properly is, with the Moon-goddess and with
   Artemis see on 34. 13.

7. **Conon,** the astronomer, was Callimachus' contemporary, a
   native of Samos who worked in Alexandria; his astronomical
   and mathematical writings are lost, but his work is known

from the references of his friend Archimedes. He was especially interested in the phenomena of eclipse (ll. 3–6); cf.
Sen. *N.Q.* vii. 3. 3 'Conon postea diligens et ipse inquisi-
tor defectiones solis seruatas ('recorded') ab Aegyptiis
collegit'.

   in lumine is Vossius's correction of the impossible *numine* of
V; cf. 59 'uario . . . in lumine caeli', where *V* again has
numine. But *in caelesti lumine fulgentem* is a strange phrase.
Callimachus has merely ἔβλεψεν ἐν ἠέρι. Baehrens's *in limine*
is perhaps a more natural expansion of that phrase here and
fits *uario* better ('the spangled floor of heaven') in 59.

8. **Beroniceo** : there seems to be no reason to suppose that the
late form *Beronice* (the -*o*- of which has been preserved in its
derivative 'Veronica') goes back to Catullus, who presumably had Βερενίκης before him in the text of Callimachus. On
the use of the adjective see on 44. 10; on the spelling of the
suffix see on 68. 109. The normal adjectival form from Βερενίκη would be Βερενικαῖος (in Latin -*aeus*); Callimachus'
Βερενίκειος (l. 62: in Latin -*eus*) must have been derived from
a by-form of the name, Βερενίκεια.

   caesariem : elsewhere *caesaries* always refers to a head of
hair; here it represents Callimachus' βόστρυχος, 'lock'.

9. **multis . . . dearum** : Catullus is dealing freely with his
original's πᾶσιν ἔθηκε θεοῖς (which seems to imply that the vow
was made to a pantheon), but the change to the feminine is
natural enough. Haupt unnecessarily proposed *cunctis . . .
deorum* to bring Catullus into conformity with Callimachus,
attributing the corruption to failure to recognize the irregular
(but not impossible) use of *cuncti* with a 'partitive' genitive.

10. **protendens brachia** : in the usual ancient attitude of prayer;
cf. Callim. *Hymn* 4. 107 πήχεις / ἀμφοτέρους ὀρέγουσα, Virg. *Aen.*
xii. 930 'dextramque precantem / protendens'.

11. **tempestate** : 'time'; for the archaic use see on 64. 73.

   nouo auctus hymenaeo : for *auctus* cf. 64. 25 'taedis
felicibus aucte'; for the lengthening of -*us* before the Greek
word *hymenaeo* see on 64. 20. The hiatus after *nouo* may be
another suggestion of Greek rhythm: Peiper's *auectus* removes it but hardly fits this context (cf. 64. 132).

12. **iuerat** : the normal perfect *ii* is not a 'contraction' of *iui*
but an independent reduplicated perfect form; the alternative *u*-perfect *iui* is rare in the classical language, but the
poets sometimes find it convenient; so Virgil has *obiuit* (*Aen.*
vi. 801), Statius *subiuit* (*Silv.* ii. 1. 155).

   Assyrios : Syrian; for this common confusion see on 68. 144.
The sister of Ptolemy Euergetes, another Berenice (C in the

stemma), was the second wife of Antiochus II of Syria; after his death in 246 she was expelled by his first wife Laodice. Ptolemy, who had just succeeded to his throne in Egypt, invaded Syria with an army to protect her but was in time only to avenge her murder.

14. de : 'over': cf. Ov. *Ibis* 169 f. 'deque tuo fiet ... / ... corpore rixa lupis'.

15. nouis nuptis : 'brides'; cf. 61. 91.

15 ff. anne ... fundunt ? : 'or are the tears false with which they disappoint their parents' pleasure on their wedding day'? The connexion of thought requires the change of *atque* to *anne*. The emphasis is on *falsis* and we need a particle which makes this question an alternative to the preceding one: 'Do they really not want love? or can it be that their tears are hypocritical? I assure you, their sighs are not sincere.' For the bride's tears cf. 61. 81 f.

16. lacrimulis : the disparaging diminutive was perhaps regularly used of 'crocodile' tears; cf. Ter. *Eun.* 67 'haec uerba una mehercle falsa lacrimula, / quam oculos terendo misere uix ui expresserit, / restinguet', Cic. *Planc.* 76.

18. non, ita me diui, uera gemunt, iuerint : i.e. *ita me di iuerint, non uera gemunt.* This bold hyperbaton may have been suggested by hellenistic practice; there are examples of violent dislocation of word-order in the remains of Alexandrian verse: e.g. Callimachus, fr. 178. 9–10 Pf. αἶνος Ὁμηρικὸς αἰὲν ὅμοιον / ὡς θεός, οὐ ψευδής, ἐς τὸν ὅμοιον ἄγει (where οὐ ψευδής belongs to αἶνος), fr. 384. 31 οὐδ' ὅθεν, οἶδεν, ὀδεύω, / θνητὸς ἀνήρ, Theoc. 29. 3 κἠγὼ μὲν τὰ φρενῶν, ἐρέω, κέατ' ἐν μυχῷ. But there are already examples in tragedy, e.g. Soph. *O.C.* 874 ἄξω βίᾳ, / κεἰ μοῦνός εἰμι, τόνδε, καὶ χρόνῳ βραδύς, *O.T.* 1251 χὥπως μὲν ἐκ τῶνδ' οὐκέτ' οἶδ', ἀπόλλυται, Eur. *Heracl.* 205 σοὶ δ' ὡς ἀνάγκη τούσδε βούλομαι φράσαι / σῴζειν. And, on the other hand, in Latin such hyperbata are not confined to verse influenced by Greek technique (e.g. Virg. *Aen.* x. 385 'Pallas ante ruentem, / dum furit, incautum, crudeli morte sodalis, / excipit', i.e. *incautum excipit dum furit crudeli morte sodalis*, Ov. *Her.* 10. 110 'illic qui silices, Thesea, uincat, habes', *A.A.* i. 399–40 'tempora qui solis operosa colentibus arua, / fallitur, et nautis aspicienda putat', *Met.* xii. 314–15 'inter duo lumina ferrum, / qua naris fronti committitur, accipis, imae'); violent dislocations are found not only in Lucretius (e.g. vi. 176 'fecit, ut ante, cauam, docui, spissescere nubem', 158 'uentus enim cum confercit, franguntur, in artum, / concreti montes') but even in comedy; such lines as Plaut. *M.G.* 862 'ne dixeritis, obsecro, huic, uostram fidem' and Ter. *Hec.* 262 'eo, domum, studeo haec, priusquam ille redeat' show that interweaving of this kind was possible even in language based on ordinary speech. These examples make the appearances of hyperbaton in the informal style of Catullus' poem 44 (8 'quam mihi meus uenter, / dum sumptuosas appeto, dedit, cenas') and Horace's *Satires* (i. 5. 72, ii. 1. 60, ii. 3. 211) less surprising. But it is not easy to see how a reader coming upon them in continuous unpunctuated writing could find them readily intelligible. (For other Latin examples see Housman, *J. Phil.* xviii, pp. 6 ff., Vollmer, *Sitz. Bay. Akad., Phil. Kl.*, 1918, 4, pp. 4 f., Platnauer, *Latin Elegiac Verse*, pp. 104 ff.)

ita me . . . iuerint : cf. 61. 189 'ita me iuuent / caelites'.

iŭerint is in origin an *s*-aorist optative formation (parallel to *faxim, ausim*: see on 44. 19), representing *iouasint*, in which the intervocalic -*s*-, by normal Latin change, became -*r*-. The form survives in other isolated instances in Plautus, (*Rud.* 305 *adiuerit*), Terence (*Ph.* 537 *adiuerit*) and Propertius (ii. 23. 22 *iuerint*). *siris* (91 below) is a formation of the same type. · The combination of vocalic *ŭ* and consonantal *u* is represented in writing by single *u*.

20. nouo . . . uiro : cf. Livy xxxvi. 17. 8 'uxorem duxit et nouus maritus . . . ad pugnam processit'. See on 61. 55.

21. et tu : the sudden apostrophe to the queen in the second person comes awkwardly after *mea regina* in the preceding sentence. For *et tu* introducing an ironical or indignant question ('and you tell me, do you, that it was not a husband but a brother that you were grieving for?') cf. Cic. *Phil.* ii. 51 'et tu apud patres conscriptos contra me dicere ausus es?', 110 'et tu in Caesaris memoria diligens?'

luxti : i.e. *luxisti*: for the syncopated form see on 14. 14.

22. fratris : Berenice and Ptolemy were not brother and sister; they were actually cousins (and *frater* is regularly used for 'cousin'), but that relationship is not in point here. The reference is to the formal honorific style which described the Egyptian king's consort as his sister: so these two are described in inscriptions (Dittenberger, *Orientis Graeci Inscr. Sel.* 60, 61) as βασιλεῖς Πτολεμαῖος Πτολεμαίου καὶ Ἀρσινόης θεῶν ἀδελφῶν καὶ βασίλισσα Βερενίκη ἡ ἀδελφὴ αὐτοῦ καὶ γυνή. The *coma* takes advantage of it to put the mischievous question 'perhaps it was *sisterly* love that made you cry?'

23. exedit cura medullas : cf. 35. 15; *cura* of the lover's pains as in 64. 72, 68. 51.

24. toto pectore may be taken either with *sollicitae* or with *mens excidit*; in the latter case cf. 68. 25.

25. ereptis : cf. 51. 6 'omnis / eripit sensus mihi'.

27. bonum . . . facinus : the reference is probably to the story told by Justin (26. 3). Berenice had been betrothed to Ptolemy by her father Magas, but after the death of Magas in 258, her mother Apame (whom Justin wrongly calls Arsinoe) invited Demetrius ὁ καλός, another cousin of Ptolemy, from Macedonia to marry Berenice and succeed to the kingdom of Cyrene. Demetrius transferred his affections from Berenice to her mother and made himself obnoxious to her subjects; with Berenice's help he was assassinated and she married Ptolemy in 247. The account of Hyginus (*Ast.* ii. 24), who professes to be explaining *magnanimam* here, wrongly makes Berenice a daughter of Ptolemy Philadelphus and says that she saved her father's life in battle: but that act could not have assisted her to attain her *regium coniugium*.

28. quod non fortior ausit alis : 'which another, though stronger, would not venture'; to take *fortior* as predicative, 'which no other would show himself braver by venturing', gives an impossibly awkward construction.

  alis : i.e. *alius*: for the form see on 29. 15.

29. mittens : letting him go on his way; so 64. 221 *mittam*.

30. tristi : i.e. *triuisti*.

  Iuppiter : for the exclamation cf. 48, 1. 7.

31. quis . . . deus ? : 'who was the great god who changed you ?', i.e. what god was so powerful as to change you ?: for this pregnant use of *tantus* and *tam* in questions cf. Virg. *Aen.* i. 539 'quaeue hunc tam barbara morem / permittit patria ?', i. 605 'quae te tam laeta tulerunt / saecula ?', ii. 282 'quae tantae tenuere morae ?'. For *quis* see on 61. 46.

  an quod : 'or can it be because'; for the ellipse cf. 40. 5 *an ut*.

33. ibi : 'then', as in 8. 6, 63. 4, 48, 76.

35. reditum tetulisset : for the epic phrase and the archaic *tetuli* cf. 63. 47.

36. Asiam : Ptolemy extended his Syrian expedition throughout Asia Minor, across the Euphrates, and up to the borders of India; so at least the official record testifies in the inscription at Adule (Dittenberger, *Orientis Graeci Inscr. Sel.* 54).

  addiderat : i.e. when he returned, he had added.

37. caelesti reddita coetu : i.e. duly rendered, as promised, to the gods; for *reddere* of payment of a vow cf. 36. 16, Hor. *Od.* ii. 7. 17 'obligatam redde Ioui dapem', Virg. *Ecl.* 5. 75 'sollemnia uota / reddemus Nymphis'.

  coetu : for the dative form cf. 64. 385.

38. pristina . . . nouo : the desire to provide a pair of balanced adjectives (cf. 68. 60; see p. 275) produces an artificial and purely formal antithesis: similarly Virg. *Aen.* iii. 181 'nouo ueterum deceptum errore locorum'.

dissolŭo : for the prosody see on 2b. 13.

39 f. inuita . . . inuita : for the emphatic epanalepsis cf. 75–76 *afore . . . afore*, 82–83 *onyx, vester onyx*.

39. Virgil borrows the line to put it into the mouth of Aeneas meeting Dido in Elysium, *Aen.* vi. 460 'inuitus, regina, tuo de litore cessi'. But to suppose that he deliberately raised the words from their trivial context in Catullus to one charged with tragic emotion may be as rash as to suspect that Ovid was parodying Virgil when he made the solemn *hoc opus, hic labor est* serve the purposes of the *Ars Amatoria* (i. 453). The one reminiscence may well be as unconscious as the other.

40. adiuro . . . caput : for the direct accusative instead of the normal *per te* cf. Virg. *Aen.* vi. 324 'iurare . . . numen', 351 'maria aspera iuro', xii. 816 'adiuro Stygii caput implacabile fontis'; the formula 'Iouem lapidem iurare' in Cic. *Fam.* vii. 12. 2 suggests that it is an old use rather than a graecism.

41. digna ferat . . . adiurarit : 'and may anyone who swears lightly by that (*quod*) receive his deserts'.

42. qui se : for the substantival use of *qui* see on 61. 46 and 17. 22.

postulet esse : 'expect, claim, to be'.

43. maximum in oris : i.e. *in oris terrarum*: so Virg. *Aen.* iii. 97 'domus Aeneae cunctis dominabitur oris', and an anonymous fragment from tragedy (43 R.: of Eleusis) 'ubi initiantur gentes orarum ultimae'; for *ora* in the sense of 'region' cf. 64. 281.

44. progenies Thiae : Pfeiffer, combining the meagre evidence of the papyrus with a lemma in Suidas, restored ἀμνάμων ('descendant') Θείης in Callimachus; the reference here is not, as Bentley naturally supposed, to the Sun as son of Thia but to Boreas, the North Wind, son of Astraeus and Eos and so grandson of Thia; *progenies* then means 'descendant' and *clarus* is used of the North Wind as it is in Virg. *Georg.* i. 460, *claro Aquilone*.

45–46. Athos, the peak of 6,350 feet in which the most easterly of the three prongs of Chalcidice terminates, is not in fact the highest mountain even in Northern Greece; not only Olympus (9,571 feet) but also Parnassus, Pindus, and Oeta are much higher. And when in 483 B.C. the Persian king

Xerxes in his second invasion of Greece dug a canal to avoid
a repetition of the disaster of 492, which had wrecked his
fleet on the point of Athos, he did not cut through the mountain (as *euersus* implies) but through the narrow neck of
the peninsula behind it.

46. classi: ablative as in 64. 212.

    nauit: cf. 64. 2.

    barbara: i.e. oriental: cf. 64. 264.

    Athon: this form may represent Ἄθων, the earlier accusa-
tive of Ἄθως, which was supplanted by Ἄθω. But Catullus may
be using the false graecism *Athōn*, as Virgil does in *Georg.* i.
332. Callimachus here has the genitive Ἄθω.

47. quid facient: there are reminiscences in Virg. *Ecl.* 3. 16
'quid domini faciant, audent cum talia fures?', and Ov. *A.A.*
iii. 655 'quid sapiens faciet? stultus quoque munere gaudet'.

48. Iuppiter, ut ... pereat: cf. Hor. *Sat.* ii. 1. 43 'o pater et rex /
Iuppiter, ut pereat positum robigine telum'. The curse on the
πρῶτος εὑρετής, the inventor of something which has turned
out to man's hurt, is a common cliché of the poets: cf. Tibullus
i. 4. 59, i. 10. 1 ff., Prop. i. 17. 13, ii. 6. 27, iv. 3. 19; the
formula is parodied in comedy, Plaut. *Men.* 451, Naeuius fr.
19 R. For examples in Greek see Eur. *Hipp.* 407, Arist.
Lys. 946, Menander, fr. 154 K.

    Chalybon: the Greek genitive plural termination is ex-
tremely rare in Latin, but clearly Catullus avoided hiatus
by taking over the Greek form from Callimachus' line: the
manuscripts agree on the termination *-um*, but they are
attempting in various ways to make a familiar word (*celerum,
celitum*, or *celorum*) out of the unintelligible proper name.

    The Chalybes were a tribe of miners and ironworkers on
the south-eastern shores of the Black Sea: in Xenophon's
itinerary they appear as a real people (*Anab.* v. 5. 1 ὁ βίος ἦν
τοῖς πλείστοις αὐτῶν ἀπὸ σιδηρείας). In later literature they become the legendary inventors of iron-working or even, as
Callimachus makes them here, the discoverers of iron; for a
lively picture of their activities see Apoll. ii. 1001–7.

49 f. principio ... institit: for the combination cf. Ter. *Hec.*
381 'hanc habere orationem mecum principio institit'; here,
as often in prose, *institit* (properly 'set about' with deter-
mination) is synonymous with *instituit*.

50. stringere is a technical term for drawing molten metal into
bars: so in Virg. *Aen.* viii. 420 f. 'striduntque cauernis /
stricturae Chalybum', 'their molten bars hiss in their caverns'.

    ferri ... duritiem: i.e. *durum ferrum*: a common device of
poetry in which the abstract idea is presented more vividly

and with more 'body' by a substantive than it would be by an epithet; cf. Virg. *Georg.* i. 143 *ferri rigor*.

51. abiunctae, as the Greek (νεότμητόν με κόμαι ποθέεσκον ἀδελφεαί) shows, is to be taken not as nominative with *comae* but as genitive with *mea* ('of me separated'); for the construction cf. Ov. *Her.* 5. 45 'nostros uidisti flentis ocellos', *Am.* i. 8. 108 'ut mea defunctae molliter ossa cubent'.

52 f. Memnonis . . . equos : *unigena Memnonis* represents Callimachus' γνωτὸς Μέμνονος and must mean 'Memnon's brother' (see on 64. 300); as the scholiast on Callimachus explains, the reference is to Zephyrus, the West Wind, who like Memnon is a son of Eos. *ales equos* appears to be confirmed by κυκλώσας βαλιὰ πτερὰ . . . ἵππος in the Greek: Zephyrus is represented not, as the winds sometimes are, as a rider but as a winged horse. Arsinoe, Ptolemy II's queen, was deified and identified with Aphrodite, and had a temple on the promontory of Zephyrium, east of Alexandria (Strabo xvii. 800), from which she had the title *Zephyritis* (57: so Call. *Epigr.* 5. 1 Pf.); hence Zephyrus, apparently, is represented as her attendant (*famulus*, 57) and he is dispatched to bring the lock from the Pantheon, where it has been dedicated, to her own temple, from which it is conveyed to the sky. Bentley's *Locridos* is confirmed by Λοκρίδος of Pap. Oxy. 2258, which seems preferable to Λοκρικός of P.S.I. 1092 (for the corruption in *V* cf. 64. 3 *fas(c)idicos* for *Phasidos*), but this epithet for Arsinoe has not been satisfactorily explained; there was another Zephyrium in south Italy in or near the territory occupied by Locrian settlers from Greece, the so-called Λοκροὶ Ἐπιζεφύριοι, but an allusion to that seems unlikely.

57. eo : 'for that purpose'.

58. incola litoribus : the unusual construction is paralleled at 64. 300.

Graiia : Arsinoe is of the Macedonian dynasty of the Ptolemies. *O*'s reading *gratia* may point to the old spelling with double *i*; so Cicero (according to Quintilian i. 4. 11) wrote *Maiia* for *Maia*. See Housman, *C.R.* v (1891), 296.

Canopitis : the Greek has Κ]ανωπίτου ναιέτις α[ἰγιαλοῦ, 'dweller on the Canopic shore'; the town of Canopus was not far from Zephyrium, but the adjective may be used as a general term for Egyptian (cf. Virg. *Georg.* iv. 287). If the Latin is to correspond, we must read *Canopeis . . . litoribus. litoribus* needs an epithet, but Statius's *Canopitis* cannot be ablative plural: Greek adjectives with masculine termination -ίτης (Latin -*ita*) and feminine -ιτις have no neuter form.

59. The sense is clear: Ariadne's crown is not to be the only adornment of a mortal head to be placed in the sky. But the beginning of the line is corrupt and has not been plausibly emended: Postgate's *inde Venus* involves a very awkward separation of *Venus* from *diua* in l. 64.

uario . . . in lumine caeli : the epithet suits *limine* better than *lumine* (see on 7; for *uarius*, 'star-spangled', cf. Ov. *Met.* ii. 193 'sparsa quoque in uario passim miracula caelo', *Fast.* iii. 449 'caeruleum uariabunt sidera caelum'), but Catullus seems to be representing φάεσ]ιν ἐν πολέεσσιν and *uario . . . lumine* ('shifting lights') may be right.

61. corona : the crown given by Dionysus to Ariadne and after their marriage taken from her head and placed in the sky as a constellation (Ov. *Fast.* iii. 459 ff.).

fulgeremus : for the spondaic ending see on 64. 3.

62. flaui : see on 64. 63.

63. uuidulam a fluctu : the temple from which the *coma* was conveyed to heaven was on the coast; presumably she is regarding the spray from the adjoining sea as a discomfort (hence the self-pitying diminutive *uuidulam*) from which her translation has rescued her. Palladius's *a fletu* does not fit the context; when Berenice made her vow she was weeping for her absent husband (21–22), but she had no reason to be tearful when she paid it on his safe return. For *a*, 'in consequence of', 'with', see on 64. 275.

uuidulam : for the pathetic diminutivè cf. 64. 60.

templa deum : 'the abodes of the gods', the *templa caeli* of Lucr. i. 1014; see on 64. 75.

65. The cluster of stars which is the *Coma* adjoins Virgo, Leo, and the Bear and sets before Bootes.

namque very rarely stands so late in the sentence, but Virgil has it in the sixth place at *Ecl.* i. 14 and in the fourth at *Aen.* v. 733; on postponement of connectives in Catullus see on 23. 7.

66. iuncta : *V*'s *iuxta* involves an unparalleled shortening of the *-a*.

Callisto : Καλλιστῷ, the only example in Latin literature of this Greek dative form. Callisto, daughter of the Arcadian king Lycaon, was changed into a bear by the jealousy of Hera, but Zeus atoned by placing her in heaven as the constellation of the Bear: for the story see Ov. *Met.* ii. 409 ff., *Fast.* ii. 155 ff.

67. 'As I wheel to my setting, I lead the way in front of slow Bootes': for *tardum . . . sero* cf. Hom. *Od.* v. 272 ὀψὲ δύοντα Βοώτην, Q. Cic. 19 'serus in alta / conditur Oceani ripa cum luce Bootes', Ov. *Fast.* iii. 405 'piger ille Bootes'.

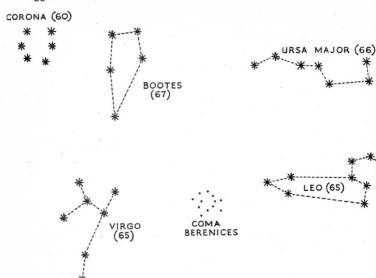

68. uix sero : for the strengthening *uix* cf. *uix tandem*, 62. 2.

69 f. She is in the sky, the floor of heaven, by night and at morning returns to Ocean.

  Tethyi : Tethys was wife of Oceanus; cf. 64. 29. For the Greek dative in *-i* cf. 64. 247 *Minoidi*.

71. An interjected prayer to Nemesis, who punishes presumption and whose displeasure the *coma* is inviting by her indifference to her new beatitude.

  pace tua : a familiar conciliatory formula, 'without offence to you': cf. Lutatius Catulus, fr. 2 Morel, 'pace mihi liceat, caelestes, dicere uestra: / mortalis uisus pulchrior esse deo', Ov. *Am.* iii. 2. 60 'pace loquar Veneris: tu dea maior eris', Cic. *Tusc.* v. 12 'pace tua dixerim'.

  hic : 'at this point'.

  Ramnusia : cf. 68. 77: there was a famous temple of Nemesis at Rhamnus in Attica.

73 : nec si : 'not even if': the earliest instance of the use of *nec* for *ne quidem* which becomes common in post-Augustan Latin; elsewhere Catullus uses *non si*—70. 2 (see note there), 48. 5, 69. 3, 88. 8.

    discerpent : 'pull to pieces', as we say; the simple *carpo* is common (cf. 62. 36) in this sense.

74. condita . . . pectoris, what is stored in my heart; cf. Plaut. *Pseud.* 575 'meo in pectore conditumst consilium'.
    euolŭam : for the prosody see on 2*b*. 13.

76. discrucior, 'I am racked by the thought that': this use with accusative and infinitive is perhaps colloquial; cf. Cic. *Att.* xiv. 6. 1 'discrucior Sextili fundum a uerberone Curtilio possideri'.

77 f. quicum . . . bibi : the sense of the Greek is clear: 'with whom I, while she was a virgin, drank many simple perfumes but had no share in those of grown womanhood'; the contrast here, as in *Hymn* 5. 15, 25, is between the χρίματα λιτά or ἄμεικτα which the girl uses and the more elaborate μεικτά of the married woman; the *coma* left Berenice's head before she could enjoy the latter. Lobel's correction *uilia*, representing λιτά, for *milia* is highly probable, but even with that correction the text as it stands does not adequately represent the Greek and would be barely intelligible without it; if *omnibus* is right, *unguentis* has not the epithet which is needed to correspond to γυναικείων and contrast with *uilia*.
    Berenice's taste for cosmetics was well known and her patronage assisted the development of the perfumery trade in Alexandria (Athen. xv. 689a): her name is appropriately perpetuated in the word 'varnish'—though that word (βερνίκη in late Greek, *ver(o)nice* in late Latin) is probably derived from it at one remove, through the name of a town called after her.

77. quicum : i.e. *cum quo* (*uertice*); see on 2. 2. The old ablative form *qui* (originally instrumental; see on 116. 3) serves for all genders; Virgil uses it as feminine, *Aen.* xi. 822. *una* goes closely with *quicum*, 'in company with which'.

79. The *coma* calls upon brides to make an offering to her, on their wedding-day, of the perfumes which she was denied in her earthly existence.

    optato . . . lumine either 'with its longed-for light' or 'on the longed-for day'; for *optatus* in this connexion cf. 64. 31.

80. unanimis : 'loving'; see on 9. 4.

80 f. non prius . . . tradite : *non*, for the normal *ne*, with an imperative occurs first here; in this case it can be justified as being attached closely to *prius* (see Kühn.–Steg. i. 203), but cf. *non siris* below (91).

82. libet implies that the *coma* is now a divinity.
    onyx is not the precious stone of that name but a yellow

marble which was used for perfume-jars (Pliny, *N.H.* xxxvi. 60 '(onyx) quem cauant et ad uasa unguentaria quoniam optime seruare incorrupta dicatur'); cf. Hor. *Od.* iv. 12. 17 'nardi paruus onyx', Prop. ii. 13. 30 'Syrio munere plenus onyx'.

83. quae : the antecedent is contained in *uester*: the construction is common, e.g. Cic. *Vat.* 29 'nostra acta quos tyrannos uocas'. Cf. 64. 369.

colitis ... iura : observe the code (see on 102. 3) of marriage; cf. Ov. *Met.* vii. 715 'iura iugalia'. Propertius has the opposite, iv. 5. 28 'frange et damnosae iura pudicitiae'.

85. irrita is proleptic: 'may the light dust drink up her wicked offering so that it is of no effect'.

87. sed magis : 'but instead'; see on 73. 4.

89. The *coma* closes with an appeal to Berenice herself.

90. festis luminibus : 'on holy days'.

91. unguinis : the archaic *unguen* provides a convenient substitute for *unguentum*; *V*'s *sanguinis* introduces an idea (cf. 34) which is irrelevant here.

non siris : for the rare use of *non* for *ne* with the perfect subjunctive in a prohibition, cf. Ov. *A.A.* i. 389 'aut non temptaris aut perfice'. *non* occasionally appears with a jussive present subjunctive both in verse and in prose: e.g. Cic. *Clu.* 155 'a legibus non recedamus' (see Kühn.–Steg. i. 192).

siris is not a contracted form of *siueris* but an *s*-aorist optative formation, parallel to *faxis*, from the stem *si-* of *sino*, *-s-* between vowels, by the development normal in early Latin, becoming *-r-*: the archaic form is found in Plautus and in old formulae in Livy. See on 18 *iuerint*.

tuam me : 'I who belong to you': the monosyllabic ending gives emphasis to the unusual combination.

92 ff. The reading of *V*, *sidera cur iterent*, can be translated: 'by your lavish gifts give the stars cause to repeat "would that I might become a royal lock; then let Orion shine next to Aquarius"'; *effice cur*, though it is not found elsewhere, may be justified by Ovid's *aut amet aut faciat cur ego semper amem* (*Am.* i. 3. 2). The other stars are represented as being jealous of the *coma*'s privileges. But while their envy may be intelligible, the pointless irresponsibility of l. 94 is not; a general upheaval in heaven in which the constellations changed their places would not assist them to acquire the *coma*'s peculiar status. With Lachmann's *corruerint*, the whole is spoken by the *coma*: 'Treat me to lavish gifts. May the stars crash. Let me become a royal lock (again) and let Orion shine next to Aquarius.' The desire to return to her old life has already been suggested in 75 (though the absence of the essential 'again' here is difficult; hence Markland proposed *iterum* for *utinam*), but the impious wish for a heavenly cataclysm comes strangely from the *coma* which has had misgivings about uttering even the cautious sentiments of 75–76 and, even if that wish were granted, the fulfilment of her desire would not follow. If either text is what Catullus wrote, he seems to have been writing without having a clear picture in his mind. The Greek is unfortunately missing; perhaps Catullus misrepresented his original here as he seems to have done at 77–78.

92. affice muneribus : a prosaic phrase: cf. Cic. *Fam.* ii. 3. 2, Nepos, *Ages.* 3. 3.

Hydrochoi may represent a Greek dative Ὑδροχοεῖ, corresponding to a nominative Ὑδροχοεύς, but the usual form of the name is Ὑδροχόος and Callimachus seems to have had Ὑδροχόος, in the nominative, here. To take *Hydrochoi* as genitive (of *Hydrochous*) involves the unparalleled graecism of giving *proximus* the construction of Callimachus' γείτων.

94. fulgeret : present subjunctive from *fulgerare*, an old form of *fulgurare*.

Oarion : Callimachus has the form Ὠαρίων for the usual Ὠρίων at *Hymn* 3. 265.

68

This poem (if it is one poem) falls into two clearly distinguishable parts—(*a*) a personal letter to a friend (lines 1–40), informal in style and indeed sometimes little more than versified prose, and (*b*) an elaborately constructed elegiac poem (41–148), opening with a formal invocation of the Muses and obviously meant to stand by itself as an artistic composition, to which are added a dozen lines of envoi (149–60). At first sight we seem to have a formal poem enclosed for transmission between a preface and an epilogue, in much the same way in which poem 66 is accompanied by the explanatory preface of poem 65. But the relation between the parts is not so simple as that between 65 and 66. In 65 Catullus writes to a friend that in spite of his private troubles he has contrived to write the poem for which his friend had asked him; 66 is the poem itself, a translation from Callimachus made for the occasion. Here the personal letter is an apology for being unable to give a friend what he has asked for; far from introducing the poem which follows, it is concerned to explain the absence of a poem. *munera Musarum*, he tells his friend in the letter, he cannot give; but what follows he describes in the envoi (149) as *confectum carmine munus*. The apparent inconsistency, if the two parts belong together, we must explain by the assumption that, having excused himself from doing what is asked of him, he finds himself moved, by the remembrance of the past and of his debt to his friend, to go on to write some lines expressive of his gratitude which turn into a formal elegiac poem, not a translation from Alexandrian poetry like 66 but not less obviously Alexandrian in its inspiration.

This assumption is not without difficulties.

1. The persons addressed in the two parts do not appear to bear the same name. The name of the addressee of (*a*) is given by the manuscripts in the form *Mali* (with the variant *Manli* in *R*), which was early emended to *Malli*; for that of the addressee of (*b*) the manuscript readings point to *Allius*. Both Mallius (i.e. Manlius) and Allius are gentile names, and the only circumstance in which at this period the two could have been borne by one person is adoption. That Catullus' friend should have acquired by adoption a name differing by one letter from that which he had by birth would be a possible, though curious, accident; that Catullus should have given him one of these names (twice) in the epistle and the other (four times) in what follows is hardly likely. Lachmann attempted to remove the difficulty by reading *Mani* for *Mali*, assuming that Catullus' friend was Manius Allius and that Catullus used first his *praenomen* and then his *nomen*. But the use of the *praenomen* in writing between intimates does not seem to have been normal practice. Cicero in his letters usually addresses his intimate friends (even Atticus) by *nomen* or by *cognomen*.[1] Catullus calls his closest friend 'Licini' or 'Calue', not 'Gai', and never uses a *praenomen* in the vocative by itself.[2] Schöll's *mi Alli* is perhaps a more likely alternative in spite of the unique elision in the sixth foot in l. 11.

2. The 'Manius' of the epistle has written in distress to Catullus, after suffering a severe blow (1 *fortuna casuque*

---

[1] *Fam.* xii. 25, where Cicero writes first *mi Cornifici* and then *mi Quinte*, is exceptional. When Tiro demurs at what seems to him excessive familiarity between master and servant, it is because Cicero has addressed a letter to him by *cognomen* (*Fam.* xvi. 18. 1); so in *Fam.* vii. 32. 1 the omission of the *praenomen* is a sign of familiarity.

[2] He uses *nomen* in the vocative fifteen times, *cognomen* five times: once (see on 49. 2) he has the formal combination of *praenomen* and *nomen*.

oppressus acerbo); he is *desertus in lecto caelibe* (6), and that
phrase would naturally refer to the loss of, or separation from,
his wife, or perhaps his mistress.[1] In the elegy there is nothing
to suggest that 'Allius' is, or has been, at all disconsolate, and
the envoi conveys good wishes (155) to him and to someone
who is called his '*uita*'. On the other hand, the elegy is an
acknowledgement of a debt to 'Allius', while in the epistle
there is nothing to suggest that Catullus is conscious of any
particular debt to 'Manius'; like Hortalus in 65, he is a friend
who has asked a favour.

3. A passage referring to the death of Catullus' brother
appears in almost identical form in both parts (20–24, 92–96),
standing at the centre of each and integral to the argument of
the first and to the structure of the second. If the two were
sent to the same person, it is difficult to think that they were
sent at the same time.

It is possible that having written the apologetic epistle,
Catullus followed it up later with the elegy. But it is open to
question whether the epistle and the elegy were addressed to
the same person. If they had stood apart in our text, they
would have been accepted as referring to two quite different
situations and there would have been no temptation to connect
them. That Catullus should have used the lines on his brother
in poems addressed, at the time of his brother's death, to different persons is not more remarkable than that he should have
used them twice over in what he sent to one person.

Catullus writes the epistle from Verona, shortly after his
brother's death in Asia. Where 'Manius' is, Catullus does not
say; presumably he is in Rome. In his distress, denied love and
unable to find distraction in older literature (5–8), he has asked
Catullus for *munera et Musarum et Veneris*—two requests
apparently, as *utriusque* in 39 shows, corresponding to the two
neque clauses of 5–8: for the pleasures of love and for poetry
from Catullus' hand, poetry (as the contrast with *ueterum*
implies) in the 'new' manner (7–8)—and has expostulated with
Catullus for cutting himself off from the pursuits of gay
society (27–29). Catullus replies that in his own sorrow he has
put love and love-making (26 *delicias animi*) out of his mind,
and that in Verona, without his books, he cannot write what
'Manius' is expecting from him.

In the elegy Catullus appears to be doing just what he has said
he has neither the heart nor the means to do, and *quod potui* in
149 is not necessarily an apology for the inadequacy of his

[1] Cf. Sen. *Agam.* 184–6 (Clytaemnestra speaking of Agamemnon),
'neue desertus foret / a paelice unquam barbara caelebs torus, /
ablatam Achilli diligit Lyrnesida'.

writing; it may be taken as well, or better, as apology for the
inadequacy of his thank-offering—poetry is all that he can
offer by way of return for what Allius has done for him. The
poem is in fact a highly finished and intricate composition. It
begins and ends with a *gratiarum actio* to Allius; between, it
pursues a series of elaborately interrelated themes, forwards
and then backwards, through a series of ingeniously contrived
connexions. The pattern is:

41–50: thanks to Allius for his service;
51–69: the story of Catullus' own love and of Allius' help
      in it, ending with the appearance of his '*candida
      diua*', who reminds him of
73–85: Laodamia and her love for the husband whom she
      sent to
87–90: Troy, later to be the scene of
91–100: his own brother's death.
101–4: Troy;
105–30: Laodamia's love, with two elaborate similes;
131–48: his own love and its vicissitudes;
[149–60: thanks to Allius].

The construction is heavy and awkward, with trailing periods
of ten lines or more (57–66, 79–86, 105–16, 119–28) and accumu-
lations of relative clauses, and there are jarring prosaic phrases
like *in quo genere* (52), *tam ualde* (77), *una atque altera* (82), *aut
nihil aut paulo* (131), *atque alia atque alia* (152). On the other
hand, the stylistic devices which appear in the narrative poem
64 (see pp. 274 f.) are exploited here also—balanced arrangement
of words within the line (e.g. 62, 63, 67, 79, 104–5), apostrophe
(93, 105), pathetic repetition (88–90, 99); alliteration runs riot
(e.g. 49, 59, 67, 81, 117–24, 137) and even the metrical mannerism of the spondaic hexameter (see on 64. 3) plays its part (65,
87, 89, 109). Alexandrian *doctrina*, romantic allusion to history
and legend, colours the whole poem and sometimes verges on
pedantry. But beneath all the studied artifice and formal
embellishment there is intense personal feeling—of friendship
for Allius, of sorrow for his brother, of love for someone who
can only be Lesbia: in that respect Catullus' two experiments
in elegy, different as they are from one another—this poem
with its uninhibited excitement and 76 with its unadorned
despair—have a quality that was never surpassed.

(For a survey of the questions raised by poem 68, with
references to earlier literature, see H. W. Prescott, *Trans.
Amer. Phil. Ass.* lxxi [1940], pp. 473 ff.)

1 f. Quod . . . mittis : 'your sending me this note', is picked up
by *id* in l. 9. *mihi* is dative of person interested, the speaker

regarding himself as recipient and not, as with the normal *ad me*, as addressee: cf. 116. 1.

2. **epistolium** : this latinization of the Greek diminutive ἐπιστόλιον occurs only here.

    conscriptum . . . lacrimis : 'written in tears', i.e. instead of ink: Seneca goes even further, *Dial.* vi. 1. 3 'libros quos uir ille fortissimus sanguine suo scripserat'.

3. **naufragum ut eiectum**, 'wrecked and cast ashore by the foaming waves': Cicero has the same combination (in a very different context, of Catiline's following of 'human wrecks') *Cat.* ii. 24 'naufragorum eiectam et debilitatam manum'.

4. **mortis limine** : cf. Lucr. ii. 960 'leti limine ab ipso'.

5. **sancta Venus** : see on 36. 3.

6. **in lecto caelibe** : in Ovid, *Her.* 13. 107 Laodamia uses the phrase of her own condition in her husband's absence: see also Sen. *Agam.* 184–6 quoted on p. 343 n. 1 above.

7. **ueterum . . . scriptorum** : the Greek poets must be meant; neither Catullus nor anyone who shared his tastes would have used *dulcis* of the older school of Latin poetry (see on poems 22 and 95).

8. **cum . . . peruigilat** : here, as in 32, the *cum*-clause can be taken as strictly temporal, 'at a time when your mind is sleepless with anxiety'.

10. **munera et Musarum . . . et Veneris** : δῶρα Μουσῶν and δῶρα Ἀφροδίτης are both familiar expressions of early Greek poetry (e.g. Theog. 250 ἀγλαὰ Μουσάων δῶρα, Archilochus, fr. 1 D. Μουσέων ἐρατὸν δῶρον ἐπιστάμενος, Hesiod, *Sc.* 47 τερπόμενος δώροισι πολυχρύσου Ἀφροδίτης) for the gift of poetry and the delights of love; Anacreon combines them, fr. 96 D. ὅστις Μουσέων τε καὶ ἀγλαὰ δῶρ' Ἀφροδίτης / συμμίσγων ἐρατῆς μνήσκεται εὐφροσύνης. But *utriusque* in l. 39 makes it clear that 'Manius' is making two requests and that the *munera Musarum* and the *munera Veneris* are distinct.

    hinc : i.e. from me.

    Catullus freely permits elision at the diaeresis of the pentameter (so 56, 82, 90 of this poem) except in poems 65 and 66.

11. **incommoda** : 'misfortunes': so 21 *commoda*, 'blessings'.

12. **odisse** : 'repudiate', 'be impatient of': as often, the implication of *odisse* is not represented by 'hate' but corresponds to our colloquial 'have no use for': cf. Hor. *Od.* i. 38. 1 'Persicos odi, puer, apparatus', iii. 1. 1 'odi profanum uulgus', *Ep.* i. 7. 20 'prodigus et stultus donat quae spernit et odit', Virg. *Aen.* xii. 431 'odit moras', Prop. i. 1. 5 '(amor) me docuit

castas odisse puellas', Cic. *Fin.* i. 32 'nemo enim ipsam uoluptatem quia uoluptas sit aspernatur aut odit aut fugit'.

14. dona beata : i.e. *dona beatorum*, 'gifts that only the happy can give': Propertius has a similar transference, iv. 7. 60 'aura beata' (of the airs of Elysium).

15. uestis . . . pura : i.e. the *toga uirilis*, the plain white toga, which the Roman boy formally assumed, at the age of 15 or 16, as the symbol of entry into manhood, in place of the child's *toga praetexta* with a purple edging. For the thought cf. Prop. iii. 15. 3 'ut mihi praetexti pudor est ablatus amictus / et data libertas noscere amoris iter'.

16. uer ageret : 'was keeping its springtime'; for the metaphor, cf. Ov. *Met.* x. 85 'aetatis breue uer'.

florida : of the fresh and vigorous charm of youth, as in 61. 57 'florida puellula', Lucr. v. 943 'nouitas . . . florida mundi': so *florens*, 64. 251, Lucr. iii. 1008 'aeuo florente puellas'.

17. lusi : of the lover's dalliance as in 156; cf. 17. 17, 61. 204.

non est dea nescia nostri : an inversion of the usual phrase (Bacchylides 5. 174 νῆϊν Κυπρίδος, Callim. fr. 75. 49 Pf. χαλεποῦ νήϊδες θεοῦ) which the author of the *Ciris* borrows, 242 'non est Amathusia nostri / tam rudis.'

18. dulcem . . . amaritiem : 'flavours her cares with a sweet bitterness': the oxymoron goes back to Sappho (47 L.-P. Ἔρος . . . γλυκύπικρον ἀμάχανον ὅρπετον) and Theognis (1353 πικρὸς καὶ γλυκύς ἐστι . . . Ἔρως): cf. Plaut. *Pseud.* 63 'dulce amarumque una nunc misces mihi'.

curis : of the sorrows of love, as in 64. 72 and often in the elegiac poets: cf. 51 *curam*.

19 ff. For Catullus' brother's death cf. 65. 5. The ending of l. 19 in a stressed monosyllable and the break after the first foot in l. 20 convey the shock of sudden sorrow and the repetitions *fraterna—frater—frater* and *tu—tecum—tecum—tuus* are pathetically eloquent.

25. interitu : for the ablative cf. 87 *raptu* and see on 14. 2.

tota de mente, i.e. entirely from my mind; for the idiom cf. 76. 22 'expulit ex omni pectore laetitias', [Tib.] iii. 1. 20 'an toto pectore deciderim' ('slipped entirely out of your heart'), Ov. *A.A.* iii. 56 'e toto pectore cessit onus'.

26. delicias animi : cf. 64. 372 *animi . . . amores.* On the meaning of *deliciae* see on 50. 3 (esp. Cic. *Cael.* 44 there quoted).

27. quare, quod scribis : the *quod*-clause ('as for your writing that . . .'), making reference to a point in his correspondent's letter to which the writer is replying, is a regular feature of

Latin epistolary style: there are hundreds of instances in
Cicero's correspondence, e.g. *Fam.* xii. 2. 2 'quare, quod
scribis te confidere aliquid profici posse, non nihil ut in tantis
malis est profectum'. For similar usages see on 10. 28, 83. 4.

If the quotation from 'Manius'' letter is, as is to be
expected after *quod scribis*, indirect, *hic* must mean 'in
Verona' ('in Rome', if 'Manius' was writing from there, would
be *istic*). With the old correction *Catullo* and the alteration
of *V*'s unmetrical *tepefacit* to the subjunctive *tepefactet*, the
sense appears to be 'It is a shame, you say, for Catullus to be
in Verona, because here in Verona a member of the smart set
cannot pursue his pleasures'; but *Veronae turpe Catullo esse*
standing for *Veronae esse turpe Catullo esse* is a very awkward
brachylogy. With *V*'s reading *Catulle*, the words *Veronae . . .
cubili* must be a direct quotation from 'Manius'' letter, *est*
being understood with *turpe*; *hic* then refers to the place from
which 'Manius' is writing, presumably Rome, and in the
following words he is giving a hint of Lesbia's unfaithfulness
—in Catullus' absence from Rome everyone is enjoying her
favours (*tepefactat*). The construction is easier, but the
direct quotation is unparalleled and improbable. For
Catullus' use of his own name see on 135.

   turpe is not to be taken too seriously: for the colloquial use
cf. Cic. *Fam.* viii. 6. 5 (Caelius has been pestering Cicero to
provide him with panthers from Cilicia, and writes 'turpe
tibi erit pantheras graecas me non habere').

28. **quisquis de meliore nota :** 'everyone of the better class'.
While the neuter *quicquid* used in the sense of *quidque* is not
uncommon, the masculine does not appear to be so used and
there is no need to take *quisquis* so here: *est* can readily be
understood, as it is in Ov. *A.A.* i. 267 'quisquis ubique, uiri,
dociles aduertite mentes'. *nota*, 'brand', is a metaphor from
the wine-cellar (cf. Hor. *Sat.* i. 10. 24 'nota Falerni'): for this
colloquial use cf. Cic. *Fam.* vii. 29. 1 (from Curius) 'Sulpici
successori nos de meliore nota commenda ('give me a better-
class introduction'), Sen. *Ben.* iii. 9. 1 '(beneficia) quaedam
non sunt ex hac uulgari nota sed maiora', Petr. 116. 5 'ur-
banioris notae homines'.

29. **tepefactet :** the verb does not occur elsewhere, but Plautus
has the corresponding *frigefactare* twice: for the prosody see
on 64. 360.

30. **magis :** 'instead', 'on the contrary': see on 73. 4.

31. **ignosces :** for this formula of courtesy cf. Prop. i. 11. 19
'ignosces igitur, si quid tibi triste libelli / attulerint', Hor.
Sat. i. 9. 72.

32. cum nequeo : 'at a time when I cannot': cf. 8.

33. nam : as often, is an elliptical connexion, relating the clause which it introduces to a thought which has not been expressed (see Kühn.–Steg., ii. 117–18): 'I cannot give you one thing you ask because of my sorrow: (and I cannot give you the other either,) for I am away from my books.' The excuse is revealing evidence of the methods and ideals of the *doctus poeta*; what is expected of him is Alexandrian poetry, translated from, or modelled on, Greek, and for that he needs his library.

34. hoc : probably ablative, 'for this reason', anticipating *quod*.

36. capsula : the *capsa* was, like the *scrinium* (see 14. 18), a cylindrical box in which *uolumina* stood on end.

    sequitur : either a general present 'goes with me to Verona whenever I go there' or perhaps 'has gone with me now to V.', the present being used of a past action whose effect extends into the present (cf. Virg. *Aen.* vii. 363 'non sic Phrygius penetrat Lacedaemona pastor', ix. 266; see on 149).

37. maligna : 'grudging': cf. 10. 18.

    id facere : the use of *id facere* to stand for a verb which has already been used (cf. 85. 1) is not uncommon (though Latin idiom makes much less use of this device for avoidance of repetition than English); here it stands for a verb (*recusare, nolle*, or the like) which has not actually been used but can be inferred from the context: cf. Cic. *Brut.* 130 'etsi . . . non deerat in causis, tamen id non saepe faciebat (i.e. causas agebat)'.

38. ingenuo : the *ingenuus animus* is the right-mindedness which comes from good birth; cf. 61. 79 *ingenuus pudor*.

39. non : negatives *posta est*—'I have not supplied you with both things'.

    posta : the syncopated form presents no difficulty (Lucretius has it four times): the phrase *copiam ponere* is unparalleled (hence Fröhlich's *praesto*, 'at your disposal') but does not seem impossible.

40. ultro : 'I should have offered it unasked': cf. Hor. *Ep.* i. 12. 22 'si quid petet, ultro ("without being pressed") defer', Cic. *Fam.* iv. 13. 2 'nec mihi quicquam in mentem uenit optare quod non ultro mihi Caesar detulerit'.

41–46. The poet tells his story to the Muses (*deae*) and invites them to transmit the record of it to posterity. The more usual convention makes the Muses speak to the poet and the poet convey their message to others (e.g. Call. *Hymn* 3. 186, Theoc. 22. 116): Apollonius has been thought to be giving

the same twist to the idea as Catullus in i. 20 f. ἐγὼ γενέην τε
καὶ οὔνομα μυθησαίμην / ἡρώων, ... Μοῦσαι δ' ὑποφήτορες εἶεν ἀοιδῆς,
but ὑποφήτορες probably is 'inspirers', not 'interpreters'.

41. non possum : 'I cannot bring myself to' as in l. 84, 62. 21,
104. 1; cf. Virg. *Aen*. ix. 482 'potuisti linquere solam?', xi. 307
'nec uicti possunt absistere ferro', Prop. i. 8. 5 'tune audire
potes uesani murmura ponti?'

43. ne : Calphurnius's correction of *V*'s *nec* (with which *tegat*
would have to be taken as potential) avoids the interruption
of the connexion between 41 and 45.

    saeclis obliuiscentibus : Quintilian has the opposite of this
striking phrase, x. 1. 104 'saeculorum memoria dignus'.

44. caeca nocte : cf. 64. 207 *caeca caligine*.

45. porro dicite : see on 45. 3.

46. carta ... anus : 'make my paper speak when it is old': for
the adjectival use cf. 78. 10 'fama loquetur anus'.

48. magis ... atque magis : the common formula; Catullus also
uses *magis magis* 38. 3, 64. 274.

49 f. 'no spider weaving her delicate web in air do her work
over Allius' neglected name': the image is that of an abandoned monument; cf. Prop. ii. 6. 35 'non immerito uelauit
aranea fanum / et mala desertos occupat herba deos'.

50. opus faciat : so the bees *opus faciunt* in Varro, *R.R.* iii. 16. 5.

51. duplex : 'treacherous', the opposite of *simplex*; the use is
rare but cf. Hor. *Od*. i. 6. 7 'cursus duplicis Ulixei', Ov. *Am*.
i. 12. 27 (to his tablets) 'ergo ego uos rebus duplices pro
nomine sensi' ('found you double in nature and not merely
in name').

    Amathusia : Venus; see on 36. 12 f.

52. in quo ... genere : 'in what matter': cf. Cic. *Att*. iv. 2. 7
'quo (relative) in genere nunc uehementer laboratur':
similarly *in omni genere* (Cic. *Att*. xii. 33. 2 'tota domus in
omni genere diligens', *Q.F.* ii. 2. 4 'innumerabiles res sunt in
quibus te cotidie in omni genere desiderem'), *in aliquo genere*
(Cic. *de Or*. ii. 17 'qui in aliquo genere inconcinnus est').

    torruerit : *V*'s *corruerit*, 'brought me crashing down', is
perhaps not in itself impossible: the rare transitive use is
found in Lucr. v. 368 'corruere hanc rerum uiolento turbine
summam'. But Turnebus's *torruerit* is confirmed by *arderem*
in the next line: for the use of the verb in this context cf.
100. 7, Hor. *Od*. iv. 1. 12.

53. Trinacria rupes : 'the Sicilian crag', i.e. Aetna: the same
comparison in Hor. *Epod*. 17. 30 ff. 'ardeo / quantum neque ...

nec Sicana feruida / uirens in Aetna flamma', Ov. *R.A.* 491
'quamuis infelix media torreberis Aetna', *Her.* 15. 12 'me
calor Aetnaeo non minor igne tenet'. Θρινακίη was Homer's
name for a western island (*Od.* xi. 107): in the form Τρινακρία
it became attached to Sicily (cf. Thuc. vi. 2. 2) by a popular
etymology which interpreted it as 'the island with three promontories' (τρία ἄκρα). The name appears here for the first
time in Latin; later poets found the noun and the adjective
convenient alternatives to *Sicilia* and *Siculus*.

54. **lymphaque**: for the use of the coordinating *-que* where
English idiom prefers the disjunctive 'or' see on 45. 6.

lympha . . . Thermopylis: i.e. the hot springs which gave
their name to the pass of Thermopylae in Malis, where the
main route connecting northern and central Greece was enclosed between Mount Oeta and the Malian Gulf.

55. **neque**: for the postponement of *neque* see on 23. 7.

tabescere lumina: cf. Hor. *Epod.* 5. 40 'cum . . . intabuis-
sent pupulae'.

56. **imbre**: of tears, as often in Ovid: e.g. *Tr.* i. 3. 18.

57 ff. **qualis . . . agros**: with the punctuation of the Oxford
text and the reading *ac* in l. 63, the simile of the mountain
stream relates to Allius' service in l. 66. In favour of this it
can be urged that the point of the simile lies in the solace
brought by the stream to the thirsty traveller and that *qualis*
(57) corresponds to *tale* (66). On the other hand, (i) this leaves
an abrupt transition between 56 and 57, where some explicit
connexion might be expected; (ii) the insertion of another
comparison for Allius in 63–65, this time with the welcome
breeze sent by Castor and Pollux, the sailor's friends, makes
the structure awkward and unwieldy; (iii) elsewhere in
Catullus a simile introduced by *qualis* relates to what precedes: compare 64. 89, 65. 13, and especially 109–16 of this
poem, where *quale* adds a comparison even longer, and in its
detail more irrelevant, than the present one. It is possible
that the lines should be punctuated with comma after 56
and colon after 62, *hic* ('thereupon') read in l. 63, and the
simile related to the poet's tears in the preceding lines 53–56.
So taken, the simile has precedent in Homer, *Il.* ix. 14 f.
(repeated in xvi. 3 f.) ἵστατο δάκρυ χέων ὥς τε κρήνη μελάνυδρος /
ἥ τε κατ' αἰγίλιπος πέτρης δνοφερὸν χέει ὕδωρ, and it is reasonable to think that Catullus had these lines in mind. There,
in the epic manner, the simile is expanded beyond the point
of relevance in the detail of steep crag and dark water: so
here Catullus develops the image for its own sake in a
vivid picture. *hic* in 63 then makes the transition from

Catullus' distress to Allius' comfort, and *tale* (66) takes up *uelut* (63).

59. de prona praeceps : 'after tumbling headlong down the sloping valley': Catullus has the same pair of adjectives again at 65. 23.

60. densi . . . iter populi : Homer's λαοφόρος κέλευθος (*Il.* xv. 682): *densi* provides a balancing adjective to *medium* (see on 66. 38) and enlivens the picture by contrasting the busy highway with the lonely heights.

61. lasso : if *lasso* is to be taken not with *uiatori* but with *sudore*, as the rhythm strongly suggests (and as it would certainly have to be taken in a later poet), the transference is like that in *piger sopor* (63. 37), *tussis anhela* (Virg. *Georg.* iii. 497).

62. hiulcat : 'when the oppressive heat makes the burned fields gape' with cracks in the soil: cf. Virg. *Georg.* ii. 353 'hiulca siti findit canis aestifer arua'. The verb is not found again till Venantius Fortunatus in the sixth century A.D.

65. iam . . . iam : an emphatic repetition, not the Virgilian use of *iam . . . iam* for *modo . . . modo* or *nunc . . . nunc.*

   prece Pollucis . . . implorata : 'besought by prayer to Pollux': for the use of the verb cf. Hor. *Ep.* ii. 1. 135 'caelestis implorat aquas': for the genitive, Virg. *Aen.* xi. 4 'uota deum', Prop. iv. 1. 101 'Iunonis uotum'. For Castor and Pollux as patrons of seafarers see on 4. 27.

67 f. is is emphatically repeated three times: 'it was he who' . . ..

   clausum . . . campum : 'opened a fenced field with a broad path': cf. Virg. *Aen.* ix. 323 'lato te limite ducam'. Catullus probably wrote *claussum*, as Quintilian (i. 7. 20) says Cicero and Virgil both did, the -*ss*- (which here represents an earlier -*ds*-: *claud-sum*, earlier *claud-tum*) not yet being reduced to -*s*-.

68. isque . . . dominae : if *domina* here bears the meaning of *amica* (i.e. presumably Lesbia), *V*'s *dominam* cannot stand and Fröhlich's *dominae* must be read, 'afforded a house to me and my mistress'. That use of *domina* is well established in the later elegiac poets, and Catullus himself uses the precisely similar *era* in 136. But, (i) it is very difficult to suppose that *domus . . . domina* are not correlatives, the house and its chatelaine, here as they are in 61. 31 (see note on that line), and the symmetry of the line, with the balanced *isque . . . isque*, demands that they should be. (ii) The antecedent of *ad quam* must then be found not in the immediately preceding *dominae* but in *domum*, and the Latin for 'the house in which' is not *domus ad quam* but *domus in qua*. If, on the other hand, *dominam* is retained with the meaning 'chatelaine', *domus* and *dominam* are properly related, the relative is not separated from its antecedent, and *dominam ad quam*, 'a chatelaine under whose roof', gives normal Latin. The sense will then be that Allius afforded the lovers a house (his own or someone else's) in which to meet and a complaisant chatelaine (his wife or someone else); there is, however, the awkwardness that *exerceremus* is only explained by the appearance of *mea diua* in the next sentence. The same problem arises in l. 156.

69. communes . . . amores : 'the love we (i.e. Catullus and Lesbia) shared': Lucretius uses *communia gaudia* in the same connexion (iv. 1195).

70 f. se . . . intulit : she walked as a goddess walks, softly (*molli pede*) and with majesty : *se inferre*, like *incedere*, has the implication of a presence.

72. innixa . . . solea : she halts, stately, on the threshold (cf. Ov. *Am.* iii. 1. 31, of the Muse of Tragedy, *pictis innixa cothurnis*) and her lover has been waiting for her step: cf. Tibullus i. 8. 65 'dum mihi uenturam fingo, quodcumque mouetur, / illius credo tunc sonuisse pedes'. *arguta* is probably best taken of sound, the sudden tap of her shoe, but it might refer to shape, 'neat'; 'quick-moving', 'twinkling' is less likely here. *argutus* and *argu?iae* can be applied to anything that makes a sharp impression on one of the senses— most often of hearing (Virg. *Ecl.* 8. 22 'argutum nemus', *Georg.* i. 143 'arguta serra', i. 294 'argutum pecten', Prop. i. 18. 30 'argutae aues') but also of sight (Cic. *Leg.* i. 27 'oculi arguti', 'quick eyes', *de Or.* iii. 220 'manus arguta', 'restless hands': Virg. *Georg.* iii. 80 'argutum caput', 'with clear-cut lines'), and even of smell (Pliny, *N.H.* xv. 18) and of taste (Palladius iii. 25. 4 'argutos sapores'): their metaphorical uses correspond—of quickness of mind, incisiveness of style, expressiveness in art.

74. Protesilāēam : *-eus* represents the Greek termination -ειος: so Propertius has *Menelaeo* (ii. 15. 14). On Catullus' use of such adjectives see on 64. 368.

74 f. domum inceptam frustra : the δόμος ἡμιτελής of Homer, *Il.* ii. 701, which Protesilaus did not live to finish. In Homer's brief reference to the story there is nothing which connects Protesilaus' untimely death at Troy, where he was killed as he came ashore, with divine anger at neglect of a sacrifice, and Catullus does not indicate what kind of sacrifice was neglected; the scholiasts and mythographers, using later Greek versions of the story which are lost to us, add much to the later part of it but nothing to the earlier except that Protesilaus had only one day of married life with Laodamia before leaving for the war. The story was no doubt handled by Alexandrian poets from whom it made its way into Latin literature: Laevius, writing about the turn of the first century, had already used it in his lyric *Protesilaodamia*, but the fragments give no indication of how he treated it.

74. Laudamia : Greek -*ao*- certainly became -*au*- in Latin in such popular borrowings as *lautumia* (from λαοτομία) and the hybrid *Laudiceni* ('Laodiceans'), but in these the -*au*- was a diphthong, as is shown by Plautine prosody for the first and by the puns in Sen. *Contr.* ix. 4. 21 and Pliny, *Ep.* ii. 14. 5. That spelling for proper names like *Laocoon* and *Laomedon* appears not infrequently in manuscripts (see Usener in *N. Jahrb.* xci. 227 ff., Palmer on Ov. *Her.* 13. 2), but whether it was maintained where metre recognized the two vowels as distinct is doubtful. The manuscripts, which consistently write *Laudomia*, may be no more trustworthy for the -*au*- than for the -*o*- and Catullus may have written *Laodamia*.

75. sanguine sacro : cf. Virg. *Georg.* iv. 542 *sacrum cruorem*.

76. pacificasset : i.e. obtained *pax*, a characteristically Roman conception. The *pax deorum*, the 'terms' between god and man which man secures by sacrifice, is one of the basic contractual notions of primitive Roman religion, exemplified in such formulae as *pacis deum exposcendae causa* (Livy vii. 2. 2), *Iouis pacem expetere* (Plaut. *Amph.* 1127), *pacem diuom exorare* (Virg. *Aen.* iii. 370).

77. For the interjected personal prayer cf. 63. 91.

   Ramnusia virgo : Nemesis, the goddess who visits human presumption with retribution (50. 20), so called (cf. 66. 71) from her famous temple at R(h)amnus in Attica.

79. pium . . . cruorem : the blood of due sacrifice: for the 'transferred' epithet cf. Hor. *Od.* iii. 23. 20 'farre pio', Virg. *Aen.* iv. 637 'pia uitta', [Ov.] *Her.* 21. 7 'pia tura'.

82. una atque altera : 'before the coming of a first and a second winter had satisfied their greedy love': so Cic. *Clu.* 72 'unus et alter dies intercesserat', But *unus et alter* is often indistinguishable in meaning from *unus alterue*, 'one or two': e.g. Hor. *Ep.* ii. 1. 74 'si uersus paulo concinnior unus et alter', Ov. *Tr.* i. 3. 16 'qui modo de multis unus et alter erat'.

84. posset : 'could bear to'; see on l. 41.

85. quod : i.e. *abruptum coniugium*, 'the breaking of the wedding-tie'.

    scibant : for the form cf. 64. 319 *custodibant*, 84. 8 *audibant*. An oracle had declared that the first Greek to land on Trojan soil would lose his life, but only the Fates knew that Protesilaus was to be the first.

87. Helenae raptu : for the ablative see on 14. 2.

89. Troia : for the pathetic repetition cf. 64. 62.

    commune sepulcrum : Lucretius uses the same phrase of earth, v. 259.

90. acerba : 'untimely', as often; for examples see Mayor's note on Juv. 11. 44.

    cinis : Catullus makes the word feminine in the singular again at 101. 4 (as Calvus also did: see note on that line), but the plural is in the normal masculine at 98 below. For the same variation with *finis* see on 64. 3.

    uirum et uirtutum : cf. Virg. *Aen.* i. 566 'quis Troiae nesciat urbem / uirtutesque uirosque ? '.

91. quaene : with Heinsius's correction of *V*'s meaningless reading the idiom is the rare (and probably colloquial) one found in Hor. *Sat.* i. 10. 21 'o seri studiorum, quine putetis / difficile et mirum Rhodio quod Pitholeonti / contigit ? '. It cannot well be separated from the much commoner usage in which a clause introduced by a relative (as in 64. 180 and often in comedy)—or by a conjunction (e.g. Plaut. *Rud.* 1063 'utine istic prius dicat?', 'for him to speak first?', Virg. *Aen.* iv. 538 'quiane auxilio iuuat ante leuatos ?')—is addressed interrogatively either to the speaker himself or to an interlocutor. In the present use the relative clause appears to be given emphasis by being put interrogatively, as though 'Troy that brought death to my brother', were replaced by 'Troy: is it not Troy that . . . ?'

93. iucundum lumen : cf. Virg. *Aen.* vi. 363 'per caeli iucundum lumen et auras'.

97 f. longe . . . compositum : for the thought of death in a strange land away from kin cf. Prop. iii. 7. 10 'nec (mater) pote cognatos inter humare rogos', Ov. *Tr.* iii. 3. 37 ff.

98. cognatos . . . cineres : cf. Prop. iii. 7. 10 quoted above.

    compositum : 'laid to rest': cf. Hor. *Sat.* i. 9. 28 'omnes composui', Prop. ii. 24. 35 'tu mea (ossa) compones'.

99. obscena . . . infelice : 'sinister and ill-omened': *obscenus* is originally a term of augural practice: so Virg. *Aen.* iii. 241 'obscenas uolucres', Ov. *Her.* 5. 119 'obscenam puppim' (of the ship which carried Helen to Troy). For the ablative in *-e* see on 43. 4.

100. extremo : 'at the end of the world': cf. 11. 2 'extremos Indos', Ov. *Tr.* iii. 3. 13 'in extremis iaceo populisque locisque'.

101. tum resumes the theme which was left at 90.
   fertur lecta . . . pubes : see on 64. 1 f. and 4.

102. penetralis . . . focos : the hearths at the heart of their homes: cf. Virg. *Aen.* v. 660 'rapiuntque focis penetralibus ignem', Cic. *Har. Resp.* 57 'deorum . . . abditos ac penetralis focos'.

103. libera : 'unchallenged': cf. 64. 402.

105. tum resumes the theme of Laodamia which was left at 85.

106. uita dulcius : see on 64. 215 'longa iucundior . . . uita'.

107 f. tanto . . . barathrum expands and explains *dulcius*: 'in such an eddy had the flood of love engulfed you and swept you into a sheer abyss'.

108 ff. barathrum . . . foret : *barathrum* is an old borrowing from Greek (βάραθρον), already a familiar word in Plautus: Virgil uses it of Charybdis in a phrase clearly recalling Catullus' words, *Aen.* iii. 421 'imo barathri ter gurgite uastos / sorbet in abruptum fluctus'. Here, in an extreme instance of the characteristically Alexandrian taste for the parade of mythological detail, Catullus particularizes his picture with a reference to the underground channels near the town of Pheneus in northern Arcadia, which drained off from the low-lying plain under Mount Cyllene the flood-waters of the river Olbius and which legend attributed to the work of Heracles, and piles up a whimsically precious mythological excursus in a string of subordinate clauses (*quale . . . quod . . . quo tempore . . . ut*), each dependent on the preceding.

109. Cyllenaeum : the principle, established by Housman (*J. Phil.* xxiii. 54 ff.), that Greek adjectives formed from 1st declension feminine names have the suffix -αῖος (represented in Latin by -aeus) and those formed from other names the suffix -ειος (represented by -eus), requires the form *Cyllenaeum* here, *Ariadnaeis* at 66. 60, *Penelopaeo* at 61. 223 (unless there was an adjective Πηνελόπειος from the alternative form of the name, Πηνελόπεια: cf. 66. 8) and, on the other hand, *Aeeteos* at 64. 3.

111. medullis : cf. Virg. *Aen.* iii. 575 *uiscera montis*.

   fodisse . . . audit : 'is said to have dug': the use of *audire* in the sense of 'be called', is a not uncommon graecism derived from a regular use of ἀκούειν (e.g. Hor. *Sat.* ii. 7. 101 'subtilis ueterum iudex et callidus audis'): the verb is only here used with an infinitive, as equivalent to *dici*, but its archaic

synonym *cluere* is so used by Plautus (*Bacch.* 925 'Atridae
. . . cluent fecisse facinus maximum') and Lucretius (iv. 53
'cluet . . . uagari').

112. falsiparens Amphitryoniades : i.e. Heracles. The circum-
locution, the compound (Callimachus has ψευδοπάτωρ, but in
a different sense, 'false father', *Hymn* 6. 98), the patronymic
form, and the rhythm make this one of the most Greek-
sounding lines in Latin. Heracles is *falsiparens Amphitryoniades* because while Amphitryon was his putative mortal
father, his real father was Zeus.

113. Stymphalia monstra : the killing of the man-eating birds
of Stymphalus, whose valley lay on the other side of Mt.
Cyllene from Pheneus, was one of the twelve labours
imposed on Heracles by Eurystheus: *deterior erus*, 'a master
inferior to his servant', represents Heracles' own description
of Eurystheus in Hom. *Od.* xi. 621, χείρων φώς. For *monstra*
see on 64. 15.

    certa : 'unerring', as in Hor. *Od.* i. 12. 23.

115 f. pluribus . . . foret : after his death Heracles was rewarded with apotheosis—and so the gods who trod the
doorway of heaven were *plures*, by one—and with marriage
to the maiden goddess Hebe: see Hom. *Od.* xi. 602 ff.

117. sed resumes the Laodamia theme after the digression and
tibi takes up the apostrophe of 105.

118. indomitam . . . docuit : i.e. her love drove her into marriage
with Protesilaus: for the metaphor from breaking in (*domare*)
an animal (cf. 63. 33), already implicit in Homer's παρθένος ἀδμής
(*Od.* vi. 109), cf. Hor. *Od.* ii. 5. 1. *tamen* takes its meaning
from *indomita*, 'unbroken as she was, taught her after all';
see Munro on Lucr. iii. 553, Housman on Luc. i. 333.

119–28. Now follow two more elaborate comparisons for
Laodamia's passion: (i) 119–24, the old man's love for his
only daughter's late-born son, who gives him an heir and
disappoints the hopes of his next-of-kin, (ii) 125–8, the
dove's devotion to its mate. In (i) there may be a distant
echo of Pindar (*Ol.* 10. 86 ff.) ἀλλ' ὧτε παῖς ἐξ ἀλόχου πατρὶ |
ποθεινὸς ἵκοντι νεότατος τὸ πάλιν ἤδη, | μάλα δέ οἱ θερμαίνει φιλότατι
νόον, ἐπεὶ πλοῦτος ὁ λαχὼν ποιμένα | ἐπακτὸν ἀλλότριον | θνάσκοντι
στυγερώτατος, and Homer (*Il.* ix. 481 f.) καὶ μ' ἐφίλησ' ὡς εἴ τε πατὴρ
ὃν παῖδα φιλήσῃ | μοῦνον τηλύγετον πολλοῖσιν ἐπὶ κτεάτεσσι, but the
colour is essentially Roman.

119. confecto aetate parenti : Virgil repeats the phrase, *Aen.* iv.
599 'confectum aetate parentem'.

119 f. carum . . . caput . . . nepotis : for the emotional periphrasis cf. Virg. *Aen.* iv. 354 'capitis iniuria cari', Hor. *Od.*

i. 24. 1 f. 'quis desiderio sit pudor aut modus / tam cari capitis ? '. *una, seri, nata* all contribute to the picture: the old man has no son or close male relative (*agnatus*)—and under the Lex Voconia of 168 B.C. the heir to a large fortune must be male; he has only one daughter; and her son is not born till his grandfather is old. The hopes of the distant kinsman are high.

121. uix tandem : 'at long last': 'with no time to spare' is the suggestion of *uix*: cf. 62. 2.

122. nomen . . . intulit : i.e. has had his name entered; for the idiom see on 64. 305.

    testatas : passive, 'witnessed', i.e. authenticated by the seals of witnesses.

123. impia : 'unnatural', conflicting with the demands of *pietas* (cf. 23. 10), because founded on hope of the old man's death.

    derisi : 'made a laughing-stock' is proleptic: cf. Hor. *Sat.* ii. 5. 57 (of a disappointed legacy-hunter) 'captatorque dabit risus Nasica'.

124. suscitat : 'scares off' the bird of prey from the old man's head; for *uolturium* cf. Sen. *Ep.* 95. 43 'amico aegro aliquis adsidet: probamus; at hoc hereditatis causa facit: uoltur est: cadauer exspectat'; Mart. vi. 62.

    capiti : the archaic ablative in -*i* is not uncommon in Lucretius, and later poets sometimes find *capiti* (Virg. *Ecl.* 6. 16, Prop. ii. 30. 39), *cineri, lateri, nemori* convenient.

126. compar : 'mate'. The dove is a model of conjugal affection not only in poetry (cf. Prop. ii. 15. 27 'exemplo iunctae tibi sint in amore columbae, / masculus et totum femina coniugium') but also in sober natural history: cf. Pliny, *N.H.* x. 104 'coniugii fidem non uiolant communemque seruant domum; nisi caelebs aut uidua nidum non relinquunt'.

    improbius : 'more outrageously': *improbus* regularly implies conduct which defies social or moral convention.

127. mordenti : cf. 2. 4 *morsus*; for the ablative in -*i* cf. 64. 99 *languenti*.

128. multiuola : i.e. *multos uolens*: the word may have belonged to popular language: for it appears again in the Vulgate (*Eccl.* 9. 3).

129. furores : the passion of love as in 64. 54, 94.

130. flauo : see on 64. 63.

    conciliata : cf. Plaut. *M.G.* 801, Lucr. v. 963.

131. tum resumes the poet's own story which he left at 74.

cui : for the postponement of the relative cf. 44. 8, 51. 5, 62. 13.

aut nihil aut paulo : 'little or not at all', a curiously prosaic phrase, and a curiously unromantic caution, in this context. Latin idiom reverses the English order of terms in such expressions: so Cic. *Fam.* xiv. 4. 1 'certe nihil aut non multum in uita mali uidissemus', *Brut.* 150 'nihil aut non fere multum differunt', *Tusc.* iv. 6 'nulla fere sunt aut pauca admodum', *in Caec.* 41 'aut nemo aut pauci', Hor. *Ep.* i. 15. 33 'nil aut paulum abstulerat'. The phrase is attached to *concedere digna* (with which strict grammar would require *paulum*), as being equivalent in sense to *minor*.

132. lux mea : cf. 160; so Cicero calls his wife *mea lux, meum desiderium, Fam.* xiv. 2. 2.

134. candidus : 'radiant': so Prop. ii. 3. 24 *candidus Amor*. Cupid hovers round these lovers as he does round Acme and Septimius in poem 45.

in tunica : for this use of *in* of costume cf. Prop. iv. 2. 38 'ibo / mundus demissis institor in tunicis' ('a pedlar dressed in a long tunic'); so of other personal accompaniments ('in hastis' Enn. 506 V., 'in iaculis' Virg. *Aen.* v. 37, 'in arcu' Man. ii. 241, 'in anulo', 'wearing a ring', Pliny, *N.H.* xxxiii. 30).

135. tamen etsi : the *tamen* in this combination belongs in sense to the main clause.

Catullo : the poet's reference to himself by name, looking at himself, as it were, from the outside, has always an emotional nuance, sometimes pathetic, as here or in 11. 1, 38. 1, 58. 2, 72. 1, 82. 1, sometimes playful, as in 13. 7, 14. 13, 44. 3. Closely akin to it is the self-address which betrays strong feeling, whether the mood is the excitement of 46. 4 or the indignation of 52. 1 or the despairing courage of 8. 1 and 76. 5. Both are characteristic of Catullus, but they are not unknown to other poets; Ovid knows the pathetic value of using his own name (e.g. *Tr.* iii. 10. 1 'si quis adhuc istic meminit Nasonis adempti', *Pont.* i. 7. 69) and Propertius occasionally addresses himself in self-conscious pride (ii. 8. 17).

136. rara uerecundae : the two words express the same idea in different aspects: 'we shall bear with her affairs since she is circumspect and they are few and far between'. *uerecundia* is the feeling that keeps one from going too far (cf. *uerecundum Bacchum*, Hor. *Od.* i. 27. 3) and offending the susceptibilities of others (Cic. *Off.* i. 99); so in Velleius ii. 33. 3 *uerecundus* is opposed to *immodicus*. Catullus here shuts his

eyes to the fact that her relation with him is as much a
furtum as any; he recognizes it in 143–5.

furta : i.e. *furtiui amores*, as in 140: the first appearance of
the word in this sense, which is common in the elegiac
poets.

erae : i.e. *amicae*: like the common *domina* in the elegiac
poets, the word implies that the relation between lover and
beloved is that between slave and mistress. (For the corresponding use of *dominus* by women cf. Ov. *Am.* iii. 7. 11,
A.A. i. 314.)

137. molesti : 'fussy'; cf. 10. 33.

138. caelicolum : see on 64. 355.

139. concoquit, 'digested her wrath': cf. Cic. *Q.F.* iii. 9. 5 'ut
eius ista odia non sorbeam solum sed etiam concoquam'.

in culpa : 'in the matter of, over, his fault': the use of *in*
is akin to that with personal objects noted on 64. 98.

140. omniuoli : i.e. *omnes uolentis*: formed like *multiuola* (128).

141. componier : for the archaic infinitive cf. 61. 42.

141 f. There does not appear to be any obvious relation between
nec in 141 and *nec* in 143: one is forced to assume a lacuna
between 141 and 142 and cannot conjecture with any assurance what 141 led up to or how 142 is to be interpreted.
142 has generally been taken as developing the thought of
137, 'have done with the unwelcome oppression of the
elderly father', i.e. 'do not be uncompromisingly intolerant'.
tolle is often so used (e.g. Virg. *Aen.* x. 451 *tolle minas*, Hor.
Ep. i. 12. 3 *tolle querellas*), but there is no evidence for the
sense assigned to *onus*, and *tolle* in combination with *onus*
would naturally mean 'take up (the burden)'.

143. nec tamen : presumably 'and anyhow (however that may
be) she is not my wedded wife'; for this common meaning of
et tamen and *nec tamen* cf. Cic. *Sen.* 16 'notum enim vobis
carmen est et tamen ('and anyhow, even if that were not
so') ipsius Appi exstat oratio': examples are collected in
Reid's note on that passage and Munro's on Lucr. v. 1177.

dextra deducta paterna : *deducta* is not used in its technical
sense here (for the bride's father did not take part in the
formal *deductio* to her new home) but in the general sense of
tradita.

144. fragrantem . . . domum : i.e. a bride's new home adorned
to receive her: so *Ciris* 512 (in a similar context) 'non
thalamus Tyrio fragrans accepit amomo'.

Assyrio : *Assyrius* is a frequent epithet of perfumes in the

poets (e.g. Virg. *Ecl.* 4. 25 'Assyrium amomum', Hor. *Od.*
ii. 11. 16 'Assyria nardus', Tib. i. 3. 7 'Assyrii odores') who,
with their usual inaccuracy in matters of oriental geography,
use it as equivalent to *Syrius*, though Syria, the coastal
region of the Levant, and Assyria, the region beyond the
Tigris (the eastern part of modern Iraq), were far apart. The
oriental perfumes and spices used in Rome were produced
not in Syria but in Arabia or farther East, but took the
name Syrian from the fact that they reached Rome from
Syrian ports to which caravans had brought them overland.

145. mira . . . nocte : romantic as the phrase sounds to modern
ears, it can hardly be genuine: Heyse's *muta* is the most
plausible correction.

  munuscula : cf. 64. 103.

147 f. si nobis . . . notat : if the days she gives to me are her red-
letter days, i.e. if I am her favourite.

148. lapide . . . candidiore : see on 107. 6.

  dies : *is datur quem illa dies notat,* for *is datur dies quem
illa notat,* is a violent (and, so far as one can judge, pointless)
hyperbaton: *is datur quem illa diem notat,* on the other hand,
is an example of the not uncommon attraction of an antecedent into the relative clause (cf. 153–4) and the old correction *diem* should probably be accepted.

149. quod potui : 'all I could do': for the parenthetical use cf.
Virg. *Ecl.* 3. 70 'quod potui, puero siluestri ex arbore lecta /
aurea mala decem misi', Ov. *Her.* 8. 5 'quod potui, renui'.

  confectum carmine munus : 'a gift wrought in verse'.

151. uestrum . . . nomen : see on 39. 20 and cf. Cic. *Scaur.* 30 'si
te omen nominis uestri forte duxit', Ov. *Tr.* ii. 65 (to
Augustus) 'inuenies uestri praeconia nominis illic'. In all
three passages a plural reference for *uester* cannot be excluded.

  scabra . . . rubigine : cf. Virg. *Georg.* i. 495 'exesa . . . scabra
rubigine pila'.

152. haec . . . alia : a very prosaic line: for *alia atque alia,* 'one
after another' cf. Lucr. v. 303 'solem . . . putandumst / ex
alio atque alio lucem iactare subortu'.

153. Themis olim : Catullus wishes Allius the blessings of the
golden age when men still observed *pietas* and Themis, i.e.
Justice, still walked the earth and rewarded them: cf. 64. 386
and Aratus *Phaen.* 112 αὐτὴ πότνια λαῶν / μυρία πάντα παρεῖχε
Δίκη, δώτειρα δικαίων.

155. tua uita must mean Allius' wife or his mistress: cf. *mea
uita* in 45. 13, 104. 1, 109. 1.

156. domus . . . domina : if *domina* means *amica* here, the supplement *ipsa* cannot stand: for *lusimus et domina* cannot mean what *lusimus ego et domina* means. ⟨*nos*⟩ *lusimus* would make it possible to take *domina* so, but this line and 68 must go together and here, as there, *domina* should probably be taken as the correlative of *domus*. See on l. 68.

157 f. The second half of l. 157 is clearly corrupt and no solution for it has been found—or is likely to be found in our ignorance of the person to whom *qui* and *quo* refer. Scaliger's ingenious *te tradidit* makes him a friend to whose introduction Catullus owed his acquaintance with Allius, but the suggestions which have been offered for the last word (*auctor*, *auspex*, *Afer*, *Anser*) are implausible. Line 158, unlike 157, is intelligible, but the hiatus at the diaeresis makes it likely that there is corruption here also. The first half of the line is repeated at 66. 49.

159. et longe ante omnes : sc. *felix sit*.
    mihi . . . me carior ipso : cf. Cic. *Att.* iii. 22. 3 'premor desiderio cum omnium rerum tum meorum qui mihi me cariores semper fuerunt', Ov. *Tr.* v. 14. 2 'o mihi me coniunx carior', *Pont.* ii. 8. 27 'patriae nomen quae te tibi carior ipso est'.

160. qua uiua uiuere dulce : cf. Hor. *Epod.* 1. 5 (to Maecenas) 'nos quibus te uita si superstite / iucunda, si contra grauis'.

70

The epigram is reminiscent of Callimachus *Epig.* 25 Pf.

> ὤμοσε Καλλίγνωτος Ἰωνίδι μήποτ' ἐκείνης
> ἕξειν μήτε φίλον κρέσσονα μήτε φίλην.
> ὤμοσεν, ἀλλὰ λέγουσιν ἀληθέα τοὺς ἐν ἔρωτι
> ὅρκους μὴ δύνειν οὔατ' ἐς ἀθανάτων,

and the repetition *dicit . . . dicit* makes it certain that Catullus had that in mind. There is an echo of the first couplet in the anonymous epigram (quoted by Suetonius, *de Gramm.* 18) on the *grammaticus* L. Crassicius Pansa, who wrote a commentary on Cinna's *Zmyrna*:

> uni Crassicio se credere Zmyrna probauit:
>   desinite, indocti, coniugio hanc petere.
> soli Crassicio se dixit nubere uelle
>   intima cui soli nota sua exstiterint.

As Kroll points out, this poem might well be taken to be a literary exercise were it not that Catullus picks up the theme in the clearly personal poem 72.

1. **mulier mea** : commentators compare Plaut. *Bacch.* 842
'meamne hic . . . ut retineat mulierem?', Hor. *Epod.* 12. 23
'magis quem/diligeret mulier sua quam te': but *mulier* here is
suggested by the general *mulier* of l. 3.

   nulli : the substantival use is rare in the republican
period (once in Cicero's letters, twice in Caesar): in Livy and
later prose *nulli* supplants *nemini*.

2. **non si** = *ne tum quidem si*, 'not even if': so again in 48. 5,
69. 3, 88. 8; cf. Lucr. vi. 1075 'dirimi qui non queat unquam, /
non si Neptuni fluctu renouare operam des', Virg. *Georg.* ii.
42 'non ego cuncta meis amplecti uersibus opto, / non mihi
si linguae centum sint', *Aen.* v. 17, Hor. *Od.* ii. 14. 5, Prop.
ii. 30. 2–4. The usage seems to be rare in prose: examples are
Livy vii. 10. 2 (in a speech) 'iniussu tuo numquam pugna-
uerim, non si certam uictoriam uideam', Tac. *Ann.* xiii. 57
'neque exstingui poterant non si imbres caderent'. For *nec
si* in this sense, which is rare in the Ciceronian period but
becomes normal in Silver Latin, see on 66. 73.

   Iuppiter ipse : for the proverbial expression cf. Ov. *Met.*
vii. 801 'nec Iouis illa meo thalamos praeferret amori', *Her.*
4. 36 'Hippolytum uideor praepositura Ioui'. Similarly
Plaut. *Cas.* 323 'negaui ipsi me concessurum Ioui, / si is
mecum oraret'.

4. **uento et rapida . . . aqua** : wind and water appear often
enough in reference to idle words; the usual type of expression is represented by Prop. ii. 28. 8 'quicquid iurarunt
uentus et unda rapit', Ov. *Am.* ii. 16. 45 'uerba puellarum /
. . . irrita qua uisum est uentus et unda ferunt'. Writing in
water (or wind) does not appear elsewhere in Latin, but
Greek uses εἰς ὕδωρ γράφειν (Soph. fr. 741 N.² ὅρκον δ' ἐγὼ γυναικὸς
εἰς ὕδωρ γράφω, Plato, *Phaedr.* 276 c).

72

Catullus tries to convey the quality of his feeling for Lesbia
by a comparison unique in ancient literature: his love for her
was like a father's affection for his children. That pure affection her unfaithfulness has destroyed.

2. **tenere** : 'possess', of an object of desire or affection: cf.
64. 28, Virg. *Ecl.* 1. 31 'dum me Galatea tenebat', Tib. i.
5. 39.

   Iouem : see on 70. 2.

4. **gnatos . . . et generos** : *nati*, like *filii*, may include daughters
even in everyday prose; whether *generi* can (as Kroll says)

include daughters-in-law is very doubtful. No example can be quoted, and the few uses of *patres* for father and mother (if that reading is right at Virg. *Aen.* ii. 579) and *soceri* for father- and mother-in-law (*Aen.* ii. 457, Ov. *Met.* iii. 132) are not parallel: *gener* / *nurus* is not a pair like *pater* / *mater* or *socer* / *socrus*. A modern poet would no doubt have said 'his children' or 'his sons and daughters'. The significant difference is not that Catullus does not do the same (for that more than one obvious reason can be suggested), but that he does include the sons-in-law: that reflects a traditional attitude which puts the sons-in-law within the head of the family's protective concern.

5. nunc te cognoui : 'now, I know you', i.e. I am not deceived any longer.

7. qui potis : 'how it can be ?': this use of the old instrumental form of the interrogative (see on 2. 2) is common in classical prose in the phrases *qui possum*, &c. (e.g. Cic. *Att.* xii. 40. 2 quoted below) and *qui fit*, 'how does it come about?' (e.g. Hor. *Sat.* i. 1. 1). For the use of the corresponding relative form in final clauses ('whereby') see on 116. 3.

   potis is here neuter (as in 76. 24, 115. 3): it is feminine in 65. 3. On the relation between *potis* and *pote* see on 45. 5. For the common ellipse of *fieri* cf. 42. 16 'si non aliud potest', 76. 16 'siue id non pote siue pote', 76. 24 'quod non potis est', Cic. *Att.* xii. 40. 2 'ne doleam? qui potest?', *Tusc.* i. 23 'cuperem utrumque si posset', *Acad.* ii. 121 'negas sine deo posse quicquam'.

   iniuria : so of a mistress's unfaithfulness in Prop. ii. 24*b*. 39 'nil ego non patiar: numquam me iniuria mutat', iv. 8. 27 'cum fieret nostro totiens iniuria lecto', Ov. *Met.* ix. 150 'quantum iniuria possit / femineusque dolor . . . testor'.

8. bene uelle : the feelings of ordinary friendship: cf. Plaut. *Pseud.* 233 'iam diu ego huic bene et hic mihi uolumus et amicitia est antiqua'.

73

The theme of betrayed friendship recalls 30 and 77, but here there is no personal address and no clue to the occasion. The editors quote expressions of the same general thought in Greek —Hom. *Od.* iv. 695, Theog. 1263—but there is no reason to suppose that Catullus had these consciously in mind.

1. quoquam quicquam : cf. 67. 11 'nec peccatum a me quisquam pote dicere quicquam'. The emphatic repetition is common in Plautus: e.g. *Pseud.* 134 'quorum numquam quic-quam quoiquam uenit in mentem ut recte faciant'.

1 f. quoquam . . . aliquem : 'any one (at all) . . . some one (or other)': for the force of the two pronouns in negative or quasi-negative sentences see on 76. 7.

2. pium : cf. 76. 2 and 26.
  fieri : 'show himself', 'turn out to be'.

3. omnia sunt ingrata : (1) 'everything (i.e. everything one does) brings no return': 64. 103 'non ingrata . . . munuscula diuis / promittens', 76. 6 'ingrato amore', Plaut. *Asin.* 136 'ingrata atque irrita esse omnia intellego / quae dedi et quod bene feci', *Epid.* 136 'miserum est ingratum esse homini id quod facias bene', Lucr. iii. 942, 'quod pereat male et in-gratum occidat omne'; or (2) 'the whole world is ungrate-ful': for the generalizing *omnia* cf. 89. 3 'omnia plena puellis', Cic. *Quinct.* 10 'cum ei . . . omnia inimica atque infesta fuerint', *Am.* 52 'omnia semper suspecta atque sollicita'.

  fecisse benigne : 'doing a kindness' so Cic. *Deiot.* 36 'dicere est solitus benigne sibi a populo Romano esse factum', *Leg.* i. 49 'ubi enim beneficus si nemo alterius causa benigne facit ?', *Fam.* xiii. 67. 1 'plurimis in ista prouincia benigne fecisti'.

4. In *V* the line is unmetrical: *immo etiam taedet obestque magisque magis*. Most editors have removed *magisque* and added another verb at the beginning of the line: the oldest supplement, Avantius's *prodest*, is commended by the fre-quent antithesis of *prodesse* and *obesse* of which Ellis gives examples (so Cic. *Mil.* 34 'non modo nihil prodest sed obest etiam Clodi mors Miloni', *Verr.* ii. 2. 169, Ov. *Met.* xi. 320); Munro's *iam iuuat* also gives good sense. But it is per-haps better to take *nihil fecisse benigne* as an independent sentence (with or without Friedrich's addition ⟨*est*⟩), and adopting Avantius's alternative supplement to read *immo etiam* ⟨*taedet*⟩, *taedet obestque magis*. *nihil est* 'it is no good' is a colloquial idiom (Plaut. *Capt.* 344 'nihil est ignotum ad illum mittere: operam luseris'; *Cas.* 286 'nihil est me cupere factum', *Truc.* 769 'de nihilo nihil est irasci') and the repe-tition of *taedet* is in Catullus' manner (cf. 38. 1 f., 107. 4 f.).

  magis : 'instead': cf. 68. 30 'non est turpe, magis miserum est'. Examples like these or Prop. ii. 3. 53 'quem non lucra, magis Pero formosa coegit', Virg. *Ecl.* 1. 11 'non equidem inuideo, miror magis', show how readily *magis* could become in later Latin an adversative particle, the ancestor of Ital. *ma* and Fr. *mais*.

6. **unum atque unicum** : the phrase has an archaic ring: it is not found in extant comedy (though Plaut. *Asin.* 208 has the similar 'me unice unum ex omnibus te atque illam amare aibas'), but recurs in the archaizing Gellius, xviii. 4. 2 'se unum et unicum lectorem esse enarratoremque Sallustii' (cf. Apul. *Met.* iv. 31 'idque unum et pro omnibus unicum').

75

The mood of disillusioned resignation is like that of 72 and Catullus repeats his pathetic paradox. He must still love Lesbia whatever her sins: he cannot have regard for her though she turn saint.

1. **huc est . . . deducta . . . ut** : 'my mind has been brought to the point that', of an unwelcome necessity; cf. Val. Max. viii. 1. abs. 6 'satis iam graues eum poenas sociis dedisse arbitrati sunt huc deductum necessitatis ut abicere se tam suppliciter . . . cogeretur'.

   mea has usually been taken with *Lesbia*; in spite of his disillusionment she is still *mea* to Catullus, as she was in 5. 1; so in the bitter 11. 15 she is still *mea puella*. But *mens* needs the epithet and the juxtaposition of *tua mea* is more effective so.

   culpa : cf. 11. 22, 68. 139.

2. **se officio perdidit . . . suo** : 'brought itself to disaster by its own devotion': Ovid makes a similar point in *Am.* iii. 3. 38 (of Semele) 'officio est illi poena reperta suo'.

3 f. **bene uelle . . . amare** : cf. 72. 8.

4. **omnia si facias** : 'though you should do anything', i.e. stop at nothing, do the worst imaginable.

76

The mental conflict which is conveyed with epigrammatic conciseness in three short poems, 72, 75, and 85, is here presented in an elegy. The soliloquy recalls that of poem 8; there also Catullus alternates between dwelling on the past and bracing himself to an effort of will. But here it is not the happiness of the past that he remembers, but his faithfulness which has been betrayed; here he has passed beyond recrimination and is obsessed by his own undeserved suffering. Here his despair is final and there is no thought of reconciliation: his only hope is that the gods will pity him and help him to master himself.

1. benefacta : i.e. his own good deeds, *fecisse benigne* of 73. 3.

2. pium : cf. 73. 2: *pietas*, 'grauissimum et sanctissimum nomen' (Cic. *Fam.* i. 9. 1), is conformity to divine will and consists both in the rendering of due service to the gods and in the due performance of those duties in human society, in a man's relations with his family, his friends, his fellow-citizens, which have divine sanction.

3. fidem . . . foedere : the same combination occurs in 87. 3 'nulla fides ullo fuit umquam foedere tanta'; but there the *fides* of the lover's contract is uppermost in Catullus' thought, while here the reference is more general. *Fides* is the principle of keeping one's word (see on 30. 11): it is *sancta*, protected by divine ordinance against violation.

    nec foedere nullo : a pleonastic negative after *neque* is not uncommon in comedy (e.g. Plaut. *Rud.* 359 'nec te aleator nullus est sapientior', *Pseud.* 136 'neque ego homines magis asinos numquam uidi': see Löfstedt, *Syntactica* ii. 210) and the simple ablative *foedere* is paralleled in 87. 3 (quoted above). But the easy corrections, *in ullo* here and *unquam in foedere* at 87. 3 are tempting. The similar pleonasm at 48. 4 *nec numquam uidear satur futurus* is more dubious, since the two negatives are not separated, and Statius's *nec mi unquam* is probable.

4. numine abusum : i.e. by swearing deceitfully: cf. Cic. *de Domo* 125 'ementiri, fallere, abuti deorum immortalium numine ad hominum timorem quid uoluisti?'. For a useful account of the meaning and usage of *numen* see Bailey, *Religion in Virgil*, 60 ff.

5 f. manent . . . tibi : 'are laid up in store for you': cf. 8. 15.

    in longa aetate seems to mean little more than 'all your life long': the implication is not that length of days is the reward of virtue but that the pleasures of conscious rectitude will fill even a long life.

6. hoc ingrato . . . amore : this love of mine which has brought no return: cf. 73. 3 'omnia sunt ingrata' and passages quoted in the note there.

7. cuiquam : 'to any single person'. The usage of *quisquam* is most neatly illustrated by (*a*) the line of Publilius quoted by Sen. *Dial.* ix. 11. 8 'cuiuis potest accidere quod cuiquam potest', 'what can happen to any single individual can happen to anyone at all' and (*b*) Cic. *post Red. in Sen.* 30 'difficile est non aliquem, nefas quemquam praeterire', 'it is difficult not to leave out someone or other; it is wrong to leave out any single person'. (See Nettleship, *Contributions to Latin Lexicography*, 126; Krebs–Schmalz i. 140; Draeger i². 89, 97.) This implication accounts for the frequency of *quisquam* in negative and quasi-negative sentences (e.g. 22. 18, 73. 1) and in conditional clauses (e.g. 96. 1, 98. 1, 102. 1, Cic. *Fam.* vi. 14. 1 'si quisquam est timidus in magnis periculosisque rebus, . . . is ego sum ').

9. **omnia quae :** Catullus has the same prosaic connexion again at 64. 66, Lucretius at ii. 321, 1033.

   perierunt credita : 'have been thrown away', 'have gone for nothing'. The metaphor is from a bad investment: cf. Sen. *Ben.* i. 1. 1 'sequitur ut male collocata (beneficia) male debeantur, de quibus non redditis sero querimur: ista enim perierunt cum darentur'. Plautus has *interire* in a similar context, *Poen.* 635 'malo si quid bene facias, beneficium interit'; cf. 14. 11 *dispereunt.*

10. **iam te cur amplius :** *cur te iam amplius* is the reading of *V*; the hiatus at the diaeresis is intolerable (especially since *iam* is elided in ll. 18 and 23 of this poem) and the fault should be removed here as it has been at 66. 48, 67. 44, and 99. 8; at 68. 158 (which has defied correction) the text is dubious on other grounds. The old transposition *iam te cur* restores the metre but unidiomatically separates *iam* and *amplius*, which are regularly placed together in verse as in prose (e.g. Cic. *Att.* ix. 7. 7, *Cat.* i. 6, Virg. *Aen.* iii. 192, 260, v. 8, xi. 807); Baehrens's *cur tete iam* respects both metre and idiom.

11. **animo offirmas :** the change to *animum*, accepted by many editors, is unnecessary. The phrase *animum offirmare* is used by Plautus (*Merc.* 82) and Pliny (*Ep.* vii. 27. 8), but *offirmare* is used intransitively in comedy (e.g. Plaut. *Stich.* 68 'quid agimus, soror, si offirmabit pater aduorsum nos?', Ter. *Eun.* 217 'censen posse me offirmare et perpeti ne redeam?') and Catullus may well have used it so with the local ablative *animo* ('stiffen in your mind'). Ovid *Met.* ix. 745 'quin animum firmas teque ipsa recolligis?' looks like a reminiscence of this line but affords no support for *animum* here since his substitution of *firmare* (which is not used intransitively) for *offirmare* made the accusative necessary for him.

   istinc teque reducis: if the text is sound, *atque* connects *offirmas* with the pair of verbs *reducis* and *desinis*, which are themselves more closely linked by *-que . . . et*, *-que* being attached to the second word in its clause as it is in 57. 2 (the only other example in Catullus, but the usage is common in

Lucretius: see Munro on Lucr. ii. 1050). Catullus has *-que . . .
et* elsewhere, joining a pair of nouns, at 28. 5 (*frigoraque et
famem*) and 44. 15 (*otioque et urtica*), but the structure which
has to be assumed here seems very unlikely. Ellis's *te ipse*
is what Catullus might be expected to have written: cf. Ov.
Tr. v. 7. 65 (below) and *Met.* ix. 745 (above).

istinc : 'from where you are', as often in comedy: for **te
reducis** cf. Ov. *Tr.* v. 7. 65 'meque ipse reduco / a contem-
platu semoueoque mali'.

12. dis inuitis . . . esse miser : i.e. to hold to this love which
causes his unhappiness is flying in the face of heaven. Ovid
repeats the phrase, *Rem. Am.* 657 'odio qui finit amorem, /
aut amat aut aegre desinet esse miser'.

14. efficias : 'this is what you must secure': so *facias* in 16; for
the jussive subjunctive taking the place of an imperative
see on 8. 1.

15. una salus haec est : 'this is your one deliverance', with the
normal 'attraction' of the pronoun as in Virg. *Aen.* vi. 129
'hoc opus, hic labor est', Ov. *Her.* 2. 56 'debuit haec meriti
summa fuisse mei', cf. 83. 2, 5.

peruincendum : the spondaic ending, which is common in
the hexameters of poem 64, where it reproduces a hellenistic
mannerism (see on 64. 3), is much less common in the
elegiacs: here it clearly conveys the notion of effort.

16. hoc . . . pote : 'this is what you must do, possible or impossible': for this 'polar expression', in which a sweeping
statement is made by the use of two opposite terms of which
only one is properly applicable, cf. Plaut. *Trin.* 360 'comedit
quod fuit quod non fuit', Sen. *Medea* 567 'incipe / quicquid
potes, Medea, quicquid non .potes'. So in Greek, Soph. *Ant.*
1108 ἴτ', ἴτ', ὀπάονες, / οἵ τ' ὄντες οἵ τ' ἀπόντες, *El.* 305 τὰς οὔσας τέ
μου / καὶ τὰς ἀπούσας ἐλπίδας διέφθορεν.

siue pote : For the form *pote* see on 45. 5; for the omission
of *fieri* see on 72. 7.

**17–26. o di, si uestrum est . . . aspicite . . . reddite mi hoc pro
pietate mea** : for the prayer formula cf. Virg. *Aen.* i. 603–5
'di tibi, si qua pios respectant numina, si quid / usquam
iustitia est et mens sibi conscia recti, / praemia digna ferant';
ii. 689–91 'Iuppiter omnipotens, precibus si flecteris ullis, /
aspice nos—hoc tantum—et, si pietate meremur, / da deinde
auxilium', v. 687–9. The *si*-clause which is regular in such
appeals, far from implying any doubt in the petitioner's
mind, expresses his confidence in the power which he invokes.

18. extremam . . . opem : 'brought aid at the last'.

19. **puriter** : the old form of the adverb is appropriate to the language of prayer: at 39. 14 it is in a solemn formula facetiously used.

20. **pestem perniciemque** : the same alliterative combination in Cic. *Rab. Perd.* 2 'pestem ac perniciem ciuitatis', *Cat.* i. 33, *Off.* ii. 51.

21. **subrepens . . . ut torpor** : 'creeping like a paralysis': cf. 77. 3 *subrepsti.*

22. **ex omni pectore** : 'from the whole of my heart', i.e. completely from my heart: for the idiom see on 68. 25.

23. **non iam** : 'at this stage I do not ask'.
    contra : 'in return': cf. Plaut. *Amph.* 655 'quae me amat, quam contra amo', *M.G.* 101.

24. **potis** may be either impersonal, with *fieri* understood (cf. 16 above), or personal, with *facere* understood: for the form see on 45. 5.

77

The theme of the false friend has already appeared in 30 and 73. Here the charge is explicit; Rufus has stolen Catullus' love from him. On the identification of Rufus with M. Caelius Rufus see Introd., pp. xv f.

1. **frustra ac nequiquam** : *frustra* usually emphasizes the disappointment of the agent, *nequiquam* the failure of his object, but no hard and fast distinction can be drawn between the words. *nequiquam* was an old-fashioned word which was disappearing from ordinary use in Catullus' time.
    credite amice : 'believed my friend', *qui creditus es amicus.* The personal use of *credor* with a complement is common: e.g. Ov. *F.* ii. 176 'quae fuerat uirgo credita, mater erat', iv. 344 'credita uix tandem teste pudica deā', *Her.* 9. 150 'cur Herculis uxor / credar', Livy i. 39. 6 'ut serua natus crederetur'. Here the predicate inevitably follows the case of *credite*: for a similar attraction cf. Prop. ii. 15. 2 'lectule deliciis facte beate meis'.

2. **frustra? immo** : 'all for nothing, did I say? No, to my own great cost and sorrow'.
    cum : cf. 40. 8 'cum longa . . . poena', Plaut. *Rud.* 710 'iniqua haec patior cum pretio tuo', *Bacch.* 503 'illa illud hercle cum malo fecit suo'.

3. **sicine** (from *si-ce-ne*: *sic* was originally a disyllable, *sice, -ce* being the deictic particle which also appears in *hic*) introduces a reproachful, disillusioned question, 'Is this how . . . ?'

cf. 64. 132 'sicine me . . . auectam . . . liquisti?', Plaut. *Rud.*
884 sicine me spernis?', *Pseud.* 320 'sicine mihi abs te bene
merenti male refertur gratia?', *Persa* 42 'sicine hoc te mi
facere?', Cic. *Flacc.* 81 'sicine tu eum cui tu in consilio
fuisses . . . in discrimen uocauisti?', Prop. ii. 15. 8 'sicine,
lente, iaces?'

subrepsti : cf. 76. 21 *subrepens*; for the syncopated form see
on 14. 14 *misti*.

4. **ei misero** : cf. 68. 92 'ei misero frater adempte mihi'. *ei
mihi* and *ei misero mihi* are common as parenthetical
exclamations in comedy, but here, as in 68. 92, *misero* comes
within the structure of the sentence and *ei* stands by itself
as an ejaculation emphasizing *misero*: *miser* is often strengthened by an interjection (64. 71 'a misera', Tib. i. 8. 23 'quid
queror heu misero carmen nocuisse ?').

omnia . . . bona : 'my whole happiness'; cf. 68. 158.

6. **pestis amicitiae** : 'blight of our friendship' (*amicitia* picking
up the *amice* of l. 1) rather than 'of my love' (for *amicitia*
taking the place of *amor* cf. 96. 4, 109. 6). *pestis* thus used of
persons is common (e.g. Cic. *Sest.* 33 'peste patriae', 65
'huius imperii pestibus'). *uenenum* is naturally used in the
same way; this use is not found elsewhere, but cf. Varr. *R.R.*
i. 2. 18.

81

For Iuventius see on 24.

1–2. 'Was no *bellus homo* to be found among all those people for
you to fall in love with?'

1. in tanto . . . populo : i.e. at Rome, an emphatic colloquialism: cf. Cic. *Rab. Post.* 45 'ecquis est e tanto populo qui . . .
uelit?', *de Domo* 108 'ciuis est nemo tanto in populo . . . qui
non . . . me defenderit?'; similarly Hor. *Sat.* i. 6. 79 'in magno
ut populo'.

2. bellus homo : cf. 24. 7 'non est homo bellus', and see on 22. 9.

nemo . . . homo : the combination is frequent in comedy and
in Cicero (e.g. *N.D.* ii. 96 'ut per biduum nemo hominem
homo agnosceret', *Fam.* xiii. 55. 1 'ut hominem neminem
pluris faciam'), the origin of *nemo* in the compound *ne-hemo*
(an alternative form of *homo*) being disregarded.

diligere inciperes : an emphatic periphrasis of familiar
language ('go and fall in love with'): similarly with *uelle* and
nolle (Virg. *Aen.* vi. 751 'incipiant . . . uelle reuerti', Sen.
Apoc. 14. 2, Petr. 98. 8).

3. **moribunda ab sede** : Pisaurum was an old Roman colony in Umbria, on the Adriatic; that it was now in decline is confirmed by the fact that a new body of settlers was sent to it in 43 B.C. *sede Pisauri* has a mock-heroic ring: cf. Virg. *Aen.* iii. 687 'ab sede Pelori / missus adest'.

4. **hospes** : i.e., presumably, a visitor to Rome: cf. Cic. *Mil.* 33 'uos soli ignoratis, uos hospites in hac urbe uersamini?', Hor. *Sat.* ii. 4. 10 'ede hominis nomen simul et Romanus an hospes'.

inaurata . . . statua : gilding of bronze statues was common: so Cic. *Cat.* iii. 19 'Romulus quem inauratum in Capitolio . . . fuisse meministis', *Pis.* 25 'me inaurata statua (Campani) donarant', *Phil.* v. 41.

pallidior : *pallidus* and *palleo* correspond to our 'pale' in representing the effect of emotion or disease on the complexion; but, unlike 'pale', they are not mere negations of colour but positive colour-words connoting a yellowish shade: their force is most clearly seen in Prop. iv. 7. 82 'numquam . . . pallet ebur', where *pallet* refers to a colour not lighter but darker than the normal, that of white ivory yellowing with age, or in Pliny, *N.H.* x. 144 'ouorum alia sunt candida, ut columbis, alia pallida, ut aquaticis', where the contrast is between pure white eggs and darkish ones. So *palleo* and *pallidus* are used of yellow pansies (Virg. *Ecl.* 2. 47), of yellow-leaved ivy (*Ecl.* 3. 39), of moss (Ov. *Met.* i. 374 'fastigia turpi / pallebant musco'), of box-wood (Pliny, *N.H.* xvi. 70), and often of gold (Ov. *Met.* xi. 110 'tollit humo saxum, saxum quoque palluit auro', 'was yellow with gold', Mart. viii. 44. 10 'arca palleat nummis', 'the cash-box is yellow with coins'). And since the tint of a sallow complexion turned pale is yellowish (Hor. *Epod.* 10. 16 'pallor luteus'), it is to gold, not to a linen sheet or to snow, that it is compared. For this comparison cf. 64. 100 'magis fulgore expalluit auri', Stat. *Silv.* iv. 7. 15 (of the gold-miner) 'pallidus fossor redit erutoque / concolor auro': the cliché *buxo pallidior* is also common.

6. **quod** : *quid* of the manuscripts is hardly supported by the rare examples in early Latin of *quid* with adjectival force in place of the normal *quod*: so Plaut. *Poen.* 829 'quid illuc est genus, quae illic hominum corruptelae fiunt!' (Observe that while the distinction between substantival *quid* and adjectival *quod* is regularly observed, there is no corresponding distinction between *quis* and *qui*: see on 61. 46.)

facinus facias : see on 110. 4.

82

Catullus appeals to Quintius not to take his love away from him. From poem 100 it appears that Quintius is a Veronese: how he comes into the story of Catullus and Lesbia we cannot guess, but the poem reads as if Lesbia were meant.

2. si quid carius est : this characteristic turn appears again at 13. 10, 22. 13, 42. 14. For *carius oculis* cf. 3. 5, 14. 1, 104. 2.

3. ei : monosyllabic, as sometimes in Plautus: elsewhere in Plautus and always in Lucretius the word is spondaic (i.e. is scanned *ēï-ï*, though only one *i* is written). The oblique cases of the colourless *is* are in general avoided in later verse, which prefers the stronger demonstratives; the dative is not used either by Virgil or by the elegiac poets. Cf. 84. 5 and see B. Axelson, *Unpoetische Wörter*, pp. 70 ff.

　ei . . . illi : referring to the same person; the change from *is* in a principal clause to *ille* in a subordinate one is normal idiom: see Reid on Cic. *Amic.* 59.

3–4. 'What is far more precious to him than his eyes or than anything there is more precious than his eyes': for the single *seu* equivalent to *uel si* see on 13. 10.

83

If Lesbia is the famous Clodia (see Introd., pp. xiv ff.), this poem must be earlier than the death of Clodia's husband, Q. Metellus Celer, in 59 B.C. For the point cf. 92.

1. mi . . . mala plurima dicit : cf. Plaut. *Cist.* 233 'mala multa dici mihi uolo', Cic. *Att.* viii. 5. 1 'multa mala cum dixisset—suo capiti ut aiunt'.

2. haec . . . laetitia est : 'this is sheer delight to him'. For the idiomatic 'attraction' of the pronoun cf. 5 below 'quae multo acrior est res', 76. 15 'una salus haec est'.

3. mule : the mule was notorious in ancient as in modern times for *tarditas indomita* (Pliny, *N.H.* viii. 171): as a type of stupidity it does not appear elsewhere, unless Juv. 16. 23 *mulino corde Vagelli*, where the meaning is uncertain, has that implication. But the reference here must be to insensibility: a reference to childlessness (though it would be true) would have no point in the context. Garrod's suggestion (*C.R.* xxxiii [1919], 67) that *mule* is intended as an easily penetrable disguise for *Metelle* is based on dubious premisses (*Metellus*, like many *cognomina*, is a common noun, but Festus's statement that it means *mercennarius* may be

right in spite of his derivation of it from *metallum* and the case
for the meaning 'pack-horse' is not proved) and assumes too
elaborate an artifice (*pulcer* at 79. 1, if it is a reference to
Clodius' cognomen, is much more obvious).

nihil sentis : 'you are not alive to anything'; cf. 17. 20.

4. **sana** : i.e. free from the *morbus* of love: cf. Tib. (Sulp.) iv.
6. 17 'uritur ut celeres urunt altaria flammae / nec, liceat
quamuis, sana fuisse uelit'; Ov. *Rem. Am.* 493 'et sanum
simula ne si quid forte dolebis / sentiat.'

gannit : properly of a dog's growl or snarl: for the use of
a human being cf. Ter. *Ad.* 556 'quid ille gannit ?', Afran. fr.
283 R. 'gannire ad aurem numquam didici dominicam', Mart.
v. 60. 2 'gannitibus improbis lacessas'; similarly *oggannire*
in Plaut. *Asin.* 422 '. . . quin centiens eadem imperem atque
ogganiam', Ter. *Phorm.* 1030.

quod gannit : the *quod*-clause is adverbial, 'as for her
snarling': cf. 10. 28, 68. 27.

6. **hoc est, uritur et loquitur** : 'that is to say' (summing up the
situation) 'she is burning with passion and so she talks'. To
modern taste *loquitur* is a weak repetition which makes the
epigram lame. Hence the correction of Dousa and Lipsius,
coquitur, accepted by some editors: for *coquo* in this sense
cf. Enn. *Ann.* 336 V. 'curam . . . quae nunc te coquit', Plaut.
Trin. 225 'egomet me coquo et macero et defetigo', Virg.
Aen. vii. 345 'femineae ardentem curaeque iraeque coque-
bant'. *hoc est* will then explain *meminit . . . iratast*: she has
not forgotten me (*meminit—uritur*) and she is worked up
about it (*irata est—coquitur*). But the repetitions in 82. 2–4
and 103. 2–4 are just as weak and *coquitur* is over-ingenious.

84

Arrius is a parvenu of humble origin who is uncertain of his
aspirates and in his efforts to imitate educated speech inserts
them in the wrong places. There is no reason to suppose that
the joke is more complicated.

The question of aspirates was exercising philologists in
Catullus' time; Gellius (xiii. 6. 3) preserves a remark of the
grammarian Nigidius Figulus, *rusticus fit sermo si aspires
perperam*, and in his work on Analogy Caesar had a section *de
uerborum aspirationibus*. Both in the matter of aspirated consonants and in that of simple aspirates they had reason for
their inquiries and Arrius for his mistakes.

1. The aspirated consonants (i.e. consonants pronounced
with an explosion of breath after them, as English stops are

pronounced by many Irish speakers of English) which were characteristic of the parent Indo-Germanic language and were preserved in Greek, were lost in primitive Latin, and borrowed Greek words which contained them were for long transliterated into Latin without the aspirate (so *Aciles, teatrum*). By Catullus' time practice had changed and the aspirate was introduced not only in borrowings from Greek but also in a number of words such as *triumphus, Gracchus, pulcher,* in which it had no justification. The change is first seen in inscriptions in the middle of the second century B.C.; in the first it was well established. Cicero (*Orator* 160) says that with reluctance and without conviction he had himself accepted the new convention in some words, though he declined to countenance such novelties as *lachrima, sepulchrum,* and *Otho,* and Quintilian (i. 5. 20), who refers to this poem as well known (*Catulli nobile epigramma*), says that in a short time after the introduction of the aspirate *nimius usus* had extended it to *corona, centurio,* and *praeco.* The unlettered had some excuse for uncertainty in a matter in which educated practice was neither consistent nor stable, and popular inscriptions show spellings like *phius* and *marithus.*

2. The initial aspirate *h-* was an original sound in Latin, representing the I.E. *gh* which is represented in Greek by χ: in Latin the guttural was lost while the aspirate survived. But it was highly volatile and in popular speech it disappeared; its traces were so uncertain that grammarians had to invoke the occurrence of *f-* in Sabine forms to prove the existence of *h-* in such words as *harena, hircus* (so Varro, quoted by Velius Longus, vii. 69. 4–10 K.), *hortus,* and *holus.* In this matter too there was inconsistency: an intrusive *h-* found its way into *umidus* (in which Varro, *L.L.* v. 24 supports it by a false etymology) and *avere* (to omit the aspirate in that word was pedantic in Quintilian's time, i. 6. 21), whereas the original *h-* of *anser* had been so completely effaced by popular usage that it was never written. The speaker of Latin who dropped aspirates which the intelligentsia pronounced incurred a social stigma, as he still did four centuries after this (hating one's fellow man, says Augustine, is less regarded than dropping the aspirate of *homo*: *Conf.* i. 18); then, as now, the man who wanted to improve his position might self-consciously overdo them and make it worse.

Theories which refer Arrius' mispronunciations to Etruscan origin (A. J. Bell in *C.R.* xxix [1915], 137) or to his having Venetic as his mother tongue (E. Harrison, ib. 198) are unconvincing and unnecessary. The status of the aspirate in Rome itself, from such evidence as we have, appears to have been not very different from its status in modern England, where most dialects (including that of the metropolis) have lost initial *h-*

but educated speech has preserved it, with a few exceptions which appear capricious to all but students of language. The English Arrius even now, in spite of the effects of education and broadcasting, is not unknown (a Scottish Arrius is impossible, since in Scotland *h-* is universally pronounced—a fact which has had considerable social implications) and Catullus' epigram, *mutatis mutandis*, would have had its appeal to social prejudice in England fifty years ago.

[See Lindsay, *Lat. Lang.* 55–59; Kühner i. 41–43; Stolz–Schmalz 130, 138; Sommer, *Handb.* 192–5, 199–201.]

Arrius was long ago identified with the ranting advocate Q. Arrius whom Cicero cites (*Brut.* 242) as an example of what a man without birth, gifts, or training can do by energy and readiness to take his opportunities: 'hic enim rebus infimo loco natus et honores et pecuniam et gratiam consecutus etiam sine doctrina sine ingenio in patronorum aliquem numerum peruenerat'. The identification is certainly possible. Q. Arrius was praetor before 63 and was still alive in 52, when Pompey's judiciary law imposed on advocates standards of relevance and restraint which put him out of business. If Catullus' Arrius was a familiar figure in the courts, *requierunt omnibus aures* would have particular point. Cicero says that Q. Arrius played second fiddle to Crassus ('fuit M. Crassi quasi secundarum'); he may have gone to the East with Crassus in 55 B.C. and, if he is Catullus' Arrius, *in Syriam misso* might be so explained. Another member of the *gens*, one C. Arrius, appears in two of Cicero's letters of 59 B.C. as one of a pair of his neighbours at Formiae who give him too much of their company. Writing to Atticus of their visits, Cicero says 'uides quibus hominibus aures sint deditae meae' (*Att.* ii. 14. 2); if he must have company, he would prefer to be 'cum rusticis potius quam cum his perurbanis' (*Att.* ii. 15. 3). 'aures' and 'perurbanis' might tempt one to find Catullus' Arrius here, but Cicero is speaking of Arrius' conversation, not of his habits of speech.

1. **chommoda . . . hinsidias :** if there is point in the choice of these particular words, both having a wide variety of meaning, it is lost on us.

    si quando . . . uellet : a number of examples of the subjunctive taking the place of the normal indicative in what appear to be frequentative clauses are adduced from republican Latin: see Kühn.–Steg. ii. 206 and literature there cited. Most of the examples follow *cum* in past time and in these the subjunctive is readily explained by the assumption that a relation not merely temporal but circumstantial was present to the author's mind. In the few examples after *si* the subjunctive is perhaps best explained as emphasizing the notion of contingency. (In some, e.g. Caes. *B.C.* iii. 110. 4 'si quis a domino prehenderetur consensu militum eripiebatur', Sall. *Iug.* 58. 3 'sin Numidae propius adcessissent ibi uero uirtutem ostendere', the subjunctive might be explained as conveying 'reported thought', but that explanation would not fit the present case and others.) It is natural to seek to relate the use with past tenses after *si* to the similar use of the present subjunctive in such cases as Cic. *Part. Or.* 72 'id fit si factis uerbis . . . aut translatis frequenter utamur'. (See Handford, *The Latin Subjunctive*, 176–9 for an attempt to reconstruct the history of the usages.) Catullus has the subjunctive after *ubi* in a frequentative clause at 63. 67.

3. sperabat : 'flattered himself'.

4. quantum poterat : with all the force of his lungs: Arrius not only gets his aspirates wrong but makes the most of them.

5. credo sic mater : as *credo* shows, the explanation is ironical. Arrius must have inherited his idiosyncracies on his mother's side, for women notoriously preserve purity of speech. For this belief see Plato, *Cratylus* 418b, Cic. *Brut.* 211, *de Or.* iii. 45 'facilius enim mulieres incorruptam antiquitatem conseruant, quod multorum sermonis expertes ea tenent semper quae prima didicerunt': Crassus's mother-in-law Laelia 'sono ipso uocis ita recto et simplici est ut nihil ostentationis aut imitationis adferre uideatur: ex quo sic locutum esse eius patrem iudico, sic maiores'.

liber : if right, must be an innuendo, implying that Arrius' maternal family was servile but that his maternal uncle made pretensions to free birth. None of the proper names which have been suggested to replace it has any probability.

eius : the genitive occurs only here in Catullus (at 64. 109 *V*'s *eius* is corrupt): as Bentley showed on Hor. *Od.* iii. 11. 18, it is avoided in epic, but Propertius twice ends an elegiac hexameter with it (iv. 2. 35, 6. 67) and Ovid once (*Tr.* iii. 4. 27). See on 82. 3 *ei*.

7. misso would naturally refer to an official journey; see p. 375.

8. leniter et leuiter : *leniter*, 'smoothly, without jarring on the ear'; *leuiter*, either 'softly, in a low tone' (see on 64. 273) or 'trippingly, without undue emphasis'. The same collocation is quoted from Gellius xviii. 9. 7 'ueteres non inseque sed insece dixerunt credo quia erat lenius leuiusque': there *leuius* (if it is *lĕu-* and not *lēu-*) must have the second meaning. For *leniter* cf. Cic. *Brut.* 259 (of Catulus) 'suauitas uocis et lenis appellatio litterarum (i.e. enunciation of sounds) bene loquendi famam confecerat'. For the idiom which attaches

to a verb of hearing an adverb which we should regard as
applicable to a verb of speaking cf. Virg. *Aen*. ii. 11 'breuiter
Troiae supremum audire laborem': so in Greek, Dem. vi. 6
ἀκοῦσαί μου διὰ βραχέων, Plato, *Hipp. Mai.* 300e ἀλλά μου σαφέ-
στερον ἄκουσον ὃ βούλομαι λέγειν.

9. **postilla** seems to have had a shorter literary life than the
parallel forms *posthac* and *postea* and appears here for the
last time.

11. **Ionios fluctus** : the Adriatic, which Arrius would cross from
Brundisium on his way to the East. It is unlikely that *Hionios*
is meant to suggest χιονέους (E. Harrison, *C.R.* xxix [1915],
198); the treatment of χ as a spirant in Greek was probably
not general by this time; and if a play on χ- and *c*-, like that on
χαλκός and *excalceare* recorded by Porph. ad Hor. *Sat*. i. 8. 39,
was possible, it follows that a play on χ- and *h*- was not. D. M.
Jones (*Proc. Class. Ass*. liii [1956], 26) suggests that the point
of the joke lies in the fact that the same words (*leuis, lenis,
asper, spiritus*) can be applied to the phenomena of weather
and to those of speech: the result of Arrius' scattering aspirates on the Adriatic is a rough sea. But the contrast is between the temporary calm which educated ears were enjoying
on Arrius' departure and the message which suddenly shatters
it with a new blast of mis-aspiration.

85

Hellenistic epigrams turn the theme of hate and love in a
variety of ingenious ways (e.g. Philodemus, *A.P.* v. 107,
Euenus, *A.P.* xii. 172), but this couplet owes nothing to these
conceits. Even if the paradox of the disillusioned lover was a
τόπος, as it may have been, the sheer simplicity of the words,
'ces paroles négligées', as Fénelon called them, 'où le cœur
saisi parle seul dans une espèce de désespoir', is worlds away
from convention. An element of formal art, of course, there is:
the anticipated question (cf. 72. 7) is a familiar part of the poet's
technique, as it is of the orator's. But the conversational idiom
of *quare id faciam* (standing for *quare oderim et amem*: cf.
Hor. *Sat*. i. 1. 63 'iubeas miserum esse, libenter / quatenus id
facit') is the guarantee of sincerity.

86

Lesbia is compared with a meaner beauty, Quintia, perhaps
a Veronese and a relative of the Quintius of 82 and 100. This

time the rival is not *pour rire*, like the provincial belle of poem 43. She has her points, but she is not in Lesbia's class; Lesbia is not only *pulcra* but *formosa*, since to her beauty is added charm.

In a study of the history of *formosus* (*Rev. de Phil.* xxi [1947], 65) A. Ernout suggests that the word came into use late, at a time when aesthetic appreciation was developing under Greek influence—he notes that Plautus has only one example of it against 32 of *pulcer*—and observes that while *pulc(h)er* is a general term which may have, and often has, non-physical and even moral applications, *formosus* is confined to physical beauty. The facts are hardly so simple. Cicero can apply the two adjectives in the same breath to an object as concrete as a cylinder or a cone (*N.D.* i. 24) or to one as abstract as *uirtus* itself (*Fam.* ix. 14. 4). The one Plautine instance of *formosus* is applied to a goat, and in Varro *formosus* is a regular term of the stockbreeder, in whose practical vocabulary horses, lambs, chickens, pigs, donkeys, and even fish are *formosi*. Here in Catullus there is a clear distinction between the words, but a very different one. *Formosus* implies *pulchritudo* and something else as well, *sal* or *uenus*, piquancy, subtlety, attractiveness. Catullus puts a new value on a word which his contemporaries could use of objects as incompatible with *uenus* as a geometrical solid or a prize sow, and gives it an esoteric implication in the aesthetic vocabulary of a sophisticated society. Seneca makes a similar point, that the quality which *formosus* represents resides in a whole person, not in details (*Ep.* 33. 5 'non est formosa cuius crus laudatur aut bracchium sed illa cuius uniuersa facies admirationem partibus singulis abstulit'); that is part of Catullus' definition, but Seneca does not think in terms of *uenus*. It is relevant to note, as Ernout does, that the sensuous *formosus* is a favourite word in the *Eclogues* (it is applied to persons more than a dozen times, *pulcher* only once) but is absent from the *Aeneid*, in which *pulcher* is worked very hard and its function is sometimes merely ornamental.

1. **multis** : 'in many people's eyes'. For this use of the dative of the person judging cf. Hor. *Ep.* i. 19. 45 'tibi pulcher', [Quint.] *Decl.* 18. 9 'quis enim non est formosus filius matri?'

1 f. **candida, longa, / recta** : she has a good complexion; she is tall (cf. Ov. *Am.* ii. 4. 33 'tu quia tam longa es ueteres heroidas aequas', iii. 3. 8 'longa decensque fuit'); she is well-made (cf. 10. 20; Prop. ii. 34. 46 'despicit et magnos recta puella deos'). Varro has the same combination, *Sat.*

432 Büch. 'amiculam . . . proceram candidam teneram formosam'; cf. Hor. *Sat.* i. 2. 123 'candida rectaque sit, munda
hactenus ut neque longa / nec magis alba uelit quam dat
natura uideri'.

2. **haec ego sic singula confiteor :** 'these points, as I have mentioned them (*sic*), I admit'. For the 'pleonastic' use of *sic*
(and *ita*) see Madvig on Cic. *Fin.* ii. 17 and examples there
cited, e.g. Cic. *Font.* 36 'si hoc ita perlatum erit in Galliam',
Mil. 31 'sin hoc nemo uestrum ita sentit', Cael. ap. Cic. *Fam.*
viii. 6. 4 'hoc sic nuntiatum est', *Att.* xvi. 9 'quod quidem ita
credo', *Verr.* ii. 4. 106 'hoc . . . sic arbitrantur', *Leg.* ii. 31
'neque uero hoc, quia sum ipse augur, ita sentio'. See also
Löfstedt, *Coniectanea* (1950), 7–9.

For *singula* of 'points' of beauty cf. Hor. *Sat.* i. 6. 30–32 'si
qui . . . haberi . . . cupiat formosus, eat quacumque, puellis /
iniciat curam quaerendi singula, quali / sit facie, sura, quali
pede, dente, capillo'; Ov. *Am.* i. 5. 23.

3. **totum illud formosa nego :** 'the description *formosa* as a
whole I disallow.' The quoted '*formosa*' stands outside the
grammatical construction, *illud* acting in the same way as
the Greek definite article (τὸ *formosa*); so Quint. i. 7. 27
(quoted on 1. 1) 'ab illo "qui"'. Latin idiom normally
brings a quoted word, when it is declinable, into the grammatical structure: so Ov. *Met.* ix. 529 'scripta soror fuerat,
uisum est delere sororem' ('I had written "sister" and decided to delete "sister"'), x. 402 'patre audito' ('hearing the
word "father"'), Virg. *Georg.* iv. 527 'Eurydicen toto
referebant flumine ripae', Cic. *Phil.* ii. 30 'Ciceronem excla-
mauit ('he called "Cicero!"'). But a quoted word is occasionally left undeclined: so Ov. *Met.* xv. 96 'aetas cui fecimus
aurea nomen' ('to which we gave the name "aurea"'), Prop.
i. 18. 31 'resonent mihi Cynthia siluae' (contrast Virg. *Ecl.*
1. 5 'formosam resonare doces Amaryllida siluas', 'teach the
woods to re-echo "formosa Amaryllis"').

4. **tam magno est corpore :** *magno* is contrasted with *mica,*
but is not in itself uncomplimentary: Propertius says in
praise of his Cynthia (ii. 2. 5) 'fulua coma est longaeque
manus et maxima toto / corpore'. When Aristotle refuses to
recognize beauty without size (*Eth. Nic.* 1123ᵇ7 τὸ κάλλος ἐν
μεγάλῳ σώματι, οἱ μικροὶ δὲ ἀστεῖοι καὶ σύμμετροι, καλοὶ δ' οὔ), he is no
doubt thinking of male beauty. But the ancients did not admire *petitesse* in women either, and stature is a mark of female
beauty in Homer (*Od.* xviii. 248 ἐπεὶ περίεσσι γυναικῶν εἶδός τε
μέγεθός τε) as it is in Xenophon (*Anab.* iii. 2. 25: one of the

attractions of the East is Περσῶν καλαῖς καὶ μεγάλαις γυναιξὶ καὶ παρθένοις ὁμιλεῖν), in Aristotle himself (*Rhet.* 1361ᵃ5 θηλειῶν δὲ ἀρετὴ σώματος μὲν κάλλος καὶ μέγεθος), and in the Greek romances (Ach. Tat. i. 4. 5: the hero says of his first sight of his beloved ἐπῄνουν τὸ μέγεθος, ἐξεπεπλήγμην τὸ κάλλος). (For other illustrations see W. J. Verdenius in *Mnem.* ii [1949], 295 ff.; μέγεθος, however, does not imply any very imposing stature by our standards: the Athenian woman who was divinely tall enough to impersonate Athena (Herod. i. 60) was only 5 ft. 10 in.)

mica salis : 'piquancy' ('spice' rather than 'salt' is our metaphor), but here without its usual reference to wit in thought or language: so in Lucretius iv. 1162 the undersized girl is to her lover's blind eye 'chariton mia, tota merum sal'. Martial (vii 25. 3) repeats Catullus' phrase but with the usual reference to verbal wit. Quintilian, discussing *salsum* (vi. 3. 18), quotes Catullus' line, somewhat heavy-handedly, to show that *salsum* need not mean *ridiculum*.

6. omnibus una : for the contrast cf. 1. 5–6, 5. 3.

surripuit Veneres : the phrase may have been suggested by an Alexandrian original: cf. Nonnus xvi. 45 παρθενικὴ γὰρ κάλλος ὅλον σύλησεν Ὀλύμπιον. For *Veneres* cf. 3. 1, Plaut. *Stich.* 278 'amoenitates omnium uenerum et uenustatum adfero'.

87

Like 72 and 75, these lines belong to the period of disillusionment, but Scaliger was wrong in attaching them to 75: that poem is clearly complete in itself. As in 76 and again in 109, Catullus turns, not in self-righteousness but in despair, to the obsessing thought of his own loyalty. In the change of person between l. 2 and l. 4 and the jingling repetition of -ta meast emotion seems to be struggling with the restrictions of form.

1 f. tantum . . . quantum : cf. 37. 12 'amata tantum quantum amabitur nulla'.

2. mea est : Scaliger's *mea es* removes the abrupt change by which Lesbia passes from the third person in l. 2 to the second in l. 4 (*tuo*), but involves an awkwardly complicated order of words (*a me, Lesbia, amata, mea, es*).

3. ullo . . . umquam foedere : the simple ablative may perhaps stand both here and in 76. 3 'foedere nullo', but ⟨in⟩ should probably be inserted after *umquam* here—the *in* is called

for to balance *in amore* in the next line—and *in ullo* read in 76. 3.

4. amore tuo : 'love for you': cf. 64. 253.

ex parte ... mea : 'on my side': cf. 17. 18 *ex sua parte*. For the diaeresis of the pentameter falling within a word-group, between preposition and noun, cf. 76. 18 *in | morte*, 111. 2 *e | laudibus*.

92

Gellius quotes the whole poem (vii. 16) in a discussion of the word *deprecor*, misunderstood, he says, by a pretentious but ill-informed critic: 'nam cum esset uerbum deprecor doctiuscule positum in Catulli carmine, quia id ignorabat, frigidissimos uersus esse dicebat, omnium quidem iudicio uenustissimos, quos subscripsi'. For the theme cf. 83.

2. dispeream nisi : for the colloquialism cf. Hor. *Sat.* i. 9. 47 'dispeream ni | summosses omnes', *Catal.* 4. 3 'dispeream si te fuerit mihi carior alter', Prop. ii. 21. 9 'dispeream si ....' Similarly 'peream (ni)si' (Varro, *R.R.* iii. 3. 9, Cic. *Fam.* xv. 19. 4), 'peream male si' (Hor. *Sat.* ii. 1. 6), 'interam si' (Hor. *Sat.* i. 9. 38).

3. quo signo? quia ... : the same ellipse in Plaut. *M.G.* 1001 '*Py.* huius sermo hau cinerem quaeritat. | *Pa.* quo argumento?—*Py.* quia enim loquitur laute et minime sordide'. For *signum* of love symptoms cf. Prop. iii. 8. 9 (of Cynthia's outbursts of rage) 'nimirum ueri dantur mihi signa caloris', Ov. *Am.* ii. 1. 8 'atque aliquis iuuenum quo nunc ego saucius arcu | agnoscat flammae conscia signa suae'.

sunt totidem mea : whatever the origin of this phrase (Ellis dubiously suggests a metaphor from a game, 'I have the same score') and whatever the noun which is to be supplied in it (which is not *signa* anyhow, as Kroll says), it must be taken in connexion with Horace's 'dixerit insanum qui me, totidem audiet' (*Sat.* ii. 3. 298, 'he will have the same said about him'). The two phrases point to a colloquial usage in which the notion of quantity has slipped into the notion of kind and from which the use of *totidem* in late Latin for *idem* or *itidem* is derived: see A. Sonny in *A.L.L.* xi. 132, Löfstedt, *Verm. Studien*, 99, who cite from the 4th century phrases like *totidem ipse fecisti, negare totidem non potes*. There may be a similar use in [Cic.] *in Sallust.* 21 'totidem putas esse bis senatorem et bis quaestorem fieri quot bis consularem et bis triumphalem?', but the text is uncertain.

deprecor : the direct object of *deprecari*, 'pray for relief', may be either (*a*) that from which relief is sought (Cic. *Verr.* ii. 5. 125 *mortem d.*), (*b*) that for which appeal is made (Cic. *Sull.* 72 *uitam d.*), (*c*) the person to whom appeal is made (Cic. *post Red. in Sen.* 37 *populum Romanum d.*). The use here is the first of these: Gellius, in whose time *deprecor* was being used as merely an intensified form of *precor*, has to explain it and paraphrases it by *detestor, exsecror, depello, abominor*.

93

The couplet looks like a rejoinder to some overture by or on behalf of Caesar, but there is nothing to determine its occasion.

1. **nil nimium :** 'not very much', a survival of the original use of *nimium* as a synonym of *ualde*: so Cic. *Fam.* xii. 30. 7 'illud non nimium probo', Mart. ix. 81. 3 'non nimium curo'. *non nimis* is similarly used in classical prose. See on 43. 4.

   studeo ... uelle placere : the 'pleonastic' *uelle* is not altogether otiose: *uelle placere* is 'make an effort to please': cf. Sen. *Apoc.* 14. 2 'incipit ... uelle respondere', Ov. *Met.* x. 132 'uelle mori statuit'. The extreme case of Cic. *Fin.* iii. 68 'uelit ... uelle' looks like an inadvertence; there is a deliberate conceit in [Ov.] *Her.* 21. 58 'me precor, ut serues, perdere uelle uelis'. (The use of *uelle* after *noli(te)*—Nep. *Att.* 4. 2 'noli me uelle ducere', Cic. *Balb.* 64 'nolite ... hunc ... nuntium uelle perferri', *Cael.* 79 'nolite ... hunc ... uelle maturius exstingui' —is the natural result of the weakening of *noli(te)* into a mere formula of prohibition.) But such pleonasms with verbs are not uncommon even in prose: cf. Cic. *Verr.* ii. 2. 45 'neque enim permissum est ut impune nobis liceat ...', *Leg. Agr.* ii. 34 'Italiam ... ut complere liceat permittitur', Tac. *Dial.* 3. 3 'maturare libri huius editionem festino', and see Löfstedt, *Synt.* ii. 181. For another common type of pleonastic expression see on 46. 1 *egelidos tepores*.

2. **scire utrum sis albus an ater :** for the proverbial phrase cf. Cic. *Phil.* ii. 41 'qui albus aterne fuerit ignoras' ('about whom you do not know the first thing'), Apul. *Apol.* 16 'libenter te nuper usque albus an ater esses ignoraui'. Quintilian (xi. 1. 38), discussing the point that the same words do not suit every speaker, quotes the line loosely and apparently has forgotten its authorship: 'negat se magni facere aliquis poetarum utrum Caesar ater an albus homo sit; insania: uerte ut idem Caesar de illo dixerit; arrogantia est'.

95

Catullus' welcome to the miniature masterpiece of his friend Cinna (see on 10. 29 f.) is at the same time a literary manifesto, a proclamation of those Alexandrian principles of poetry to which Cinna and he were pledged—elaborate technique on a small scale, pursuit of the unobvious in matter and in manner, appeal to the cultivated taste of an esoteric circle—and a condemnation of those who, like the Volusius of this poem and 36, or Suffenus of 14 and 22, followed the old, 'dull' tradition and had less exacting standards in technique. So Callimachus had hailed the work of Aratus (*Ep.* 27 Pf.), χαίρετε λεπταὶ / ῥήσιες, Ἀρήτου σύντονος ἀγρυπνίη, and had proclaimed his own poetic creed and his intolerance of the old school (*Ep.* 28 Pf.) ἐχθαίρω τὸ ποίημα τὸ κυκλικόν, οὐδὲ κελεύθῳ / χαίρω τις πολλοὺς ὧδε καὶ ὧδε φέρει . . . οὐδ' ἀπὸ κρήνης / πίνω· σικχαίνω πάντα τὰ δημόσια; so, among his Italian devotees, the work of Valerius Cato, the pioneer of the new poetry, was greeted by Ticidas (fr. 2 Morel 'Lydia doctorum maxima cura liber') and by Cinna himself (fr. 14 Morel 'saecula permaneat nostri Dictynna Catonis'). The Oxford text follows Statius in detaching ll. 9–10 to form a separate poem. But the couplet is not inappropriate as a finale to the praise of the *Zmyrna*: Cinna's poem, says Catullus, is a masterpiece of patient craftsmanship—unlike Hortensius' work (1–4); it is destined to live —unlike Volusius' (5–8); it has the admiration of the discriminating critic—and can do without that of the man in the street. But see on l. 9.

Cinna's *Zmyrna* was a narrative poem in the style in favour of which Callimachus and his followers had renounced the epic and in which Catullus himself wrote poem 64. His subject was a more recondite one than Catullus'—the Cyprian legend of the passion of Smyrna (or Myrrha) for her father Cinyras, a story which, as Ovid's version of it in *Met.* x. 298 ff. shows, gave ample scope for Alexandrian erudition and romanticism in the elaboration of mythological detail and the exploration of morbid emotion. Cinna's treatment was such that within a few generations it needed a commentary from the *grammaticus* Crassicius Pansa (see on 70).

1. **Zmyrna** : the *z* in this word (and in *zmaragdus*) conforms to contemporary Greek spelling, in which ζ by this time has come to represent the sound of voiced *s*.

1 f. **nonam post . . . hiemem** : 'published nine summers and nine winters after it was begun': that is, Cinna had worked on his poem for nine years. For the construction, cf. Cic. *Fam.* xvi. 21. 1 'post diem quadragesimum et sextum quam a vobis discesserant'.

2. **editã** : the main verb, *mittetur*, is in l. 5, where the subject *Zmyrna* is emphatically repeated after the intervening parenthesis.

3. **cum interea** : the general sense of the missing pentameter is clear; *cum interea*, as often, conveys a contrast (as 'while' often does in English), and Cinna's fastidiousness is contrasted with the fluent facility of another poet. That *uno* agrees with *anno* or *mense* in the missing line is an easy guess and the likeliest supplement is something like Fröhlich's *uersiculorum anno quolibet ediderit* (though his *quolibet* is not happy); Parthenius's *in pede stans fixo carmina ructat hians*, though it is not itself very plausible, reminds one that there are other possibilities. But the appearance of Hortensius is surprising. The Hortensius of this poem and the (H)ortalus of poem 65 must be Q. Hortensius Hortalus, Cicero's rival in the courts and the leading exponent of the Asianic style in Roman oratory. Now in 65 Catullus sends to (H)ortalus, at his prompting, his own translation from Callimachus. Of Hortensius' verse we have only one word surviving, but we know that he wrote *nugae* of the same sort as Catullus and his friends; Ovid (*Tr.* ii. 441) speaks of his *improba carmina* along with Catullus, Calvus, Cinna, and Memmius, and Pliny (*Ep.* v. 3. 5) puts him in the same company. He did write a work called *Annales*, but the references of Cicero and Velleius to it suggest that it was a prose work, and the passing reference in Plutarch (*Luc.* I. 1) to a work on the Marsic War, if it concerns a poem at all, concerns a *jeu d'esprit* of his youth. Though he belonged to an older generation (he was some thirty years older than Catullus), all that we hear of him suggests sympathy with the tastes and ideals of the neoteric school; we do not know enough either of him or of Catullus' personal relátions to conjecture how he comes to appear here on the other side.

5. **cauas** : 'deep-channelled': cf. Virg. *Georg.* i. 326, iv. 427, *caua flumina*.

Satrachi : Satrachus was a river in Cyprus which Nonnus (xiii. 458) connects with the legend of Adonis, Smyrna's son. Cinna's poem will be known even in that distant part of the world where its scene is laid.

6. **cana . . . saecula** : the generations will go on reading it till they are old and grey: for the same illogical notion cf. *Ciris* 41 *senibus saeclis*.

peruolŭent : quadrisyllabic: see on 2b. 13 *soluit*.

7. **Volusi annales** : see on 36.

Paduam . . . ipsam : the meaning must be that Volusius'

verses will not get beyond the place of their (or their author's) origin. Padua is the branch of the Po which Polybius (ii. 16. 11) calls Παδόα: the river-name balances *Satrachi* in l. 5.

8. **scombris . . . tunicas** : i.e. paper to wrap mackerel in. *saepe* and *laxas* have their point: when Volusius' works are available, there is no need to be thrifty with paper. Martial borrows the phrase (iv. 86. 8 'nec scombris tunicas dabis molestas': cf. iii. 50. 9, Pers. 1. 43) and Horace has a similar use for literary waste-paper, *Ep.* ii. 1. 269–70 'deferar in uicum uendentem tus et odores / et piper et quicquid chartis amicitur ineptis'.

9. **monimenta** : see on 11. 10. If this line refers to Cinna, the Aldine's supplement *sodalis* is very suitable (Cinna is Catullus' *sodalis* in 10. 29), but the loss of the word is not easily explained. Bergk and Munro thought that the name of an Alexandrian poet was called for to balance *Antimacho* and proposed *Philetae* and *Phalaeci* respectively: but *mei* with such a name would be patronizing. If the couplet is a separate poem, the missing word must be taken to be a proper name, presumably that of a friend of Catullus: Leo's *Catonis* was suggested by Cinna's own line quoted above.

10. **Antimacho** : here Catullus finds his contrast not in a contemporary but in a famous literary figure of the fifth century, Antimachus of Colophon, who wrote a long epic *Thebaid*: his contemporary Plato admired his work and so did later critics (cf. Quint. x. 1. 53), but he fell under the condemnation of Callimachus, who called his *Lyde* παχὺ γράμμα ⸱καὶ οὐ τορόν (fr.398 Pf.). Catullus ends with a defiant challenge to literary tradition and conventional criticism; like Cinna and his friends, he is concerned only with the verdict of the *docti*, their fellow-innovators.

96

An acknowledgement to Calvus (see on 14) of his elegy on the early death of his wife Quintilia: for a penetrating discussion of the poem see E. Fraenkel in *Wiener Studien* lxix (1956), 282 ff. We know of the elegy from Propertius, ii. 34. 89–90

> haec etiam docti confessa est pagina Calui
> cum caneret miserae funera Quintiliae,

and two of the fragments of Calvus may be ascribed to it:

fr. 15 (Morel) cum iam fulua cinis fuero,

fr. 16 forsitan hoc etiam gaudeat ipsa cinis.

That Calvus' verses told the story of other loves we are explicitly told by Ovid, *Tr.* ii. 431–2:

> par fuit exigui similisque licentia Calui
> detexit uariis qui sua furta modis.

Fraenkel concludes that in his elegy Calvus had made the dead
Quintilia herself reproach him for his infidelities, as Propertius
(iv. 7. 13 ff.) makes the dead Cynthia charge him with his forgetfulness; *cum iam fulua cinis fuero*, she had said, you will be
sorry for your *furta*, and he had hoped that his repentance would
comfort her shade (*gaudeat ipsa cinis*). Using his own words,
Catullus gently reassures him; *ueteres amores* and *missae
amicitiae* are the love that Calvus had lightly abandoned and
the generalizing plural tenderly spares his feelings. The structure of the poem closely resembles that of the first six lines of 76.

1. **si quicquam** : for the opening cf. 102, 107. For the thought
   compare Sulpicius' words to Cicero on the dead Tullia,
   Fam. iv. 5. 6 'si qui etiam inferis sensus est, qui illius in te
   amor fuit pietasque in omnis suos, hoc certe illa te facere
   non uult'.

   mutis : cf. 101. 4.

   gratum acceptumue : the combination is regular: e.g.
   Plaut. *Stich.* 50 'mihi grata acceptaque est huius benignitas',
   Truc. 617 'accepta et grata', Cic. *Phil.* xiii. 50 'rem . . .
   gratam acceptamque', *Tusc.* v. 45.

3. **quo desiderio** : a development of the idiom, common in early
   Latin and surviving in classical prose especially with *dies* and
   locus, by which the antecedent is repeated in a relative clause:
   e.g. Plaut. *Epid.* 41 'est caussa qua caussa simul mecum ire
   ueritust', Ter. *Heaut.* 20 'habet bonorum exemplum quo
   exemplo sibi / licere facere quod illi fecerunt putat'. Here
   desiderio takes the place of a repeated *dolore* and defines
   dolore more precisely.

3 f. **amores . . . amicitias** have the same reference: so 109. 1 and
   6.

4. **missas** is not equivalent to *amissas* and must imply voluntary
   abandonment: cf. Plaut. *Pseud.* 685 'certa mittimus dum
   incerta petimus' and the common *missum facere*.

5. **certe**, as often, emphasizing the apodosis of a condition: cf.
   Cic. *Fam.* iv. 5. 6 quoted on 1 above.

5 f. **tanto . . . quantum** : for adjectival *tanto* correlative to
   adverbial *quantum* cf. Lucan i. 259 ff. 'sed quantum, uolucres
   cum bruma coercet, / rura silent, . . . / tanta quies'.

   amore : Calvus has shown his *amor* now in *dolor* and
   desiderium.

100

These lines are connected with Verona on the one hand (l. 2), with Rome on the other, if this Caelius and this Quintius are the Caelius and the Quinctius who appear elsewhere in the poems. Caelius, who is here thanked for service rendered to Catullus in his love (and *uesana flamma* can hardly refer to anyone but Lesbia), is told the story of Lesbia's degradation in poem 58: Quintius is reproached for taking Catullus' love from him in 82. Aufillena appears again in 110: the name seems to be of Etruscan origin and to be associated with north Italy (Schulze, *Lat. Eigennamen*, 114).

2. flos: cf. 24. 1 *flosculus Iuuentiorum*, 63. 64 *gymnasi flos*.
   depereunt: cf. 35. 12.

3. hic . . . ille: the reversal of the normal roles of *hic* and *ille*, *hic* referring to the more remote subject and *ille* to the nearer, is occasionally found elsewhere: e.g. Ov. *Tr.* i. 2. 23 f. 'nihil est nisi pontus et aer, / fluctibus hic tumidus, nubibus ille minax'. (For a list of examples see Shackleton Bailey, *Propertiana*, p. 279.) But the juxtaposition of *hic . . . ille* and *hoc . . . illud* is awkward, and *uere* and *dulce* are mere stopgaps.

   quod dicitur illud: 'that is what is meant by the phrase brotherly friendship'. Catullus mischievously gives a new meaning to a familiar phrase (cf. Ov. *Tr.* i. 3. 65 'quosque ego dilexi fraterno more sodales'): the *sodalicium* of these good friends may be called *fraternum* in the sense that they are in love with brother and sister. For *illud* cf. 86. 3 n.

5. cui faueam . . . tibi: for the formula of question and answer cf. 1. 1–3.

6. The text is uncertain. *perfecta exigitur* cannot stand: apart from the dubious meaning and the arbitrary lengthening of *-ur* at the diaeresis, the combination of the conflicting tenses in *exigitur . . . torreret* is impossible. The old correction *perspecta* is certain; for the rest Palmer's *est igni tum* is probably right ('was tried by fire in those days when . . .'). Schoell's *ex igni* involves an unlikely use of the preposition. 'Tried by fire' is a common cliché: cf. Cic. *post Red. in Sen.* 23 'ut . . . amicitias igni perspectas tuear', *Fam.* ix. 16. 2 'ut quasi aurum igni sic beneuolentia fidelis periculo aliquo perspici possit', *Off.* ii. 38 'quod in quo uiro perspectum sit hunc igni spectatum arbitrantur'.

7. uesana . . . flamma: the bold transposed epithet recalls 7. 10 *uesano Catullo*.

101

Catullus' brother had died in the Troad, in the North-western corner of Asia Minor (cf. 65. 7, 68. 91–92), and it is a reasonable conjecture that on his journey to Bithynia, the adjoining province, in 57 B.C. Catullus took the opportunity to visit his tomb and make the traditional offerings there. The sepulchral epigram in the strict sense—verses written, or purporting to be written, for inscription on a tomb—was a long-established genre going back to Simonides in the fifth century, and Book vii of the Greek Anthology presents some hundreds of examples of it from Plato onwards, many of them highly stylized and developed with ingenious fancy and conceit. Unlike most of these Catullus' poem is not an epitaph. Here as elsewhere he has turned a recognized literary form into something more intimate and personal; in Wilamowitz's phrase, it is a short elegy (*Hell. Dicht.* i. 234). Nearest to it in spirit, perhaps, among the epigrams of the Anthology, are Meleager's moving lines (*A.P.* vii. 476):

> δάκρυα σοὶ καὶ νέρθε διὰ χθονός, Ἡλιοδώρα,
> δωροῦμαι στοργᾶς λείψανον εἰς Ἀίδαν,
> δάκρυα δυσδάκρυτα· πολυκλαύτῳ δ' ἐπὶ τύμβῳ
> σπένδω μνᾶμα πόθων, μνᾶμα φιλοφροσύνας.
> οἰκτρὰ γὰρ οἰκτρὰ φίλαν σε καὶ ἐν φθιμένοις Μελέαγρος
> αἰάζω, κενεὰν εἰς Ἀχέροντα χάριν.
> αἰαῖ, ποῦ τὸ ποθεινὸν ἐμοὶ θάλος; ἅρπασεν Ἅιδας,
> ἅρπασεν, ἀκμαῖον δ' ἄνθος ἔφυρε κόνις.
> ἀλλά σε γουνοῦμαι, γᾶ πάντροφε, τὰν πανόδυρτον
> ἠρέμα σοῖς κόλποις, μᾶτερ, ἐναγκαλίσαι.

For all their simplicity Catullus' lines have a distinction of form, both in language and ·metre, which makes them outstanding among his elegiacs: the alliteration on *m* which runs through the poem is a piece of studied technique.

2. aduenio : 'I have come': for this use, which is common in comedy, cf. Plaut. *Most.* 440 'Aegypto aduenio domum' ('here I am, home from Egypt'), *Men.* 287 'numero ("opportunely") huc aduenis ad prandium', Ter. *Eun.* 976 'saluom te aduenire, ere, gaudeo'.

ad : final as in l. 8, 'to make this offering'.

inferias : an offering made to the *di manes*, the spirits of the departed, at the tomb; wine, milk, honey, and flowers were the usual gifts. The Romans themselves connected the word with *inferi*: in fact it is probably related to *fero*, and Cato (132. 2) uses the adjective *inferium* (*uinum*) of a sacrifice to Jupiter. The *inferiae* are *miserae* because they call out feelings of sadness: cf. Ovid, *F*. vi. 492 (of a funeral offering) 'dederat miseris omnia iusta rogis', Prop. i. 15. 21 'miseros delata per ignes' (of a pyre).

3. **donarem :** the historic sequence is determined by the past intention implied in *uectus aduenio*; cf. Plaut. *Persa* 537–8 'tua ego hoc facio gratia, / ut tibi recte conciliandi primo facerem copiam' ('to give you the chance of a good bargain').

postremo ... munere mortis : cf. Virg. *Aen*. xi. 25 'egregias animas . . . decorate supremis / muneribus'. The defining genitive *mortis* ('gift connected with death, death-gift') takes the place of an adjective like *funereus* or *feralis*.

4. **mutam ... cinerem :** cf. 96. 1 'mutis sepulcris', Tib. ii. 6. 34 'mea cum muto fata querar cinere', Prop. ii. 1. 77 'taliaque illacrimans mutae iace uerba fauillae': so *A.P.* vii. 467. 7 (Antipater Sid.) ἀντὶ δὲ σεῖο / στάλα καὶ κωφὰ λείπεται ἄμμι κόνις.

cinerem : *cinis* is feminine as in 68. 90 and in Lucretius (iv. 926) and Calvus (fr. 15, 16 Morel): see on 1. 2.

nequiquam is explained by *muta*; his words are vain because he can have no answer.

5. **quandoquidem :** a prosaic word whose metrical form (with the ō reduced to ŏ by iambic shortening: see on 10. 27) commends it to dactylic poets (Lucr. ii. 980, Virg. *Ecl*. 3. 55).

6. **indigne :** of a death which is 'shocking' because of its prematureness (Cic. *Clu*. 42 'acerbe indigneque moreretur', Plin. *Ep*. vi. 6. 7 'immatura morte indignissime abreptum', Virg. *Aen*. vi. 163 'indigna morte peremptum': so in sepulchral inscriptions, *Carm. Epigr*. 69 Büch. 'parentibus praesidium amicis gaudium / pollicita pueri uirtus indigne occidit') or its circumstances (Caes. *B.G*. vii. 38. 8 [of the victims of a massacre] 'qui indignissime interierunt'). So a *facinus indignum* is an act which is 'shocking' or 'a shame' because it conflicts with accepted notions of what is right and proper: cf. Virg. *Georg*. i. 491 'nec fuit indignum superis', 'the gods did not find it shocking'. The second half of the line is repeated in 68. 20 and 92.

7. **nunc tamen interea :** there is no implication that this is a provisional offering and that Catullus hopes to do more at another time, and no suggestion that he is likely to see the grave again. *interea* is 'in the present situation', confirming the hopelessness of *nunc*—usually the meaning of *interea* is limited by a *dum*-clause expressed or implied: here, to Catullus' sorrow, there can be no 'until'—and *tamen* expresses a contrast with the thought of the preceding lines: 'things being as they are, (though my offering is vain and you are lost to me), for all that let me give it to you'.

more parentum : 'the custom of our forefathers': so in Virgil's description of the funeral rites for Misenus, *Aen.* vi. 223 'subiectam more parentum / auersi tenuere facem'.

8. **tradita sunt . . . ad inferias :** 'which I have presented for my offering'.

　　tristi munere : for the modal ablative cf. 65. 19 'missum furtiuo munere'.

9. **manantia fletu :** the exaggeration is a commonplace of Latin poetry: so in similar contexts Tib. ii. 6. 31 'illius dona sepulcro / et madefacta meis serta feram lacrimis', Ov. *Tr.* iii. 3. 82 'deque tuis lacrimis umida serta dato'.

10. **aue atque uale :** so Aeneas bids farewell to the dead Pallas, Virg. *Aen.* xi. 97 f. 'salue aeternum mihi, maxime Palla, / aeternumque uale'. The formula is not uncommon in sepulchral inscriptions (e.g. *C.I.L.* ii. 3506, 3512, 3519), and Virgil's phrase *nouissima uerba, Aen.* vi. 231, is probably (in spite of Servius) to be referred to it.

102

Who the Cornelius was whose confidence Catullus pledges himself to respect we do not know; he may or may not be Cornelius Nepos of poem 1. The lines are clumsy and crabbed even for Catullan elegiacs. As they stand, they are little more than doggerel, and the substantival *tacito*, the awkwardly placed relative clause, the coordination of indicative and imperative, the repeated *me esse* are infelicities which cannot all be due to faults in transmission.

1. **si quicquam :** *quisquam* is not confined to the negative and quasi-negative clauses in which it is regular: its 'exclusive' force ('any single one', 'one if there is only one') makes it equally appropriate in hypothetical clauses and it is often so used both in comedy and in classical prose: cf. 96. 1, 98. 1, 107. 1, and see on 76. 7. *si quid quoi* (Baehrens's improvement on Maehly's *si quoi quid*) removes the awkwardness of *tacito*, standing alone as a substantive, by providing a substantival dative for it to qualify (for corruption of *quoi* see on 1. 1); Munro's *tacite* weakens the sense by attaching *cuius fides nota sit* to *amico* and so removing all reference to the recipient of the confidence.

1 f. **fido ab amico . . . fides :** i.e. there is *fides* on both sides: confidence is mutual.

3. **meque esse inuenies :** most modern editors have taken *meque* as equivalent to *me quoque* ('you will find that I too . . .'), but for this usage, accepted by Kühner–Stegmann (ii. 2. 15) and

Leumann–Hofmann (657), there is little evidence. In later
prose (from Velleius onwards) there are undoubted instances
of *hodieque* with the sense of *etiam hodie* (however that idiom
may be supposed to have arisen), but the other examples
cited for this use of *-que* with personal pronouns are extremely
dubious. At Cat. 31. 13 *uosque* is an emendation: in all the
rest (Prop. iii. 1. 35 'meque inter seros laudabit Roma nepotes',
iii. 21. 15 'ualeatis amici: / qualiscumque mihi tuque,
puella, uale', iii. 19. 21, ii.33. 31) *-que* can be taken as a connective and the force of 'also' which is imputed to it actually
inheres in the emphatic position of the personal pronoun.
Voss with *me aeque* removes the *-que*, and perhaps neither the
inelegant elision nor the otiose adverb need be objected to
here.

   illorum iure sacratum : 'bound by their code'. *illorum*
refers generally to the persons described in ll. 1–2, those who
are parties to a friendship of this kind. *ius* is the code or
system of rights and duties which is accepted and assumed
in some human relationship (cf. 66. 83): so Cic. *Am.* 35 'ius
amicitiae deserere', 63, *Fam.* xiii. 14. 1 'iura necessitudinis',
Quinct. 53 'ius amicitiae societatis affinitatis', Ov. *Tr.* iv. 10.
46 'iure sodalicii', Virg. *Aen.* iv. 27 'tua (*sc.* pudoris) iura
resoluo'. No example of the personal genitive can be cited,
but it seems possible. Ellis is probably right in interpreting
sacratum as 'bound under sanction'. *lex sacrata* is the regular
technical term for a covenant to which such a sanction
(making one who breaks it *sacer*) is attached; a person who
enters into a covenant so sanctioned may perhaps be described
as *sacratus*.

4. **puta :** the co-ordination of indicative and imperative, *inuenies
et puta*, is impossible but *puta* may perhaps be taken in its
parenthetic use, 'say', 'for instance'. Both infinitives will
then depend on *inuenies*: 'you will find that I am bound by
their code and have turned into—say, an Arpocrates'. Pleitner
proposed *putum* ('an out-and-out A.'), but the old word
putus, 'pure', is elsewhere used in this colloquial sense only
in the combination *purus putus*.

   Arpocratem : (H)arpocrates is the graecized form of one of
the names of Horus, 'Horus the child', associated in Egyptian
mythology and cult with Isis and Serapis, his mother and
father. In art he was often represented as a child holding his
finger to his lips (August. *Ciu. Dei* xviii. 5 'fere in omnibus
templis ubi colebantur Isis et Serapis erat etiam simulacrum
quod digito labiis impresso admonere uideretur ut silentium
fieret'; Varro, *L.L.* v. 57, Ov. *Met.* ix. 692); large numbers
of such representations have survived.

103

An ultimatum to Silo, who is told either to give back the
money he has had or, if he means to be a *leno*, to moderate his
rudeness. The name Silo makes it doubtful whether *leno* is to be
taken literally; it is a common cognomen and so points to its
owner's being a freeborn citizen, whereas a professional *leno*
is unlikely to have been such. The appearance of Silo as a
cognomen among the Iuventii on a Roman inscription of the
late Republic (*C.I.L.* i². 1322) is not enough to relate this Silo
to the Iuventius of poems 24, 48, 81, and 99, nor can any conclusion be drawn from the fact that the sum mentioned, ten
thousand sesterces, is that which the *Ameana puella* asks for
in 41. 2.

As in 82, the second half of the two pentameters is the same.

1. **aut . . . aut :** for the idiom cf. 12. 10.

2. **quamuis saeuus :** 'as savage as you like': see on 12. 5 *quamuis sordida*.

3. **nummi :** 'cash', as in Hor. *Ep.* i. 1. 54 (the materialist's
   slogan) 'uirtus post nummos'.

4. **atque idem :** 'and at the same time': for *idem* emphasizing
   an inconsistency see on 22. 14.

104

A reply to someone who has taken Catullus to task for hard
words about Lesbia or has supposed that they mean a change
of heart.

1. **meae . . . uitae :** Lesbia, as in 109. 1: cf. 45. 13, 68. 155.
   potuisse : 'had the heart to'; see on 68. 41.

2. **carior . . . oculis :** cf. 3. 5, 14. 1, 82. 4.

3. **perdite amarem :** cf. 45. 3 n. The harsh elision of a long
   syllable in the fifth foot of the hexameter is unparalleled not
   only in Virgil but even in Lucretius.

4. **omnia monstra facis :** probably 'you shrink from no enormity' rather than 'you make a sensation out of anything' (for
   monstrum in this sense cf. Cic. *Att.* iv. 7. 1 'mera monstra
   nuntiarat', 'his story was sheer sensationalism'; for the implications of the word see on 64. 15); Catullus turns the tables
   on his critic by accusing him of unmentionable doings. But
   we have no clue to the reference of *cum Tappone*. The name
   Tappo is found in Livy, as a cognomen of Valerii, and in
   inscriptions of north Italy: Schulze (*Lat. Eigennamen*, 95)

explains it as Etruscan; Walde accepts the suggestion that
it is a nickname from a stock character in south Italian farce,
perhaps derived from a Doric θαπῶν, corresponding to Attic
θηπῶν which Hesychius glosses by θαυμάζων, ἐξαπατῶν, κολακεύων.
A certain Valerius, who seems to have borne the cognomen
Tappo and to have been the author of the burlesque Lex
Tappula of which a fragment has been preserved (Dessau,
I.L.S. 8761), wrote verses so shameless that the recitation of
them in court was enough to secure the acquittal, against the
evidence, of the man he was prosecuting (Val. Max. viii. 1. 8),
but the date of the incident is uncertain.

105

Mentula here and in 94, 114, and 115 has generally been
taken to be an offensive nickname for Caesar's favourite officer
Mamurra (see 29 int.), who appears under his own name in
29 and 57. His literary pretensions are ridiculed again in 57. 7
where he and Caesar are *uno in lectulo erudituli ambo*.

1. **Pipleium . . . montem** : the hill of the Muses in Pieria, where
   the spring Pipla and the region about it, on the northern
   foothills of Olympus, were sacred to them: so the Muse is
   Piplea (or *Pipleis*) in Hor. *Od.* i. 26. 9. For the aspirant to
   poetry represented as climbing the Muses' hill cf. Ennius,
   Ann. 215 V. 'neque Musarum scopulos ⟨quisquam superarat⟩'.
2. **furcillis . . . eiciunt** : for the proverbial expression cf. Hor.
   Ep. i. 10. 24 'naturam expelles furca, tamen usque recurret',
   Cic. *Att.* xvi. 2. 4 'quoniam furcilla extrudimur, Brundisium
   cogito'.

107

A jubilant outburst after a reconciliation with Lesbia, in
which excitement struggles with the restraint of form and
language and the artifice of verbal repetition (*cupido—cupido—
cupido, optanti—optandam* (?), *insperanti—insperanti, gratum—
gratum*) runs riot.

1. **si quicquam** : the manuscripts have *quicquid* or *quid quid*;
   Ribbeck's *si quoi quid* eases the construction by providing a
   substantive for *cupido* and *optanti*, but the early correction
   quicquam is supported by Catullus' partiality for this combination, with which two other poems open (96 and 102);
   cf. 15. 3). For the use of *quicquam* see on 76. 7; for the emphatic *quicquam . . . unquam* cf. Naev. *com.* 14 R. 'secus si
   unquam quicquam feci', 96 R. 'si unquam quicquam filium

resciuero argentum . . . sumpse mutuum', Cic. *Verr*. ii. 2. 17 'si cuiquam denique ulla in re unquam temperarit'.

cupido : the Aldine rightly added *-que* to remove the hiatus.

2. **insperanti** : 'if something that a man desires and longs for happens to him beyond his hopes': the dative is awkward after the pair of adjectival datives in l. 1, but it is confirmed by the repetition in l. 5 and Heinsius's *insperati* (*quicquam insperati*, 'anything unhoped for') is unnecessary. For the predicative use cf. Cic. *de Or*. i. 96 'insperanti mihi et Cottae sed ualde optanti utrique nostrum cecidit'.

proprie : 'personally', 'individually' or perhaps, with *gratum*, 'in the strict sense'.

3. **nobis quoque carius auro** : the manuscript reading can just be translated as 'welcome, also more precious to me than gold'; *quoque* cannot qualify *auro* ('more precious even than gold'; *quoque* is 'as well', not 'even'), but it may belong to the whole clause. But if that reading is right, it is better construed with a pause after *quoque*, *carius auro* being added by asyndeton as parallel to *gratum*, and *quoque* ('to me as well', καὶ ἐμοί) serving to emphasize the particular case as opposed to the general maxim expressed in ll. 1 and 2. Haupt's *nobisque est* and Statius's *nobisque hoc* both have the effect of attaching *nobis* to the second clause only and suggesting a contrast which does not exist.

carius auro : the commonplace appears in Cic. *Rep*. iii. 8 'iustitiam rem omni auro cariorem' ('than any gold'), Tib. i. 8. 31, and often elsewhere.

3 f. **nobis . . . mi** : cf. 68. 132 'lux mea se nostrum contulit in gremium', 91. 1–2 'mihi . . . nostro', 100. 5–7 'nobis . . . meas'. 'Catullus seems to have thought it' (*nos*) 'more tender than the singular' (Munro, *Crit. and Eluc*., p. 185); 'in the case of relatives or close associates' the use of *noster* instead of *meus* in Cicero's letters 'implies either a suppression or an absence of intimate personal feeling' (R. S. Conway in *Trans. Camb. Phil. Soc*. v [1899], p. 14). One who seeks to determine the nuance which in any particular context justifies the substitution of *nos* or *noster* for *ego* or *meus* may take warning from these conclusions. Most discussions of the matter are vitiated by a tendency to look for a universal pattern and an unwillingness to recognize that in many cases, if there is a psychological explanation of the variation, it may be one that our intuition cannot discover. There are cases in which an explanation can be offered with some confidence, those, in particular, in which the speaker, for one reason or another, desires to associate others with himself;

there are some such in which the usage is more or less conventional (e.g. the plural of modesty, the official plural, the author's plural). But cases in which, as here, singular and plural are combined in one sentence are not at all uncommon and may defy the most casuistical attempts at finding a psychological motive. It must be recognized that the cause of the shift from singular to plural may lie no deeper than the level of expression; it may be due to desire for variety on the one hand or to assimilation, conscious or unconscious, on the other, or to considerations of metre in poetry or rhythm in prose. It is no disparagement of Catullus to suppose that he found the plural a metrically convenient substitute for the singular. (See F. Slotty in *Indo-Germ. Forsch.* xliv [1927], 288; W. S. Maguinness in *Mnem.* vii [1939], 148 [Catullus], *C.Q.* xxxv [1941], 127 [Virgil]; R. Waltz in *Rev. de Phil.* l [1926], 219; Hofmann, *Lat. Umgangsp.*[2] 135; Marouzeau, *Traité de Stylistique*, 210.)

5. **ipsa** : 'of your own accord'.

  refers te : cf. Prop. i. 18. 11 (in a similar context) 'sic mihi te referas'.

6. **candidiore nota** : cf. 68. 148 'lapide illa diem candidiore notat'. The white mark for a lucky day appears in various forms: so Pliny, *Ep.* vi. 11. 3 'o diem laetum notandumque mihi candidissimo calculo', Mart. ix. 52. 5 'diesque nobis / signandi melioribus lapillis', viii. 45. 2 'hanc lucem lactea gemma notet', Hor. *Od.* i. 36. 10 'cressa [i.e. chalk] ne careat pulchra dies nota': the cliché was popularly connected with the habit imputed to some primitive tribes (Thracians in Pliny's version, *N.H.* vii. 131) of putting a white or a black pebble every day in a jar to represent the happiness or unhappiness of each individual and by a final count assessing the happiness of his life, but it probably goes back to the practice of marking lucky days on a primitive calendar, and so has a similar origin to our 'red-letter day'.

7. **me uno . . . felicior** : the addition of *unus* in this idiom is logically unjustified: it is presumably due to the analogy of the equivalent *ego unus felicissimus uiuo*, 'I am uniquely the luckiest of men'. Cf. Cic. *Att.* xi. 2. 3 'quis me miserior uno iam fuit?', *Fam.* vii. 16. 3 'constat inter omnis neminem te uno . . . iuris peritiorem esse', [Virg.] *Catal.* 4. 9 'quis te in terris loquitur iucundior uno', Mart. iv. 56. 3 'nihil est te spurcius uno': see R. P. Winnington-Ingram in *C.R.* v [1955], 140.

  hac (*O* : me *GR*) **est optandus uita** : the manuscript readings are untranslatable and none of the proposed emendations commends itself; Muretus's comment is still true, 'tres postremi uersus . . . ita uarie leguntur ut appareat eam uarietatem non aliunde quam ex corrigere uolentium temeritate extitisse'. It is one thing to believe that Catullus' expression may have been awkward, as it is elsewhere in this poem and in his other elegiacs, and another to impute a particular awkwardness to him. *hac re optandam uitam* (Riese), 'who can call life more to be desired than this event?', gives tolerable sense but no more; the same may be said of *hac res optandas uita* (Lachmann), 'who can mention things more desirable than this life?', i.e. the life Catullus now enjoys. *hac rem optandam in uita* (Postgate) is based, like Kroll's surprising *hac re optandam in uita*, on the supposition that *in uita* means 'in the world' (Kroll): but in Cic. *Fam.* xv. 4. 16 'qua nec mihi carior ulla unquam res in uita fuit' (which Kroll quotes in support), as in Prop. ii. 9. 43 'te nihil in uita nobis acceptius unquam', *in uita* means 'in the course of my life' (cf. Cic. *Fam.* xiv. 4. 1).

108

Some of the details of this wild and gruesome invective reappear in Ovid's *Ibis*, 165–72:

> carnificisque manu populo plaudente traheris
> infixusque tuis ossibus uncus erit. . . .
> unguibus et rostro tardus trahet ilia uultur
> et scindent auidi perfida corda canes.
> deque tuo fiet—licet hac sis laude superbus—
> insatiabilibus corpore rixa lupis;

and the resemblance has suggested that Catullus was drawing on reminiscences of the *Ibis* of Callimachus, the masterpiece of learned abuse which was Ovid's model. It may be so, but such commonplace vituperation perhaps need not have so distinguished an ancestry.

One Publius Cominius, an *eques* from Spoletum, twice prosecuted an ex-tribune, C. Cornelius, on charges of *maiestas*, in 66 B.C., when he and his brother were mobbed by the *populares* and (it was said) bribed into dropping the case, and again in 65, when Cornelius was defended by Cicero and acquitted. It is unlikely that this poem is directly connected with incidents of that date and *populi arbitrio*, 'universal verdict', is too vague a phrase to support a connexion. The name Cominius was common in Rome—and in Cisalpine Gaul: Catullus' quarrel, whatever it amounted to, may belong to his days in Verona.

1. **cana senectus** : cf. 61. 155 *cana anilitas*: reference to a malefactor's grey hairs which his conduct disgraces is a familiar device to excite odium.

4 f. **sit data . . . uoret**: the periphrastic future subjunctive does not lend itself to verse, and the present subjunctive may replace it even in prose: cf. Cic. *Clu.* 158 'non debeo dubitare quin si qua ad uos causa eius modi delata sit eius qui lege non teneatur, etiam si is inuidiosus aut multis offensus esse uideatur, . . . tamen absoluatis et religioni potius uestrae quam odio pareatis'; similarly in past time Cic. *Quir.* 14 'nec si illa restitueretur dubitaui quin me secum ipsa reduceret'.

5. **effossos** : *effodere* is the regular word for gouging out the eye: so in the threats of comedy, Plaut. *Aul.* 53 'oculos hercle ego istos, improba, ecfodiam tibi'.

109

Not without misgivings Catullus clutches at Lesbia's promises; his desperate intensity of feeling is reflected in the piling up of synonyms—*hunc nostrum | inter nos, uere | sincere | ex animo, tota vita | aeternum.*

1. **mea uita** : cf. 104. 1 n., 45. 13.

    proponis : 'you declare', with almost the same meaning as *promittere* in l. 3. For *proponere* of a formal undertaking cf. Vell. ii. 6. 5 'pretium se daturum idque auro repensurum proposuit'.

    iucundum . . . perpetuumque must be taken together. Baehrens takes *iucundum* as object of *proponis* and *amorem . . . fore* as epexegetic of it, *inter nos* being equivalent to *mutuum*: but *nostrum amorem inter nos fore* is an impossible expression.

3. **di magni** : a prayer here, like *o di* in 76. 17, not the conversational ejaculation of 14. 12, 53. 5.

    uere promittere possit : 'that she be capable of promising sincerely'.

3 f. **uere . . . sincere . . . ex animo** : cf. Ter. *Eun.* 175 ff. 'utinam istuc uerbum ex animo et uere diceres! / . . . si istuc crederem / sincere dici, quiduis possem perpeti'.

5. **tota . . . uita** : the earliest example of the use of the ablative of duration of time in place of the normal accusative: so Varro, *R.R.* ii. 2. 16 'toto die cursantes', Caes. *B.G.* i. 26. 5 'ea tota nocte continenter ierunt', Prop. i. 6. 7 'totis argutat noctibus ignis'. For the development of the use see Löfstedt, *Per. Aeth.* 52 ff.

perducere : 'carry through': with *perducere* in this sense an
end is usually specified (e.g. *res ad noctem perducitur*). Hence
Lachmann proposed *producere*—unnecessarily, since here the
end is sufficiently implied in *tota uita* and *aeternum*.

6. **aeternum** : 'everlasting' or, it may be, 'lifelong': *aeternus*
(from *aeuiternus*) often has reference to the span of human
life; cf. Ter. *Eun.* 872 'spero aeternam inter nos gratiam
fore', Cic. *Sull.* 28 'cum mihi uni cum omnibus improbis
aeternum uideam bellum esse susceptum', Sall. *Iug.* 31. 22.

sanctae foedus amicitiae : Catullus conceives of love, to his
own sorrow, as an inviolable contract: cf. 76. 3, 87. 3.

110

Aufillena (see on 100) is accused of taking money for her
favours and then breaking her bargain.

1 f. **bonae . . . instituunt** : 'decent *amicae*' (cf. Tib. ii. 4. 45
'bona quae nec auara fuit') 'regularly get the credit they
deserve: they take their fee for what they set about performing'. Aufillena's behaviour, on the other hand, would dis-
grace a professional *meretrix*.

2. **accipiunt pretium quae facere instituunt** : i.e. 'eorum quae
facere instituunt'. The ellipse of an antecedent in a case
other than nominative or accusative (cf. 62. 60) is common in
Plautus, e.g. *Aul.* 605 'is speculatum huc misit me ut quae
fierent fieret particeps (i.e. eorum quae)', *Curc.* 581 'ego
illam reddidi qui argentum a te attulit (i.e. ei qui)', *Poen.*
764 'ita mihi renuntiatum est quibus credo satis', but rare
later.

3 f. **tu . . . facinus** : the construction is involved and awkward:
it is most natural to take *facis facinus* as the main clause,
with two parallel *quod*-clauses attached to it and a relative
quod-clause subordinate to the first of them (*quod inimica
mentita es quod promisisti, quod nec das et fers, facinus facis*).

3. **promisti** (and **promisse** below): for the syncopated form see
on 14. 14.

quod promisti . . . mentita . . . es : for the construction cf.
Prop. ii. 17. 1 (in a similar context) 'mentiri noctem, pro-
missis ducere amantem, / hoc erit infectas sanguine habere
manus'.

4. **nec das et fers** : Guarinus's correction is necessary: while *dare*
and *ferre* can in some uses be practically synonyms (so *dona*

dare and *dona ferre* may be applied to the same action), the
context here points clearly to the antithesis of *dare* and *ferre*,
'give' and 'take': cf. Plaut. *Most.* 614 'quin feram si quid
datur'.

facis facinus : for the idiomatic use without an adjective,
'do wrong', cf. 81. 6 'quod facinus facias', Cic. *Fin.* ii. 95
'uide ne facinus facias cum mori suadeas'. Ovid has a
rhetorical development of the same idea, *A.A.* iii. 463–6
'illa potest uigiles flammas exstinguere Vestae / et rapere
e templis, Inachi, sacra tuis / . . . accepto Venerem munere si
qua negat' (the *amica* who does not keep her bargain is
capable of any enormity).

5 f. aut . . . fuit : there is a natural but illogical compression:
the thought would be fully expressed by *aut facere debes,
quod ingenuae est, aut non promittere debebas, quod pudicae
fuit. est . . . fuit*: note the change of tense. She can still show
herself *ingenua* by keeping her promise; she cannot now,
after making it, be *pudica* (cf. 76. 23 f. 'non iam illud quaero,
contra ut me diligat illa, / aut, quod non potis est, esse pudica
uelit').

5. ingenuae : as often, the adjective, properly meaning 'free-
born', refers to the proper feeling which may be supposed to
go with good birth (the development of our 'gentlemanly' is
very similar): cf. 61. 79 *ingenuus pudor*.

6 f. data . . . auarae : 'to snap up presents' (cf. Prop. iii. 15. 6
'nullis capta Lycinna datis') 'while evading your obligation
is worse than the behaviour of a grasping *meretrix*'. The text
is very uncertain. With this reading *fraudando* must be
taken in a loose modal connexion with *corripere*: that use of
the ablative of the gerund becomes common in later Latin,
but earlier examples generally show at least a vestige of the
instrumental force which is entirely absent here. Bergk's
officiis, 'cheating (the donor) of your obligations' or 'of your
compliances' gives tolerable sense: Ellis's *effectis* seems impossible, since it could only refer to actual results, not to the
anticipated but unrealized results which are in question here.

7. plus quam : for *plus quam* implying that the following description is inadequate cf. Cic. *Phil.* ii. 31 'confiteor eos . . .
plus quam sicarios, plus quam homicidas esse', Livy x. 28. 4
'proelia plus quam uirorum', xxi. 4. 9 'perfidia plus quam
Punica', xxi. 2. 4 'quae (opes) apud militem plebemque plus
quam modicae erant', Ov. *Met.* xiii. 451 'fortis et infelix
et plus quam femina uirgo', Lucan i. 1 'bella . . . plus quam
ciuilia'.

113

Written in 55 B.C. In Pompey's first consulship Maecilia
had two lovers; now, fifteen years later, when he is consul
again, she has two thousand. On Catullus' friend Cinna see on
10. 29 f. and on 95.

1. **solebant :** for the euphemistic ellipse of a verb cf. Plaut.
   Cist. 36 'uiris cum suis praedicant nos solere'.

2. **Maeciliam :** Maecilia is unknown, but the name is a well
   authenticated gentile name. Pleitner's *Mucillam* is meant to
   be a disparaging reference to Pompey's third wife Mucia (the
   lawyer Scaevola's daughter and half-sister of Clodia's husband Metellus), whom he divorced in 62 B.C., on his return
   from the East, on the ground of misconduct with Caesar
   (Suet. *Iul.* 50, Plut. *Pomp.* 42). That was a notorious
   scandal at the time (Cic. *Att.* i. 12. 3), but when this poem
   was written, it was an old story; Pompey had been four
   years married to Julia, and Mucia was the wife of M. Aemilius
   Scaurus. Pompey's repeated consulship is enough in itself to
   give the epigram its point.

3 f. **manserunt . . . singula :** the sense is made clear by the
   'prolific growth' of l. 4—'there are still two, but a thousand
   has accumulated for each one'. *in unum* and *singula* both
   convey the distributive notion: there has been an increase of
   'a thousand per one'. For the distributive use of *in* cf. Livy
   ix. 41. 7 'binae tunicae in militem exactae.' ('two tunics per
   soldier'), Suet. *Nero* 30. 3 'quadringenis in punctum sestertiis
   aleam lusit' (of Nero's high stakes, 'four hundred sesterces
   a pip'). It is not implied that Maecilia's original pair of
   admirers has remained constant over fifteen years (though
   duo can mean 'the two of them': cf. Sen. *Dial.* ii. 16. 2 with
   Gertz's note): *duo* is 'the number two', 'the 2'.

114

This poem and the next are lame and laboured epigrams on
the pretensions and extravagance of Mentula—that is, probably, Mamurra (see on 105), the 'bankrupt of Formiae' (43. 5)
who has run through three fortunes (29. 17–19).

1. **Firmano saltu :** 'M. has the name of being rich for his estate
   at Firmum'. If *Firmanus saltus*, to which *V*'s reading points,
   is retained, *Mentula* must be taken as vocative and *egeas*
   must be read in 6; but the poem reads more easily if Mentula
   is the subject throughout, as in 115.

Firmano : near Firmum in Picenum.

saltu : here in the general sense of 'estate'. Technically *saltus* is properly applied to rough country of wood, scrub, and hill pasture: Varro, *L.L.* v. 36 'quos agros non colebant propter siluas aut id genus ubi pecus possit pasci . . . saltus nominauerunt'.

3. **aucupium omne genus** : 'all sorts of fowl': for this limiting accusative attached to a noun cf. Cato 8. 2 'sub urbe hortum omne genus, coronamenta omne genus (serito)', Varro, *R.R.* iii. 5. 11 'auibus omne genus', Lucr. iv. 735 'omne genus simulacra feruntur', Petr. 71. 7 'omne genus poma'. Similar uses of *hoc genus* and *id genus* are common.

   aucupium, like *uenatio* and *piscatus*, is regularly transferred from the pursuit of hunting to its object: so Cic. *Fin.* ii. 23 'optimis cocis, pistoribus, piscatu, aucupio, uenatione', Celsus ii. 26. 2 'minima inflatio ("flatulence") fit ex uenatione, aucupio, piscibus, pomis'; Sen. *Dial.* i. 3. 6 'felicior esset si in uentrem suum . . . peregrina aucupia congereret'. A striking example of the change of meaning is Livy xxv. 9. 8 'capta uenatio' ('game caught').

   prata : 'meadow land'; **arua**, 'ploughed land'; **ferae**, 'game', i.e. deer and boar. *aucupium, pisces, ferae* are mentioned not as sporting possibilities but as sources of food supply: Italian hunting was essentially practical.

4. **exsuperat** : 'he exceeds its returns with his outlays'—i.e. he spends more than the estate brings in.

5. **concedo** : 'I don't mind his being rich (i.e. being called rich) so long as he has no assets at all': not 'I agree that he is rich' (*concedo diuitem esse*: see Reid on Cic. *Amic.* 18).

6. **ipse** : the owner; cf. 2. 9 *ipsa*.

   dum modo ipse : the hiatus makes the second half of the line suspect. Lachmann's *dum domo* does not make the metre sound: for 'prosodic hiatus', in which a final open vowel is shortened, following Homeric practice, before a following vowel, is not found in Catullus, or anywhere in a pentameter.

115

Like 114, on the estate of Mentula (Mamurra).

1. **habet instar** : *V*'s reading is suspect on two grounds, the construction of *instar* and the irrational lengthening of the second syllable of *habet*. *instar*, which is normally followed by a genitive (see on 17. 12), seems to be used here appositionally with *triginta* ('has something like, as many as, thirty

iugera'). The only evidence for this use with expressions of quantity is two passages of Columella: iv. 8. 2 'recedere . . . instar unius digiti spatio conueniet' (where the genitive depends on *spatio,* 'a distance of something like one finger's breadth'), xii. 28. 1 'irim cribratam quae sit instar pondo quincuncem et trientem'. (Elsewhere Columella has the usual genitive.) The lengthening of a short final syllable under the ictus is an epic artifice not uncommon in Virgil, who took it from Ennius. Catullus has it three times in the long poems: each time it occurs before a form of the Greek word *hymenaeus* (62. 4, 64. 20, 66. 11) and clearly echoes a Greek rhythm. Its appearance here seems entirely arbitrary and has been suspected with reason, but no convincing correction has been made; Avantius proposed *noster* for *instar,* but the corruption is unlikely and Catullus would not apply the affectionate *noster* to his arch-enemy Mamurra.

   triginta : the figures are not to be taken more seriously here than in 26. 4: the point is that they are low. Mentula has some 20 acres of meadow and some 27 acres under cultivation: the rest is swamp. The *maria* must be the *paludes* of l. 5; the town of Firmum was only six miles from the Adriatic.

3. **potis sit** : see on 45. 5.

4 f. **saltu . . . saltusque paludesque** : if the text is sound, Catullus (*a*) is so careless as to say that the *saltus* (singular: i.e. the estate, as in 114. 1) contains *saltus* (plural: 'rough country') as one of its assets, and (*b*) resorts here, as in 64. 298, to the device (nowhere else found in elegiacs) of hypermetric *-que* elided into the following line. (*b*) is not in itself impossible, though it is fanciful to find here the dramatic intention which can be plausibly ascribed to some Virgilian instances of hypermeter (Virgil often puts the second of a pair of *-que*s in this position) and conjecture that Catullus means to suggest the infinite expanse of Mentula's estate, going on and on. But even in lines which may have been thrown off on the spur of the moment, the slovenliness implied in (*a*) cannot be imputed to Catullus. The old correction *altasque paludes* removes both faults and restores concinnity by providing the adjective which is needed to balance *ingentes*.

6. **ad Hyperboreos . . . Oceanum** : stretching to the fabulous ends of the earth. The Hyperboreans, mythical inhabitants of the far north, go back to the Homeric Hymn to Dionysus (29) and to Pindar (*Isth.* 6. 23). For the apposition *mare Oceanus* cf. Caesar, *B.G.* iii. 7. 2 'proximus mare Oceanum'.

7. **ipse** : the owner, as in 114. 6.

ultro : for the emphatic colloquial use ('actually') cf.
Plaut. *Aul.* 530 'ubi disputata est ratio cum argentario,
etiam ipsus ultro debet argentario', *Men.* 843 'insanire me
aiunt ultro quom ipsi insaniunt', Cic. *Quinct.* 74 'Naeuius qui
cum ipse ultro deberet . . . cupidissime contenderet ut . . .'.

8. non homo sed : a common colloquial turn: cf. Cic. *Att.* i. 18. 1
'non homo sed litus atque aer et solitudo mera', vii. 13*a*. 2
'non hominem sed scopas solutas'. So in Petronius 'phan-
tasia non homo' (38. 15), 'discordia non homo' (43. 3), 'piper
non homo' (44. 6), 'codex non mulier' (74. 13).

    homŏ : as in 24. 7; on the 'iambic shortening' see on 10.
27. Catullus has *homō* at 17. 12, 81. 2.

    sed uero : 'but in fact': for *uero* strengthening *sed* cf. Lucr.
iv. 986 'non homines solum sed uero animalia cuncta', Cic.
Verr. ii. 5. 14 'praeclarum imperatorem nec iam cum M'.
Aquilio . . . sed uero cum Paulis Scipionibus Mariis con-
ferendum'.

116

    In poem 91 Gellius is a friend whom Catullus denounces for
playing him false over his love. In this poem Catullus says that
he had meant to make a move towards better relations by
dedicating a translation from Callimachus to Gellius (as in
poem 65 he dedicated the *Coma Berenices* (66) to Hortalus);
realizing that his hopes of changing Gellius by a compliment
to his interest in poetry are vain, he now declares war. The
five short poems (74, 80, 88–90) in which Gellius is viciously
abused may represent this new offensive. The lumbering first
sentence, trailing over six lines, the metrical crudity of l. 3,
and the unique ecthlipsis of -*s* in l. 8, make this angry outburst
the roughest of all Catullus' elegiac poems.

    Gellius has generally been identified with L. Gellius Popli-
cola: our information about his not very creditable career
belongs to a time long after this—he was consul in 36 B.C. and
commanded a wing for Antony at Actium—but there are
indications that he was associated with Clodia and her circle
at the time of the trial of Caelius in 56 B.C.—the prosecutor's
sister was his wife and the Palla whom Caelius was accused of
defrauding may have been his stepmother (see R. G. Austin on
Cic. *Cael.* 23)—and the scandal reported of him by Valerius
Maximus (v. 9. 1) bears some resemblance to the charges which
Catullus flings. (See Münzer in P.–W. vii. 1003 ff.)

1. tibi : to dedicate a piece of writing to someone is normally
ad aliquem mittere (so regularly in Cicero; e.g. *Sen.* 3, *Ac.* i. 2,

Fin. i. 8, *N.D.* i. 16, *Att.* viii. 12. 6) but Varro has the dative, *R.R.* i. 1. 10; cf. 68. 1–2.

studioso animo uenante : for the combination of adjective and participle cf. Virg. *Aen.* iii. 70 'lenis crepitans uocat auster', v. 764 'creber . . . aspirans . . . auster', *Georg.* iv. 370. *studioso uenante* might well refer to the work of the translator, but Catullus may be thinking rather of the effort of composing the conciliatory letter which was to accompany it.

1 f. **requirens . . . uti :** 'looking about to see how': for the 'timeless' use of the present participle cf. *Aen.* i. 305 'per noctem plurima uoluens, / ut primum lux alma data est, exire . . . / constituit'.

2. **Battiadae :** the title which Callimachus gave himself: see on 65. 16.

3. **qui:** 'whereby': the old instrumental form of the relative, the use of which with an antecedent can be seen, for example, in Varro, *R.R.* ii. *pr.* 3 'frumentum qui saturi fiamus', Plaut. *Stich.* 292 'mittere ad me . . . quadrigas / qui uehar' has already in Plautus become practically a conjunction equivalent to *ut* in final clauses: cf. *Amph.* 339 'certumst confidenter hominem contra conloqui / qui possim uideri huic fortis', *Pseud.* 826 'diuinis condimentis utere / qui prorogare uitam possis hominibus'. (The classical use of the ablative form *quo* as a final conjunction, usually with a comparative but sometimes without one—e.g. Cic. *Clu.* 9 'corrupisse dicitur Cluentius iudicium pecunia quo inimicum innocentem Albium condemnaret', *Sest.* 93, *Verr.* ii. 1. 17—represents the same development.) So here, where *neu* is coordinate with *qui*. The same form survives in *quicum* (see on 2. 2, 66. 77); for the corresponding interrogative use see on 72. 7.

qui . . . conarere : the only hexameter consisting entirely of spondees to be found outside Ennius.

4. **tela . . . caput:** Muretus's correction *tela* is necessary to supply *mittere* with an object; *tela infesta* is a common phrase both in verse (Virg. *Aen.* v. 582) and in prose.

in usque caput : Propertius has a very similar phrase, ii. 8. 15 'an usque / in nostrum iacies uerba superba caput ?'. For the inversion of normal order cf. 4. 24 'hunc ad usque limpidum lacum'. For *caput* cf. 15. 16 'ut nostrum insidiis caput lacessas'.

6. **hic:** i.e. *in hac re*: Muretus's *huc*, 'to this point', with *ualuisse*, is probably unnecessary.

7. **contra :** adverb, 'on my side', 'in reply', rather than preposition governing *nos* (*ista tua contra nos tela*).

euitabimus †amitha: so *O*; *GR* had *amicta*. Most editors have accepted the old corrections *euitamus amictu*, taking Catullus to mean 'in reply (*contra*) I parry your missiles by wrapping my garment round my arm (or my head)' and referring to such passages as Pacuvius 186 R. 'chlamyde contorta astu clupeat bracchium' ('makes his arm into a shield'), Petronius 80. 2 'intorto circa bracchium pallio composui ad proeliandum gradum', Sen. *Dial.* ii. 7. 4 'non minus latro est cuius telum opposita ueste elusum est'. But the future *euitabimus*, though it is not indispensable, is not out of place, and the bald *amictu*, without *opposito* or the like, is a surprisingly compressed way of referring to a gesture of defence. If *euitamus amictu* had been the reading of the manuscripts, the awkwardness of the expression might be condoned in a poem which bears the marks of hasty composition; as a correction it is highly dubious. Baehrens's (*euitabimus*) *acta* gives excellent sense, 'I shall evade those missiles of yours launched against me', but his explanation of the corruption, an adscript *mi* (expanding *dabis*) intruded into *acta*, is not very convincing.

8. dabis : the only instance in Catullus of the suppression of final *-s* after a short vowel before a word beginning with a consonant. The regular suppression of *-s* in that position in Plautus clearly indicates that it was silent, or faintly pronounced, in the ordinary speech of his time, and the omission of it in the spelling of early inscriptions points in the same direction. The practice of the early poets, Ennius and Lucilius, who disregard *-s* in prosody at will, was continued as late as Lucretius, and Cicero still takes advantage of it in his verse. But in Cicero's time, as he writes in 44 B.C. (*Orator* 161), the fashion had changed: the dropping of *-s*, which had been an elegant pronunciation, had become provincial ('iam subrusticum uidetur, olim autem politius') and the *poetae noui* had broken with the convention of disregarding *-s* in prosody. (See P. W. Harsh in *T.A.P.A.* lxxxiii [1952], 267 ff.)

APPENDIX I

GREEK POEMS TRANSLATED BY CATULLUS

(a) Sappho, frag. 31 (E. Lobel and D. L. Page, *Poetarum Lesbiorum Fragmenta*: Oxford, 1955).

φαίνεταί μοι κῆνος ἴσος θέοισιν
ἔμμεν' ὤνηρ, ὄττις ἐνάντιός τοι
ἰσδάνει καὶ πλάσιον ἆδυ φωνεί-
σας ὑπακούει

καὶ γελαίσας ἰμέροεν, τό μ' ἦ μὰν   5
καρδίαν ἐν στήθεσιν ἐπτόαισεν,
ὡς γὰρ ἔς σ' ἴδω βρόχε', ὤς με φώναι-
σ' οὐδ' ἒν ἔτ' εἴκει,

ἀλλ' ἄκαν μὲν γλῶσσα †ἔαγε, λέπτον
δ' αὔτικα χρῶι πῦρ ὑπαδεδρόμηκεν,   10
ὀππάτεσσι δ' οὐδ' ἒν ὄρημμ', ἐπιρρόμ-
βεισι δ' ἄκουαι,

κὰδ δέ μ' ἴδρως κακχέεται, τρόμος δὲ
παῖσαν ἄγρει, χλωροτέρα δὲ ποίας
ἔμμι, τεθνάκην δ' ὀλίγω 'πιδεύης   15
φαίνομ' †αι ...
ἀλλὰ πὰν τόλματον ἐπεὶ †καὶ πένητα ....

(b) Callimachus, frag. 110 (R. Pfeiffer, *Callimachus*, vol. i: Oxford, 1949).

1   πάντα τὸν ἐν γραμμαῖσιν ἰδὼν ὅρον ᾗ τε φέρονται

7   †η με Κόνων ἔβλεψεν ἐν ἠέρι τὸν Βερενίκης
        βόστρυχον ὃν κείνη πᾶσιν ἔθηκε θεοῖς

13/14   [σύμβολον ἐννυχίης ... ἀεθλοσύνης ?]

40   ... σήν τε κάρην ὤμοσα σόν τε βίον

        ἀμνά]μω[ν Θείης ἀργὸς ὑ]περφέρεται,
45   βουπόρος Ἀρσινόης μητρὸς σέο, καὶ διὰ μέ[σσου
        Μηδείων ὀλοαὶ νῆες ἔβησαν Ἄθω.
        τί πλόκαμοι ῥέξωμεν, ὅτ' οὔρεα τοῖα σιδή[ρῳ
        εἴκουσιν; Χαλύβων ὡς ἀπόλοιτο γένος,
        γειόθεν ἀντέλλοντα, κακὸν φυτόν, οἵ μιν ἔφ[ηναν

50   πρῶτοι καὶ τυπίδων ἔφρασαν ἐργασίην.

ἄρτι νεότμητόν με κόμαι ποθέεσκον ἀδε[λφεαί,
καὶ πρόκατε γνωτὸς Μέμνονος Αἰθίοπος
ἵετο κυκλώσας βαλιὰ πτερὰ θῆλυς ἀήτης,
ἵππος ἰοζώνου Λοκρίδος Ἀρσινόης,

55   ἥρπ]ασε δὲ πνοιῇ με, δι᾽ ἠέρα δ᾽ ὑγρὸν ἐνείκας
Κύπρ]ιδος εἰς κόλπους . . . [ἔθηκε] . . .
αὐτή μιν Ζεφυρῖτις ἐπὶ χρέος . . .
. . . Κανωπίτου ναιέτις α[ἰγιαλοῦ.
ὄφρα δὲ] μὴ νύμφης Μινωίδος ο[. . .

60   . . .]ος ἀνθρώποις μοῦνον ἐπι[. . .
φάεσ]ιν ἐν πολέεσσιν ἀρίθμιος ἀλλ[ὰ γένωμαι
καὶ Βερ]ενίκειος καλὸς ἐγὼ πλόκαμ[ος,
ὕδασι] λουόμενόν με παρ᾽ ἀθα[νάτους ἀνιόντα
Κύπρι]ς ἐν ἀρχαίοις ἄστρον [ἔθηκε νέον.

. . . .

75   οὐ τάδε μοι τοσσήνδε φέρει χάριν ὅσσον ἐκείνης
ἀ]σχάλλω κορυφῆς οὐκέτι θιξόμεν[ος,
ἧς ἄπο, παρθενίη μὲν ὅτ᾽ ἦν ἔτι, πολλὰ πέπωκα
λιτά, γυναικείων δ᾽ οὐκ ἀπέλαυσα μύρων.

. . . .

THE ARRANGEMENT OF THE POEMS

THE poems as we have them fall into three divisions. Poems 1–60 are short poems in iambic or lyric metres, the majority in hendecasyllables; poems 61–68 are long poems (except for 65, which is a preface to 66), one in glyconics, one in galliambics, two in hexameters, and three in elegiacs; poems 69–116 are elegiac, all (with one exception) short and of the nature of epigrams.

Catullus certainly made a collection of his poems and prefixed a dedication to Nepos (poem 1), who some time before (1. 5 *iam tum*) had been kind to his verses. The terms of the dedication do not imply that only short occasional poems were included in that collection. But they do imply a single *uolumen*, and the whole corpus as we have it, equal in number of lines to three books of Virgil, is too long to have been contained in one roll. Besides, it is unlikely that poems so different in scale and manner as the short poems 1–60 on the one hand and the long formal poems 61–66 on the other were included together there; poems 66 and 68 have their own dedicatory epistles and 64 would naturally be supposed to have stood by itself, as Catullus implies that Cinna's *Zmyrna* did. Whether the *libellus* offered to Nepos included all of the poems 1–60 or only some of them we cannot tell; it can only be said that if it contained any of the poems 11, 29, and 55, it must have been put together towards the end of Catullus' life, since none of these poems was written before 55 B.C., and that it is difficult to believe that Catullus offered the inconsequent 58*b* to Nepos as it stands. Evidence that the order of the poems at some points represents Catullus' own arrangement has been sought on two contrary premisses— that he deliberately placed poems on the same subject together and that he deliberately separated such related poems by an unrelated and contrasting one. He may indeed have used both principles, but to attempt to reconstruct the working of his taste in combining them is a hazardous proceeding and the cases in which either is evident are too few to be clearly significant. As for the whole collection the likeliest hypothesis is that it took its present form long after his death. His friends may have collected some of his work for publication (and 58*b* may be a draft which they found among his papers); the final edition which our manuscript tradition represents was probably later, and some features in that tradition suggest that the archetype of our manuscripts, or an ancestor of it, was put together from separate *libelli*[1] in the period when texts were being transferred from *uolumen* to *codex* form.

[1] See B. L. Ullman, *Studies in the Italian Renaissance* (Rome, 1955) pp. 102 ff.; one such feature is O's *explicit epithalamium* at the end of 61, which suggests that that poem had once stood by itself.

APPENDIX III

BIBLIOGRAPHY

(a) Commentaries

BAEHRENS (E.): 2nd ed., Leipzig, 1885.

BENOIST (E.), THOMAS (E.): Paris, 1882–90.

ELLIS (R.): 2nd ed., Oxford, 1889.

FRIEDRICH (G.): Leipzig, 1908.

KROLL (W.): Leipzig, 1923; reprinted with additions 1929 and 1959.

LENCHANTIN DE GUBERNATIS (M.): Turin, 1928; reprinted 1953.

MERRILL (E. T.): Boston, 1893; reprinted 1951.

MUNRO (H. A. J.), *Criticisms and Elucidations of Catullus*: 2nd ed., London, 1905.

(b) Other Works

BARDON (H.), *L'art de la composition chez Catulle*: Paris, 1943.

BAYET (J.), 'Catulle' in *L'influence grecque sur la poésie latine de Catulle à Ovide*, (Entretiens Hardt, tome ii): Geneva, 1956.

BRAGA (D.), *Catullo e i poeti greci*: Messina, 1950.

CUTT (T.), *Meter and Diction in Catullus' Hendecasyllabics*: Chicago, 1936.

FERRERO (L.), *Un' introduzione a Catullo*: Turin, 1955.

—— *Interpretazione di Catullo*: Turin, 1955.

FRANK (T.), *Catullus and Horace*: Oxford, Blackwell, 1928.

HAVELOCK (E. A.), *The Lyric Genius of Catullus*: Oxford, Blackwell, 1939.

HERESCU (N. I.), *Catullo*: Rome, 1943.

HEUSCH (H.), *Das Archaische in der Sprache Catulls*: Bonn, 1954.

HEZEL (O.), *Catull und das griechische Epigramm*: Stuttgart, 1932.

LEVENS (R. G. C.), 'Catullus' in *Fifty Years of Classical Scholarship*: Oxford, Blackwell, 1954.

NEUDLING (C. L.), *A Prosopography to Catullus*. (Iowa Studies in Classical Philology, xii.) Privately printed, 1955.

PASCAL (C.), *Poeti e personaggi catulliani*: Catania, 1916.

SCHNELLE (I.), *Untersuchungen zu Catulls dichterischer Form*: Leipzig, 1933.

SVENNUNG (J.), *Catulls Bildersprache*: Uppsala, 1945.

VAN GELDER (J.), *De Woordherhaling bij Catullus*: The Hague, 1933.

VON WILAMOWITZ-MOELLENDORFF (U.), *Hellenistische Dichtung*, vol. ii, ch. 8, 'Catull': Berlin, 1924.

WEINREICH (O.) *Die distichen des Catull*: Tübingen, 1926.

WHEELER (A. L.), *Catullus and the Traditions of Ancient Poetry*: Berkeley, 1934.

INDEXES TO THE NOTES

(1) INDEX VERBORUM

(2) INDEX NOMINUM

(3) INDEX RERUM

PRINTED IN GREAT BRITAIN
AT THE UNIVERSITY PRESS, OXFORD
BY VIVIAN RIDLER
PRINTER TO THE UNIVERSITY